DK FRENCH DICTIONARY

FRENCH · ENGLISH
ENGLISH · FRENCH

DK PUBLISHING, INC.

A DK PUBLISHING BOOK
www.dk.com

First American Edition, 1999

4 6 8 10 9 7 5

This book was originally published in the
DK Pockets series in 1999.

Published in the United States by
DK Publishing, Inc.
95 Madison Avenue
New York, New York 10016

Published in Great Britain by
Dorling Kindersley Limited.

ISBN 0-7894-4494-1

This edition revised by DK Publishing, Inc.

Printed and bound in Italy by Legoprint

THE IMITATED PRONUNCIATION

If the syllables given are pronounced as if they formed part of an English word, the speaker will probably be understood. However, the real sounds of the French language can be achieved by remembering a few simple rules:

r   (italic) not to be pronounced at all.

ng   (italic) not to be pronounced at all. It merely indicates that the preceding vowel has a nasal sound; ah*ng* is pronounced like **au** in "aunt", a*ng* like **ang** in "fang," o*ng* like **ong** in "wrong," and u*ng* like **ung** in "lung."

r   (bold type) pronounced more strongly than in English – rrroll it on the tongue.

sh   (bold) like **s** in "measure."

eh   like **e** in "bed."

er   like **u** in "fur."

er   (bold) is the same sound, but longer and with the **r** sounded.

er   like **e** in "her." but more closed.

ah   like **a** in "far." but shorter.

ai or ay   like **ai** in "fair."

E, EE   represent the sound of the French **u**: say "tree" with lips rounded as when whistling, and the terminal sound of **ee** is the one required.

oo   like **oo** in "book," "look," "took."

There is practically **no stress** in French words; the same value should be given to all syllables.

LA PRONONCIATION FIGURÉE

Prononcer chaque syllabe comme si elle appartenait à un mot français, mais en tenant compte des indications suivantes:

a   a extrèmement bref. Dans certains mots (**have, had, has, man, hat** etc.), entre l'**a** de "bal" et l'**è** de "complète."

a, eu,   o son indistinct et sourd, analogue à celui d'**e** dans "me," "de," "que." Ce son est souvent indiqué par une apostrophe dans la prononciation figurée de certaines finales anglaises: **lesson**, less -'n.

o   son très bref, entre **eu** dans "fleur" et **a** dans "lac." Par exemple: **but**, botte (son presque comme "batte").

oa   désigne un son qu'on reproduira avec une exactitude suffisante en prononçant à peu près, et d'une seule émission de voix, comme **au** dans "laure," "Fauré."

r   à la fin d'un mot ou d'une syllabe, ne se fait sentir que très faiblement, à moins qu'il ne soit immédiatement suivi d'une voyelle.

h   cette lettre s'aspire toujours distinctement.

th   (dur=*ts*, et doux=*dz*). Prononcer *is* et *dz* en mettant le bout de la langue entre les dents comme lorsqu'on zézaie.

L'**e** muet à la fin d'une syllabe ne doit jamais se prononcer.

ACCENT TONIQUE

En anglais, l'accentuation d'une syllabe est donnée dans la prononciation figurée par le symbole ´ placé après la syllabe accentuée.

ABBREVIATIONS

a	adjective	poss	possessive
abbr	abbreviation	pp	past participle
adv	adverb	prep	preposition
art	article	pres part	present participle
auto	car	pron	pronoun
Brit	British	psych	psychology
chem	chemistry	refl	reflexive
com	commercial	s	singular
comput	computing	TM	trademark
conj	conjunction	v	verb
eccl	ecclesiastical	vulg	vulgar
f	feminine noun		
fam	familiar		
fin	financial		
fig	figurative sense		
geog	geographical		
hair	hairdressing		
inf	infinitive		
interj	interjection		
interrog	interrogative		
jur	legal		
m	masculine noun		
mech	mechanical		
med	medical		
mil	military		
mus	musical		
n	noun		
naut	nautical		
num	numeral		
pers	persons		
phr	phrase		
pl	plural		
pop	popular		

ABRÉVIATIONS

abbr	abréviation	poss	possessif
adj	adjectif	pp	participe passé
adv	adverbe	prep	préposition
art	article	pres part	participe présent
auto	auto	pron	pronom
Brit	britanique	psych	psychologie
chem	chimie	refl	réflechi
com	commercial	s	singulier
comput	informatique	v	verbe
conj	conjonction	vulg	vulgaire
eccl	ecclésiastique	TM	marque déposée
f	nom féminin		
fam	familier		
fig	figuré		
fin	financier		
geog	géographique		
hair	coiffure		
inf	infinitif		
interj	interjection		
interrog	interrogatif		
jur	juridique		
m	nom masculin		
mech	mécanique		
med	médical		
mil	militaire		
mus	musical		
n	nom		
naut	nautique		
num	chiffre		
pers	personnes		
phr	expression		
pl	pluriel		
pop	populaire		

FRENCH · ENGLISH
FRANÇAIS · ANGLAIS

For an explanation
of the imitated
pronunciation please
read page 4.

A

à, ăh, *prep* to; at; in; within; on; by; for; from.

a, ăh, *v* has.

abaissement, ăh-bayss-mah*ng, m* lowering; fall; diminution; disgrace.

abaisser, ăh-bayss-eh, *v* to lower; to pull down. **s'–,** to humble oneself; to stoop.

abandon, ăh-bah*ng*-dong, *m* abandonment; desertion; ease. **àl'–,** neglected state.

abandonné, e, ăh-bah*ng*-donn-eh, *p p* & *a* deserted; neglected; disused.

abandonner, ăh-bah*ng*-donn-eh, *v* to abandon; to desert; to give up; to let go. **s'–,** to indulge (à, in); to let oneself go.

abasourdir, ăh-băh-zoohr-deer, *v* to stun.

abatage, abattage, ăh-băh-tăhsh, *m* cutting down; slaughter.

abâtardir, ăh-bah-tăhr-deer, *v* to debase. **s'–,** to degenerate.

abat-jour, ăh-băh-shoohr, *m* reflector; lampshade.

abattement, ăh-băht-mah*ng, m* prostration.

abattis, ăh-băh-te, *m* felling; giblets.

abattoir, ăh-băh-to'ăhr, *m* slaughterhouse.

abattre, ăh-băh-tr, *v* to bring down; to cut down. **s'–,** to fall.

abattu, e, ăh-băh-tE, *pp* & *a* brought down; depressed.

abbaye, ăh-bay-yee, *f* abbey.

abbé, ăh-beh, *m* abbot; priest.

abbesse, ăh-bess, *f* abbess.

abcès, ăhb-say, *m* abscess.

abdiquer, ăhb-de-keh, *v* to abdicate.

abdomen, ăhb-doh-menn, *m* abdomen.

abeille, ăh-bay'e, *f* bee.

abhorrer, ăh-bor-eh, *v* to abhor; to loathe.

abîme, ăh-beem, *m* abyss.

abîmer, ăh-bee-meh, *v* to spoil; to damage.

abject, e, ăhb-sheckt, *a* base; mean.

abjection, ăhb-sheck-se-ong, *f* vileness.

abjurer, ăhb-shE-reh, *v* to renounce.

ablution, ăhb-lE-se-ong, *f* washing.

abnégation, ăhb-neh-găh-se-ong, *f* self-denial.

aboi, ăh-boăh, *m*
aboiement, ăh-boăh-mah*ng, m* bark; barking.

abois, ăh-boăh, *mpl* **aux abois,** oh-z'–, at bay; desperate situation.

abolir, ăh-bol-eer, *v* to abolish.

abominable,* ăh-bomm-e-năh-bl, *a* abominable.

abomination, ăh-bomm-e-năh-se-ong, *f* abomination.

A
B
C
D
E
F
G
H
I
J
K
L
M
N
O
P
Q
R
S
T
U
V
W
X
Y
Z

abondamment, ăh-bong-dăh-mahng, *adv* plentifully.

abondant, e, ăh-bong-dahng, *a* abundant.

abonder, ăh-bong-deh, *v* to abound (**en, in,** with).

abonné, e, ăh-bonn-eh, *mf* subscriber.

abonnement, ăh-bonn-mahng, *m* subscription. **carte d'–,** kăhrt d–, season ticket.

abonner (s'–), săh-bonn-eh, *v* to subscribe.

abord, ăh-bor, *m* access. **d'–,** at first.

aborder, ăh-bor-deh, *v* to land; to approach; to accost; to tackle; to collide with.

aborti-f, ve, ăh-bor-tiff, *a* abortive.

aboucher, ăh-boo-sheh, *v* to bring together. **s'–,** to confer.

aboutir, ăh-boo-teer, *v* to end; to abut; to lead.

aboutissant, ăh-boo-tiss-ahng, *m* abuttal. **tenants et –s,** ter-nahng z'eh–, ins and outs.

aboyer, ăh-bo'ăh-yeh, *v* to bark.

abrégé, ăh-breh-sheh, *m* summary; synopsis.

abréger, ăh-breh-sheh, *v* to shorten.

abreuver, ăh-brer-veh, *v* to water animals; (fig.) to soak. **s'–,** to drink plentifully.

abreuvoir, ăh-brer-vo'ăhr, *m* watering place.

abréviation, ăh-breh-ve-ah-se-ong, *f* abbreviation; shortening.

abri, ăh-bre, *m* shelter.

abricot, ăh-bre-ko, *m* apricot.

abriter, ăh-bre-teh, *v* to shelter.

abroger, ăh-bro-sheh, *v* to repeal.

abrupt, e,* ăh-brEpt, *a* abrupt; steep; rugged.

abrutir, ăh-brE-teer, *v* to stupefy. **s'–,** to make a beast of oneself.

absent, e, ăhb-sahng, *a* absent.

absenter(s'), săhb-sahng-teh, *v* to absent oneself

abside, ăhb-seed, *f* apse.

absinthe, ăhb-sangt, *f* wormwood; absinth.

absolument, ăhb-sol-E-mahng, *adv* absolutely.

absolution, ăhb-sol-E-se-ong, *f* absolution; pardon.

absorber, ăhb-sor-beh, *v* to absorb; to engross.

absorption, ăhb-sorp-se-ong, *f* absorption.

absoudre, ăhb-soo-dr, *v* to absolve.

abstenir(s'), săbhs-ter-neer, *v* to abstain.

abstinence, ăhbs-te-nahngss, *f* abstinence; fasting.

abstraire, ăhbs-trair, *v* to abstract.

abstrait, e,* ăhbs-tray, *a* abstract; abstruce; obscure.

absurde,* ăhbss-EErd, *a* absurd; silly.

absurdité, ăhbss-EEr-de-teh, *f* absurdity; nonsense.

abus, ăh-bE, *m* abuse.

abuser, ăh-bE-zeh, *v* to deceive; to abuse.

abusi-f, ve,* ăh-bE-ziff, *a* improper (use of word).

académie, ăh-kăh-deh-mee, *f* academy.

acajou, ăh-kăh-shoo, *m* mahogany.

acariâtre, ăh-kăh-re-ah-tr, *a* sour-tempered.

accablant, e, ăh-kăh-blahng, *a* overwhelming; oppressive; unbearable.

accablement, ăh-kăh-bler-mahng, *m* depression; dejection.

accabler, ăh-kăh-bleh, *v* to overwhelm; to crush; to overcome (**de,** with).

accaparer, ăh-kăh-păh-reh, v to monopolize; to forestall.

accéder, ăhck-seh-deh, v to accede; to comply (à, with).

accélérateur, ăhck-seh-leh-răh-ter, m accelerator.

accélérer, ăhck-seh-leh-reh, v to hasten.

accent, ăhck-sahng, m accent; tone; stress.

accentuer, ăhck-sahng-tE-eh, v to accentuate; to emphasize.

acceptation, ăhck-sehp-tăh-se-ong, f acceptance.

accepter, ăhck-sehp-teh, v to accept.

acception, ăhck-sehp-se-ong, f regard; meaning (of word).

accès, ăhck-say, m access; fit.

accessoire, ăhck-sess-o'ăhr a secondary; of minor interest.

accident, ăhck-se-dahng, m accident; mishap.

accidenté, e, ăhck-se-dahng-teh, a eventful; checkered; victim (of accident).

accise, ăhck-seez, f excise.

acclamer, ăh-klăh-meh, v to acclaim.

acclimater, ăh-kle-măh-teh, v to acclimatize.

accolade, ăh-kol-ăhd, f embrace.

accommodant, e, ăh-komm-odd-ahng, a easy to deal with.

accommodement, ăh-komm-odd-mahng, m settlement.

accommoder, ăh-komm-od-eh, v to suit; to do up (food); s' –à, to adapt oneself to; s' –de, to put up with.

accompagnement, ăh-kong-păhn'yer-mahng, m attendance; accessory; accompaniment.

accompagner, ăh-kong-păhn'yeh, v to accompany.

accompli, e, ăh-kong-ple, pp & a accomplished; thorough.

accomplissement, ăh-kong-pliss-mahng, m completion; fulfillment.

accord, ăh-kor, m agreement; consent; tuning; d'–, agreed; tomber d' –, tong-beh d–, to come to an agreement; mettre d' –, met-tr-d–, to conciliate.

accordage, ăh-kor-dăhsh, m tuning.

accorder, ăh-kor-deh, v to accord; to grant; to tune; to reconcile; s'–,to agree.

accoster, ăh-koss-teh, v to accost (a person); to come alongside.

accoter, ăh-kot-eh, v to stay; s' –,to lean.

accoucher, ăh-koo-sheh, v to give birth; to deliver a child.

accoucheur, ăh-koo-sher, m obstetrician.

accoucheuse, ăh-koo-sher-z, f midwife.

accouder (s'), săh-koo-deh, v to lean on one's elbow.

accoupler, ăh-koo-pleh, v to couple; to yoke; to pair.

accourir, ăh-koo-reer, v to run up; to hasten.

accoutrement, ăh-koo-trer-mahng, m garb.

accoutrer, ăh-koo-treh, v to rig out.

accoutumer, ăh-koo-tE-meh, v to accustom; s'– à, to get used to.

accréditer, ăh-kreh-de-teh, v to accredit; to credit.

accroc, ăh-kro, m tear; hitch.

accrocher, ăh-kro-sheh, v to hook on; to catch; s'–,to cling.

accroire, ăh-kro'ăhr, v

A
B
C
D
E
F
G
H
I
J
K
L
M
N
O
P
Q
R
S
T
U
V
W
X
Y
Z

(used infinitive only and with **faire**), to make believe; **en faire –,** ahng fayr –, to impose (à, upon).

accroissement, ăh-kro'ahss-mahng, *m* increase.

accroître, ăh-kro'ăh-tr, *v* to increase; **s'–,** to grow.

accroupir, (s'), săh-kroo-peer, *v* to squat.

accru, e, ăh-krE, *pp* increased.

accueil, ăh-ker'e, *m* reception; welcome.

accueillir, ăh-ker-yeer, *v* to receive; to welcome.

accumulateur, ăh-kE-mE-lăh-ter, *m* accumulator; storage battery.

accumuler, ăh-kE-mE-leh, *v* to accumulate; to heap.

accusation, ăh-kE-zăh-se-ong, *f* accusation; charge.

accusé, e, ăh-kE-zeh, *mf* accused person; **–de réception,** – der reh-sep-se-ong, acknowledgment.

accuser, ăh-kE-zeh, *v* to accuse; to indict.

acerbe, ăh-sairb, *a* sour; harsh.

acéré, e, ăh-seh-reh, *a* sharp; steeled.

achalandé, e, ăh-shăh-lahng-deh, *a* well-stocked.

acharnement, ăh-shăhr-ner-mahng, *m* relentlessness; desperate eagerness.

acharner (s'), săh-shăhr-neh, *v* to be relentless; to persist in something.

achat, ăh-shăh, *m* purchase.

acheminement, ăsh-meen-mahng, *m* step.

acheminer, ăhsh-me-neh, *v* to dispatch; to convey; to route. **s'–,** to set out, to proceed.

acheter, ăhsh-teh, *v* to buy; **s'–,** to be bought; to be purchased.

acheteur, ăhsh-ter, *m* purchaser; buyer.

achever, ăhsh-veh, *v* to finish.

achoppement, ăh-shop-mahng, *m* stumbling; **pierre d'–,** pe'air d–, stumbling- block.

acide, ăh-seed, *m* acid; *a* sour; sharp.

acier, ăh-se-eh, *m* steel.

aciérie, ăh-se-eh-ree, *f* steelworks.

acné, ăhck-neh, *f* acne.

acolyte, ăh-kol-eet, *m* acolyte; accomplice.

acompte, ăh-kongt, *m* installment; deposit.

à-côtés, ăh-koht-eh *mpl* perk.

acoustique, ăh-kooss-tick, *f* acoustics; *a* acoustic.

acquérir, ăh-keh-reer, *v* to acquire.

acquiescer, ăh-ke-ess-eh, *v* to acquiesce (à, in).

acquis, e, ăh-ke, *pp* acquired; *m* knowledge; experience.

acquisition, ăh-ke-ze-se-ong, *f* acquisition; purchase.

acquit, ăh-ke, *m* receipt; **– à caution,** – t'ah koh-se-ong, permit (customs).

acquittement, ăh-kit-mahng, *m* payment; acquittal; discharge.

acquitter, ăh-ke-teh, *v* to clear; to pay; to receipt; to acquit (an accused person); **s' –de,** to carry out.

âcre, ahkr, *a* acrid; sour.

âcreté, ah-krer-teh, *f* acridity; pungency.

acrimonie, ăh-kre-monn-ee, *f* acrimony.

acrobate, ăh-kro-baht, *mf* acrobat.

acrobatie, ăh-krob-ăh-see, *f* acrobatics.

acte, ăhckt, *m* act; action; deed; certificate; **faire – de,** fair – de, to show proof of.

ac-teur, -trice, ăhck-ter, *mf* actor; actress.

actif, ăhck-tiff, *m* assets.

acti-f, ve, * ăhck-tiff, *a* active.

action, ăhck-se-ong, *f* act; deed; share; *pl* stock.

actionnaire, ăhck-se-onn-air, *mf* shareholder.

actionner, ăhck-se-onn-eh, *v* to set in motion; to sue.

activer, ăhck-te-veh, *v* to urge on; to activate.

activité, ăhck-te-ve-teh, *f* activity.

actualité, ăhck-tE-ăh-lee-teh, *f* reality; event; **les–s,** leh z–, the news; newsreel.

actuel, le, * ăhck-tE-ell, *a* present; real.

acuité, ăh-kE-e-teh, *f* acuteness.

adage, ăh-dăhsh, *m* saying; adage.

adapter, ăh-dăhp-teh, *v* to adapt; to fit; to apply; **s'–,** to be suitable (**à,** for).

addition, ăh-de-se-ong, *f* addition; bill (restaurant).

additionnel, le, ăh-de-se-onn-ell, *a* additional.

adepte, ăh-dept, *a* adept.

adhérer, ăh-deh-reh, *v* to

adhere; to join (party).

adhésion, ăh-deh-se-ong, *f* adhesion; joining (of party).

adieu, ăh-de-er, *m* farewell; *adv* good-bye; farewell.

adjacent, ăhd-shăh-sahng, *a* adjacent; contiguous.

adjoindre, ăhd-sho'ang-dr, *v* to adjoin; **s'–,** to take as an associate; to join.

adjoint, ăhd-sho'ang, *m* assistant; deputy mayor.

adjudant, ăhd-shE-dahng, *m* adjutant.

adjudicataire, ăhd-shE-de-kăh-tair, *m* highest bidder.

adjugé! ăhd-shE-sheh, *pp* gone! (in auctions).

adjuger, ăhd-shE-sheh, *v* to award; to knock down (at auctions); **s'–,** to appropriate to one's use.

adjurer, ăhd-shE-reh, *v* to adjure; to beseech.

admettre, ăhd-met-tr, *v* to admit; to allow.

administrateur, ăhd-me-niss-trăh-ter, *m* administrator; manager; director; trustee.

administré, e, ăhd-me-niss-treh, *pp & n* administered; person under one's jurisdiction.

administrer, ăhd-me-niss-treh, *v* to administrate; to administer.

admira-teur, -trice, ăhd-me-răh-ter, *mf* admirer.

admirer, ăhd-me-reh, *v* to admire.

admission, ăhd-miss-e-ong, *f* admission; admittance.

admonester, ăhd-monn-ess-teh, *v* to reprimand.

admonition, ăhd-monn-e-se-ong, *f* warning.

adolescent, e, ăh-doll-ess-sahng, *mf* youth, lad; girl.

adonner (s'), săh-donn-eh, *v* to addict oneself to; to devote oneself to.

adopter, ăh-dop-teh, *v* to adopt.

adorable, ăh-do-răh-bl, *a* adorable; charming.

adora-teur, -trice, ăh-dor-ăh-ter, *mf* worshipper.

adorer, ăh-do-reh, *v* to adore; to be passionately fond of.

adosser, ăh-dohss-eh, *v* to lean (against).

adoucir, ăh-doo-seer, *v* to soften; **s'–,** to grow softer.

adoucissement, ăh-doo-siss-mahng, *m* softening; alleviation.

adresse, ăh-dress, *f*

a
b
c
d
e
f
g
h
i
j
k
l
m
n
o
p
q
r
s
t
u
v
w
x
y
z

address; skill.

adresser, ăh-dress-eh, *v* to
address; to direct; **s'–,**to
apply; to be directed.

adroit, e,* ăh-dro'ăh, *a*
handy; skillful; artful.

aduler, ăh-dE-leh, *v* to
fawn upon, to adulate.

adulte, ăh-dEElt, *a* adult;
grown-up.

adultère, ăh-dEEl-tair, *a*
and *n* adulterous;
adulterer; adultery.

advenir, ăhd-ver-neer,
impers v to happen; to
befall.

adversaire, ăhd-vair-sair,
m opponent; foe.

adverse, ăhd-vairss, *a*
adverse.

adversité, ăhd-vair-se-teh,
f misfortune; adversity.

aéré, ăh-eh-reh, *a* aired;
airy; aerated.

aérodrome, ăh-eh-ro-
drohm, *m* airfield;
airport.

aérogare, ăh-eh-ro-gahr, *f*
air terminal.

aéroport, ăh-eh-ro-por, *m*
airport.

affable,* ăh-făh-bl, *a*
affable.

affaiblir, ăh-fay-bleer, *v* to
weaken.

affaire, ăh-fair, *f* affair;
business; matter; thing;
action; work; scrape;

avoir –à, ăh-vo'ăhr –
ăh, *v* to have to do with;
faire des –s, fair day z'–,
to do business; **faire
l'–de,** fair l– der, to suit;
homme d'–s, omm d–,
businessman; **se tirer
d'–,**ser tereh d–, to get
out of a scrape; **j'en fais
mon –,**shahng fay monn
–, I take it upon myself.

affairé, e, ăh-fay-reh, *a*
busy.

affaissé, e, ăh-fess-eh, *pp*
sunk down; depressed.

affaisser (s'), săh-fess-eh,
v to sink; to flag.

affamé, e, ăh-făh-meh, *pp*
& *a* starved; starving.

affamer, ăh-făh-meh, *v* to
starve.

affectation, ăh-feck-tăh-
se-ong, *f* affectation;
simulation; assignment.

affecté, e, ăh-feck-teh, *a*
affected, conceited.

affecter, ăh-feck-teh, *v* to
feign; to set apart; to
allocate; **s'–,**to be
moved; affected.

affection, ăh-feck-se-ong, *f*
affection; fondness;
disease.

affectionner, ăh-feck-se-
onn-eh, *v* to be fond of.

afférent, e, ăh-feh-rahng,
a pertaining to.

affermer, ăh-fair-meh, *v*

to rent; to lease.

affermir, ăh-fair-meer, *v*
to strenghten.

afféterie, ăh-feh-tree, *f*
affectation.

affichage, ăh-fe-shăhsh, *m*
bill-posting.

affiche, ăh-feesh, *f*
placard; poster.

afficher, ăh-fe-sheh, *v* to
stick up; to make a show
of; to expose.

affiler, ăh-fe-leh, *v* to
sharpen.

affilié, e, ăh-fe-le-eh, *a*
affiliated.

affiner, ăh-fe-neh, *v* to
refine.

affirmer, ăh-feer-meh, *v*
to assert; to affirm.

affleurer, ăh-fler-reh, *v* to
level; to crop out.

affliger, ăh-fle-sheh, *v* to
afflict; to grieve.

affluent, ăh-flE-ahng, *m*
tributary; *a* affluent.

affluer, ăh-flE-eh, *v* to
flow; to run; to abound.

affolé, e, ăh-foll-eh, *a*
distracted; panic-
stricken; spinning
(compass).

affoler, ăh-foll-eh, *v* to
drive mad; to panic.

affranchi, e, ăh-frahng-
she, *pp* & *a* freed;
prepaid.

affranchir, ăh-frahngsheer, *v* to free; to prepay; to stamp (letter).

affranchissement, ăh-frahng-shiss-mahng, *m* emancipation; prepayment; postage.

affréter, ăh-freh-teh, *v* to charter; to freight.

affreu-x, se,* ah-frer, *a* horrible; dreadful; hideous.

affriander, ăh-free-ahng-deh, *v* to attract; to entice.

affront, ăh-frong, *m* insult; disgrace.

affronter, ăh-frong-teh, *v* to confront; to dare; to face.

affubler, ăh-fE-bleh, *v* to muffle up; **s'–,** to rig oneself out.

affût, ăh-fE, *m* lying in wait (for game); carriage (gun); **être à l'–,** ay-tr ăh l–, to be on the watch (**de,** for).

affûter, ăh-fE-teh, *v* to sharpen.

afin, ăh-fang, *conj* **–de,** in order to; **–que,** in order that.

agacement, ăh-găhss-mahng, *m* annoyance.

agacer, ăh-găh-seh, *v* to set on edge; to irritate; to provoke; to tease.

agacerie, ăh-găhss-ree, *f* provocation; *pl* allurement.

âge, ahsh, *m* age; old age; period; generation.

âgé, e, ah-sheh, *a* aged; old.

agence, ăh-shahngss, *f* agency.

agencement, ăh-shahngss-mahng, *m* arrangement (of house); *pl* fittings; fixtures.

agenda, ăh-shang-dăh, *m* memorandum book; diary.

agenouiller (s'), săhsh-noo'e-yeh, *v* to kneel.

agent, ăh-shahng, *m* agent; middleman; policeman.

agent de voyages, ăh-shahng-der-vo'ăh-yăhsh *m* travel agent.

agglomérer (s'), săh-glomm-eh-reh, *v* to agglomerate.

aggravation, ăh-grăh-văh-se-ong, *f* aggravation; worsening.

aggraver, ăh-grăh-veh, *v* to aggravate; to make worse; to increase; **s'–,** to become worse.

agile,* ăh-shill, *a* nimble; quick.

agir, ăh-sheer, *v* to act; to do; to work; **de quoi**

s'agit-il? der kwăh săh-she-till? what is the matter? **il s'agit de ...,** ill săh-she der ... the matter, thing, or question is (about, to) ...

agiter, ăh-she-teh, *v* to agitate; to shake; to toss; to wave; **s'–,** to exert oneself; to fret; to swell; to get disturbed.

agneau, ăhn-yoh, *m* lamb.

agonie, ăh-gonn-ee, *f* death struggle; anguish; great pain. **à l'–,** ăh-l–, dying.

agonisant, ăh-gonn-e-zahng, *a* dying.

agrafe, ăh-grăhf, *f* hook; clasp; staple.

agrafeuse, ăh-grăh-ferz, *f* stapler.

agraire, ăh-grair, *a* agrarian.

agrandir, ăh-grahng-deer, *v* to enlarge; **s'–,** to become larger; to expand.

agrandissement, ăh-grahng-diss-mahng, *m* enlargement.

agréable,* ăh-greh-ăh-bl, *a* agreeable; pleasing; acceptable.

agréé, ăh-greh-eh, *m* solicitor; attorney.

agrégation, ăh-greh-găh-se-ong, *f* high level

A
B
C
D
E
F
G
H
I
J
K
L
M
N
O
P
Q
R
S
T
U
V
W
X
Y
Z

competitive exam.

agrégé, ăh-greh-**sheh,** *m*
holder of the
"agrégation."

agrément, ăh-greh-mah*ng*,
m consent; favor;
pleasure; *pl* charms.

agrès, ăh-gray, *m pl*
rigging; tackle.

agresseur, ăh-grayss-**er,** *m*
aggressor.

agreste, ăh-gresst, *a* rustic.

agricole, ăh-gre-kol, *a*
agricultural.

agriculteur, ăh-gree-kEEl-
ter, *m* agriculturist;
farmer.

agripper, ăh-gre-peh, *v* to
clutch.

aguerrir, ăh-ghay-reer, *v*
to harden; to accustom;
s'–, to become inured to
war^. *a* hardened;
accustomed.

aguets, ăh-ghay, *mpl* **aux
–,** oh z'–, on the watch.

ahurir, ăh-E-reer, *v* to
astound; to confuse.

ahurissement, ăh-E-riss-
mah*ng*, *m* flurry;
bewilderment.

aide, ayd, *m* helper;
assistant.

aide, ayd, *f* help;
assistance; **à l'–!** ăh l–!
help!

aider, ay-deh, *v* to assist;
to help.

aïe, ăh-e, *int* oh dear! oh!
(pain).

aïeul, ăh-yerl, *m*
grandfather; *f* **aïeule,**
ăh-yerl, grandmother.

aïeux, ăh-yer, *mpl*
ancestors; forefathers.

aigle, ay-gl, *m* eagle;
lectern; *f* standard.

aiglon, ay-glo*ng*, *m* eaglet.

aigre,* ay-gr, *a* sour; acid;
tart.

aigrefin, ay-grer-fa*ng*, *m*
crook.

aigrelet, te, ay-grer-lay, *a*
sourish.

aigrette, ay-grett, *f* egret;
tuft.

aigreur, ay-grer, *f*
sourness; acrimony; ill-
feeling; spite.

aigrir, ay-greer, *v* to sour;
to irritate; to envenom;
s'–, to become sour; to
become embittered.

aigu, ë, ay-ghE, *a* sharp;
pointed; acute; shrill.

aiguille, ay-gwee-yer, *f*
needle; hand (of clock,
watch); index; spire;
switch; point (rail).

aiguillette, ay-gwee-yet, *f*
tag covering lace ends;
slice of flesh.

aiguilleur, ay-gwee-yer, *m*
point man.

aiguillon, ay-gwee-yo*ng*, *m*
goad; sting; prickle;

thorn; spur.

aiguillonner, ay-gwee-
yonn-eh, *v* to goad; to
spur on.

aiguiser, ay-gwee-zeh, *v* to
whet; to sharpen.

ail, ăh'e, *m* garlic.

aile, ayl, *f* wing; sail; aisle;
flank (of army or fleet).

ailé, e, ay-leh, *a* winged.

aileron, ayl-ro*ng*, *m*
pinion; small wing; fin.

ailette, ay-lehtt, *f* winglet.

ailleurs, ăh'e-yer, *adv*
elsewhere; **d'–,**
moreover.

aimable,* ay-măh-bl, *a*
amiable; lovable; kind;
pleasing.

aimant, ay-mah*ng*, *m*
loadstone; magnet.

aimant, e, ay-mah*ng*, *a*
loving; affectionate.

aimanter, ay-mah*ng*-teh, *v*
to magnetize.

aimer, ay-meh, *v* to love;
to like; to be fond of; to
enjoy; **s'–,** to love each
other.

aine, ayn, *f* groin.

aîné, e, ay-neh, *a & n*
elder; eldest;

aînesse, ayness, *f*
primogeniture; **droit
d'–,** dro'ăh d–,
birthright.

ainsi, ang-se, *adv & conj*
so; thus; therefore,

–que, – ker, as well as; **–de suite,** – der sweet, so on; **–soit-il,** – so'ăh-till, amen!

air, air *m* air; wind; look; appearance; likeness; tune; **avoir l'air de,** ăh-vo'ăhr lair der, to look like; **en l'–,** ahng l–, in the air; upward; at random.

airain, ay-rang, *m* brass; **d'–,** d–, pitiless; hard.

aire, air, *f* area; threshing-floor; zone; aerie.

ais, ay, *m* plank; board.

aisance, ay-zahngss, *f* ease; comfort; competency; **être dans l'–,** ay-tr dahng l–, to be well off.

aise, ayz, *f* ease; comfort; enjoyment; **à l'–,** ăh l–, comfortable.

aise, ayz, *a* glad; pleased (**de,** of, with).

aisé, e,* ay-zeh, *a* easy; well-off.

aisselle, ayss-ell, *f* armpit.

ajonc, ăh-**sh**ong, *m* gorse.

ajourner, ăh-**sh**oohr-neh, *v* to postpone; to put off; to defer; to summon; **s'–,** to adjourn.

ajouter, ăh-**sh**oo-teh, *v* to add; **s'–,** to be added.

ajuster, ăh-**sh**EEs-teh, *v* to adjust; to fit; to arrange; to reconcile; to aim at;

s'–, to be adjusted; adapted; to adapt oneself; to fit.

alanguir, ăh-lahng-gheer, *v* to make languid; to enfeeble; to weaken.

alarme, ăh-lăhrm, *f* alarm.

alarmer, ăh-lăhr-meh, *v* to alarm; **s'–,** to take fright.

albâtre, ăhl-bah-tr, *m* alabaster; snowy whiteness.

albumine, ăhl-bE-meen, *f* albumen.

alcali, ăhl-kăh-le, *m* alkali.

alcool, ăhl-kohl, *m* alcohol; spirits; *fam* booze.

alcoolisme, ăhl-koh-lissm, *m* alcoholism.

alcôve, ăhl-kohv, *f* alcove; recess.

alcyon, ăhl-se-ong, *m* kingfisher; halcyon.

aléa, ăh-leh-ăh, *m* risk; chance.

aléatoire, ăh-leh-ăh-to'ăhr, *a* risky; hazardous.

alêne, ăh-laynn, *f* awl.

alentour, ăh-lahng-toohr, *adv* around; about.

alentours, ăh-lahng-toohr, *mpl* neighborhood; surroundings; outskirts.

alerte, ăh-layrt, *f* alarm; alert.

alerte, ăh-layrt, *a* alert; sharp; quick; nimble.

algue, ăhl-gh, *f* alga; seaweed.

aliénable, ăh-le-eh-năh-bl, *a* transferable.

aliénation, ăh-le-eh-năh-se-ong, *f* transfer; estrangement; madness.

aliéné, e, ăh-le-eh-neh, *n* & *a* lunatic; mad(man).

aliéner, ăh-le-eh-neh, *v* to transfer; to alienate; to estrange.

aligner, ăh-leen-yeh, *v* to set in a line; **s'–,** to fall in.

aliment, ăh-le-mahng, *m* food.

alimentaire, ăh-le-mahng-tair, *a* dietary; nutritious; alimentary.

alinéa, ăh-le-neh-ăh, *m* paragraph.

alité, e, ăh-le-teh, *pp* & *a* laid up; bedridden.

aliter, ăh-le-teh, *v* to confine to bed; **s'–,** to take to one's bed.

allaiter, ăh-lay-teh, *v* to suckle; to nurse.

allant, ăh-lahng, *pres part* & *a* going; active; stirring.

allécher, ăh-leh-sheh, *v* to allure; to entice.

allée, ăh-leh, *f* going; alley; passage; lane;

B
C
D
E
F
G
H
I
J
K
L
M
N
O
P
Q
R
S
T
U
V
W
X
Y
Z

path; **–s et venues,** –z'eh ver-nE, going and coming; running about.

allège, ăh-laysh, *f* lighter (nav.); tender; sill (window).

alléger, ăh-leh-**sheh,** *v* to lighten; to unload; to ease.

allègre, * ăhl-lay-gr, *a* lively; cheerful.

allégresse, ăhl-leh-gress, *f* cheerfulness; glee.

alléguer, ăhl-leh-gheh, *v* to allege.

allemand, e, ăhl-mahng, *a* & *n* German.

aller, ăh-leh, *v* to go; to get on; to become; to fit; to suit; **comment allez-vous?** komm-ahng t'ăh-leh voo? how are you?; **cet habit vous va bien,** set ăh-be voo văh b'ang, this clothing suits you (or fits you) well; **s'en –,** sahng n'–, to go away.

aller, ăh-leh, *m* **billet d'–et retour,** bee-yay d–eh rer-toor, return ticket.

allergie, ăh-lair-shee, *f* allergy.

allergique, ăh-lair-shick, *a* allergic.

alliage, ăh-le-ăhsh, *m* alloy.

alliance, ăh-le-ahngss, *f* alliance; match; wedding ring.

allier, ăh-le-eh, *v* to ally; to match; to blend; to mix; to alloy; **s'– to combine;** to unite (**à,** with); to intermarry; to harmonize with.

allô!, ăh-loh *int* hello (on phone).

allocation, ăh-lock-ăh-se-ong, *f* allowance; grant.

allocution, ăh-lock-E-se-ong, *f* short speech.

allonge, ăh-longsh, *f* (table); extension.

allonger, ăh-long-sheh, *v* to lengthen; to prolong; **s'–,** to grow longer; to lie down.

allouer, ăh-loo-eh, *v* to allow; to grant.

allumer, ăh-lE-meh, *v* to light; to kindle; **s'–,** to light up; to catch fire.

allumette, ăh-lE-mett, *f* match.

allumeur, ăh-lE-mer, *m* igniter; lamplighter.

allure, ăh-lEEr, *f* gait; pace; manner; aspect.

allusion, ăhl-lE-ze-ong, *f* allusion; **faire –à,** fayr – ăh, to allude to.

aloi, ăh-lo'ăh, *m* **de bon –** respectable; worthy; **de mauvais –** unsavoury; unworthy.

alors, ăh-lor, *adv* then; at that time; in that case.

alouette, ăh-loo-ett, *f* lark.

alourdir, ăh-loor-deer, *v* to render heavy; **s' –,** to become heavy.

aloyau, ăh-lo'ăh-e-oh, *m* sirloin.

alpestre, ăhl-pess-tr, *a* Alpine.

alpinisme, ăhl-pe-nism *m* mountaineering.

altérable, ăhl-teh-răh-bl, *a* liable to change.

altérant, e, ăhl-teh-rahng, *a* alterative; producing thirst.

altération, ăhl-teh-răh-se-ong, *f* change; deterioration; misrepresentation; falsification; faltering.

altercation, ăhl-tayr-se-ong, *f* wrangling.

altéré, e, ăhl-teh-reh, *a* altered.

altérer, ăhl-teh-reh, *v* to alter; to impair; to debase; to misrepresent; to falsify; **s'–,** to become worse.

alternati-f, -ive, * ăhl-tair-năh-tiff, *a* alternative; alternating; **-ive,** *nf* alternative.

alterner, ăhl-ter-neh, *v* to alternate; to take turns.

altesse, ăhl-tess, *f*

highness (title).

altitude, ăhl-tee-tEEd, *f* altitude.

alto, ăhl-to, *m* tenor violin.

alun, ăh-lung, *m* alum.

alvéole, ăl-veh-ol, *f* cell; socket.

amabilité, ăh-măh-be-le-teh, *f* pleasantness; kindness.

amadouer, ăh-măh-doo-eh, *v* to coax.

amaigrir, ăh-may-greer, *v* to make thin; to emaciate.

amaigrissant, e, ăh-may-gree-ssahng-té, *a* regime; cure; diet; **amaigrissement** *m* loss of weight.

amande, ăh-mahngd, *f* almond.

amandier, ăh-mahng-de-eh, *m* almond tree.

amant, e, ăh-mahng, *mf* lover; suitor; sweetheart.

amarrer, ăh-măh-reh, *v* to moor; to fasten; to lash.

amas, ăh-mah, *m* heap; pile; mass.

amasser, ăh-măhss-eh, *v* to amass; to heap up; **s'–,** to gather.

ama-teur, ăh-mahter, *a mf* amateur; lover; dilettante.

amazone, ăh-măh-zohn, *f* amazon; female rider; riding-habit; *m* the Amazon river.

ambassade, ăhng-băhss-ăhd, *f* embassy.

ambassa-deur, -drice, ahng-băhss-ăh-der, *mf* ambassador; ambassadress.

ambiance, ahng-be-ahngss, *f* atmosphere (of surroundings, of environment, etc.).

ambiant, e, ahng-be-ahng, *a* surrounding; ambient.

ambigu, ë, ahng-be-ghE, *a* ambiguous; obscure.

ambitieu-x, se, * ahng-be-se-er, *a* ambitious; pretentious; *n* ambitious person.

ambition, ahng-be-se-ong, *f* ambition.

ambre, ahng-br, *m* amber.

ambulance, ahng-bE-lahngss, *f* ambulance.

ambulancier, ahng-bE-lahngss-e-eh, *m* ambulance man; orderly.

ambulant, e, ahng-bE-lahng, *a* itinerant; strolling; traveling (circus, etc.).

âme, ahmm, *f* soul; mind; spirit; life; feeling; ghost; heart; essence; core; creature; bore (of gun); valve.

améliorer, ăh-meh-le-o-reh, *v* to improve; to make better; **s'–,** to get better.

aménagement, ăh-meh-năhsh, *m* fitting out; disposition; *pl* fittings; accommodation.

aménager, ăh-meh-năh-sheh, *v* to arrange.

amende, ăh-mahngd, *f* fine; penalty; costs; **–honorable,** –onn-or-ăh-bl, apology.

amendement, ăh-mahngd-mahng, *m* amendment; improvement.

amender, ăh-mahng-deh, *v* to improve.

amener, ăhm-neh, *v* to bring; to introduce; to bring in; on or about; **mandat d'–,** mahng-dăh d–, warrant for arrest; capias.

am-er, ère, * ăh-mair, *a* bitter.

américain, e, ăh-meh-re-kang, *a* & *mf* American.

amertume, ăh-mair-tEEm, *f* bitterness.

ameublement, ăh-mer-bler-mahng, *m* furniture.

ameuter, ăh-mer-teh, *v* to train to hunt together; to excite; to draw a crowd; **s'–,** to rebel; to riot.

a
b
c
d
e
f
g
h
i
j
k
l
m
n
o
p
q
r
s
t
u
v
w
x
y
z

A
B
C
D
E
F
G
H
I
J
K
L
M
N
O
P
Q
R
S
T
U
V
W
X
Y
Z

ami, e, ăh-me, *mf* friend; **chambre d'–,** shahng-br d–, spare room; *a* friendly to; fond of.

amiable, ăh-me-ăh-bl, *a* amicable; **à l' –,** ăh l–, amicably; by private contract.

amiante, ah-me-ahngte, *f* asbestos.

amical, e, * ăh-me-kăhl, *a* friendly; kind.

amidon, ăh-me-dong, *m* starch.

amincir, ăh-mang-seer, *v* to make thinner; **s'–,** to become thinner.

amiral, ăh-me-răhl, *m* admiral; **contre –,** kong-tr' –, rear admiral.

amirauté, ăh-me-roh-teh, *f* admiralty.

amitié, ăh-me-te-eh, *f* friendship; *pl* kind regards; compliments; love.

ammoniaque, ăh-monn-e-ăhck, *f* ammonia.

amnésie, ăhm-neh-zee, *f* loss of memory; amnesia.

amnistie, ăhm-niss-tee, *f* amnesty.

amoindrir, ăh-mo'ang-dreer, *v* to diminish.

amollir, ăh-moll-eer, *v* to soften; to mollify; to enervate.

amonceler, ăh-mongss-leh, *v* to heap up.

amont, ăh-mong, *m* upriver; upstream; uphill.

amorce, ăh-morss, *f* bait; allurement; priming; cap.

amortir, ăh-mor-teer, *v* to deaden; to pay off; to redeem; **s'–,** to grow weak or faint.

amortissable, ăh-mor-tiss-ăh-bl, *a* redeemable.

amortissement, ăh-mor-tiss-mahng, *m* paying off; redemption; (wireless) damping.

amortisseur, ăh-mor-tiss-er, *m* shock absorber.

amour, ăh-moohr, *m* love; passion; **–-propre, –** pro-pr, self-love; self-esteem.

amourette, ăh-moo-rett, *f* passing love affair.

amoureu-x, se, * ah-moo-rer, *a* in love; enamored.

amovible, ăh-mov-ee-bl, *a* removable.

ampère. ahng-pair, *m* ampere.

ampèremètre, ahng-pair-met-tr, *m* ammeter.

amphibie, ahng-fe-bee, *a* amphibious.

ample, * ahng-pl, *a* ample; spacious; large; copious.

ampleur, ahng-pler, *f* ampleness; largeness; fullness.

ampliation, ahng-ple-ăh-se-ong, *f* duplicate; true copy; **pour –,** poohr –, a true copy.

amplification, ahng-ple, fe-kăh-se-ong, *f* enlargement.

amplifier, ahng-ple-fe-eh, *v* to enlarge upon.

amplitude, ahng-ple-tEEd, *f* amplitude.

ampoule, ahng-pool, *f* blister; phial; (electric light) bulb.

ampoulé, e, ahng-pool-eh, *a* blistered; bombastic.

amputer, ahng-pE-teh, *v* to amputate.

amuser, ăh-mE-zeh, *v* to amuse; to entertain; to deceive; **s'–,** to enjoy oneself.

amuse-gueule, ăh-mEEz-gherl, *m* cocktail snack.

amygdale, ăh-meegh-dăhl, *f* tonsil.

an, ahng, *m* year, **jour de l'–,** shoohr der l–, New Year's day.

analogue ăh-năh-log, *a* analogous.

analyser, ăh-năh-le-zeh, *v* to analyze; to parse; to criticize.

ananas, ăh-năh-năh, *m* pineapple.

anarchie, ăh-năhr-shee, *f* anarchy.

anathème, ăh-năh-taym, *m* anathema.

ancêtre, ahng-say-tr, *m* ancestor.

anchois, ahng-sho'ăh, *m* anchovy.

ancien, ahng-se-ang, *m* elder; senior.

ancien, ne, * ahng-se-ang, *a* ancient; old; past; former; retired.

ancienneté, ahng-se-enn-teh, *f* antiquity; seniority; age.

ancre, ahng-kr, *f* anchor; **lever l'–,** ler-veh l–, to weigh anchor; **–de salut,** – der săh-lE, sheet anchor.

andouille, ahng-doo'e-yer, *f* chitterlings; idiot (familiar)

andouillette, ahng-doo'e-yette, *f* small sausage.

âne, ahn, *m* donkey; dunce.

anéantir, ăh-neh-ahng-teer, *v* to annihilate; to destroy; to tire out.

anéantissement, ăh-neh-ahng-tiss-mahng, *m* annihilation; utter exhaustion; self-humiliation.

anémie, ăh-neh-mee, *f* anemia.

ânerie, ahn-ree, *f* stupidity; gross ignorance; blunder.

anesthésie, ăh-ness-teh-ze, *f* anesthesia.

anesthésiste, ăh-ness-teh-zist, *m* anesthetist.

anévrisme, ăh-neh-vrissm, *m* aneurysm.

ange, ahngsh, *m* angel; **être a ux–s,** ay-tr oh z' –, to be overjoyed.

angine, ahng-**sheen,** *f* sore throat.

anglais, ahng-glay, *a* English (language); *n* English *m.*

angle, ahng-gl, *m* angle; corner.

Angleterre, ahng-gler-tair, *f* England.

angliciser, ahng-gle-se-zeh, *v* to anglicize.

anglicisme, ahng-gle-sissm, *m* anglicism.

angoisse, ahng-gwăhss, *f* anguish; pang.

anguille, ahng-ghee-yer, *f* eel; **–sous roche,** – soo rosh, a snake in the grass.

anicroche, ăh-ne-krosh, *f* hitch.

animal, ăh-ne-măhl, *n* & *a* animal; sensual; brutal.

animer, ăh-ne-meh, *v* to animate; to enliven; to

cheer; to excite; **s'–,** to become excited; warm; angry; to encourage each other.

anis, ăh-ne, *m* aniseed.

ankylose, ahng-ke-lohz, *f* stiffness.

anneau, ăh-noh, *m* ring.

année, ăh-neh, *f* year; crop; vintage.

annelé, e, ăhn-leh, *a* ringed.

annexe, ăh-nex, *f* annex; rider; schedule.

annihilation, ăhn-ne-ee-lăh-se-ong, *f* annihilation.

anniversaire, ăh-ne-vair-sair, *n* & *a* anniversary; birthday.

annonce, ăh-nongss, *f* announcement; advertisement.

annoncer, ăh-nong-seh, *v* to announce; to foretell; **s'–bien,** s– be-ang, to look promising.

annoter, ăhn-no-teh, *v* to annotate.

annuaire, ăhn-nE-air, *m* yearbook; directory.

annulaire, ăhn-nE lair, *m* ring finger, *a* annular.

annulation, ăhn-nE-lăh-se-ong, *f* canceling.

annuler, ăhn-nE-leh, *v* to annul; to cancel.

anoblir, ăh-nob-leer, *v* to

ennoble.

anodin, e, ăh-nod-an*g, a* mild; unmeaning; painkiller.

anomalie, ăh-nomm-ăh-lee, *f* anomaly.

ânon, ah-non*g, m* little donkey.

ânonner, ah-nonn-eh, *v* to falter; to mumble.

anonyme, * ăh-nonn-eem, *a* anonymous; **société –,** soss-e-eh-teh –, joint-stock company.

anormal, e, * ăh-nor-măhl, *a* abnormal.

anse, ahnn*g*ss, *f* handle; creek.

antan, ahn*g*-tahn*g, m* yesteryear.

antécédent, ahng-teh-seh-dahng, *a & m* antecedent; previous.

antenne, ahn*g*-tenn, *f* antenna; feeler, horn; (wireless) aerial.

antérieur, e, * ahn*g*-teh-re-er, *a* former, past; front.

antériorité, ahng-teh-re-o-re-teh, *f* priority.

anthère, ahn*g*-tair, *f* anther; **tip.**

anthropophage, ahng-trop-of-ăhsh, *a & m* cannibal.

antibiotique, ahng-te-be-oh-tick, *a & m,*

antibiotic.

anticonceptionnel, le ahng-te-kon*g*-sep-se-on*g*-nell, *a* contraceptive.

antidérapant, ahng-te-deh-răh-pahn*g, a* nonskid (tire).

antidote, ahng-te-dott, *m* antidote.

antienne, ahng-te-enn, *f* anthem.

antiquaire, ahng-te-kair, *m* antique dealer; antiquarian.

antiquité, ahng-te-ke-teh, *f* antiquity; *pl* antiques.

antiseptique, ahng-te-sayp-tick, *a & m* antiseptic.

antre, ahng-tr, *m* cave; den.

anxiété, ahn*g*k-se-eh-teh, *f* anxiety.

anxieu-x, se, * ahn*g*k-se-er, *a* anxious; uneasy.

août, ăh'oo, or oo, *m* August.

apaiser, ăh-pay-zeh, *v* to appease; **s' –,** to subside; to abate; to compose oneself.

apanage, ăh-păh-năhsh, *m* appanage; attribute; lot.

aparté, ăh-păhr-teh, *m* words spoken aside.

apercevoir, ăh-pair-ser-vo'ăhr, *v* to perceive; **s'–**

(de or **que),** to notice.

aperçu, ăh-pair-SE, *m* glance; summary view.

apéritif, ăh-peh-re-tiff, *m* appetizer; aperitif.

aphte, ăhft, *m* mouth ulcer.

apitoyer, ăh-pe-to'ah-e-eh, *v* to move to compassion; **s' –,** to pity.

aplanir, ăh-plăh-neer, *v* to level; to smooth.

aplatir, ăh-plăh-teer, *v* to flatten.

aplomb, ăh-plong, *m* perpendicularity; self-possession; audacity; **d' –,** upright.

apogée, ăh-po-sheh, *m* apogee; greatest height; peak.

apologie, ăh-poll-o-shee, *f* apology; vindication.

apostat, ăh-poss-tăh, *m* apostate.

aposter, ăh-poss-teh, *v* to set on a watch.

apostolat, ăh-poss-toll-ăh, *m* apostleship.

apostrophe, ăh-poss-trof, *f* apostrophe; address; reproach.

apostropher, ăh-poss-trof-eh, *v* to address; to challenge.

apothicaire, ăh-po-te-kair, *m* apothecary; **compte d' –,** kon*g*t d–, exorbitant bill.

apôtre, ăh-poh-tr, *m* apostle.

apparaître, ăh-păh-ray-tr, *v* to appear.

apparat, ăh-păh-răh, *m* pomp; state; **d' –,** formal.

appareil, ăh-păh-ray'e, *m* preparation; display; apparatus; appliance.

appareiller, ăh-păh-ray'e-eh, *v* to match; to set sail.

apparemment, ăh-păh-răh-mah*ng*, *adv* apparently.

apparence, ăh-păh-rah*ng*ss, *f* appearance.

apparent, e, ăh-păh-rah*ng*, *a* apparent.

apparenté, e, ăh-păh-rah*ng*-teh, *a* related.

apparition, ăh-păh-re-se-*ong*, *f* appearance; publication; ghost.

appartement, ăh-păhr-ter-mah*ng*, *m* apartment; flat.

appartenir, ăh-păhr-ter-neer, *v* to belong to; to concern.

appas, ăh-pah, *mpl* attractions; charms.

appât, ăh-pah, *m* bait; allurement.

appauvrir, ăh-poh-vreer, *v* to impoverish.

appel, ăh-pell, *m* call; appeal; muster.

appeler, ăhp-leh, *v* to call; to appeal; to name; **s' –,** to be called.

appendice, ăh-pa*ng*-diss, *m* appendix; appendage.

appendicite, ăh-pa*ng*-de-sit, *f* appendicitis.

appesantir, ăh-per-zah*ng*-teer, *v* to make heavy; **s' –,** to become heavy; to dwell (**sur,** upon).

appesantissement, ăh-per-zah*ng*-tiss-mah*ng*, *m* heaviness; dullness.

appétissant, e, ăh-peh-tiss-ah*ng*, *a* appetizing; tempting.

appétit, ăh-peh-te, *m* appetite; hunger; **l' –vient en mangeant,** l–ve-a*ng* t'ah*ng* mah*ng*-shah*ng*, the more one has, the more one wants.

applaudir, ăh-ploh-deer, *v* to applaud; to commend; **s' – (de,** on), to congratulate oneself.

applaudissement, ăh-ploh-diss-mah*ng*, *m* applause; cheering.

application, ăh-ple-kăh-se-*ong*, *f* application; attention; diligence; appropriation.

applique, ăh-pleek, *f*

bracket.

appliqué, e, ăh-ple-keh, *pp & a* applied; studious; diligent.

appliquer, ăh-ple-keh, *v* to apply; to lay on; to adapt; to devote; **s' –,** to be applied; to be applicable to; to apply oneself.

appoint, ăh-po'a*ng*, *m* balance; odd money.

appointements, ăh-po'a*ng*t-mah*ng*, *mpl* salary.

apport, ăh-por, *m* share of capital; *pl* vendor's shares.

apporter, ăh-por-teh, *v* to bring (something portable).

apposer, ăh-poh-zeh, *v* to affix; to append; to add.

apposition, ăh-poh-ze-se-*ong*, *f* affixing; apposition.

apprécier, ăh-preh-se-eh, *v* to appreciate; to value.

appréhender, ăh-preh-ah*ng*-deh, *v* to apprehend; to arrest; to fear.

appréhension, ăh-preh-ah*ng*-se-*ong*, *f* apprehension; fear.

apprendre, ăh-prah*ng*-dr, *v* to learn; to hear; to teach; to inform.

A
B
C
D
E
F
G
H
I
J
K
L
M
N
O
P
Q
R
S
T
U
V
W
X
Y
Z

apprenti, ăh-prah*ng*-te, *m* apprentice; novice.

apprentissage, ăh-prah*ng*-tiss-ăh**sh,** *m* apprenticeship.

apprêt, ăh-pray, *m* preparation; dressing of food; affectation.

appris, e, ăh-pre, *pp* learnt; taught; **malappris,** măh-lăh-pre, ill-bred.

apprivoiser, ăh-pre-vo'ăh-zeh, *v* to tame.

approba-teur, trice, ăh-pro-băh-**ter,** *mf* approver. *a* approving; of approval.

approbati-f, ve,* ăh-pro-băh-tiff, *a* approbatory; of approval.

approbation, ăh-pro-băh-se-o*ng*, *f* approval.

approchant, e, ăh-pro-shah*ng*, *a* near; like; approximate; *adv* thereabouts.

approche, ăh-prosh, *f* approach; access.

approcher, ăh-pro-sheh, *v* to approach; to bring near **s' –,** to come near.

approfondi, e, ăh-pro-fo*ng*-de, *a* profound; thorough.

approfondir, ăh-pro-fo*ng*-deer, *v* to deepen; to sift.

approprier, ăh-pro-pre-eh, *v* to appropriate; to adapt; to suit; **s' –,** to appropriate to oneself.

approuver, ăh-proo-veh, *v* to approve.

approvisionnement, ăh-pro-ve-ze-onn-mah*ng*, *m* victual; supply; stores.

approvisionner, ăh-pro-ve-ze-onn-eh, *v* to provide; **s'–,** to provide oneself (**de,** with); to lay in store.

approximati-f, ve,* ăh-prock-se-măh-tiff, *a* approximate; rough.

appui, ăh-pwe, *m* support; sill.

appuyer, ăh-pwe-yeh, *v* to support; to prop; to insist; **s'–,** to lean; to rely (**sur,** on).

âpre, ah-pr, *a* rough; harsh; severe.

après, ăh-pray, *prep* after; *adv* afterwards; **d'–,** from, according to; **et–?eh–?** what then?

après-demain, ăh-prayd-mang, *adv* the day after tomorrow.

après-dîner, ăh-pray-de-neh, *m* after dinner.

après-midi, ăh-pray-me-de, *m & f* afternoon.

âpreté, ah-prer-teh, *f* roughness; harshness;

greediness.

apte, ăh-pt, *a* fit; capable; qualified (**à,** of, for).

aptitude, ăhp-te-tEEd, *f* aptitude; fitness (**à,** to; **pour,** for).

apurer, ăh-pE-reh, *v* to audit.

aquarelle, ăh-ko'ăh-rell, *f* watercolor.

aquarium, ăh-ko'ăh-re-omm, *m* aquarium.

aquatique, ăh-ko'ăh-tick, *a* aquatic.

aqueduc, ăhck-dEEk, *m* aqueduct.

aquilin, ăh-ke-la*ng*, *a* aquiline.

aquilon, ăh-ke-lo*ng*, *m* north wind; cold wind.

arable, ăh-răh-bl, *a* arable; tillable.

arachide, ăh-răh-sheed, *f* peanut.

araignée, ăh-rayn-yeh, *f* spider.

aratoire, ăh-răh-to'ăhr, *a* agricultural.

arbalète, ăhr-băh-lett, *f* crossbow.

arbitrage, ăhr-be-trăh**sh,** *m* arbitration.

arbitraire,* ăhr-be-trayr, *a* arbitrary; despotic.

arbitre, ăhr-bee-tr, *m* arbitrator; umpire; master; **libre –,** lee-br' –, free will.

arborer, ăhr-bor-eh, *v* to set up; to hoist; to don.

arbre, ăhr-br, *m* tree; shaft; axle.

arbrisseau, ăhr-bre-soh, *m* small tree.

arbuste, ăhr-bEEst, *m* shrub.

arc, ăhrk, *m* bow; arc; arch.

arcade, ăhr-kăhd, *f* row of arches; arcade.

arc-boutant, ăhrk-boo-tahng, *m* buttress.

arceau, ăhr-soh, *m* arch; vault.

arc-en-ciel, ăhr-kahng-se-ell, *m* rainbow.

archange, ăhr-kahngsh, *m* archangel.

arche, ăhrsh, *f* arch; ark.

archéologue, ăhr-keh-o-log, *m* archeologist.

archer, ăhr-sheh, *m* bowman.

archet, ăhr-shay, *m* bow, fiddlestick.

archevêque, ăhr-sher-vayk, *m* archbishop.

archidiacre, ăhr-she-de-ăh-kr, *m* archdeacon.

archiduc, ăhr-she-dEEk, *m* archduke.

archiduchesse, ăhr-she-dE-shess, *f* archduchess.

archipel, ăhr-she-pell, *m* archipelago.

architecte, ăhr-she-teckt, *m* architect.

architecture, ăhr-she-teck-tEEr, *f* architecture.

archives, ăhr-sheev, *fpl* archives;records; recording office.

arçon, ăhr-song, *m* saddlebow; **cheval d'–,** sher-văhl-d, vault; vaulting horse.

ardemment, ăhr-dăh-mahng, *adv* ardently; eagerly; passionately.

ardent, e, ăhr-dahng, *a* burning; glowing; eager.

ardeur, ăhr-der, *f* ardor; eagerness; heat; spirit.

ardoise, ăhr-do'ăhz, *f* slate.

ardoisière, ăhr-do'ăh-ze-air, *f* slate quarry.

ardu, e, ăhr-dE, *a* arduous; difficult.

are, ăhr, *m* (unit of land measure in the French metrical system, equal to 100 square meters, or 119.60 square yards).

arène, ăh-rain, *f* arena; ring.

arête, ăh-rayt, *f* fishbone; edge; ridge.

argent, ăhr-shahng, *m* silver; money; cash; **–comptant,** –kong-tahng, ready money;– **fou,**– foo, lots of money.

argenté, e, ăhr-shahng-teh, *a* silvered; silver-white.

argenter, ăhr-shahng-teh, *v* to plate.

argenterie, ăhr-shahng-tree, *f* silver plate; plate.

argille, ăhr-sheel, **f** clay.

argileu-x, se, ăhr-she-ler, *a* clayey.

argot, ăhr-gho, *m* slang.

arguer, ăhr-ghE-eh, *v* to argue; to infer.

argument, ăhr-ghE-mahng, *m* argument; reasoning; summary.

argumenter, ăhr-ghE-mahng-teh, *v* to argue; to infer (**de,** from).

argutie, ăhr-ghE-see, *f* quibble.

aride,* ăh-reed, *a* arid; dry; barren.

aridité, ăh-re-de-teh, *f* aridity; dryness; barrenness.

aristocratie, ăh-riss-to-krăh-see, *f* aristocracy.

arithmétique, ăh-reet-meh-tick, *f* arithmetic.

arlequin, ăhr-ler-kang, *m* harlequin.

arlequinade, ăhr-ler-ke-năhd, *f* harlequinade; buffoonery.

armateur, ăhr-măh-ter, *m* shipowner.

armature, ăhr-măh-tEEr, *f* ironwork; framework;

A
B
C
D
E
F
G
H
I
J
K
L
M
N
O
P
Q
R
S
T
U
V
W
X
Y
Z

fittings.

arme, ăhrm, *f* weapon; arm; **maître d'–,** may-tr d–, fencing master; **faire des–s,** fair day z'–, to fence.

armée, ăhr-meh, *f* army; multitude.

armement, ăhr-mer-mahng, *m* armament.

armer, ăhr-meh, *v* to arm (**de,** with); to set against (**contre,** kong-tr); to cock; to equip; **s'–,** to arm oneself (**de,** with); to summon up.

armoire, ăhr-mo'ăhr, *f* cupboard; wardrobe.

armoiries, ăhr-mo'ăh-ree, *fpl* arms; coat of arms.

armorial, ăhr-mo-re-ăhl, *m* book of heraldry.

armure, ăhr-mEEr, *f* armor.

armurier, ăhr-mE-re-eh, *m* gunsmith; armorer.

arnica, ăhr-ne-kăh, *mf* arnica.

aromatiser, ăh-ro-măh-te-zeh, *v* to aromatize; to perfume.

arome, ăh-rohm, *m* aroma.

aronde, ăh-rongd, *f* (obs.) swallow; **en queue d'–,** ahng ker d–, dovetailed.

arpège, ăhr-paish, *m* arpeggio.

arpent, ăhr-pahng, *m* acre.

arpentage, ăhr-pahng-tăhsh, *m* land surveying.

arpenter, ăhr-pahng-teh, *v* to survey; to stride along.

arpenteur, ăhr-pahng-ter, *m* land surveyor.

arquer, ăhr-keh, *v* to arch; to bend; **s' –,** to become curved.

arrache-pied (d'), dăh-răhsh-pe-eh, *adv* at a stretch; without interruption.

arracher, ăh-răh-sheh, *v* to force out; to pull out; to pluck out; to snatch; to tear away; to wrest; **s' –,** to tear oneself, to break away (**à,** from).

arrangement, ăh-rahngsh-mahng, *m* arrangement; preparation; adjustment; accommodation.

arranger, ăh-rahng-sheh, *v* to arrange; to settle; to repair; to suit; to trim up; **s' –,** to make shift (**de,** with); to come to an arrangement (**avec,** with).

arrérages, ăh-reh-răhsh, *mpl* arrears.

arrestation, ăh-ress-tăh-se-ong, *f* arrest; custody.

arrêt, ăh-ray, *m* decree; stop; catch.

arrêt d'autobus, ăh-re-doh-toh-bEs, *m* bus stop.

arrêté, ăh-ray-teh, *m* decision; order, decree.

arrêter, ăh-ray-teh, *v* to stop; to detain; to restrain; to arrest; to fix; to resolve; to book; to engage; to conclude; **s' –,** to stop; to resolve (**à,** on).

arrhes, ăhr, *fpl* deposit (of money).

arrière, ăh-re-air, *m* back part; stern; *adv* behind; *interj* away! **en –,** ahng n' –, backward; **–-pensée** – pahng-seh, *f* ulterior motive; **–-plan,** – plahng, *m* background; **–-saison,** – say-zong, *f* end of autumn; closing season.

arriéré, ăh-re-eh-reh, *m* arrears.

arriéré, e, ăh-re-eh-reh, *a* in arrears; backward (mentally).

arrimer, ăh-re-meh, *v* to stow.

arrimeur, ăh-re-mer, *m* stevedore.

arrivage, ăh-re-văhsh, *m* arrival (of cargo, goods).

arrivée, ăh-re-veh, *f* arrival.

arriver, ăh-re-veh, *v* to arrive (**à,** at); to come;

to reach; to occur; to succeed (**avec** with); to become of. **arrive que pourra,** ăh-reev ker poo-răh, happen what may.

arriviste, ăh-re-visst, *m* & *f* pushy person; climber (social).

arrogamment, ăh-ro-găh-mahng, *adv* arrogantly.

arrogance, ăh-ro-gahngss, *f* arrogance.

arrogant, e, ăh-ro-gahng, *a* arrogant; haughty.

arroger (s'), săh-ro-**sheh**, *v* to arrogate to oneself; to assume.

arrondir, ăh-rong-deer, *v* to round; **s' –,** to become round; to increase.

arrondissement, ăh-rong-diss-mahng, *m* rounding; administrative district; borough.

arrosage, ăh-ro-zăhsh, *m* watering.

arroser, ăh-ro-zeh, *v* to water; to sprinkle; to wet; to baste.

arrosoir, ăh-ro-zo'ăhr, *m* watering can; sprinkler.

arsenal, ăhr-ser-năhl, *m* arsenal; dockyard.

arsenic, ăhr-ser-nick, *m* arsenic.

art, ăhr, *m* art.

artère, ăhr-tair, *f* artery.

artériole, ăhr-teh-re-ol, *f* small artery.

artésien, ăhr-teh-ze-ang, *a* artesian.

arthrite, ăhr-treet, *f* arthritis.

artichaut, ăhr-te-shoh, *m* artichoke.

article, ăhr-tee-kl, *m* article; thing; paragraph; item; goods; **–de fond, –** der fong, leading article.

articulation, ăhr-te-kE-lăh-se-ong, *f* articulation; joint.

articulé, e, ăhr-te-kE-leh, *a* articulated.

articuler, ăhr-te-kE-leh, *v* to utter; to pronounce; to set forth.

artifice, ăhr-te- fiss, *m* contrivance; deceit; **feu d' –,** fer d –, fireworks.

artificiel, le, * ăhr-te-fe-se-ell, *a* artificial.

artificieu-x, se, * ăhr-te-fe-se-er, *a* artful.

artillerie, ăhr-tee-yer-ree, *f* artillery.

artilleur, ăhr-tee-yer, *m* artilleryman.

artisan, ăhr-te-zahng, *m* artisan; craftsman.

artiste, ăhr-tisst, *m* artist; actor; performer.

as, ahss, *m* ace; (fig.) one who excels in some part.

ascendance, ăhss-sahng-dahngss, *f* ascending line; ascendancy.

ascendant, ăhss-sahng-dahng, *m* ascendancy; *pl* fore-fathers.

ascendant, e, ăhss-sahng-dahng, *a* ascending.

ascenseur, ăhss-sahng-ser, *m* lift; hoist; elevator.

ascension, ăhss-sahng-se-ong, *f* ascension; ascent; Ascension day.

ascète, ăhss-sett, *m* ascetic; hermit.

ascétisme, ăhss-seh-tism, *m* asceticism.

à sens unique, ăh-sahngss-E-neeck *a* one-way (*street*).

asile, ăh-zeel, *m* asylum; shelter; refuge; sanctuary.

aspect, ăhss-pay, *m* aspect; view; appearance.

asperge, ăhss-pair**sh**, *f* asparagus.

asperger, ăhss-pair-**sheh**, *v* to sprinkle (**de,** with).

aspérité, ăhss-peh-re-teh, *f* roughness.

aspersion, ăhss-pair-se-ong, *f* aspersion; sprinkling.

asphalte, ăhss-făhlt, *m* asphalt.

asphyxier, ăhss-feek-se-eh, *v* to asphyxiate; to suffocate.

A B C D E F G H I J K L M N O P Q R S T U V W X Y Z

aspic, ăhss-pick, *m* asp; spike lavender; cold meat in jelly.

aspirant, ăhss-pe-rahng, *m* candidate.

aspirant, e, ăhss-pe-rahng, *a* suction (pump, etc.).

aspirateur, ăhs-pe-răh-ter *m* vacuum cleaner.

aspiration, ăhss-pe-răh-se-ong, *f* inhalation; suction; (fig.) longing.

aspirer, ăhss-pe-reh, *v* to inhale; to exhaust; to suck up; (fig.) to long for.

aspirine, ăhss-pe-reen, *f* aspirin.

assaillant, e, ăhss-sah'e-ahng, *n* & *a* assailant.

assaillir, ăhss-sah'eer, *v* to assail; to attack.

assainir, ăhss-ay-neer, *v* to make healthy.

assaisonnement, ăhss-ay-zonn-mahng, *m* seasoning; salad dressing.

assaisonner, ăhss-ay-zonn-eh, *v* to season; to dress (salad).

assassin, ăhss-ăh-sang, *m* murderer.

assaut, ăhss-oh, *m* assault; attack; fencing match.

assemblage, ăhss-ahng-blăsh, *m* assemblage; gathering; medley; joining.

assemblée, ăhss-ahng-bleh, *f* assembly; congregation; party; meeting.

assembler, ăhss-ahng-bleh, *v* to collect; to convoke; to join together; **s' –,** to meet; **qui se ressemble s'assemble,** kee ser rerss-ahng-bl săhss-ahng-bl, birds of a feather flock together.

asséner, ăhss-eh-neh, *v* to strike; to deal (a blow).

assentiment, ăhss-ahng-te-mahng, *m* assent.

asseoir, ăhss-o'ăhr, *v* to seat; **s' –,** to sit down.

assermenter, ăhss-air-mahng-teh, *v* to swear in.

assertion, ăhss-air-se-ong, *f* assertion.

asservir, ăhss-air-veer, *v* to enslave; to subdue.

asservissement, ăhss-air-viss-mahng *m* enslavement; slavery.

assesseur, ăhss-ess-er, *m* assessor; assistant; judge.

assez, ăhss-eh, *adv* enough; fairly; rather.

assidu, e, ăhss-e-dE, *a* assiduous; diligent; attentive.

assiduité, ăhss-e-dwe-teh, *f* assiduity; regular attendance; *pl* assiduous attentions.

assidûment, ăhss-e-dE-mahng, *adv* assiduously; diligently.

assiégeant, e, ăhss-e-eh-shahng, *n* & *a* besieger.

assiéger, ăhss-e-eh-sheh, *v* to besiege; to dun (**de,** with).

assiette, ăhss-e-ett, *f* plate; situation; assessment.

assignable, ăhss-een-yăh-bl, *a* assignable.

assignation, ăhss-een-yăh-se-ong, *f* assignment; summons; writ; subpoena; appointment.

assigner, ăhss-een-yeh, *v* to assign; to allot; to summon; to appoint.

assimiler, ăhss-e-me-leh, *v* to assimilate (**to,** with).

assis, e, ăhss-e, *pp* seated.

assise, ăhss-eez, *f* course; layer; basis; foundation; *pl* assizes.

assistance, ăhss-iss-tahngss, *f* attendance; audience; help.

assistant, e, ăhss-iss-tahng *n* & *a* person present; helper; *pl* those present.

assister, ăhss-iss-teh, *v* to attend; to be present; to help.

association, ăhss-o-se-ăh-se-ong, *f* association;

partnership.

associé, e, ăhss-o-se-eh, *mf* associate; partner.

associer, ăhss-o-se-eh, *v* to associate; **s' –,** to join (**à, avec,** with); to enter into partnership; to share (**à,** in).

assombrir, ăhss-ong-breer, *v* to darken; **s' –,** to become gloomy.

assommant, e, ăhss-omm-ahng, *a* boring.

assommer, ăhss-omm-eh, *v* to knock down; to bore to death.

assommoir, ăhss-ommo'ăhr, *m* bludgeon; (fig.) sleazy bar.

assomption, ăhss-ongp-seong, *f* Assumption.

assortiment, ăhss-or-temahng, *m* assortment; set; stock; match.

assortir, ăhss-or-teer, *v* to assort; to stock; to match; **s' –,** to harmonize (**à, avec,** with).

assoupir, ăhss-oo-peer, *v* to make drowsy; to hush up **s' –,** to doze; to die away.

assoupissant, e, ăhss-oopiss-ahng, *a* soporific.

assoupissement, ăhss-oopiss-mahng, *m* drowsiness; indolence.

assouplir, ăhss-oo-pleer, *v* to make supple; **s' –,** to become supple.

assourdir, ăhss-oohr-deer, *v* to deafen; to muffle.

assourdissant, e, ăhssoohr-diss-ahng, *a* deafening.

assouvir, ăhss-oo-veer, *v* to satiate; to glut.

assujettir, ăhss-E-shayteer, *v* to subdue; to bind; to fasten; **s' –,** to subject oneself.

assujettissement, ăhss-Eshayt-iss-mahng, *m* subjection.

assumer, ăhss-E-meh, *v* to assume.

assurance, ăhss-E-rahngss, *f* assurance; reliance; boldness; insurance.

assuré, e, ăhss-E-reh, *pp* & *a* assured; insured; secured; confident.

assurément, ăhss-E-rehmahng, *adv* certainly; assuredly.

assurer, ăhss-E-reh, *v* to assure; to insure; to secure; to assert; **s' –,** to make sure (**de,** of; **que,** that).

assureur, ăhss-E -rer, *m* insurer; underwriter.

asthme, ăhssm, *m* asthma.

asticot, ăhss-te-ko, *m* maggot.

asticoter, ăhss-te-kot-eh, *v* (fam.) to worry; to tease.

astiquer, ăhss-te-keh, *v* to polish.

astral, e, ăhss-trăhl, *a* stellar; astral.

astre, ăhss-tr, *m* star.

astreindre, ăhss-trang-dr, *v* to subject; to compel.

astringent, e, ăhss-trangshahng, *a* astringent.

astrologue, ăhss-troll-og, *m* astrologer.

astronome, ăhss-tronnomm, *m* astronomer.

astuce, ăhss-tEEss, *f* cunning; astuteness; witticism.

astucieu-x, se,* ăhss-tEse-er, *a* artful; crafty; witty.

atelier, ăh-ter-le-eh, *m* workshop; studio; gang; **chef d'–,** shayf d–, overseer.

à temps partiel, ăh-tahngpăhr-se-ell *a, adv* parttime.

atermoiement, ăh-tairmo'ăh-mahng, *m* respite.

athée, ăh-teh, *m* atheist.

athlète, ăht-lett, *m* athlete; champion.

atlas, ăht-lăhss, *m* atlas.

atmosphère, ăht-mossfair, *f* atmosphere.

atome, ăh-tom, *m* atom.

atomique, ăh-to-mick, *a*

atomic.

atomiseur, ăh-to-me-zer, *m* atomizer; spray.

atours, ăh-toohr, *mpl* attire; finery.

atout, ăh-too, *m* trump card.

âtre, ah-tr, *m* hearth.

atroce,* ăh-tross, *a* atrocious; heinous; excruciating.

atrocité, ăh-tross-e-teh, *f* atrocity; (archit.) eyesore.

atrophié, e, ăh-trof-e-eh, *a* wasted; withered.

attabler (s'), săh-tăh-bleh, *v* to sit down to table.

attachant, e, ăh-tăh-shahng, *a* engaging.

attache, ăh-tăhsh, *f* tie; bond; fastening; leash.

attaché, ăh-tăh-sheh, *m* attaché (of an embassy).

attaché, e, ăh-tăh-sheh, *pp* & *a* attached.

attachement, ăh-tăhsh-mahng, *m* affection.

attacher, ăh-tăh-sheh, *v* to attach; to fasten; to bind; to interest; to endear; **s'–,** to cling.

attaque, ăh-tăhck, *f* attack; fit; stroke.

attaquer, ăh-tăh-keh, *v* to attack; to begin; to sue; **s'–à,** to attack.

atteindre, ăh-tang-dr, *v* to reach; to attain; to strike; to injure.

atteinte, ăh-tangt, *f* blow; injury; violation.

attelage, ăht-lăhsh, *m* team; harness; coupling.

atteler, ăht-leh, *v* to put to; to yoke.

attenant, e, ăht-nahng, *a* adjoining.

attendant (en), ahng n'ăh-tahng-dahng, *adv* meanwhile.

attendre, ăh-tahng-dr, *v* to wait for; to expect; to look forward to; **s'–à,** to expect; to rely upon.

attendrir, ăh-tahng-dreer, *v* to make tender; to move; **s'–,** to be moved.

attendrissement, ăh-tahng-driss-mahng, *m* emotion.

attendu, e, ăh-tahng-dE, *pp* expected; *prep* considering.

attentat, ăht-tahng-tăh, *m* criminal attempt; outrage.

attente, ăh-tahngt, *f* waiting; expectation.

attenter, ăh-tahng-teh, *v* to make a criminal attempt.

attenti-f,-ve,* ăh-tahng-tiff, *a* attentive.

attention, ăh-tahng-se-ong, *f* attention; care; kindness.

atténuer, ăht-teh-nE-eh, *v* to weaken; to extenuate.

atterrer, ăh-tay-reh, *v* to throw down; to astound.

atterrir, ăh-tay-reer, *v* to land.

atterrissage, ăh-tay-riss-ăhsh, *m* landing.

attestation, ăh-tess-tăh-se-ong, *f* certificate; testimonial.

attester, ăh-tess-teh, *v* to attest; to take to witness.

attiédir, ăh-te-eh-deer, *v* to cool; **s'–,** to cool down.

attirail, ăh-te-rah'e, *m* apparatus; paraphernalia.

attirant, e, ăh-te-rahng, *a* attractive; alluring.

attirer, ăh-te-reh, *v* to attract; to draw; to bring on; **s' –,** to bring on oneself; to attract each other.

attiser, ăh-te-zeh, *v* to stir up; to poke.

attitré, e, ăh-te-treh, *a* regular; appointed; official.

attitude, ăh-te-tEEd, *f* attitude.

attouchement, ăh-toosh-mahng, *f* touch; feeling.

attraction, ăh-trăhck-se-

ong, *f* attraction.

attrait, ăh-tray, *m*
attraction; charm.

attrape, ăh-trăhp, *f* catch;
trick; hoax; trap; —
nigaud, – ne-goh, con
game.

attraper, ăh-trăh-peh, *v* to
entrap; to catch; to
cheat; to get.

attrayant, e, ăh-tray'e-
ahng, *a* attractive.

attribuer, ăht-tre-bE-eh, *v*
to attribute; to assign; to
impute; **s' –,** to claim.

attribution, ăht-tre-bE-se-
ong, *f* attribution;
prerogative.

attrister, ăh-triss-teh, *v* to
sadden; **s' –,** to grieve.

attroupement, ăh-troop-
mahng, *m* gathering;
mob.

attrouper, ăh-troo-peh, *v*
to assemble; **s' –,** to
crowd.

au (*sing*), **aux** (*pl*), oh,
contraction of **à le, à
les.**

aubaine, oh-bayn, *f*
windfall; godsend.

aube, ohb, *f* dawn.

aubépine, oh-beh-peen, *f*
hawthorn.

auberge, oh-bairsh, *f* inn;
–de jeunesse, der **sher-**
ness, youth hostel.

aubergine, oh-bair-sheen,
f aubergine; eggplant.

aubergiste, oh-bair-**shi**sst,
m innkeeper.

aucun, e, oh-kung, *a* any;
no; none; *pron* anyone;
no one.

aucunement, oh-kEEn-
mahng, *adv* by no
means; not at all.

audace, oh-dăhss, *f*
audacity; insolence;
daring.

audacieu-x, se*, oh-dăh-
se-**er**, *a* audacious;
impudent; bold.

au-dessous, oh-der-soo,
adv below; underneath.

au-dessus, oh-der-sEE, *adv*
above.

audience, oh-de-ahngss, *f*
audience; hearing;
court; sitting.

audiencier, oh-de-ahngss-
e-eh, *m* usher; crier of a
court.

audi-teur, trice, oh-de-
ter, *mf* hearer.

auditi-f, ve, oh-de-tiff, *a*
auditory.

audition, oh-de-se-ong, *f*
hearing; audition.

auditoire, oh-de-to'ăhr, *m*
audience.

au fond, oh-fong, *a*
basically.

auge, ohsh, *f* trough; hod.

augmentation, og-mahng-
tăh-se-ong, *f* increase;

rise.

augmenter, og-mahng-teh,
v to increase; to raise; **s'**
–, to increase.

augure, oh-ghEEr, *m*
augury; omen; augur.

augurer, oh-ghE-reh, *v* to
augur; to surmise.

auguste, oh-ghEEst, *a*
august.

aujourd'hui, oh-**shoo**hr-
dwe, *adv* today;
nowadays.

aumône, oh-mohn, *f* alms;
charity.

aumônier, oh-moh-ne-eh,
m chaplain.

aune, ohn, *m* alder; *f* ell.

auparavant, oh-păh-răh-
vahng, *adv* before;
previously; once; first.

auprès, oh-pray, *adv* near;
close; hard by.

auprès de, oh-pray der,
prep near; close to; in
comparison with.

auréole, oh-reh-ol, *f* halo;
glory; crown; nimbus.

auriculaire, oh-re-kE-lair,
m the little finger; *a*
auricular.

aurifère, oh-re-fair, *a*
auriferous.

aurifier, oh-re-fe-eh, *v* to
fill with gold.

aurore, oh-ror, *f* dawn.

ausculter, ohss-kEEl-teh, *v*
to auscultate; to sound

a
b
c
d
e
f
g
h
i
j
k
l
m
n
o
p
q
r
s
t
u
v
w
x
y
z

the chest of.

auspice, oss-piss, *m* auspice.

aussi, ohss-e, *adv* too; also; likewise; so; as; as much. *conj* therefore; consequently; –...**que,** –ker, as...as.

aussitôt, ohss-e-toh, *adv* immediately; –**que,** –ker, as soon as.

austère,* ohss-tair, *a* stern; rigid.

autant, oh-tah*ng*, *adv* as much; as many; so much; so many; **d'**–**mieux,** d– me-er, all the better; **d'** –**moins,** d– mo'a*ng*, all the less; **d'** –**que,** d– ker, more especially as.

autel, oh-tell, *m* altar.

auteur, oh-ter, *m* author; writer; **droit d'**–, dro'ăh d–, copyright.

authenticité, oh-tah*ng*-te-se-teh, *f* authenticity; genuineness.

autobiographe, oh-toh-be-oh-grăhf, *m* autobiographer.

autobiographie, oh-toh-be-oh-grăh-fee, *f* autobiography.

autobus, oh-toh-bEEs, *m* bus.

autocratie, oh-toh-krăh-sec, *f* autocracy.

autographe, oh-toh-grăhf, *m* autograph.

automate, oh-toh-măht, *m* automation.

automatique,* oh-toh-măh-tick, *a* automatic.

automne, oh-tonn, *m* autumn.

automobile, oh-toh-mo-beel, *f* car; *a* self-moving; **canot** –, kăh-no –, motorboat.

automobilisme, oh-toh-mo-be-lissm, *m* motoring.

automobiliste, oh-toh-mo-be-lisst, *mf* motorist.

autopsie, oh-top-see, *f* post-mortem examination; autopsy.

autorisation, oh-toh-re-zăh-se-ong, *f* authority; permission.

autoriser, oh-toh-re-zeh, *v* to authorize.

autorité, oh-toh-re-teh, *f* authority; power; control.

autoroute, oh-toh-root, *f* highway; freeway.

autoroute qui contourne, oh-toh-root-ke-kong-toohrn, *f auto* bypass.

autour, oh-toohr, *adv* round about.

autour de, oh-toohr der, *prep* around; about.

autre, oh-tr, *pron* another;

a other; different; **tout** –, too t'–, quite different; anybody else; **nous** –**s, vous** –**s,** noo z'–, voo z'–, we; you; ourselves; yourselves; **à d'**– **s,** ăhd d–, nonsense!

autrefois, oh-trer-fo'ăh, *adv* formerly.

autrement, oh-trer-mah*ng*, *adv* otherwise.

autruche, oh-trEEsh, *f* ostrich.

autrui, oh-trwe, *pron* others.

auvent, oh-vah*ng*, *m* penthouse; shed.

aux, oh, *m* & *fpl* to the; at the.

auxiliaire, ohk-se-le-air, *a* & *m* auxiliary.

aux seins nus, oh-sang-nE *a* topless.

aval, ăh-văhl, *m* guarantee; endorsement; lower part; **en** –, ahng n'–, down the river.

avaler, ăh-văh-leh, *v* to swallow; (fig.) to pocket.

avance, ăh-vah*ng*ss, *f* advance; money advanced; **d'**–, d–, beforehand.

avancement, ăh-vah*ng*ss-mah*ng*, *m* progress; rise.

avancer, ăh-vah*ng*ss-eh, *v* to advance; to promote;

to hasten; to hold forth; to proceed; to progress; to be fast (clock); **s'–,** to come forward.

avanie ăh-văh-nee, *f* outrage; affront.

avant, hă-vah*ng*, *adv* far; deep; forward; *prep* before; *m* forepart; bow; **en –,** ahng n'–,in front; **–de** or **que,** before; **– dernier,** dair-ne-se-eh, last but one; **–-hier,** – t'e-air, the day before yesterday; **–-propos,** – pro-poh, foreword; **– veille,** –vay'e, two days before.

avantage, ăh-vahng-tăhsh *m* advantage; benefit.

avantageu-x, se,* ăh-vahng-tăhsh-er, *a* advantageous.

avant-première, ăh-vahng-prer-me-air *f* preview.

avare, ăh-văhr, *m* miser; *a* avaricious.

avarice, ăh-văh-riss, *f* avarice.

avarie, ăh-văh-ree, *f* damage; average.

avarier, ăh-văh-re-eh, *v* to damage; to spoil; **s'–,** to get damaged.

avec, ăh-veck, *prep* with; by.

avenant, ăh—nahng, *m*

additional clause (to an insurance policy).

avenant, e, ăhv-nahng, *a* prepossing; **à l'–,** ăh-l– in keeping with.

avènement, ăh-vane-mahng, *m* accession; coming.

avenir, ăhv-neer, *m* future; prospects; posterity; **à l' –,** ăhl–, in future.

avent, ăh-vahng, *m* advent.

aventure, ăh-vahng-tEEr, *f* adventure; love affair; **à l'–,** ăhl–, at random.

aventuré, e, ăh-vahng-tE-reh, *a* hazardous.

aventurer, ăh-vahng-tE-reh, *v* to venture; **s'–,** to take a chance.

aventureu-x, se,* ăh-vahng-tE-rer, *a* adventuresome.

aventuri-er, ère, ăh-vahng-tE-re-eh, *mf* adventurer; adventuress.

avenue, ăhv-nE, *f* avenue.

avérer, ăh-veh-reh, *v* to aver; **s'–,** to be proved.

averse, ăh-vairss, *f* heavy shower.

aversion, ăh-vair-se-ong, *f* dislike (**pour,** of, for).

averti, e, ăh-vair-te, *a* experienced, wide-awake.

avertir, ăh-vair-teer, *v* to warn; to inform.

avertissement, ăh-vair-tiss-mahng, *m* warning; notice; preface.

aveu, ăh-ver, *m* admission; avowal; confession; **homme sans–,** omm sahng z'–, vagabond.

aveugle, ăh-ver-gl, *a* blind.

aveuglément, ăh-ver-gleh,mahng, *adv* blindly; implicitly.

aveugler, ăh-ver-gleh, *v* to blind; **s'–,** to be blind (**sur,** to).

aveuglette, (à l'), ăh-lăh-ver-glett, *adv* in the dark; blindly.

aviateur, ăh-ve-ăh-ter, *m* airman.

aviation, ăh-ve-ăh-se-ong, *f* flying; Air Force.

avide,* ăh-veed, *a* greedy; eager.

avilir, ăh-ve-leer, *v* to degrade; **s'–,** to degrade oneself; to depreciate.

avilissement, ăh-ve-liss-mahng, *m* degradation; debasement.

avion, ăh-ve-ong, *m* airplane.

aviron, ăh-ve-rong, *m* oar; **l'–,** rowing (sport).

avis, ăh-ve, *m* opinion;

a
b
c
d
e
f
g
h
i
j
k
l
m
n
o
p
q
r
s
t
u
v
w
x
y
z

A B C D E F G H I J K L M N O P Q R S T U V W X Y Z

advice; caution; news.

avisé, e, ăh-ve-zeh, *a* advised; wise; circumspect.

aviser, ăh-ve-zeh, *v* to perceive; to advise; to see to it; **s'−,** to take it into one's head (**de,** to).

aviver, ăh-ve-veh, *v* to brighten; to quicken; to polish.

avocat, ăh-vo-kăh, *m* barrister; counsel; lawyer.

avocat, ăh-vo-kăh, *m* avocado.

avoine, ăh-vo'ăhn, *f* oats.

avoir, ăh-vo'ăhr, *v* to have; to get; to be; *m* property; **qu'avez-vous?** kăh-veh voo? what is the matter with you? **j'ai chaud,** shay shoh, I am warm; **il y a,** ill e ăh, there is; there are; ago; **j'ai 20 ans,** sheh-vang-ahng, I am 20.

avoisiner, ăh-vo'ăh-ze-neh, *v* to be near.

avortement, ăh-vor-ter-mahng, *m* abortion.

avorter, ăh-vor-teh, *v* to miscarry; **se faire −,** to have an abortion.

avorton, ăh-vor-tong, *m* abortive child or animal.

avoué, ăh-voo-eh, *m* solicitor; attorney.

avouer, ăh-voo-eh, *v* to confess; to acknowledge.

avril, ăh-vreel, *m* April.

axe, ăhks, *m* axis; axle.

ayant-droit, ay-yahng-dro'ăh, *m* rightful owner; beneficiary.

azote, ăh-zot, *m* nitrogen.

azur, ăh-zEEr, *m* azure; blue.

azyme, ăh-zeem, *a* unleavened.

baba, băh-băh, *m* baba; spongy plum cake **–au rhum,** – oh romm, sponge cake moistened with rum syrup.

babillage, băh-bee-yăsh, *m* prattling.

babiller, băh-bee-yeh, *v* to prattle; to babble.

babine, băh-been, *f* lip of animal; chops(of animals).

babiole, băh-be-ol, *f* bauble; toy; knickknack.

bâbord, bah-bor, *m* port side.

babouin, băh-boo-ang, *m* baboon.

bac, băhck, *m* ferryboat.

baccalauréat, băh-kăh-loh-reh-ăh, *m* high school diploma.

bâche, bahsh, *f* canvas cover.

bachelier, băh-sher-le-eh, *m* one who has passed high school.

bachot, băh-sho, *m* "baccalauréat"; small boat.

bacille, băh-sill, *m* bacillus.

bâcler, bah-kleh, *v* to do hastily.

badaud, e, băh-doh, *mf* idler; saunterer.

badigeonner, băh-de-shonn-eh, *v* to whitewash; to paint.

badin, e, băh-dang, *a* & *mf* playful; joker.

badinage, băh-de-năhsh, *m* banter; lighthearted tone.

badiner, băh-de-neh, *v* to joke.

bafouer, băh-foo-eh, *v* to scoff at.

bagage, băh-găhsh, *m* luggage; **plier –,** ple-eh –, to pack up; to make off.

bagarre, băh-găhr, *f* fight; scuffle; brawl.

bagatelle, băh-găh-tell, *f* trifle; trinket.

bagne, băhn-yer, *m* convicts' prison.

bague, băhg, *f* ring.

baguette, băh-ghett, *f* wand; rod; stick; long stick of bread.

bah! băh, *interj* nonsense! pooh! indeed!

bahut, băh-E, *m* chest; cupboard.

bai, e, bay, *a* bay.

baie, bay, *f* bay; berry; opening.

baigner, bain-yeh, *v* to bathe; **se –,** to bathe.

baignoire, bain-yo'ăhr, *f* bathtub; (theater) box.

bail, bah'e, *m* lease; *pl* **baux,** boh.

bâillement, bah'e-mahng, *m* yawning; gaping.

bâiller, bah'e-eh, *v* to yawn; to gape.

bailleur, bah'e-er, *m* lessor.

bailli, bah'e-yee, *m* bailiff.

bâillon, bah'e-yong, *m* gag.

bâillonner, bah'e-yonn-eh, *v* to gag.

bain, ba*ng*, *m* bath; **salle de –,** săhl-*der* –, *f* bathroom.

bain-marie, ba*ng*-măh-ree, *m* double saucepan (cooking).

baïonnette, băh'e-onn-ett, *f* bayonet.

baiser, bay-zeh, *m* kiss.

baisse, bess, *f* fall; decline; drop.

baisser, bess-eh, *v* to lower; to let down; to decline; **se –,** to stoop.

bal, băhl, *m* ball.

balade, băh-lăhd, *f* stroll; ramble.

balader (se), ser băh-lăh-deh, *v* (fam.) to take a stroll.

baladin, băh-lăh-da*ng*, *m* mountebank; buffoon.

balafre, băh-lăh-fr, *f* gash; scar.

balai, băh-lay, *m* broom; brush.

balance, băh-lah*ng*ss, *f* scale; pair of scales.

balancer, băh-lah*ng*-seh, *v* to balance; to weigh; to hesitate; to swing; (fam.) to turn out; to dismiss.

balancier, băh-lah*ng*-se-eh, *m* pendulum; pole; beam.

balançoire, băh-lah*ng*-so'ăhr, *f* seesaw; swing.

balayer, băh-lay-yeh, *v* to sweep.

balayures, băh-lay-yEEr, *fpl* sweepings.

balbutier, băhl-bE-se-eh, *v* to stammer; to mumble.

balcon, băhl-ko*ng*, *m* balcony.

baldaquin, băhl-dăh-ka*ng*, *m* canopy.

baleine, băh-lain, *f* whale.

baleinier, băh-lay-ne-eh, *m* whaler; **–de sauvetage,** – der sohv-t ăhsh, lifeboat.

balise, băh-leez, *f* beacon; buoy.

ballade, băh-lăhd, *f* ballad; ballade.

ballant, e, băh-lah*ng*, *a* swinging; dangling.

balle, băhl, *f* ball; bullet; bale; **prendre la –au bond** prah*ng*-dr lăh – oh bo*ng*, to seize the opportunity.

ballet, băh-lay, *m* ballet.

ballon, băh-lo*ng*, *m* balloon; football.

ballot, băh-loh, *m* bale.

ballottage, băh-lot-ăhsh, *m* second ballot; shaking.

ballotter, băh-lot-eh, *v* to toss; to ballot.

balnéaire, băhl-neh-air, *a* bathing; **station –,** stăh-

se-*ong* –, seaside; health resort.

balourdise, băh-loohr-deez, *f* stupid thing; blunder.

balsamique, băhl-zăh-mick, *a* balsamic.

balustre, băh-lEEs-tr, *m* railing; balustrade.

bambin, e, bah*ng*-ba*ng*, *mf* little child; tiny tot.

bambocheur, bah*ng*-boh-sher, *m* debauchee.

bambou, bah*ng*-boo, *m* bamboo.

ban, bah*ng*, *m* proclamation; banishment.

banal, e,* băh-năhl, *a* commonplace; banal.

banane, băh-năhn, *f* banana.

banc, bah*ng*, *m* bench.

bancal, e, bah*ng*-kăhl, *a* & *n* bandy-legged.

bandage, bah*ng*-dăhsh, *m* bandaging; truss; tire.

bande, bah*ng*d, *f* strip; wrapper; gang; lot; tire.

bandeau, bah*ng*-doh, *m* headband; bandage.

bandolette, bah*ng*d-lett, *f* narrow band; small bandage.

bander, bah*ng*-deh, *v* to bandage; to bind up; to stretch; to blindfold.

banderole, bah*ng*d-rol, *f*

streamer.

bandit, bah*ng*-de, *m* bandit.

bandoulière, bah*ng*-doo-le-air, *f* shoulder belt; **en –,** ah*ng* –, slung over the shoulder.

banlieue, bah*ng*-le-*er*, *f* suburbs.

bannière, băh-ne-air, *f* banner; flag.

bannir, băh-neer, *v* to banish.

banque, bah*ng*k, *f* bank; banking.

banqueroute, bah*ng*k-root, *f* bankruptcy.

banquet, bah*ng*-kay, *m* feast; banquet.

banquette, bah*ng*-kett, *f* bench; seat.

banquier, bah*ng*-ke-eh, *m* banker.

banquise, bah*ng*-keez, *f* ice-shelf, -floe.

baptême, băh-taym, *m* baptism.

baptiser, băh-te-zeh, *v* to christen.

baquet, băh-kay, *m* tub; bucket.

baragouiner, băh-răh-gwee-neh, *v* to talk gibberish.

baraque, băh-răhck *f* shed; hovel; hut.

baratter, băh-răh-teh, *v* to churn.

barbare, băhr-băhr, *a* & *mf* barbarian; barbarous.

barbe, băhrb, *f* beard.

barbelé, băhr-ber-leh, *a* barbed; *m* barbed wire.

barbiche, băhr-beesh, *f* tuft of beard.

barbier, băhr-be-eh, *m* barber.

barboter, băhr-bot-eh, *v* to dabble; to paddle.

barbouiller, băhr-boo'e-yeh, *v* to daub; to scribble.

barbu, e, băhr-b*E*, *a* bearded.

barème, băh-raym, *m* scale of change.

barguigner, băhr-gheen-yeh, *v* to hum and haw; to hesitate.

baril, băh-re, *m* barrel; cask; keg.

bariolage, băh-re-o-lăhsh, *m* medley (of colors).

bariolé, băh-re-o-leh, *a* gaudy; of many colors.

baromètre, băh-roh-met-tr, *m* barometer.

baron, băh-rong, *m* baron; *f* **baronne,** băh-ronn.

baronnet, băh-ro-nay, *m* baronet.

baroque, băh-rock, *a* odd; baroque (style).

barque, băhrk, *f* boat.

barrage, băh-răhsh, *m* stoppage; dam; barrage.

barre, băhr, *f* bar; tiller; stroke.

barreau, băh-roh, *m* bar; law profession.

barrer, băh-reh, *v* to bar; to cross out.

barrette, băh-rehtt, *f* hair slide; barrette.

barrière, băh-re-air, *f* barrier; gate.

bas, bah, *adv* low down; *m* bottom; stocking.

bas, se,* bah, *a* low; mean; base.

basané, e, băh-zăh-neh, *a* sunburnt; swarthy.

bas-côté, bah-koh-teh, *m* aisle (side).

bascule, băhss-k*EEl*, *f* seesaw; weighing machine.

base, bahz, *f* basis; base.

baser, bah-zeh, *v* to base; to ground.

bas-fond, bah-fong, *m* low ground.

basque, băhsk, *f* flap (coat, etc.); *a* & *mf* Basque.

basse, bahss, *f* bass; violoncello.

basse-cour, bahss-koohr, *f* poultry yard.

bassesse, bahss-ess, *f* baseness; meanness.

bassin, băhss-ang, *m* basin; dock; pelvis.

bassiner, băhss-e-neh, *v* to

warm (a bed); to bathe (wound, etc.).

bassinoire, băhss-e-no'ăhr, *f* warming pan.

basson, bahss-ong, *m* bassoon.

baste! băhsst! *interj* pooh! bosh! nonsense!

bastingage, băhss-tang-găhsh, *m* netting.

bastringue, băhss-trang-gh, *m* sleazy dancing place.

bas-ventre, bah-vahng-tr, *m* lower abdomen.

bât, bah, *m* packsaddle.

bataille, băh-tah'e, *f* battle.

bataillon, băh-tah'e-ong, *m* battalion; host.

bâtard, e, bah-tăhr, *n & a* illegitimate; French loaf of bread.

bateau, băh-toh, *m* boat.

bateleur, băht-ler, *m* tumbler; buffoon.

batelier, băh-ter-le-eh, *m* boatman.

bâti, bah-te, *m* tacking; frame; *pp* built.

batifoler, băh-te-foll-eh, *v* to play; to romp.

bâtiment, bah-te-mahng, *m* building; ship.

bâtir, bah-teer, *v* to build; to erect.

bâtisse, bah-tiss, *f* building; masonry.

batiste, băh-tisst, *f* cambric; lawn.

bâton, bah tong, *m* stick; club; **à —s rompus,** ăh—rong-pE, by fits and starts; **mettre des —s dans les roues,** met-tr day–dahng lay roo, to put a spoke in one's wheel.

bâtonner, bah-tonn-eh, *v* to cudgel.

battage, băh-tăhsh, *m* beating; churning; threshing.

battant, băh-tahng, *m* leaf (door); clapper (bell).

battant, e, băh-tahng, *a* beating; pelting.

battement, băht-mahng, *m* beat(ing); throb(bing); clapping.

batterie, băht-ree, *f* fight; battery; set; **—de cuisine,** —de kwee-zeen, kitchen utensils; percussion; drums.

battoir, băh-to'ăhr, *m* beater; paddle; bat.

battre, băh-tr, *v* to beat; to thrash; to coin; to churn; to thresh; to shuffle; **se—,** to fight.

baudet, boh-day, *m* donkey; sawhorse.

bauge, bohsh, *f* lair (of wild boar); dirty hovel; squirrel's nest.

baume, bohm, *m* balm; balsam.

bavard, e, băh-văhr, *mf* chatterbox; *a* talkative.

bavardage, băh-văhr-dăhsh, *m* chitchat.

bavarder, băh-văhr-deh, *v* to chatter.

baver, băh-veh, *v* to dribble.

bavoir, băh-vo'ăhr, *m* bib.

bazar, băh-zăhr, *m* bazaar.

béant, e, beh-ahng, *a* gaping; **bouche —e,** boosh —ahngt, agape.

béat, e,* beh-ăh, *a* sanctimonious; blissful.

beau, boh, *m* beautiful; beauty; fine weather.

beau (before vowel or a mute *h*: **bel,** bell), boh, *m*; **belle,*** bell, *f, a* beautiful; handsome; fine fair; **avoir–,** ăh-vo'ăhr–, to... in vain; **de plus belle,** with renewed ardor.

beaucoup, boh-koo, *adv* much; many; a great deal.

beau-fils, boh-fiss, *m* stepson; son-in-law.

beau-frère, boh-frair, *m* brother-in-law.

beau-père, boh-pair, *m* father-in-law; stepfather.

beauté, boh-teh, *f* beauty.

beaux-parents, boh-păh-rahng, *mpl* parents-in-law.

bébé, beh-beh, *m* baby.

bec, beck, *m* beak; snout.

bécarre, beh-kăhr, *m* natural (music).

bécasse, beh-kăhss, *f* woodcock.

bécassine, beh-kăhss-een, *f* snipe; silly girl.

bec-de-lièvre, beck der le-ay-vr, *m* harelip.

béchamel, beh-shăh-mell, *f* cream sauce.

bêche, baish, *f* spade.

bêcher, bay-sheh, *v* to dig.

becqueter, bayk-teh, *v* to peck; to kiss.

bedaine, ber-denn, *f* paunch; belly.

bedeau, ber-doh, *m* beadle.

bée, beh, *af* open; gaping; **bouche –,** boosh –, open-mouthed.

beffroi, beh-fro'ăh, *m* belfry.

bégayer, beh-ghay-yeh, *v* to stammer; to stutter.

bègue, baygh, *n & a* stammerer; stammering.

bégueule, beh-gherl, *f* haughty; prude.

beige, baish, *a* beige.

beignet, bayn-yay, *m* fritter.

bêler, bay-leh, *v* to bleat.

bélier, beh-le-eh, *m* ram;

battering ram.

belle-fille, bell fee-ye, *f* daughter-in-law; stepdaughter.

belle-mère, bell mair, *f* mother-in-law; stepmother.

belle-soeur, bell ser, *f* sister-in-law.

belliqueu-x, se,* bell-le-ker, *a* warlike.

bémol, beh-mol, *m* flat (music).

bénédicité, beh-neh-de-se-teh, *m* grace before meals.

bénédiction, beh-neh-dick-se-ong, *f* blessing.

bénéfice, beh-neh-fiss, *m* benefit, profit; living.

benêt, ber-nay, *a & m* booby; simpleton; silly.

bénévole,* beh-neh-vol, *a* voluntary; unpaid.

béni, e, beh-ne, *a* blessed.

béni-n, gne, beh-nang, *a* benign; kind.

bénir, beh-neer, *v,* to bless.

bénitier, beh-ne-te-eh, *m* holy-water basin.

benzine, bang-zeen, *f* benzine.

béquille, beh-kee-ye, *f* crutch.

bercail, bair-kah'e, *m* (sing, only) sheepfold; fold.

berceau, bair-soh, *m* cradle; arbor; cradle vault.

bercer, bair-seh, *v* to rock; to lull; to delude.

berceuse, bair-serz, *f* rocking chair; lullaby.

béret, beh-ray, *m* beret.

berge, bairsh, *f* steep bank of a river.

berg-er, ère, bair-sheh, *mf* shepherd.

bergère, bair-shair, *f* easy chair.

bergerie, bair-sher-ree, *f* sheepfold.

berlue, bair-lE, *f* dimness of sight; false vision.

berner, bair-neh, *v* to toss in a blanket; to fool.

besace, ber-zăhss, *f* beggar's bag.

besogne, ber-zon-yer, *f* work; task; labor.

besogneu-x, se, ber-zon-yer, *a* needy; necessitous.

besoin, ber-zo-ang, *m* need; want; necessity; **au –,** oh –, in case of need.

bestial, e,* bess-te-ăhl, *a* beastly; brutish.

bestiaux, bess-te-oh, *mpl* cattle.

bétail, beh-tah'e, *m* cattle; livestock.

bête, bayt, *f* beast; animal;

a
b
c
d
e
f
g
h
i
j
k
l
m
n
o
p
q
r
s
t
u
v
w
x
y
z

a* stupid; **–noire,**
–no'ăhr, aversion.

bêtise, bay-teez, *f*
stupidity; stupid thing.

béton, beh-*tong*, *m*
concrete.

betterave, bett-răhv, *f*
beetroot.

beugler, ber-gleh, *v* to
bellow; to bawl.

beurre, ber, *m* butter.

beurrer, ber-reh, *v* to
butter.

bévue, beh-vE, *f* blunder;
mistake.

biais, be-ay, *m* slant;
expedient; **en –,** ahng–,
on the cross.

biaiser, be-ay-zeh, *v* to
slope; to shuffle.

bibelot, beeb-lo, *m*
trinket; knicknack.

biberon, beeb-rong, *m*
feeding bottle.

bible, bee-bl, *f* bible.

bibliophile, be-ble-off-eel,
m lover of books.

bibliothécaire, be-ble-o-
teh-kair, *m* librarian.

bibliothèque, be-ble-o-
teck, *f* library; bookcase.

biche, bish, *f* hind; doe.

bicoque, be-kock, *f* paltry
house; hut; hovel.

bicyclette, be-se-klett, *f*
bicycle.

bidon, be-dong, *m* can.

bidonville, be-dong-veel,

m shantytown.

bielle, be-ell, *f*
connectingrod.

bien, be-ang, *adv* well;
quite; very; *m* good;
property; welfare; **–que,**
–ker, although; **tout va
–,** too văh–, all is well.

bien-aimé, e, be-ang n'ay-
meh, *a* beloved.

bien-être, be-ang n'ay-tr,
m comfort; welfare.

bienfaisant, e, be-ang-fer-
zahng, *a* kind;
charitable.

bienfait, be-ang-fay, *m*
kindness; favor; boon.

bienfai-teur, trice, be-ang-
fay-ter, *mf* benefactor;
benefactress.

bien-fonds, be-ang-fong, *m*
real estate.

bienheureu-x, se, be-ang-
ner,rer, *a* blessed; happy.

bienséance, be-ang-seh-
ahngss, *f* decorum;
propriety.

bientôt, be-ang-toh; *adv*
soon; shortly.

bienveillance, be-ang-
vay'e-yahngss, *f*
kindness; goodwill.

bienveillant, e, be-ang-
vay'e-yahng, *a* kind;
benevolent.

bienvenu, e, be-angv-nEE,
a & *n* welcome.

bienvenue, be-angv-nEE, *f*

welcome.

bière, be-air, *f* beer;
coffin; bier.

biffer, be-feh, *v* to strike
out; to cancel.

bifteck, beef-teck, *m*
beefsteak.

bifurquer (se), ser be-
fEEr-keh, *v* to fork.

bigarré, e, be-găh-reh, *a*
motley; streaked.

bigorneau, be-gor-noh, *m*
winkle (periwinkle).

bigot, e, be-gho, *mf* bigot;
a bigoted.

bigoudi, be-goo-de, *m*
curler (hair).

bijou, be-shoo, *m* jewel;
trinket; (fig.) darling.

bijouterie, be-shoot-ree, *f*
jewelry.

bijoutier, be-shoo-te-eh,
m jeweler.

bikini, be-ke-ne, *m* bikini.

bilan, be-lahng, *m*
balancesheet; schedule.

bile, beel, *f* bile; gall;
anger.

bilieu-x, se, be-le-er, *a*
bilious; irritable.

billard, bee-yăhr, *m*
billiards; billiards room.

bille, bee-ye, *f* ball;
marble; log.

billet, bee-yay, *m* bill;
note; ticket; **–de
banque,** – der bahngk,
banknote; **–simple,** –

sang-pl, single ticket;
–d'aller et retour, –
dăh-leh-eh rer-toohr,
return ticket.

billevesée, bill-ver-zeh, *f*
nonsense.

billion, bill-e-ong, *m*
thousand millions.

billot, bee-yo, *m* block.

bimensuel, -le, be-măhng-
sE-ell, *a* bimonthly.

binette, be-nett, *f* hoe;
(pop.) face.

binocle, be-nock-kl, *m*
pince-nez.

biographie, be-og-răh-fee,
f biography.

bipède, be-payd, *a* & *m*
biped; two-legged.

biplan, be-plahng, *m*
biplane.

bique, bick, *f* nanny-goat.

bis, biss, *adv* twice; again;
encore!

bis, e, be, *a* brown.

bisaïeul, e, be-zăh-yerl, *mf*
great-grandfather; great-
grandmother.

biscornu, e, biss-kor-nE, *a*
odd; queer.

biscotte, biss-kot, *f* rusk.

biscuit, biss-kwe, *m*
biscuit.

bise, beez, *f* north wind;
cold blast; *fam* kiss.

biseau, be-zoh, *m* bevel.

bisque, beesk, *f* shellfish
soup; vexation.

bisquer, bees-keh, *v*
(fam.) to be vexed.

bisser, biss-eh, *v* to
encore.

bissextile, be-secks-teel, *af*
used only in **Année –,**
Leap Year.

bistré, e, biss-treh, *a*
tawny; swarthy.

bizarre,* be-zăhr, *a* odd;
whimsical; eccentric.

blafard, e, blăh-făhr, *a*
dim; wan; pale.

blague, blăhg, *f*
tobaccopouch; (fam.)
joke.

blaguer, blăh-gheh, *v*
(fam.) to joke; to hoax.

blaireau, blay-roh, *m*
badger; shaving brush.

blâme, blahm, *m* blame;
censure.

blâmer, blah-meh, *v* to
blame; to find fault
with.

blanc, blahng, *m* white;
white man; blank.

blan-c, che, *a* white;
clean; blank; pale; **nuit
blanche** nwe blahngsh,
sleepless night.

blanchaille, blahng-
shah'e, *f* whitebait.

blanchâtre, blahng-shah-
tr, *a* whitish.

blancheur, blahng-sher, *f*
whiteness.

blanchir, blahng-sheer, *v*

to whiten; to bleach; to
grow white.

blanchissage, blahng-
shiss-ăhsh, *m* washing.

blanchisserie, blahng-
shiss-re, *f* laundry;
laundering.

blanquette, blahng-kett, *f*
stew with white sauce.

blaser, blah-zeh, *v* to
blunt; to pall; **se–,** ser–,
to get tired of **(de)**; to
become blasé.

blason, blah-zong, *m*
heraldry; coat-of-arms.

blasphème, blăhss-faym,
m blasphemy.

blé, bleh, *m* corn; wheat;
grain.

blême, blaym, *a* pallid;
ghastly; wan.

blémir, bleh-meer, *v* to
grow pale.

blessant, e, bless-ahng, *a*
offensive **(pour,** to);
hurtful.

blessé, bless-eh, *m*
wounded man; *pp* & *a*
wounded.

blesser, bless-eh, *v* to
wound; to hurt; to
injure; to offend; **se –,** to
hurt oneself; to be
offended **(de,** at, with).

blessure, bless-EEr, *f*
wound; injury.

blet, te, blay, *a* overripe.

bleu, e, bler, *a* blue; *m*

bruise.

bleuâtre, bler-ah-tr, *a* bluish.

bleuet, bluet, bler-ay, blE-ay, *m* cornflower.

bleuir, bler-eer, *v* to make blue; to turn blue.

blindé, blang-deh, *a* steelplated; ironclad.

bloc, block, *m* block; lump; log; **en –,** ahng –, in the lump.

blocus, block-EEss, *m* blockade.

blond, e, blong, *a* fair; light; blond.

bloquer, block-eh, *v* to blockade; to block up.

blottir (se), serblot-eer, *v* to crouch; to snuggle down.

blouse, blooz, *f* frock; smock-frock; pinafore; pocket (billiards).

blouser, bloo-zeh, *v* to dupe; **se –,** ser –, (fam.) to blunder.

bluette, blE-ayt, *f* spark; literary trifle.

boa, bo'ăh, *m* boa; fur tippet.

bobard, bo-bahr, *m* (fam.) lie; fib.

bobine, bob-een, *f* bobbin; spool; reel; coil.

bobo, bob-o, *m* slight hurt.

bocage, bock-ăhsh, *m* grove; copse.

bocal, bock-ăhl, *m* glass bowl; wide-mouthed bottle.

bock, bock, *m* beerglass; glass of beer.

bœuf, berf, *m* bullock; beef.

bohémien, ne, bo-eh-me-ang, *mf* Bohemian; gypsy.

boire, bo'ăhr, *v* to drink; to soak up (paper, etc.).

bois, bo'ăh, *m* wood; timber; horns (deer).

boisé, e, bo'ăh-zeh, *a* wooded; wainscoted.

boiserie, bo'ăhz-ree, *f* wainscot.

boisseau, bo'ăhss-oh, *m* bushel.

boisson, bo'ăhss-ong, *f* drink; beverage; drinking.

boisson non alcoolisée, bo'ăhss-ong-ăhl-koll-e-seh *f* soft drink.

boîte, bo'ăht, *f* box; case; tin;**–aux lettres,** –oh lay-tr, mailbox; **–de vitesses,** –derve-tess, gearbox.

boiter, bo'ăh-teh, *v* to limp.

boiteu-x, -se, bo'ăh-ter, *mf* cripple; *a* lame; limping.

bol, boll, *m* bowl; basin.

bombance, bong-bahngss, *f* feasting.

bombarder, bong-băhr-deh, *v* to bombard.

bombe, bongb, *f* bomb; shell.

bomber, bong-beh, *v* to make convex; to bulge out.

bon, bong, *m* good; good quality; bond; order; check.

bon, ne, bong, *a* good; kind; advisable; right.

bonasse, bonn-ăhss, *a* meek.

bonbon, bong-bong, *m* sweet; candy.

bonbonnière, bong-bonn-e-air, *f* candy box.

bond, bong, *m* bound; leap; jump; **faire faux –,**fair foh –, to fail.

bonde, bongd, *f* bunghole; sluice; plughole.

bondir, bong-deer, *v* to bound; to spring; to skip.

bonheur, bonn-er *m* happiness; delight; luck.

bonhomie, bonn-omm-ee, *f* good nature; simplicity.

bonhomme, bonn-omm, *m* good-natured man; old man; fellow.

bonification, bonn-e-fe-kăh-se-ong, *f* improvement; allowance.

bonifier, bonn-e-fe-eh, *v* to improve.

boniment, bonn-e-mah*ng*, *m* sales talk; tall story.

bonjour, bong- shoor, *m* good morning.

bonne, bonn, *f* maid.

bonnement, bonn-mah*ng*, *adv* simply; plainly.

bonnet, bonn-ay, *m* cap; cup (bra); **gros –,**groh –, big wig; magnate.

bonneterie, bonn-tree, *f* hosiery.

bonnetier, bonn-te-eh, *m* hosier.

bonsoir, bong-so'ăhr, *m* good evening; good night.

bonté, bong-teh, *f* goodness; kindness (**pour,** to).

bord, bor, *m* border; edge; rim; side; bank; shore.

bordée, bor-deh, *f* volley; broadside.

border, bor-deh, *v* to border; to edge; to hem; to tuck up.

bordereau, bor-de*r*-roh, *m* schedule; detailed account; memorandum.

bordure, bor-dEEr, *f* border; edge; curb.

bord du trottoir, bor-de*r*-trot-o'ăhr *m* curb.

boréal, e, bor-eh-ăhl, *a* northern.

borgne, born-ye*r*, *a* blind in one eye; (fig.) shady.

borne, born, *f* boundary; milestone; terminal.

borné, e, bor-neh, *pp* & *a* limited; narrow; shortsighted.

borner, bor-neh, *v* to bound; to limit; to confine.

bosquet, boss-kay, *m* grove; thicket.

bosse, boss, *f* hump; bump; embossment.

bosseler, boss-leh, *v* to emboss; to dent; to batter.

bossu, e, boss-E, *mf* hunchback; *a* hunchbacked.

bot, bo, *n* & *a* used only in **pied-bot,** pe-eh-bo, clubfoot; clubfooted.

botanique, bot-ăh-nick, *f* botany; *a* botanical.

botte, bott, *f* boot; high boot; bundle; hank; thrust; **à propos de –s,** ăh pro-poh de –, without any reason.

botter, bott-eh, *v* to help one with his boots; (*fam*) to suit; to boot; to kick.

bottier, bott-e-eh, *m* bootmaker.

bottin, bott-ang, *m* French Post-Office Directory; telephone directory.

bottine, bott-een, *f* half-boot; lady's boot; boot.

bouc, book, *m* goat; – **émissaire,** –eh-miss-air, scapegoat.

boucanier, boo-kăh-ne-eh, *m* buccaneer.

bouche, boosh, *f* mouth; opening.

bouchée, boo-sheh, *f* mouthful.

boucher, boo-sheh, *v* to stop; to obstruct; to cork.

bouch-er, èr, boo-sheh, *mf* butcher.

boucherie, boosh-ree, *f* butcher's shop or trade; shambles; slaughter.

bouchon, boo-shong, *m* cork; stopper.

boucle, boo-kl, *f* buckle; ring; curl; **–d'oreille,** –doh-ray'e, earring.

bouclé, e, boo-kleh, *a* curly.

boucle d'oreille, book-ler-do-ray, *f* earring.

boucler, boo-kleh, *v* to buckle; to ring; to curl.

bouclier, boo-kle-eh, *m* shield; buckler.

bouder, boo-deh, *v* to pout; to sulk.

boudin, boo-dang, *m* blood sausage.

boue, boo, *f* mud; mire;

dirt.

bouée, boo-eh, *f* buoy.

boueur, or **boueux,** boo-er, *m* garbage collector.

boueu-x, se, boo-er, *a* muddy.

bouffant, e, boo-fahng, *a* puffed; baggy.

bouffée, boo-feh, *f* puff; whiff.

bouffer, boo-feh, *v* to puff out; (*pop*) to eat greedily.

bouffi, e, boo-fe, *pp* & *a* puffed up; inflated; (**de,** with).

bouffon, boo-fong, *m* buffoon; jester.

bouffon, ne, boo-fong, *a* comical; droll.

bouge, boosh, *m* hovel; den; bulge.

bougeoir, boo-sho'ăhr, *m* candlestick.

bouger, boo-sheh, *v* to stir; to budge; to move.

bougie, boo-shee, *f* candle; sparkplug.

bougonner, boo-ghonn-eh, *v* to grumble.

bougran, boo-grahng, *m* buckram.

bouillabaisse, boo'e-yăh-bess, *f* highly seasoned fish soup.

bouillant, e, boo'e-yahng, *a* boiling; hot-tempered.

bouilli, e, –, boo'e-yee, *a*

boiled.

bouillie, boo'e-yee, *f* baby cereal; gruel.

bouillir, boo'e-yeer, *v* to boil.

bouilloire, boo'e-yo'ăhr, *f* kettle.

bouillon, boo'e-yong, *m* broth; soup; stock; bubble.

bouillonner, boo'e-yonn-eh, *v* to bubble up; to boil.

bouillotte, boo'e-yot, *f* hot water bottle; bouillotte (card game).

boulangerie, boo-lahng sh-ree, *f* bakery.

boule, bool, *f* ball.

bouleau, boo-loh, *m* birch tree.

boulet, boo-lay, *m* cannonball; shot; small ovoid coal.

boulette, boo-lett, *f* meatball; pellet; blunder.

boulevard, bool-văhr, *m* boulevard.

bouleversement, bool-vair-ser-mahng, *m* overthrow; confusion.

bouleverser, bool-vair-seh, *v* to overthrow; to upset.

boulier, boo-lee-eh, *m* abacus; scoring board.

boulon, boo-long, *m* bolt;

pin.

boulonner, boo-lonn-eh, *v* to bolt; (*fam*) to work hard.

bouquet, boo-kay, *m* bunch; nosegay; aroma; crowning piece; prawn.

bouquin, boo-kang, *m* (*fam*) book.

bouquiner, boo-ke-neh, *v* (*fam*) to read.

bouquiniste, boo-ke-nisst, *m* dealer in secondhand books.

bourbe, boohrb, *f* mud; mire; dirt.

bourbier, boohr-be-eh, *m* slough; mire.

bourde, boohrd, *f* fib; sham; (*fam*) mistake.

bourdon, boohr-dong, *m* bumblebee; great bell; drone bass.

bourdonner, boohr-donn-eh, *v* to hum; to buzz.

bourg, boohr, *m* market town; village.

bourgade, boohr-găhd, *f* small town or large village.

bourgeois, -e, boohr-sho'ăh, *mf* citizen; middle-class man or woman; Bourgeois; **les petits –,** lay per te –, the lower middle class; master; *a** citizenlike; middle-class; common.

bourgeoisie, boohr-sho'ăh-zee, *f* middleclass.

bourgeon, boohr-shong, *m* bud; shoot; (fam.) pimple.

bourgeonner, boohr-shonn-eh, *v* to come into bud; (*fam*) to have pimples.

bourgogne, boohr-gonn-yer, *m* Burgundy wine.

bourrade, boo-răhd, *f* cuff; hard blow.

bourrasque, boo-răhsk, *f* gust of wind.

bourre, boohr, *f* flock; wadding.

bourreau, boo-roh, *m* executioner; tormentor.

bourrelet, boohr-lay, *m* pad; padding; cushion; (*fam*) rolls of fat.

bourrelier, boohr-le-eh, *m* harness-maker.

bourrer boo-reh, *v* to stuff; to cram; (**de,** with); to thrash.

bourriche, boo-reesh, *f* basket; hamper.

bourru, e, boo-rE, *a* surly; rough.

bourse, boohrs, *f* purse; scholarship; stock exchange.

boursier, boohr-se-eh, *a* & *n* exhibitioner; speculator on the stock exchange.

boursoufler, boor-soo-ßeh, *v* to bloat; to puff up.

bousculer, boos-kE-leh, *v* to jostle; to hustle; to shove.

bouse, booz, *f* manure.

boussole, boo-sol, *f* compass.

bout, boo, *m* end; tip; à –, ăh –, exhausted; **au –du compte,** oh – dE kongt, after all.

boutade, boo-tăhd, *f* whim; freak; sally.

boute-en-train, boot-ahng-trang, *m* life and soul of a party.

bouteille, boo-tay'e, *f* bottle.

boutique, boo-teeck, *f* shop; boutique; store.

boutiqui-er, -ère, boo-te-ke-eh, *mf* storekeeper.

bouton, boo-tong, *m* bud; button; handle; knob; stud; pimple; **–de manchettes,** – der mahng-shett, *m* cufflink.

boutonner, boo-tonn-eh, *v* to button; to bud.

boutonnière, boo-tonn-e-air, *f* buttonhole.

bouture, bou-tEEr, *f* cutting (of plant).

bouvreuil, boo-vrer'e, *m* bullfinch.

boxe, box, *f* boxing.

boyau, bo'ăh-yoh, *m* bowel; gut; hose; long narrow passage.

bracelet, brăhss-lay, *m* bracelet.

braconnier, brăh-konn-e-eh, *m* poacher.

braguette, brah-ghett, *f* fly (of pants).

brailler, brah'e-yeh, *v* to bawl; to squall.

braire, brair, *v* to bray.

braise, brayz, *f* embers; live coals.

braisé, e, bray-zeh, *a* stewed; braised.

brancard, brahng-kăhr, *m* stretcher; shaft.

brancardier, brahng-kăhr-de-eh, *m* stretcher-bearer.

branche, brahngsh. *f* branch; bough; division.

brancher, brahng-sheh, *v* to branch; to plug in, to connect; to put through.

branchies, brahng-shee, *fpl* gills.

brandir, brahng-deer, *v* to brandish.

branlant, e, brahng-lahng, *a* shaking; tottering; loose.

branle, brangl, *m* swinging; impulse; motion; **donner le –,** donn-eh ler –, to set

a
b
c
d
e
f
g
h
i
j
k
l
m
n
o
p
q
r
s
t
u
v
w
x
y
z

A
B
C
D
E
F
G
H
I
J
K
L
M
N
O
P
Q
R
S
T
U
V
W
X
Y
Z

going.

branle-bas, brah*n*gl-bah, *m* upset; clearing the decks for action.

branler, brah*n*g-leh, *v* to swing; to totter; to be loose.

braquer, brăh-keh, *v* to aim (**sur,** at); to change direction (of car, etc.); (*fam*) to hold up a bank.

bras, brăh, *m* arm; handle; bracket; power; labor; –**dessus –dessous,** – der-sE – der-soo, arm in arm.

brasier, brăh-ze-eh, *m* red-hot coal-fire; brazier.

brassard, brăhss-ăhr, *m* armlet; armband.

brasse, brăhss, *f* fathom; stroke; breaststroke.

brassée, brăhss-eh, *f* armful; stroke.

brasser, brăhss-eh, *m* to brew; to concoct.

brasserie, brăhss-ree, *f* brewery; cafe; restaurant.

brasseur, brăhss-er, *m* brewer

bravade, brăh-văhd, *f* bravado; bluster.

brave, * brăhv, *a* brave; honest; good; smart; **un homme –,** u*n*g n'omm –, a brave man; **un –homme,** u*n*g – omm, a worthy man.

braver, brăh-veh, *v* to brave; to face; to dare.

bravoure, brăh-voohr, *f* bravery; courage; gallantry.

brebis, brer-be, *f* sheep; ewe;– **galeuse,** – găh-ler*z*, black sheep.

brèche, braysh, *f* breach; gap; notch.

bredouille, brer-doo'e-yer, *a* empty-handed; être –, to have failed.

bredouiller, brer-doo'e-yeh, *v* to mumble.

bref, brayf, *adv* briefly; in short; **bref, ève,** *a* brief; short.

breloque, brer-lock, *f* trinket; charm.

brème, braym, *f* bream.

bretelle, brer-tell, *f* strap; sling; *pl* suspenders.

breuvage, brer-văhsh, *m* drink; beverage.

brevet, brer-vay, *m* patent; licence; warrant; commission; diploma.

breveter, brerv-teh, *v* to patent; to grant a patent; to commission.

bréviaire, breh-ve-air, *m* breviary.

bribe, breeb, *f* scrap.

bric-à-brac, brick-ăh brăhk *m* junk.

bricole, bree-kol, *f* breast harness; *fpl* odds and

ends; little bits; trifles.

bricoler, bree-ko-leh, *v* to put breast harness on horse; to do odd jobs; to putter about.

bricoleur, bree-ko-ler, *a* & *n* handy; handyman.

bride, breed, *f* bridle; reins; string (of bonnet, etc.); triple (crochet); **tourner –,** toohr-neh – to turn back.

brider, bre-deh, *v* to bridle; to restrain; to tie up.

brie, bree, *m* Brie cheese.

brièvement, bre-ayv-mah*n*g, *adv* briefly.

brièveté, bre-ayv-teh, *f* briefness.

brigade, bre-găhd, *f* brigade; gang; –**de sûreté,** –der sEEr-teh, detective force.

brigadier, bre-găh-de-eh, *m* corporal; bombardier; sergeant; foreman.

brigand, bre-ghah*n*g, *m* thief; robber.

brigue, breegh, *f* intrigue; cabal.

briguer, bre-gheh, *v* to aspire to; to solicit.

brillamment, bree-yăh-mah*n*g, *adv* brilliantly.

brillant, e, bree-yah*n*g, *a* bright; brilliant; shining. *n* brilliancy; shine;

diamond.

briller, bree-yeh, *v* to shine; to be conspicuous.

brimborion, bra*ng*-bo-re-*ong*, *m* bauble; trinket.

brimer, bree-meh, *v* to victimize; to persecute.

brin, bra*ng*, *m* bit; blade; sprig.

brioche, bre-osh, *f* bun.

brique, brick, *f* brick.

briquet, bre-kay, *m* cigarette lighter; **pierre à –,** pe-ayr ah–, *f* lighter flint.

briqueterie, brick-tree, *f* brickworks.

bris, bre, *m* wreck.

brisant, bre-zah*ng*, *m* breaker; reef.

brise, breez, *f* breeze.

briser, bre-zeh, *v* to break; **se –,** to break up.

broc, brock, *m* jug; jar.

brocanter, brock-ah*ng*-teh, *v* to deal in secondhand goods.

brocant-eur, -euse, brock-ah*ng*-ter, *mf* secondhand storekeeper; broker.

brocard, brock-ăhr, *m* taunt; jeer; scoff.

brocart, brock-ăhr, *m* brocade.

broche, brosh, *f* spit; brooch.

broché, e, brosh-eh, *pp* &

a paperback (books).

brochet, brosh-ay, *m* pike.

brochette, bro-shett, *f* skewer; small spit.

brochure, brosh-EEr, *f* pamphlet; brochure.

broder, brod-eh, *v* to embroider; (*fig*) to embellish (a story).

broderie, brod-ree, *f* embroidery; (*fig*) embellishment.

broiement, bro'ăh-mah*ng*, *m* pounding; crushing.

broncher, bro*ng*-sheh, *v* to stumble; to trip; **sans –,** sah*ng* –, without flinching.

bronches, bro*ng*sh, *fpl* bronchial tubes.

bronchite, bro*ng*-sheet, *f* bronchitis.

bronzage, bro*ng*-zăh*sh* *m* suntan.

bronze, bro*ng*z, *m* bronze.

bronzer, bro*ng*-zeh, *v* to bronze; to tan.

brosse, bross, *f* brush.

brosser, bross-eh, *v* to brush.

brou, broo, *m* husk; hull.

brouet, broo-ay, *m* thin broth.

brouette, broo-ett, *f* wheelbarrow; hand cart.

brouhaha, broo-ăh-ăh, *m* uproar; hubbub.

brouillamini, broo'e-yăh-

me-ne, *m* (*fam*) confusion.

brouillard, broo'e-yăhr, *m* fog; haze.

brouille, broo'e-ye, *f* disagreement; quarrel.

brouiller, broo'e-yeh, *v* to mix up; to confuse; **se –,** to fall out; to quarrel.

brouillon, broo'e-yo*ng*, *m* rough draft; rough book.

brouillon, ne, broo'e-yo*ng*, *n* & *a* blundering; muddleheaded.

broussailles, broo-sah'e, *fpl* brushwood.

brouter, broo-teh, *v* to graze.

broyer, bro'ăh-yeh, *v* to pound; to crush.

bru, brE, *f* daughter-in-law.

bruine, brween, *f* drizzling rain.

bruire, brweer, *v* to rustle; to murmur.

bruissement, brweess-mah*ng*, *m* rustling; rumbling.

bruit, brwee, *m* noise; din; rumor; sound.

brûlant, e, brE-lah*ng*, *a* burning; scorching; fervent; impassioned.

brûle-pourpoint (à), ăh brEEl poohr-po'a*ng*, *adv* point-blank.

brûler, brE-leh, *v* to burn;

to blow; to pass without stopping.

brûlure, brE-lEEr, *f* burn; scald.

brume, brEEm, *f* mist; haze.

brun, e, bru*n*g, brEEn, *a* & *n* brown; dusky; dark.

brunâtre, brE-nah-tr, *a* brownish.

brune, brEEn, *f* dusk; dark-complexioned woman.

brunir, brE-neer, *v* to brown; to burnish; to tan.

brusque,* brEEsk, *a* blunt; rough; abrupt; sudden.

brusquer, brEEss-keh, *v* to be blunt with; hurry on (with events).

brusquerie, brEEss-ker-ree, *f* bluntness; abruptness.

brut, e, brEt, *a* raw; rough; abrupt; coarse; gross.

brutal, e,* brE-tăhl, *a* brutal; brutish.

brutaliser, brE-tăhl-e-zeh, *v* to treat brutally; to bully.

brutalité, brE-tăhl-e-teh, *f* roughness; brutishness.

brute, brEt, *f* brute.

bruyamment, brE-yăh-mah*n*g, *adv* noisily; loudly.

bruyant, e, brE-yah*n*g, *a* noisy; loud.

bruyère, brE-yair, *f* heather.

buanderie, bÜ-ahngd-ree, *f* laundry (place).

bûche, bEEsh, *f* log; (*fig*) blockhead; Christmas cake.

bûcher, bEE-sheh, *m* woodshed; funeral pyre; stake.

bûcheron, bEEsh-ro*n*g, *m* lumberjack; logger.

bûch-eur, -euse, bEE-sher, *mf* (*fam*) hard-working person.

budget, bEEd-**shay,** *m* budget.

buée, bE-eh, *f* steam; vapor; blur.

buffet, bE-fay, *m* sideboard; buffet; refreshment cart.

buffle, bEE-ß *m* buffalo; buff-leather.

buis, bwe, *m* boxwood; box tree.

buisson, bweess-o*n*g, *m* bush; thicket; **faire l'école buissonière,** fair leh-kol bweess-onn-e-air, to play truant.

bulle, bEEl, *f* bubble.

bulletin, bEEl-ta*n*g, *m* report; bulletin; ticket.

buraliste, bE-răh-lisst, *mf* tobacconist.

bureau, bE-roh, *m* office; desk; department.

bureaucrate, bE-roh-

krăht, *m* bureaucrat.

bureaucratie, bE-roh-krăhss-ee, *f* bureaucracy; (*fam*) red tape.

burette, bE-rayt, *f* cruet; oilcan.

burlesque, bEEr-lessk, *a* burlesque; ludicrous.

buse, bEEz, *f* buzzard; (*fig*) blockhead.

buste, bEEst, *m* bust.

but, bE, *m* mark; aim; goal; end; purpose.

buter, bE-teh, *v* to butt; to prop; to stumble; **se –, ser –,** to be bent (**à**, on).

buté, bE-teh, *a* fixed; obstinate.

butin, bE-ta*n*g, *m* plunder; booty.

butor, bE-tor, *m* (*fig*) lout.

butte, bEEt, *f* mound; knoll; **en –à,** ahng – ăh, exposed to.

buvable, bE-văh-bl, *a* drinkable.

buvard, bE-văhr, *m* blotting-pad; **papier –,** păh-pe-eh –, blotter.

buveu-r, -se, bE-ver, *mf* drinker.

ça, săh, *pron* contraction of **cela,** ser-lăh, that.

çà, săh, *adv* hither; **–et là,** – eh lăh, here and there.

cabale, kăh-băhl, *f* cabal.

cabane, kăh-băhnn, *f* hut; cabin.

cabanon, kăh-băh-nong, *m* cell; padded cell.

cabaret, kăh-băh-ray, *m* cabaret.

cabas, kăh-bah, *m* rush basket; shopping bag.

cabestan, kăh-bess-tahng, *m* capstan.

cabillaud, kăh-bee-yoh, *m* codfish (fresh).

cabine, kăh-been, *f* cabin; beach house; telephone booth.

cabinet, kăh-be-ney, *m* small room; closet; office; practice; bathroom; chambers; cabinet (pol.).

cabine téléphonique, kăh-been-teh-leh-fonn-eeck *f* pay-phone.

câble, kah-bl, *m* cable; rope.

câbler, kah-bleh, *v* to cable; to twist (strands).

câblogramme, kah-blo-grahmm, *m* cablegram.

caboche, kăh-bosh, *f* (*fam.*) head.

cabosser, kăh-bo-sseh, *v* to bump; to dent.

cabotage, kăh-bot-ăhsh, *m* coasting.

caboter, kăh-bot-eh, *v* to coast.

cabotin, kăh-bot-ang, *m* bad actor; show off.

cabrer (se), ser kăh-breh, *v* to rear; to fire up.

cabriole, kăh-bre-ol, *f* caper; leap; somersault.

cabriolet, kăh-bre-oll-ay, *m* convertible.

cacahuète, kăh-kăh-wait, *f* peanut.

cacao, kăh-kăh-o, *m* cocoa.

cacatoès, kăh-kăh-to'es, *m* cockatoo.

cachalot, kăh-shă-lo, *m* sperm-whale.

cache, kăhsh, *f* hiding-place; **cache-cache,** *m* hide-and-seek.

cache-nez, kăhsh-neh, *m* muffler; scarf.

cacher, kăh-sheh, *v* to hide; to conceal.

cachet, kăh-shay, *m* seal; style; tablet (med); fee (show bus).

cacheter, kăhsh-teh, *v* to seal (up).

cachette, kăh-shett, *f* hiding-place; **en –,** ahng –, secretly.

cachot, kăh-sho, *m* cell; dungeon; prison.

cachotterie, kăh-shot-ree, *f* little secret.

cadavre, kăh-dah-vr, *m* corpse; dead body.

cadeau, kăh-doh, *m* present; gift.

cadenas, kăhd-nah, *m* padlock.

cadenasser, kăhd-năhss-

A
B
C
D
E
F
G
H
I
J
K
L
M
N
O
P
Q
R
S
T
U
V
W
X
Y
Z

eh, *v* to padlock.

cadence, kăh-dahngss, *f* cadence; rhythm.

cadet, te, kăh-day, *a & n* younger; least; youngest.

cadran, kăh-drahng, *m* dial.

cadre, kah-dr, *m* frame; plan; managerial staff; staff.

cadrer, kah-dreh, *v* to conform; to tally.

cadu-c, que, kăh-dEEk, *a* null and void.

cafard, kăh-făhr, *m* cockroach; (*fam*) "the blues".

cafardage, kăh-făhz-dăhshe, *m* hypocrite.

cafarder, kăh-făhr-deh, *v* to tattletale.

café, kăh-feh, *m* coffee; coffeehouse; café; – **au lait,** – oh lay, coffee with milk, –**noir,** – no'ăhr, black coffee.

cafetière, kăhf-te-air, *f* coffeepot.

cage, kăhsh, *f* cage; coop; frame.

cagneu-x, se, kăhn-yer, *a* knock-kneed.

cagoule kăh-geol, *f* hood; balaclava.

cahier, kăh-yeh, *m* notebook; workbook.

cahin-caha, kăh-ang kăh-ăh, *adv* so-so; middling.

cahot, kăh-o, *m* jolt; bump.

cahoter, kăh-ot-eh, *v* to jolt; to bump along.

cahute, kăh-EEt, *f* hut; hovel.

caille, kah'e, *f* quail.

cailler, kah'e-yeh, *v* to curdle; to clot.

caillot, kah'e-o, *m* clot.

caillou, kah'e-yoo, *m* pebble; flint; stone.

caisse, kess, *f* case; box; chest; cashregister; fund; checkout; (carriage) body; drum; –**d'épargne,** – deh-păhrn'yer, savings bank.

caissi-er, ére, kess-e-eh, *mf* cashier.

cajoler, kăh-**sh**oll-eh, *v* to wheedle; to coax.

calamité, kăh-lăh-me-teh, *f* calamity.

calandre, kăh-lahng-dr, *f* calender; mangle.

calcaire, kăhl-kair, *m* limestone. *a* calcareous.

calciner, kăhl-se-neh, *v* to calcine; to burn up.

calcul, kăhl-kEEl, *m* calculation; arithmetic; calculus; stone (in bladder, etc.).

calculer, kăhl-kE-leh, *v* to calculate; to reckon; to compute.

cale, kăhl, *f* wedge; hold (ship).

calé e, kăh-leh, *a* wedged up; stalled; (*fam.*) learned.

caleçon, kăhl-song, *m* men's pants; bathing trunks; leggings.

calembour, kăh-lahng-boohr, *m* pun.

calembredaine, kăh-lahng-brer-dayn, *f* joke; nonsense.

calendrier, kăh-lahng-dre-eh, *m* calendar.

calepin, kăhl-pang, *m* notebook.

caler, kăh-leh, *v* to wedge up; to jam; to stall.

calfeutrer, kăhl-fer-treh, *v* to stop up weatherstrip; **se –,** to to make oneself snug.

calibre, kăh-lee-br, *m* caliber; size; diameter.

calice, kăh-liss, *m* chalice; calyx.

calicot, kăh-le-ko, *m* calico.

califourchon (à), ăh kăh-le-foohr-shong, *adv* astride.

câlin, e, kah-lang, *a* caressing; tender. *m*, cuddle.

câliner, kah-le-neh, *v* to caress; to fondle; to cuddle.

calleu-x, se, kăh-ler, *a*

callous; horny.

calmant, kăhl-mah*ng, m*
sedative.

calmant, e, kăhl-mah*ng, a*
soothing.

calmar, kăhl-măhr *m*
squid.

calme, kăhlm, *m* calm;
stillness. *a* quiet; calm.

calmer, kăhl-meh, *v* to
calm; to quiet; to still.

calomnie, kăh-lomm-nee,
f calumny; slander.

calomnier, kăh-lomm-ne-
yeh, *v* to calumniate; to
slander.

calorie, kăh-lo-re, *f*
calorie.

calorifère, kăh-lor-e-fair,
a heat-conveying. *m*
heating installation.

calorifuger, kăh-lo-re-fE-
sheh, *v* to insulate.

calotte, kăh-lott, *f*
skullcap; cap; (*slang*)
box on the ears;
priesthood; (*fam.*) slap.

calotter, kăh-lott-eh, *v* to
box the ears of.

calque, kăhlk, *m* tracing;
copy.

calquer, kăhl-keh, *v* to
trace; to copy.

calvaire, kăhl-vair, *m*
calvary; (*fig.*)
martyrdom.

calvitie, kăhl-vee-see, *f*
baldness.

camarade, kăh-măh-răhd,
m comrade; pal; friend.

camaraderie, kăh-măh-
răhd-ree, *f* close
friendship; comradeship.

camard, e, kăh-măhr, *a*
flat-nosed.

cambouis, kah*ng*-boo-e, *m*
dirty oil or grease.

cambrer, kah*ng*-breh, *v* to
bend; to arch; **se –,** se*r*
–, to arch one's back.

cambriolage, kah*ng*-bre-
ol-ăhsh, *m* burglary.

cambrioleur, kah*ng*-bre-
ol-er, *m* burglar.

came, kăhm, *f* cam; (*fam.*)
junk; drug; **arbre à –,**
ahr-br ăh–,*m* camshaft.

camée, kăh-meh, *m*
cameo.

camelote, kăhm-lot, *f*
cheap goods; trash; stuff.

caméra, kăh-meh-răh, *f*
movie camera.

camion, kăh-me-ong, *m*
truck; wagon.

camionnage, kăh-me-onn-
ăhsh, *m* carting;
haulage.

camionnette, kăh-me-
onn-ett, *f* van.

camisole, kăh-me-zol, *f*
camisole; straitjacket.

camouflet, kăh-moo-flay,
m affront; insult.

camoufler, kăh-moo-fleh,
v to disguise; to

camouflage; **se –,** to
hide.

camp, kah*ng, m* camp.

campagnard, e, kah*ng*-
păhn-yăhr, *n & a*
countryman;
countrywoman; rustic.

campagne, kah*ng*-păhn-
yer, *f* country;
campaign.

campement, kah*ng*p-
mah*ng, m* encampment;
camping.

camper, kah*ng*-peh, *v* to
camp.

camphre, kah*ng*-fr, *m*
camphor.

camping, kah*ng*-pee, *m*
camping; campground.

camus, e, kăh-mE, *a* flat-
nosed.

canaille, kăh-nah'e, *f*
scoundrel; crook.

canal, kăh-năhl, *m* canal;
channel; pipe; conduit.

canapé, kăh-năh-peh, *m*
sofa; open sandwich.

canard, kăh-năhr, *m* duck;
drake; false news; rag
(newspaper).

cancan, kah*ng*-kah*ng, m*
cancan; (*fam.*) gossip.

cancaner, kah*ng*-kăh-neh,
v (*fam.*) to gossip.

cancer, kah*ng*-sair, *m*
cancer.

cancéreu-x, se kah*ng*-seh-
re*r, a* cancerous; *n*

a
b
c
d
e
f
g
h
i
j
k
l
m
n
o
p
q
r
s
t
u
v
w
x
y
z

A
B
C
D
E
F
G
H
I
J
K
L
M
N
O
P
Q
R
S
T
U
V
W
X
Y
Z

cancer patient.

cancre, kahng-kr, *m* (*fig.*) dunce.

candélabre, kahng-deh-läh-br, *m* candelabra; streetlight.

candeur, kahng-der, *f* candor; frankness.

candidat, kahng-de-däh, *m* candidate.

candide, * kahng-deed, *a* candid; open; frank.

cane, käh, *f* duck (female).

caneton, käh-tong, *m* duckling.

canevas, käh-vah, *m* canvas; sketch.

caniche, käh-neesh, *m* poodle.

canif, käh-niff, *m* penknife.

canin, käh-nang, *a* canine.

canine, käh-neen, *f* canine tooth.

caniveau, käh-ne-voh, *m* gutter.

canne, käh, *f* cane; walking stick; rod.

cannelle, käh-nell, *f* cinnamon.

cannelure, käh-lEEr, *f* groove.

canon, käh-nong, *m* cannon; gun.

canot, käh-no, *m* canoe; –de sauvetage, der sohvtahsh, lifeboat.

canotage, käh-not-ähsh, *m* boating.

canotier, käh-not-e-eh, *m* oarsman; boater (hat).

cantaloup, kahng-täh-loo, *m* cantaloupe.

cantatrice, kahng-täh-triss, *f* professional singer; cantatrice.

cantharide, kahng-täh-reed, *f* Spanish fly.

cantine, kahng-teen, *f* canteen.

cantique, kahng-tick, *m* canticle; sacred song.

canton, kahng-tong, *m* subdistrict; canton.

cantonade, kahng-tonn-ähd, *f* wings (theater); à la –, äh läh –, a way of speaking to everyone in general.

cantonnier, kahng-tonn-e-eh, *m* trackman.

canule, käh-nEEl, *f* cannula.

caoutchouc, käh-oot-shoo, *m* rubber; **bottes de –,** rubber boots.

cap, kähp, *m* cape.

capable, käh-päh-bl, *a* able; efficient; qualified.

capacité, käh-päh-se-teh, *f* capacity; capaciousness; qualification.

cape, kähp, *f* cape; cloak with a hood.

capitaine, käh-pe-tayn, *m* captain.

capital, e, käh-pe-tähl, *a* capital; principal; chief.

capital, käh-pe-tähl, *m* capital; stock.

capitale, käh-pe-tähl, *f* capital (city).

capiteu-x, se, käh-pe-ter, *a* heady; strong (of wines).

capitonner, käh-pe-tonn-eh, *v* to stuff; to pad.

capituler, käh-pe-tE-leh, *v* to capitulate; to come to terms.

capon, käh-pong, *m* coward.

caporal, käh-por-ähl, *m* corporal.

capote, käh-pot, *f* great coat; hooded cloak; hood (of car).

câpre, käh-pr, *f* caper.

caprice, käh-priss, *m* caprice; whim; fancy.

capsule, kähp-sEEl, *f* capsule; cap.

capter, kähp-teh, *v* to capture; to pick up.

captieu-x, se, * kähp-se-er, *a* captious.

capti-f, ve, kähp-tiff, *a* captive. *n* prisoner.

capture, kähp-tEEr, *f* capture; booty; arrest.

capturer, kähp-tE-reh, *v* to capture; to arrest.

capuchon, käh-pE-shong,

m hood; cover.

capucin, kăh-pE-*sang*, *m* capuchin; friar.

capucine, kăh-pE-seen, *f* nasturtium.

caque, kăhck, *f* keg; barrel.

caquet, kăh-kay, *m* cackle.

caqueter, kăhck-teh, *v* to cackle; to chatter.

car, kăhr, *conj* for; because; as.

car, kăhr, *m* bus.

carabine, kăh-răh-been, *f* rifle.

carabinier, kăh-răh-be-ne-eh, *m* rifleman.

caracoler, kăh-răh-koll-eh, *v* to wheel about; to prance.

caractère, kăh-răhck-tair, *m* character; temper; type; print.

carafe, kăh-răhf, *f* decanter; water bottle; carafe.

carafon, kăh-răh-*fong*, *m* small decanter.

carambolage, kăh-rah*ng*-boh-lăhsh *m* pileup.

caramel, kăh-răh-mell, *m* burnt sugar; caramel; toffee.

carapace, kăh-răh-păhss, *f* carapace; shell.

carat, kăh-răh, *m* carat.

caravane, kăh-răh-văhn, *f* caravan.

carbonate, kăhr-bonn-ăht, *m* carbonate.

carbone, kăhr-bonn, *m* carbon.

carboniser, kăhr-bonn-e-zeh, *v* to carbonize; to char.

carburateur, kăhr-bE-rah-ter, *m* carburetor.

carbure, kăhr-bEEr, *m* carbide.

carcasse, kăhr-kăhss, *f* carcass; framework.

cardiaque, kăhr-de-ăhck, *a & mf* cardiac.

cardigan, kăhr-de-gah*ng*, *m* cardigan.

cardinal, e, kăhr-de-năhl, *a* cardinal; principal; chief.

carême, kăh-raym, *m* Lent.

carence, kăh-rah*ng*ss, *f* deficiency; inadequacy.

carène, kăh-rain, *f* keel; bottom; careen.

caressant, e, kăh-rayss-ah*ng*, *a* caressing; tender.

caresser, kăh-rayss-eh, *v* to caress; to stroke.

cargaison, kăhr-gay-*zong*, *f* cargo; freight.

cari, kăh-re *m* curry.

caricature, kăh-re-kăh-tEEr, *f* caricature.

carie, kăh-ree, *f* decay; –**dentaire,** dah*ng*-tair,

dental decay; cavity.

carillon, kăh-ree-*ong*, *m* chime; peal.

carmin, kăhr-mang, *m* crimson.

carnage, kăhr-năhsh, *m* slaughter.

carnassier, kăhr-năhss-e-eh, *a* carnivorous.

carnaval, kăhr-năh-văhl, *m* carnival.

carnet, kăhr-nay, *m* notebook.

carnivore, kăhr-ne-vor, *a* carnivorous.

carotte, kăh-rot, *f* carrot.

carotter, kăh-rot-eh, *v* (*fam.*) to dupe; to cheat.

carpe, kăhrp, *f* carp.

carpette, kăhr-pett, *f* rug.

carré, kăh-reh, *m* square; landing.

carré, e, kăh-reh, *a* square; straight; peremptory.

carreau, kăh-roh, *m* square; pane; tile; diamonds (cards).

carrefour, kăhr-foohr, *m* crossroads.

carreler, kăhr-leh, *v* to pave with brick or tile.

carrément, kăh-reh-mah*ng*, *adv* squarely; boldly; straightforwardly.

carrer, kăh-reh, *v* to square; **se** – to strut.

a
b
c
d
e
f
g
h
i
j
k
l
m
n
o
p
q
r
s
t
u
v
w
x
y
z

carrière, kăh-re-air, *f* quarry; career.

carriole, kăh-re-ol, *f* light covered cart.

carrosse, kăh-ross, *m* coach (horse-drawn).

carrosserie, kăh-ross-re, *f* body work (of car).

carrure, kăh-rEEr, *f* breadth of shoulders.

cartable, kăhr-tabl, *m* school bag.

carte, kăhrt, *f* card; ticket; map; menu; **–blanche,** blahngsh, full power.

carte des vins, kăhrt-er-deh-vang *f* wine list.

carte routière, kăhr-ter-roo-te-air *m* road-map.

cartilage, kăhr-te-lăhsh, *m* cartilage; (*fam.*) gristle.

carton, kăhr-tong, *m* pasteboard; cardboard; cartoon; hatbox; bandbox; cardboard box.

cartouche, kăhr-toosh, *f* cartridge; carton (of cigarettes); refill.

cas, kah, *m* case; matter; event; **en cas de,** ahng kah der, in case of.

casani-er, ère, kăh-zăh-ne-eh, *a* home-loving.

cascadeur, kăhss-kăh-der, *m* stuntman.

case, kahz, *f* hut; cabin; pigeonhole; square (on game board).

caser, kah-zeh, *v* to place; to find a situation for.

caserne, kăh-zairn, *f* barracks.

casier, kah-ze-eh, *m* pigeonhole; rack; filing cabinet; **–judiciaire,** **–shE-de-se-air,** police record.

casque, kăhssk, *m* helmet.

casquette, kăhss-kett, *f* cap.

cassant, e, kăhss-ahng, *a* brittle; blunt; sharp.

cassation, kăhss-ah-se-ong, *f* annulment; quashing; appeal.

casse, kahss, *f* breakage.

casse-cou, kahss-koo, *m* daredevil.

casse-noisettes, kahss-no'ăh-zett, *m* nutcracker.

casse-tête, kahss-tayt, *m* club; tomahawk; puzzle; brainteaser.

casser, kahss-eh, *v* to break; to crack; to quash; to discharge.

casserole, kăhss-rol *f* saucepan; casserole.

cassette, kăhss-ett, *f* casket; cassette.

cassis, kahss-iss, *m* black currant.

cassure, kahss-EEr, *f* broken place; crack; fracture.

caste, kăhsst, *f* caste.

castor, kăhss-tor, *m* beaver.

casuel, kăh-zE-ell, *m* perquisites.

casuel, le,* kăh-zE-ell, *a* casual; accidental.

catalogue, kăh-tăh-log *m* catalog; list.

cataplasme, kăh-tăh-plăhssm, *m* poultice.

catarrhe, kăh-tăhr, *m* catarrh.

catastrophe, kăh-tăhss-trof, *f* catastrophe.

catéchisme, kăh-teh-shissm, *m* catechism.

catégorie, kăh-teh-go-re, *f* category; order; class.

cathédrale, kăh-teh-drăhl, *f* cathedral.

catholique, kăh-toll-eeck, *a* & *mf* Catholic.

cauchemar, kohsh-măhr, *m* nightmare.

cause, kohz, *f* cause; motive; case; trial; **à –de,** ăh – der, on account of.

causer, koh-zeh, *v* to cause; to chat.

causerie, kohz-ree, *f* talk; chat; chattering.

causeuse, koh-zerz, *f* settee.

caustique, kohss-tick, *a*

caustic.

cauteleu-x, se,* koht-ler, *a* cunning; crafty.

cautériser, koh-teh-re-zeh, *v* to cauterize; to burn.

caution, koh-se-ong, *f* bail; security; **sujet à —,** SE-shay t'ăh –, not to be trusted.

cautionnement, koh-se-onn-mahng, *m* bail; surety; security.

cautionner, koh-se-onn-eh, *v* to post bail for.

cavalerie, kăh-văhl-ree, *f* cavalry.

cavali-er, ère, kăh-văh-le-eh, *mf* horseman; horsewoman; rider; partner; *a* blunt, offhand.

cavalièrement, kăh-văh-le-air-mahng, *adv* bluntly; unceremoniously.

cave, kăhv, *f* cellar; vault; wine-cellar. *a* hollow.

caveau, kăh-voh, *m* cellar; vault.

caverne, kăh-vairn, *f* cavern; cave; den.

cavité, kăh-ve-teh, *f* cavity; hollow.

ce, cet, *m*; **cette,** *f* ser, sett, *a* this, that.

ceci, ser-se, *pron* this; this thing.

cécité, seh-se-teh, *f* blindness.

céder, seh-deh, *v* to yield; to give up; to hand over.

cédille, seh-dee-ye, *f* cedilla.

cèdre, say-dr, *m* cedar.

ceindre, sang-dr, *v* to enclose; to surround; to gird; to wreathe (**de,** with).

ceinture, sang-tEEr, *f* girdle; belt; waist; enclosure; zone; circle.

cela, ser-lăh, or slăh, *pron* that.

célèbre, seh-lay-br, *a* celebrated; famous.

célébrer, seh-leh-breh, *v* to celebrate.

celer, ser-leh, *v* to hide; to conceal (**à,** from).

céleri, seh-ler-re, *m* celery.

célérité, seh-leh-re-teh, *f* speed; swiftness.

céleste, seh-laist, *a* celestial, heavenly.

célibat, seh-le-băh, *m* celibacy.

célibataire, seh-le-băh-tair, *m* bachelor. *a* unmarried.

cellier, say-le-eh, *m* cellar; storeroom.

cellulaire, say-lE-lair, *a* cellular.

cellule, say-lEEl, *f* cell.

celui, *m* **celle,** *f* ser-lwe,

sell; *pron* he; she; him; her; the one; that.

cendre, sahng-dr, *f* ash; ashes; cinder.

cendré, e, sahng-dreh, *a* ash-colored.

cendrier, sahng-dre-eh, *m* ash-hole; ashtray.

cendrillon, sahng-dree-yong, *f* Cinderella.

cène, sayn, *f* Lord's Supper.

censé, e, sahng-seh, *a* reputed; supposed.

censeur, sahng-ser, *m* censor; critic.

censure, sahng-sEEr, *f* censorship; censure.

censurer, sahng-sE-reh, *v* to censure; to blame.

cent, sahng, *m* & *a* one hundred; hundred.

centaine, sahng-tain, *f* hundred; **une–,** EEn–, about a hundred.

centenaire, sahngt-nair, *m* centenary; *a* & *mf* centenarian.

centiare, sahng-te-ăhr *m* centiare (a square meter).

centième, sahng-te-aym, *m* the hundredth part; *a* hundredth.

centigrade, sahng-te-grăhd, *a* centigrade.

centigramme, sahng-te-grăhm, *m* centigram.

centime, sahng-teem, *m* one centime.

centimètre, sahng-te-may-tr, *m* centimeter; (*fam.*) tape measure; (hundredth part of a meter).

central, e, sahng-trăhl, *a* central.

centralisation, sahng-trăh-le-zăh-se-ong, *f* centralization.

centre, sahng-tr, *m* center; middle.

centre de la ville, sahng-tr-der-lăh-veel *m* town center.

centre de zone urbaine, sahng-tr-der-zohn-EEr-bayn *m* inner city.

centre-ville, sahng-tr-veel *m* town center.

centrifuge, sahng-tre-fEE sh, *a* centrifugal.

centupler, sahng-tE-pleh, *v* to increase a hundredfold.

cependant, ser-pahng, *adv* meanwhile; *conj* yet; however.

céramique, seh-răh-meek, *a* ceramic. *f* ceramics; pottery.

cerceau, sair-soh, *m* hoop.

cercle, sair-kl, *m* circle; ring; hoop; club.

cercueil, sair-ker-e, *m* coffin.

céréales, seh-reh-ăhl, *fpl* cereals; corn crops.

cérébral, e, seh-rch-brăhl, *a* a cerebral.

cérémonial, seh-reh-monn-e-ăhl, *m* ceremonial.

cérémonie, seh-reh-monn-ee, *f* ceremony.

cérémonieu-x, se,* seh-reh-monn-e-er, *a* ceremonious; formal.

cerf, sair, or sairf, *m* stag; deer; —volant, – voll-ahng, kite.

cerfeuil, sair-fer'e, *m* chervil.

cerise, ser-reez, *f* cherry.

cerisier, ser-re-ze-eh, *m* cherry tree.

cerneau, sair-noh, *m* green walnut.

cerné, e, sair-neh, *pp* & *a* surrounded; black-ringed (eyes).

cerner, sair-neh, *v* to surround; to trap.

certain, e,* sair-tang, *a* certain; sure; *pl* (before a noun) some.

certes, sairt, *adv* most certainly.

certificat, sair-te-fe-kăh, *m* certificate; testimonial.

certifier, sair-te-fe-eh, *v* to certify; to testify.

certitude, sair-te-tEEd, *f* certitude; certainty; assurance.

cerveau, sair-voh, *m* brain; mind; intellect.

cervelas, sair-ver-lah, *m* sausage.

cervelle, sair-vell, *f* brains; head; intelligence.

ces, say (*pl* of ce), *mf a* these; those.

cessation, sess-ăh-se-ong, *f* discontinuance.

cesse, sayss, *f* ceasing; respite.

cesser, sayss-eh, *v* to cease; to come to an end.

cessible, sayss-ee-bl, *a* transferable (*law.*).

cession, sayss-e-ong, *f* transfer (*law.*).

c'est-à-dire, sayt-ah-deer, *conj* that is to say.

chacal, shăh-kăhl, *m* jackal.

chacun, e, shăh-kung, *pron* everyone; each; each one.

chafouin, e, shăh-foo-ang, *n* & *a* mean-looking; mean; sly-looking (person).

chagrin, shăh-grang, *m* grief; sorrow; trouble; shagreen (leather).

chagrin, e, shăh-grang, *a* sorrowful; gloomy; peevish.

chagrinant, e, shăh-gre-nah*ng*, *a* grievous; sad; vexing.

chagriner, shăh-gre-neh, *v* to grieve; to vex.

chahut, shăh-EE, *m* rowdyism; noise; **faire du –,** fair DE –, to cause a rumpus; to cause an uproar.

chaîne, shain, *f* chain; line; *pl* fetters.

chaînon, shay-no*ng*, *m* link (of chain).

chair, shair, *f* flesh; meat; pulp; **–de poule,** – der pool, goose-pimples.

chaire, shair, *f* pulpit; desk; professorship.

chaise, shayz, *f* chair; seat.

chaise longue, shayz long-gh, *f* deck-chair; chaise-longue; couch.

chaland, shăh-lah*ng*, *m* lighter; barge.

châle, shahl, *m* shawl.

chalet, shah-lay, *m* Swiss cottage; chalet.

chaleur, shăh-ler, *f* heat; warmth; zeal; heat (of animals).

chaleureu-x, se,* shăh-ler-rer, *a* warm; ardent.

chaloupe, shăh-loop, *f* rowboat; launch.

chalumeau, shăh-lE-moh, *m* reed; blowtorch.

chalut, shăh-lE, *m* trawl.

chalutier, shăh-lE-te-eh, *m* trawler.

chamailler (se), ser shăh-mah'e-yeh, *v* to squabble; to quarrel.

chambranle, shah*ng*-brah*ng*l, *m* door frame.

chambre, shah*ng*-br, *f* bedroom; chamber.

chambre à un lit, chah*ng*-brăh-u*ng*-lee *f* single room.

chambrée, shah*ng*-breh, *f* roomful.

chameau, shăh-moh, *m* camel.

chamelier, shăh-mer-le-eh, *m* camel driver.

chamois, shăh-mo'ăh, *m* chamois, wild goat; chamois leather; *a* buff.

champ, shah*ng*, *m* field; ground; subject; scope; **sur le–,** sEEr ler –, immediately; **à tout bout de –,** ăh-too-boo der –, every moment.

champagne, shah*ng*-păhn-yer, *m* champagne.

champêtre, shah*ng*-pay-tr, *a* rural; rustic.

champignon, shah*ng*-peen-yo*ng*, *m* mushroom.

champion, shah*ng*-pe-o*ng*, *m* champion.

chance, shah*ng*ss, *f* chance; luck.

chancelant, e, shah*ng*s-lah*ng*, *a* tottering.

chanceler, shah*ng*ss-leh, *v* to totter; to stagger.

chancelier, shah*ng*-ser-le-eh, *m* chancellor.

chancellerie, shah*ng*-sell-ree, *f* chancellery.

chanceu-x, se, shah*ng*-ser, *a* lucky; risky.

chancre, shah*ng*-kr, *m* canker.

chandeleur, shah*ng*d-ler, *f* Candlemas.

chandelier, shah*ng*-der-le'eh, *m* candlestick.

chandelle, shah*ng*-dell, *f* candle.

change, shah*ng*sh, *m* exchange; **agent de –,** ăh-**shah*ng*** der –, stockbroker; exchange broker.

changeant, e, shah*ng*-shah*ng*, *a* changeable; fickle.

changement, shah*ng*sh-mah*ng*, *m* change; alteration.

changer, shah*ng*-sheh, *v* to change; to alter; to exchange; to shift.

changeur, shah*ng*sh-er, *m* moneychanger.

chanoine, shăh-no'ăhn, *m* canon.

chanson, shah*ng*-so *ng*, *f* song; ballad.

a
b
c
d
e
f
g
h
i
j
k
l
m
n
o
p
q
r
s
t
u
v
w
x
y
z

chansonnette, shahng-sonn-ett, *f* simple song; ditty.

chansonnier, shahng-sonn-e-eh, *m* songwriter (*esp.* satirical); songbook.

chant, shahng, *m* singing; song; strain; canto.

chantage, shahng-tǎhsh, *m* blackmail.

chantant, e, shahng-tahng, *a* singing; tuneful.

chanter, shahng-teh, *v* to sing; to celebrate; (*fam.*) to say; **faire –, fair –,** to blackmail.

chanteu-r, se, shahng-ter, *mf* singer.

chantier, shahng-te-eh, *m* yard; lumberyard; dockyard; building site.

chantonner, shahng-tonn-eh, *v* to hum a tune.

chanvre, shahng-vr, *m* hemp.

chaos, kǎh-o, *m* chaos.

chape, shǎhp, *f* cope; cover.

chapeau, shǎh-poh, *m* hat; bonnet; derby.

chapelain, shǎhp-lang, *m* chaplain.

chapelet, shǎhp-lay, *m* chaplet; rosary.

chapeli-er, ère, shǎh-per-le-eh, *mf* hatter.

chapelle, shǎh-pell, *f* chapel.

chapellerie, shǎh-pell-ree, *f* hatmaking; hat shop.

chapelure, shǎhp-lEEr, *f* bread crumbs.

chaperon, shǎhp-rong, *m* hood; chaperon.

chaperonner, shǎhp-ronn-eh, *v* to chaperon; to put a hood on.

chapiteau, shǎh-pe-toh, *m* top; capital; crest; marquee.

chapitre, shǎh-pe-tr, *m* chapter; heading.

chapitrer, shǎh-pe-treh, *v* to lecture; to reprimand.

chapon, shǎh-pong, *m* capon.

chaque, shǎhck, *a* each; every.

char, shǎhr, *m* car; chariot; hearse.

charabia, shǎh-rǎh-be-ǎh, *m* gibberish.

charbon, shǎhr-bong, *m* coal; charcoal; carbuncle.

charbonnage, shǎhr-bonn-ǎhsh, *m* coal mine.

charbonner, shǎhr-bonn-eh, *v* to blacken; to char.

charbonneu-x, se, shǎhr-bonn-er, *a* coal-black; coal-like.

charbonnier, shǎhr-bonn-e-eh, *m* coal-man; charcoal-burner.

charcuterie, shǎhr-kEEt-ree, *f* delicatessen.

chardon, shǎhr-dong, *m* thistle.

chardonneret, shǎhr-donn-ray, *m* goldfinch.

charge, shǎhrsh, *f* load; burden; expense; office; charge.

chargement, shǎhr-sher-mahng, *m* loading; cargo.

chargé, e, shǎhr-sheh, *pp* & *a* full; laden; heavy (of stomach); **–d'affaires, –** dǎh-fair, deputy ambassador.

charger, shǎhr-sheh, *v* to load; to charge; to entrust (**de,** with); **se –, ser –,** to take upon oneself.

chargeur, shǎhr-sher, *m* loader; shipper.

chariot, shǎh-re-o, *m* wagon; cart; truck; carriage (of typewriter).

charitable,* shǎh-re-tǎh-bl, *a* charitable.

charité, shǎh-re-teh, *f* charity; alms; benevolence.

charivari, shǎh-re-vǎh-re, *m* hurly-burly; deafening noise.

charlatan, shǎhr-lǎh-

tahng, *m* quack;
charlatan.

charmant, e, shăhr-
mahng, *a* charming;
delightful.

charme, shăhrm, *m*
charm; spell; attraction.

charmer, shăhr-meh, *v* to
charm.

charmille, shăhr-mee-ye, *f*
arbor.

charnel, le, shăhr-nell, *a*
carnal; sensual.

charnière, shăhr-ne-air, *f*
hinge.

charnu, e, shăhr-nE, *a*
fleshy.

charogne, shăh-ronn-yer,
f carrion.

charpente, shăhr-pahngt, *f*
framework.

charpentier, shăhr-pahng-
te-eh, *m* carpenter.

charpie, shăhr-pee, *f*
shredded linen.

charretée, shăhr-teh, *f*
cartload.

charretier, shăhr-te-eh, *m*
carter.

charrette, shăh-rett, *f* cart.

charrier, shăh-re-eh, *v* to
cart; to drift; (*fam.*) to
poke fun at; to
exaggerate.

charroi, shăh-ro'ăh, *m*
carting.

charron, shăh-rong, *m*
wheelwright.

charrue, shăh-rE, *f* plow;
**mettre la – devant les
bœufs,** met-tr lăh–der-
vahng lay ber, to put the
cart before the horse.

charte, shăhrt, *f* charter.

chartreuse, shăhr-trerz, *f*
chartreuse (liqueur).

chas, shah, *m* eye of a
needle.

châsse, shahss, *f* shrine;
frame.

chasse, shăhss, *f* chase;
hunting; shooting sport;
pursuit.

chasse-neige, shăhss-
naysh, *m* (*inv in pl*)
snowplow; stem
(skiing).

chasser, shăhss-eh, *v* to
hunt; to drive away; to
shoot; to discharge.

chasseur, shăhss-er, *m*
hunter; sportsman;
footman.

châssis, shahss-e, *m* frame;
sash; chassis.

chaste,* shăhsst, *a* chaste;
pure; modest.

chasteté, shăhss-ter-teh, *f*
chastity; purity.

chat, te, shăh, *mf* cat;
–huant, –E-ahng, *m*
tawny owl; brown owl.

châtaigne, shah-tain-yer, *f*
sweet chestnut.

châtain, e, shah-tang, *a*
chestnut.

château, shah-toh, *m*
castle; mansion.

châteaubriant, shah-toh-
bre-ahng *m* thick grilled
steak.

châtelain, e, shaht-lang,
mf owner of a manor or
castle.

châtier, shah-te-eh, *v* to
chastise; to punish; to
correct.

châtiment, shah-te-
mahng; *m* chastisement;
punishment.

chatoiement, shăh-to'ăh-
mahng, *m* glistening;
shimmer (colors).

chaton, shăh-tong, *m*
kitten; setting of stone.

chatouiller, shăh-too'e-
yeh, *v* to tickle.

chatouilleu-x, se, shăh-
too'e-yer, *a* ticklish;
touchy.

chatoyer, shăh-to'ăh-yeh,
v to glisten; to shimmer.

châtrer, shah-treh, *v* to
castrate; to prune.

chatterie, shăht-ree, *f*
usually *pl* coaxing way.

chaud, shoh, *m* heat;
warmth; **avoir –,** ăh-
vo'ăhr –, to be warm.

chaud, e,* *a* hot; warm;
new (of news).

chaudière, shoh-de-air, *f*
copper; boiler.

chaudron, shoh-drong, *m*

kettle; caldron; (*fam.*) bad piano.

chaudronnier, shoh-dronn-e-eh, *m* boilermaker; brazier.

chauffage, shoh-făsh, *m* warming; heating; **–central,** – sahng-trăhl, *m* central heating.

chauffe, shohf, *f* heating; furnace.

chauffe-eau, shohf-oh, *m* water heater.

chauffer, shoh-feh, *v* to warm; to heat; to get hot.

chauffeur, shoh-fer, *m* chauffeur; stoker; driver.

chaume, shohm, *m* stubble; thatch.

chaumière, shoh-me-air, *f* thatched house; cottage.

chausse-pied, shohss-pe-eh, *m* shoehorn.

chaussée, shohss-eh, *f* road; pavement.

chausser, shohss-eh, *v* to put shoes or boots on; to supply with shoes or boots.

chaussette, shohss-ett, *f* sock.

chausson, shohss-ong, *m* slipper; babies' bootees; **–de dance,** der dahngss, ballet shoes.

chaussure, shohss-EEr, *f* shoes; footwear.

chauve, shohv, *a* bald.

chauve-souris, shohv-soo-re, *f* bat.

chauvin, e, shoh-vang, *mf* chauvinist.

chauvinisme, shoh-ve-nissm, *m* chauvinism.

chaux, shoh, *f* lime; **blanc de –,** blahng der –, whitewash.

chavirer, shăh-ve-reh, *v* to capsize.

chef, sheff.; *m* chef; chief; boss; **de son –,** der song –, on one's responsibility.

chef-d'œuvre, shay-der-vr, *m* masterpiece.

chef-lieu, sheff-le-er, *m* chief town (of country).

chemin, sher-mang, *m* way; road; path; **–de fer,** – der fair, railroad; **en –,** ahng –, on the way.

chemineau, sher-me-no, *m* tramp.

cheminée, sher-me-neh, *f* chimney; fireplace; mantel-piece; funnel.

cheminer, sher-me-neh, *v* to walk; to jog on.

cheminot, sher-me-no, *m* railroad worker.

chemise, sher-meez, *f* shirt; case; folder; **–de nuit,** – der nwe, nightdress.

chemisier, sher-me-ze-eh, *m* shirtmaker; woman's blouse or shirt.

chenal, sher-năhl, *m* channel.

chenapan, sher-năh-pahng, *m* rascal.

chêne, shain, *m* oak.

chéneau, sheh-noh, *m* eaves; gutter.

chenet, sher-nay, *m* andiron.

chenil, sher-ne, *m* kennel.

chenille, sher-nee-ye, *f* caterpillar.

chèque, sheck, *m* check; **–barré,** – băh-reh, check for deposit only.

chèque de voyage, sheck-der-voăh-yăhsh *m* traveler's check.

cher, shair, *adv* dear; at a high price.

ch-er, ère,* shair, *a* dear; beloved; costly.

chercher, shair-sheh, *v* to seek; to look for; **envoyer –,** ahng-vo'ăh-yeh –, to send for.

chercheur, shair-sher, *m* seeker; inquirer.

chère, shair, *f* living; fare; cheer; **faire bonne –,** fair bonn –, to live well; to feast.

chéri, e, sheh-re, *a* darling; beloved; favorite. *m* dear one; dearest.

chérir, sheh-reer, *v* to cherish; to love.

cherté, shair-teh, *f* high price; dearness.

chérubin, sheh-rE-bang, *m* cherub.

chéti-f, ve,* sheh-tiff, *a* puny; paltry; weak.

cheval, sher-văhl, *m* horse; **–vapeur,** – văh-per, horsepower.

chevaleresque, sher-văhl-resk, *a* chivalrous.

chevalerie, sher-văhl-ree, *f* chivalry; knighthood.

chevalet, sher-văh-lay, *m* support; stand.

chevalier, sher-văh-le-eh, *m* knight; **–d'industrie,** –dang-dEes-tree, wheeler-dealer.

chevaucher, sher-voh-sheh, *v* to ride; to overlap.

chevelu, e, sherv-lE, *a* hairy.

chevelure, sherv-lEEr, *f* head of hair.

chevet, sher-vay, *m* bolster; bedside.

cheveu, sher-ver, *m* hair (a single); **les –x,** lay –, the hair.

cheville, sher-vee-ye, *f* ankle; peg; pin; bolt.

chèvre, shay-vr, *f* nanny-goat; **ménager la –et le chou,** meh-năh-sheh

lăh – eh ler shoo, to run with the hare and hunt with the hounds.

chevreau, sher-vroh, *m* kid (goat).

chèvrefeuille, shay-vrer-fer'e, *m* honeysuckle.

chevrette, sher-vrett, *f* young doe; young nanny goat.

chevreuil, sher-vrer'e, *m* roe deer.

chevrier, sher-vre-eh, *m* goatherd.

chevron, sher-vrong, *m* rafter.

chevrotant, sher-vrot-ahng, *a* quivering; tremulous.

chevrotin, sher-vrot-ang, *m* kid leather.

chez, sheh, *prep* at; to; with; among; in; at or to the house of.

chic, sheeck, *m* stylishness; knack. *a* smart; stylish; (*fam.*) fine! a sport (of person).

chicane, she-kăhn, *f* chicanery; pettifogging.

chicaner, she-kăh-neh, *v* to quarrel with; to shuffle; to quibble.

chicanerie, she-kăhn-ree, *f* chicanery.

chiche,* sheesh, *a* stingy; *interj* I dare you!

chicorée, she-kor-eh, *f*

chicory; endive.

chicot, she-ko, *m* stump.

chien, she-ang, *m* dog; cock (gun).

chienne, she-enn, *f* bitch (dog).

chiffe, sheef, *f* flimsy stuff; weak man.

chiffon, she-fong, *m* rag; scrap; duster; *pl* finery.

chiffonné, e, she-fonn-eh, *pp* & *a* rumpled; of irregular but agreeable features.

chiffonner, she-fonn-eh, *v* to crumple; to vex.

chiffonnier, she-fonn-e-eh, *m* ragman; chiffonnier.

chiffre, shee-fr, *m* figure; number; total; cipher; **en –s connus,** ahng – konn-E, in plain figures; **–d'affaires,** – dăh-fair, turnover.

chiffrer, she-freh, *v* to cipher; to assess.

chignon, sheen-yong, *m* bun.

chimère, she-mair, *f* chimera; idle fancy.

chimérique, she-meh-reeck, *a* chimerical.

chimie, she-mee, *f* chemistry.

chimique,* she-meeck, *a* chemical.

chimiste, she-meesst, *m*

a
b
c
d
e
f
g
h
i
j
k
l
m
n
o
p
q
r
s
t
u
v
w
x
y
z

A
B
C
D
E
F
G
H
I
J
K
L
M
N
O
P
Q
R
S
T
U
V
W
X
Y
Z

chemist (scientific).

chimpanzé, shang-pahng-zeh, *m* chimpanzee; chimp.

chinois sheeno'ăh, *a* Chinese.

chiot sheo, *m* puppy.

chiper she-peh, *v* to steal.

chipie, she-pee, *f* shrew.

chipoter she-pot-eh, *v* to quibble; to nibble.

chique, sheeck, *f* wad of tobacco.

chiquenaude, sheeck-nohd, *f* flick of finger.

chiquer she-keh, *v* to chew (tobacco).

chirurgie, she-rEEr-shee, *f* surgery.

chirurgien, she-rEEr-she-ang, *m* surgeon.

chlore, klor, *m* chlorine.

chlorure, klor-EEr, *m* chloride.

choc, shock, *m* shock; collision; clash; knock.

chocolat, shock-oll-ăh, *m* chocolate. *a* chocolate colored.

chœur, ker, *m* choir; chorus; chancel.

choir, sho'ăhr, *v* to fall.

choisi, sho'ăh-ze, *pp* & *a* chosen; selected; choice.

choisir, sho'ăh-zeer, *v* to choose; to select (**dans, entre, parmi,** from).

choix, sho'ăh, *m* choice;

selection; election.

choléra, koll-eh-răh, *m* cholera.

chômage, shoh-măhsh, *m* unemployment; time spent without work.

chômer, shoh-meh, *v* to stand idle; to be out of work.

chômeur, shoh-mer, *m* unemployed.

chopper, shop-eh, *v* to stumble; to trip up.

choquant, e, shock-ahng, *a* offensive (**pour,** to); shocking; unpleasant.

choquer, shock-eh, *v* to shock; to strike; to touch; to displease; **se –,** to take offense (**de,** at); to be shocked.

chose, shohz, *f* thing; matter; affair; **bien des – s à,** be-ang deh – ăh, my best regards to.

chou, shoo, *m* cabbage; dear; pet;**– fleur,** –fler cauliflower.

choucroute, shoo-kroot, *f* sauerkraut.

chouette, shoo-ait, *f* owl; *a* (*fam.*) fantastic; great; marvelous.

choyer, sho'ăh-yeh, *v* to fondle; to pet.

chrétien, ne,* kreh-te-ang, *a* & *mf* Christian.

chrétienté, kreh-te-ang-

teh, *f* Christendom.

christ, krisst, *m* Christ; crucifix.

christianisme, krisst-e-ăh-nissm, *m* Christianity.

chrome, krohm, *m* chromium; chrome.

chronique, kronn-eeck, *f* chronicle. *a* chronic.

chronomètre, kronn-omm-ay-tr, *m* chronometer.

chrysalide, kre-zăh-leed, *f* chrysalis.

chrysanthème, kre-zahng-taym, *m* chrysanthemum.

chuchoter, shE-shot-eh, *v* to whisper.

chut, shEEt, *interj* hush!

chute, shEEt, *f* fall; downfall; failure.

ci, se, *adv* here; this; –- **joint,** –sho'ang, enclosed; **comme –, comme ça,** komm – komm săh, so-so, middling.

cible, see-bl, *f* target.

ciboulette, se-boo-lett, *f* chives.

cicatrice, se-kăh-triss, *f* scar.

cidre, see-dr, *m* cider.

Cie (for **Compagnie**), kong-păhn-yee, *f* "Co."

ciel, se-ell, *m* heaven; sky.

cierge, se-airsh, *m* altar

candle.

cigale, se-găhl, *f* cicada.

cigare, se-găhr, *m* cigar.

cigarette, se-găh-rett, *f* cigarette.

cigogne, se-gonn-yer, *f* stork.

cigüe, se-ghE, *f* hemlock.

cil, seel, *m* eyelash.

cime, seem, *f* summit; top; crest.

ciment, se-mahng, *m* cement.

cimenter, se-mahng-teh, *v* to cement.

cimetière, seem-te-air, *m* cemetery; churchyard; graveyard.

cinéaste, se-neh-ăhsst, *m* moviemaker.

cinéma, se-neh-măh, *m* movie theater; **faire du –, fair dE –,** to act in films.

cingler, sang-gleh, *v* to lash; to sail.

cinglé, sang-gleh, *a* (*fam.*) nuts; cracked.

cinq, sangk, *a* five.

cinquantaine, sang-kahng-tain, *f* about fifty.

cinquante, sang-kahngt, *a* fifty.

cinquantenaire, sang-kahng-nair, *m* fiftieth anniversary.

cinquantième, sang-kahng-te-aym, *a* fiftieth.

cinquième, sang-ke-aym, *m* & *a* fifth.

cintre, sang-tr, *m* semicircle; arch; coat hanger.

cintré, e, sang-treh, *pp* & *a* arched; fitted (of coat, etc.).

cirage, se-răhsh, *m* polishing; shoe polish.

circoncire, seer-kong-seer, *v* to circumcise.

circoncision, seer-kong-se-ze-ong, *f* circumcision.

circonférence, seer-kong-feh-rahngss, *f* circumference.

circonflexe, seer-kong-flex, *a* circumflex.

circonscription, seer-kongss-krip-se-ong, *f* district.

circonscrire, seer-kongss-kreer, *v* to circumscribe.

circonspect, e, seer-kongss-peckt, or seer-kongss-pay, *a* circumspect; wary.

circonspection, seer-kongss-peck-se-ong, *f* cautiousness.

circonstance, seer-kongss-tahngss, *f* circumstance; occasion.

circonstancier, seer-kongss-tahng-se-eh, *v* to state fully.

circonvenir, seer-kongv-neer, *v* to circumvent; to deceive.

circonvoisin, seer-kong-vo'ăh-zang, *a* surrounding; neighboring.

circuit, seer-kwe, *m* circuit; roundabout way.

circulaire, seer-kE-lair, *f* circular. *a* circular.

circulation, seer-kE-lăh-se-ong, *f* circulation; currency; traffic.

circuler, seer-kE-leh, *v* to circulate; to move.

cire, seer, *f* wax.

cirer, se-reh, *v* to wax; to polish (shoes, floors, etc.); to spread about.

cirque, seerk, *m* circus.

ciseau, se-zoh, *m* chisel; *pl* scissors; shears.

ciseler, seez-leh, *v* to carve; to chisel.

citadelle, se-tăh-dell, *f* citadel.

citadin, e, se-tăh-dang, *mf* townsman; townswoman.

citation, se-tăh-se-ong, *f* quotation; subpoena.

cité se-teh, *f* city; town.

citer, se-teh, *v* to quote; to mention; to summon; to subpoena.

citerne, se-tairn, *f* cistern; tank; reservoir.

a
b
c
d
e
f
g
h
i
j
k
l
m
n
o
p
q
r
s
t
u
v
w
x
y
z

A
B
C
D
E
F
G
H
I
J
K
L
M
N
O
P
Q
R
S
T
U
V
W
X
Y
Z

cithare, se-tăhr, *f* zither.

citoyen, ne, se-to'ăh-yang, *mf* & *a* citizen; freeman.

citrate, se-trăht, *m* citrate.

citron, se-trong, *m* lemon; citron. *a* lemon-colored.

citronade, si-tro-năhd, *f* lemonade.

citrouille, see-troo'e-yer, *f* pumpkin; gourd.

cive, seev, *fpl* chives.

civet, se-vay, *m* game stew; **–de lièvre,** – der le-ay-vr, rabbit stew.

civière, se-ve-air, *f* stretcher.

civil, se-vill, *m* civilian; layman.

civil, e,* se-vill, *a* polite; civil.

civilisation, se-ve-le-zăh-se-ong, *f* civilization.

civiliser, se-ve-le-zeh, *v* to civilize.

civilité, se-ve-le-teh, *f* civility.

civique, se-veeck, *a* civic.

civisme, seeveesm, *m* public responsibility; public-spiritedness.

clafoutis, klăh-footee, *m* dessert made with fruit and batter.

claie, klay, *f* hurdle; screen.

clair, klair, *m* light; light part.

clair, e,* klair, *a* clear; bright; light; evident.

claire-voie, klair-vo'ăh, *f* opening; lattice; skylight.

clairière, klai-re-air, *f* glade.

clairon, klai-rong, *m* clarion; bugle; bugler.

clairsemé, e, klair-ser-meh, *a* thinly sown; sparse; scattered.

clairvoyance, klair-vo'ăh-yahngss, *f* clairvoyance; clear-sightedness.

clairvoyant, e, klair-vo'ăh-yahng, *n* & *a* clear-sighted; judicious; clairvoyant.

clameur, klăh-mer, *f* clamor; outcry.

clan, klahng, *m* clan; clique.

clandestin, e,* klahng-dess-tang, *a* clandestine.

clapet, klăh-pay, *m* clapper; valve.

clapier, klăh-pe-eh, *m* burrow; warren; hutch.

clapoter, klăh-pot-eh, *v* to chop, to ripple.

clapotis, klăh-pot-e, *m* ripple; splashing.

clapper, klăh-peh, *v* to smack; to clack.

claque, klăhck, *m* opera hat; *f* slap; hired applauders.

claquemurer, klăhck-mE-reh, *v* to shut up; to confine.

claquer, klăh-keh, *v* to clap; to smack.

claqueur, klăh-ker, *m* hired applauder.

clarifier, klăh-re-fe-eh, *v* to clarify; **se –,** to make clear.

clarinette, klăh-re-nett, *f* clarinet.

clarté, klăhr-teh, *f* clearness; light; brightness.

classe, klahss, *f* class; order; rank; form; school; classroom.

classement, klahss-mahng, classification; filing.

classeur, klăhss-er, *m* files; filing cabinet.

classifier, klăhss-e-fe-eh, *v* to classify.

classique, klăhss-eeck, *m* classic; *a* classical.

clause, klohz, *f* clause; condition.

claustration, klohs-trăh-se-ong, *f* cloistering; confinement.

clavecin, klăhv-sang, *m* harpsichord.

clavicule, klăh-ve-kEEl, *f* collarbone.

clavier, klăh-ve-eh, *m* keyboard.

clef, or **clè,** kleh, *f* key; wrench; lever; keystone.

fermer à –, fair-meh ăh –, to lock.

clémence, kleh-mahngss, *f* clemency; mercy.

clerc, klair, *m* clerk; cleric; scholar. **faire un pas de –,** fair ung pah der –, to blunder.

clergé, klair-sheh, *m* clergy.

clérical, e, kleh-re-kăhl, *a* clerical.

cliché, kle-sheh, *m* stereotype; negative (photo); stereotyped phrase.

client, e, kle-ahng, *mf* client; patient; customer.

clientèle, kle-ahng-tell, *f* clients; customers.

cligner, clignoter, kleen-yeh, kleen-yot-eh, *v* to wink; to blink; to flicker.

clignotant, kleen-yot-ahng, *m* turn signal.

climat, kle-măh, *m* climate; clime; atmosphere.

climatérique, kle-măh-teh-reeck, *a* climatic.

climatisé, kle-măh-te-zeh, *a* air-conditioned.

climatiseur, kle-măh-te-zer, *m* air conditioner.

clin d'œil, klang-der'e, *m* wink.

clinique, kle-neeck, *f* nursing home; clinic. *a* clinical.

clinquant, klang-kahng, *m* tinsel; glitter.

clique, kleeck, *f* gang; set; clan.

cliquetis, kleeck-te, *m* clank; clashing; jingle.

clivage, kle-văhsh, *m* cleavage.

clochard, klo-shar, *m* tramp; homeless.

cloaque, klo'ăhck, *m* sewer; cesspool.

cloche, klosh, *f* bell; dish cover; (*fam.*) idiot.

cloche-pied (à), ăh klosh-pe-eh, *adv* hopping on one leg.

clocher, klosh-eh, *v* to limp; to go wrong somewhere.

clocher, klosh-eh, *m* steeple; church tower.

clocheton, klosh-tong, *m* pinnacle; turret.

clochette, klosh-ett, *f* small bell; bellflower; bluebell.

cloison, klo'ăh-zong, *f* partition.

cloître, klo'ăh-tr, *m* cloister; monastery.

clopin-clopant, klop-ang klop-ahng, *adv* hobbling along.

cloque, clock, *f* blister.

clos, e, klo, *pp* & *a* closed; finished.

cloque, klock, *f* blister.

clos, klo, *m* close; enclosure; vineyard.

clôture, kloh-tEEr, *f* enclosure; seclusion; closing.

clôturer, kloh-tE-reh, *v* to enclose; to close down.

clou, kloo, *m* nail; boil; chief attraction; **–de girofle,** – der she-rofl, clove.

clouer, kloo-eh, *v* to nail; to rivet; to clench.

clouter, kloo-teh, *v* to stud.

clown, kloon, *m* clown.

club, klEEb, *m* club.

clystère, kliss-tair, *m* enema.

coacquéreur, ko'ăh-kehrer, *m* joint purchaser.

coadministrateur, ko'ăhd-me-niss-trăh-ter, *m* codirector.

coaguler, ko'ăh-ghE-leh, *v* to coagulate; **se –,** to curdle.

coaliser (se), ser ko'ăh-le-zeh, *v* to unite; to form a coalition.

coasser, ko'ăhss-eh, *v* to croak.

coassocié, e, ko'ăh-soss-e-eh, *mf* co-partner.

cocagne (pays de), pay-

yee der kock-ăhn-yer, *m*
land of plenty; **mât de –,**
mah der –, greasy pole.
cocarde, kock-ăhrd, *f*
cockade.
cocasse, kock-ăhss, *a*
funny; droll.
coccinelle, kock-se-nell, *f*
ladybug.
coche, kosh, *m* coach;
barge; *f* notch; sow.
cocher, kosh-eh, *m*
coachman; driver.
cochon, kosh-ong, *m* hog;
pig; porker; swine; pork;
–de lait, – der lay,
sucking pig; **–d'Inde,** –
dangd, guinea pig.
cochonnerie, kosh-onn-
ree, dirtiness; indecent
action or language;
(*fam.*) dirty trick.
coco, kock-o, *m* coconut;
(*fam.*) pet.
cocon, kock-ong, *m*
cocoon.
cocotier, kock-ot-e-eh, *m*
coconut palm.
cocotte, kock-ot, *f*
stewpan; darling; child's
word for chicken;
–minute, – me-nEEt,
pressure cooker.
code, kod, *m* code; law.
coefficient, ko-eh-fe-se-
ahng, *m* coefficient.
coercition, ko-air-se-se-
ong, *f* coercion.

cœur, ker, *m* heart; soul;
love; courage; core;
avoir mal au –, ăh-
vo'ăhr măhl oh –, to
feel sick.
coffre, kofr, *m* trunk;
chest; box; **–fort, –** for,
safe.
coffrer, kof-reh, *v* (*fam.*)
to lock up.
coffret, kof-ray, *m* small
chest; jewelry box.
cognac, kon-yăhck, *m*
brandy.
cognée, kon-yeh, *f*
hatchet.
cogner, kon-yeh, *v* to
knock; to strike; to drive
in.
cohérent, e, ko-eh-rahng,
a coherent.
cohéritier, ko-eh-re-te-eh,
mf jointheir.
cohésion, ko-eh-ze-ong, *f*
cohesion.
cohue, koE, *f* crowd; mob;
rout; uproar.
coi, coite, *f* ko'ăh, ko'ăht,
a quiet; still.
coiffe, ko'ăhf, *f* headdress.
coiffer, ko'ăhf-eh, *v* to put
on the head. **se –,** to
brush one's hair; to
comb.
coiffeur, -euse, ko'ăhf-er,
mf hairdresser.
coiffeuse, ko'ăh-ferz,
dressing table.

coiffure, ko'ăhf-EEr, *f*
headdress; hairstyle;
hairdo.
coin, ko-ang, *m* corner;
angle; wedge.
coincer, ko-ang-seh, *v* to
wedge up; to jam.
coïncider, ko-ang-se-deh,
v to coincide.
coing, ko-ang, *m* quince.
col, kol, *m* collar; neck;
pass.
colère, koll-air, *f* anger;
wrath; ire.
colérique, koll-eh-reeck, *a*
angry; irascible.
colibri, koll-e-bre, *m*
hummingbird.
colifichet, koll-e-fe-shay,
m knickknack; trinket;
bauble.
colimaçon, koll-e-măh-
song, *m* snail.
colin-maillard, koll-ang-
mah'e-yăhr, *m*
blindman's buff.
colique, koll-eeck, *f* pain
in the stomach; stomach
cramp.
colis, koll-e, *m* package;
parcel.
collabora-teur, trice, kol-
lăh-bor-ăh-ter, *mf*
collaborator; assistant;
contributor.
collaborer, kol-lăh-bor-
eh, *v* to work together.
collage, koll-ăhsh, *m*

sticking; pasting; gluing.

collant, e, koll-ah*ng*, *a*
sticking; tight; *m* pair of
tights.

collation, koll-ăh-se-o*ng*, *f*
collation; light meal.

collationner, koll-ăh-se-
onn-eh, *v* to collate; to
compare; to lunch.

colle, kol, *f* paste; glue;
size.

collecte, koll-leckt, *f*
collection.

collecti-f, ve,* koll-leck-
teeff, *a* collective.

collectionner, koll-leck-
se-onn-eh, *v* to collect.

collège, koll-ay**sh**, *m*
school; junior high
school.

collégien, koll-eh-**she**-
a*ng*, *m* schoolboy;
collegian.

collégiennne , koll-eh-
she-angn *f* schoolgirl.

coller, koll-eh, *v* to stick;
to glue; to adhere.

collet, koll-ay, *m* collar;
snare; **–monté,** – mo*ng*-
teh, strait-laced.

colleur, koll-er, *m*
paperhanger.

collier, koll-e-eh, *m* collar;
necklace; ring.

colline, koll-een, *f* hill;
hillock.

colloque, koll-lock, *m*
colloquium; conference.

collusoire, koll-lE-zo'ăhr,
a collusive.

colombe, koll-o*ng*b, *f*
dove.

colombier, koll-o*ng*-be-eh,
m dovecote; pigeonhole.

colon, koll-o*ng*, *m*
colonist; planter.

côlon, kohll-o*ng*, *m* colon.

colonel, koll-onn-ell, *m*
colonel.

colonie, koll-onn-ee, *f*
colony; settlement.

colonnade, koll-onn-ăhd,
f colonnade.

colonne, koll-onn, *f*
column; pillar;
–vertébrale, – vair-teh-
brăhl, spine; backbone.

coloquinte, koll-ock-a*ng*t,
f bitter apple.

colorer, koll-or-eh, *v* to
color; to stain.

coloris, koll-or-e, *m*
coloring; hue.

colosse, koll-oss, *m*
colossus; giant.

colporter, koll-por-teh, *v*
to hawk about; to spread
(news).

colporteur, koll-por-ter,
m peddler; hawker.

combat, ko*ng*-bâh, *m*
fight; battle; contest;
hors de –, or der –,
disabled.

combattre, ko*ng*-bâh-tr, *v*
to fight; to contest; to

contend (**contre,** with).

combien, ko*ng*-be-a*ng*, *adv*
how much; how many;
how; **–de temps,** – der
tah*ng*, how long?

combinaison, ko*ng*-be-
nay-zo*ng*, *f* combination;
slip; contrivance.

combinaison de plongée,
ko*ng*-be-nay-zo*ng*-der-
plo*ng*-**sheh** *f* wetsuit.

combine, ko*ng*-been, *f*
(*fam.*) scheme;
arrangement; fiddle.

combiner, ko*ng*-be-neh, *v*
to combine; to contrive.

comble, ko*ng*-bl, *m*
heaping (measure);
summit; acme; *pl* gables;
de fond en –, der fo*ng*
t'ah*ng* –, from top to
bottom; **pour –de,**
poohr – der, to crown;
to complete.

comble, ko*ng*-bl, *a*
crowded; full; heaped
up.

combler, ko*ng*-bleh, *v* to
fill; to heap; to cover; to
overwhelm (**de,** with);
to fulfill.

combustible, ko*ng*-bEEs-
tee-bl, *m* fuel; *a*
combustible.

comédie, komm-eh-dee, *f*
comedy; play; theater.

comédien, ne, komm-eh-
de-a*ng*, *mf* actor; actress;

comedian.

comestible, komm-ess-tee-bl, *a* edible.

comestibles, komm-ess-tee-bl, *mpl* provisions; food.

comète, komm-ett, *f* comet.

comice, komm-iss, *m* agricultural or electoral meeting.

comique, komm-eeck, *m* comic actor; comic art; *a* comic; comical.

comité, komm-e-teh, *m* board; committee.

commandant, komm-ahng-dahng, *m* commander; major; commanding officer.

commande, komm-ahngd, *f* order.

commander, komm-ahng-deh, *v* to command; to order; to overlook.

commanditaire, komm-ahng-de-tair, *m* silent partner.

commandite, komm-ahng-deet, *f* limited partnership.

comme, komm, *adv* as; like; as if; almost; how; *conj* as; since; because.

commençant, e, komm-ahng-sahng, *mf* beginner.

commencement, komm-ahngss-mahng, *m* beginning.

commencer, komm-ahngss-eh, *v* to begin.

comment, komm-ahng, *adv* how; why! what! —donc! – dong! to be sure!

commentaire, komm-mahng-tair, *m* commentary; comment; remark.

commenter, komm-ahng-teh, *v* to comment; to criticize; to pass remarks.

commerçant, komm-air-sahng, *m* trader; tradesman; dealer. *a* commercial; business.

commerce, komm-airss, *m* trade; business.

commère, komm-air, *f* gossip; busybody.

commettre, komm-et-tr, *v* to commit; to entrust; to appoint; to make (a mistake).

commis, komm-e, *m* clerk; shop assistant; —voyageur, –vo'ăh-yăh-sher, commercial traveler.

commissaire, komm-iss-air, *m* commissioner; commissary; steward; superintendent (police); —priseur, – pre-zer,

auctioneer.

commissariat, komm-iss-săh-re-ăh, *m* station (police).

commission, komm-iss-e-ong, *f* commission; message; errand; committee; commission agency; —ner *v* to commission.

commissionnaire, komm-iss-e-onn-air, *m* agent; porter; messenger; broker.

commode, komm-odd, *f* chest of drawers. *a* convenient; suitable; handy.

commodité, komm-odd-e-teh, *f* convenience.

commotion, komm-moss-e-ong, *f* disturbance; concussion.

commun, komm-ung, *m* generality; commonplace; lower class; domestic servant; *pl* domestic offices.

commun, e, komm-ung, komm-EEn, *a* common; ordinary; trivial; vulgar.

communal, e, komm-E-năhl, *a* communal.

communauté, komm-E-noh-teh, *f* community; convent; corporation.

commune, komm-EEn, *f* commune; parish.

communément, komm-E-neh-mah*ng, adv* commonly.

communicant, e, komm-E-ne-kah*ng, a* communicating.

communication, komm-E-ne-kăh-se-o*ng, f* communication; message; cognizance; telephone call.

communier, komm-E-ne-eh, *v* to receive the sacrament.

communion, komm-E-ne-o*ng, f* communion; sacrament; fellowship.

communiqué, komm-E-ne-keh, *m* official statement.

communiquer, komm-E-ne-keh, *v* to communicate; to impart; to infuse.

compact, e, ko*ng*-păhckt, *a* compact; dense.

compagne, ko*ng*-păhn-yer, *f* female companion; mate; partner; playmate.

compagnie, ko*ng*-păhn-yee, *f* company; society; companionship; **fausser** –, foh-seh –, to sneak away from someone.

compagnon, ko*ng*-păhn-yo*ng, m* companion; partner; mate; playmate.

comparable, ko*ng*-păh-răh-bl, *a* comparable.

comparaison, ko*ng*-păh-ray-zo*ng, f* comparison.

comparaître, ko*ng*-păh-ray-tr, *v* to appear (in court).

comparant, ko*ng*-păh-rah*ng, a* appearing (in court).

comparer, ko*ng*-păh-reh, *v* to compare.

compartiment, ko*ng*-păhr-te-mah*ng, m* compartment; division.

comparution, ko*ng*-păh-rE-se-o*ng, f* appearance (in court).

compas, ko*ng*-pah, *m* compass; compasses.

compassé, e, ko*ng*-păhss-eh, *a* formal; stiff.

compasser, ko*ng*-păhss-eh, *v* to measure; to regulate; to lay out.

compassion, ko*ng*-păhss-e-o*ng, f* compassion; pity.

compatible, ko*ng*-păhstee-bl, *a* compatible.

compatir, ko*ng*-pah-teer, *v* to sympathize (à, with).

compatissant, ko*ng*-pah-tiss-ah*ng, a* compassionate.

compatriote, ko*ng*-păh-tre-ot, *mf* fellow-countryman, fellow-countrywoman.

compenser, ko*ng*-pahng-seh, *v* to compensate.

compère, ko*ng*-pair, *m* announcer (theater); accomplice; chum.

compétence, ko*ng*-peh-tah*ng*ss, *f* competence; jurisdiction.

compétent, e, ko*ng*-peh-tah*ng; a* competent; suitable.

compéti-teur, trice, ko*ng*-peh-te-ter, *mf* competitor.

compétition, ko*ng*-peh-te-se-o*ng, f* competition; rivalry; contest.

compilateur, ko*ng*-pe-lăh-ter, *m* compiler.

compiler, ko*ng*-pe-leh, to compile.

complainte, ko*ng*-plangt, *f* lament; ballad.

complaire (à), ko*ng*-plair ăh, *v* to please; **se** –, to delight (**à, dans,** in).

complaisamment, ko*ng*-play-zăh-mah*ng, adv* obligingly.

complaisance, ko*ng*-play-zah*ng*ss, *f* obligingness; kindness; complacency.

complaisant, ko*ng*-play-zah*ng, m* flatterer.

complaisant, e, ko*ng*-play-zah*ng, a* obliging; kind.

complément, ko*ng*-pleh-mah*ng, m* complement;

object (grammar); remainder.

complet, kong-play, *m* full number; suit (of clothes).

compl-et, ète,* kong-play, *a* complete; full; utter.

compléter, kong-pleh-teh, *v* to complete; to make complete.

complexe, kong-plex, *a* complex; complicated.

complexion, kong-plex-e-ong, *f* constitution; disposition.

complexité kong-plex-e-teh, *f* complexity.

complication, kong-ple-kăh-se-ong, *f* complication.

complice, kong-pliss, *mf & a* accomplice; corespondent.

compliment, kong-ple-mahng, *m* compliment; *pl* congratulations.

complimenter, kong-ple-mahng-teh, *v* to congratulate.

compliqué, e, kong-ple-keh, *a* complicated.

compliquer, kong-ple-keh, *v* to complicate.

complot, kong-plo, *m* plot; conspiracy; scheme.

comploter, kong-plot-eh, *v* to plot.

comporter, kong-por-teh,

v to permit; to admit; to comprise; **se –,** to behave.

composé, kong-poz-eh, *m* compound.

composé, e, kong-poz-eh, *a* composed; compound.

composer, kong-poz-eh, *v* to compose; to compound; to settle.

composi-teur, trice, kong-poz-e-ter, *m* composer; compositor.

composition, kong-poz-e-se-ong, *f* composition; agreement; examination; essay; **de bonne–,** der bonn –, easy to deal with.

compote, kong-pot, *f* stewed fruit; **en –,** ahng –, stewed; (*fig.*) bruised.

compréhensible, kong-preh-ahng-see-bl, *a* understandable.

compréhensi-f, ve, kong-preh-ahng-siff, *a* comprehensive.

compréhension, kong-preh-ahng-se-ong, *f* comprehension.

comprendre, kong-prahng-dr, *v* to understand; to include.

compression, kong-press-e-ong, *f* compression.

comprimé, kong-pre-meh, *m* tablet.

comprimé, e, kong-pre-meh, *pp & a* compressed.

comprimer, kong-pre-meh, *v* to compress; to condense; to restrain.

compris, e, kong-pre, *pp & a* understood; included; **y –, e –,** including; **non –,** nong –, excluding.

compromettant, e, kong-promm-ett-ahng, *a* compromising.

compromettre, kong-promm-et-tr, *v* to compromise; to imperil.

compromis, kong-promm-e, *m* compromise.

comptabilité, kong-tăh-be-le-teh, *f* accountancy; bookkeeping; accounts; accountant's office.

comptable, kong-tăh-bl, *m* accountant; **expert –** ecks-pair –, *m* licensed accountant. *a* accountable; responsible.

comptant, kong-tahng, *a* ready (money); cash; **au – oh –,** for cash.

compte, kongt, *m* account; reckoning; amount; right number; **en fin de –,** ahng fangd –, after all; **se rendre –de,** ser rahng-dr –, to realize.

compte en banque, kongt-ăh*ng*-bă*ngk, m bank account.

compter, kong-teh, *v* to count; to reckon; to intend; to rely.

compte-rendu, kongt rah*ng*-dE, *m* account; report; minutes (of meeting).

compteur, kong-ter, *m* speedometer; meter; recorder.

comptoir, kong-to'ăhr, *m* counter; trading syndicate branch; bar.

compulser, kong-pEEl-seh, *v* to examine (documents, etc).

compulsi-f, ve, kong-pEEl-seef, *a psych* compulsive.

comte, kongt, *m* count; earl.

comté, kong-teh, *m* county; earldom.

concasser, kong-kăhss-seh, *v* to pound; to crush.

concave, kong-kăhv, *a* concave.

concéder, kong-seh-deh, *v* to concede; to grant; to allow.

concentration, kong-sah*ng*-trăh-se-o*ng*, *f* concentration.

concentré, kong-sah*ng*-treh, *m* extract; concentration.

concentrer, kong-sah*ng*-treh, *v* to concentrate; to hold back (feelings).

conception, kong-sep-se-ong, *f* conception; thought.

concernant, kong-sair-nah*ng*, *prep* relating to.

concerner, kong-sair-neh, *v* to concern; to belong to.

concert, kong-sair, *m* concert; concord; **de –,** der–. in concert; jointly.

concerter, kong-sair-teh, *v* to concert; to contrive; **se–,** to plan together.

concession, kong-sess-e-ong, *f* concession; grant; claim.

concessionnaire, kong-sess-e-onn-air, *m* concessionnaire; contractor; grantee.

concevable, kongss-văh-bl, *a* conceivable.

concevoir, kongss-vo'ăhr, *v* to conceive; to understand; to imagine.

concierge, kong-se-airsh, *mf* concierge; janitor; doorman.

conciergerie, kong-se-air-sher-ree, *m* janitor's lodge.

conciliable, kong-se-le-ăh-bl, *a* reconcilable.

conciliabule, kong-se-le-ăh-bEEl, *m* secret assembly; secret meeting.

conciliant, e, kong-se-le-ah*ng*, *a* conciliatory.

concilia-teur, trice, kong-se-le-ăh-ter, *mf & a* peacemaker; conciliator; conciliatory.

concilier, kong-se-le-eh, *v* to reconcile; **se –,** to win over.

concis, e, kong-se, *a* concise; brief.

concision, kong-se-ze-ong, *f* conciseness.

concitoyen, ne, kong-se-to'ăh-yang, *mf* fellow citizen.

conclave, kong-klăv, *m* conclave.

concluant, e, kong-klE-ah*ng*, *a* conclusive.

conclure, kong-klEEr, *v* to conclude; to close; to infer; to prove; to move.

conclusi-f, ve, * kong-klE-zeeff, *a* conclusive.

conclusion, kong-klE-ze-ong, *f* conclusion; inference; motion; verdict.

concombre, kong-kong-br, *m* cucumber.

concordance, kong-kor-dah*ng*ss, *f* agreement; concord; concordance (Bible).

A
B
C
D
E
F
G
H
I
J
K
L
M
N
O
P
Q
R
S
T
U
V
W
X
Y
Z

concorder, kong-kor-deh, *v* to live in agreement; to agree; to compound.

concourir, kong-koo-reer, *v* to concur; to converge; to compete; to cooperate.

concours, kong-koohr, *m* cooperation; concourse; competition; meeting.

concre-t, ète, kong-kray, *a* concrete.

concupiscence, kong-kE-piss-ahngss, *f* concupiscence; sexual desire.

concurremment, kong-kEEr-răh-mahng, *adv* concurrently; in competition.

concurrence, kong-kEEr-rahngss, *f* competition; concurrence; **jusqu'à** –de,shEEs-kăh – der, to the amount of.

concurrent, e, kong-kEEr-rahng, *mf* competitor.

condamnable, kong-dăh-năh-bl, *a* reprehensible; condemnable.

condamnation, kong-dăh-năh-se-ong, *f* condemnation; sentence; conviction.

condamné, e, kong-dăh-neh, *pp & mf* condemned; convict.

condamner, kong-dăh-

neh, *v* to condemn; to convict; to sentence; to block up.

condenser, kong-dahng-seh, *v* to condense.

condescendance, kong-dess-sahng-dahngss, *f* condescension.

condescendre, kong-dess-sahng-dr, *v* to condescend; to yield; to comply.

condiment, kong-de-mahng, *m* condiment.

condisciple, kong-de-see-pl, *m* schoolmate.

condition, kong-de-se-ong, *f* condition; position; term.

conditionnel, le, * kong-de-se-onn-ell, *a* conditional.

conditionner, kong-de-se-onn-eh, *v* to condition; **air conditionné, air** kong-de-se-onn-eh, air-conditioned.

condoléance, kong-doll-eh-ahngss; *f* condolence.

conduc-teur, trice, kong-dEEk-ter, *mf* conductor; leader; guide; driver. *a* conducting; leading.

conduire, kong-dweer, *v* to conduct; to lead; to guide; to drive; to steer; to carry; to manage; **se** –, to behave.

conduit, kong-dwe, *m* pipe; tube; way.

conduite, kong-dweet, *f* conduct; behavior; management; care; driving; channel; **changer de** –, shahng-sheh der –, to turn a new leaf.

cône, kohn, *m* cone.

confection, kong-feck-se-ong, *f* making; manufacture; clothing industry; **–neur,** *m* readymade manufacturer; maker.

confédération, kong-feh-deh-răh-se-ong *f* confederacy.

confédéré e, kong-feh-deh-reh, *a* confederate.

confédérer, kong-feh-deh-reh, *v* to unite.

conférence, kong-feh-rahngss, *f* lecture; conference; **maître de** –s, may-tr der –, college professor.

conférencier, kong-feh-rahng-se-eh, *m* lecturer.

conférer, kong-feh-reh, *v* to confer (à, upon); to grant; to compare; to consult together.

confesser, kong-fayss-eh, *v* to confess; to acknowledge.

confession, kong-fayss-e-

ong, f confession.

confiance, kong-fe-ahngss, *f* confidence; trust; reliance.

confiant, e, kong-fe-ahng, *a* confident; confiding; assured.

confidemment, kong-fe-dăh-mahng, *adv* in confidence.

confidence, kong-fe-dahngss, *f* confidence; secret.

confidentiel, le, * kong-fe-dahng-se-ell, *a* confidential.

confier, kong-fe-eh; *v* to confide; to entrust; **se –,** to confide (**à, in**).

confiner, kong-fe-neh, *v* to confine; to border upon.

confins, kong-fang, *mpl* confines; borders.

confire, kong-feer, *v* to preserve; to pickle.

confirmati-f, ve, kong-feer-măh-teeff, *a* confirmatory.

confirmer, kong-feer-meh, *v* to confirm; **se –, ser–,** to be confirmed.

confiscation, kong-fiss-kăh-se-ong, *f* confiscation; forfeiture.

confiserie, kong-feez-ree, *f* confectionery; preserving; candy store.

confiseur, kong-fe-zer, *m* confectioner.

confisquer, kong-fiss-keh, *v* to confiscate.

confit, kong-fe, *a* preserved; candied.

confiture, kong-fe-tEEr, *f* preserves; jam.

conflagration, kong-flăh-grăh-se-ong, *f* conflagration.

conflit, kong-fle, *m* conflict; clash.

confluent, kong-flE-ahng, *m* confluence.

confondre, kong-fong-dr, *v* to confound; to confuse; to overwhelm; **se–,ser–,** to become indistinct; to be mistaken.

conformation, kong-for-măh-se-ong, *f* conformation.

conforme, kong-form, *a* in accordance; conformable; consistent (**à, with**); **pour copie–,** poohr kop-e –, certified copy.

conformément, kong-for-meh-mahng, *adv* in accordance (**à, with**).

conformer, kong-for-meh, *v* to conform; **se–, ser–,** to comply (**à, with**).

conformité, kong-for-me-teh, *f* conformity.

confort, kong-for, *m* comfort; ease.

confortable, * kong-for-tăh-bl, *a* comfortable; easy.

conforter, kong-for-teh, *v* to comfort; to strengthen.

confraternité, kong-frăh-tair-ne-teh, *f* brotherhood.

confrère, kong-frair, *m* colleague; fellow member (of profession, etc.); brother.

confronter, kong-frong-teh, *v* to confront; to compare.

confus, e, kong-fE, *a* confused; embarrassed; overwhelmed.

confusion, kong-fE-ze-ong, *f* confusion; disorder; trouble; shame.

congé, kong-sheh, *m* leave; resignation; dismissal; holiday.

congédier, kong-sheh-de-eh, *v* to discharge; to dismiss; to pay off.

congélateur, kong-sheh-lăh-ter, *m* deep-freeze machine.

congélation, kong-sheh-lăh-se-ong, *f* freezing.

congeler, kongsh-leh, *v* to congeal; to freeze.

congestion, kong-shess-te-ong, *f* congestion.

a
b
c
d
e
f
g
h
i
j
k
l
m
n
o
p
q
r
s
t
u
v
w
x
y
z

congre, kong-gr, *m* conger eel.

congrégation, kong-greh-găh-se-*ong*, *f* congregation.

congrés, kong-gray, *m* congress.

conique, koh-neeck, *a* conic; conical.

conjecturer, kong-sheck-tE-reh, *v* to conjecture; to surmise; to guess.

conjoindre, kong-sho'*ang*-dr, *v* to join; to unite.

conjoint, e, * kongsho'*ang*, *pp* & *a* joined; united; **–s,** *mpl* husband and wife.

conjonction, kong-shongk-se-*ong*, *f* conjunction; union.

conjugaison, kong-shE-gay-*zong*, *f* conjugation.

conjugal, e, * kong-shE-găhl, *a* conjugal; married.

conjuguer, kong-shE-gheh, *v* to conjugate.

conjuration, kong-shE-răh-se-*ong*, *f* conspiracy; entreaty (in *pl*).

conjuré, kong-shE-reh, *m* conspirator, plotter.

conjurer, kong-shE-reh, *v* to conspire; to implore; to ward off.

connaissance, konn-ayss-ahngss, *f* knowledge; acquaintance; senses; learning; **sans –,** sahng–, unconscious.

connaisseur, konn-ess-er, *m* connoisseur.

connaître, konn-ay-tr, *v* to know; to be acquainted with; to be aware of; **se – (à or en),** to be a good judge (of); **chiffres connus,** shee-fr konn-E, plain figures.

connexe, konn-ecks, *a* connected (**à,** with).

connexion, konn-eck-se-*ong*, *f* connection.

connivence, konn-ne-vahngss, *f* connivance.

conquérant, kong-keh-rahng, *m* conqueror.

conquérant, e, kong-keh-rahng, *a* conquering.

conquérir, kong-keh-reer, *v* to conquer; to gain.

conquête, kong-kayt, *f* conquest.

consacrer, kong-săh-kreh, *v* to consecrate; to devote.

conscience, kong-se-ahngss, *f* conscience; conscientiousness; consciousness; awareness.

conscription, kongs-krip-se-*ong*, *f* conscription.

conscrit, kongs-kre, *m* conscript.

consécration, kong-seh-krăh-se-*ong*, *f* consecration; dedication.

consécuti-f, ve, * kong-seh-kE-teeff, *a* consecutive.

conseil, kong-say'e, *m* advice; council; counsel; adviser; **–d'administration,** –dăhd-me-niss-trăh-se-ong, board of directors; **–de guerre,** – der ghair, court-martial.

conseiller, kong-say'e-eh, *m* councillor; adviser.

conseiller, kong-say'e-eh, *v* to advise; to counsel.

consentement, kong-sahngt-mahng, *m* consent; assent.

consentir, kong-sahng-teer, *v* to consent; to agree.

conséquemment, kong-seh-kăh-mahng, *adv* consequently; accordingly.

conséquence, kong-seh-kahngss, *f* consequence; inference; importance; **en –,** ahng –, consequently; **sans –,** sahng –, immaterial.

conséquent, e, kong-seh-kahng, *a* consequent; consistent; **par –,** păhr

–, in consequence.

conserva-teur, trice, kong-sair-văh-**ter,** *mf* & *a* guardian; keeper; commissioner; preservative; conservative.

conservation, kong-sair-văh-se-*ong, f* preservation; guardianship; registration (mortgages).

conservatoire, kong-sair-văh-to'ăhr, *m* conservatory; museum; music school.

conserve, kong-sairv, *f* preserve; pickled food; tinned food.

conserver, kong-sair-veh, *v* to preserve; to conserve (food); to take care of; to retain.

considérable,* kong-se-deh-răh-bl, *a* considerable.

considération, kong-se-deh-răh-se-*ong, f* consideration; regard; esteem; **en – de,** ahng – der, out of regard for.

considérer, kong-se-deh-reh, *v* to consider; to examine; to value; to regard.

consignataire, kong-seen-yăh-tair, *m* consignee; trustee.

consignation, kong-seen-yăh-se-*ong, f* consignment; deposit.

consigne, kong-seen-yer, *f* orders; checkroom; confinement.

consigner, kong-seen-yeh, *v* to deposit; to record; to confine.

consistance, kong-siss-tahngss, *f* firmness; consistency; stability; credit.

consister, kong-siss-teh, *v* to consist (**à, dans,** of).

consolation, kong-soll-ăh-se-*ong, f* consolation; comfort.

console, kong-sol, *f* bracket; console.

consoler, kong-soll-eh, *v* to console; to comfort.

consomma-teur, trice, kong-somm-ăh-ter, *mf* consumer; customer.

consommation, kong-somm-ăh-se-*ong, f* consummation; consumption; a drink (in café, etc).

consommé, kong-somm-eh, *m* stock; clear soup; consommé.

consommer, kong-somm-eh, *v* to consume; to complete.

consomption, kong-songp-se-*ong, f* consumption.

consonne, kong-sonn, *f* consonant.

conspirateur, kongs-pe-răh-ter, *m* conspirator.

conspiration, kongs-pe-răh-se-*ong, f* conspiracy; plot.

conspirer, kongs-pe-reh, *v* to conspire.

conspuer, kongs-pE-eh, *v* to hoot; to hiss.

constamment, kongs-tăh-mahng, *adv* constantly.

constance, kongs-tangss, *f* constancy; persistence.

constant, e, kongs-tahng, *a* constant; steadfast.

constatation, kongs-tăh-tăh-se-*ong, f* establishment (of fact, etc.); certified statement.

constater, kongs-tăh-teh, *v* to ascertain; to prove; to state; to report.

constellation, kongs-tell-lăh-se-*ong, f* constellation.

consternation, kongs-tair-năh-se-*ong, f* consternation.

consterné, e, kongs-tair-neh, *a* dismayed.

consterner, kongs-tair-neh, *v* to dismay.

constipation, kongs-te-păh-se-*ong, f* constipation.

a
b
c
d
e
f
g
h
i
j
k
l
m
n
o
p
q
r
s
t
u
v
w
x
y
z

A
B
C
D
E
F
G
H
I
J
K
L
M
N
O
P
Q
R
S
T
U
V
W
X
Y
Z

constipé, e, kongs-te-peh, *a* constipated.

constituant, e, kongs-te-tE-ahng, *a* constituent.

constituer, kongs-te-tE-eh, *v* to constitute; to appoint; to assign; **se –prisonnier,** ser – pre-zonne-eh, to give oneself up.

constitution, kongs-te-tE-se-ong, *f* constitution; composition.

constitutionnel, le, kongs-te-tE-se-onn-ell, *a* constitutional.

constricteur, kongs-trick-ter, *m* constrictor.

constructeur, kongs-trEEk-ter, *m* builder; **–mécanicien,** – meh-käh-ne-se-ang, engineer.

construction, kongs-trEEk-se-ong, *f* construction; building; structure.

construire, kongs-trE-eer, *v* to construct; to build; to construe.

consul, kong-sEEl, *m* consul.

consulaire, kong-sE-lair, *a* consular.

consulat, kong-sE-läh, *m* consulate.

consultant, kong-sEEl-tahng, *a* consulting; **médecin –,** mehd-sang –, consulting physician.

consultation, kong-sEEl-täh-se-ong, *f* consultation.

consulter, kong-sEEl-teh, *v* to consult; to refer to; to give consultations; **se–,** to consider.

consumer, kong-sE-meh, *v* to consume; to destroy; to squander.

contact, kong-tähckt, *m* contact; touch; connection.

contagieu-x, se, kong-täh-she-er, *a* contagious; infectious; catching.

contagion, kong-täh-she-ong, *f* contagion; infection.

contaminer, kong-täh-me-neh, *v* to contaminate.

conte, kongt, *m* tale; story; **–à dormir debout,** –äh-dor-meer der-boo, cock and bull story; **–de fées,** – der feh, fairy tale.

contemplation, kong-tahng-pläh-se-ong, *f* contemplation; meditation.

contempler, kong-tahng pleh, *v* to contemplate; to meditate.

contemporain, e, kong-tahng-por-ang, *a* contemporary.

contenance, kongt-nahngss, *f* countenance; look; capacity.

contenir, kongt-neer, *v* to hold; to contain; to restrain.

content, kong-tahng, *a* contented; satisfied; pleased.

contentement, kong-tahngt-mahng, *m* satisfaction.

contenter, kong-tahng-teh, *v* to satisfy; to please.

contentieux, kong-tahng-se-er, *m* disputed claims; legal business. *a* in dispute; litigious.

contenu, kongt-nE, *m* contents; subject.

conter, kong-teh, *v* to tell; to relate; **en – (à),** to tell a tall story.

contestable, kong-tess-täh-bl, *a* debatable; questionable.

contestation, kong-tess-täh-se-ong, *f* contest; dispute.

contester, kong-tess-teh, *v* to contest; to dispute.

conteu-r, se, kong-ter, *mf* storyteller.

contexte, kong-text, *m* context.

contexture, kong-tex-tEEr, *f* contexture; structure.

contigu, ë, kong-te-ghE, *a* adjoining; contiguous.

contiguité, kong-te-gwe-teh, *f* contiguity.

continent, kong-te-nahng, *m* continent.

continental, e, kong-te-nahng-tăhl, *a* continental.

contingent, kong-tang-shahng, *m* share; proportion; quota.

contingent, e, kong-tang-shahng, *a* contingent.

continu,* e, kong-te-nE, *a* continued; continuous.

continuel, le, * kong-te-nE-ell, *a* continual.

continuer, kong-te-nE-eh, *v* to continue; to go on.

continuité, kong-te-nwe-teh, *f* continuity.

contondant, e, kong-tong-dahng, *a* blunt.

contorsion, kong-tor-se-ong, *f* contortion.

contour, kong-toohr, *m* outline; circuit.

contourner, kong-toohr-neh, *v* to outline; to distort; to twist; to go round.

contractant, e, kong-trăhck-tahng, *mf* & *a* contracting party; contracting.

contracter, kong-trăck-teh, *v* to contract; to acquire; to catch; **se –,** to shrink; to be

contracted.

contradictoire, kong-trăh-dick-to'ăhr, *a* contradictory.

contraindre, kong-trang-dr, *v* to constrain; to compel; **–en justice,** –ahng **sh**EE**s**-teess, to sue.

contraint, e, kong-trang, *a* constrained; unnatural.

contrainte, kong-trangt, *f* compulsion; restraint.

contraire, kong-trair, *a* & *n* contrary; reverse; **au –,** oh –, on the contrary; on the other hand.

contrariant, e, kong-trăh-re-ahng, *a* vexing; provoking.

contrariété, kong-trăh-re-eh-teh, *f* contrariness; annoyance.

contraste, kong-trăhst, *m* contrast; opposition.

contrat, kong-trăh, *m* contract; deed; agreement; indenture; covenant.

contravention, kong-trăh-vahng-se-ong, *f* offense; breach of regulations; fine.

contre, kong-tr, *prep* against; versus; near. *adv* **par –,** păhr –, on the other hand. *m* opposite side.

contre-amiral, kong-trăh-me-răhl, *m* rear admiral.

contrebalancer, kong-trer-băh-lahng-seh, *v* to counterbalance.

contrebande, kong-trer-bahngd, *f* smuggling; smuggled goods.

contrebandier, kong-trer-bahng-de-eh, *m* smuggler.

contrebas (en), ahng kong-trer-bah, *adv* downwards; at lower level.

contrebasse, kong-trer-bahss, *f* double bass.

contrecarrer, kong-trer-kăh-reh, *v* to thwart.

contrecœur (à), ăh kong-trer-ker, *adv* reluctantly.

contrecoup, kong-trer-koo, *m* rebound; consequence.

contredire, kong-trer-deer, *v* to contradict.

contredit (sans), sahng kong-trer-de, *adv* unquestionably.

contrée, kong-treh, *f* country; region; district; land.

contre-épreuve, kongtr-eh-prerv, *f* countercheck.

contrefaçon, kong-trer-făh-song, *f* forgery; counterfeit; piracy;

a
b
c
d
e
f
g
h
i
j
k
l
m
n
o
p
q
r
s
t
u
v
w
x
y
z

A
B
C
D
E
F
G
H
I
J
K
L
M
N
O
P
Q
R
S
T
U
V
W
X
Y
Z

infringement.

contrefacteur, kong-trer-făhck-ter, *m* forger; counterfeiter.

contrefaire, kong-trer-fair, *v* to counterfeit; to imitate; to mimic; to disguise; to infringe.

contrefait, kong-trer-fay, *pp* & *a* counterfeited; deformed.

contrefort, kong-trer-for, *m* buttress; spur; stiffener.

contre-jour (à), ăh kong-trer-shoohr, *adv* in a false light.

contremaître, kong-trer-may-tr, *m* foreman.

contremander, kong-trer-mahng-deh, *v* to countermand.

contremarque, kong-trer-măhrk, *f* check.

contrepartie, kong-trer-păhr-tee, *f* counterpart; opposite view.

contre-pied, kong-trer-pe-eh, *m* contrary; reverse.

contrepoids, kong-trer-po'ăh, *m* counterbalance.

contrepoil (à), ăh kong-trer-po'ăhl, *adv* against the grain; the wrong way.

contrepoint, kong-trer-po'ang, *m* counterpoint.

contrepoison, kong-trer-po'ăh-zong, *m* antidote.

contresens, kong-trer-sahngss, *m* misinterpretation; wrong way.

contresigner, kong-trer-seen-yeh, *v* to countersign.

contretemps, kong-trer-tahng, *m* mishap; disappointment; out of time; **à** –, ăh –, inopportunely.

contre-torpilleur, kong-trer-tor-pee-yer, *m* destroyer.

contrevenant, kong-trerv-nahng, *m* offender.

contrevenir, kong-trerv-neer, *v* to infringe; to transgress.

contrevent, kong-trer-vahng, *m* shutter.

contre-vérité, kong-trer-veh-re-teh, *f* falsehood; irony; satire.

contribuable, kong-tre-bE-ăh-bl, *m* taxpayer; *a* tax-paying.

contribuer, kong-tre-bE-eh, *v* to contribute; to be conducive.

contribution, kong-tre-bE-ong, *f* contribution; tax; rate; part.

contrister, kong-triss-teh, *v* to grieve; to sadden.

contrit, e, kong-tre, *a* contrite; penitent.

contrôle, kong-trohl, *m* register; list; checking; censure; control.

contrôler, kong-troh-leh, *v* to inspect; to control; to verify; to monitor; **se** –, to control oneself.

contrôleu-r, se, kong-troh-ler, *mf* inspector; ticket collector.

controuvé, e, kong-troo-veh, *pp* & *a* invented; false.

controverse, kong-trov-airs, *f* controversy.

contumace, kong-tE-măhss, *f* contumacy; default. *m* defaulter. *a* rebellious.

contusion, kong-tE-ze-ong, *f* bruise.

convaincant, e, kong-vang-kahng, *a* convincing.

convaincre, kong-vang-kr, *v* to convince; to convict.

convaincu, e, kong-vang-kE, *pp* & *a* convinced; convicted.

convalescence, kong-văh-layss-ahngss, *f* convalescence.

convenable, * kongv-năh-bl, *a* proper; fit; suitable.

convenance, kongv-nahngss, *f* fitness; convenience; *pl* good manners; propriety.

convenir, kongv-neer, *v* to agree (**avec,** with; **de,** on); to acknowledge; to suit; to be agreeable to.

convention, kong-vahng-se-*ong*, *f* convention; agreement; condition.

conventionnel, le, * kong-vahng-se-onn-ell, *a* conventional.

convenu, kongv-nE, *pp* agreed.

converger, kong-vair-sheh, *v* to converge.

conversation, kong-vair-săh-se-ong, *f* conversation.

converser, kong-vair-seh, *v* to converse; to talk.

conversion, kong-vair-se-ong, *f* conversion.

converti, e, kong-vair-te, *mf* & *a* convert; converted.

convertir, kong-vair-teer, *v* to convert; to turn; **se –,** to become converted (**à,** to).

convexe, kong-vex, *a* convex.

conviction, kong-vick-se-ong, *f* conviction; convincing proof.

convier, kong-ve-eh, *v* to invite; to prompt.

convive, kong-veev, *m* guest (at meal).

convocation, kong-vock-ăh-se-*ong*, *f* convocation; requisition; summons.

convoi, kong-vo'ăh, *m* funeral procession; train; convoy.

convoiter, kong-vo'ăh-teh, *v* to covet.

convoitise, kong-vo'ăh-teez, *f* covetousness.

convoquer, kong-vock-eh, *v* to convoke; to call; to summon.

convulsion, kong-vEEl-se-ong, *f* convulsion.

convulsi-f, ve, * kong-vEEl-seef, *a* convulsive.

coopéra-teur, trice, ko-op-eh-răh-**ter,** *mf* cooperator.

coopérer, ko-op-eh-reh, *v* to cooperate.

coordonner, ko-or-donn-eh, *v* to arrange; to coordinate.

copain, kop-ang, *m* chum.

copeau, kop-oh, *m* chip; shaving.

copie, kopee, *f* copy; manuscript; reproduction; imitation.

copier, kop-e-eh, *v* to copy; to imitate; to mimic.

copieu-x, se, * kop-e-er, *a* copious; plentiful.

copropriétaire, kop-rop-re-eh-tair, *m* joint-owner; co-owner.

coq, kock, *m* cock; cockerel; weathercock; **–à l'âne, –** ăh lahn, abrupt change of subject.

coque, kock, *f* shell; cockle; hull.

coquelicot, kock-le-ko, *m* poppy.

coqueluche, kock-lEEsh, *f* whooping cough; favorite (person); idol.

coquerico, kock-re-ko, *m* cock-a-doodle-doo.

coquet, te, * kock-ay, *a* flirtatious; elegant.

coquetier, kock-te-eh, *m* eggcup; egg merchant.

coquetterie, kock-ett-ree, *f* coquetry; flirtation; stylishness (in dress).

coquillage, kock-ee-yăhsh, *m* empty shell; shellfish.

coquille, kock-ee-ye, *f* shell.

coquin, e, kock-ang, *a* rogue; rascal; (fam) naughty.

coquinerie, kock-een-ree, *f* mischievousness; roguishness.

cor, kor, *m* horn; corn (on the foot).

a b c d e f g h i j k l m n o p q r s t u v w x y z

corail, kor-ah'e, *m* coral.

coran, kor-ahng, *m* Koran.

corbeau, kor-boh, *m* raven; crow.

corbeille, kor-bay'e, *f* basket; wedding presents; flowerbed; **– à papier,** – ăh pah-pe-eh, wastepaper basket.

corbillard, kor-bee-yăhr, *m* hearse.

cordage, kor-dăhsh, *m* rope.

corde, kord, *f* string; cord; rope; **la –sensible,** lăh – sahng-see-bl, the tender spot; **tenir la –,** ter-neer lăh –, to have the best chance.

cordeau, kor-doh, *m* line; cord.

corder, kor-deh, *v* to string; to twist.

cordial, e, * kor-de-ăhl, *a* hearty.

cordon, kor-dong, *m* twist; string; cord; **–bleu,** –bler, first-rate cook.

cordonnerie, kor-donn-ree, *f* shoemaking; shoemaker's.

cordonnet, kor-donn-ay, *m* twist; small string; braid.

cordonnier, kor-donn-e-eh, *m* cobbler.

coriace, kor-e-ăhss, *a* tough (of meat, etc);

(fam) hard (person).

cormoran, kor-mor-ahng, *m* cormorant.

cornaline, kor-năh-leen, *f* cornelian stone.

corne, korn, *f* horn; feeler (of snail); dog-ear (book page).

corneille, kor-nay'e, *f* crow.

cornemuse, kor-ner-mEEz, *f* bagpipe.

cornet, kor-nay, *m* horn; cornet; ice cream cone.

corniche, kor-neesh, *f* cornice; ledge (of rock).

cornichon, kor-ne-shong, *m* gherkin; pickle; ninny (person).

cornu, e, kor-nE, *a* horned.

corollaire, kor-oll-lair, *m* corollary.

corps, kor, *m* body; corps; corpse; substance.

corpulent, e, kor-pE-lahng, *a* stout; corpulent.

correct, e, * kor-reckt, *a* correct; proper.

correcteur, kor-reck-ter, *m* proofreader.

correction, kor-reck-se-ong, *f* correction; accuracy; correctness; punishment.

corrélati-f, ve,* kor-reh-lăh-teeff, *a* correlative.

correspondance, kor-ress-pong-dahngss, *f* correspondence; connection (between trains); **petite –,** per-teet –, personal column.

correspondant, e, kor-ress-pong-dahng, *mf & a* correspondent; pen pal; guardian; corresponding.

corridor, kor-e-dor, *m* corridor; passage; hallway.

corrigé, kor-e-sheh, *m* corrected version.

corriger, kor-e-sheh, *v* to correct; to grade; to chastise.

corroboration, kor-rob-or-ăh-se-ong, *f* strengthening.

corroder, kor-rod-eh, *v* to corrode.

corrompre, kor-ong-pr, *v* to corrupt; to bribe.

corrompu, e, kor-ong-pE, *pp & a* corrupted; bribed; putrid.

corrup-teur, trice, kor-EEp-**ter,** *mf & a* corrupter; corrupting; briber.

corruptible, kor-EEp-tee-bl *a* corruptible.

corruption, kor-EEp-se-ong, *f* corruption.

corsage, kor-săsh, *m* bodice.

corsé, e, kor-seh, *a* full-bodied.

corser, kor-seh, *v* to give volume to; (*fig*) to thicken.

corset, kor-say, *m* corset.

cortège, kor-taysh, *m* procession; retinue.

corvée, kor-veh, *f* chore; drudgery; unpleasant job.

coryphée, kor-e-feh, *m* leader; chief.

cosaque, koz-ăhck, *m* cossack; brutal man.

cosmétique, koss-meh-teeck, *m* & *a* cosmetic.

cosmique, koss-meeck, *a* cosmic.

cosmopolite, koss-mop-oll-eet, *mf* & *a* cosmopolitan.

cosse, koss, *f* shell; husk; pod.

cossu, e, koss-E, *a* opulent; well-off.

costume, koss-tEEm, *m* costume; suit (man's); **grand –,** grahng –, full dress.

costumier, koss-tE-me-eh, *m* costumier; wardrobe master or mistress.

cote, kot, *f* mark; share; quota.

côte, koht, *f* rib; hill; coast; shore; **–à–, –ăh–,** side by side.

côté, koht-eh, *m* side; way; part; direction; **à –,** ăh –, near; **de ce –,** der ser –, this way; **mauvais –,** moh-vay –, wrong side.

coteau, kot-oh, *m* hillside; slope.

côtelette, koht-lett, *f* cutlet; chop.

coter, kot-eh, *v* to assess; to quote; to number.

coterie, kot-ree, *f* set; circle; clique.

côtier, koh-te-eh, *m* coasting vessel. *a* coasting; coastal.

cotillon, kot-ee-yong, *m* petticoat; cotillon.

cotisation, kot-e-zăh-se-ong, *f* contribution; subscription.

cotiser, kot-e-zeh, *v* to rate; **se–,** to club together; to open a subscription.

coton, kot-ong, *m* cotton; down; cotton thread.

cotonnade, kot-onn-ăhd, *f* cotton fabric; cotton goods.

côtoyer, koh-to'ăh-yeh, *v* to skirt; to border on.

cottage, kot-ăhsh, *m* cottage.

cou, koo, *m* neck.

couard, koo-ăhr, *mf* & *a* coward; cowardly.

couchant, koo-shahng, *m* sunset; west; decline. *a* setting.

couche, koosh, *f* couch; bed; layer; confinement; diaper.

couché, koo-sheh, *pp* & *a* lying down; in bed.

couche-culotte, koosh-kE-lot, *f* disposable diaper.

coucher, koo-sheh, *m* bedtime; sunset.

coucher, koo-sheh, *v* to lay down; to put to bed; **se–** to go to bed.

couchette, koo-shett, *f* crib; berth; sleeper (on trains, etc.).

couci-couça, koo-se-koo-sah, *adv* (*fam*) so-so.

coucou, koo-koo, *m* cuckoo; cuckoo clock; cowslip; peek-a-boo!.

coude, kood, *m* elbow; bend; angle.

coudée, kood-eh, *f* **–s franches,** – frahngsh, elbow room.

cou-de-pied, kood-pe-eh, *m* instep.

coudoyer, koo-do'ăh-yeh, *v* to elbow; to jostle.

coudre, koo-dr, *v* to sew; to stitch; to tack.

couenne, koo-ăhn, *f* rind (of bacon).

couette, ko'ett, *f* comforter.

coulage, koo-lăhsh, *m*
leakage; pouring;
casting.

coulant, e, koo-lahng, *a*
flowing; running; fluent;
accommodating
(person).

coulée, koo-leh, *f* flow;
casting.

couler, koo-leh, *v* to flow;
to glide; to run (of
liquid); to cast; to sink.

couleur, koo-ler, *f* color;
paint; suit (cards).

couleuvre, koo-ler-vr, *f*
grass snake; (*fig*) bitter
pill.

coulis, koo-le, *m* jelly;
meat or vegetable broth;
puree. *a* **vent** –, vahng –,
draft.

coulisse, koo-leess, *f*
groove; slide; wing of
theater; unofficial stock
market.

couloir, koo-lo'ăhr, *m*
passage; corridor; lobby.

coup, koo, *m* blow; stroke;
hit; kick; knock; rap;
thrust; cast; cut; stab;
lash; wound; shot;
report; toll; beat; clap;
peal; throw; haul; event;
deed; outburst; trick.

coupable, koo-păh-bl, *mf*
& *a* culprit; guilty.

coupage, koo-păhsh, *m*
mixing; diluting;
cutting.

coupant, e, koo-pahng, *a*
cutting; sharp.

coup de soleil, koo-der-
soll-a'ye *m* sunburn.

coup de téléphone, koo-
der-teh-leh-fonn *m*
telephone call.

coupe, koop, *f* cut; cup;
section.

couper, koo-peh, *v* to cut;
to mix; to dilute; to cut
off.

couperet, koop-ray, *m*
chopper; knife (for
meat).

couperose, koop-rohz, *f*
copperas; blotchiness (of
complexion).

coupeur, koo-per, *m*
cutter.

couplage, koo-plăhsh, *m*
coupling; connecting.

couple, koo-pl, *m* pair;
couple; brace.

coupler, koo-pleh, *v* to
couple.

couplet, koo-play, *m* verse;
stanza.

coupole, koo-pol, *f*
cupola.

coupon, koo-pong, *m*
remnant; short length;
coupon; ticket.

coupure, koo-pEEr, *f* cut;
suppression; bill; note;
cutting.

cour, koohr, *f* yard; court;
courtship.

courage, koo-răhsh, *m*
courage; guts.

courageu-x, se,* koo-
răhsh-er, *a* courageous;
spirited; brave.

couramment, koo-răh-
mahng, *adv* fluently;
generally.

courant, koo-rahng, *m*
current; stream; course;
au–de, oh – der,
conversant with; **mettre
au–** met-tr-oh–, to
inform; *a* current;
running; ordinary;
present.

courbature, koohr-băh-
tEEr, *f* stiffness in the
joints; ache.

courbaturé, koohr-băh-tE-
reh, *a* stiff; aching.

courbe, koohrb, *f* curve;
bend; curb.

courbé, koohr-beh, *pp* &
a curved; bent; crooked.

courbette, koohr-bett, *f*
servile bow; cringing.

courbure, koohr-bEEr, *f*
curvature; bend.

coureur, koo-rer, *m*
runner; racer; (*fam*)
womanizer; *a* running.

courge, koohrsh, *f* squash.

courgette, koohrsh-ett, *f*
zucchini.

courir, koo-reer, *v* to run;
to hunt; to flow.

courlis, koohr-le, *m*
curlew.

couronne, koo-ronn, *f*
crown; coronet; wreath.

couronné, koo-ronn-eh,
pp & *a* crowned;
rewarded with a prize.

couronnement, koo-ronn-mahng, *m* coronation;
crowning.

courrier, koo-re-eh, *m*
courier; mail; post;
messenger.

courrier électronique,
koo-re-eh-eh-leck-tro-neeck, *m* e-mail.

courroie, koo-ro'ăh, *f*
strap; belt.

courroucer, koo-roo-seh,
v to irritate; to incense.

courroux, koo-roo, *m*
wrath.

cours, koohrs, *m* course;
flow; vent; currency;
market price; course (of
lectures, etc.); lesson.

course, koohrs, *f* running;
run; race; drive; errand;
pl shopping.

coursier, koohr-se-eh, *m*
steed.

court, e, koohr, *a* short;
limited; *m* court.

courtage, koohr-tăhsh, *m*
brokerage.

courtaud, e, koohr-toh, *a*
thickset.

court-circuit, koohr-seer-

kwe, *m* short circuit.

court de tennis, koor-der-teh-neess *m* **tennis
court.**

courtepointe, koohr-ter-po'angt, *f* quilt.

courtier, koohr-te-eh, *m*
broker.

courtisan, koohr-te-zahng,
m courtier.

courtiser, koohr-te-zeh, *v*
to court.

courtois, e, * koohr-to'ăh,
a courteous.

courtoisie, koohr-to'ăh-zee, *f* courtesy.

couru, e, koo-rE, *pp* & *a*
run; sought after;
popular; (*fam*) dead
certainty.

cousin, koo-zang, *m* gnat.

cousin, e, koo-zang, *mf*
cousin.

coussin, kooss-ang, *m*
cushion; bolster.

coussinet, kooss-e-nay, *m*
pad; small cushion;
bearing.

cousu, e, koo-zE, *pp*
sewed; sewn.

coût, koo, *m* cost;
expense; charge.

coûtant, koo-tahng, *a* used
only in **à prix –,** ăh pre
–, at cost.

couteau, koh-toh, *m*
knife.

coutelas, koot-lah, *m*

cutlass; knife (kitchen).

coutellerie, koo-tell-ree, *f*
cutlery (industry).

coûter, koo-teh, *v* to cost.

coûteu-x, se, * koo-ter, *a*
expensive.

coutil, koo-te, *m* ticking
twill.

coutume, koo-tEEm, *f*
custom; practice.

coutumier, koo-tEE-me-eh, *a* customary; usual.

couture, koo-tEE, *f* seam;
needlework; sewing.

couturi-er, ère, koo-tE-re-eh, *mf* dressmaker.

couvée, koo-veh, *f* covey;
brood.

couvent, koo-vahng, *m*
convent.

couver, koo-veh, *v* to
brood; to sit on; to
hatch; to smolder; **–des
yeux, –** day z'e-er, to
look fondly on.

couvercle, koo-vair-kl, *m*
cover; lid; cap.

couvert, koo-vair, *m* place
setting; cover charge (in
restaurant); cover;
shelter; **mettre le –,**
met-tr ler –, to set the
table.

couvert, koo-vair, *a*
covered; overcast
(weather); clad.

couverture, koo-vair-tEEr,
f cover; blanket; rug;

a
b
c
d
e
f
g
h
i
j
k
l
m
n
o
p
q
r
s
t
u
v
w
x
y
z

A
B
C
D
E
F
G
H
I
J
K
L
M
N
O
P
Q
R
S
T
U
V
W
X
Y
Z

security.

couvre-chef, koo-vrer-sheff, *m* hat; (*fam*) cap.

couvre-feu, koo-vrer-fer, *m* curfew.

couvre-lit, koo-vrer-le, *m* bedspread.

couvreur, koo-vrer, *m* roofer.

couvrir, koo-vreer, *v* to cover (**de,** with); to conceal; to screen; se –, to put one's hat on; to clothe oneself.

crabe, krahb, *m* crab.

crachat, krăh-shăh, *m* saliva; spit.

craché, krăh-sheh, *pp* & *a*; **tout** –, too –, the spitting image of.

cracher, krăh-sheh, *v* to spit; (*fam*) to cough up.

crachoir, krăh-sho'ăhr, *m* spittoon.

craie, kray, *f* chalk.

craindre, krang-dr, *v* to fear; to dread.

crainte, krangt, *f* fear; dread.

crainti-f, ve, * krang-teeff, *a* timorous; fearful.

cramoisi, e, krăh-mo'ăh-ze, *a* crimson.

crampe, krahngp, *f* cramp.

crampon, krahng-pong, *m* clamp; stud; crampon; (*fam*) bore.

cramponner, krahng-

ponn-eh, *v* to cramp; se – à, to cling to.

cran, krahng, *m* notch; cog; peg; (*fam*) pluck.

crâne, krahn, *m* skull; *a* plucky; swaggering.

crânerie, krahn-ree, *f* pluck; swagger.

crapaud, krăh-poh, *m* toad.

crapule, krăh-pEEl, *f* debauchery; (*fam*) crook.

crapuleu-x, se, krăh-pE-ler, *a* villainous; dishonest.

craque, krăhck, *f* (*fam*) fib.

craquer; krăhck-leh, *v* to crack.

craquement, krăhck-mahng, *m* cracking; crackling.

craquer, krăh-keh, to crack; to crackle.

crasse, krăhss, *f* dirt; filth; stinginess. *a* gross; crass.

crasseu-x, se, krăhss-er, *a* filthy; nasty; sordid.

cratère, krăh-tair, *m* crater.

cravache, krăh-văhsh, *f* riding crop.

cravate, krăh-văht, *f* necktie.

crayeu-x, se, kray-e-er, *a* chalky.

crayon, kray-yong, *m*

pencil.

crayonner, kray-yonn-eh, *v* to sketch; to draw.

créance, kre-ahngss, *f* credit; trust; right to a debt; credence.

créancier, kreh-ahngss-e-eh, *m* creditor.

créateur, kreh-ăh-ter, *m* creator; maker; *a* creative.

création, kreh-ăh-se-ong, *f* creation; production.

créature, kreh-ăh-tEEr, *f* creature.

crécelle, kreh-sell, *f* rattle.

crèche, kraysh, *f* crib; manger; nursery.

crédence, kreh-dahngss, *f* sideboard.

crédit, kreh-de, *m* credit; trust; loan; influence; esteem.

créditer, kreh-de-teh, *v* to credit (**de,** with).

credo, kreh-do, *m* creed; belief.

crédule, kreh-dEEl, *a* credulous.

crédulité, kreh-dE-le-teh, *f* credulity.

créer, kreh-eh, *v* to create; to invent; to establish.

crémaillère, kreh-mah'e-air, *f* rack; (*fam*) **pendre la** –, pahng-dr lăh –, to have a housewarming.

crémation, kreh-măh-se-ong, *f* cremation.

crème, kraym, *f* cream; custard; best.

crèmerie, krehm-ree, *f* creamery; dairy.

crémi-er, ère, kreh-me-eh, *mf* dairyman; dairywoman.

créneau, kreh-noh, *m* battlement.

crénelé, e, krehn-leh, *a* notched; crenellated.

créneler, krehn-leh, *v* to cog; to mill.

crénelure, krehn-lEEr, *f* indentation.

crêpe, krayp, *m* crepe; mourning veil. *f* pancake.

crêper, kray-peh, *v* to frizz; to crisp.

crépi, kreh-pe, *m* roughcast.

crépir, kreh-peer, *v* to roughcast; to crimp.

crépine, kreh-peen, *f* fringe (on upholstery).

crépiter, kreh-pe-teh, *v* to crackle.

crépu, e, kreh-pE, *a* woolly; fuzzy.

crépuscule, kreh-pEEss-kEEl, *m* twilight; decline.

cresson, krehss-ong, *m* cress; watercress.

crétacé, e, kreh-tăhss-eh, *a* cretaceous.

crête, krayt, *f* crest; top; ridge; comb (of a cock).

crétin, kreh-tang, *m* idiot.

crétinisme, kreh-te-nissm, *m* idiocy.

cretonne, krer-tonn, *f* cretonne.

creuser, krer-zeh, *v* to dig; to hollow; to scoop out; to fathom.

creuset, krer-zay, *m* crucible; (*fam*) test.

creux, krer, *m* hollow cavity; bass voice.

creu-x, se, krer, *a* hollow; empty; unsubstantial; off-peak.

crevaison, krer-veh-zong, *f* puncture; bursting.

crevasse, krer-văhss, *f* crevice; chink; crack.

crève-cœur, krayv-ker, *m* heartbreaking thing.

crever, krer-veh, *v* to burst; to pierce; to puncture; **se –,** to burst.

crevette, krer-vett, *f* shrimp; prawn.

cri, kre, *m* cry; shout; shriek; scream; clamor; **le dernier –,** ler dair-ne-eh –, the latest fashion.

criailler, kree-ah'e-yeh, *v* to bawl.

criant, e, kree-ahng, *a* crying; glaring.

criard, e, kree-ăhr, *a* clamorous; shrill; loud; gaudy.

crible, kree-bl, *m* sieve; riddle.

cribler, kree-bleh, *v* to sift; to riddle; to pierce with holes.

cric, kre, *m* jack (car).

cricket, kre-kay, *m* cricket (game).

cri-cri, kre-kre, *m* cricket (insect).

criée, kree-eh, *f* auction.

crier, kree-eh, *v* to cry; to shout; to shriek; to proclaim.

crieur, kree-er, *m* crier; auctioneer; town-crier.

crime, kreem, *m* crime.

criminalité, kre-me-năh-le-teh, *f* criminality.

criminel, le, kre-me-nell, *mf & a** criminal; culprit.

crin, krang, *m* horsehair; **les –s,** lay –, mane and tail.

crinière, kre-ne-air, *f* mane; (*fam*) thick head of hair.

crique, kreeck, *f* creek; cove.

criquet, kre-kay, *m* locust; (*fam*) cricket.

crise, kreez, *f* crisis; fit; attack.

crisper, kriss-peh, *v* to shrivel; to clench; to irritate; **se –,** to contract.

a
b
c
d
e
f
g
h
i
j
k
l
m
n
o
p
q
r
s
t
u
v
w
x
y
z

crisser, kriss-eh, *v* to grate; to grind.

cristal, kriss-tăhl, *m* crystal; cut-glass.

cristallin, kriss-tăh-la*n*g, *a* crystalline.

cristalliser, kriss-tăh-le-zeh, *v* to crystallize.

critérium, kre-teh-re-omm, *m* criterion.

critique, kre-teeck, *m* critic; *f* criticism; censure; *a** critical.

critiquer, kre-te-keh, *v* to criticize.

croasser, kro'ăhss-eh, *v* to croak; to caw.

croc, kro, *m* hook; canine tooth; tusk; fang.

croche, krosh, *f* quaver; eigth (*mus*).

crochet, krosh-ay, *m* hook; picklock; clasp; bend; crochet.

crocheter, krosh-teh, *v* to pick (a lock).

crochu, e, krosh-E, *a* hooked; crooked.

crocodile, krock-odd-eell, *m* crocodile.

crocus, krock-EEss, *m* crocus; saffron.

croire, kro'ăhr, *v* to believe; to think; to trust to.

croisade, kro'ăh-zăhd, *f* crusade.

croisé, kro'ăh-zeh, *m* crusader; twill; *pp* & *a* crossed; double-breasted.

croisée, kro'ăh-zeı, *f* crossing; casement window; transept.

croisement, kro'ăhz-mah*n*g, *m* crossing.

croiser, kro'ăh-zeh, *v* to cross; to interbreed (animal); to cruise.

croiseur, kro'ăh-zer, *m* cruiser.

croisière, kro'ăh-ze-air, *f* cruise.

croissance, krwăhss-ahngss, *f* growth; increase.

croissant, krwăhss-ah*n*g, *m* crescent; French crescent roll.

croissant, e, krwăhss-ah*n*g, *a* growing.

croître, kro'ah-tr, *v* to grow; to increase; to lengthen.

croix, kro'ăh, *f* cross.

croquant, krock-ah*n*g, *m* (*fam*) peasant; poor wretch; *a* crisp.

croque-mitaine, krock-me-tain, *m* (*fam*) bogeyman.

croque-mort, krock-mor, *m* pallbearer.

croquer, krock-eh, *v* to crunch; to munch; to sketch.

croquette, krock-ett, *f* croquette.

croquis, krock-e, *m* sketch; outline.

crosse, kross, *f* crosier; butt-end; hockey sticks.

crotte, krot, *f* dung; dropping of animal dirt.

crotté, e, krot-eh, *a* dirty; muddy.

crotter, krot-eh, *v* to dirty.

crottin, krot-ang, *m* horse or sheep dung.

croulant, e, kroo-lah*n*g, *a* sinking; tottering; tumbledown.

crouler, kroo-leh, *v* to fall; to sink; to crumble.

croup, kroop, *m* croup.

croupe, kroop, *f* rump; buttocks.

croupier, kroo-pe-eh, *m* croupier.

croupière, kroo-pe-air, *f* crupper.

croupion, kroo-pe-ong, *m* rump; butt; (*fam*) pope's nose.

croupir, kroo-peer, *v* to stagnate; to wallow.

croupissant, e, kroo-piss-ah*n*g, *a* stagnating; putrescent.

croustillant, e, krooss-tee-yah*n*g, *a* crisp.

croûte, kroot, *f* crust; scab; (*fam*) daub; old fogy; **casser une –,**

kăhss-ehEEn –, to take a snack.

croûton, kroo-tong, *m* crust end; crouton.

croyable, kro'ăh-yăh-bl, *a* credible; likely.

croyance, kro'ăh-yahngss, *f* belief; creed; faith.

croyant, e, kro'ăh-yahng, *mf* believer; *pl* the faithful.

cru, krE, *m* vineyards; vintage.

cru, e, krE, *a* raw; crude; coarse.

cruauté, krE-oh-teh, *f* cruelty.

cruche, krEEsh, *f* pitcher; blockhead.

cruchon, krE-shong, *m* jug; stone bottle.

crucial, e, krE-se-ăhl, *a* cross-shaped; crucial; fundamental.

crucifier, krE-se-fe-eh, *v* to crucify.

crucifix, krE-se-fe, *m* crucifix.

crudité, krE-de-teh, *f* crudity; crudeness; rawness; coarseness.

crue, krEE, *f* rise; swelling; flood.

cruel, le,* krE-ell, *a* cruel; sore; annoying.

crûment, krEE-mahng, *adv* bluntly.

crustacé, krEEss-tăhss-eh,

m & *a* crustacean; crustaceous.

crypte, kree-pt, *f* crypt.

cubage, kE-băhsh, *m* cubic measurement; cubage.

cube, kEEb, *m* cube; toy building block; *a* cubic.

cueillette, ker'e-yett, *f* picking; gathering; mixed cargo.

cueillir, ker'e-yeer, *v* to gather; to pick; to pluck.

cuiller or **cuillère,** kwee-yair, *f* spoon.

cuillerée, kwee-yer-reh, *f* spoonful.

cuir, kweer, *m* skin; hide; leather.

cuirasse, kwee-răhss, *f* breast plate; armor-plating.

cuirassé, kwee-răhss-eh, *m* battleship.

cuirassé, e, kwee-răhss-eh, *a* armored.

cuirassier, kwee-răhss-e-eh, *m* cuirassier.

cuire, kweer, *v* to cook; to bake; to roast; to stew; to smart.

cuisant, e, kwee-zahng, *a* sharp; acute; burning.

cuisine, kwee-zeen, *f* kitchen; cooking; cookery.

cuisiner, kwee-ze-neh, *v* to cook; (*fam*) to concoct (scheme, etc).

cuisini-er, ère, kwee-ze-ne-eh, *mf* cook; *f* stove.

cuisse, kweess, *f* thigh; leg of bird.

cuisson, kweess-ong, *f* cooking; baking; firing (of bricks, etc); smarting.

cuissot, kweess-o, *m* haunch.

cuit, e, kwee, *pp* & *a* cooked; done; drunk; done for.

cuivre, kwee-vr, *m* copper; –**jaune,** –shohn, brass.

cuivreu-x, se, kwee-vrer, *a* coppery.

cul, kE, *m* (vulgar, except in compounds), bottom; back; rump.

culbute, kEEl-bEEt, *f* somersault; fall; tumble; failure; ruin.

culbuter, kEEl-bE-teh, *v* to topple over; to tumble down.

culinaire, kE-le-nair, *a* culinary.

culminant, e, kEEl-me-nahng, *a* highest; prominent.

culot, kE-lo, *m* bottom; plug; (*fam*) cheek; [to have a] lot of nerve.

culotte, kE-lot, *f* buttock (of beef); underpants; pants; breeches.

culotter, kE-lot-eh, *v* to

breech.

culpabilité, kEEl-păh-be-le-reh, *f* guilt.

culte, kEElt, *m* worship; creed; cult; veneration.

cultivateur, kEEl-te-văh-ter, *m* grower; agriculturist; farmer.

cultiver, kEEl-te-veh, *v* to cultivate.

culture, kEEl-tEEr, *f* cultivation; culture.

cumuler, kE-mE-leh, *v* to hold several offices; to cumulate.

cupide, kE-peed, *a* covetous; greedy.

curage, kE-răhsh, *m* picking (of teeth); clearing; cleaning.

curatelle, kE-răh-tell, *f* guardianship; trusteeship.

cura-teur, trice, kE-răh-ter, *mf* guardian; curator; trustee.

cure, kEEr, *f* cure; treatment; living; vicarage; parish.

curé, kE-reh, *m* priest.

cure-dent, kEEr-dahng, *m* toothpick.

curer, kE-reh, *v* to pick (teeth, etc); to clean out.

curieux, kE-re-er, *m* inquisitive person; bystander; curious thing

or fact.

curieu-x, se, * kE-re-er, *a* curious; inquisitive; singular.

curiosité, kE-re-ohz-e-teh, *f* curiosity; inquisitiveness; curio.

cutané, e, kE-tăh-neh, *a* cutaneous.

cuve, kEEv, *f* vat; tub; copper.

cuvée, kE-veh, *f* vatful; **bonne –,** bon –, quality.

cuver, kE-veh, *v* to ferment; to settle; – **son vin,** – song vang, to sleep oneself sober.

cuvette, kE-vett, *f* basin; washing-up bowl.

cuvier, kE-ve-eh, *m* wash-tub.

cyanure, se-ăh-nEEr, *m* cyanide.

cycle, see-kl, *m* cycle.

cycliste, see-kleest, *mf* cyclist.

cygne, seen-yer, *m* swan.

cylindre, se-lang-dr, *m* cylinder; roller.

cymbale, sang-băhl, *f* cymbal.

cynique, se-neeck, *m* cynic; *a* * cynical.

cynisme, se-nissm, *m* cynicism.

cyprès, se-pray, *m* cypress.

cytise, se-teez, *m* laburnum.

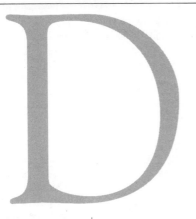

dactylographe, dăhck-te-log-răhf, *mf & a* typist.

dactylographie, dăhck-te-log-răh-fee, *f* typing.

dada, dăh-dăh, *m* hobbyhorse; hobby; pet subject.

dadais, dăh-day, *m* ninny; simpleton.

dague, dăhg, *f* dagger.

daigner, dayn-yeh, *v* to deign.

daim, dang, *m* deer; buck; suede.

dais, day, *m* canopy.

dalle, dăhl, *f* flagstone; slab.

daltonisme, dăhl-tonn-issm, *m* color-blindness.

damas, dăh-mah, *m* damask.

dame, dăhm, *f* lady; queen (cards); a king in checkers; *pl* game of checkers.

dame! dăhm! *interj* why! well! indeed!

damer, dăh-meh, *v* to crown (in checkers); (*fam*) –**le pion à,** – ler pe-*ong* ăh, to outdo.

damier, dăh-me-eh, *m* checkerboard.

damner, dah-neh, *v* to damn.

dandiner (se), ser dahng-de-neh, *v* to waddle; to strut.

danger, dahng- sheh, *m* danger.

dangereu-x, se,* dahng-sher-rer, *a* dangerous.

dans, dahng, *prep* in, into; within; according to.

danse, dahngss, *f* dance; dancing.

danseu-r, se, dahng-ser, *mf* dancer.

dard, dăhr, *m* dart; sting.

darder, dăhr-deh, *v* to dart; to shoot; to beam.

darne, dăhrn, *f* fish steak.

dartre, dăhr-tr, *f* sore.

date, dăht, *f* date.

dater, dăh-teh, *v* to date.

datif, dăh-tiff, *m* dative.

datte, dăht, *f* (fruit) date.

dattier, dăh-te-eh, *m* date tree.

daube, dohb, *f* stew.

dauber, doh-beh, *v* to cuff; to jeer; to stew.

dauphin, doh-fang, *m* dolphin.

davantage, dăh-vahng-tăhsh, *adv* more.

de, der, *prep* of; from; out of; by; with; as; than; to; upon; since; some; any.

dé, deh, *m* thimble; die.

débâcle, deh-bah-kl, *f* breaking up; downfall.

déballage, deh-băh-lăhsh, *m* unpacking; (*fam*) show-down.

déballer, deh-băh-leh, *v* to unpack.

débandade, deh-bahng-dăhd, *f* stampede; **à la** –, ăh lăh –, helter-skelter.

débander, deh-bahng-deh, *v* to unbend; to disband; **se–,** to disband; to

a
b
c
d
e
f
g
h
i
j
k
l
m
n
o
p
q
r
s
t
u
v
w
x
y
z

disperse; to run away.

débaptiser, deh-băh-te-zeh, *v* to change the name of.

débarbouiller, deh-băhr-boo'e-yeh, *v* to wash the face of; to clean; **se –,** to wash one's face; to extricate oneself.

débarcadère, deh-băhr-kăh-dair, *m* wharf; pier.

débarder, deh-băhr-deh, *v* to unload.

débardeur, deh-băhr-der, *m* longshoreman.

débarquement, deh-băhr-ker-mahng, *m* landing; arrival; unloading.

débarquer, deh-băhr-keh, *v* to land; to disembark; to unload.

débarras, deh-băh-răh, *m* riddance; junk closet; **bon –! bong –!** good riddance! **chambre de –,** shahng-br der –, storeroom.

débarrasser, deh-băh-răhss-eh, *v* to clear; to rid; **se –,** to get rid (**de,** of).

débat, deh-băh, *m* debate; *pl* pleadings; trial; case.

débattre, deh-băh-tr, *v* to debate; to discuss; **se –,** to struggle.

débauche, deh-bohsh, *f* debauch; debauchery.

débaucher, deh-boh-sheh, *v* to debauch; to entice away; **se –,** to go astray.

débile,* deh-beell, *a* weak; feeble.

débilité, deh-be-le-teh, *f* stupidity; weakness.

débiliter, deh-be-le-teh, *v* to weaken.

débine, deh-been, *f* (*fam*) destitution; straits; **il est tombé dans la –,** il ai tongbeh dahng lă–, he has fallen into poverty.

débiner, deh-be-neh, *v* (*fam*) to disparage; **se –,** to make off; to run away.

débit, deh-be, *m* sale; market; retail store; flow; utterance; output; delivery.

débit, deh-be, *m* debit.

débitant, deh-be-tahng, *m* dealer.

débiter, deh-be-teh, *v* to retail; to sell; to cut up; to recite; to debit (**de,** with).

débi-teur, trice, deh-be-ter, *mf* & *a* debtors .

déblai, deh-blay, *m* excavation; clearing; *pl* rubble.

déblatérer, deh-blăh-teh-reh, *v* to rail at.

déblayer, deh-blay-yeh, *v* to clear away.

débloquer, deh-block-eh,

v to raise the blockade of; to free.

déboire, deh-bo'ăhr, *m* vexation; disappointment.

déboiser, deh-bo'ăh-zeh, *v* to deforest.

déboîter, deh-bo'ăh-teh, *v* to dislocate; to disconnect.

de bonne réputation, der-bong-reh-pE-tăh-se-ong *a* reputable.

débonnaire, deh-bonn-air, *a* good-natured; meek; gentle.

débordement, deh-bor-der-mahng, *m* overflowing; (*fam*) dissoluteness.

déborder, deh-bor-deh, *v* to overflow; to project; to untuck.

débotter, deh-bot-eh, *v* to pull boots off; **au –,** oh –, immediately on arrival.

débouché, deh-boo-sheh, *m* outlet; market; issue.

déboucher, deh-boo-sheh, *v* to open; to uncork; to unblock; to emerge; to run into.

déboucler, deh-boo-kleh, *v* to unbuckle; to uncurl.

débourber, deh-boohr-beh, *v* to clean; to extricate from the mud.

déboursés, débours, deh-boohr-seh, deh-boohr, *mpl* expenses; disbursements.

débourser, deh-boohr-seh, *v* to disburse; to lay out.

debout, der-boo, *adv* upright; standing.

débouter, deh-boo-teh, *v* to dismiss.

déboutonner, deh-boo-tonn-eh, *v* to unbutton.

débraillé, e, deh-brah'e-yeh, *a* untidy; disarrayed.

débrayage, deh-bre-yash, *m* disengaging (of clutch); declutching.

débrayer, deh-bray-yeh, to declutch; to disengage.

débrider, deh-bre-deh, *v* to unbridle; to stop; **sans** –, without stopping.

débris, deh-bre, *m* remains; debris; rubbish.

débrouillard, e, deh-broo'e-yăhr, *mf* & *a* (*fam*) resourceful; capable.

débrouiller, deh-broo'e-yeh, *v* to disentangle; to unravel; **se** –, to cope.

début, deh-bE, *m* beginning; first appearance; lead.

débutant, e, deh-bE-tahng, *mf* & *a* beginner;

performer appearing for the first time.

débuter, deh-bE-teh, *v* to begin; to make one's first appearance.

deçà, der-săh, *adv* on this side.

décacheter, deh-kăhsh-teh, *v* to unseal.

décadence, deh-kăh-dahngss, *f* decay; decline.

décaisser, deh-kayss-eh, *v* to unpack; to disburse.

décaler, deh-cah-leh, *v* to unwedge; to alter (time); to displace.

décalquer, deh-kăhl-keh, *v* to transfer a tracing; to trace.

décamper, deh-kahng-peh, *v* to move off; to bolt.

décanter, deh-kahng-teh, *v* to decant.

décapiter, deh-kăh-pe-teh, *v* to behead.

décéder, deh-seh-deh, *v* to die; to decease.

déceler, dehss-leh, *v* to discover; to detect; to guess.

décembre, deh-sahng-br, *m* December.

décemment, deh-săh-mahng, *adv* decently.

décence, deh-sahngss, *f* decency; propriety.

décent, e, deh-sahng, *a*

decent; becoming; proper.

déception, deh-sep-se-ong, *f* disappointment; setback.

décerner, deh-sair-neh, *v* to award; to issue (writ, etc).

décès, deh-say, *m* death; decease.

décevant, deh-ser-vahng, *a* misleading; disappointing.

décevoir, deh-ser-vo'ăhr, *v* to disappoint.

déchaîné, deh-shay-neh, *pp* & *a* unchained; furious; mad.

déchaîner, deh-shay-neh, *v* to unchain; to let loose.

déchanter, deh-shahng-teh, *v* to become disillusioned.

décharge, deh-shăhrsh, *f* discharge; discharging; unloading; acquittal; **à** –, ăh –, for the defense.

décharger deh-shăhr-sheh, *v* to unload; to relieve; to clear.

déchargeur, deh-shăhr-sher, *m* longshoreman.

décharné, e, deh-shăhr-neh, *a* emaciated.

déchaussé, e, deh-shohss-eh, *pp* & *a* barefooted; shrinking (of gums).

a
b
c
d
e
f
g
h
i
j
k
l
m
n
o
p
q
r
s
t
u
v
w
x
y
z

A
B
C
D
E
F
G
H
I
J
K
L
M
N
O
P
Q
R
S
T
U
V
W
X
Y
Z

dèche, daysh, *f (pop)* destitution.

déchéance, deh-sheh-ahngss, *f* forfeiture; downfall.

déchet, deh-shay, *m* waste; loss.

décheveler, deh-sherv-leh, *v* to dishevel; to tousle.

déchiffrer, deh-she-freh, *v* to decipher; to sight-read (music).

déchiqueter, deh-shick-teh, *v* to cut up; to slash; to tear.

déchirant, e, deh-she-rahng, *a* piercing; heartrending.

déchirement, deh-sheer-mahng, *m* tearing; anguish; excruciating pain.

déchirer, deh-she-reh, *v* to tear; to rend; to break.

déchirure, deh-she-rEEr, *f* tear; rip.

déchoir, deh-sho'ăhr, *v* to fall; to decline; to decay.

décidé, e, deh-se-deh, *pp* & *a* decided; determined.

décidément, deh-se-deh-mahng, *adv* decidedly.

décider, deh-se-deh, *v* to decide; to determine; to persuade; **se –,** to make up one's mind.

décimal, deh-se-mahl, *a* decimal.

décimale, deh-se-mahl, *f* decimal (fraction).

décisi-f, ve,* deh-se-zeeff, *a* decisive.

décision, deh-se-ze-ong, *f* decision; resolution.

déclamer, deh-klăh-meh, *v* to declaim; to recite.

déclaration, deh-klăh-răh-se-ong, *f* declaration; affidavit.

déclarer, deh-klăh-reh, *v* to declare; to proclaim; to certify.

déclassé, e, deh-klăhss-eh, *mf* & *a* one who has lost social position.

déclencher, deh-klahng-sheh, *v* to unlock; to disconnect; *(fam)* to launch; to set in motion.

déclinaison, deh-kle-nay-zong, *f* declination (of compass, star, etc); declension.

décliner, deh-kle-neh, *v* to decline; to deviate.

déclivité, deh-kle-ve-teh, *f* declivity.

déclouer, deh-kloo-eh, *v* to pry open.

décocher, deh-kosh-eh, *v* to shoot; to let fly.

décoiffer, deh-ko'ăh-feh, *v* to take off hat; to disarrange hair.

décollage, deh-ko-lash, *m* unsticking; takeoff (of plane).

décoller, deh-koll-eh, *v* to unstick; to take off (of plane).

décolleté, deh-koll-teh, *a* low-cut; low-necked. *m* neckline.

décolorer, deh-koll-or-eh, *v* to discolor; to bleach.

décombres, deh-kong-br, *mpl* rubbish.

décommander, deh-komm-ahng-deh, *v* to countermand; to cancel.

décomposer, deh-kong-poz-eh, *v* to decompose.

décomposition, deh-kong-poz-e-se-ong, *f* decomposition; discomposure; analyzing.

décompte, deh-kongt, *m* deduction; disappointment.

décompter, deh-kong-teh, *v* to deduct; to be disappointed.

déconcerter, deh-kong-sair-teh, *v* to disconcert; to confuse; to baffle.

décongeler, deh-kong-sher-leh, to thaw; to defrost (food).

déconseiller, deh-kong-say'e-yeh, *v* to advise against.

déconsidérer, deh-kong-se-deh-reh, *v* to discredit.

décontenancer, deh-ko*ng*t-nah*ng*ss-eh, *v* to disconcert; to unsettle.

décontracté, deh-ko*ng*-trahck-teh, *a* relaxed.

décontracter (se), ser deh-ko*ng*-trahck-teh, *v* to relax.

déconvenue, deh-ko*ng*gv-nE, *f* mishap; ill luck; disappointment.

décor, deh-kor, *m* decoration; *pl* stage-scenery.

décorateur, deh-kor-ăh-ter, *m* decorator; set designer.

décoration, deh-kor-ăh-se-o*ng*, *f* decoration; medal.

décoré, e, deh-kor-eh, *a* decorated; wearing a decoration.

décorer, deh-kor-eh, *v* to embellish; to confer a decoration on.

découcher, deh-koo-sheh, *v* to sleep out; to stay out all night.

découdre, deh-koo-dr, *v* to unstitch.

découler, deh-koo-leh, *v* to drop; to trickle; to follow (**de,** from).

découper, deh-koo-peh, *v* to cut up; to cut out; to carve.

découplé, deh-koo-pleh, *pp* & *a* uncoupled; **bien** –, be-a*ng* –, strapping.

découpure, deh-koo-pEEr, *f* workmanship; indentations.

décourageant, deh-koo-rah-**sha**h*ng*, *a* discouraging; disheartening.

découragement, deh-koo-răhsh-mah*ng*, *m* discouragement; despondency.

décourager, deh-koo-răh-**sheh**, *v* to discourage; to deter; **se** –, to lose heart.

décousu, e, deh-koo-zE, *pp* & *a* unsewed; unconnected; desultory.

découvert, deh-koo-vair, *m* deficit; overdraft.

découvert, e, deh-koo-vair, *pp* & *a* uncovered; open; **à** –, ăh –, openly; unsecured; exposed.

découverte, deh-koo-vairt, *f* discovery.

découvrir, deh-koo-vreer, *v* to uncover; to discover; to unmask; to find out; **se** –, to take off one's hat; to come to light; to clear up (weather).

décrasser, deh-krăhss-eh, *v* to clean; to get dirt off.

décréditer, deh-kreh-de-teh, *v* to discredit.

décrépit, e, deh-kreh-pe, *a* decrepit; senile.

décret, deh-kray, *m* decree; order.

décréter, deh-kreh-teh, *v* to decree.

décrier, deh-kre-eh, *v* to run down; to decry.

décrire, deh-kreer, *v* to describe.

décrocher, deh-krosh-eh, *v* to unhook; to take off.

décroissance, deh-kro'ăhss-ah*ng*ss, *f* decrease.

décroître, deh-kro'ăh-tr, *v* to decrease; to diminish.

décrotter, deh-krot-eh *v* to clean mud off (boots, etc); to brush.

décrottoir, deh-krot-o ăhr, *m* scraper.

déçu, e, deh-sE, *pp* & *a* disappointed.

décupler, deh-kE-pleh, *v* to increase tenfold.

dédaigner, deh-dayn-yeh, *v* to disdain.

dédaigneu-x, se,* deh-dayn-yer, *a* disdainful; scornful.

dédain, deh-dah*ng*, *m* disdain; scorn.

dedans, der-dah*ng*, *adv* inside; in; in it; in them.

m inside; interior.

dédicace, deh-de-kăhss, *f* dedication.

dédier, deh-de-eh, *v* to dedicate.

dédire, deh-deer, *v* to retract a statement.

dédit, deh-de, *m* forfeit.

dédommagement, deh-domm-ăhsh-mahng, *m* compensation; indemnification.

dédommager deh-domm-ăh-sheh, *v* to compensate; (**de,** for).

dédouaner, deh-doo-ah-neh, *v* to clear; to clear through customs.

dédoubler, deh-doo-bleh, *v* to take the lining out of; to diminish by half; to divide in two.

déduction, dah-dEEk-se-ong, *f* deduction; inference; **–faite de, –** fayt der, after deducting.

déduire, deh-dweer, *v* to deduct; to deduce; to infer.

déesse, deh-ess, *f* goddess.

défaillance, deh-fah'e-yahngss, *f* faintness; faltering; failing.

défaillir, deh-fah'e-yeer, *v* to faint; to falter; to fail.

défaire, deh-fair, *v* to undo; to break; to defeat; **se –de,** to get rid

of.

défait, e, deh-fay, *pp* & *a* undone; defeated; meager.

défaite, deh-fayt, *f* defeat; pretext.

défalcation, deh-făhl-kăh-se-ong, *f* deduction.

défalquer, deh-făhl-keh *v* to deduct.

défaut, deh-foh, *m* defect; fault; default; **à –de,** ăh – der, for want of; **faire –,** fair –, to fail; to be missing.

défaveur, deh-făh-ver, *f* disgrace; disfavor.

défavorable, * deh-făh-vor-ăh-bl, *a* unfavorable.

défecti-f, ve, deh-feck-teeff, *a* defective.

défection, deh-feck-se-ong, *f* desertion; disloyalty.

défectueu-x, se, * deh-feck-tE- er, *a* defective; faulty.

défectuosité, deh-feck-tE-oz-e-teh, *f* defect; blemish; flaw.

défend-eur, eresse, deh-fahng-der, *mf* defendant.

défendre, deh-fahng-dr, *v* to defend; to forbid.

défense, deh-fahngss, *f* defense; prohibition; *pl* tusks.

défenseur, deh-fahng-ser,

m defender.

défensi-f, ve, * deh-fahng-seeff, *a* defensive.

déférence, deh-feh-rahngss, *f* deference.

déférer, deh-feh-reh, *v* to bestow; to bring before; to comply (**à,** with); to defer; to tender (oath).

déferler, deh-fair-leh, *v* to unfurl; to break.

défi, deh-fe, *m* defiance; challenge.

défiance, deh-fe-ahngss, *f* distrust; diffidence.

défiant, e, deh-fe-ahng, *a* distrustful; suspicious.

déficeler, deh-fiss-leh, *v* to untie.

défier, deh-fe-eh, *v* to challenge; to defy; **se –** (**de**), to mistrust.

défigurer, deh-fe-ghE-reh, *v* to disfigure.

défilé, deh-fe-leh, *m* straight; march past.

défini, e, deh-fe-ne, *pp* & *a* defined; definite; precise.

définir, deh-fe-neer, *v* to define.

définissable, deh-fe-niss-ăh-bl, *a* definable.

définiti-f, ve, * deh-fe-ne-teeff, *a* definitive; positive; **en –ve,** ahng –, finally.

définition, deh-fe-ne-se-ong, *f* definition; clue (of crossword puzzle).

défoncer, deh-fongss-eh, *v* to smash in; to break up.

déformer, deh-for-meh, *v* to put out of shape; to distort.

défraîchi, e, deh-fray-she, *a* no longer fresh; tatty.

défrayer, deh-fray-yeh, *v* to defray the expense of.

défricher, deh-fre-sheh, *v* to clear; to reclaim (of land).

défroque, deh-frock, *f* cast-off clothes (usu in *pl*; of monk, etc).

défroqué, deh-frock-eh, *a* & *m* unfrocked (priest, etc); ex-priest.

défunt, e, deh-fung, *a* deceased.

dégagé, e, deh-găh-sheh, *pp* & *a* redeemed; free; easy; offhand.

dégager, deh-găh-sheh, *v* to redeem; to clear; to release.

dégaine, deh-gain, *f* ungainliness; awkward gait.

dégainer, deh-gay-neh, *v* to unsheathe.

dégarnir, deh-găhr-neer, *v* to strip; to dismantle; **se –de,** to part with.

dégât, deh-gah, *m* damage; havoc; waste.

dégel, deh-shell, *m* thaw.

dégénérer, deh-sheh-neh-reh, *v* to degenerate.

dégingandé, e, deh-shang-gahng-deh, *a* & *mf* ungainly; disjointed.

dégivrer, deh-she-vreh, *v* to deice; to defrost.

dégivreur, deh-she-vrer, *m* defroster.

dégommer, deh-gomm-eh, *v* to ungum; (*fam*) to give the sack to.

dégonfler, deh-gong-fleh, *v* to reduce; to bring down; to defiate; **se –,** to collapse (tire, balloon, etc); (*fam*) to get into a funk.

dégorger, deh-gor-sheh, *v* to disgorge; to clear; to scour.

dégourdi, e, deh-goohr-de, *a* sharp; acute (of person).

dégourdir, deh-goohr-deer, *v* to revive; to stretch; to sharpen; **se –,** to get sharp.

dégoût, deh-goo, *m* dislike; disgust; loathing.

dégoûtant, e, deh-goo-tahng, *a* sickening; disgusting.

dégoûté, e, deh-goo-teh, *pp* & *a* disgusted; fastidious; squeamish.

dégoutter, deh-goot-eh, *v* to drip; to trickle.

dégrader, deh-grăh-deh, *v* to degrade; to debase; to damage.

dégrafer, deh-grăh-feh, *v* to unhook; to unclasp.

dégraisser, deh-grayss-eh, *v* to scour; to clean; to remove the grease from; to skim fat off; to dry clean.

degré, der-greh, *m* degree; step; stage.

dégringoler, deh-grang-goll-eh, *v* to tumble down.

dégriser, deh-gre-zeh, *v* to sober up.

dégrossir, deh-gross-eer, *v* to smooth rough edges of.

déguenillé, e, deh-gher-nee-yeh, *a* ragged.

déguerpir, deh-gair-peer, *v* to pack off; to clear out quickly.

déguisement, deh-gheez-mahng, *m* disguise.

déguiser, deh-ghee-zeh, *v* to disguise; to conceal.

déguster, deh-ghEEs-teh, *v* to taste; to sample; to eat or drink with relish.

déhanché, deh-ahng-sheh, *a* swaying; ungainly.

dehors, der-or, *adv* without; outside; *m* outside; exterior;

a
b
c
d
e
f
g
h
i
j
k
l
m
n
o
p
q
r
s
t
u
v
w
x
y
z

appearances.

déjà, deh-**shăh,** *adv* already; yet; then; before; as far back as; to begin with.

déjeuner, deh-**sher**-neh, *m* lunch; **petit –,** per-te –, breakfast.

déjeuner, deh-**sher**-neh, *v* to breakfast; to lunch.

déjouer deh-**shoo**-eh, *v* to foil; to outsmart; to thwart.

déjuger (se), ser deh-**shE**-sheh, *v* to change one's opinion.

delà der-**lăh,** *prep* beyond; on the other side of; farther than; **au –de** oh – der beyond.

délabré, e, deh-**lăh**-breh, *a* tattered; dilapidated; in ruins.

délabrement, deh-**lăh**-brer-mahng, *m* ruin; decay; dilapidation.

délai, deh-**lay,** *m* interval; delay; **dans un –de,** dahng z'ung – der, within.

délaissement, deh-**layss**-mahng, *m* abandonment; relinquishment.

délaisser, deh-**layss**-eh, *v* to forsake; to abandon.

délassement, deh-**lăhss**-mahng, *m* relaxation;

rest.

déla-teur, trice, deh-**lăh**-ter, *mf* informer; spy.

délation, deh-**lăh**-se-ong, *f* information; denunciation.

délayer, deh-**lay**-yeh, *v* to mix with water; to thin out; to spin out.

délecter (se), ser deh-**leck**-teh, *v* to delight (à, in).

délégation, deh-**leh**-găh-se-ong, *f* delegation; assignment; proxy.

délégué, deh-**leh**-gheh, *m* delegate; deputy; union representative.

déléguer, deh-**leh**-gheh, *v* to delegate; to assign.

délétère, deh-**leh**-tair, *a* deleterious.

délibérément, deh-**le**-beh-reh-mahng, *adv* deliberately.

délibérer, deh-**le**-beh-reh, *v* to deliberate; to resolve.

délicat, e, * deh-**le**-kăh, *a* delicate; dainty; scrupulous; tricky; difficult.

délicatesse, deh-**le**-kăh-tess, *f* delicacy; nicety; scrupulousness.

délicieu-x, se, * deh-**le**-se-er, *a* delicious; delightful.

délictueu-x, se, deh-**lick**-tE- er, *a* unlawful; offensive; felonious.

délié, deh-**le**-eh, *pp* & *a* untied; loose; easy; slender; sharp.

délier, deh-**le**-eh, *v* to untie; to unbind; to release; to absolve.

délimiter, deh-**le**-me-teh, *v* to fix the limits of.

délinquant, deh-**lang**-kahng, *m* offender; delinquent.

délirant, e, deh-**le**-rahng, *a* delirious; frenzied; rapturous.

délire, deh-**leer,** *m* delirium; frenzy.

délit, deh-**le,** *m* misdemeanor; offense; **en flagrant –,** ahng flăh-grahng –, in the very act; **le corps du –,** ler kor dE –, the charge.

délivrance, deh-**le**-vrahngss, *f* deliverance; release; rescue; confinement.

délivrer, deh-**le**-vreh, *v* to deliver; to rid; to release; to set free.

déloger, deh-**losh**-eh, *v* to dislodge; to turn out; (*fam*) to clear out; **–sans tambour ni trompette, –** sahng tahng-boohr ne trong-payt, to steal away.

déloyal, e, * deh-lo'ăh-yăhl, *a* disloyal; dishonest; unfair.

déloyauté, deh-lo'ăh-yoh-teh, *f* dishonesty.

déluge, deh-lEE sh, *m* flood.

déluré, e, deh-lE-reh, *a* sharp; resourceful; sassy.

demain, der-mang, *adv* tomorrow; **après** –, ăh-pray –, the day after tomorrow.

démancher, deh-mahng-sheh, *v* to take the handle off; to dislocate.

demande, der-mahngd, *f* question; request; prayer; *pl* inquiries; orders.

demander, der-mahng-deh, *v* to ask; to beg; to claim; to want; to demand; to require; se –, to wonder.

demand-eur, eresse, der-mahng-der, *mf* plaintiff; applicant.

démangeaison, deh-mahng- shay-zong, *f* itching; longing.

démanger, deh-mahng-sheh, *v* to itch; to long.

démantibuler, deh-mahng-te-bE-leh, *v* to put out of order.

démaquillant, deh-măh-kee-yahng, *m* cleansing cream; makeup remover.

démaquiller, deh-măh-kee-yeh, *v* to remove makeup.

démarche, deh-mahrsh, *f* gait; walk; step; measure; attempt.

démarquer, deh-măhr-keh, *v* to unmark; to mark down (goods).

démarrage, deh-măh-răhsh, *m* unmooring; start.

démarrer, deh-măh-reh, *v* to start up; to cast off.

démarreur, deh-mah-rer, *m* starter (in car).

démasquer, deh-măhss-keh, *v* to unmask; to show up.

démêlé, deh-may-leh, *m* (usu *pl*) dispute; differences.

démêler, deh-may-leh, *v* to disentangle.

démêloir, deh-may-lo'ăhr, *m* large-tooth comb.

démembrer, deh-mahng-breh, *v* to dismember.

déménagement, deh-meh-năhsh-mahng, *m* removal. *v* moving.

déménager, deh-meh-năh-sheh, *v* to remove; to move (house).

démence, deh-mahngss, *f* madness; insanity.

démener (se), ser deh-mer-neh, *v* to struggle.

démenti, deh-mahng-te, *m* flat denial.

démentir, deh-mahng-teer, *v* to deny; to contradict.

démérite, deh-meh-reet, *m* demerit.

démériter, deh-meh-re-teh, *v* to deserve censure.

démesuré, e, deh-mer-ZEE-reh, *a* immoderate; excessive.

démettre, deh-met-tr, *v* to dislocate; to dismiss; se –, to resign.

démeubler, deh-mer-bleh, *v* to unfurnish.

demeurant, der-mer-rahng, *pp* residing; **au** –, oh –, after all; nevertheless.

demeure, der-mer, *f* residence; **à** –, ăh –, fixed; **mettre en** –, met-tr'ahng –, to call upon; to summon; **péril en la** –, peh-reel ahng lăh –, danger in delay.

demeurer, der-mer-reh, *v* to reside; to live; to stay; to stand; **en** –**là,** ahng –lăh, to go no farther.

demi, der-me, *m* & *a* half; (*fam*) a glass of beer.

démission, deh-miss-e-ong, *f* resignation;

donner sa démission, donn-eh săh –, to give one's resignation.

démobiliser, deh-mob-e-le-zeh, *v* to demobilize.

démocratie, deh-mock-răh-see, *f* democracy.

démodé, e, deh-mod-eh, *a* old-fashioned.

demoiselle, der-mo'ăh-zell, *f* young lady; single woman; **–d'honneur, –** donn-er, bridesmaid.

démolir, deh-moll-eer, *v* to pull down.

démon, deh-mong, *m* demon; devil; an imp (of child).

démonétiser, deh-monn-eh-te-zeh, *v* to demonetize.

démoniaque, deh-monn-e-ăhck, *a* demonic.

démonstration, deh-mongss-trăh-se-ong, *f* demonstration.

démontable, deh-mong-tăh-bl, *a* that can be dismantled.

démonter, deh-mong-teh, *v* to dismount; to take apart; to put out; **se –,** to lose face.

démontrer, deh-mong-treh, *v* to demonstrate; to prove.

démoraliser, deh-mor-ăh-le-zeh, *v* to demoralize.

démordre, deh-mor-dr, *v* to let go; to desist.

démouler, deh-moo-leh, *v* to remove from mold.

démunir (se), ser deh-mE-neer, *v* to part (**de,** with).

dénaturé, e, deh-năh-tE-reh, *pp* & *a* altered; distorted; unnatural; depraved.

dénégation, deh-neh-găh-se-ong, *f* denial.

dénicher, deh-ne-sheh, *v* to take out of its nest; to find out.

dénier, deh-ne-eh, *v* to deny.

dénigrer, deh-ne-greh, *v* to disparage.

dénombrement, deh-nong-brer-mahng, *m* numbering; enumeration; census.

dénommer, deh-nomm-eh, *v* to name.

dénoncer, deh-nongss-eh, *v* to denounce.

dénonciateur, deh-nongss-e-ăh-ter, *m* informer.

dénoter, deh-not-eh, *v* to denote; to show.

dénouement, deh-noo-mahng, *m* outcome; issue; end; ending.

dénouer, deh-noo-eh, *v* to untie; to undo; to unravel; to loose; to

solve.

denrée, dahng-reh, *f* ware; provision; *pl* produce; commodities; **–s alimentaires, –** ăh-le-mahngt-air, food products.

dense, dahngss, *a* dense.

densité, dahng-se-teh, *f* thickness; density.

dent, dahng, *f* tooth; notch; cog; prong.

dentaire, dahng-tair, *a* dental.

dentelé, e, dahngt-leh, *a* indented; notched; jagged.

dentelle, dahng-tell, *f* lace; lacework.

dentier, dahng-te-eh, *m* denture.

dentifrice, dahng-te-freess, *m* toothpaste.

dentiste, dahng-teesst, *m* dentist.

dentition, dahng-te-se-ong, *f* teeth; dentition.

dénuder, deh-nE-deh, *v* to denude; to strip.

dénué, e, deh-nE-eh, *pp* & *a* destitute; devoid of.

de nuit, der-nwee *a, train* overnight train.

dénûment, deh-nEE-mahng, *m* destitution; penury.

déodorant, deh-oh-doh-rahng, *m* deodorant.

dépannage, deh-pah-nash, *m* road repairs; repair service.

dépanner, deh-pah-neh, *v* to repair (broken-down cars); (*fam*) to help out.

dépaqueter, deh-păck-teh, *v* to unpack.

dépareillé, e, deh-păh-ray'e-yeh, *pp* & *a* unmatched; odd; incomplete.

déparer, deh-păh-reh, *v* to strip; to disfigure; to spoil the look of.

départ, deh-păhr, *m* departure.

département, deh-păhr-ter-mahng, *m* department; county.

départir, deh-păhr-teer, *v* to allot; to bestow; **se –de,** to give up.

dépasser, deh-păhss-eh, *v* to pass; to go beyond; to exceed; to outrun; to rise above.

dépayser, deh-pay-yee-zeh, *v* to send from home.

dépaysé, deh-pay-yee-zeh, *a* out of one's element; **se sentir –,** not to feel at home.

dépêche, deh-paysh, *f* despatch; telegram.

dépêcher, deh-pay-sheh, *v* to dispatch; **se –,** to make haste.

dépeindre, deh-pang-dr, *v* to depict.

dépendance, deh-pahng-dahngss, *f* dependence; dependency; *pl* out buildings.

dépendre, deh-pahng-dr, *v* to depend; to result; to belong to; to unhang.

dépens, deh-pahng, *mpl* expenses (legal), costs; **au –de,** at the expense of.

dépense, deh-pahngss, *f* expense; expenditure.

dépenser, deh-pahngss-eh, *v* to spend (money or time).

dépensi-er, iére, deh-pahngss-e-eh, *mf* spendthrift; *a* extravagant; prodigal.

déperdition, deh-pair-de-se-ong, *f* loss; waste.

dépérir, deh-peh-reer, *v* to fade away.

dépêtrer, deh-pay-treh, *v* to disentangle; to extricate.

dépeupler, deh-per-pleh, *v* to depopulate.

dépister, deh-piss-teh, *v* to track; to throw off the scent.

dépit, deh-pe, *m* spite; resentment; vexation; **en –de,** ahng – der, in spite of.

dépiter, deh-pe-teh, *v* to vex; to spite.

déplacé, e, deh-plăhss-eh, *pp* & *a* in the wrong place; improper; uncalled for; displaced (of person).

déplacement, deh-plăhss-mahng, *m* removal; change of place; **frais de –,** fray der –, traveling expenses.

déplacer, deh-plăhss-eh, *v* to displace **se –,** to move; to travel.

déplaire, deh-plair, *v* to displease; to offend; **se –à,** to dislike (a place, etc).

déplaisant, e, deh-play-zahng, *a* disagreeable; unpleasant.

déplier, deh-ple-eh, *v* to unfold.

déplisser, deh-pliss-eh, *v* to unpleat.

déploiement, deh-plo'ăh-mahng, *m* unfolding; display.

déplorer, deh-plor-eh, *v* to deplore.

déployer, deh-plo'ăh-yeh, *v* to unfold; to display; to exert; to deploy.

déplumer, deh-plE-meh, *v* to pluck; to pick.

déporté, deh-por-teh, *m*

A B C **D** E F G H I J K L M N O P Q R S T U V W X Y Z

& *a* deported; transported convict.

déportements, deh-por-ter-mahng, *mpl* misconduct.

déporter, deh-por-teh, *v* to deport; to transport.

déposant, deh-poh-zahng, *m* depositor; witness.

déposer, deh-poh-zeh, *v* to deposit; to put down; to lodge; to give evidence; to depose; to leave; **marque –ée,** mahrk –, registered trademark.

dépositaire, deh-poh-ze-tair, *m* depositary; trustee.

déposition, deh-poh-ze-se-ong, *f* evidence.

déposséder, deh-poss-eh-deh, *v* to dispossess.

dépôt, deh-poh, *m* deposit; depositing; trust; store; warehouse; jail; sediment.

dépouille, deh-poo'e-ye, *f* skin; remains; *pl* spoils.

dépouillement, deh-poo'e-yer-mahng, *m* deprivation; stripping; abstract; perusal; counting.

dépouiller, deh-poo'e-yeh, *v* to deprive; to strip; to skin.

dépourvoir, deh-poohr-vo'ăhr, *v* to leave unprovided for; to strip.

dépourvu, e, deh-poohr-VE, *pp* & *a* destitute; unprovided; **au –,** oh –, unprepared.

dépraver, deh-prăh-veh, *v* to deprave.

déprécier, deh-preh-se-eh, *v* to depreciate; to undervalue.

dépression, deh-preh-se-ong, *f* depression; dejection; **–nerveuse,** – nair-verz, nervous breakdown.

déprimé, e, deh-pre-meh, *a* depressed.

déprimer, deh-pre-meh, *v* to depress; to disparage.

depuis, der-pwe, *adv* & *prep* since; ever since; from; **–peu,** – per, lately; **–quand?** – kahng, how long?

député, deh-pE-teh, *m* representative; member of the French Parliament.

députer, deh-pE-teh, *v* to send; to delegate.

déraciner, deh-răh-se-neh, *v* to uproot.

déraillement, deh-rah'e-mahng, *m* derailment.

dérailler, deh-rah'e-yeh, *v* to derail.

déraisonnable, deh-ray-zonn-ăh-bl, *a* unreasonable.

déraisonner, deh-ray-zonn-eh, *v* to rave; to talk nonsense.

dérangement, deh-rahng sh-mahng, *m* derangement; disturbance; trouble; disorder; upset.

déranger, deh-rahng-sheh, *v* to displace; to put out of order; to disturb; to upset; **se –,** to put oneself out.

déraper, deh-răh-peh, *v* to trip; to skid.

déréglé, e, deh-reh-gleh, *pp* & *a* put out of order; irregular; disorderly; dissolute.

dérèglement, deh-ray-gler-mahng, *m* disorder; irregularity; dissoluteness.

dérégler, deh-reh-gleh, *v* to unsettle; to put out of order; **se –,** to get out of order; to lead a disorderly life.

dérider, deh-re-deh, *v* to unwrinkle; to cheer; **se –** to brighten up.

dérision, deh-re-ze-ong, *f* derision; mockery.

dérisoire, * deh-re-zo'ăhr, *a* derisive.

dérive, deh-reev, *f* drift; leeway; **à la –,** ăh lăh –, adrift.

dériver, deh-re-veh, *v* to drift; to come from.

derni-er, ère, dair-ne-eh, *a* last; latter; utmost; final; youngest; latest.

dernièrement, dair-ne-air-mah*ng*, *adv* lately.

dérobé, e, deh-rob-eh, *pp* & *a* stolen; concealed; **à la dérobée,** ăh lăh–, stealthily.

dérober, deh-rob-eh, *v* to steal; to rob; to hide; to shield; **se –,** to steal away; to shun.

dérouiller, deh-roo'e-yeh, *v* to rub the rust off; **se –,** to polish up (a subject).

dérouler, deh-roo-leh, *v* to unroll.

déroute, deh-root, *f* rout; disorder.

dérouter, deh-root-eh, *v* to lead astray; to baffle; to divert.

derrière, dayr-e-air, *adv* & *prep* behind; at the back.

derrière, dayr-e-air, *m* back; hindquarters; (*fam*) bottom; rear.

dès, day, *prep* from; since; on; even; in; **–que, –** ke*r*, as soon as.

désabuser, deh-zăh-bE-zeh, *v* to disillusion.

désaccord, deh-zăh-kor, *m* disagreement; discord.

désaccorder, deh-zăh-kor-deh, *v* to put out of tune; to set at variance.

désaccoutumer, deh-zăh-koo-tE-meh, *v* to cause to lose a habit.

désaffection, deh-zăh-feck-se-o*ng*, *f* disaffection.

désagréable, * deh-zah-greh-ăhbl, *a* disagreeable; unpleasant.

désagréger, deh-zăh-greh-sheh, *v* to disintegrate.

désagrément, deh-zăh-greh-mah*ng*, *m* unpleasantness; inconvenience; defect; nuisance.

désaltérer, deh-zăhl-teh-reh, *v* to quench the thirst of.

désapproba-teur, trice, deh-zăh-prob-ăh-ter, *a* disapproving.

désapprouver, deh-zăh-proo-veh, *v* to disapprove of.

désarmer, deh-zăhr-meh, *v* to disarm; to appease.

désarroi, deh-zăh-ro'ăh, *m* disarray; confusion.

désastre, deh-zăhss-tr, *m* disaster.

désavantage, deh-zăh-vahng-tăhsh, *m* disadvantage.

désaveu, deh-zăh-ve*r*, *m* disavowal.

désaveugler, deh-zăh-ve*r*-gleh, *v* to disabuse.

désavouer, deh-zăh-voo-eh, *v* to disavow; to disown.

desceller, deh-sell-eh, *v* to unseal.

descendance, deh-sahng-dahngss, *f* descent; lineage.

descendre, deh-sahng-dr, *v* to descend; to come or go down; to dismount; to alight; to stop or stay; to put up (at hotel, etc); to search; to take down.

descente, deh-sahngt, *f* descent; taking down; rupture; run (skiing).

description, dehss-kreep-se-o*ng*, *f* description.

désembarquer, deh-zahng-băhr-keh, *v* to disembark; to land.

désemparer, deh-zahng-păh-reh, *v* to quit; to disable; **sans –,** sah*ng* –, without stopping.

désenchanter, deh-zahng-shahng-teh, *v* to disenchant; to disillusion.

désenfler, deh-zahng-fleh, *v* to become less swollen.

a
b
c
d
e
f
g
h
i
j
k
l
m
n
o
p
q
r
s
t
u
v
w
x
y
z

désennuyer, deh-zahng-nwe-yeh, *v* to amuse; to enliven.

déséquilibré, deh-zeh-ke-le-breh, *a* mentally unbalanced; out of balance.

désert, deh-zair, *m* wilderness; desert.

déserter, deh-zair-teh, *v* to desert; to forsake.

désespéré, e, deh-zess-peh-reh, *mf* & *a* desperate; desperado.

désespérer, deh-zess-peh-reh, *v* to despair.

désespoir, deh-zess-po'ăhr, *m* despair.

déshabiller, deh-zăh-bee-yeh, *v* to undress.

déshabituer, deh-zăh-be-tE-eh, *v* to disaccustom.

déshériter, deh-zeh-re-teh, *v* to disinherit.

des heures creuses, deh-zer-krerz *a* off-peak (time).

déshonnête, deh-zonn-ayt, *a* indecent; immodest.

déshonneur, deh-zonn-**er**, *m* dishonor; disgrace.

déshonorer, deh-zonn-or-eh, *v* to dishonor; to disgrace.

désignation, deh-zeen-yăh-se-ong, *f* designation; indication; nomination.

désigner, deh-zeen-yeh, *v* to point out; to denote; to appoint.

désillusion, deh-zill-lE-ze-ong, *f* disillusion.

désinfecter, deh-zang-feck-teh, *v* to disinfect.

désintéressement, deh-zang-teh-ress-mahng, *m* disinterestedness.

desintéresser, deh-zang-teh-ress-eh, *v* to indemnify; **se** –, to lose interest.

désintéressé, deh-zang-teh-ress-eh, *a* not involved; unbiased; unselfish.

désinvolte, deh-zang-vollt, *a* casual, free and easy.

désinvolture, deh-zang-voll-tEEr, *f* free and easy manner.

désir, deh-zeer, *m* desire; wish.

désirer, deh-ze-reh, *v* to desire; to wish.

désister (se), ser deh-ziss-teh, *v* to desist; to waive.

désobéir, deh-zob-eh-eer, *v* to disobey.

désobéissance, deh-zob-eh-iss-ahngss, *f* disobedience.

désobligeance, deh-zob-le-shahngss, *f* unkindness.

désobliger, deh-zob-le-sheh, *v* to disoblige.

désœuvré, e, deh-zer-vreh, *a* idle.

désolant, e, deh-zoll-ahng, *a* distressing; grievous; very annoying.

désolation, deh-zoll-ăh-se-ong, *f* grief; desolateness.

désoler, deh-zoll-eh, *v* to distress; **se** –, to lament; to grieve.

désopilant, e, deh-zop-e-lahng, *a* funny; laughable.

désopiler (se – la rate), ser deh-zop-ee-leh lăh răht, (*fam*) to laugh immoderately.

désordonné, e, deh-zor-donn-eh, *pp* & *a* disorderly; untidy.

désordre, deh-zor-dr, *m* disorder; disturbance; licentiousness.

désorienter, deh-zor-e-ahng-teh, *v* to put out; to bewilder.

désormais, deh-zor-may, *adv* henceforth.

désosser, deh-zohss-eh, *v* to bone.

dessaisir, deh-say-zeer, *v* to dispossess; **se** –, to part (**de**, with).

dessaler, deh-săh-leh, *v* to remove salt; to soak; to capsize.

dessécher, deh-seh-sheh, *v* to dry up.

dessein, deh-*sang*, *m* design; plan.

desserrer, deh-say-reh, *v* to loosen.

dessert, deh-sair, *m* dessert.

desservant, deh-sair,-vah*ng*, *m* officiating priest or clergyman.

desservir, deh-sair, *v* to clear the table; to play a dirty trick on; to officiate; to serve (of trains, etc).

dessiller (les yeux), deh-see-yeh lay ze'er, *v* to open someone's eyes.

dessin, deh-*sang*, *m* drawing; design; pattern.

dessinateur, deh-se-näh-ter, *m* drawer; sketcher.

dessiner, deh-se-neh, *v* to draw; to sketch; to outline; **se –,** to become perceptible.

dessous, der-soo, *m* underpart; disadvantage; worst.

dessous, der-soo, *adv* & *prep* under; underneath.

dessus, der-sE, *adv* & *prep* on; above; uppermost; upon; over.

dessus, der-sE, *m* upper part; top; right side; advantage.

destin, dess-tan*g*, *m* destiny; fate; lot.

destinataire, dess-te-näh-tair, *m* receiver; consignee; addressee.

destination, dess-te-näh-se-ong, *f* destination; object; end.

destinée, dess-te-neh, *f* destiny; fate.

destiner, dess-te-neh, *v* to destine; to intend; to fate.

destitué, e, dess-te-tE-eh, *pp* & *a* dismissed; devoid.

destituer, dess-te-tE-eh, *v* to dismiss.

destitution, dess-te-tE-se-ong, *f* dismissal; removal.

destruction, dess-trEEk-se-ong, *f* destruction.

désuétude, deh-sE-eh-tEEd, *f* disuse.

désunion, deh-zE-ne-ong, *f* separation; disunion.

désunir, deh-zE-neer, *v* to separate; to disunite.

détaché, e, deh-täh-sheh, *pp* & *a* detached; unconnected; indifferent; disinterested.

détachement, deh-tähsh-mahng, *m* detachment; indifference.

détacher, deh-täh-sheh, *v* to untie; to detach; to undo; to separate; **se –,** to break away (**de,** from).

détail, deh-tah'e, *m* detail; particulars; trifle; retail.

détailler, deh-tah'e-yeh, *v* to cut up; to sell retail; to relate in detail.

déteindre, deh-tang-dr, *v* to take the color out of; to discolor; to fade; to run (of color).

détendre, deh-tahng-dr, *v* to unbend; to relax; to slacken.

détendu, e, deh-tahng-dEE, *a* slack; relaxed.

détenir, deh-ter-neer, *v* to detain; to keep back.

détente, deh-tahngt, *f* relaxation; slackening; expansion; trigger.

déten-teur, trice, deh-tahng-ter, *mf* holder.

détention, deh-tahng-se-ong, *f* detention; imprisonment.

détenu, deh-ter-nE, *m* prisoner.

détériorer, deh-teh-re-or-eh, *v* to damage; to impair; to deface.

déterminé, e, deh-tair-me-neh, *pp* & *a* determined; resolute.

déterminer, deh-tair-me-neh, *v* to determine; to

a
b
c
d
e
f
g
h
i
j
k
l
m
n
o
p
q
r
s
t
u
v
w
x
y
z

A
B
C
D
E
F
G
H
I
J
K
L
M
N
O
P
Q
R
S
T
U
V
W
X
Y
Z

decide; to bring on; **se –**, to resolve.

déterrer, deh-tay-reh, v to dig up; to unearth; to discover.

détester, deh-tess-teh, v to detest; to hate; to abhor.

détoner, deh-tonn-eh, v to detonate; to explode.

détonner, deh-tonn-eh, v to be out of tune; to clash.

détordre, deh-tor-dr, v to untwist.

détour, deh-toohr, m turn; bend; winding; wile; roundabout way; subterfuge; **sans –**, sahng –, straightforward.

détourné, e, deh-toohr-neh, pp & a out of the way; embezzled.

détournement, deh-toohr-ner-mahng, m turning aside; embezzlement; abduction; hijacking.

détourner, deh-toohr-neh, v to lead astray; to turn away; to avert; to divert; to deter; to embezzle; to abduct; to hijack.

détracteur, deh-trăhck-ter, m slanderer.

détraquer, deh-trăh-keh, v to put out of order.

détrempe, deh-trahngp, f

distemper.

détremper, deh-trahng-peh, v to water; to dilute; to soften.

détresse, deh-trayss, f distress.

détriment, deh-tre-mahng, m detriment; prejudice.

détritus, deh-tre-tEEss, m detritus; garbage.

détroit, deh-tro'ăh, m strait; straits; pass.

détromper, deh-trong-peh, v to disabuse; to correct someone's mistake.

détrôner, deh-troh-neh, v to dethrone.

détrousser, deh-trooss-eh, v to rob; to untuck.

détruire, deh-trweer, v to destroy.

dette, dett, f debt.

deuil, der, e, m mourning; sorrow; grief; **personnes en –**, pairsonn ahng, mourners.

deux, der, m & a two; both; second (the).

deuxième,* der-ze-aym, a &m second.

dévaler, deh-văh-leh, v to descend; to rush down.

dévaliser, deh-văh-le-zeh, v to rob; to plunder.

devancer, der-vahng-seh, v to get ahead of; to outrun; to precede; to anticipate.

devanci-er, ère, der-vahng-se-eh, mf predecessor.

devant, der-vahng, prep & adv before; opposite; in front; ahead; m front; forepart; **aller au –de,** ăh-leh oh – der, to go to meet.

devanture, der-vahng-tEEr, f front; facade.

dévaster, deh-văhss-teh, v to devastate.

déveine, deh-vain, f bad luck.

développement, deh-ver-lop-mahng, m unfolding; development; growth.

développer, deh-ver-lop-eh, v to unfold; to develop; to expand; to explain; **se –**, to spread out.

devenir, derv-neer, v to become.

dévergondage, deh-vair-gong-dăhsh, m shamelessness; licentiousness.

dévergondé, e, deh-vair-gong-deh, a openly profligate.

dévergonder (se), ser deh-vair-gong-deh, v to lose all sense of shame.

déverser, deh-vair-seh, v to incline; to pour; to throw.

dévêtir, deh-vay-teer, *v* to undress.

déviation, deh-ve-a-se-ong, deviation.

dévider, deh-ve-deh, *v* to wind; to reel.

dévier, deh-ve-eh, *v* to deviate.

deviner, der-ve-neh, *v* to guess.

devinette, der-ve-nett, *f* puzzle; riddle.

devis, der-ve, *m* estimate.

dévisager, deh-ve-zăh-sheh, *v* to stare at.

devise, der-veez, *v* device; motto; currency.

deviser, der-ve-zeh, *v* to chat.

dévisser, deh-viss-eh, *v* to unscrew.

dévoiler, deh-vo'ăh-leh, *v* to unveil; to reveal.

devoir, der-vo'ăhr, *v* to owe; to be bound to; to have to; **je crois** –,sher kro'ăh –, I think it my duty to.

devoir, der-vo'ăhr, *m* duty; task; exercise; *pl* homework; **se mettre en –de,** ser met-tr'ahng–der, to set about.

dévorant, e, deh-vor-ahng, *a* devouring; ravenous; burning.

dévorer, deh-vor-eh, *v* to devour.

dévot, e, * deh-vo, *a & mf* devout; pious person.

dévotion, deh-vos-e-ong, *f* devotion; piety.

dévoué, e, deh-voo-eh, *pp & a* devoted; loving; **votre tout –,** vot-rer too –, sincerely yours.

dévouement, deh-voo-mahng, *m* devotedness; self-sacrifice.

dévouer, deh-voo-eh, *v* to devote.

dévoyé, e, deh-vo'ăh-yeh, *pp & a* misled; astray.

dextérité, decks-teh-re-teh, *f* dexterity; skill.

d'habitude, dăh-be-tEEd *a* **usually.**

diabète, de-ăh-bett, *m* diabetes.

diable, de-ăh-bl, *m* devil; mischievous child; **tirer le –par la queue,** te-reh ler – păhr lăh ker, to struggle hard for a living; **un bon –,** ung bong –, not a bad fellow.

diablement, de-ăh-bler-mahng, *adv (fam)* fiendishly; devilishly.

diabolique, * de-ăh-boll-eeck, *a* diabolical.

diacre, de-ăh-kr, *m* deacon.

diagnostic, de-ăhg-noss-teeck, *m* diagnosis.

diagonal, e,* de-ăh-gonn-

ăhl, *a* diagonal.

diagnostique, de-ăhg-noss-teeck, *a* diagnostic.

dialecte, de-ăh-leckt, *m* dialect.

dialogue, de-ăh-log, *m* dialogue.

diamant, de-ăh-mahng, *m* diamond.

diamètre, de-ăh-met-tr, *m* diameter.

diapason, de-ăh-păh-zong, *m* pitch; tuning fork.

diaphane, de-ăh-făhn, *a* transparent.

diapositive, de-ah-poh-ze-teev, *f* transparency (photo).

diarrhée, de-ăh-reh, *f* diarrhea.

dictateur, dick-tăh-ter, *m* dictator.

dictature, dick-tăh-tEEr, *f* dictatorship.

dictée, dick-teh, *f* dictation.

dicter, dick-teh, *v* to dictate.

dictionnaire, dicks-e-onn-air, *m* dictionary.

dicton, dick-tong, *m* saying.

dièse, de-ayz, *m* sharp (music).

diète, de-ett, *f* diet.

dieu, de-er, *m* God.

diffamant, e, de-făh-mahng, *a* defamatory.

A
B
C
D
E
F
G
H
I
J
K
L
M
N
O
P
Q
R
S
T
U
V
W
X
Y
Z

diffamation, de-făh-măh-se-*ong*, *f* libel; slander.

diffamer, de-făh-meh, *v* to defame; to slander.

différence, de-feh-rah*ng*ss, *f* difference.

différencier, de-feh-rah*ng*-se-eh, *v* to distinguish.

différend, de-feh-rah*ng*, *m* difference; dispute.

différent, de-feh-rah*ng*, *a* different; unlike; various.

différentiel, le, de-feh-rah*ng*-se-ell, *mf* & *a* differential.

différer, de-feh-reh, *v* to defer; to postpone; to differ (**de**, from).

difficile, * de-fe-seell, *a* difficult; particular; (*fam*) choosy.

difficulté, de-fe-kEEl-teh, *f* difficulty; obstacle; objection.

difforme, de-form, *a* deformed; ugly.

difformité, de-for-me-teh, *f* deformity.

diffus, e, de-fE, *a* diffuse; prolix.

diffuser, de-fE-zeh, *v* to diffuse; to broadcast.

diffusion, de-fE-ze-*ong*, *f* diffusion; diffuseness; **radio –,** răh-de-o –, broadcasting.

digérer, de-sheh-reh, *v* to assimilate; to digest.

digestion, de-shess-te-*ong*, *f* digestion.

digital, e, de-she-tăhl, *a* digital.

digitale, de-she-tăhl, *f* foxglove.

digne, * deen-yer, *a* worthy; deserving; dignified.

dignité, deen-yee-teh, *f* dignity; title; stateliness.

digue, deeg, *f* dike; dam; embankment.

dilapider, de-lăh-pe-deh, *v* to dilapidate; to squander.

dilater, de-lăh-teh, *v* to dilate; to enlarge.

dilatoire, de-lăh-to'ăhr, *a* dilatory.

dilemme, de-lemm, *m* dilemma.

diligence, de-le-shah*ng*ss, *f* diligence; speed; stage-coach.

diluer, de-lE-eh, *v* to dilute; to water down.

dimanche, de-mah*ng*sh, *m* Sunday.

dimension, de-mah*ng*-se-*ong*, *f* dimension; size; measurement.

diminuer, de-me-nE-eh, *v* to diminish; to lessen; to abate.

diminution, de-me-nE-se-*ong*, *f* decrease; abatement.

dinde, da*ng*d, *f* female turkey.

dindon, da*ng*-do*ng*, *m* turkey-cock; (*fig*) goose.

dindonneau, da*ng*-donn-o, *m* young turkey.

dîner, de-neh, *v* to dine.

dîner, de-neh, *m* dinner.

dînette, de-nett, *f* informal meal; doll's tea party.

diocèse, de-oss-ayz, *m* diocese.

diplomate, de-plomm-ăht, *m* diplomat.

diplomatie, de-plomm-ăh-see, *f* diplomacy.

diplômé, de-ploh-meh, *mf* & *a* graduate.

dire, deer, *v* to say; to tell; to speak; **dites donc!** deet do*ng*, that's enough!

dire, deer, *m* saying; statement.

direct, e, * de-reckt, *a* direct; straight; through express (of train); live (of television).

direc-teur, trice, de-reck-ter, *mf* director; manager; headmaster; headmistress; principal.

direction, de-reck-se-*ong*, *f* management; manager's office; steering; direction.

dirigeable, de-re-shăh-bl, *m* dirigible; *a* manageable.

diriger, de-re-sheh, *v* to direct; to manage; to run; to guide; **se –,** to go (**vers, sur,** towards).

discerner, diss-air-neh, *v* to discern; to distinguish.

disciple, diss-ee-pl, *m* disciple; follower.

discipline, diss-e-pleen, *f* discipline.

discontinuer, diss-kong-te-nE-eh, *v* to discontinue.

disconvenance, diss-kongv-nahngss, *f* unsuitableness; incongruity; disproportion.

discorde, diss-kord, *f* discord; disagreement.

discourir, diss-koo-reer, *v* to converse.

discours, diss-koohr, *m* conversation; speech; lecture; talk.

discourtois, e, * diss-koohr-to'ăh, *a* discourteous.

discrédit, diss-kreh-de, *m* discredit; disrepute.

discréditer, diss-kreh-de-teh, *v* to discredit.

discr-et, ète, * diss-kray, *a* discreet; quiet.

discrétion, diss-kreh-se-ong, *f* discretion.

disculper, diss-kEEl-peh, *v* to exonerate.

discussion, diss-kEEss-e-ong, *f* discussion; debate; dispute.

discuter, diss-kE-teh, *v* to discuss; to debate.

disert, e, de-zair, *a* fluent; eloquent.

disette, de-zett, *f* dearth; scarcity.

disgrâce, diss-grahss, *f* disgrace; misfortune.

disgracié, e, diss-grăhss-e-eh, *pp & a* unfortunate; out of favor.

disgracier, diss-grăhss-e-eh, *v* to put out of favor.

disgracieu-x, se, * diss-grăhss-e-e-er, *a* ungraceful.

disjoindre, diss-sho-ang-dr, *v* to disjoint; to separate.

disloquer, diss-lock-eh, *v* to dislocate.

disparaître, diss-păh-ray-tr, *v* to disappear.

disparate, diss-păh-răht, *f* incongruity; *a* incongruous; dissimilar.

disparition, diss-păh-re-se-ong, *f* disappearance.

disparu, e, diss-păh-rE, *pp & a* disappeared; missing.

dispensaire, diss-pahng-sair, *m* clinic; outpatients' department (of hospital).

dispense, diss-pahngss, *f* dispensation; exemption; license.

disperser, diss-pair-seh, *v* to scatter; to disperse.

disponibilité, diss-ponn-e-be-le-teh, *f* availability; *pl* funds available.

disponible, diss-ponn-ee-bl, *a* disposable; available; disengaged.

dispos, diss-poh, *a* active; nimble; lively.

disposé, e, diss-poz-eh, *pp & a* disposed; inclined; willing.

disposer, diss-poz-eh, *v* to dispose; to have at command; to induce.

dispositif, diss-poz-e-tiff, *m* purview (law); contrivance (technology); apparatus.

disposition, diss-poz-e-se-ong, *f* arrangement; frame of mind; tendency; aptitude.

disproportionné e, diss-prop-or-se-onn-eh, *a* disproportionate.

dispute, diss-pEEt, *f* dispute; quarrel.

disputer, diss-pE-teh, *v* to dispute; **se –,** to quarrel;

to vie.

disque, deesk, *m* disk; record.

dissemblable, diss-sahng-blăh-bl, *a* dissimilar.

dissension, diss-sahng-se-ong, *f* dissension.

dissentiment, diss-sahng-te-mahng, *m* dissent.

disséquer, diss-seh-keh, *v* to dissect.

dissertation, de-sair-tăh-se-ong, *f* dissertation; essay.

dissident, diss-se-dahng, *m* dissenter.

dissimulé, e, diss-se-mE-leh, *pp* & *a* dissembled; dissembling; deceptive.

dissimuler, diss-se-mE-leh, *v* to dissimulate; to conceal; to pretend ignorance of.

dissiper, diss-se-peh, *v* to dissipate; to waste; to dispel; **se –,** to vanish; to misbehave (at school).

dissolu, e, diss-soll-E, *a* dissolute.

dissoluble, diss-soll-EE-bl, *a* dissolvable; soluble.

dissolvant, diss-soll-vahng, *m* & *a* solvent; nail-polish remover.

dissoudre, diss-soo-dr, *v* to dissolve.

dissuader, diss-sE-ăh-deh,

v to dissuade.

distance, diss-tahngss, *f* distance.

distancer, diss-tahngss-eh, *v* to distance.

distant, e, diss-tahng, *a* distant; remote.

distendre, diss-tahng-dr, *v* to distend.

distillerie, diss-till-ree, *f* distillery.

distinct, e,* diss-tang-kt, *a* distinct.

distinction, diss-tangk-se-ong, *f* distinction; refinement.

distingué, e, diss-tang-gheh, *a* distinguished; refined.

distinguer, diss-tang-gheh, *v* to distinguish; to perceive.

distraction, diss-trăhck-se-ong, *n* inattention; absence of mind; absentmindedness; amusement.

distraire, diss-trayr, *v* to distract; to separate; to amuse.

distrait, e,* diss-tray, *a* inattentive; absentminded; scatterbrained.

distribuer, diss-tre-bE-eh, *v* to distribute.

distributeur, diss-tre-bE-ter, *m* deliverer;

distributor; **–automatique,** – oh-tomm-ăh-teeck –, vending machine.

distributeur automatique de billets, diss-tre-bE-ter-oh-toh-măh-teeck-der-bee-yay, *m* automatic teller machine.

distribution, diss-tre-bE-se-ong, *f* distribution; delivery; handling.

dit, dee, *m* saying.

dit, e, dee, *pp* & *a* told; agreed; alias; **autrement –,** oh-trer-mahng–, in other words.

dito, de-to, *adv* ditto.

divaguer, de-văh-gheh, *v* to wander; to ramble.

divan, de-vahng, *m* divan; sofa; couch.

diverger, de-vair-sheh, *v* to diverge.

divers, de-vair, *mpl* sundries.

divers, e, de-vair, *a* different; various; several; varied.

divertir, de-vair-teer, *v* to amuse; to divert.

divertissant, e, de-vair-tiss-ahng, *a* entertaining.

divertissement, de-vair-tiss-mahng, *m* amusement; entertainment.

dividende, de-ve-dah*n*gd, *m* dividend.

divin, e,* de-va*n*g, *a* divine; heavenly; exquisite.

diviniser, de-ve-ne-zeh, *v* to deify.

diviser, de-ve-zeh, *v* to divide.

divisionnaire, de-ve-ze-onn-air, *a* divisional; of a division.

divorce, de-vorss, *m* divorce; separation.

divulguer, de-vEEl-gheh, *v* to divulge.

dix, deess, (before a consonant, dee), *m & a* ten; tenth.

dixième, de-ze-aym, *m & a* tenth.

dizaine, de-zain, *f* ten; about ten.

do, do, *m* the note C.

docile,* doss-eell, *a* docile; tractable.

docteur, dock-ter, *m* doctor.

doctorat, dock-tor-ăh, *m* doctorate.

doctrine, dock-treen, *f* doctrine.

document, dock-E-mah*n*g, *m* document.

documentaire, dock-E-mah*n*g-tair, *m & a* documentary.

documenter, dock-E-mah*n*g-teh, *v* to document.

dodo, dod-o, *m* sleep (in baby talk); **aller faire –,** ăh-leh-fair–, to go to bye bye.

dodu, e, dod-E, *a* plump.

dogmatiser, dog-măh-te-zeh, *v* to dogmatize.

dogme, dogm, *m* dogma.

dogue, dog, *m* large watchdog.

doigt, do'ăh, *m* finger; **à deux –s de,** ăh der – der, within an inch of.

doigter, doigté, do'ăh-teh, *m* fingering; tact.

doit, do'ăh, *m* debit.

doléance, doll-eh-ah*n*gss, *f* complaint; grievance.

dolent, e, doll-ah*n*g, *a* doleful; painful.

domaine, domm-ain, *m* domain; estate; property; (*fam*) province; sphere.

dôme, dohm, *m* dome; canopy.

domesticité, domm-ess-te-se-teh, *f* servants; domesticity.

domestique, domm-ess-teeck, *mf & a* servant; domestic; private; tame.

domicile, domm-e-seell, *m* domicile; residence; home.

domicilié, e, domm-e-se-le-eh, *pp & a* domiciled; resident.

dominant, e, domm-e-nah*n*g, *a* dominant; ruling; prevailing.

dominer, domm-e-neh, *v* to rule; to domineer; to govern; to overlook.

dominical, e, domm-e-ne-kăhl, *a* dominical **oraison –e,** or-ay-zo*n*g –, the Lord's Prayer.

dommage, domm-ăhsh, *m* damage; loss; **c'est – say –,** it is a pity.

dompter, dong-teh, *v* to tame; to subdue.

dompteu-r, se, dong-ter, *mf* trainer (of animals).

don, dong, *m* gift; present; talent.

dona-teur, trice, donn-ăh-ter, *mf* donor.

donc, dong (and dongk at the beginning of a sentence and before a vowel), *conj* then; therefore.

donjon, dong- sho*n*g, *m* dungeon; keep; turret.

donne, donn, *f* deal (cards).

donnée, donn-eh, *f* notion; *pl* data.

donner, donn-eh, *v* to give; to strike; to look; to shine; to yield (of trees, etc); to deal; to

a b c d e f g h i j k l m n o p q r s t u v w x y z

charge; **s'en –,** sah*ng* –; to enjoy oneself.

dont, do*ng*, *pron* whose; of whom; from whom; by whom; of which; with whom or which.

doré, e, dor-eh, *pp* & *a* gilded; gilt; golden.

dorénavant, dor-eh-năh-vah*ng*, *adv* henceforth.

dorer, dor-eh, *v* to gild; to glaze (pastry).

dorloter, dor-lot-eh, *v* to coddle; to pamper.

dormant, e, dor-mah*ng*, *a* sleeping; dormant; dull.

dormeur, dor-mer, *m* sleeper.

dormir, dor-meer, *v* to sleep; to be dormant.

dorsal, e, dor-săhl, *a* dorsal.

dortoir, dor-to'ăhr, *m* dormitory.

dorure, dor-EEr, *f* gilding; glaze (of pastry).

dos, doh, *m* back.

dosage, doh-zăhsh, *m* dosage.

dose, dohz, *f* dose.

doser, doh-zeh, *v* to dose.

dossier, doh-se-eh,, *m* back (of chair, etc) brief; file of notes, dossier.

dot, dott, *f* dowry; marriage settlement.

dotal, e, dot-ăhl, *a* of the dowry.

doter, dot-eh, *v* to endow (**dc,** with).

douairière, doo-ay-re-air, *f* & *a* dowager.

douane, doo-ăhn, *f* customs.

douanier, doo-ăh-ne-eh, *m* customs officer.

doublage, doo-blăhsh, *m* doubling; dubbing (film).

double,* doo-bl, *a* double; *m* duplicate; replica; double.

doubler, doo-bleh, *v* to double; to line (**de,** with); to dub (film); to understudy; to pass (on road).

doublure, doo-blEEr, *f* lining; substitute.

douceâtre, dooss-ah-tr, *a* sweetish.

douceur, dooss-er, *f* sweetness; softness; charm; gentleness; *pl* sweets; pleasant things.

douche, doosh, *f* shower.

doué, doo-eh, *a* gifted.

douer, doo-eh, *v* to endow (with qualities).

douille, doo-ye, *f* socket (electricity).

douillet, te,* doo'e-yay, *a* delicate; tender.

douleur, doo-ler, *f* pain; grief; sorrow.

douloureu-x, se,* doo-loo-rer, *a* painful; mournful; grievous.

doute, doot, *m* doubt.

douter, doo-teh, *v* to doubt; **se –,** to suspect; to have some notion (**de** or **que,** of or that).

douteu-x, se,* doo-ter, *a* doubtful; questionable.

douve, doov, *f* trench; moat; open ditch.

dou-x, ce,* doo, dooss, *a* sweet; soft; kind; gentle; smooth; mild.

douzaine, doo-zain, *f* dozen.

douze, dooz, *a* twelve; twelfth (the).

douzième, doo-ze-aym, *mf* & *a* twelfth.

doyen, do'ah-yang, *m* dean; senior; elder.

dragée, drăh-sheh, *f* sugared almond; sugar-coated pill.

dragon, drăh-go*ng*, *m* dragon; termagant; dragoon.

draguer, drăh-gheh, *v* to dredge.

drainer, dray-neh, *v* to drain.

dramaturge, drăh-măh-tEEsh, *mf* dramatist; playwright.

drame, drăhm, *m* drama; (*fam*) catastrophe.

drap, drăh, *m* cloth; sheet.

drapeau, drăh-poh, *m* flag; colors; **sous les − x,** soo lay −, in the army.

draper, drăh-peh, *v* to cover with cloth; **se−,** to drape; to wrap oneself up.

draperie, drăhp-ree, *f* drapery; cloth manufacturer.

drapier, drăh-pe-eh, *m* draper; clothier.

dressage, dress-ăhsh, *m* training.

dresser, dress-eh, *v* to erect; to pitch; to lay out; to train; **se −,** to stand up.

dressoir, dress-o'ăhr, *m* sideboard; dresser.

drogue, drog, *f* drug; (*fam*) garbage.

droguer, drogh-eh, *v* to drug; **se −,** to take drugs.

droguiste, drogh-eesst, *m* druggist; retailer in chemicals.

droit, dro'ăh, *m* right; authority; law; title;duuty; tax; franchise; **faire son −,** fair song −, to study law; **qui de −,** ke der −, those whom it may concern.

droit, e, dro'ăh, *adv* straight; directly; **tout −,** too −, straight on. *a* straight; right; erect; straightforward; righteous.

droite, dro'ăht, *f* right hand; right side.

droiture, dro'ăh-tEEr, *f* straightforwardness.

drôle, drohl, *m* rogue; scamp. *a** funny; queer.

dru, e, drE, *adv* thick; hard. *a* fledged; dense; close; thick.

du, dE, contraction of **de le.**

dû, dE, *pp* & *a* owed; been obliged.

duc, dEEk, *m* duke.

duché, dE-sheh, *m* dukedom; duchy.

duchesse, dE-shess, *f* duchess.

duel, dE-ell, *m* duel.

dûment, dE-mahng, *adv* duly.

dune, dEEn, *f* dune.

d'une nuit, dEn-nwee *a, stay* overnight stay.

duo, dE-o, *m* duet.

dupe, dEEp, *f* dupe.

duper, dE-peh, *v* to dupe.

duperie, dEp-ree, *f* trickery.

duplicata, dE-ple-kăh-tăh, *m* duplicate.

duplicité, dE-ple-se-teh, *f* duplicity; double-dealing.

duquel, dE-kell, *pron* contraction of **de lequel;** whose; from whom; of which; from which.

dur, dEEr, *m* hardness; (*fam*) tough guy.

dur, e,* dEEr, *a* hard; harsh; rough; stiff.

durable, dE-răh-bl, *a* lasting.

durant, dE-rahng, *prep* during.

durcir, dEEr-seer, *v* to harden; to set.

durcissement, dEEr-siss-mahng, *m* hardening.

durée, dE-reh, *f* duration.

durer, dEE-reh, *v* to last; to hold out.

dureté, dEEr-teh, *f* hardness; harshness.

duvet, dE-vay, *m* down.

dynamite, de-năh-meet, *f* dynamite.

a
b
c
d
e
f
g
h
i
j
k
l
m
n
o
p
q
r
s
t
u
v
w
x
y
z

A B C D E F G H I J K L M N O P Q R S T U V W X Y Z

eau, oh, *f* water; rain; **–de vie,** –der vee, spirit; brandy.

ébahir (s'), seh-băh-eer, *v* to be amazed (**de,** at).

ébats, eh-băh, *mpl* frolics.

ébattre (s'), seh-băh-tr, *v* to frolic.

ébauche, eh-bohsh, *f* sketch; outline.

ébaucher, eh-boh-sheh, *v* to sketch; to roughcast.

ébène, eh-bain, *f* ebony.

ébéniste, eh-beh-neesst, *m* cabinetmaker.

éblouir, eh-bloo-eer, *v* to dazzle.

éblouissement, eh-blooiss-mahng, *m* dazzling; dizziness.

éboulement, eh-boolmahng, *m* falling rocks; crumbling.

ébouriffé, e, eh-boo-refeh, *a* disheveled; tousled (hair); flurried.

ébranlement, eh-brahnglmahng, *m* shaking; commotion.

ébranler, eh-brahng-leh, *v* to shake; to disturb; to put in motion; **s' –,** to totter; to begin to move.

ébrécher, eh-breh-sheh, *v* to notch; to indent; to chip.

ébruiter, eh-brwe-teh, *v* to divulge; **s' –,** to become known.

ébullition, eh-bE-le-seong, *f* boiling.

écaille, eh-kah'e, *f* scale; tortoiseshell.

écailler, eh-kah'e-eh, *v* to scale; to open (of shellfish).

écarlate, eh-kăhr-lăht, *a* & *f* scarlet.

écarquiller, eh-kăhr-keeyeh, *v* to open wide (eyes); to straddle.

écart, eh-kăhr, *m* step aside; separation; digression; discrepancy; error, *m adv phr* à l'–, ah l'–, aside.

écarté, eh-kăhr-teh, *a* remote; lonely.

écartement, eh-kăhr-termahng, spacing; putting aside.

écarter, eh-kăhr-teh, *v* to separate; to keep off; **s' –,** to deviate; to move aside.

ecclésiastique, eh-kleh-zeăhss-teeck, *m* clergyman. *a* ecclesiastical.

écervelé, e, eh-sair-verleh, *a* harebrained.

échafaud, eh-shăh-foh, *m* scaffolding; stage; scaffold.

échafaudage, eh-shăhfoh-dăhsh, *m* scaffolding; building up.

échafauder, eh-shăh-fohdeh, *v* to erect scaffolding; to pile up.

échalote, eh-shăh-lot, *f* shallot.

échancrer, eh-shahngkreh, *v* to indent; to

hollow out.

échange, eh-shah*ng*sh, *m* exchange; barter; **libre –** lee-br –, free trade.

échanger, eh-sah*ng*-sheh, *v* to exchange.

échantillon, eh-shah*ng*-tee-yong, *m* sample; pattern.

échappatoire, eh-shăh-pah-to'ăhr, *f* evasion; loophole.

échappée, eh-shăh-peh, *f* escapade; vista.

échappement, eh-shăhp-mah*ng*, *m* escape; leakage; exhaust.

échapper, eh-shăh-peh, *v* to escape; to avoid; to slip; **s' –,** to steal away.

écharde, eh-shahrd, *f* splinter.

écharpe, eh-shăhrp, *f* scarf; sling; sash; **en –** ah*ng* n'–, slanting.

écharper, eh-shăhr-peh, *v* to cut to pieces.

échasse, eh-shăhss, *f* stilt.

échassier, eh-shăhss-e-eh, *m* wading bird.

échauder, eh-shoh-deh, *v* to scald.

échauffement, eh-shohf-mah*ng*, *m* heating; over-heating; overexcitement.

échauffer, eh-shoh-feh, *v* to heat; to overheat; to

excite.

échauffourée, eh-shoh-foo-reh, *f* skirmish; fray.

échéance, eh-sheh-ah*ng*ss, *f* falling due; expiration; maturity.

échéant, eh-sheh-ah*ng*, *pp* falling due; occurring; **le cas –,** ler kah z'–, should it so happen.

échec, eh-shayk, *m* check; failure; blow; *pl* chess; chessmen.

échelle, eh-shell, *f* ladder; steps; scale.

échelon, ehsh-lo*ng*, *m* rung; step; degree.

échelonner, ehsh-lonn-eh, *v* to stagger; to arrange by degrees; to space out.

écheveau, ehsh-voh, *m* hank; skein.

échevelé, e, eh-sher*v*-leh, *a* disheveled.

échine, eh-sheen, *f* spine; backbone.

échiner, eh-she-neh, *v* to work to death.

échiquier, eh-she-ke-eh, *m* chessboard.

écho, eh-ko, *m* echo.

échoir, eh-sho'ăhr, *v* to fall due; to fall to the lot of.

échoppe, eh-shop, *f* stall.

échouer, eh-shoo-eh, *v* to run aground; to fail.

échu, e, eh-shE, *pp* fallen

due; outstanding.

éclabousser, eh-klăh-booss-eh, *v* to splash.

éclair, eh-klayr, *m* lightning; flash; éclair.

éclairage, eh-klay-răhsh, *m* lighting; illumination.

éclaircie, eh-klayr-see, *f* clearing; glade opening.

éclaircir, eh-klayr-seer, *v* to clear up; to elucidate.

éclairer, eh-klay-reh, *v* to light; to enlighten.

éclaireur, eh-klay-rer, *m* scout.

éclat, eh-klăh, *m* splinter; explosion; clap; splendor; uproar; scandal.

éclatant, e, eh-klăh-tah*ng*, *a* bright; brilliant; resounding; flagrant; loud.

éclater, eh-klăh-teh, *v* to burst; to explode; to shine; **– de rire,** d-reer, to burst out laughing.

éclisse, eh-kleess, *f* wedge; splint.

éclopé, e, eh-klop-eh, *a* lame; cripple.

éclore, eh-klor, *v* to hatch; to dawn; to open.

éclosion, eh-kloh-ze-ong, *f* hatching; opening.

écluse, eh-klEEz, *f* lock.

écœurer, eh-ker-reh, *v* to sicken.

école, eh-kol, *f* school.

écoli-er, ère, eh-koll-e-eh, *mf* schoolboy; schoolgirl.

éconduire, eh-kong-dweer, *v* to get rid of; to deny.

économat, eh-konn-omm-äh, *m* treasureship; bursar's office.

économe, eh-konn-omm, *m* steward; bursar; *a* economical; saving.

économie, eh-konn-omm-ee, *f* economy; saving; *pl* savings.

économique,* eh-konn-omm-eeck, *a* economic(al).

économiser, eh-konn-omm-e-zeh, *v* to economize; to save.

économiste, eh-konn-omm-eesst, *m* economist.

écorce, eh-korss, *f* bark; rind; peel; skin; outside.

écorcher, eh-kor-sheh, *v* to skin; to graze; to fleece.

écorchure, eh-kor-shEEr, *f* graze.

écosser, eh-koss-eh, *v* to shell; to hull.

écot, eh-ko, *m* share; quota; reckoning.

écoulement, eh-kool-mahng, *m* flow; drainage; turnover.

écouler, eh-koo-leh, *v* to flow out; to elapse; to sell off.

écoute, eh-koot, *f* listening place; wiretapping.

écouter, eh-koo-teh, *v* to listen; to pay attention to.

écouteu-r, se, eh-koo-ter, *mf* listener; *m* receiver (telephone); earphone.

écran, eh-krahng, *m* screen; smokescreen.

écrasant, e, eh-kräh-zahng, *a* crushing; overwhelming.

écraser, eh-kräh-zeh, *v* to crush; to overwhelm; to run over.

écrémer, eh-kreh-meh, *v* to skim.

écrevisse, eh-krer-veess, *f* crayfish.

écrier (s'), seh-kre-eh, *v* to exclaim.

écrin, eh-krang, *m* box; case; casket.

écrire, eh-kreer, *v* to write.

écriteau, eh-kre-toh, *m* board.

écriture, eh-kre-tEEr, *f* writing; handwriting; scripture; *pl* accounts.

écrivain, eh-kre-vang, *m* writer; author.

écrou, eh-kroo, *m* screwnut.

écrouer, eh-kroo-eh, *v* to put in jail.

écroulement, eh-krool-mahng, *m* falling down; collapse; ruin.

écrouler (s'), seh-kroo-leh, *v* to fall down; to collapse.

écru, e, eh-krE, *a* unbleached; raw.

écueil, eh-ker'e, *m* rock; reef; stumbling block.

écuelle, eh-kE-ell, *f* bowl.

écume, eh-kEEm, *f* foam; froth; scum.

écumer, eh-kE-meh, *v* to skim; to foam.

écureuil, eh-kE-rer'e, *m* squirrel.

écurie, eh-kE-ree, *f* stable; stud.

écusson, eh-kEEss-ong, *m* coat of arms.

écuyer, eh-kwee-yeh, *m* squire; riding master; rider.

édenté, e, eh-dahng-teh, *a* toothless.

édicter, eh-dick-teh, *v* to decree; to exact.

édification, eh-de-fe-käh-se-ong, *f* edification; building.

édifice, eh-de-feess, *m* building; structure.

édifier, eh-de-fe-eh, *v* to

edify; to erect; to enlighten.

édit, eh-de, *m* edict; decree.

éditer, eh-de-teh, *v* to publish; to edit.

éditeur, eh-de-ter, *m* publisher.

édition, eh-de-se-ong, *f* edition; publishing.

édredon, eh-drer-dong, *m* eiderdown.

éducation, eh-dE-kăh-se-ong, *f* education; breeding; training.

éduquer, eh-dE-keh, *v* to educate; to bring up.

effacer, eh-făhss-eh, *v* to efface; to rub out; to wipe out; to eclipse.

effaré, e, eh-făh-reh, *pp* & *a* scared.

effaroucher, eh-făh-roo-sheh, *v* to scare away; **s'–,** to take fright at.

effectif, eh-fehck-teeff, *m* strength; size; number of.

effecti-f, ve, eh-fehck-teeff, *a* effective; actual.

effectivement, eh-fehck-teev-mahng, *adv* effectively; actually; that is so.

effectuer, eh-fehck-tE-eh, *v* to effect; to carry out.

efféminé, e, eh-feh-me-neh, *a* effeminate.

effervescence, eh-fair-vayss-ahngss, *f* effervescence; excitement.

effet, eh-fay, *m* effect; impression; bill; *pl* goods; effects; bills.

effeuiller, eh-fer'e-yeh, *v* to strip off leaves or petals.

efficace,* eh-fe-kăhss, *a* efficacious; effective.

effilé, e, eh-fe-leh, *a* slender; slim; sharp; frayed.

efflanqué, e, eh-flahng-keh, *a* lean; thin; lank.

effleurer, eh-fler-reh, *v* to skim; to touch slightly; to glance over.

effluve, eh-flEEv, *m* effluvium; smell.

effondrement, eh-fong-drer-mahng, *m* falling down; collapse.

effondrer (s'), seh-fong-dreh, *v* to fall down; to collapse.

efforcer (s'), seh-for-seh, *v* to strive; to endeavor.

effort, eh-for, *m* effort; endeavor; strain; exertion.

effrayant, e, eh-fray-yahng, *a* dreadful; frightful; (*fam*) awful.

effrayer, eh-fray-yeh, *v* to frighten.

effréné, e, eh-freh-neh, *a* unbridled; unrestrained.

effriter (s'), seh-fre-teh, *v* to crumble away.

effroi, eh-fro'ăh, *m* fright; terror.

effronté, e, eh-frong-teh, *a* impudent.

effrontément, eh-frong-teh-mahng, *adv* impudently.

effronterie, eh-frongt-ree, *f* impudence; insolence.

effroyable,* eh-fro'ăh-yăh-bl, *a* frightful; (*fam*) tremendous.

effusion, eh-fE-ze-ong, *f* effusion; overflowing; shedding.

égal, e, eh-găhl, *a* equal; even; like; same; level; **cela m'est –,** slăh may t' **–,** it is all the same to me.

également, eh-găhl-mahng, *adv* equally; alike; both; likewise; also.

égaler, eh-găh-leh, *v* to equal; to match.

égaliser, eh-găh-le-zeh, *v* to equalize; to level; to smooth.

égalitaire, eh-găh-le-tair, *a* leveling.

égalité, eh-găh-le-teh, *f* evenness; equality; uniformity; deuce (in tennis).

égard, eh-găhr, *m* regard; respect; consideration.

égaré, e, eh-găh-reh, *a* stray; bewildered; out of the way; erring.

égarement, eh-găhr-mahng, *m* distraction; misconduct; wandering.

égarer, eh-găh-reh, *v* to mislead; to mislay; to bewilder; **s'–,** to lose one's way.

égayer, eh-gay-yeh, *v* to enliven; to cheer up.

églantine, eh-glahng-teen, *f* sweetbriar; dog rose.

église, eh-gleez, *f* church.

egoïsme, eh-go-issm, *m* selfishness.

égoïste, eh-go-isst, *m* selfish person; egoist. *a* selfish.

égorger, eh-gor-sheh, *v* to cut the throat of; to kill.

égosiller (s'), seh-goz-ee-yeh, *v* to make oneself hoarse.

égout, eh-ghoo, *m* drain; sewer; drip.

égoutter, eh-ghoot-eh, *v* to drain; to drip.

égratigner, eh-grăh-teen-yeh, *v* to scratch.

égrener, eh-grer-neh, *v* to pick.

éjaculer, eh-shah-kEE-leh, *v* to ejaculate.

éjecter, eh-sheck-teh, *v* to eject.

élaborer, ch-lăh-bor-eh, *v* to elaborate; to work out.

élaguer, eh-lăh-gheh, *v* to lop; to prune.

élan, eh-lahng, *m* spring; start; dash; impetus.

élancé, e, eh-lahngss-eh, *a* slender; slim.

élancer, eh-lahngss-eh, *v* to dart; **s'–,** to rush.

élargir, eh-lăhr-sheer, *v* to widen; to extend; to release.

élastique, eh-lăhss-teeck, *a* & *m* elastic; springy.

électeur, eh-leck-ter, *m* elector.

élection, eh-leck-se-ong, *f* election; polling.

électricien, eh-leck-tre-se-ang, *m* electrician.

électricité, eh-leck-tre-se-teh, *f* electricity.

électriser, eh-leck-tre-zeh, *v* to electrify.

électrophone, eh-leck-tro-fon, *m* record player.

élégamment, eh-leh-găh-mahng, *adv* elegantly.

élégance, eh-leh-gahngss, *f* elegance.

élégie, eh-leh-shee, *f* elegy.

élément, eh-leh-mahng, *m* element; unit(of

furniture).

élémentaire, eh-leh-mahng-tair, *a* elementary; rudimentary.

éléphant, h-leh-fahng, *m* elephant.

élevage, ehl-văhsh, *m* breeding; animal husbandry.

élévation, eh-leh-văh-se-ong, *f* elevation; raising; rise.

élève eh-layv, *mf* pupil; scholar; student; *f* breeding (of cattle).

élevé, e, ehl-veh, *pp* & *a* raised; lofty; brought up; bred.

élever, ehl-veh, *v* to raise; to build; to extol; to bring up; **s' –,** to rise; to amount.

élider, eh-le-deh, *v* to omit; to cut off.

éliminer, eh-le-me-neh, *v* to eliminate; to get rid of.

élire, eh-leer, *v* to elect; to choose.

élision, eh-le-ze-ong, *f* omission.

élite, eh-leet, *f* pick; elite.

elle, ell, *pron* she; her; it; **elles,** they; them.

ellipse, eh-lips, *f* ellipsis; ellipse.

éloge, eh-losh, *m* praise;

commendation.

élogieu-x, se,* eh-losh-e-er, *a* eulogistic.

éloigné, e, eh-lo'ăhn-yeh, *a* removed; distant; out of the way; disinclined.

éloignement, eh-lo'ăhn-yer-mahng, *m* distance; absence; aversion.

éloigner, eh-lo'ăhn-yeh, *v* to remove; to keep away; to delay; to estrange.

éloquemment, en-lock-ăh-mahng, *adv* eloquently.

éloquence, eh-lock-ahngss, *f* eloquence.

élu, e, eh-lE, *pp* & *a* elected.

éluder, eh lE deh, *v* to elude; to evade.

émail, eh-mah'e, *m* enamel; glaze; *pl* **émaux,** ehmoh.

émaner, eh-măh-neh, *v* to emanate.

émarger, eh-măhr-sheh, *v* to annotate; to draw a salary.

emballage, ah-*ng*-băh-lăhsh, *m* packing; wrapping.

emballer, ahng-băh-leh, *v* to pack; to pack up; to wrap; **s'–,** to bolt; (*fam*) to get carried away (excitement, anger, etc).

embarcadère, ahng-băhr-kăh-dair, *m* pier; departure platform.

embarcation, ahng-băhr-kăh se-ong, *f* small boat; craft.

embarquer, ahng-băhr-keh, *v* to embark; to ship; to board (a plane).

embarras, ahng-băh-răh, *m* encumbrance; difficulty; perplexity; embarrassment; fuss.

embarrassant, ahng-băh-răhss-ahng, *a* cumbersome; awkward; embarrassing.

embarrasser, ahng-băh-răhss-eh, *v* to encumber; to perplex; to embarrass.

embaucher, ahng-boh-sheh, *v* to hire; to engage; to enlist; to entice away.

embaumer, ahng-boh-meh, *v* to perfume; to embalm.

embellir, ahng-bay-leer, *v* to embellish; to improve (in looks).

embêtant, e, ahng-bay-tahng *a* (*fam*) annoying; bothering.

embêter, ahng-bay-teh, *v* (*fam*) to bother; to bore; **s'–,** to be bored.

embêtement, ahng-bayt-mahng, *m* bother;

trouble.

emblée (d'), dahng-bleh, *adv* at the first attempt.

emblème, ahng-blaym, *m* emblem; badge.

emboîter, ahng-bo'ah-teh, *v* to encase; to interlock.

embolie, ahng-bo-le, *f* embolism; blood clot.

embonpoint, ahng-bong-po'ang, *m* plumpness.

embouchure, ahng-boo-shEEr, *f* mouth; mouthpiece.

embourber (s'), sahng-boohr-beh, *v* to get stuck in the mud; (*fam*) to become involved in trouble.

embouteillage, ahng-boo-tay-yăhsh, *m* bottling; traffic congestion.

embranchement, ahng-brahngsh-mahng, *m* branching-fork (classification); junction; branch-line.

embrancher (s'), sahng-brahng-sheh, *v* to branch off.

embrasé, e, ahng-brăh-zeh, *pp* & *a* in flames; burning.

embraser, ahng-brăh-zeh, *v* to set on fire; to kindle.

embrasser, ahng-brăhss-eh, *v* to embrace; to kiss.

a
b
c
d
e
f
g
h
i
j
k
l
m
n
o
p
q
r
s
t
u
v
w
x
y
z

A
B
C
D
E
F
G
H
I
J
K
L
M
N
O
P
Q
R
S
T
U
V
W
X
Y
Z

embrasure, ahng-brǎh-zEEr, *f* door-frame; window frame; opening.

embrayage, ahng-bray-yash, *m* clutch.

embrayer, ahng-bray-yeh, *v* to engage the clutch.

embrouillé, e, ahng-broo'e-yeh, *pp & a* entangled; intricate.

embrouiller, ahng-broo'e-yeh, *v* to tangle; to confuse.

embrumé, e, ahng-brE-meh *a* foggy; misty.

embryon, ahng-bree-yong, *m* embryo.

embûche, ahng-bEEsh, *f* snare; trap.

embuscade, ahng-bEss-kǎhd, *f* ambush.

émeraude, ehm-rohd, *f* emerald.

émeri, ehm-re, *m* emery.

émerveiller, eh-mair-vay'e-yeh, *v* to astonish; to fill with wonder.

émétique, eh-meh-teeck, *m* emetic.

émet-teur, trice, *m* transmitter. *a* transmitting; broadcasting.

émettre, eh-met-tr, *v* to issue; to express; to broadcast.

émeute, eh-mert, *f* riot; disturbance; outbreak.

émietter, eh-me-ayt-eh, *v* to crumble.

émigrer, eh-me-greh, *v* to emigrate.

émincé, eh-mang-seh, *m* thin slices of meat.

éminemment, eh-me-nǎh-mahng, *adv* eminently.

éminence, eh-me-nahngss, *f* eminence.

émissaire, eh-miss-air, *m* emissary.

émission, eh-miss-e-ong, *f* issue; uttering; transmission; program (radio).

emmagasiner, ahng-mǎh-gǎh-ze-neh, *v* to store.

emmancher, ahng-mahng-sheh, *v* to put a handle on; to haft; to begin; **s'–,** to fit together.

emmêler, ahng-may-leh, *v* to entangle.

emménager, ahng-meh-nǎh-**sheh,** *v* to move in.

emmener, ahngm-neh, *v* to take away; to lead away.

emmitoufler, ahng-me-too-fleh, *v* to wrap up.

émoi, eh-mo'ǎh, *m* agitation; anxiety; flurry; emotion.

émolument, eh-moll-E-mahng, *m* emolument; gain; profit; *pl* salary; fees.

émotion, eh-mohss-e-ong, *f* emotion.

émousser, eh-mooss-eh, *v* to blunt; to dull.

émouvant, e, eh-moo-vahng, *a* touching; stirring.

émouvoir, eh-moo-vo'ǎhr, *v* to move; to stir up; to rouse; to affect.

empailler, ahng-pah'e-yeh, *v* to pack in straw; to stuff (animals).

empaqueter, ahng-pǎhck-teh, *v* to pack up.

emparer (s'), sahng-pǎh-reh, *v* to take possession.

empêché, e, ahng-pay-sheh, *pp & a* prevented; embarrassed; in a difficulty.

empêchement, ahng-paysh-mahng, *m* impediment; hindrance; obstacle.

empêcher, ahng-pay-sheh, *v* to prevent; to hinder; to keep from.

empereur, ahngp-rer, *m* emperor.

empeser, ahng-per-zeh, *v* to starch.

empester, ahng-pess-teh, *v* to infect; to stink.

empêtrer, ahng-pay-treh, *v* to entangle.

emphase, ahng-fahz, *f* emphasis; bombast;

pomposity.

emphatique,* ahng-făh-teeck, *a* emphatic; bombastic.

empierrer, ahng-pe-ay-reh, *v* to gravel; to pave.

empiéter, ahng-pe-eh-teh, *v* to encroach; to trespass.

empiler, ahng-pe-leh, *v* to pile up; to stack.

empire, ahng-peer, *m* empire; rule; control.

empirer, ahng-pe-reh, *v* to make worse; to get worse.

emplacement, ahng-plăhss-mahng, *m* site; place.

emplâtre, ahng-plah-tr, *m* plaster; helpless person.

emplette, ahng-plett, *f* purchase.

emplir, ahng-pleer, *v* to fill up (**de,** with).

emploi, ahng-plo'ăh, *m* employment; use; occupation; situation.

employé, ahng-plo'ăh-yeh, *m* employee; clerk.

employer, ahng-plo'ăh-yeh, *v* to employ; to use.

employeur, ahng-plo'ăh-yer, *m* employer.

empocher, ahng-posh-eh, *v* to pocket.

empoigner, ahng-po'ăhn-yeh, *v* to grasp; to arrest.

empois, ahng-po'ăh, *m* starch.

empoisonner, ahng-po'ăh-zonn-eh, *v* to poison; to infect; (*fam*) to annoy; to irritate.

emporté, e, ahng-por-teh, *a* quick-tempered.

emportement, ahng-por-ter-mahng, *m* transport; outburst; fit.

emporter, ahng-por-teh, *v* to carry away; **s'–,** to lose one's temper.

empourprer (s'), sahng-poohr-preh, *v* to flush; to turn red.

empreinte, ahng-prangt, *f* impress; mark; stamp; print; **–digitale, –** de-she-tăhl, fingerprint.

empressé, e, ahng-press-eh, *a* eager; assiduous; obliging.

empressement, ahng-press-mahng, *m* earnestness; assiduous attention.

empresser (s'), sahng-press-eh, *v* to hasten (**de,** to).

emprisonner, ahng-pre-zonn-eh, *v* to imprison.

emprunt, ahng-prung, *m* loan; borrowing.

emprunté, e, ahng-prung-teh, *pp* & *a* borrowed;

self-conscious.

emprunter, ahng-prung-teh, *v* to borrow.

ému, e, eh-mE, *pp* & *a* moved (by emotion).

émule, eh-mEEl, *m* rival; competitor.

en, ahng, *pron* some; any; of it; of them; of, from or about him, her, it; there. *prep* in; into; within; at; in the; like a; by; while.

en avoir marre (de), ahng-ăh-vo'ăhr-măhr-der, *v* fed-up (with).

en boîte, ahng-bo'ăht *a* canned.

encadrer, ahng-kăh-dreh, *v* to frame; to encircle.

encaisse, ahng-kayss, *f* cash in hand; cash balance.

encaissé, ahng-kayss-eh, *a* embanked.

encaissement, ahng-kayss-mahng, *m* packing; payment; cashing; embankment.

encaisser, ahng-kayss-eh, *v* to pack; to collect; to receive; to embank.

en-cas, ahng-kah, *m* snack.

encastrer, ahng-kăhss-treh, *v* to fit in; to embed.

encaustique, ahng-kohs-

teeck, *f* wax polish;
furniture polish.

encaver, ahng-kăh-veh, *v*
to store in a cellar.

enceinte, ahng-sangt, *f*
enclosure; precincts. *a*
pregnant.

encens, ahng-sahng, *m*
incense; (*fam*) praise;
flattery.

encenser, ahng-sahngss-
eh, *v* to flatter.

enchaînement, ahng-
shain-mahng, *m*
chaining up; train (of
events).

enchaîner, ahng-shay-neh,
v to chain up; to fetter;
to connect.

enchanté, ahng-shahng-
teh, *pp* & *a* enchanted;
spellbound; delighted.

enchantement, ahng-
shahngt-mahng, *m*
enchantment; spell;
delight.

enchanter, ahng-shahng-
teh, *v* to enchant; to
delight; to charm.

enchant-eur, eresse,
ahng-shahng-ter, *mf*
enchanter; *a*
bewitching; enchanting.

enchâsser, ahng-shahss-
eh, *v* to enshrine; to set.

enchère, ahng-shair, *f*
bidding; auction.

enchérir, ahng-sheh-reer,

v to outbid.

enchevêtrer, ahngsh-vay-
treh, *v* to entangle.

enclaver, ahng-klăh-veh, *v*
to enclose; to wedge in.

enclin, e, ahng-klang, *a*
inclined; prone.

enclore, ahng-klor, *v* to
enclose; to fence in.

enclos, ahng-kloh, *m*
enclosure; pen; paddock.

enclume, ahng-klEEm, *f*
anvil.

encoche, ahng-kosh, *f*
notch.

encoignure, ahng-konn-
yEEr, *f* corner; corner
cupboard.

encolure, ahng-koll-EEr, *f*
neckline.

encombrement, ahng-
kong-brer-mahng, *m*
obstruction; traffic jam.

encombrer, ahng-kong-
breh, *v* to encumber; to
obstruct; to crowd.

en conserve, ahng-kong-
sairv *a* canned.

encontre (à l'– de), ăh
lahng-kong-trer der, *prep*
against; contrary to.

encore, ahng-kor, *adv* still;
again; yet; **pas–,**păh z' –,
not yet.

encourager, ahng-koo-
răh-sheh, *v* to
encourage.

encourir, ahng-koo-reer, *v*

to incur.

encre, ahng-kr, *f* ink.

encrier, ahng-kre-eh, *m*
inkstand.

encroûté, e, ahng-kroo-
teh, *a* to be a stick in
the mud; to be stuck in
a rut.

encyclopédie, ahng-se-
klop-eh-dee, *f*
encyclopedia.

en désordre, ahng-deh-
zor-dr *a* messy.

endetter, ahng-day-teh, *v*
to get (a person) into
debt; **s'–,** to run into
debt.

endiablé, ahng-de-ăh-
bleh, *pp* & *a* furious;
wicked; reckless.

endiguer, ahng-de-gheh, *v*
to dam in; to bank up.

endimancher (s'), sahng-
de-mahng-sheh, *v* to put
on one's Sunday best.

endoctriner, ahng-dock-
tre-neh, *v* to gain over.

endolori, e, ahng-doll-or-
e, *a* aching; tender.

endommager, ahng-
domm-ăh-**sheh**, *v* to
damage.

endormi, e, ahng-dor-me,
pp & *a* gone to sleep;
sleeping; sleepy;
sluggish; numb.

endormir, ahng-dor-meer,
v to put to sleep; to lull;

(fam) to deceive; **s'**–, to fall asleep; to lie idle.

endos, endossement, ah*ng*-doh, ah*ng*-dohss-mah*ng*, *m* endorsement.

endosser, ah*ng*-dohss-eh, *v* to put on; to endorse.

endroit, ah*ng*-dro'ăh, *m* place; spot; part; right side.

enduire, ah*ng*-dweer, *v* to coat.

enduit, ah*ng*-dwe, *m* coat; layer.

endurant, e, ah*ng*-dE-rah*ng*, *a* enduring; patient; tolerant.

endurcir, ah*ng*-dEEr-seer, *v* to harden; to inure.

endurcissement, ah*ng*-dEEr-siss-mah*ng*, *m* hardening; toughness.

endurer, anhg-dEEr-eh, *v* to bear; to endure.

énergie, eh-nair-**sh**ee, *f* energy; force.

énergique,* eh-nair-**sh**eeck; *a* energetic.

énergumène, eh-nair-ghE-main, *m* fanatic; frantic person.

énervant, eh-nair-vah*ng*, *a (fam)* aggravating; irritating.

énerver, eh-nair-veh, *v* to get on one's nerves.

enfance, ah*ng*-fah*ng*ss, *f* childhood; infancy.

enfant, ah*ng*-fah*ng*, *mf* child; infant.

enfanter, ah*ng*-fah*ng*-teh, *v* to give birth to.

enfantillage, ah*ng*-fah*ng*-tee-yăh**sh**, *m* childishness.

enfantin, e, ah*ng*-fah*ng*-tang, *a* childish.

enfariner, ah*ng*-făh-re-neh, *v* to flour.

enfer, ah*ng*-fair, *m* hell.

enfermer, ah*ng*-fair-meh, *v* to shut in; to lock up; to enclose.

enfilade, ah*ng*-fe-lăhd, *f* row; line; long string.

enfiler, ah*ng*-fe-leh, *v* to thread; to string; to run through.

enfin, ah*ng*-fang, *adv* at last; finally; in short; on the whole; after all.

enflammer, ah*ng*-flăh-meh, *v* to set on fire; to rouse.

enfler, ah*ng*-fleh, *v* to swell; to inflate; to puff up.

enfoncé, ah*ng*-fong-seh, *pp & a* smashed in; sunk; done for.

enfoncer, ah*ng*-fong-seh, *v* to sink into; to drive in; to smash; to surpass.

enfouir, ah*ng*-foo-eer, *v* to bury; to hide in the ground.

enfourcher, ah*ng*-foohr-**sh**eh, *v* to straddle; to mount; to get on.

enfreindre, ah*ng*-frang-dr, *v* to infringe.

enfuir (s'), sah*ng*-fweer, *v* to run away; to vanish; to leak.

enfumer, ang-fE-meh, *v* to smoke out.

engagement, ah*ng*-gah**sh**-mah*ng m* engagement; contract; agreement; commitment.

engager, ah*ng*-găh-**sh**eh, *v* to engage; to pawn; to invite; to hire; **s'**–, to enlist; to undertake.

engelure, ah*ng***sh**-lEEr, *f* frostbite.

engendrer, ah*ng*-**sh**ah*ng*-dreh, *v* to beget; to engender; to father.

engin, ah*ng*-**sh**ang, *m* engine; machine; tackle.

englober, ah*ng*-glob-eh, *v* to lump together; to unite.

engloutir, ah*ng*-gloo-teer, *v* to swallow up; to engulf.

engloutissement, ah*ng*-gloo-tiss-mah*ng*, *m* swallowing up; sinking.

engorger, ah*ng*-gor-**sh**eh, *v* to obstruct; to block up.

engouement, ah*ng*-goo-

a b c d e f g h i j k l m n o p q r s t u v w x y z

mahng, *m* infatuation.

engouffrer, ahng-goo-freh, *v* to wolf down; to cram in.

engourdi, e, ahng-goohr-de, *pp* & *a* numbed; dull; torpid.

engrais, ahng-gray, *m* manure.

engraisser, ahng-grayss-eh, *v* to fatten; to fertilize.

engrener, ahng-grer-neh, *v* to throw into gear.

engueuler, ahng-gher-leh, *v (fam)* to scold; to blow up; to abuse.

enhardir, ahng-ăhr-deer, *v* to embolden.

énigme, eh-neegm, *f* enigma; riddle.

enivrer, ahng-ne-vrehh, *v* to intoxicate; to enrapture; **s'–,** to get drunk.

enjamber, ahng-shahng-beh, *v* to stride over.

enjeu, ahng-sher, *m* stake.

enjoindre, ahng-sho'ang-dr, *v* to enjoin; to order.

enjôler, ahng-shoh-leh, *v* to wheedle.

enjoliver, ahng-sholl-e-veh, *v* to embellish.

enjoué, e, ahng-shoo-eh, *a* playful; lively; sprightly.

enlacer, ahng-lăhss-eh, *v* to lace; to entwine; to interweave; to clasp; to

embrace.

enlaidir, ahng-lay-deer, *v* to disfigure; to grow ugly.

enlèvement, ahng-layv-mahng, *m* carrying away; removal; kidnapping.

enlever, ahngl-veh, *v* to lift; to take away; to run away with; to collect; to kidnap; **s'–,** to rise; to come off; to be sold.

ennemi, ain-me, *m* enemy.

ennemi, e, ain-me, *a* hostile; adverse.

ennoblir, ahng-nob-leer, *v* to ennoble.

ennui, ahng-nwe, *m* tediousness; boredom; annoyance;

ennuyer, ahng-nwee-yeh, *v* to worry; to tire; to annoy; to bore; **s'–,** to feel bored.

ennuyeu-x, se,* ahng-nwee-yer, *a* tiresome; annoying; vexing; bothering.

énoncer, eh-nong-seh, *v* to state; to articulate.

enorgueillir (s'), sahng-nor-gher-yeer, *v* to be proud.

énorme, eh-norm, *a* enormous; huge.

énormément, eh-nor-meh-mahng, *adv* enormously; *(fam)*

tremendously.

en phase terminale, ahng-fáliz-tair-me-năhl *a med* terminal illness.

en poudre, ahng-poo-dr, *a* dehydrated (milk, eggs, etc).

enquérir (s'), sahng-keh-reer, *v* to inquire.

enquête, ahng-kayt, *f* inquiry; inquest.

enraciner, ahng-răhss-e-neh, *v* to root.

enragé, e, ahng-răh-sheh, *a* mad; enraged; furious; desperate.

enrager, ahng-răh-sheh, *v* to be mad; to be in a rage; **faire –,** fair **–,** to drive mad.

enrayer, ahng-ray-yeh, *v* to stop; to jam; to check.

enregistrement, ahng-rer-shiss-trer-mahng, *m* registration; entry; recording (record, etc).

enregistrer, ahng-rer-shiss-treh, *v* to register; to record.

enrhumer (s'), sahng-rE-meh, *v* to catch a cold.

enrichi, e, ahng-re-she, *a* & *mf* upstart.

enrichir, ahng-re-sheer, *v* to enrich; to embellish.

enrôler, ahng-roh-leh, *v* to enroll; to enlist.

enroué, e, ahng-roo-eh, *a* hoarse.

enrouler, ahng-roo-leh, *v* to roll up.

ensanglanter, ahng-sahng-glahng-teh, *v* to stain with blood.

enseigne, ahng-sayn-yer, *m* ensign; midshipman; junior lieutenant; *f* neon sign; *pl* (flag) colors.

enseignement, ahng-sayn-yer-mahng, *m* teaching; instruction; tuition; education.

enseigner, ahng-sayn-yeh, *v* to teach; to inform; to direct.

ensemble, ahng-sahng-bl, *m* whole; ensemble; mass; general appearance; harmony; *adv* together; at the same time.

ensevelir, ahng-serv-leer, *v* to shroud; to bury.

ensoleillé, ahng-soll-ay-yeh, *a* sunny; sunlit.

ensorceler, ahng-sor-ser-leh, *v* to bewitch.

ensuite, ahng-sweet, *adv* afterwards; after; then; next.

ensuivre (s'), sahng-swee-vr, *v* to follow; to ensue.

entailler, ahng-tah'e-yeh, *v* to notch.

entamer, ahng-tăh-meh, *v* to make the first cut in; to begin.

entasser, ahng-tăhss-eh, *v* to pile up; to stack.

entendement, ahng-tahngd-mahng *m* understanding; sense; judgment.

entendre, ahng-tahng-dr, *v* to hear; to understand; to mean; **bien entendu,** be-ang n'ahng-tahng-dE, of course.

entente, ahng-tahngt, *f* understanding; sense; meaning.

enterrement, ahng-tair-mahng, *m* burial; funeral.

enterrer, ahng-tay-reh, *v* to bury; (*fam*) to outlive.

en-tête, ahng-tayt, *m* heading.

entêté, e, ahng-tay-teh, *a* obstinate; stubborn.

entêter, ahng-tay-teh, *v* to make giddy; **s'–,** to be obstinate.

enthousiasme, ahng-too-ze-ăhssm, *m* enthusiasm.

entier, ahng-te-eh, *m* entirety; whole.

enti-er, ère,* ahng-te-eh, *a* whole; perfect; full.

entonner, ahng-tonn-eh, *v* to strike up.

entonnoir, ahng-tonn-o'ăhr, *m* funnel.

entorse, ahng-torss, *f* sprain; strain; twist.

entortiller, ahng-tor-tee-yeh, *v* to twist; to wind; to entangle; to get round.

entourage, ahng-too-răhsh, *m* environment; setting; circle.

entourer, ahng-too-reh, *v* to surround (**de,** with).

entracte, ahng-trăhckt, *m* intermission.

entraider (s'), sahng-tray-deh, *v* to help one another.

entrailles, ahng-trah'e, *fpl* entrails; bowels; feelings.

entrain, ahng-trang, *m* spirits; life; animation.

entraînant, e, ahng-tray-nahng, *a* captivating; winning.

entraînement, ahng-train-mahng, *m* force; impulse; sway; training; coaching.

entraîner, ahng-tray-neh, *v* to carry away; to attract; to involve; to bring about; to train.

entraîneur, ahng-tray-ner, *m* trainer; coach.

entrant, ahng-trahng, *m* person coming in. *a* coming in; entering.

a
b
c
d
e
f
g
h
i
j
k
l
m
n
o
p
q
r
s
t
u
v
w
x
y
z

entrave, ah*ng*-trăhv, *f* impediment; *pl* fetters.

entre, ah*ng*-tr, *prep* between; among; into; in.

entrebâiller, ah*ng*-trer-bah'e-yeh, *v* to half-open; to set ajar.

entrechoquer (s'), sah*ng*-trer-shock-eh, *v* to clash.

entrecôte, ah*ng*-trer-koht, *f* steak (from ribs).

entrecouper, ah*ng*-trer-koo-peh, *v* to intercept; to intersect.

entrecroiser (s'), sah*ng*-trer-kro'ăh-zeh, *v* to intertwine.

entre-deux, ah*ng*-trer-der, *m* space between; insertion.

entrée, ah*ng*-treh, *f* entrance; admission; beginning; entry; entrée.

entrefaites, ah*ng*-trer-fayt, *fpl* **sur ces –,** sEEr say z' –, meanwhile.

entrelacement, ah*ng*-trer-lăhss-mah*ng*, *m* intertwining.

entrelardé, e, ah*ng*-trer-lăhr-deh, *pp* & *a* interlarded; streaky.

entremêler, ah*ng*-trer-may-leh, *v* to intermingle; **s' –,** to interpose.

entremets. ah*ng*-trer-may, *m* sweet; dessert.

entremetteur, ah*ng*-trer-met-er, *m* go-between.

entremettre (s'), sahng-trer-met-tr, *v* to intervene.

entrepont, ah*ng*-trer-pong, *m* steerage.

entreposer, ah*ng*-trer-poh-zeh, *v* to store; to put in warehouse.

entrepôt, ah*ng*-trer-poh, *m* warehouse.

entreprenant, e, ah*ng*-trer-prer-nah*ng*, *a* enterprising; pushing; bold; venturous.

entreprendre, ah*ng*-trer-prahng-dr, *v* to undertake; to contract for; to attempt.

entrepreneur, ah*ng*-trer-prer-ner, *m* contractor; builder; **–de pompes funèbres,** – der pong fE-nay-br, undertaker.

entreprise, ah*ng*-trer-preez, *f* enterprise; undertaking; contract; attempt.

entrer, ah*ng*-treh, *v* to enter (**dans, en,** into); to begin; to bring in; **faire –,** fair –, to show in.

entresol, ah*ng*-trer-sol, *m* mezzanine.

entretenir, ah*ng*-trert-neer, *v* to keep up; to maintain; to cherish; **s'–,** to converse; to keep fit.

entretien, ah*ng*-trer-te-ang, *m* upkeep; maintenance; conversation; interview.

entrevoir, ah*ng*-trer-vo'ăhr, *v* to have a glimpse of; to foresee.

entrevue, ah*ng*-trer-vE, *f* interview.

entrouvert, e, ah*ng*-troo-vair, *a* ajar; half-open.

entrouvrir, ah*ng*-troo-vreer, *v* to half-open.

énumérer, eh-nE-meh-reh, *v* to enumerate.

envahir, ah*ng*-văh-eer, *v* to invade; to encroach on; to overrun.

enveloppe, ah*ng*gv-lop, *f* wrapper; cover; envelope.

envelopper, ah*ng*gv-lop-eh, *v* to envelop; to wrap up; to cover.

envenimer, ah*ng*gv-ne-meh, *v* to poison; **s'–,** to fester.

envergure, ah*ng*-vair-ghEEr, *f* span; width.

envers, ah*ng*-vair, *prep* towards; to; *m* wrong side; **à l' –,** ăh l'–, inside out.

envi (à l'), ăh lahng-ve, *adv* in emulation (**de,** of).

envie, ahng-vee, *f* envy; inclination; wish.

envier, ahng-ve-eh, *v* to envy; to long for.

environ, ahng-ve-rong, *adv* about; *pl* environs; surroundings; outskirts; vicinity.

environner, ahng-ve-ronn-eh, *v* to surround.

envisager, ahng-ve-zăh-sheh, *v* to look at; to face; to consider.

envoi, ahng-vo'ăh, *m* sending; dispatch; consignment; goods; parcel; remittance.

envoler (s'), sahng-voll-eh, *v* to fly away.

envoyé, ahng-vo'ăh-yeh, *m* messenger; envoy.

envoyer, ahng-vo'ăh-yeh, *v* to send; to forward; to dispatch.

envoyer par télécopie, ahng-vo'ăh-yeh-păhr-teh-leh-ko-pee, *v* to fax.

épagneul, eh-păhn-yerl, *m* spaniel.

épais, se, eh-pay, *a* thick.

épaisseur, eh-payss-er, *f* thickness.

épaissir, eh-payss-eer, *v* to thicken.

épanchement, eh-pahngsh-mahng, *m* effusion; discharge.

épancher, eh-pahng-sheh, *v* to pour out; to vent; **s'** –, to overflow; to open one's heart.

épandre, eh-pahng-dr, *v* to spread; to scatter.

épanouir (s'), seh-păh-noo-eer, *v* to bloom; to open up; to light up.

épargne, eh-păhrn-yer, *f* economy; saving.

épargner, eh-păhrn-yeh, *v* to save; to spare; to have mercy on.

éparpiller, eh-păhr-pee-yeh, *v* to scatter.

épars, e, eh-păhr, *a* scattered; disheveled.

épatant, e, eh-păh-tahng, *a* (*fam*) wonderful; super; great.

épater, eh-păh-teh, *v* to flatten; (*fam*) to amaze.

épaule, eh-pohl, *f* shoulder.

épave, eh-păhv, *f* wreck; waif; remnant.

épée, eh-peh, *f* sword.

épeler, eh-pleh, *v* to spell (word).

éperdu, e, * eh-pair-dE, *a* distracted; aghast; desperate.

éperlan, eh-pair-lahng, *m* smelt.

éperon, eh-prong, *m* spur; buttress.

épervier, eh-pair-ve-eh, *m* hawk; casting net.

épi, eh-pe, *m* ear; spike; cluster.

épice, eh-peess, *f* spice; **pain d'**–, pang d –, gingerbread

épicerie, eh-peess-ree, *f* grocery; grocer's store.

épici-er, ère, eh-peess-e-eh, *mf* grocer.

épidémie, eh-pe-deh-mee, *f* epidemic.

épiderme, eh-pe-dairm, *m* epidermis.

épier, eh-pe-eh, *v* to spy; to watch.

épiler, eh-pe-leh, *v* to remove superfluous hair; to pluck (eyebrows).

épiloguer, eh-pe-logh-eh, *v* to carp.

épinards, eh-pe-năhr, *mpl* spinach.

épine, eh-peen, *f* thorn; spine.

epineu-x, se, eh-pe-ner, *a* thorny; prickly; ticklish.

épingle, eh-pang-gl, *f* pin; clothespin; **–de sûreté,** – der sEEr-teh, safety pin.

épingler, eh-pang-gleh, *v* to pin; to fasten with a pin.

épisode, eh-pe-zod, *m* episode.

a
b
c
d
e
f
g
h
i
j
k
l
m
n
o
p
q
r
s
t
u
v
w
x
y
z

épître, eh-pee-tr, *f* epistle.

éploré, e, eh-plor-eh, *a* in tears; weeping.

éplucher, eh-plE-sheh, *v* to pick; to peel; (*fam*) to examine.

épointer, eh-po'ang-teh, *v* to blunt.

éponge, eh-pongsh, *f* sponge.

éponger, eh-pong-sheh, *v* to sponge up; to mop.

épopée, eh-pop-eh, *f* epic poem.

époque, eh-pock, *f* epoch; time; date; period.

épouse, eh-pooz, *f* wife; spouse.

épouser, eh-poo-zeh, *v* to marry; to take up.

épousseter, eh-pooss-teh, *v* to dust.

épouvantable, * eh-poo-vahng-tăh-bl, *a* frightful; terrible.

épouvantail, eh-poo-vahng-tah'e, *m* scarecrow; (*fam*) bogeyman.

épouvante, eh-poo-vahngt, *f* fright; terror.

épouvanter, eh-poo-vahng-teh, *v* to frighten; to terrify.

époux, eh-poo, *m* husband; spouse; *pl* married couple.

éprendre (s'), seh-prahng-dr, *v* to fall in love (**de,** with).

épreuve, eh-prerv, *f* trial; test; proof; print (photo).

épris, e, eh-pre, *pp* & *a* taken; smitten.

éprouver, eh-proo-veh, *v* to try; to experience; to feel.

épuisement, eh-pweez-mahng, *m* draining; exhaustion.

épuisé, eh-pwee-zeh, *a* exhausted; tired out.

épuiser, eh-pwee-zeh, *v* to drain; to exhaust; to use up.

épurer, eh-pe-reh, *v* to purify; to refine.

équateur, eh-kwăh-ter, *m* equator.

équerre, eh-kair, *f* square set.

équestre, eh-kess-tr, *a* equestrian.

équilibre, eh-ke-lee-br, *m* equilibrium; poise; balance.

équipage, eh-ke-păhsh, *m* equipage; equipment; carriage; crew.

équipe, eh-keep, *f* gang; team; set; crew.

équipée, eh-ke-peh, *f* prank; lark.

équiper, eh-ke-peh, *v* to equip; to fit out.

équipement, eh-keep-mahng, *m* equipment; supplies; outfit.

équitable, * eh-ke-tăh-bl, *a* equitable; fair.

équitation, eh-ke-tăh-se-ong, *f* riding.

équité, eh-ke-teh, *f* equity.

équivalent, e, eh-ke-văh-lahng, *a* & *m* equivalent.

équivoque, eh-ke-vock, *f* ambiguity. *a* equivocal; dubious.

érable, eh-răh-bl, *m* maple.

éraflure, eh-răh-flEEr, *f* slight scratch.

éraillé, eh-rah'e-eh, *pp* & *a* frayed; bloodshot; hoarse.

ère, air, *f* era; epoch.

érection, eh-reck-se-ong, *f* raising; erection.

éreinté, e, eh-rang-teh, *a* tired out; harassed.

éreinter, eh-rang-teh, *v* to break the back of (horse); to exhaust; to criticize; **s'–,** to tire oneself out.

ergot, air-go, *m* spur (of cock, etc).

ermite, air-meet, *m* hermit.

errant, e, air-rahng, *a* wandering; roaming.

errer, air-reh, *v* to wander; to stray; to err.

erreur, air-**rer**, *f* error; mistake.

erroné, e, * air-ronn-eh, *a* erroneous.

escabeau, ess-kăh-boh, *m* stool; steps.

escadre, ess-kăh-dr, *f* squadron.

escadron, ess-kăh-dro*ng*, *m* squadron; **chef d'–,** shaif d–, major.

escalade, ess-kăh-lăhd, *f* scaling; climb.

escale, ess-kăhl, *f* port of call; stop over; touch down.

escalier, ess-kăh-le-eh, *m* stairs; staircase; steps.

escalope, ess-kăh-lop, *f* thin slice of meat (usually veal); escalope.

escamoter, ess-kăh-mot-eh, *v* to juggle; to filch.

escapade, ess-kăh-păhd, *f* prank; escapade.

escargot, ess-kăhr-go, *m* snail.

escarpé, e, ess-kăhr-peh, *a* steep; abrupt.

esclaffer (s'), sess-clăh-feh, *v* to shake with laughter.

esclandre, ess-klah*ng*-dr, *m* scandal; scene.

esclavage, ess-klăh-văh**sh**, *m* slavery.

esclave, ess-klăhv, *mf* slave; *a* slavish.

escompte, ess-ko*ng*t, *m* discount; rebate.

escompter, ess-ko*ng*-teh, *v* to discount; (*fam*) to expect.

escorter, ess-kor-teh, *v* to escort; to convoy; to accompany.

escouade, ess-koo-ăhd, *f* squad; gang.

escrime, ess-kreem, *f* fencing.

escrimer (s'), sess-kree-meh, *v* to endeavor; to try hard.

escroc, ess-kro, *m* swindler; crook.

escroquer, ess-krock-eh, *v* to swindle.

espace, ess-păhss, *m* space; room; infinity; vacancy.

espacer, ess-păhss-eh, *v* to space; to leave space between.

espadrille, ess-păh-dree-ye, *f* canvas shoe with rope sole.

espagnol, e, ess-păhn-yol, *a & mf* Spanish; Spaniard; *m* Spanish.

espalier, ess-păh-le-eh, *m* espalier.

espèce, ess-payss, *f* species; kind; sort; case; *pl* specie.

espérance, ess-peh-rah*ng*ss, *f* hope; expectation.

espérer, ess-peh-reh, *v* to hope; to expect; to trust.

espiègle, ess-pe-ay-gl, *a* frolicsome; mischievous.

espion, ess-pe-o*ng*, *m* spy.

espoir, ess-po'ahr, *m* hope; expectation.

esprit, ess-pre, *m* spirit; soul; ghost; mind; intellect; wit; feeling.

esquif, ess-keeff, *m* skiff.

esquinter, ess-kang-teh, *v* (*fam*) to exhaust; to smash; to ruin; to spoil.

esquisse, ess-keess, *f* sketch; outline.

esquiver, ess-ke-veh, *v* to avoid; to elude; **s'–,** to slip away.

essai, eh-say, *m* trial; attempt; essay; try; **coup d'–,** koo d–, first attempt.

essaim, eh-sa*ng*, *m* swarm; host.

essayer, eh-say-yeh, *v* to try; to try on; to attempt; **s'–,** to try one's skill (**à, dans,** at).

essence, eh-sah*ng*ss, *f* gasoline; spirits; essence.

essentiel, eh-sah*ng*-se-ell, *m* main thing.

essentiel, le, * eh-sah*ng*-se-ell, *a* essential.

essieu, eh-se-er, *m* axletree; axle.

essor, eh-sor, *m* flight;

scope; play; impulse.

essorer, eh-sor-eh, *v* to wring (clothes); to squeeze.

essoreuse, eh-sor-erz, *f* spin-dryer.

essouffler, eh-soo-fleh, *v* to make breathless.

essuie-glace, eh-swee-glăhss, *m* wiper.

essuie-mains, eh-swee-mang, *m* hand towel.

essuyer, eh-swee-yeh, *v* to wipe; to dry; to sustain; to go through.

est, esst, *m* east.

estampe, ess-tahngp, *f* print; engraving.

estampille, ess-tahng-pee-ye, *f* stamp; mark; trademark.

estimation, ess-tee-măh-se-*ong*, *f* estimate; valuation.

estime, ess-teem, *f* esteem; regard.

estimer, ess-tee-meh, *v* to estimate; to consider.

estomac, ess-tomm-ăh, *m* stomach.

estrade, ess-trăhd, *f* platform.

estragon, ess-trăh-gong, *m* tarragon.

estropier, ess-trop-e-eh, *v* to cripple; to maim.

esturgeon, ess-tEEr-shong, *m* sturgeon.

et, eh, *conj* and.

étable, eh-tăh-bl, *f* stable; cowshed. *m* bench.

établi, e, eh-tăh-ble, *pp* & *a* established.

établir, eh-tăh-bleer, *v* to establish; to set; to institute; to prove.

établissement, eh-tăh-bliss-mahng, *m* establishment; institution; setting up.

étage, eh-tăhsh, *m* story; floor.

étagère, eh-tăh-**shair**, *f* set of shelves; shelf.

étai, eh-tay, *m* stay; prop.

étain, eh-tang, *m* tin; pewter.

étalage, eh-tăh-lăhsh, *m* window display.

étaler, eh-tăh-leh, *v* to display; to spread out; to lay out; **s'–,** to sprawl; to show off; to fall down.

étalon, eh-tăh-long, *m* stallion; standard (of weights etc).

étamine, eh-tăh-meen, *f* sieve; stamen.

étanche, eh-tahngsh, *a* watertight.

étancher, eh-tahng-sheh, *v* to staunch; to make water-tight; to stop; to quench.

étang, eh-tahng, *m* pond; pool.

étape, eh-tăhp, *f* stopover; stage.

état, eh-tăh, *m* state; plight; profession; trade; list; statement; nation.

état-major, eh-tăh măh-**shor,** *m* staff; headquarters.

étau, eh-toh, *m* vice.

étayer, eh-tay-yeh, *v* to prop up.

été, eh-teh, *m* summer.

éteindre, eh-tang-dr, *v* to extinguish; to turn off (light, etc); **s'–,** to die out.

éteint, e, eh-tang, *pp* & *a* put out; extinct; faint.

étendard, eh-tahng-dăhr, *m* standard; flag.

étendre, eh-tahng-dr, *v* to extend; to spread; to stretch; to expand; **s'–,** to reach; to expatiate.

étendu, e, eh-tahng-dE, *pp* & *a* extended; spread; extensive.

étendue, eh-tahng-dEE, *f* extent.

éternel, le, * eh-tair-nell, *a* eternal; unending.

éternuer, eh-tair-nE-eh, *v* to sneeze.

éther, eh-tair, *m* ether.

étinceler, eh-tangss-leh, *v* to sparkle; to gleam.

étincelle, eh-tang-sell, *f* spark.

étioler (s'), seh-te-oll-eh, to grow emaciated.

étique, eh-teeck, *a* lean; hectic; emaciated.

étiquette, eh-te-kett, *f* label; tag; etiquette; ceremony.

étirer, eh-te-reh, *v* to stretch; to draw.

étoffe, eh-tof, *f* stuff; cloth; material.

étoile, eh-to'ăhl, *f* star; asterisk.

étole, eh-tol, *f* stole.

étonnant, eh-tonn-ahng, *a* astonishing; wonderful; surprising.

étonner, eh-tonn-eh, *v* to astonish; to astound; to surprise.

étouffer, eh-too-feh, *v* to suffocate; to stiffle; to smother; to choke; to hush up.

étourderie, eh-toohr-der-ree, *f* thoughtlessness; blunder.

étourdi, e, eh-toohr-de, *pp* & *a* stunned; heedless; scatterbrained; giddy.

étourdir, eh-toohr-deer, *v* to stun; to deafen; s'–, to escape from oneself.

étourdissant, e, eh-toohr-diss-ahng, *a* deafening.

étourdissement, eh-toohr-diss-mahng, *m* giddiness; stupefaction.

étourneau, eh-toohr-noh, *m* starling; scatterbrain.

étrange, * eh-trahngsh, *a* strange; odd; queer.

étranger, eh-trahng-sheh, *m* stranger; foreigner; foreign countries; à l'–, ăh l'–, abroad.

étrang-er, ère, eh-trahng-sheh, *a* strange; foreign.

étranglé, eh-trahng-gleh, *pp* & *a* strangled; narrow; tight.

étrangler, eh-trahng-gleh, *v* to strangle; to compress.

être, ay-tr, *v* to be; to exist; to belong; *m* being; existence; individual.

étreindre, eh-trang-dr, *v* to bind; to clasp; to grasp.

étreinte, eh-trangt, *f* fastening; grasp; embrace.

étrenne, eh-trenn, *f* (usually *pl*) New Year's gifts.

étrier, eh-tre-yeh, *m* stirrup; **le coup de l'–,** ler koo der l'–, stirrup cup.

étrille, eh-tree-ye, *f* currycomb.

étriqué, e, eh-tre-keh, *a* tight; skimpy.

étroit, e, * eh-tro'ăh, *a* narrow; tight; close; strict; à l'–, ăh l'–, cramped.

étroitesse, eh-tro'ăh-tess, *f* narrowness; tightness; closeness.

étude, eh-tEEd, *f* study; chambers; practice; survey; **faire ses –s à,** fair seh zeh-tEEd-ăh, to be educated at.

étudiant, eh-tE-de-ahng, *m* student.

étudier, eh-tE-de-eh, *v* to study; to observe; s' –, to endeavor (à, to).

étui, eh-twee, *m* case; box; sheath.

étuvée, eh-tE-veh, *f* braised; à l' –, ăhl –, steamed.

eucharistie, er-kăh-riss-tee, *f* Eucharist.

euphonie, er-fon-ee, *f* euphony.

euh! er, *interj* hum! well!

eux, er, *pron* them; they.

évacuer, eh-văh-kE-eh, *v* to evacuate; to vacate.

évader (s'), seh-văh-deh, *v* to escape; to get away.

évaluer, eh-văh-lE-eh, *v* to value; to estimate.

évangile, eh-vahng-sheel, *m* Gospel.

évanouir (s'), seh-văh-noo-eer, *v* to faint; to vanish.

A
B
C
D
E
F
G
H
I
J
K
L
M
N
O
P
Q
R
S
T
U
V
W
X
Y
Z

évanouissement, eh-văh-noo-iss-mah*ng*, *m* fainting; swoon.

évaporer (s'), seh-văh-por-eh, *v* to evaporate.

évasé, e, eh-vah-zeh, *pp* & *a* widened.

évasi-f, ve,* eh-vah-zeeff, *a* evasive.

évasion, eh-vah-se-o*ng*, *f* escape; flight.

éveil, eh-vay'e, *m* awakening; warning; **en –,** ah*ng* n'–, on the alert.

éveillé, e, eh-vay'e-yeh, *pp* & *a* awakened; wide awake; vigilant; alert.

éveiller, eh-vay'e-yeh, *v* to awaken.

événement, eh-venn-mah*ng*, *m* event; occurrence; issue.

éventail, eh-vah*ng*-tah'e, *m* fan.

éventer, eh-vah*ng*-teh, *v* to fan; to air; to make flat; **s' –,** to go flat.

éventrer, eh-vah*ng*-treh, *v* to rip up; to disembowel.

éventualité, eh-vah*ng*-tE-ăh-le-teh, *f* contingency; possibility.

éventuel, le,* eh-vah*ng*-tE-ell, *a* contingent; possible; eventual.

évêque, eh-vayk, *m* bishop.

évertuer (s'), seh-vair-tE-eh, *v* to exert oneself; to do one's utmost.

évidemment, eh-ve-dăh-mah*ng*, *adv* evidently; obviously.

évidence, eh-ve-dahng*ss, *f* evidence.

évident, e, eh-ve-dah*ng*, *a* evident; clear.

évider, eh-ve-deh, *v* to scoop out.

évier, eh-ve-eh, *m* sink.

évincer, eh-vang-seh, *v* to turn out; to oust.

éviter, eh-ve-teh, *v* to avoid; to dodge.

évolué, eh-vol-E-eh, *a* advanced;developed.

évolution, eh-voll-E-se-o*ng*, *f* evolution.

évoquer, eh-vock-eh, *v* to conjure up; to call up.

exact, e,* egg-zăhckt, *a* exact; accurate; true; punctual.

exaction, egg-zăhck-se-o*ng*, *f* extortion.

exactitude, egg-zăhck-te-tEEd, *f* exactness; accuracy; punctuality.

exagérer, egg-zăh-**sheh**-reh, *v* to exaggerate; to go too far.

exalté, e, egg-zăhl-teh, *pp* & *a* exalted; elated; enthusiastic; fanatic.

exalter, egg-zăhl-teh, *v* to

glorify; to praise; to excite.

examen, egg-zăh-mia*ng*, *m* examination; scrutiny.

examinateur, egg-zăh-me-năh-ter, *m* examiner.

examiner, egg-zăh-me-neh, *v* to examine; to inquire into.

exaspérer, egg-zăhss-peh-reh, *v* to exasperate; to provoke.

exaucer, egg-zoh-seh, *v* to hear; to grant.

excédent, eck-seh-dah*ng*, *m* surplus; excess.

excéder, eck-seh-deh, *v* to exceed; to exasperate.

excellemment, eck-say-lăh-mah*ng*, *adv* excellently.

excellence, eck-say-lahng*ss, *f* excellence.

excellent, e, eck-say-lah*ng*, *a* excellent.

exceller, eck-say-leh, *v* to excel.

excentrique,* eck-sah*ng*-treeck, *a* eccentric.

excepté, eck-sayp-teh, *prep* except.

excepter, eck-sayp-teh, *v* to except.

exception, eck-sayp-se-o*ng*, *f* exception.

excès, eck-say, *m* excess.

excessi-f, ve,* eck-sayss-eeff, *a* excessive;

exorbitant.

excitant, e, eck-se-tah*ng*, *a* exciting; stimulating.

excitation, eck-se-tăh-se-o*ng*, *f* excitement.

exciter, eck-se-teh, *v* to excite; to rouse.

exclamer (s'), secks-klăh-meh, *v* to exclaim.

exclure, ecks-klEEr, *v* to exclude.

exclusi-f, ve,* ecks-klE-zeeff, *a* exclusive.

exclusivité, ecks-klE-ze-ve-teh, *f* exclusiveness; sole rights.

excommunier, ecks-komm-E-ne-eh, *v* to excommunicate.

excroissance, ecks-kro'ăh-sah*ng*ss, *f* excrescence; growth.

excursion, ecks-kEEr-se-o*ng*, *f* excursion; tour; outing.

excuse, ecks-kEEz, *f* excuse; *pl* apology.

excuser, ecks-kE-zeh, *v* to excuse; **s'**–, to apologize; to decline (offer, etc).

exécrer, ecks-eh-kreh, *v* to loathe.

exécutant, egg-zeh-kE-tah*ng*, *m* performer.

exécuter, egg-zeh-kE-teh, *v* to execute; to perform; to carry out; to distrain; **s'**–, to yield.

exécution, egg-zeh-kE-se-o*ng*, *f* execution; performance; distraint.

exemplaire, egg-zah*ng*-plair, *m* copy. *a* exemplary.

exemple, egg-zah*ng*-pl, *m* example; instance; copy; **par** –, păhr –, for instance; *interj* really!

exempt, e, egg-zah*ng*, *a* exempt; exempted; free.

exempter, egg-zah*ng*-teh, *v* to exempt; to dispense.

exercer, egg-zair-seh, *v* to exercise; to train; to practice; to follow (a profession).

exercice, egg-zair-seess, *m* exercise; practice; fiscal year; drill.

exhaler, egg-zăh-leh, *v* to exhale; to vent.

exhausser, egg-zohss-eh, *v* to raise.

exhiber, egg-ze-beh, *v* to exhibit; to show.

exhorter, egg-zor-teh, *v* to exhort.

exhumer, egg-zE-meh, *v* to exhume; to bring to light.

exigeant, e, egg-ze-shah*ng*, *pp* & *a* exacting; hard to please.

exigence, egg-ze-**shah*ng*ss**, *f* exigency; demand.

exiger, egg-ze-**sheh**, *v* to exact; to demand; to insist upon.

exigu, ë, egg-ze-ghE, *a* scanty; small; slender.

exiguïté, egg-ze-ghE-e-teh, *f* scantiness.

exil, egg-zeel, *m* exile.

exiler, egg-ze-leh, *v* to exile; to banish.

existence, egg-ziss-tah*ng*ss, *f* existence; life; stock in hand.

exister, egg-ziss-teh, *v* to exist; to live.

exode, egg-zod, *m* exodus.

exonérer, egg-zonn-eh-reh, *v* to exonerate.

exorbitant, e, egg-zor-be-tah*ng*, *a* exorbitant.

exorciser, egg-zor-se-zeh, *v* to exorcise.

expansi-f, ve, ecks-păh*ng*-seeff, *a* expansive; exuberant; effusive.

expédient, ecks-peh-de-ah*ng*, *m* resource; *a* expedient; advisable.

expédier, ecks-peh-de-eh, *v* to post; to expedite; to dispatch; to draw up.

expéditeur, ecks-peh-de-ter, *m* sender; shipper; forwarding agent.

expéditi-f, ve, ecks-peh-de-teeff, *a* expeditious.

expédition, ecks-peh-de-se-o*ng*, *f* expedition;

a
b
c
d
e
f
g
h
i
j
k
l
m
n
o
p
q
r
s
t
u
v
w
x
y
z

forwarding; consignment; copy.

expérience, ecks-peh-re-ahngss, *f* experience; experiment.

expérimenter, ecks-peh-re-mahng-teh, *v* to experiment; to try; to test.

expert, ecks-pair, *m* expert; specialist; surveyor. *a* skilled; — **comptable,** – kong-tăh-bl, *m* certified accountant.

expertise, ecks-pair-teez, *f* valuation; survey.

expier, ecks-pe-eh, *v* to atone for.

expirer, ecks-pe-reh, *v* to expire; to breathe out; to die.

explicati-f, ve, ecks-ple-kăh-teeff, *a* explanatory.

explication, ecks-ple-kăh-se-ong, *f* explanation.

expliquer, ecks-ple-keh, *v* to explain; to construe; to account for.

exploit, ecks-plo'ăh, *m* deed; feat; writ.

exploitation, ecks-plo'ăh-tăh-se-ong, *f* working; cultivation; exploitation.

exploiter, ecks-plo'ăh-teh, *v* to work; to cultivate; to turn to account; to take advantage of.

exploiteur, ecks-plo'ăh-ter, *m* exploit; exploiter; (*fam*) swindler.

explorer, ecks-plor-eh, *v* to explore.

exploser, ecks-plo-zeh, *v* to explode; to blow up.

explosion, ecks-plo-ze-ong, *f* explosion; outbreak.

exportation, ecks-por-tăh-se-ong, *f* export.

exporter, ecks-por-teh, *v* to export.

exposant, ecks-po-zahng, *m* exhibitor; petitioner.

exposé, ecks-po-zeh, *m* statement; account.

exposer, ecks-po-zeh, *v* to expose; to exhibit; to explain.

exposition, ecks-po-ze-se-ong, *f* exposure; exhibition; statement.

exprès, ecks-pray, *adv* on purpose.

exprès, ecks-pray, *a & m* special delivery.

expr-ès, esse, ecks-pray, *a* express; explicit.

express, ecks-press, *m* express train. *a* express.

expression, ecks-prayss-e-ong, *f* expression; utterance; expressiveness.

exprimer, ecks-pre-meh, *v* to squeeze out; to express; **s' –,** to express oneself.

expulser, ecks-pEEl-seh, *v* to expel; to turn out.

exquis, e,* ecks-ke, *a* exquisite.

extase, ecks-tahz, *f* ecstasy.

extasier (s'), secks-tah-ze-eh, *v* to be enraptured.

exténuer, ecks-teh-nE-eh, *v* to extenuate; to exhaust.

extérieur, ecks-teh-re-er, *m* exterior; outside.

extérieur, e,* ecks-teh-re-er, *a* external; outward; foreign.

exterminer, ecks-tair-me-neh, *v* to destroy.

externe, ecks-tairn, *m* day student; non-resident medical student. *a* external.

extincteur, ecks-tangk-ter, *m* fire extinguisher.

extinction, ecks-tangk-se-ong, *f* extinction; suppression; paying off.

extirper, ecks-teer-peh, *v* to root out.

extorquer, ecks-tor-keh, *v* to extort.

extra, ecks-trăh, *m* extra. *a inv* extra special; first class.

extrader, ecks-trăh-deh, *v* to extradite.

extraire, ecks-trair, *v* to extract.

extrait, ecks-tray, *m* extract; abstract; certificate.

extraordinaire,* ecks-trǎh-or-de-nair, *a* unusual; extraordinary.

extravagant, ecks-trǎh-vǎh-gah*ng, a* extravagant; eccentric.

extrême,* ecks-traym, *a* extreme; utmost. *m* extreme limit.

extrémité, ecks-treh-me-teh, *f* extremity; end; last moments.

a
b
c
d
e
f
g
h
i
j
k
l
m
n
o
p
q
r
s
t
u
v
w
x
y
z

fable, făh-bl, *f* fable; story.

fabricant, făh bre-kah*ng*, *m* manufacturer.

fabrication, făh-bre-kăh-se-*ong*, *f* manufacturing; production.

fabrique, făh-breeck, *f* factory.

fabriquer, făh-bre-keh, *v* to manufacture; to make; to forge.

fabuleu-x, se,* făh-bE-ler, *a* fabulous.

façade, făhss-ăhd, *f* front; facade.

face, făhss, *f* face (of something); front; aspect; side; **en –,** ah*ng* –, opposite.

facétie, făh-seh-see, *f* facetiousness; jest.

facétieu-x, se,* făh-seh-se-*er*, *a* jocular.

fâché, fah-sheh, *a* sorry (**de,** for); angry (**contre,** with); on bad terms (**avec,** with).

fâcher, fah-sheh, *v* to offend; to grieve; to anger; **se –,** to take offense; to get angry.

fâcheu-x, se,* fah-sher, *a* grievous; troublesome; annoying; unfortunate.

facile,* făh-seell, *a* easy; fluent; ready.

facilité, făh-se-le-teh, *f* ease; fluency; readiness; *pl* abilities.

faciliter, făh-se-le-teh, *v* to facilitate.

façon, făh-song, *f* making; make; shape; manner; *pl* affectation.

façonner, făh-sonn-eh, *v* to shape; to form.

facteur, făhck-**ter,** *m* maker (of musical instruments); mailman; agent; factor.

factice, făhck-teess, *a* artificial.

factieu-x, se,* făhck-se-*er*, *a* factious; seditious.

factionnaire, făhck-se-onn-air, *m* sentry.

facture, făhck-tEEr, *f* invoice; bill.

facultati-f, ve,* făh-kEEl-tah-teeff, *a* optional.

faculté, făh-kEEl-teh, *f* faculty; power; right.

fadaise, făh-dayz, *f* drivel; nonsense.

fade, făhd, *a* insipid; flat; dull.

fagot, făh-go, *m* faggot; bundle.

fagoter, făh-got-eh, *v* to bundle up; to rig out; **se –,** to dress in a slovenly way.

faible, fay-bl, *m* weak spot; partiality. *a** weak; feeble; poor.

faiblesse, fay-bless, *f* weakness; deficiency; indulgence; fainting fit.

faiblir, fay-bleer, *v* to weaken; to relax.

faïence, făh-yahngss, *f* earthenware; crockery.

failli, fah'e-yee, *pp* & *a* fallen; bankrupt.

faillir, fah'e-yeer, *v* to err; to fail.

faillite, fah'e-yeet, *f* failure; bankruptcy; **faire – fair –,** to go bankrupt.

faim, fang, *f* hunger.

fainéant, e, fay-ney-ah*ng*, *mf* & *a* idler; idle; slothful.

faire, fair, *v* to make; to do; to be; to form; to arrange.

faire du jogging, fair-der-dsho-geng *v* jog.

faire-part, fair-par, *m* death notice; wedding announcement.

faisable, fer-zăh-bl, *a* feasible.

faisan, fer-zah*ng*, *m* pheasant.

faisandé, e, fer-zah*ng*-deh, *a* bad (flavor); gamy.

faisceau, fayss-oh, *m* bundle; pile.

faiseur, fer-zer, *m* maker; doer; jobber; fussy person.

fait, fay, *pp* & *a* made; done; full-grown; accustomed; dressed up; **c'est bien –,** say be-a*ng* –, serve (him, her, them, you, us, etc) right.

fait, fay, *m* fact; act; deed; doing; making; feat; **–s divers,** – de-vair,

miscellaneous news.

faîte, fayt, *m* summit; ridge.

faix, fay, *m* burden.

falaise, făh-layz, *f* cliff.

fallacieu-x, se,* făhl-lăh-se-er, *a* fallacious.

falloir, făh-lo'ăhr, *v* to be necessary; must; to be obliged; should; ought; to want; **il faut que je ...,** ill foh ker sher ..., I must; **il me faut,** ill mer foh, I want.

falot, făh-lo, *m* lantern.

falot, e, făh-lo, *a* colorless (pers); wan.

falsifier, făhl-se-fe-eh, *v* to counterfeit; to adulterate.

famé, e, făh-meh, *a* famed; **bien –,** be-a*ng* –, of good repute.

famélique, făh-meh-leeck, *a* starving.

fameu-x, se,* făh-mer, *a* famous; first-rate.

familiariser, făh-me-le-ăh-re-zeh, *v* to familiarize.

familier, făh-me-le-eh, *m* intimate; conversant (with, avec).

famili-er, ère,* făh-me-le-eh, *a* familiar.

famille, făh-mee-ye, *f* family; household.

famine, făh-meen, *f* famine; starvation.

fan, făhn, *mf* fan.

fanal, făh-năhl, *m* lantern; beacon.

fanatisme, făh-năh-tissm, *m* fanaticism.

faner, făh-neh, *v* to make hay; to wither; **se –,** to fade away.

faneur, făh-ner, *m* haymaker.

fanfare, fah*ng*-făhr, *f* flourish (of trumpets); brass band.

fanfaron, fah*ng*-făh-ro*ng*, *m* boaster; blusterer.

fange, fah*ng*sh, *f* mire; mud; dirt.

fanion, fah-ne-o*ng*, *m* flag.

fantaisie, fah*ng*-tay-zee, *f* imagination; whim.

fantasque, fah*ng*-tăhsk, *a* odd; whimsical.

fantassin, fah*ng*-tăhss-a*ng*, *m* infantryman.

fantastique,* fah*ng*-tass-teeck, *a* fantastic.

fantôme, fah*ng*-tohm, *m* phantom; specter; ghost.

faon, fah*ng*, *m* fawn.

farce, făhrss, *f* stuffing; farce; practical joke.

farcir, făhr-seer, *v* to stuff; to cram.

fard, făhr, *m* paint; rouge.

fardeau, făhr-doh, *m* burden; load.

farder, făhr-deh, *v* to paint; to make up.

a
b
c
d
e
f
g
h
i
j
k
l
m
n
o
p
q
r
s
t
u
v
w
x
y
z

A
B
C
D
E
F
G
H
I
J
K
L
M
N
O
P
Q
R
S
T
U
V
W
X
Y
Z

farfouiller, făhr-foo-yeh, *v* to rummage.

farine, făh-reen, *f* flour; meal.

farineu-x, se, făh-re-ner, *a* floury.

farouche, făh-roosh, *a* wild; fierce; sullen; shy.

fascicule, făhss-se-kEEl, *m* part; installment; booklet.

fasciner, făhss-se-neh, *v* to fascinate.

fastidieu-x, se,* făhss-te-de-er, *a* tedious.

fastueu-x, se,* făhss-tE-er, *a* pompous; ostentatious.

fatal, e,* făh-tăhl, *a* fatal; inevitable.

fatalisme, făh-tăh-lissm, *m* fatalism.

fatigant, e, făh-te-ghahng, *a* tiring; tedious.

fatigue, făh-teegh, *f* fatigue; stress; wear and tear.

fatiguer, făh-te-gheh, *v* to tire out; to annoy.

fatras, făh-trah, *m* clutter; hodgepodge.

fatuité, făh-tE-e-teh, *f* conceit.

faubourg, foh-boohr, *m* outskirt; suburb; quarter.

fauché, foh-sheh, *a* broke.

faucher, foh-sheh, *v* to mow; to cut; to reap (field, corn, etc); to mow down.

faucille, foh-see-ye, *f* sickle.

faucon, foh-kong, *m* falcon.

faufiler, foh-fe-leh, *v* to tack; to baste; to insert; se –, to creep in.

faune, fohn, *f* fauna.

faussaire, fohss-air, *m* forger.

fausser, fohss-eh, *v* to bend; to strain; to pervert; to falsify; to be out of tune; to distort; to sneak away.

fausset, fohss-ay, *m* spigot; falsetto.

fausseté, fohss-teh, *f* falseness; falsehood; insincerity.

faute, foht, *f* fault; error; mistake; lack; –de, – der, for want of.

fauteuil, foh-ter'e, *m* armchair; orchestra seat; rocking chair; wheelchair.

fauti-f, ve,* foh-teeff, *a* faulty; guilty.

fauve, fohv, *m* fawn color; wild beast; *a* tawny, buff.

fauvette, foh-vett, *f* warbler.

faux, foh, *adv* falsely; *m* falsehood; imitation; forgery.

fau-x, sse,* foh, *a* false; sham; base; bad; imitated.

faux, foh, *f* scythe.

faux-fuyant, foh-fwee-yahng, *m* evasion; subterfuge.

faveur, făh-ver, *f* favor; interest.

favorable,* făh-vor-ăh-bl, *a* favorable.

favori, te, făh-vor-e, *a* & *mf* favorite.

favoris, făh-vor-e, *mpl* sideburns.

favoriser, făh-vor-e-zeh, *v* to favor; to befriend; to aid.

fébrile, feh-breell, *a* feverish.

fécond, e, feh-kong, *a* fecund; fruitful; productive; teeming.

féconder, feh-kong-deh, *v* to fertilize.

fédéré, feh-deh-reh, *a* federated.

fée, feh, *f* fairy.

féerie, feh-ree, *f* fairytale; enchantment.

féerique, feh-reeck, *a* magical; enchanting.

feindre, fang-dr, *v* to feign; to pretend.

feint, e, fang, *pp* & *a* feigned; pretended; mock.

feinte, fangt, *f* pretense;

sham; dodge.

fêler, fay-leh, *v* to crack (glass, etc).

félicitation, feh-le-se-tăh-se-*ong, f* congratulation.

félicité, feh-le-se-teh, *f* happiness.

féliciter, feh-le-se-teh, *v* to congratulate; **se –,** to be pleased (**de,** with).

félin, e, feh-lang, *a* feline.

félon, feh-long, *m* traitor. *a* felonious; traitorous.

félonie, feh-lonn-ee, *f* treason.

félure, fay-lEEr, *f* crack; split.

femelle, fer-mell, *f* & *a* female.

féminin, feh-me-nang, *m* feminine gender.

féminin, e, feh-me-nang, *a* feminine; womanly.

femme, făhmm, *f* woman; wife; **–de chambre, –** der shahng-br, chambermaid; **–de charge, –** der shăhrsh, housekeeper; **–de ménage, –** der meh-năhsh, cleaning woman.

fémur, feh-mEEr, *m* thighbone; femur.

fenaison, fer-nay-zong, *f* haymaking.

fendre, fahng-dr, *v* to cleave; to split; to crack; to break through; **se –,**

to split; to lunge; to "fork out".

fendu, e, fahng-dE, *pp* & *a* slit; cracked.

fenêtre, fer-nay-tr, *f* window.

fente, fahngt, *f* split, crack; slot.

fer, fair, *m* iron; horseshoe; sword; *pl* fetters.

fer-blanc, fair-blahng, *m* tin plate.

ferblanterie, fair-blahngt-ree, *f* platemaking.

férié, e, feh-re-eh, *a* **jour –,shoo**r **–,** holiday (general); bank holiday.

fermage, fair-măhsh, *m* tenant farming.

ferme, fairm, *f* farm; farmhouse; farming.

ferme, fairm, *adv* firmly; hard. *a** firm; steady; strong; stiff.

ferment, fair-mahng, *m* leaven; ferment.

fermenter, fair-mahng-teh, *v* to ferment; to rise.

fermer, fair-meh, *v* to shut; to close; **–à clef, –** ăh kleh, to lock.

fermeté, fair-mer-teh, *f* firmness; steadfastness; strength.

fermeture, fair-mer-tEEr, *f* closing; shutting.

fermeture éclair, fair-mer-tEEr eh-klayr, *f* zipper.

fermi-er, ère, fair-me-eh, *mf* farmer.

fermoir, fair-mo'ăhr, *m* clasp.

féroce,* feh-ross, *a* ferocious; wild; very strict.

ferraille, fay-rah'e *f* scrap iron; old iron.

ferrailleur, fay-rah'e-yer, *m* scrap-iron dealer.

ferré, e, fay-reh, *pp* & *a* iron-shod; versed; skilled.

ferrer, fay-reh, *v* to bind with iron; to shoe; to metal.

ferrure, fay-rEEr, *f* metal hinge; horseshoes.

fertile, fayr-teel, *a* fertile; productive; eventful.

fervent, e, fair-vahng, *a* fervent.

ferveur, fair-ver, *f* fervor.

fesse, fayss, *f* buttock; bottom.

fessée, fayss-eh, *f* spanking.

fesser, fayss-eh, *v* to spank.

festin, fayss-tang, *m* feast; banquet.

feston, fayss-tong, *m* festoon.

fête, fayt, *f* feast; festivity; festival; saint's day;

birthday; holiday.

fêter, fay-teh, *v* to celebrate; to observe as a holiday; to welcome.

fétide, feh-teed, *a* fetid.

feu, fer, *m* fire; fireplace; passion; **–d'artifice, –** dăhr-te-fiss, fireworks.

feu, e, fer, *a* late; deceased.

feuillage, fer'e-yăhsh, *m* foliage.

feuille, fer'e, *f* leaf; sheet; paper.

feuilleter, fer'e-yer-teh, *v* to leaf through; to run through; to make puff pastry.

feuilleton, fer'e-yer-to*ng*, *m* serial installment; literary or scientific article; installment.

feutre, fer-tr, *m* felt; felt hat.

fève, fayv, *f* bean.

février, feh-vre-eh, *m* February.

fiacre, fe-ăh-kr, *m* horse-drawn carriage.

fiançailles, fe-ah*ng*-sah'e, *fpl* betrothal; engagement.

fiancé, e, fe-ah*ng*-seh, *mf* fiancé; fiancée.

fiancer (se), ser fe-ah*ng*-seh, *v* to become engaged.

fibre, fee-br, *f* fiber;

feeling; constitution.

ficeler, fis-leh, *v* to tie up.

ficelle, fe-sell, *f* string; twine; (*fam*) dodge; trick; long thin loaf of bread.

fiche, feesh, *f* label; slip; index card; peg.

ficher, fee-sheh, *v* to drive in; to fix; to put; to give; **se –,** (*fam*) not to care less (**de,** about).

fichu, fee-shE, *m* small shawl; scarf.

fichu, e, fee-shE, *a* (*pop*) wretched; got up; done for.

ficti-f, ve,* fick-teeff, *a* fictitious.

fiction, fick-se-o*ng*, *f* invention; fiction.

fidèle,* fe-dell, *a* faithful; true; exact; *m* believer.

fidélité, fe-deh-le-teh, *f* fidelity; loyalty.

fiel, fe-ell, *m* gall; bitterness; hatred.

fiente, fe-ah*ng*t, *f* droppings.

fier (se), ser fe-eh, *v* to trust; to count on.

fi-er, ère,* fe-air, *a* proud; haughty.

fierté, fe-air-teh, *f* pride; dignity.

fièvre, fe-ay-vr, *f* fever; restlessness; excitement; **avoir de la –,** ăh-vo'ăhr

der lăh –, to have a temperature.

fifre, fee-fr, *m* fife player.

figer, fe-sheh, *v* to congeal; to curdle.

figue, feeg, *f* fig.

figuier, fe-ghe-eh, *m* fig tree.

figurant, fe-ghE-rah*ng*, *m* walk-on actor; extra.

figure, fe-ghEEr, *f* figure; form; face; countenance.

figuré, e, fe-ghE-reh, *a* figurative.

figurer, fe-ghE-reh, *v* to figure; to represent; **se –,** to imagine.

fil, feel, *m* thread; yarn; wire; edge; grain; current.

filament, fe-lăh-mah*ng*, *m* filament; thread; string.

filandreu-x, se, fe-lah*ng*-drer, *a* stringy; tough; longwinded.

filant, e, fe-lah*ng*, *a* shooting (stars).

file, feel, *f* file; row; line.

filer, fe-leh, *v* to spin; to shadow; to run; to slip away; pay out.

filet, fe-lay, *m* thread; net; snare; fillet; trickle.

filial, e,* fe-le-ăhl, *a* filial.

filiale, fe-le-ăhl, *f* subsidiary company.

filigrane, fe-le-grăhn, *m* filigree; watermark.

fille, fee-ye, *f* girl; maid; daughter; servant; **petite –,** per-teet –, granddaughter.

filleul, e fee-yerl, *mf* godson; goddaughter.

film, feelm, *m* film; movie.

filon, fe-long, *m* lode; vein.

filou, fe-loo, *m* pickpocket; crook; cheat.

filouter, fe-loo-teh, *v* to cheat.

fils, feess, *m* son; **petit –,** per-te –, grandson.

filtre, feel-tr, *m* filter; percolator; **bout –,** boo –, filter-tip.

filtrer, feel-treh, *v* to filter; to strain.

fin, fang, *f* end; close; aim; purpose.

fin, e,* fang, *a* fine; thin; refined; sly; sharp (financier).

final, e,* fe-nǎhl, *a* final.

finance, fe-nahngss, *f* finance.

financer, fe-nahngss-eh, *v* to lay out money.

financier, fe-nahngss-e-eh, *m* financier.

financi-er, ère,* fe-nahngss-e-eh, *a* financial.

finaud, e, fe-noh, *a* cunning.

finesse, fe-ness, *f* fineness; nicety; delicacy; acuteness.

fini, fe-ne, *m* finish.

fini, e, fe-ne, *pp & a* finished; consummate; finite.

finir, fe-neer, *v* to finish; to put an end to.

fiole, fe-ol, *f* phial; flask.

firmament, feer-mǎh-mahng, *m* firmament.

fisc, feessk, *m* treasury; IRS.

fissure, feess-EEr, *f* fissure; crack.

fixation, feek-sǎh-se-ong, *f* fastening.

fixe,* feeks, *a* steady; firm; regular.

fixer, feek-seh, *v* to fix; to determine; to set.

fixité, feek-se-teh, *f* unchangeableness; stability.

flacon, flǎh-kong, *m* flask; small bottle; perfume bottle.

flageoler, flǎh-sholl-eh, *v* to shake; to tremble.

flageolet, flǎh-sholl-ay, *m* flageolet; small kidney bean.

flagrant, e, flǎh-grahng, *a* flagrant; **en –délit,** ahng – deh-le, in the very act.

flair, flayr, *m* scent; flair.

flamant, flǎh-mahng, *m* flamingo.

flambeau, flahng-boh, *m* torch; light.

flamber, flahng-beh, *v* to flame; to singe; to blaze.

flamboyer, flahng-bo'ǎh-e-eh, *v* to flare up; to glow.

flamme, flǎhmm, *f* flame.

flammèche, flǎh-maish, *f* spark; flake.

flan, flahng, *m* custard tart; flan.

flanc, flahng, *m* flank; side.

flancher, flahng-sheh, *v* to flinch; to give in.

flâner, flah-neh, *v* to lounge; to hang about.

flanquer, flahng-keh, *v* to flank; to throw; to hit.

flaque, flǎhck, *f* puddle.

flasque, flǎhssk, *a* flabby; weak.

flatter, flǎh-teh, *v* to flatter; to pat; to fawn upon.

flatteu-r, se,* flǎh-ter, *mf* flatterer. *a* flattering.

flatuosité, flǎh-tE-o-ze-teh, *f* flatulency.

fléau, fleh-oh, *m* scourge; curse; beam; bar.

flèche, flaish, *f* arrow; beam; spire.

fléchir, fleh-sheer, *v* to bend; to give way; to bow; to fall.

fléchissement, fleh-shiss-

mahng, *m* bending;
giving way.

flegme, flegm, *m*
composure; impassivity.

flemme, flem, *f* laziness.

flétrir, fleh-treer, *v* to
wither; to fade; to
brand; **se –,** to fade.

flétrissure, fleh-triss-EEr, *f*
withering; stigma.

fleur, fler, *f* flower;
blossom; prime; **à –de,**
ăh – der, on the surface
of.

fleurette, fler-rett, *f* small
flower; sweet nonsense.

fleurir, fler-reer, *v* to
flower; to bloom; to
thrive; to adorn with
flowers.

fleuve, flerv, *m* river.

flexion, fleck-se-ong, *f*
bending.

flirter, fleer-teh, *v* to flirt.

flocon, flock-ong, *m* flake;
flock.

floraison, flor-ay-zong, *f*
flowering; blooming.

florissant, e, flor-iss-ahng,
a flourishing.

flot, flo, *m* wave; stream;
crowd; floating.

flottant, e, flot-ahng, *a*
floating; wavering.

flotte, flot, *f* fleet; float;
(*fam*) water; rain.

flotter, flot-eh, *v* to float;
to waft; to waver; (*fam*)

to rain.

flou, e, floo, *a* hazy.

fluctuer, flEEk-tE-eh, *v* to
fluctuate.

fluet, te, flE-ay, *a* slender;
thin.

fluide, flE-eed, *m* & *a*
fluid.

flûte, flEEt, *f* flute; long
loaf of bread; tall
champagne glass.

flux, flE, *m* flux; flow.

fluxion, flEEk-se-ong, *f*
inflammation; swelling.

foi, fo'ăh, *f* faith; trust;
belief.

foie, fo'ăh, *m* liver.

foin, fo'ang, *m* hay.

foire, fo'ăhr, *f* fair.

fois, fo'ăh, *f* time;
occasion; **une –,**EEn –,
once; **à la –,** ăh lăh –, at
once; both.

foison, fo'ăh-zong, *f*
plenty; **à –,** ăh –,
abundantly.

foisonner, fo'ăh-zonn-eh,
v to abound.

fol, fol, *a* (see **fou**).

folâtre, foll-ah-tr, *a*
playful; frolicsome.

folâtrer, foll-ah-treh, *v* to
play around.

folie, foll-ee, *f* madness;
extravagance; mania.

folio, foll-e-o, *m* folio.

folle, fol, *f* (see **fou**).

follet, foll-ay, *a* merry; **feu**

–, fer –, will o' the wisp.

foncé, e, fong-seh, *a* dark
(color).

foncer, fong-seh, *v* to
deepen; to sink; to dash;
to rush (**sur,** at).

fonci-er, ère, fong-se-eh, *a*
landed; thorough;
fundamental.

foncièrement, fong-se-air-
mahng, *adv* thoroughly;
fundamentally.

fonction, fongk-se-ong, *f*
function; *pl* office;
duties.

fonctionnaire, fongk-se-
onn-air, *m* official; civil
servant.

fonctionner, fongk-se-
onn-eh, *v* to work; to
function.

fond, fong, *m* bottom;
foundation; depth;
ground; substance; **à –,**
ăh –, thoroughly.

fondamental, e,* fong-
dăh-mahng-tăhl, *a*
fundamental.

fondant, fong-dahng, *m*
fondant candy.

fondant, e, fong-dahng, *a*
melting.

fonda-teur, trice, fong-
dăh-ter, *mf* & *a* founder.

fondé, e, fong-deh, *pp* & *a*
founded; justified; **–de**
pouvoir, – der poo-
vo'ăhr, proxy.

fondement, fongd-mahng, *m* foundation; ground.

fonder, fong-deh, *v* to found; to build; to establish; **se –,** to be based on; to rely.

fonderie, fongd-ree, *f* foundry.

fondeur, fong-der, *m* founder.

fondre, fong-dr, *v* to melt; to cast; to disappear; to pounce.

fondrière, fong-dree-air, *f* quagmire; bog.

fonds, fong, *m* land; property; fund; funds; cash; *pl* securities; **–de commerce,** – der komm-airss, business.

fontaine, fong-tain, *f* fountain; spring; cistern.

fonte, fongt, *f* melting; casting; cast iron; holster.

fonts, fong, *mpl* font; **–baptismaux,** – băh-tiss-moh, christening font.

football, footbăhl; *m* soccer.

for, for, *m* **–intérieur,** – ang-teh-re-er, conscience.

forain, e, for-ang, *a* foreign; traveling (of theater, fair, etc).

forban, for-bahng, *m* pirate.

forçat, for-săh, *m* convict.

force, forss, *a* plenty of. *f* strength; power.

forcé, e, for-seh, *pp & a* forced; **travaux –s,** trăh-voh –, penal servitude.

forcément, for-seh-mahng, *adv* forcibly; necessarily.

forcené, e, for-ser-neh, *mf & a* mad; furious.

forcer, for-seh, *v* to force; to break open; to compel.

forer, for-eh, *v* to bore; to drill.

forestier, for-ayss-te-eh, *m* forester.

foret, for-ay, *m* drill; borer.

forêt, for ay, *f* forest.

forfait, for-fay, *m* crime; forfeit; contract; **à –,** ăh –, by contract.

forfanterie, for-fahng-tree, *f* bragging.

forge, forsh, *f* forge; ironworks.

forger, for-sheh, *v* to forge; to hammer; to make up; **se –,** to earn.

forgeron, for-sher-rong, *m* blacksmith.

formaliser (se), ser for-măh-le-zeh, to take offense (**de,** at).

formalité, for-măh-le-teh, *f* formality; ceremony.

format, for-măh, *m* size.

formation, fo-măh-se-ong, *f* formation; structure.

forme, form, *f* form; shape; mold; *pl* manners.

formel, le,* for-mell, *a* formal; express.

former, for-meh, *v* to form; to train; **se –,** to take form.

formidable, for-me-dăhbl, *a* fearsome; (*fam*) tremendous.

formulaire, for-mE-lair, *m* form.

formule, for-mEEl, *f* formula; prescription; form.

formuler, for-mE-leh, *v* to draw up.

fort, for, *adv* very; extremely. *m* strongest part; thickest; height; fort; forte.

fort, e,* for, *a* strong; stout; clever; thick; loud; severe; hard.

forteresse, fort-rayss, *f* fortress.

fortifiant, e, for-te-fe-ahng, *a* strengthening; tonic.

fortifier, for-te-fe-eh, *v* to strengthen; to fortify.

fortuit, e,* for-twee, *a* accidental; fortuitous.

fortune, for-tEEn, *f* fortune; chance; luck.

fortuné, e, for-tE-neh, *a*

a
b
c
d
e
f
g
h
i
j
k
l
m
n
o
p
q
r
s
t
u
v
w
x
y
z

fortunate; well-off.

fosse, fohss, *f* pit; hole; grave.

fossé, fohss-eh, *m* ditch.

fossette, fohss-ett, *f* dimple.

fossile, foss-eell, *m* & *a* fossil.

fossoyeur, fohss-o'ăh-yer, *m* gravedigger.

fou, folle, foo, fol, *mf* lunatic; fool; bishop (chess); *a* * crazy; mad; foolish. (Before a masculine noun beginning with a vowel or **h** mute, the masculine is **fol,** fol, instead of **fou**).

foudre, foo-dr, *f* lightning; thunderbolt; thunder; **coup de** –, coo der –, love at first sight.

foudroyant, e, foo-dro'ăh-yahng, *a* crushing; startling.

foudroyé, foo-dro'ăh-yeh, *pp* & *a* thunderstruck.

foudroyer, e, foo-dro'ăh-yeh, *v* to strike by lightning.

fouet, foo-ay, *m* whip; flogging.

fouetter, foo-ay-teh, *v* to whip; to flog; to lash; to whisk.

fougère, foo-shair, *f* fern.

fougue, foogh, *f* fire;

impetuosity; spirit.

fouille, foo'e-ye, *f* excavation; digging.

fouiller, foo'e-yeh, *v* to excavate; to dig; to search; to rummage.

fouillis, foo'e-yee, *m* confusion; jumble.

fouine, foo-een, *f* marten.

foulant, e, foo-lahng, *a* pressing.

foulard, foo-lăhr, *m* silk handkerchief.

foule, fool, *f* crowd; throng; mob.

fouler, foo-leh, *v* to press; to tread; to trample; to sprain.

foulure, foo-lEEr, *f* sprain.

four, foohr, *m* oven; kiln; furnace; (*fig*) failure.

fourbe, foohrb, *m* cheat; *a* tricky; deceitful.

fourberie, foohr-ber-ree, *f* cheat; trickery.

fourbir, foohr-beer, *v* to furbish.

fourbu, e, foohr-bE, *a* foundered; tired out.

fourche, foohrsh, *f* fork; pitchfork.

fourcher, foohr-sheh, *v* to branch off; to dig with pitchfork.

fourchette, foohr-shett, *f* fork (utensil); wishbone.

fourchu, e, foohr-shE, *a* forked; split.

fourgon, foohr-gong, *m* van; wagon; hearse.

fourgonner, foohr-gonn-eh, *v* to poke; to rake.

fourmi, foohr-me, *f* ant; **avoir des –s,** ah-vo'ăhr deh –, to have pins and needles in one's legs.

fourmilière, foohr-me-le-air, *f* anthill.

fourmiller, foohr-mee-yeh, *v* to teem; to swarm (**de,** with).

fourneau, foohr-noh, *m* stove; furnace; boiler.

fournée, foohr-neh, *f* ovenful; batch; lot.

fourni, e, foohr-ne, *pp* & *a* furnished; thick.

fournir, foohr-neer, *v* to supply; to provide; to stock.

fournisseur, foohr-niss-er, *m* supplier; tradesman.

fourniture, foohr-ne-tEEr, *f* supply; *pl* fittings; supplies.

fourrage, foo-răhsh, *m* fodder.

fourré, foo-reh, *m* thicket.

fourré, foo-reh, *a* lined; fur-lined; filled (of chocolates, etc).

fourreau, foo-roh, *m* sheath; scabbard; cover; tight-fitting dress.

fourrer, foo-reh, *v* to stuff; to cram; to line with fur.

fourreur, foo-**rer,** *m* furrier.

fourrière, foo-re-**air,** *f* pound.

fourrure, foo-**rEEr,** *f* fur.

fourvoyer, foohr-vo'ăh-yeh, *v* to lead astray.

foyer, fo'ăh-yeh, *m* hearth; home; center; foyer.

frac, frăhck, *m* tailcoat.

fracas, frăh-kah, *m* noise; din; crash; roar; fuss.

fracasser, frăh-kăhss-eh, *v* to shatter; to smash.

fraction, frăhck-se-o*ng*, *f* fraction.

fractionner, frăhck-se-onn-eh, *v* to divide into fractions.

fracture, frăhck-**tEEr,** *f* fracture; breaking.

fracturer, frăhck-**tE**-reh, *v* to fracture; to break.

fragile,* frăh-**sheel,** *a* fragile; brittle; frail.

fragilité, frăh-**she**-le-teh, *f* brittleness; frailty.

fragment, frăhg-mah*ng*, *m* fragment; piece; scrap.

frai, fray, *m* spawn; spawning.

fraîcheur, fray-sher, *f* freshness.

fraîchir, fray-sheer, *v* to freshen.

frais, fray, *mpl* expenses; charges; efforts.

frais, fraîche,* fray; fraysh, *a* fresh; cool; new.

fraise, frayz, *f* strawberry.

framboise, frah*ng*-bo'ăhz, *f* raspberry.

franc, frah*ng*, *m* franc.

franc, franche,* frah*ng*, frah*ng*sh, *a* free; open; frank; genuine.

français, e, frah*ng*-sseh, *a* French. *mf* Frenchman; Frenchwoman; *m* French language.

franchir, frah*ng*-sheer, *v* to clear; to leap over; to overstep; to overcome.

franchise, frah*ng*-sheez, *f* freedom; openness; exemption.

franciser, frah*ng*-se-zeh, *v* to gallicize.

franco, frah*ng*-ko, *adv* free of charge; paid.

frange, frah*ng*sh, *f* fringe.

franglais, frah*ng*-gleh, *m* mixture of French and English.

franquette, frah*ng*-kett, *f*; **à la bonne –,** ăh lăh bonn –, without ceremony.

frappant, e, frăh-pah*ng*, *a* striking.

frapper, frăh-peh, *v* to strike; to knock; to rap; to ice; **se –,** to get flustered.

fraternel, le,* frăh-tair-nell, *a* brotherly; fraternal.

fraterniser, frăh-tair-ne-zeh, *v* to fraternize.

fraternité, frăh-tair-ne-teh, *f* brotherhood; fraternity.

fraude, frohd, *f* fraud; deceit; smuggling.

frauder, froh-deh, *v* to defraud; to smuggle.

frauduleu-x, se,* froh-dE-ler, *a* fraudulent.

frayer, fray-yeh, *v* to open up; to clear a path; to spawn.

frayeur, fray-yer, *f* fright; dread; terror.

fredaine, frer-dayn, *f* prank; escapade.

fredonner, frer-donn-eh, *v* to hum.

frégate, freh-găht, *f* frigate; frigate bird.

frein, fra*ng*, *m* bit; bridle; brake; check.

freiner, freh-neh, *v* to brake; to put on the brakes.

frelater, frer-lăh-teh, *v* to adulterate.

frêle, frehl, *a* weak; frail.

frelon, frer-lo*ng*, *m* hornet; drone.

frémir, freh-meer, *v* to shudder; to tremble; to rustle; to simmer.

a
b
c
d
e
f
g
h
i
j
k
l
m
n
o
p
q
r
s
t
u
v
w
x
y
z

frémissement, freh-miss-mahng, *m* shuddering; quivering, rustling.

frêne, frain, *m* ash tree.

frénésie, freh-neh-zee, *f* frenzy.

frénétique,* freh-neh-teeck, *a* frantic.

fréquemment, freh-kăh-mahng, *adv* frequently.

fréquence, freh-kahngss, *f* frequency; quickness.

fréquent, e, freh-kahng, *a* frequent.

fréquenter, freh-kahng-teh, *v* to frequent; to associate with.

frère, frair, *m* brother; friar.

fresque, fressk, *f* fresco.

fret, fray, *m* freight; chartering.

fréter, freh-teh, *v* to charter; to freight.

frétiller, freh-tee-yeh, *v* to frisk; to wriggle; to quiver.

freux, frer, *m* rook.

friable, fre-ăh-bl, *a* crumbly.

friand, e, fre-ahng, *a* fond of delicacies.

friandise, fre-ahng-deez, *f* delicacy; tidbit.

fricandeau, fre-kahng-doh, *m* larded veal.

fricassée, fre-kăhss-eh, *f* fricassée.

fricasser, fre-kăhss-eh, *v* to fricassee; (*pop*) to fritter away.

friche, freesh, *f* wasteland.

fricot, fre-ko, *m* (*pop*) stew.

fricoter fre-kot-eh, *v* (*pop*) to cook.

friction, frick-se-ong, *f* friction; rub down.

frictionner, frick-se-onn-eh, *v* to rub.

frigidaire, fre-she-dair, *m* refrigerator.

frigide, fre-**sh**eed, *a* frigid.

frigorifier, fre-gor-e-fe-eh, *v* to chill; to refrigerate.

frileu-x, se,* fre-ler, *a* chilly; sensitive to cold.

frime, freem, *f* sham.

frimousse, fre-mooss, *f* (*fam*) face.

fringale, frang-găhl, *f* sudden hunger.

fringant, e, frang-ghang, *a* frisky; smart; lively.

fripé, e, fre-peh, *pp* & *a* rumpled.

friper, fre-peh, *v* to rumple; to crease.

fripi-er, ère, fre-pe-eh, *mf* secondhand clothes dealer.

fripon, ne, fre-pong, *mf* & *a* rogue; rascal; mischievous; roguish.

frire, freer, *v* to fry.

frise, freez, *f* frieze.

friser, free-zeh, *v* to curl; to touch; to skim; to border upon.

frisson, friss-ong, *m* shiver; shudder; thrill.

frissonner, friss-onn-eh, *v* to shiver; to quiver; to shudder.

frit, e, free, *pp* & *a* fried; (*pop*) done for; squandered.

friture, free-tEEr, *f* frying; dripping; fried fish; crackling noises (of telephone, etc).

frivole, free-vol, *a* frivolous.

froc, frock, *m* frock (of monk, etc).

froid, fro'ăh, *m* cold; coldness.

froid, e,* fro'ăh, *a* cold; cool; indifferent.

froideur, fro'ăh-der, *f* coldness; coolness; indifference.

froissement, fro'ăhss-mahng, *m* bruising; rumpling; offense.

froisser, fro'ăhss-eh, *v* to rumple; to offend; se –, to take offense (**de,** at).

frôlement, frohl-mahng, *m* light rubbing or touching.

frôler, froh-leh, *v* to touch slightly; to graze.

fromage, from-ăh**sh**, *m*

cheese.

froment, from-ahng, *m* wheat.

froncer, frongss-eh, *v* to pucker; to frown; to gather.

fronde, frongd, *f* sling; catapult.

fronder, frongd-eh, *v* to jeer at.

front, frong, *m* forehead; brow; impudence; front; **faire–,** fair–, to face.

frontière, frong-te-air, *f* frontier; border.

fronton, frong-tong, *m* pediment.

frottement, frot-mahng, *m* rubbing; friction.

frotter, frot-eh, *v* to rub; to polish.

frottoir, frot-o'ăhr, *m* rubbing cloth; scrubbing brush.

frou-frou, froo-froo, *m* rustling.

frousse, froos, *f* (*fam*) fear; **avoir la –,** ăh-vo'ăhr-lăh –, to be scared.

fructifier, frEEk-te-fe-eh, *v* to bear fruit.

fructueu-x, se,* frEEk-tE-er, *a* fruitful; profitable.

frugal, e,* frE-ghăl, *a* frugal.

fruit, frwee, *m* fruit; offspring; profit.

fruiti-er, ère, frwee-te-eh,

mf fruitseller. *a* fruit-bearing.

frusques, frEEsk, *fpl* (*fam*) clothes; effects; gear.

fruste, frEEst, *a* crude; defaced.

frustrer, frEEs-treh, *v* to frustrate; to defraud.

fugiti-f, ve, fE- she-teeff, *a* fugitive; transient.

fugue, fEEgh, *f* fugue; spree.

fuir, fweer, *v* to flee; to shun; to leak; to escape.

fuite, fweet, *f* flight; escape; evasion; leakage.

fulgurant, e, fEEl-ghE-rahng, *a* flashing.

fumée, fE-meh, *f* smoke; fume.

fumer, fE-meh, *v* to smoke; to steam; to fertilize.

fumet, fE-may, *m* pleasant smell of cooking; scent; bouquet.

fumier, fE-me-eh, *m* manure; manure heap.

fumiger, fE-me-sheh, *v* to fumigate.

fumiste, fE-meesst, *m* heating engineer; (*fam*) lazy person; fraud.

fumivore, fE-me-vor, *a* smoke-absorbing.

fumoir, fE-mo'ăhr, *m* smokehouse.

funambule, fe-nahng-bEEl,

m tightrope walker.

funèbre, fE-nay-br, *a* funeral; mournful; dismal.

funérailles, fE-neh-rah'e, *fpl* funeral.

funeste, fE-naysst *a* fatal; disastrous.

funiculaire, fE-ne-kE-lair, *m* & *a* funicular.

fur, fEEr, *m* **au –et à mesure,** oh – eh ăh merzEEr, in proportion; gradually as.

furet, fE-ray, *m* ferret.

fureter, fEEr-teh, *v* to ferret out; to rummage.

fureur, fE-rer, *f* fury; rage; mania; **faire–,** fair – to be all the rage.

furibond, e, fE-re-bong, *a* furious.

furie, fE-ree, *f* fury; rage.

furieu-x, se,* fE-re-er, *a* furious; mad; raging.

furoncle, fE-rong-kl, *m* boil.

furti-f, ve,* fEEr-teeff, *a* furtive; stealthy.

fusain, fE-zang, *m* spindle tree; charcoal pencil.

fuseau, fE-zoh, *m* spindle; taper; *pl* skiing pants.

fusée, fE-zeh, *f* fuse; rocket.

fuselage, fEEz-lăhsh, *m* fuselage; body.

fuselé, e, fEEz-leh, *a*

A
B
C
D
E
F
G
H
I
J
K
L
M
N
O
P
Q
R
S
T
U
V
W
X
Y
Z

tapering.

fusible, fE-zee-bl, *a* fusible.

fusible, fE-zee-bl, *m* fuse.

fusil, fE-ze, *m* rifle; gun.

fusillade, fE-zee-yăhd, *f* rifle fire; fusillade; shooting; execution.

fusiller, fe-zee-yeh, *v* to shoot.

fusion, fE-ze-ong, *f* fusion; melting; amalgamation.

fusionner, fE-ze-onn-eh, *v* to amalgamate.

fût, fE, *m* cask; stock; shaft.

futaille, fE-tah'e, *f* cask; barrel.

futé, e, fE-teh, *a* sly; cunning; crafty.

futile,* fE-teel, *a* futile; frivolous.

futilité, fE-te-le-teh, *f* futility; frivolousness.

futur, e, fE-tEER, *m* future; future tense; (**fam**) *mf* intended (husband, wife); *a* future; the life to come.

fuyant, e, fwee-yahng, *a* fleeting; fleeing; receding.

fuyard, e, fwee-yăhr *mf* runaway; *a* runaway; fugitive.

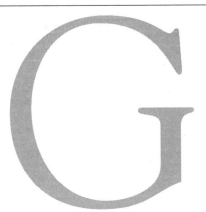

gabarit, găh-băh-re, *m* template; gauge; size.

gâcher, gah-sheh, *v* to mix; to make a mess of; to spoil.

gâchette, gah-sheh-t, *f* trigger.

gâchis, gah-she, *m* slush; mess; confusion; waste.

gadget, gah-dshe-t, *m* gadget; gimmick.

gaffe, găhf, *f* boathook; (*fam*) blunder; **faire une – fair** EEn **–,** to put one's foot in it; (*fam*) **faire –,** to be careful.

gage, găhsh, *m* pledge; pawn; forfeit; *pl* wages.

gager, găh-sheh, to bet.

gageure, găh-sh EEr, *f* wager; the impossible.

gagnant, gah-nee-ahng, *a* winning; *mf* winner.

gagne-pain, găhn-yer-pang, *m* livelihood.

gagner, găhn-yeh, *v* to earn; to win; to persuade; **se –,** to be catching.

gai, e, gheh, *a* gay; lively; cheerful.

gaiement, gheh-mahng, *adv* gaily.

gaieté, gheh-teh, *f* gaiety; cheerfulness.

gaillard, e, gah'e-yăhr, *a* lively; strong; free. *m* chap.

gain, ghang, *m* gain; profit; advantage.

gaine, ghain, *f* sheath; case; corset; girdle.

galamment, găh-lăh-mahng, *adv* courteously.

galant, găh-lahng, *m* lover; ladies' man; wooer.

galant, e, găh-lahng, *a* courteous; polite; worthy.

galanterie, găh-lahngt-ree, *f* love affair; politeness.

galbe, găhlb, *m* curve; contour.

gale, găhl, *f* mange.

galère, găh-lair, *f* galley; *pl* penal servitude.

galerie, găhl-ree, *f* gallery; spectators.

galet, găh-lay, *m* pebble; shingle.

galetas, găhl-tah, *m* attic.

galette, găh-lett, *f* pancake; biscuit; (*slang*) cash.

galeu-x, se, găh-ler, *a* scabby; mangy.

gallicisme, găhl-le-sissm, *m* French idiom.

galoche, găh-losh, *f* galosh; clog.

galon, găh-long, *m* braid; *pl* stripes.

galop, găh-lo, *m* gallop; great haste; scolding.

galoper, găh-lop-eh, *v* to gallop; to run on.

galopin, găh-lop-ang, *m* urchin; rogue.

gambader, gahng-băh-deh, *v* to leap; to skip.

gamelle, găh-mell, *f* lunch box.

gamin, e, găh-mang, *mf* kid; youngster.

a
b
c
d
e
f
g
h
i
j
k
l
m
n
o
p
q
r
s
t
u
v
w
x
y
z

gamme, găhm, *f* gamut; scale.

ganglion, gahng-gle-ong, *m* ganglion.

ganse, ghahngss, *f* cord; braid.

gant, ghahng, *m* glove; **–de toilette,** – der to'ăhlett, washcloth.

garage, găh-răhsh, *m* garage.

garant, e, găh-rahng, *mf* guarantor; surety; bail.

garantie, găh-rahng-tee, *f* guarantee; warranty; safeguard.

garantir, găh-rahng-teer, *v* to guarantee; to secure; to protect.

garçon, găhr-song, *m* boy; lad; bachelor; waiter.

garçonnière, găhr-sonn-e-air, *f* bachelor's apartment.

garde, găhrd, *m* guard; watchman; warden.

garde, găhrd, *f* guard; care; keeping; watch; protection; nurse.

garder, găhr deh, *v* to guard; to watch; to look after; to keep.

gardien, ne, găhr-de-ang, *mf* guardian; keeper; trustee.

gare, găhr, *f* station; terminus.

gare! găhr, *interj* look out!

garenne, găh-rain, *f* warren.

garer, găh-reh, *v* to park (car); to shunt; **se –,** to get out of the way.

gargarisme, găhr-găh-reessm, *m* gargle.

garnement, găhr-ner-mahng, *m* scamp; rascal.

garnir, găhr-neer, *v* to furnish (**de,** with); to adorn; to line; to decorate; to garnish.

garnison, găhr-ne-zong, *f* garrison.

garniture, găhr-ne-tEEr, *f* set; trimming; ornaments; garnishing.

garrot, găh-roh, *m* tourniquet.

garrotter, găh-rott-eh, *v* to tie down; to garrote.

gars, gah, *m* lad.

gaspiller, găhss-pee-yeh, *v* to squander; to waste.

gastronome, găhss-tronn-omm, *m* gourmet.

gâteau, gah-toh, *m* cake; **petit—,** pertee—, cookie.

gâter, gah-teh, *v* to spoil; to damage; to spoil (person).

gauche, gohsh, *f* left side. *a* left; clumsy.

gauchement, gohsh-mahng, *adv* awkwardly.

gauch-er, ère, goh-sheh, *a* left-handed.

gaucherie, gohsh-ree, *f* awkwardness.

gaufre, ghoh-fr, *f* wafer; waffle.

gaule, gohl, *f* long pole; switch.

gave, găhv, *m* stream; torrent.

gaver, gahv-eh, *v* to cram (with food); to stuff.

gavroche, găh-vrosh, *m* street urchin.

gaz, gahz, *m* gas; gaslight.

gaze, gahz, *f* gauze.

gazeu-x, se, gah-zer, *a* sparkling; fizzy.

gazon, gah-zong, *m* grass; turf; green.

gazouiller, găh-zoo'e-yeh, *v* to warble; to chirp.

geai, shay, *m* jay.

géant, e, sheh-ahng, *mf* & *a* giant; giantess; gigantic.

geindre, shang-dr, *v* to whimper; to whine.

gel, shehl, *m* frost; freezing.

gelée, sher-leh, *f* frost; jelly.

geler, sher-leh, *v* to freeze.

gémir, sheh-meer, *v* to groan; to lament; to grieve.

gémissement, sheh-miss-mahng, *m* groan; lamentation.

gemme, shaym, *f* gem. *a*
sel –, sell –, rock salt.

gênant, e, shay-nah*ng*, *a*
troublesome; awkward;
embarrassing.

gencive, shah*ng*-seev, *f*
gum.

gendarme, shah*ng*-dăhrm,
m policeman.

gendre, shah*ng*-dr, *m* son-
in-law.

gêne, shayn, *f* hindrance;
embarrassment; want.

gêner, shay-neh, *v* to
hinder; to
inconvenience; se –, to
put oneself out.

général, e,* sheh-neh-
răhl, *a* & *mf* general;
dress rehearsal.

générale, sheh-neh-răhl, *f*
alarm.

généreu-x, se,* sheh-neh-
rer, *a* generous.

générosité, sheh-neh-roz-
e-teh, *f* generosity.

genèse, sher-nayz, *f*
genesis; birth; origin.

genêt, sher-nay, *m* broom.

génial, e,* sheh-ne-ăhl, *a*
inspired; full of genius.

génie, sheh-nee, *m* genius;
spirit; engineers.

genièvre, sher-ne-ay-vr, *m*
juniper; gin.

génisse, sheh-neess, *f*
heifer.

génitif, sheh-ne-teeff, *m*
genitive case.

genou, sher-noo, *m* knee.

genre, shah*ng* r, *m* kind;
species; gender; manner.

gens, shah*ng*, *mf pl*
people; men; servants.

gent, shah*ng*, *f* brood;
race; tribe.

gentil, le, shah*ng*-tee, *a*
nice; kind; good.

gentilhomme, shah*ng*-tee-
yomm, *m* nobleman;
gentleman.

gentillesse, shah*ng*-tee-
yess, *f* kindness.

gentiment, shah*ng*-te-
mah*ng*, *adv* nicely.

géographie, sheh-ogh-răh-
fee, *f* geography.

geôli-er, ère, shoh-le-eh,
mf jailer.

géologue, sheh-oll-ogh, *m*
geologist.

géométrie, sheh-omm-eh-
tree, *f* geometry.

gérance, sheh-rah*ng*ss, *f*
management.

gérant, e, sheh-rah*ng*, *mf*
manager.

gerbe, shairb, *f* sheaf;
bundle; bunch.

gercé, shair-seh, *a*
chapped.

gerçure, shair-sEEr, *f*
crack; chap (of hands).

gérer, sheh-reh, *v* to
manage; to run.

germain, e, shair-mang, *a*
German; first (first
cousin).

germe, shairm, *m* germ;
shoot; seed.

gérondif, sheh-ro*ng*-deeff,
m gerund.

gésier, sheh-ze-eh, *m*
gizzard.

geste, shesst, *m* gesture;
motion; sign.

gesticuler, shess-te-kE-leh,
v to gesticulate.

gestion, shess-te-o*ng*, *f*
management;
administration.

gibecière, sheeb-se-air, *f*
shoulder bag.

gibelotte, sheeb-lot, *f*
rabbit stewed in wine.

gibet, shee-bay, *m* gallows.

gibier, she-be-eh, *m* game
(birds, animals).

giboulée, she-boo-leh, *f*
sudden shower.

giboyeu-x, se, she-bo'ah-
yer, *a* well stocked with
game.

gicler, she-kleh, *v* to spurt
out.

gifle, shee-fl, *f* slap in the
face.

gigantesque, she-gah*ng*-
tayssk, *a* gigantic.

gigot, she-go, *m* leg of
lamb.

gigoter, she-got-eh, *v* to
kick about.

gilet, she-lay, *m* vest.

gingembre, shang-shahng-br, *m* ginger.

girafe, she-răhf, *f* giraffe.

girofle, she-rofl, *m* clove.

giroflée, she-rof-leh, *f* gilly flower; wallflower.

girouette, she-roo-ayt, *f* vane; weathercock.

gisant, she-zahng, *a* lying.

gisement, sheez-mahng, *m* layer; deposit; stratum.

gît, she, *v* lies; **ci –, se –,** here lies.

gîte, sheet, *m* shelter; lair; leg of beef.

givre, shee-vr, *m* frost.

glabre, glah-br, *a* clean-shaven.

glace, glăhss, *f* ice; icecream; mirror; car window.

glacé, e, glăhss-eh, *pp* & *a* frozen; icy; glazed.

glacial, e, glăhss-e-ăhl, *a* icy; freezing.

glacière, glăhss-e-air, *f* cold room; refrigerator.

glaçon, glăhss-ong, *m* icicle; ice cube.

glaieul, glăh-yerl, *m* gladiolus; iris.

glaise, glayz, *f* clay.

glaive, glayv, *m* sword.

gland, glahng, *m* acorn; tassel.

glaner, glăh-neh, *v* to glean.

glapir, glăh-peer, *v* to yelp.

glas, glah, *m* knell; toll.

glissant, e, gliss-ahng, *a* slippery; sliding.

glisser, gliss-eh, *v* to slip; to slide; to glide; to touch lightly; **se –,** to creep.

globe, glob, *m* globe; ball; orb.

gloire, glo'ăhr, *f* glory; pride; halo.

glorieu-x, se, * **glor-e-er,** *a* glorious; vain-glorious.

glorifier, glor-e-fe-eh, *v* to glorify; **se –,** to glory **(de,** in).

gloser, glohz-eh, *v* to gloss; to criticize.

glousser, glooss-eh, *v* to cluck.

glouton, ne, gloo-tong, *mf* glutton; *a* gluttonous.

glu, glE, *f* birdlime.

gluant, e, glE-ahng, *a* sticky; slimy.

glycine, glee-seen, *f* wisteria.

gober, gob-eh, *v* to gulp down; to swallow; (*fam*) to believe anything; to adore (someone).

gobeu-r, se, gob-er, *mf* simpleton; credulous person.

godet, god-ay, *m* saucer (for painters); bowl.

godiche, godichon, ne, god-eesh, god-e-shong, *mf* & *a* simpleton; awkward.

goéland, gweh-lahng, *m* seagull.

goélette, gweh-lett, *f* schooner.

gogo, gogh-o, *adv phr fam;* **à –, ăh –,** in abundance.

goguenard, e, gog-năhr, *mf* & *a* jeering; sarcastic person.

goinfre, gwang-fr, *m* (*fam*) guzzler.

golf, golf, *m* golf; golfcourse.

golfe, golf, *m* gulf.

gomme, gomm, *f* gum; rubber.

gond, gong, *m* hinge.

gondole, gong-dol, *f* gondola.

gondoler, gong-do-leh, *v* to warp; to buckle; **se –,** (slang) to shake wiht laughter.

gonfler, gong-fleh, *v* to swell; to inflate.

gorge, gorsh, *f* throat; breast; pass; groove.

gorgée, gor-sheh, *f* mouthful; gulp; sip.

gorger, gor-sheh, *v* to gorge; to cram.

gosier, goz-e-eh, *m* throat; gullet.

gosse, goss, *m* (*fam*) kid; youngster.

goudron, goo-drong, *m* tar.

gouffre, goo-fr, *m* gulf; abyss.

goujat, goo-shăh, *m* boor.

goulot, goo-lo, *m* neck (of a bottle).

goulu, e, goo-lE, *mf* & *a* glutton; greedy.

goulûment, goo-lEE-mahng, *adv* greedily.

gourd, e, goohr, *a* numb.

gourde, goohrd, *f* gourd; flask; (*fam*) fool.

gourdin, goohr-dang, *m* cudgel.

gourer (se), ser goohr-eh, *v* (*fam*) to be mistaken.

gourmand, e, goohr-mahng, *mf* & *a* being fond of (food); greedy.

gourmandise, goohr-mahng-deez, *f* love of food; *pl* delicacies.

gourmé, e, goohr-meh, *pp* & *a* stiff; starched.

gourmet, goohr-may, *m* epicure; gourmet.

gousse, gooss, *f* pod; husk; shell; clove.

goût, goo, *m* taste; flavor; liking; style.

goûter, goo-teh, *v* to taste; to relish; to try. *m* afternoon tea.

goutte, goot, *f* drop; sip.

gouttière, goo-te-air, *f* gutter; drainpipe.

gouvernail, goo-vair-nah'e, *m* rudder; helm.

gouvernant, goo-vair-nahng, *m* ruler.

gouvernante, goo-vair-nahngt, *f* governess; housekeeper.

gouverne, goo-vairn, *f* guidance; rule of conduct.

gouvernement, goo-vair-ner-mahng, *m* government; management.

gouverneur, goo-vair-ner, *m* governor; tutor.

grabat, grăh-băh, *m* pallet.

grâce, grahss, *f* grace; mercy; thanks; charm.

gracier, grăh-se-eh, *v* to pardon.

gracieu-x, se,* grăh-se-er, *a* gracious; kind; courteous; pleasant; grateful.

grade, grăhd, *m* grade; rank; degree.

gradé, grăh-deh, *m* noncommissioned officer.

gradin, grăh-dang, *m* tier; step.

gradué, grăh-dE-eh, *m* graduate.

graduel, le,* grăh-dE-ell, *a* gradual.

grain, grang, *m* grain; corn; squall.

graine, grayn, *f* seed; berry; grain.

graissage, grayss-ăsh, *m* greasing; lubrication.

graisse, grayss, *f* grease; fat; drippings.

graisser, grayss-eh, *v* to grease.

graisseu-x, se, grayss-er, *a* greasy.

grammaire, grăh-mair, *f* grammar.

grammatical, e,* grăh-măh-te-kăhl, *a* grammatical.

gramme, grăhm, *m* gram.

grand, grahng, *m* grown-up.

grand, e,* grahng, *a* great; big; tall; grown-up; much.

grandeur, grahng-der, *f* greatness; size; magnitude; dignity.

grandiose, grahng-de-ohz, *m* grandeur. *a* grand.

grandir, grahng-deer, *v* to grow; to increase; to exaggerate.

grand magasin, grahng-măh-găh-zang, *m* department store.

grand-mère, grahng-mair, *f* grandmother.

grand-oncle, grahng-t'ong-kl, *m* great-uncle.

grand-père, grahng-pair, *m* grandfather.

grandroute, grahng-root, *f*

a
b
c
d
e
f
g
h
i
j
k
l
m
n
o
p
q
r
s
t
u
v
w
x
y
z

highway; main road.

grand-tante, grahng-tahngt, f great-aunt.

grange, grahngsh, f barn.

granit, grăh-neet, or grăh-nee, m granite.

granule, grăh-nEEl, m granule.

graphique, grăh-feeck, m graph; diagram. a* graphic.

graphite, grăh-feet, m graphite.

grappe, grăhp, f bunch; cluster.

grappin, grăh-pang, m hook; grappling iron.

gras, grah, m fat part; (legs) calf; fat (on meat).

gras, se, grah, a fat; plump; greasy; rich.

grassement, grahss-mahng, adv plentifully.

grasseyer, grăhss-ay-yeh, v to roll one's r's.

grassouillet, te, grăhss-oo'e-yay, a plump; chubby.

gratification, grăh-te-fe-kăh-se-ong, f bonus.

gratifier, grăh-te-fe-eh, v to favor; to confer; to bestow.

gratin, grăh-tang, m burnt part; **au** –, oh –, (cooked) with breadcrumbs.

gratis, grăh-tiss, adv gratis.

gratitude, grăh-te-tEEd, f gratitude.

gratte-ciel, grăht-se-ell, m skyscraper.

gratter, grăh-teh, v to scratch; to scrape.

grattoir, grăh-to'ăhr, m scraper.

gratuit, e,* grăh-twee, a gratuitous; free.

gratuité, grăh-twee-teh, f gratuitousness.

grave,* grăhv, a grave; serious; deep.

gravelle, grăh-vell, f stones (in bladder, etc).

gravelure, grăhv-lEEr, f obscenity.

graver, grăh-veh, v to engrave.

graveur, grăh-ver, m engraver; etcher.

gravier, grăh-ve-eh, m gravel; grit.

gravir, grăh-veer, v to climb.

gravité, grăh-ve-teh, f gravity; weight; sedateness; seriousness.

graviter, grăh-ve-teh, v to gravitate.

gravure, grăh-vEEr, f engraving; print.

gré, greh, m will; liking; thankfulness.

gredin, e, grer-dang, mf villain; scoundrel.

gréer, greh-eh, v to rig.

greffe, grayf, m clerk's office.

greffe, grayf, f graft; grafting.

greffier, gray-fe-eh, m registrar.

grêle, grayl, f hail; a slender; slim.

grêlon, gray-long, m hailstone.

grelot, grer-lo, m small round bell.

grelotter, grer-lot-eh, v to shiver.

grenade, grer-năhd, f grenade; pomegranate.

grenadier, grer-năh-de-eh, m grenadier; pomegranate tree.

grenadine, grer-năh-deen, f pomegranate syrup; grenadine.

grenat, grer-năh, m garnet; a garnet-red.

grenier, grer-ne-eh, m attic; granary.

grenouille, grer-noo'e-ye, f frog.

grenu, e, grer-nE, a grainy; clotted (oil).

grès, gray, m sandstone; stoneware.

grève, grayv, f strand; beach; strike.

grever, grer-veh, v to burden.

gréviste, greh-veesst, m

striker.

gribouiller, gre-boo'e-yeh, *v* to scrawl; to scribble.

grief, gree-eff, *m* grievance; ground for complaint.

grièvement, gree-ayv-mahng, *adv* severely; grievously.

griffe, greeff, *f* claw; clutch; signature; stamp.

griffer, greeff-eh, *v* to scratch.

griffonner, greeff-onn-eh, *v* to scribble.

grignoter, green-yot-eh, *v* to nibble.

grigou, gre-goo, *m* miser; skinflint.

gril, gree, *m* grid; grill.

grillade, gree-yăhd, *f* grilling; grilled meat.

grillage, gree-yăhsh, *m* grilling; latticework; iron-railing; grate.

grille, gree-ye, *f* iron gate; railing.

griller, gree-yeh, *v* to grill; to toast.

grillon, gree-yong, *m* cricket.

grimace, gree-măhss, *f* grimace; wry face.

grimper, grang-peh, *v* to climb; to creep up.

grincement, grangss-mahng, *m* gnashing; grating; grinding (of teeth).

grincer, grang-seh, *v* to grate; to gnash; to creak.

grincheu-x, se,* grang-sher, *a* grumpy; bad-tempered.

gringalet, grang-găh-lay, *m* thin man.

grippe, greep, *f* influenza.

gripper, greep-eh, *v* to gripe; to clutch; to snatch up.

grippe-sou, greep-soo, *m* skinflint; miser.

gris, gre, *m* gray.

gris, e, gre, *a* gray; dull.

grisâtre, gre-zah-tr, *a* grayish.

griser, gre-zeh, *v* (*fam*) to make tipsy; to excite.

grisonner, gre-zonn-eh, *v* to go gray.

grive, greev, *f* thrush.

grogner, gronn-yeh, *v* to grunt; to growl; to grumble.

grognon, e, gronn-yong, *a* & *mf* (*f inv*) grumpy; grumbler.

groin, grwang, *m* snout.

grommeler, gromm-leh, *v* to grumble; to mutter.

grondement, grongd-mahng, *m* growling; snarl; rumbling.

gronder, grong-deh, *v* to growl; to roar; to rumble; to scold.

gros, groh, *m* main part; bulk.

gros, groh, *adv* much; a great deal; **en –,** wholesale.

gros, se,* groh, *a* big; large; fat; coarse; pregnant.

groseille, groh-zay'e, *f* currant; **–à maquereau,** – ăh măhck-roh, gooseberry.

grossesse, gross-ayss, *f* pregnancy.

grosseur, gross-er, *f* size; tumor.

grossi-er, ère,* gross-e-eh, *a* coarse; rough; vulgar.

grossièreté, gross-e-air-teh, *f* coarseness; rudeness; rude thing.

grossir, gross-eer, *v* to enlarge; to put on weight.

grossissant, e, gross-iss-ahng, *a* magnifying.

grotesque, grot-essk, *m* grotesque. *a** grotesque; absurd.

grotte, grot, *f* grotto.

grouiller, groo'e-yeh, *v* to stir; to swarm; to rumble.

groupe, groop, *m* group; clump; cluster.

groupement, groop-mahng, *m* group.

grouper, groo-peh, *v* to

a
b
c
d
e
f
g
h
i
j
k
l
m
n
o
p
q
r
s
t
u
v
w
x
y
z

group.

gruau, grE-oh, *m* wheat flour; oatmeal;.

grue, grE, *f* crane.

grumeau, grE-moh, *m* clot; lump; curd.

gruyère, grE-yair, *m* Gruyère cheese.

guenille, gher-nee-ye, *f* rag; tattered garment.

guenon, gher-nong, *f* female monkey; ugly woman.

guêpe, ghayp, *f* wasp.

guêpier, ghay-pe-eh, *m* wasps' nest.

guère (ne...), ner ...ghair, *adv* hardly; not much.

guéret, gheh-ray, *m* fallow land.

guéridon, gheh-re-dong, *m* small pedestal table.

guérir, gheh-reer, *v* to cure; to heal; to recover.

guérison, gheh-re-zong, *f* cure; recovery.

guerre, ghair, *f* war; strife.

guerri-er, ère, ghair-e-eh, *mf* warrior. *a* warlike.

guerroyer, ghair-o'ăh-yeh, *v* to wage war.

guet, gay, *m* watch; **au –,** oh –, on the watch.

guet-apens, gay t'ăh-pahng, *m* ambush; trap.

guetter, ghay-teh, *v* to watch for; to look for.

gueule, gherl, *f* mouth (of animal); jaws; (*pop*) mug; **avoir la –de bois,** ăh-vo'ăhr lah – der bo'ăh, to have a hangover.

gueuler, gher-leh, *v* (*fam*) to bawl.

gueu-x, se, gher, *a* beggarly; wretched. *mf* beggar; tramp.

gui, ghe, *m* mistletoe.

guichet, ghe-shay, *m* wicket; booking office; box office.

guide, gheed, *m* guide; guidebook; *f* rein.

guider, ghe-deh, *v* to guide.

guidon, ghe-dong, *m* handlebar.

guigne, gheen-yer, *f* black cherry; bad luck.

guignol, gheen-yol, *m* puppet show.

guillemet, gheel-may, *m* inverted comma.

guillotine, ghee-yot-een, *f* guillotine.

guimauve, ghe-mohv, *f* marshmallow.

guindé, e, ghang-deh, *pp* & *a* hoisted; strained; stiff.

guinée, ghe-neh, *f* guinea.

guinguette, ghang-gayt, *f* open air café; dance hall.

guirlande, gheer-lahngd, *f* garland; wreath.

guise, gheez, *f* fancy; à la –, ah teh, as you please.

guitare, ghe-tăhr, *f* guitar.

gymnase, sheem-nahz, *m* gymnasium.

gymnaste, shem-năhs-t, *mf* gymnast.

gymnastique, shem-nahs-tik, *f* physical education; gymnastics.

gynécologue, shee-nehck-o-log, *mf* gynecologist.

There is no liaison with or elision before words marked thus; §

§**ha!** ăh, *interj* ha! ah!

habile, * ăh-beell, *a* clever; qualified.

habileté, ăh-beell-teh, *f* ability; cleverness.

habillement, ăh-bee-yer-mah*n*g, *m* clothing; dress; suit of clothes.

habiller, ăh-bee-yeh, *v* to dress.

habit, ăh-be, *m* coat; dress-coat; *pl* clothes.

habitant, e, ăh-be-tah*n*g, *mf* inhabitant; resident; inmate.

habitation, ăh-be-tăh-se-ong, *f* dwelling; house.

habiter, ăh-be-teh, *v* to inhabit; to live in; to reside.

habitude, ăh-be-tEEd, *f* habit; use; practice.

habitué, e, ăh-be-tE-eh, *mf* regular customer.

habituel, le, * ăh-be-tE-ell, *a* customary.

habituer, ăh-be-tE-eh, *v* to accustom; to inure.

§**hache,** ăhsh, *f* ax; hatchet.

§**hacher,** ăh-sheh, *v* to chop; to cut to pieces; to mince (meat, etc).

§**hachette,** ăh-shett, *f* hatchet.

§**hachis,** ăh-she, *m* hash; minced meat.

§**hagard, e,** ăh-găhr, *a* haggard.

§**haie,** ay, *f* hedge; line; row.

§**haillon,** ah'e-yong, *m* rag; tatter.

§**haine,** ain, *f* hatred; hate; spite.

§**haineu-x, se,** * ay-ne*r*, *a* hateful; spiteful.

§**haïr,** ăh'e-eer, *v* to hate.

§**haïssable,** ăh-eess-ăh-bl, *a* odious; hateful.

§**halage,** ah-lăh**sh**, *m* towing.

§**hâlé, e,** ah-leh, *a* sunburnt.

haleine, ăh-lain, *f* breath; wind.

§**haler,** ah-leh, *v* to tow; to brown; to tan.

§**haleter,** ăhl-teh, *v* to pant.

§**halle,** ăhl, *f* market; marketplace.

§**hallebarde,** ăhl-băhrd, **il pleut des –,** ill ple*r* day –, it rains cats and dogs.

§**hallier,** ăh-le-eh, *m* thicket.

hallucination, ăhl-lE-se-năh-se-o*n*g, *f* hallucination.

§**halte,** ăhlt, *f* halt; stop; haltingplace; **–là!** – lăh, stop!

§**haltère,** ăhl-tair, *f* barbell.

§**hamac,** ăh-măhck, *m* hammock.

§**hameau,** ăh-moh, *m* hamlet.

hameçon, ăhm-song, *m* fishhook; (*fig*) bait.

§**hampe,** ahngp, *f* staff; handle.

§**hanche,** ahngsh, *f* hip; haunch.

§**hangar,** ahng-găhr, *m* shed; hangar.

§**hanneton,** ăhn-tong, *m* bug.

§**hanter,** ahng-teh, *v* to frequent; to haunt.

§**happer,** ăh-peh, *v* to snap up; to snatch; to catch.

§**harangue,** ăh-rahng-gh, *f* harangue; address; speech.

§**haras,** ăh-rah, *m* stud farm.

§**harasser,** ăh-răhss-eh, *v* to tire out.

§**harceler,** ăhr-ser-leh, *v* to harass.

§**harde,** ăhrd, *f* leash; *pl* old clothes.

§**hardi, e,** ăhr-de, *a* bold; impudent.

§**hardiment,** ăhr-de-mahng, *adv* boldly.

§**hardiesse,** ăhr-de-ess, *f* boldness; assurance; impudence.

§**hareng,** ăh-rahng, *m* herring.

§**hargneu-x, se,** ăhrn-yer, *a* surly; peevish.

§**haricot,** ăh-re-ko, *m* kidney bean; **–vert, –vair,** French bean.

harmonie, ăhr-monn-ee, *f* harmony; harmonics.

harmonieu-x, se,* ăhr-monn-e-er, *a* harmonious.

§**harnachement,** ăhr-năhsh-mahng, *m* harnessing; harness.

§**harnais,** ăhr-nay, *m* harness.

§**haro,** ăh-ro, *m* outcry.

harpagon, ăhr-păh-gong, *m* (*fam*) miser.

§**harpe,** ăhrp, *f* harp.

§**harpon,** ăhr-pong, *m* harpoon.

§**hasard,** ăh-zăhr, *m* luck; chance; risk.

§**hasardeu-x, se,*** ăh-zăhr-der, *a* hazardous; unsafe.

§**hâte,** aht, *f* haste; hurry.

§**hâter,** ah-teh, *v* to hasten; to urge on; to expedite.

§**hâti-f, ve,*** ah-teeff, *a* forward; early; hasty.

§**hausse,** ohss, *f* block; rise.

§**hausser,** ohss-eh, *v* to arise; to lift; to increase; to advance; **–les épaules,** – leh zeh-pohl, to shrug one's shoulders.

§**haussier,** ohss-e-eh, *m* bull (stock exchange).

§**haut,** oh, *m* height; summit.

§**haut,** oh, *adv* high up; loudly.

§**haut, e,*** oh, *a* high; lofty; tall; erect.

§**hautain, e,*** oh-tang, *a* haughty.

§**hautbois,** oh-bo'ăh, *m* oboe.

§**hauteur,** oh-ter, *f* height; eminence; haughtiness.

§**haut-parleur,** oh-pahr-ler, *m* loudspeaker; amplifier.

§**havane,** ăh-văhn, *m* Havana cigar.

§**hâve,** ahv, *a* wan; emaciated.

§**havre,** ah-vr, *m* harbor.

§**havresac,** ah-vrer-săhck, *m* knapsack.

§**hé!** eh, *interj* hey! well! stop it! I say!

hebdomadaire, ehb-domm-ăh-dair, *a* weekly; (*fam*) weekly paper.

héberger, eh-bair-sheh, *v* to lodge; to offer a home to.

hébété, e, eh-beh-teh, *a* dazed; vacant.

hébreu, eh-brer, *m* & *a* Hebrew.

hectare, eck-tăhr, *m* hectare.

§**hein!** ang, *interj* eh? what?

hélas! eh-lăhss, *interj* unfortunately!

§héler, eh-leh, *v* to hail.

hélice, eh-leess, *f* propeller; screw.

hélicoptère, eh-li-coptair, *m* helicopter.

hémisphère, eh-miss-fair, *m* hemisphere.

hémorragie, eh-mor-ăh-shee, *f* hemorrhage.

hémorroïdes, eh-mor-o-eed, *fpl* hemorrhoids.

§hennir, ăh-neer or eh-neer, *v* to neigh.

herbage, air-băhsh, *m* grass; pasture.

herbe, airb, *f* grass; herb; weed.

herboriste, air-bor-eest, *m* herbalist.

§hère, air, *m* wretch; poor devil.

héréditaire, eh-reh detair, *a* hereditary.

hérédité, eh-reh-de-teh, *f* heredity.

hérésie, eh-reh-zee, *f* heresy.

§hérisser, eh-riss-eh, *v* to bristle up; **se –,** to stand on end (of hair).

§hérisson, eh-riss-ong, *m* hedgehog.

héritage, eh-re-tăhsh, *m* inheritance; heritage.

hériter, eh-re-teh, *v* to inherit; to get.

hériti-er, ère, eh-re-te-eh, *mf* heir; heiress.

hermétique,* air-meh-teeck, *a* hermetic.

hermine, air-meen, *f* ermine.

§hernie, air-nee, *f* hernia; rupture.

héroïne, eh-ro-een, *f* heroine; heroin.

héroïque,* eh-ro-eeck, *a* heroic.

§héron, eh-rong, *m* heron.

§héros, eh-ro, *m* hero.

§herse, airss, *f* harrow.

hésiter, eh-ze-teh, *v* to hesitate.

hétéroclite, eh-teh-rock-leett, *a* heterogeneous; assorted.

§hêtre, ay-tr, *m* beech tree.

heure, er, *f* hour; time; moment; o'clock.

heureu-x, se,* er- rer, *a* happy; lucky; successful; favorable; blessed.

§heurt, er, *m* shock; blow.

§heurter, er-teh, *v* to knock; to jostle; to offend.

hiberner, e-bair-neh, *v* to hibernate.

§hibou, e-boo, *m* owl.

§hic, eeck, *m* (*fam*) rub; difficulty.

§hideu-x, se,* e-der, *a* hideous.

hier, e-air, *adv* yesterday.

hilarité, e-lăh-re-teh, *f* hilarity; mirth.

hippique, ip-peeck, *a* of horses; racing.

hippocampe, ip-pock-ahngp, *m* seahorse.

hippodrome, ip-pod-romm, *m* racecourse.

hirondelle, e-rong-dell, *f* swallow.

§hisser, iss-eh, *v* to hoist.

histoire, iss-to'ăhr, *f* history; story; tale; fib; **faire des –s,** fair deh-z –, to make a fuss.

historien, iss-tor-e-ang, *m* historian.

historique,* iss-tor-eeck, *a* historical.

hiver, e-vair, *m* winter.

hiverner, e-vair-neh, *v* to winter; to go into winter quarters.

§hocher, osh-eh, *v* to shake; to toss; to nod.

§hochet, osh-eh, *m* child's rattle.

§holà! oll-ăh, *interj* hey!

§homard, omm-ăhr, *m* lobster.

homicide, omm-ee-seed, *m* murder; *mf* murderer; *a* murderous.

hommage, omm-ăhsh, *m* homage; token; *pl* respects.

homme, omm, *m* man; (*fam*) husband.

homosexuel, le, ommo-

secks-Eel, *a* & *m*
homosexual.

honnête, onn-ayt, *m*
honesty; *a** honest;
decent; respectable.

honnêteté, onn-ayt-teh, *f*
honesty; decency.

honneur, onn-er, *m*
honor; credit; respect.

honorable,* onn-or-ăh-bl,
a honorable;
respectable; proper;
creditable.

honoraire, onn-or-air, *a*
honorary.

honoraires, onn-or-air,
mpl fee; fees.

honorer, onn-or-eh, *v* to
honor (**de,** with).

honorifique, onn-or-e-
feeck, *a* honorary.

§honte, ongt, *f* shame;
disgrace; scandal.

§honteu-x, se,* ong-ter, *a*
shameful; ashamed;
bashful.

hôpital, op-e-tăhl, *m*
hospital.

§hoquet, ock-ay, *m*
hiccup.

§horde, ord, *f* horde.

horaire, or-air, *m*
timetable (rail, etc).

horizon, or-e-zong, *m*
horizon.

horizontal, e,* or-e-zong-
tăhl, *a* horizontal.

horloge, or-losh, *f* clock.

horloger, or-losh-eh, *m*
watchmaker;
clockmaker.

horlogerie, or-losh-ree, *f*
watchmaking;
mouvement d'–, moov-
mahng d –, clockwork.

§hormis, or-me, *adv* but;
except.

horreur, or-rer, *f* horror;
frightful thing; dread;
awe; abhorrence.

horrible,* or-ree-bl, *a*
horrible; awful;
shocking.

horripilant, or-ree-pee-
lahng, *a* hair-raising;
(*fam*) exasperating.

§hors, or, *prep* out;
beyond; past; except;
–de combat, – der kong-
băh, disabled.

§hors-d'œuvre, or der-vr,
m hors d'œuvre; starter.

horticulteur, or-te-kEEl-
ter, *m* horticulturist.

hospice, oss-peess, *m*
asylum; hospital for old
and poor people;
hospice.

hospitali-er, ère,* oss-pe-
tăh-le-eh, *a* hospitable.

hostie, oss-tee, *f* victim;
host (holy bread).

hostile,* oss-teel, *a*
hostile; adverse.

hôte, oht, *m* host; guest.

hôtel, oh-tell, *m* hotel;

mansion; townhouse.

hôteli-er, ère, oh-ter-le-
eh, *mf* hotelier;
landlord.

hôtellerie, oh-tell-ree, *f*
inn; hostelry.

hôtesse, oh-tess, *f* hostess;
landlady; guest; **–de
l'air,** – der lair, flight
attendant; stewardess.

§houblon, oo-blong, *m*
hop.

§houille, oo'e-ye, *f* coal.

§houillère, oo'e-yair, *f*
coal-mine; colliery; *a*
coalbearing.

§houle, ool, *f* surge; swell
(of sea).

§houleu-x, se, oo-ler, *a*
swelling; rough.

§houppe, oop, *f* tuft;
powderpuff.

§hourra! oo-răh, *interj*
hurrah!.

§houspiller, oos-pee-yeh,
v to handle roughly; to
abuse.

§housse, ooss, *f* slipcover.

§houx, oo, *m* holly.

§hublot, E-bloh, *m*
porthole.

§huer, E-eh, *v* to hoot; to
boo.

huile, weel, *f* oil.

huis, wee, *m*: à **–clos,** ăh –
kloh, behind closed
doors; in camera (jud.).

huissier, weess-e-yeh, *m*

usher; bailiff.

§**huit,** weet, *a* eight; eighth.

§**huitaine,** weet-ain, *f* about eight; a week.

§**huitième,** weet-e-aym, *m* & *a* eighth.

huître, wee-tr, *f* oyster.

humain, e,* E-mang, *a* human; humane.

humains, E-mang, *mpl* mankind.

humanité, E-măh-ne-teh, *f* humanity; human nature; *pl* humanities.

humble,* ung-bl, *a* humble; lowly.

humecter, E-meck-teh, *v* to moisten.

humer, E-meh, *v* to inhale; to sip up.

humeur, E-mer, *f* humor; temper; mood; fancy.

humide * E-meed, *a* humid; damp; moist.

humiliant, e, E-me-le-ahng, *a* humiliating.

humilier, E-me-le-eh, *v* to humble.

humoriste, E-mor-isst, *m* humorist.

§**huppé, e,** E-peh, *a* crested; (*fam*) best; well-off.

§**hurler,** EEr-leh, *v* to howl; to yell.

hutte, EEt, *f* hut; shed.

hybride, e-breed, *a* hybrid.

hydravion, e-drăh-ve-ong, *m* seaplane.

hydrogène, e-drosh-ain, *m* hydrogen.

hyène, e-ain, *f* hyena.

hygiène, e-she-ain, *f* hygiene.

hymne, eemn, *m* hymn; anthem.

hypertension, e-pair-tahng-se-ong, *f* hypertension; high blood pressure.

hypnotiser, ep-not-e-zeh, *v* to hypnotize.

hypocrisie, e-pock-re-zee, *f* hypocrisy.

hypocrite, e-pock-reet, *m* hypocrite; *a** hypocritical.

hypothécaire, e-pot-eh-kair, *a* mortgage.

hypothèque, e-pot-eck, *f* mortgage.

hypothèse, e-pot-ayz, *f* hypothesis.

hystérique, ees-teh-reeck, *a* hysterical.

a
b
c
d
e
f
g
h
i
j
k
l
m
n
o
p
q
r
s
t
u
v
w
x
y
z

I

ici, e-se, *adv* here; **par –,**
pǎhr –, this way.

idéal, e-deh-ǎhl, *m* ideal;
a* ideal.

idée, e-deh, *f* idea; notion;
plan; outline; conceit;
opinion.

identifier, e-dahng-te-fe-
eh, *v* to identify.

identique,* e-dahng-
teeck, *a* identical.

identité, e-dahng-te-teh, *f*
identity.

idiome, e-de-omm, *m*
dialect; language.

idiot, e, e-de-o, *mf* idiot; *a*
idiotic.

idiotie, e-de-oss-ee, *f*
idiocy.

idiotisme, e-de-o-tissm, *m*
idiom; idiocy.

idolâtre, e-doll-ah-tr, *m*
idolater; *a* idolatrous.

idolâtrer, e-doll-ah-treh, *v*
to idolize.

idole, e-dol, *f* idol.

if, eef, *m* yew.

ignare, een-yǎhr, *a*
ignoramus, ignorant.

ignoble, een-yob-l, *a*
ignoble; base.

ignominie, een-yomm-e-
nee, *f* ignominy.

ignominieu-x, se,* *a* een-
yomm-een-e-er,
ignominious.

ignorant, e, een-yor-ahng,
mf ignorant person; *a*
ignorant.

ignoré, e, een-yor-eh, *a*
unknown; hidden;
secret.

ignorer, een-yor-eh, *v* to
be ignorant of; not to
know.

il, ill, *pron* he; it; there; *pl*

they; **– y a, – e** ǎh, there
is; there are.

île, eel, *f* island; isle.

illégal, e,* ill-leh-gǎhl, *a*
illegal.

illégitime,* ill-leh-she-
teem, *a* illegitimate;
unlawful.

illettré, e, ill-lay-treh, *a*
illiterate.

illicite,* ill-le-seet, *a*
unlawful; illegal.

illimité, ill-le-me-teh, *a*
unlimited.

illisible,* ill-le-zee-bl, *a*
illegible.

illogique,* ill-losh-eeck, *a*
illogical.

illumination, ill-lE-me-
nǎh-se-ong, *f*
illumination.

illuminé, e, ill-lE-me-neh,
mf visionary; *a*
illuminated;
enlightened.

illusion, ill-lE-ze-ong, *f*
illusion; delusion.

illusoire, ill-lE-zo'ǎhr, *a*
illusory; fallacious.

illustration, ill-lEs-trǎh-se-
ong, *f* illustration;
celebrity.

illustre, ill-lEEs-tr, *m*
illustrious man; *a*
illustrious.

illustré, ill-lEEs-treh, *a*
illustrated; *m* magazine
(with pictures).

illustrer, ill-lEs-treh, *v* to illustrate.

îlot, ee-lo, *m* small island; plot; beat; block (of houses).

image, e-măhsh, *f* image; picture; likeness.

imagination, e-măh-**she**-năh-se-*ong*, *f* imagination; invention.

imaginer, e-măh-**she**-neh, *v* to imagine; to conceive; to contrive; **s'** –, to fancy.

imbécile, ang-beh-seell, *mf* idiot; fool; *a** imbecile; silly.

imberbe, ang-bairb, *a* beardless.

imbiber, ang-be-beh, *v* to soak; to imbibe.

imbroglio, ang-bro'e-lee-o, *m* confusion.

imbu, e, ang-bE, *a* imbued (**de,** with).

imbuvable, ang-bE-văh-bl, *a* undrinkable.

imiter, e-me-teh, *v* to imitate; to mimic.

immaculé, e, im-măh-kE-leh, *a* immaculate.

immanquable,* ang-mahng-kăh-bl, *a* infallible.

immatériel, le, im-măh-teh-re-ell, *a* immaterial; intangible.

immatriculer, im-măh-tre-kE-leh, *v* to register (car, etc); to enroll.

immédiat, e,* im-meh-de-ăh, *a* immediate.

immensément, im-mahng-seh-mahng, *adv* immensely.

immensité, im-mahng-se-teh, *f* immensity.

immeuble, im-mer-bl, *m* real estate; fixture; building; apartment building.

immiscer (s'), sim-miss-eh, *v* to meddle (**dans,** with, in).

immobile, im-mob-eell, *a* motionless; unmovable.

immobili-er, ère, im-mob-e-le-eh, *a* of real estate; landed; **agence –ère,** ăh-**shahng**s –, real estate office.

immobiliser, im-mob-e-le-zeh, *v* to realize.

immodéré, e, im-mod-eh-reh, *a* immoderate.

immodérément, im-mod-eh-reh-mahng, *adv* immoderately.

immodeste, im-mod-esst, *a* immodest.

immonde, im-mongd, *a* unclean; foul.

immoral, e,* im-mor-ăhl, *a* immoral.

immortel, le,* im-mor-tell, *a* immortal.

immuable,* im-mE-ăh-bl, *a* immutable.

immuniser, im-mE-ne-zeh, *v* to immunize.

immunité, im-mE-ne-teh, *f* immunity; exemption.

immutabilité, im-mE-tăh-be-le-teh, *f* immutability.

impair, e, ang-pair, *a* odd; uneven.

impardonnable, ang-păhr-donn-ăh-bl, *a* unforgivable.

imparfait, ang-păhr-fay, *m* imperfect tense; *a** imperfect.

impartial, e,* ang-păhr-se-ăhl, *a* impartial.

impasse, ang-pahss, *f* dead end; "no through road"; dilemma; fix.

impassible,* ang-păhss-ee-bl, *a* impassive; unmoved.

impatiemment, ang-păhss-e-ăh-mahng, *a* impatiently; eagerly.

impatient, e, ang-păhss-e-ahng, *a* impatient; eager; fidgety.

impatienter, ang-păhss-e-ahng-teh, *v* to make impatient; to provoke; **s'** –, to fret.

impayable, ang-pay-yăh-bl, *a* invaluable; (*fam*) very funny.

impénétrable,* *ang*-peh-neh-trǎh-bl, *a* inscrutable; impenetrable.

impératif, *ang*-peh-rǎh-teeff, *m* imperative mood.

impérati-f, ve,* *ang*-peh-rǎh-teeff, *a* imperative.

impératrice, *ang*-peh-rǎh-treess, *f* empress.

imperceptible,* *ang*-pair-sep-tee-bl, *a* imperceptible.

imperfection, *ang*-pair-feck-se-*ong*, *f* imperfection.

impérial, e,* *ang*-peh-re-ǎhl, *a* imperial.

impériale, *ang*-peh-re-ǎhl, *f* outside top (of a bus).

impérieu-x, se,* *ang*-peh-re-*er*, *a* imperious; urgent.

impérissable,* *ang*-peh-riss-ǎh-bl, *a* imperishable.

imperméable, *ang*-pair-meh-ǎh-bl, *m* raincoat; *a** impervious; waterproof.

impersonnel, le,* *ang*-pair-sonn-ell, *a* impersonal.

impertinemment, *ang*-pair-te-nǎh-mah*ng*, *adv* impertinently.

impertinence, *ang*-pair-te-nah*ng*ss, *f* impertinence; insolence; rudeness.

impertinent, e, *ang*-pair-te-nah*ng*, *mf* impertinent person; *a* impertinent.

imperturbable,* *ang*-pair-tEEr-bǎh-bl, *a* imperturbable.

impétueu-x, se,* *ang*-peh-tE-*er*, *a* impetuous.

impétuosité, *ang*-peh-tE-oz-e-teh, *f* impetuosity; vehemence.

impie, *ang*-pee, *mf* impious person; *a* impious; ungodly.

impiété, *ang*-pe-eh-teh, *f* impiety.

impitoyable,* *ang*-pe-to'ǎh-yǎh-bl, *a* pitiless.

implacable,* *ang*-plǎh-kǎh-bl, *a* implacable.

implanter, *ang*-plah*ng*-teh, *v* to implant.

implicite,* *ang*-ple-seett, *a* implicit.

impliquer, *ang*-ple-keh, *v* to implicate; to involve; to imply.

implorer, *ang*-plor-eh, *v* to implore.

impoli,* e, *ang*-poll-e, *a* uncivil; rude; impolite.

impolitesse, *ang*-poll-e-tayss, *f* impoliteness; rudeness; incivility.

impopulaire, *ang*-pop-E-lair, *a* unpopular.

importance, *ang*-por-tah*ng*ss, *f* importance.

important, *ang*-por-tah*ng*, *m* main point.

important, e, *ang*-por-tah*ng*, *a* important.

importa-teur, trice, *ang*-por-tǎh-ter, *mf* importer.

importer, *ang*-por-teh, *v* to import.

importer, *ang*-por-teh, *v* to matter (only used in 3rd person, infinitive and participles).

importun, e, *ang*-por-tung, *mf* intruder; *a* importunate.

importuner, *ang*-por-tE-neh, *v* to importune; to pester.

imposable, *ang*-pohz-ǎh-bl, *a* taxable.

imposant, e, *ang*-pohz-ah*ng*, *a* imposing.

imposer, *ang*-pohz-eh, *v* to impose; to tax.

imposition, *ang*-pohz-e-se-*ong*, *f* imposition; tax; assessment.

impossible, *ang*-poss-ee-bl, *m* impossibility; *a* impossible.

imposteur, *ang*-poss-ter, *m* impostor; *a* deceitful.

impôt, *ang*-poh, *m* tax; taxation; duty.

impotent, e, ang-pot-ahng, *mf* disabled; *a* infirm; impotent.

imprégner, ang-prehn-yeh, *v* to impregnate.

imprenable, ang-prer-năhl-bl, *a* impregnable.

impression, ang-press-e-ong, *f* impression; printing.

impressionner, ang-press-e-onn-eh, *v* to impress; to move (feelings).

imprévoyance, ang-preh-vo'ăh-yahngss, *f* improvidence.

imprévu, ang-preh-vE, *m* the unexpected.

imprévu, e, ang-preh-vE, *a* unforeseen; unexpected.

imprimé, ang-pre-meh, *m* printed paper; *pl* printed matter.

imprimer, ang-pre-meh, *v* to impress; to print; to stamp.

imprimerie, ang-preem-ree, *f* printing; printing-office.

imprimeur, ang-pre-mer, *m* printer.

improbable, ang-prob-ăh-bl, *a* unlikely.

improbe, ang-prob, *a* dishonest.

producti-f, ve,* ang-prod-EEk-teeff, *a* unproductive.

impromptu, ang-prongp-tE, *m* & *adv* impromptu.

impropriété, ang-prop-re-e-teh, *f* impropriety (of language).

improvisa-teur, trice, ang-prov-e-zăh-ter, *mf* & *a* improviser.

improvisé, e, ang-prov-e-zeh, *pp* & *a* improvised; unprepared.

improviser, ang-prov-e-zeh, *v* to improvise.

improviste (à l'), ăh lang-prov-isst, *adv* unawares; suddenly.

imprudemment, ang-prE-dăh-mahng, *adv* imprudently.

imprudence, ang-prE-dahngss, *f* imprudence.

imprudent, e, ang-prE-dahng, *a* imprudent.

impudemment, ang-pE-dăh-mahng, *adv* impudently.

impudence, ang-pE-dahngss, *f* impudence.

impudent, e, ang-pE-dahng, *a* impudent.

impudique, ang-pE-deeck, *a* lewd; indecent.

impuissance, ang-pweess-ahngss, *f* impotence; powerlessness.

impuissant, e, ang-pweess-ahng, *a* impotent; ineffectual.

impulsi-f, ve,* ang-pEEl-seeff, *a* impulsive.

impulsion, ang-pEEl-se-ong, *f* impulse; impetus.

impunément, ang-pE-neh-mahng, *adv* with impunity.

impuni, e, ang-pE-ne, *a* unpunished.

impur, e, ang-pEEr, *a* impure; unclean.

impureté, ang-pEEr-teh, *f* impurity.

imputer, ang-pE-teh, *v* to impute; to ascribe; to charge.

inabordable, e-năh-bor-dăh-bl, *a* inaccessible.

inacceptable, e-năhck-sep-tăh-bl, *a* unacceptable.

inaccessible, e-năhck-sess-ee-bl, *a* unapproachable.

inaccoutumé, e, e-năh-koo-tE-meh, *a* unaccustomed; unusual.

inachevé, e, e-năhsh-veh, *a* unfinished.

inacti-f, ve,* e-năhck-teeff, *a* inactive.

inadéquat, e,* e-năh-deh-kwăh, *a* inadequate.

inadmissible, e-năhd-me-se-bl, *a* inadmissible.

inadvertance, e-năhd-vair-tahngss, *f* inadvertence; oversight.

inaltérable,* e-năhl-teh-răh-bl, *a* unalterable.

inamovible, e-năh-mov-ee-bl, *a* irremovable.

inanité, e-năh-ne-teh, *f* inanity; futility.

inaperçu, e, e-năh-pair-sE, *a* unseen; unnoticed.

inappliqué, e, e-năh-ple-keh, *a* inattentive.

inappréciable, e-năh-preh-se-ăh-bl, *a* invaluable.

inattaquable, e-năh-tăh-kăh-bl, *a* unassailable.

inattendu, e, e-năh-tahng-dE, *a* unexpected.

inauguration, e-noh-ghE-răh-se-ong, *f* opening; unveiling.

incandescent, e, ang-kahng-dayss-sahng, *a* incandescent.

incapable, ang-kăh-păh-bl, *a* incapable; unfit; incompetent.

incapacité, ang-kăh-păh-se-teh, *f* incapacity; incompetence.

incarcérer, ang-kăhr-seh-reh, *v* to imprison.

incarnat, e, ang-kăhr-năh, *a* flesh-colored; rosy.

incarné, e, ang-kăhr-neh, *a* incarnate.

incendie, ang-sahng-dee, *m* fire; conflagration.

incendier, ang-sahng-de-eh, *v* to set on fire.

incertain, e, ang-sair-tang, *a* uncertain; undecided; wavering.

incertitude, ang-sair-te-tEEd, *f* uncertainty; instability.

incessamment, ang-sayss-săh-mahng, *adv* immediately.

incessant, e, ang-sayss-ahng, *a* incessant.

incidemment, ang-se-dăh-mahng, *adv* incidentally.

incident, ang-se-dahng, *m* incident; occurrence.

incident, e, ang-se-dahng, *a* incidental.

incinérer, ang-se-neh-reh, *v* to incinerate; to cremate.

incision, ang-se-ze-ong, *f* incision; lancing.

incitation, ang-se-tăh-se-ong, *f* incitement; instigation.

inciter, ang-se-teh, *v* to incite; to urge.

incivil, e, ang-se-veell, *a* uncivil; rude.

inclinaison, ang-kle-nay-zong, *f* tilting; incline.

inclination, ang-kle-năh-se-ong, *f* inclination; propensity; attachment.

incliner, ang-kle-neh, *v* to incline; to bend; **s'–,** to bow.

inclus, e, ang-klE, *a* enclosed; included; **ci-–, se –,** enclosed; herewith.

inclusi-f, ve,* ang-klE-zeeff, *a* inclusive.

incognito, ang-konn-yee-to, *m* & *adv* incognito.

incolore, ang-koll-or, *a* colorless.

incomber, ang-kong-beh, *v* to be incumbent (**à,** on).

incombustible, ang-kong-bEs-tee-bl, *a* incombustible; fireproof.

incommode, ang-komm-od, *a* inconvenient; troublesome.

incommoder, ang-komm-odd-eh, *v* to inconvenience; to annoy; to disturb.

incommodité, ang-komm-odd-e-teh, *f* inconvenience; discomfort.

incomparable, * ang-kong-păh-răh-bl, *a* matchless.

incompatible, * ang-kong-păh-tee-bl, *a* incompatible; inconsistent.

incompétent, ang-kong-peh-tahng, *a* incompetent.

incompl-et, ète, * ang-kong-play, *a* incomplete.

incompréhensible, ang-kong-preh-ahng-see-bl,

incomprehensible.

incompris, e, ang-kong-pre, *pp* & *a* not understood; unappreciated.

inconcevable, ang-kongss-văh-bl, *a* inconceivable.

inconciliable, ang-kong-se-le-ăh-bl, *a* irreconcilable.

inconduite, ang-kong-dweet, *f* misconduct.

incongru, e, ang-kong-grE, *a* incongruous; improper.

inconnu, e, ang-konn-E, *mf* unknown; stranger; *a* unknown.

inconsciemment, ang-kong-se-ăh-mahng, *adv* unconsciously.

inconscience, ang-kong-se-ahngss, *f* unconsciousness.

inconscient, e, ang-kong-se-ahng, *a* unconscious.

inconséquence, ang-kong-seh-kahngss, *f* inconsistency.

inconséquent, e, ang-kong-seh-kahng, *a* inconsistent.

inconstance, ang-kongss-tahngss, *f* inconstancy; fickleness.

inconstant, e, ang-kongss-tahng, *a* inconstant; unsteady; variable.

incontestable, * ang-kong-tess-tăh-bl, *a* unquestionable.

incontesté, e, ang-kong-tess-teh, *a* undisputed.

incontinent, e, ang-kong-te-nahng, *a* incontinent.

inconvenance, ang-kongv-nahngss, *f* impropriety.

inconvenant, e, ang-kongv-nahng, *a* improper; unbecoming.

inconvénient, ang-kong-veh-ne-ahng, *m* inconvenience; disadvantage.

incorporer, ang-kor-poh-reh, *v* incorporate.

incorrect, e, * ang-kor-reckt, *a* incorrect.

incrédule, ang-kreh-dEEl, *a* incredulous.

incroyable, * ang-kro'ăh-yăh-bl, *a* incredible; unbelievable.

incruster, ang-krEEs-teh, *v* to encrust (**de,** with); to inlay.

inculper, ang-kEEl-peh, *v* to charge; to accuse (**de,** with; of).

inculquer, ang-kEEl-keh, *v* to inculcate.

inculte, ang kEElt, *a* uncultivated; uneducated; rough.

incurable, ang-kE-răh-bl, *mf* & *a* incurable.

indécemment, ang-deh-săh-mahng, *adv* indecently.

indécent, e, ang-deh-sahng, *a* indecent.

indéchiffrable, ang-deh-she-frăh-bl, *a* undecipherable; incomprehensible.

indécis, e, ang-deh-se, *a* undecided; wavering.

indéfendable, ang-deh-fahng-dăh-bl, *a* indefensible.

indéfini, e, ang-deh-fe-ne, *a* indefinite.

indéfiniment, ang-deh-fe-ne-mahng, *adv* indefinitely.

indéfinissable, ang-deh-fe-niss-ăh-bl, *a* indefinable.

indélébile, ang-deh-leh-beell, *a* indelible.

indélicat, e, * ang-deh-le-kăh, *a* indelicate; unscrupulous.

indélicatesse, ang-deh-le-kăh-tayss, *f* indelicacy.

indemne, ang-daymn, *a* unhurt.

indemniser, ang-daym-ne-zeh, *v* to indemnify (**de,** for); to compensate.

indemnité, ang-daym-ne-teh, *f* indemnity; allowance.

indépendamment, ang-deh-pahng-dăh-mahng,

a
b
c
d
e
f
g
h
i
j
k
l
m
n
o
p
q
r
s
t
u
v
w
x
y
z

A B C D E F G H I J K L M N O P Q R S T U V W X Y Z

adv independently.

indépendant, e, ang-deh-pahng-dahng, *a* independent.

indescriptible, ang-dess-kreep-tee-bl, *a* indescribable.

indéterminé, e, ang-deh-tair-me-neh, *a* indeterminate; irresolute.

index, ang-dex, *m* index; forefinger.

indicateur, ang-de-kăh-ter, *m* indicator; timetable.

indica-teur, trice, ang-de-kăh-ter, *a* indicating; indicatory.

indicatif, ang-de-kăh-teeff, *m* indicative mood.

indicati-f, ve, ang-de-kăh-teeff, *a* indicative.

indice, ang-deess, *m* indication; sign; clue.

indicible, ang-deess-ee-bl, *a* inexpressible.

indifféremment, ang-de-feh-răh-mahng, *adv* indifferently; indiscriminately.

indifférent, e, ang-de-feh-rahng, *a* indifferent; immaterial.

indigène, ang-de-shain, *mf* & *a* native; indigenous.

indigent, ang-de-shahng, *m* pauper.

indigent, e, ang-de-shahng, *a* indigent; needy.

indigeste, ang-de-shaysst, *a* indigestible.

indigne,* ang-deen-yer, *a* unworthy; undeserving.

indigné, e, ang-deen-yeh, *a* indignant.

indigner, ang-deen-yeh, *v* to make indignant.

indignité, ang-deen-yee-teh, *f* unworthiness; indignity.

indiquer, ang-de-keh, *v* to indicate.

indirect, e,* ang-de-reckt, *a* indirect.

indiscipliné, ang-diss-e-plee-neh, *a* unruly.

indiscr-et, éte,* ang-diss-kray, *a* indiscreet.

indispensable,* ang-diss-pahng-săh-bl, *a* indispensable.

indisponible, ang-diss-ponn-ee-bl, *a* unavailable.

indisposer, ang-diss-poz-eh, *v* to upset; to antagonize.

indistinct, e,* ang-diss-tangkt, *a* indistinct.

individu, ang-de-ve-dE, *m* individual, person.

individuel, le,* ang-de-ve-dE-ell, *a* individual.

indocile, ang-doss-eell, *a* untractable; disobedient.

indolemment, ang-doll-ăh-mahng, *adv* indolently.

indolent, e, ang-doll-ahng, *a* indolent; sluggish; lazy.

indolence, ang-doll-ahngss, *f* indolence; laziness.

indolore, ang-doll-or, *a* painless.

indomptable,* ang-dong-tăh-bl, *a* indomitable; ungovernable.

indompté, e, ang-dong-teh, *a* untamed; unsubdued.

indubitable,* ang-dE-be-tăh-bl, *a* indubitable.

induire, ang-dweer, *v* to induce; to lead; to infer.

indulgence, ang-dEEl-shahngss, *f* leniency.

indûment, ang-dEE-mahng, *adv* unduly.

industrie, ang-dEEs-tree, *f* industry; skill; trade.

industriel, ang-dEEs-tre-ell, *m* industrialist.

industriel, le,* ang-dEEs-tre-ell, *a* industrial.

industrieu-x, se,* ang-dEEs-tre-er, *a* industrious; skillful.

inébranlable,* e-neh-brahng-lăh-bl, *a* immovable; resolute.

inédit, e, e-neh-dee, *a* unpublished; new.

ineffable,* e-neh-făh-bl, *a* unspeakable.

ineffaçable, e-neh-făh-săh-bl, *a* indelible.

inefficace,* e-neh-fe-kăhss, *a* inefficient.

inégal, e,* e-neh-găhl, *a* unequal; irregular; uneven.

inélégant, e, e-neh-leh-gahng, *a* inelegant.

inénarrable, e-neh-năhr-răh-bl, *a* indescribable.

inepte, * e-nehpt, *a* inept; silly.

ineptie, e-nehp-see, *f* ineptitude; absurdity.

inépuisable,* e-neh-pwee-zăh-bl, *a* inexhaustible.

inerte, e-nairt, *a* inert; lifeless; passive.

inertie, e-nair-see, *f* inertia.

inespéré, e, e-ness-peh-reh, *a* unhoped for.

inestimable, e-ness-te-măh-bl, *a* invaluable.

inévitable,* e-neh-ve-tăh-bl, *a* unavoidable.

inexact, e,* e-negg-zăckt, *a* inaccurate; unpunctual.

inexcusable,* e-necks-kE-zăh-bl, *a* inexcusable.

inexécutable, e-negg-zeh-kE-tăh-bl, *a* impracticable.

inexercé, e, e-negg-zair-seh, *a* unskilled; untrained.

inexigible, e-negg-ze-shee-bl, *a* not demandable.

inexorable,* e-negg-zor-ăh-bl, *a* inexorable.

inexpérimenté, e, e-necks-peh-re-mahng-teh, *a* inexperienced; untried.

inexprimable,* e-necks-pre-măh-bl, *a* inexpressible.

inextinguible, e-necks-tang-gwee-bl, *a* inextinguishable; uncontrollable.

infaillible,* ang-fah'e-ee-bl, *a* infallible.

infaisable, ang-fer-zăh-bl, *a* infeasible.

infamant, e, ang-făh-mahng, *a* ignominious.

infame, ang-fahm, *mf* infamous person; *a* infamous; vile; filthy.

infamie, ang-făh-mee, *f* infamy; infamous thing.

infanterie, ang-fahngt-ree, *f* infantry.

infatigable, ang-făh-te-găh-bl, *a* indefatigable.

infatuer (s'), sang-făh-tE-eh, *v* to become infatuated (**de,** with).

infécond, e, ang-feh-kong, *a* infertile; barren.

infect, e, ang-feckt, *a* stinking; foul.

infecter, ang-feck-teh, *v* to infect; to taint; to stink.

infection, ang-feck-se-ong, *f* infection.

inférer, ang-feh-reh, *v* to infer.

inférieur, e,* ang-feh-re-er, *a* inferior; lower.

infernal, e,* ang-fair-năhl, *a* hellish.

infertile, ang-fair-teell, *a* unfruitful.

infester, ang-fess-teh, *v* to infest.

infidèle, ang-fe-dell, *mf* infidel; unbeliever.

infidèle, ang-fe-dell, *a* unfaithful; untrue; dishonest; unbelieving.

infiltrer (s'), sang-fill-treh, *v* to infiltrate.

infime, ang-feem, *a* lowest; (*fam*) tiny.

infini, e, ang-fe-ne, *a* infinite; endless; boundless.

infiniment, ang-fe-ne-mahng, *adv* infinitely; extremely.

infirme, ang-feerm, *a* infirm; disabled.

infirmerie, ang-feerm-re, *f* infirmary; sick room.

infirmi-er, ère, ang-feer-me-eh, *mf* nurse.

a
b
c
d
e
f
g
h
i
j
k
l
m
n
o
p
q
r
s
t
u
v
w
x
y
z

A
B
C
D
E
F
G
H
I
J
K
L
M
N
O
P
Q
R
S
T
U
V
W
X
Y
Z

inflammable, ang-flăh-măh-bl, *a* inflammable.

inflammation, ang-flăh-măh-se-ong, *f* inflammation.

inflexible,* ang-fleck-see-bl, *a* inflexible.

infliger, ang-fle-sheh, *v* to inflict (**à,** on).

influent, e, ang-flE-ahng *a* influential.

influer, ang-flE-eh, *v* to exert an influence.

information, ang-for-măh-se-ong, *f* information; inquiry; *pl* news bulletin.

informe, ang-form, *a* shapeless.

informer, ang-for-meh, *v* to inform; to acquaint; **s'** –, to inquire.

infortune, ang-for-tEEn, *f* misfortune; adversity.

infortuné, e, ang-for-tE-neh, *mf* unfortunate person; *a* unfortunate.

infraction, ang-frăhck-se-ong, *f* infraction; breach.

infranchissable, ang-frahng-shiss-ăh-bl, *a* impassable; insuperable.

infructueu-x, se,* ang-frEEk-tE- er, *a* unfruitful.

infus, e, ang-fE, *a* innate.

infuser, ang-fE-zeh, *v* to infuse; to steep.

infusion, ang-fEE-she-ong, *f* herb tea.

ingénier (s'), sang- sheh-ne-eh, *v* to strive.

ingénieur, ang- sheh-ne-er, *m* engineer.

ingénieu-x, se,* ang-sheh-ne-er, *a* ingenious.

ingénu, e, ang- sheh-nE, *mf* & *a* ingenuous person; ingenuous; candid.

ingénument, ang- sheh-nE-mahng, *adv* ingenuously.

ingérer (s'), sang- sheh-reh, *v* to meddle (**dans,** with).

ingrat, e, ang-grăh, *mf* & *a* ungrateful person; ungrateful; unprofitable; unpleasant.

ingrédient, ang-greh-de-ahng, *m* ingredient.

inguérissable, ang-greh-riss-ăh-bl, *a* incurable.

inhabile,* e-năh-beell, *a* unskillful.

inhabitable, e-năh-be-tăh-bl, *a* uninhabitable.

inhabité, e, e-năh-be-teh, *a* uninhabited.

inhaler, e-năh-leh, *v* to inhale.

inhérent, e, e-neh-rahng, *a* inherent.

inhumain, e,* e-nE-mang, *a* inhuman; cruel.

inhumation, e-nE-măh-se-ong, *f* interment; burial.

inhumer, e-nE-meh, *v* to bury; to inter.

inimitié, e-ne-me-te-eh, *f* enmity; antipathy.

inique,* e-neeck, *a* iniquitous; unfair.

iniquité, e-ne-ke-teh, *f* iniquity; unfairness.

initial, e, e-ne-se-ăhl, *a* initial.

initiale, e-ne-se-ăhl, *f* initial.

initiative, e-ne-se-ăh-teev, *f* initiative.

initier, e-ne-se-eh, *v* to initiate; to instruct; to admit.

injecter, ang- shayk-teh, *v* to inject.

injure, ang- shEEr, *f* injury; wrong; insult.

injurieu-x, se,* ang- shE-re-rr, *a* injurious; offensive.

injurier, ang- shE-re-eh, *v* to abuse.

injuste,* ang- shEEst, *a* unjust; unfair; wrong.

inné, e, een-neh, *a* innate; inborn.

innocemment, e-noss-ăh-mahng, *adv* innocently.

innocent, e, e-noss-ahng, *mf* innocent person; simpleton; innocent; not guilty; harmless.

innombrable,* e-nong-brăh-bl, *a* innumerable.

inoccupé, e, e-nock-E-peh, *a* unoccupied.

inoculer, e-nock-E-leh, *v* to inoculate.

inoffensi-f, ve,* e-noff-ahng-seeff, *a* inoffensive.

inondation, e-nong-dăh-se-ong, *f* flood.

inonder, e-nong-deh, *v* to overflow; to flood.

inopiné, e, e-nop-e-neh, *a* unforeseen.

inopinément, e-nop-e-neh-mahng, *adv* unexpectedly.

inouï, e, e-noo-e, *a* unheard of; unprecedented.

inqui-et, ète, ang-ke-ay, *a* anxious; uneasy; worried.

inquiétant, e, ang-ke-eh-tahng, *a* alarming; worrying.

inquiéter, ang-ke-eh-teh, *v* to make uneasy; to alarm; to worry.

inquiétude, ang-ke-eh-tEEd, *f* anxiety; worry.

insalubre,* ang-săh-lEE-br, *a* unhealthy.

insatiable,* ang-săh-se-ăh-bl, *a* insatiable.

inscription, angss-krip-se-ong, *f* inscription; registration.

inscrire, angss-kreer, *v* to inscribe; to enter; to register.

insecte, ang-say-kt, *m* insect.

insensé, e, ang-sahng-seh, *mf* & *a* madman; madwoman; insane; senseless.

insensible,* ang-sahng-see-bl, *a* insensitive; unconscious; callous; imperceptible.

insérer, ang-seh-reh, *v* to insert; to put in.

insigne, ang-seen-yer, *a* notable.

insigne, ang-seen-yer, *m* badge; *pl* insignia.

insignificant, e, ang-seen-yee-fe-ahng, *a* insignificant.

insinuant, e, ang-se-nE-ahng, *a* insinuating.

insinuer, ang-se-nE-eh, *v* to insinuate; to hint.

insipide, ang-se-peed, *a* insipid.

insistance, ang-siss-tahngss, *f* insistence.

insociable, ang-soss-e-ăh-bl, *a* unsociable.

insolation, ang-sol-ăh-se-ong, *f* sunstroke.

insolemment, ang-soll-ăh-mahng, *adv* insolently.

insolence, ang-soll-ahngss, *f* insolence.

insolent, e, ang-soll-ahng, *mf* & *a* insolent person; insolent; impertinent.

insoluble, ang-soll-EE-bl, *a* insoluble.

insolvable, ang-soll-văh-bl, *a* insolvent.

insomnie, ang-somm-nee, *f* sleeplessness.

insondable, ang-song-dăh-bl, *a* unfathomable.

insouciance, ang-soo-se-ahngss, *f* insouciance.

insouciant, e, ang-soo-se-ahng, *a* insouciant.

insoucieu-x, se, ang-soo-se-er, *a* heedless.

insoutenable, ang-soot-năh-bl, *a* indefensible; unbearable.

inspecter, angss-peck-teh, *v* to inspect; to examine.

inspec-teur, trice, angss-peck-ter, *mf* inspector; examiner; surveyor.

inspiration, angss-pe-rah-se-ong, *f* inspiration.

inspirer, angss-pe-reh, *v* to inspire.

instable, angss-tăh-bl, *a* unstable.

installation, angss-tăh-lăh-se-ong, *f* installation; setting up; plant.

instamment, angss-tăh-mahng, *adv* earnestly; urgently.

instance, angss-tahngss, *f* entreaty; degree of

jurisdiction; suit.

instant, angss-tahng, *m*
instant; **à l' –,** ăh l –,
immediately; a moment
ago.

instinct, angss-tang, *m*
instinct.

instincti-f, ve,* angss-
tangk-teeff, *a*
instinctive.

instituer, angss-te-tE-eh, *v*
to institute; to establish;
to appoint.

institut, angss-te-tE, *m*
institute; institution;
school.

institu-teur, trice, angss-
te-tE-**ter,** *mf* elementary
schoolteacher; *f*
governess.

institution, angss-te-tE-se-
ong, *f* institution;
school.

instruction, angss-trEEk-
se-ong, *f* instruction;
judicial investigation.

instruire, angss-trweer, *v*
to instruct; to
investigate; to teach.

instruit, e, angss-trwee, *pp*
& *a* instructed; learned.

instrument, angss-trE-
mahng, *m* instrument;
tool.

instrumenter, angss-trE-
mahng-teh, *v* to draw
deeds, writs, etc.

instrumentiste, angss-trE-

mahng-teesst, *m*
instrumentalist.

insu (à l' – de), ăh lang-
sE-der, *prep* unknown to.

insuffisamment, ang-sE-fe-
zăh-mahng, *adv*
insufficiently.

insuffisant, e, ang-sE-fe-
zahng, *a* insufficient.

insulaire, ang-sE-lair, *mf*
& *a* islander; insular.

insulte, ang-sEElt, *f* insult;
abuse.

insulter, ang-sEEl-teh, *v* to
insult; to abuse.

insupportable,* ang-sE-
por-tăh-bl, *a*
unbearable; badly
behaved.

insurgé, e, ang-sEEr-**sheh,**
mf & *a* insurgent.

insurger (s'), sang-sEEr-
sheh, *v* to revolt; to
rebel.

insurmontable, ang-sEEr-
mong-tăh-bl, *a*
insurmountable.

insurrection, ang-sEEr-
rayk-se-ong, *f* uprising;
insurrection; revolt.

intact, e, ang-tăhckt, *a*
intact; whole;
undamaged.

intarissable,* ang-tăh-riss-
ăh-bl, *a* inexhaustible.

intègre,* ang-tay-gr, *a*
upright; just; honest.

intégrité, ang-tah-gze-tay,

f integrity; honesty.

intellectuel, le,* ang-tell-
leck-tE-ell, *a*
intellectual.

intelligemment, ang-tell-
le-**shăh-**mahng, *adv*
intelligently.

intelligence, ang-tell-le-
shahngss, *f* intelligence;
knowledge; skill;
harmony.

intelligent, e, ang-tell-le
shahng, *a* intelligent;
clever.

intempérie, ang-tahng-
peh-ree, *f* inclemency.

intempesti-f, ve,* ang-
tahng-pess-teeff, *a*
untimely.

intendant, ang-tahng-
dahng, *m* steward;
comptroller.

intense, ang-tahngss, *a*
intense.

intensi-f, ve, ang-tahng-
seeff, *a* intensive.

(s')intensifier, sang-tahng-
se-fe-eh, *v* escalate.

intenter, ang-tahng-teh, *v*
to institute
(proceedings); to sue.

intention, ang-tahng-se-
ong, *f* intention;
purpose.

intentionné, e, ang-tahng-
se-onn-eh, *a;* **bien** or
mal –, be-ang, măhl –,
well–, ill-disposed.

intercaler, ang-tair-kăh-leh, *v* to insert; to wedge in.

intercéder, ang-tair-seh-deh, *v* to intercede (**auprès de,** with).

intercepter, ang-tair-sep-teh, *v* to intercept.

interdire, ang-tair-deer, *v* to prohibit; to suspend; to forbid; (*fam*) to bewilder.

interdit, ang-tair-de, *m* interdict; ban.

interdit, e, ang-tair-de, *a* speechless.

intéressant, e, ang-teh-rayss-ahng, *a* interesting.

intéressé, e, ang-teh-rayss-eh, *pp* & *a* interested; selfish.

intéresser, ang-teh-rayss-eh, *v* to interest; to concern.

intérêt, ang-teh-ray, *m* interest; profit; share; concern.

intérieur, ang-teh-re-er, *m* inside; home.

intérieur, e,* ang-teh-re-er, *a* interior; inner.

intérimaire, ang-teh-re-mair, *a* temporary.

interjeter, ang-tair-sher-teh, *v* to lodge an appeal.

interlocu-teur, trice, ang-tair-lock-E-ter, *mf*

interlocutor,

interloquer, ang-tair-lock-eh, *v* to disconcert.

intermède, ang-tair-mayd, *m* interlude.

intermédiaire, ang-tair-meh-de-air, *m* & *a* medium; middleman; intermediate.

intermittence, ang-tair-mit-tahngss, *f* intermission.

internat, ang-tair-năh, *m* boarding school.

international, e, ang-tair-năh-se-on-ăhl, *a* international.

interne, ang-tairn, *mf* & *a* boarder; intern; internal.

interner, ang-tair-neh, *v* to intern.

interpeller, ang-tair-pel-leh, *v* to put a question to; to call upon.

interposer, ang-tair-poz-eh, *v* to interpose.

interprète, ang-tair-prayt, *m* interpreter.

interroga-teur, trice, ang-tair-rogh-ăh-ter, *mf* & *a* examiner; inquiring.

interrogation, ang-tair-rogh-ăh-se-ong, *f* interrogation; question.

interrogatoire, ang-tair-rogh-ăh-to'ăhr, *m* examination; cross-

examination.

interroger, ang-tair-rosh-eh, *v* to question; to examine.

interrompre, ang-tair-rong-pr, *v* to interrupt; to stop; **s' –,** to break off.

interrupteur, ang-tair-rEEp-ter, *m* switch.

intervalle, ang-tair-văhl, *m* interval.

intervenir, ang-tair-ver-neer, *v* to intervene; to interfere; to occur.

intervention, ang-tair-vahng-se-ong, *f* intervention.

intervertir, ang-tair-vair-teer, *v* to invert.

intestin, ang-tayss-tang, *m* intestine; bowel.

intimation, ang-te-măh-se-ong, *f* notification.

intime,* ang-teem, *mf* & *a* intimate friend; intimate; close; cozy.

intimer, ang-te-meh, *v* to notify.

intimider, ang-te-me-deh, *v* to intimidate.

intimité, ang-te-me-teh, *f* intimacy.

intitulé, e, ang-te-tE-leh, *pp* & *a* entitled.

intolérable,* ang-toll-eh-răh-bl, *a* insufferable.

intolérant, e, ang-toll-eh-

a
b
c
d
e
f
g
h
i
j
k
l
m
n
o
p
q
r
s
t
u
v
w
x
y
z

rahng, *a* intolerant.

intoxiquer, ang-tox-ick-eh, *v* to poison (food, etc).

intraduisible, ang-trăh-dwe-zee-bl, *a* untranslatable.

intraitable, ang-tray-tăh-bl, *a* intractable.

intransigeant, e, ang-trahng-ze-**shahng**, *a* intransigent.

intrépide,* ang-treh-peed, *a* undaunted; fearless.

intrigant, e, ang-tre-gahng, *mf* & *a* schemer; intriguing.

intriguer, ang-tre-gheh, *v* to perplex; to plot; to intrigue.

intrinsèque,* ang-trang-sayk, *a* intrinsic.

introduc-teur, trice, ang-trod-EEk-ter, *mf* introducer.

introduire, ang-trod-weer, *v* to introduce; **s'** –, to get into.

introuvable, ang-troo-văhl-bl, *a* not to be found.

intrus, e, ang-trE, *mf* intruder.

intuiti-f, ve,* ang-tE-e-teeff, *a* intuitive.

inusable, e-nE-zăh-bl, *a* everlasting.

inutile,* e-nE-teel, *a*

useless; unnecessary.

inutilité, e-nE-te-le-teh, *f* uselessness; *pl* useless things.

invalide, ang-văh-leed, *a* & *mf* invalid; infirm; pensioner.

invalider, ang-văh-le-deh, *v* to invalidate.

invariable,* ang-văh-re-ăh-bl, *a* invariable.

invasion, ang-văh-se-ong, *f* invasion; irruption.

invectiver, ang-vayk-te-veh, *v* to inveigh.

invendable, ang-vahng-dăh-bl, *a* unsalable.

invendu, e, ang-vahng-dE, *a* unsold.

inventaire, ang-vahng-tair, *m* stocktaking; inventory.

inventer, ang-vahng-teh, *v* to invent.

inven-teur, trice, ang-vahng-ter, *mf* inventor; discoverer; *a* inventive.

inventi-f, ve, ang-vahng-teeff, *a* inventive.

inventorier, ang-vahng-tor-e-eh, *v* to make an inventory of.

inverse,* ang-vairss, *a* inverse; inverted.

investigation, ang-vayss-te-gah-se-ong, *f* investigation; inquiry.

investir, ang-vayss-teer, *v*

to invest.

invétéré, e, ang-veh-teh-reh, *a* inveterate.

invisible,* ang-vee-zee-bl, *a* invisible; unseen.

invité, e, ang-ve-teh, *mf* guest.

inviter, ang-ve-teh, *v* to invite; to urge; to request.

involontaire,* ang-voll-ong-tair, *a* involuntary.

invoquer, ang-vock-eh, *v* to invoke.

invraisemblable,* ang-vrayss-ahng-blăh-bl, *a* unlikely; unbelievable.

invraisemblance, ang-vrayss-ahng-blahngss, *f* unlikelihood.

invulnérable,* ang-vEEl-neh-răh-bl, *a* invulnerable.

iode, e-od, *m* iodine.

irascible, e-răhss-ee-bl, *a* irritable.

irisé, e, e-re-zeh, *a* iridescent.

irlandais, e, eer-lahng-deh, *a* Irish; *mf* Irishman; Irishwoman; Irish.

ironie, e-ronn-ee, *f* irony.

ironique,* e-ronn-eeck, *a* ironical.

irréalisable, eer-reh-ăh-le-zăh-bl, *a* unrealizable.

irréductible, eer-reh-

dEEk-tee-bl, *a*
irreducible.

irréfléchi, e, eer-reh-fleh-she, *a* thoughtless.

irréflexion, eer-reh-fleck-se-o*ng, f*
thoughtlessness.

irréguli-er, ère,* eer-reh-ghE-le-eh, *a* irregular.

irrémissible,* eer-reh-miss-ce-bl, *a*
unpardonable.

irrésolu, e,* eer-reh-zoll-E, *a* irresolute.

irrespectueu-x, se,* eer-ress-peck-tE- er, *a*
disrespectful.

irresponsable,* eer-ress-pong-săh-bl, *a*
irresponsible

irrévocable,* eer-eh-vock-ăh-bl, *a*
irrevocable.

irrigateur, eer-re-găh-**ter,**
m hose (garden).

irriguer, eer-re-gheh, *v* to
irrigate.

irriter, eer-re-teh, *v* to
irritate; to provoke.

isolé, e, e-zoll-eh, *a*
isolated; lonely;
detached.

isolement, e-zoll-mah*ng,*
m loneliness; seclusion.

issu, e, iss-E, *a* born;
sprung from.

issue, iss-E, *f* issue; outlet;
end.

isthme, issm, *m* isthmus.

itinéraire, e-te-neh-rair,
m itinerary; route;
guidebook.

ivoire, e-vo'ăhr, *m* ivory;
whiteness.

ivre, e-vr, *a* drunk;
intoxicated.

ivresse, e-vress, *f*
drunkenness; rapture.

ivrogne, e-vronn-ye*r, m*
drunkard.

J

jabot, shăh-bo, *m* frill; crop (of a bird).

jacasser, shăh-kăhss-eh, *v* to chatter; to yak.

jacinthe, shăh-sangt, *f* hyacinth.

jadis, shăh-deess, *adv* formerly; of old.

jaillir, shah'e-eer, *v* to spout; to gush out; to spring forth.

jalon, shăh-long, *m* stake; pole; landmark.

jalouser, shăh-loo-zeh, *v* to envy.

jalousie, shăh-loo-zee, *f* jealousy; Venetian blind.

jalou-x, se, * shăh-loo, *a* jealous.

jamais, shăh-may, *adv* ever; never.

jambe, shahngb, *f* leg; shank.

jambon, shahng-bong, *m* ham.

jante, shahngt, *f* rim.

janvier, shahng-ve-eh, *m* January.

japonais, e, shah-po-neh, *a* Japanese; *mf* Japanese man, woman; Japanese.

japper, shăh-peh, *v* to yelp.

jaquette, shăh-kayt, *f* jacket.

jardin, shăhr-dang, *m* garden.

jardini-er, ère, shăhr-de-ne-eh, *mf* gardener.

jargon, shăhr-gong, *m* gibberish; jargon.

jarre, shăhr, *f* jar.

jarret, shăh-ray, *m* hamstring; hock; knuckle (veal).

jarretelle, shăhr-tell, *f* garter.

jaser, shah-zeh, *v* to chatter; to gossip.

jasmin, shăhss-mang, *m* jasmine.

jatte, shăht, *f* bowl.

jauge, shohsh, *f* gauge; tonnage.

jaunâtre, shoh-nah-tr, *a* yellowish.

jaune, shohn, *a* yellow.

jaunir, shoh-neer, *v* to make yellow; to turn yellow.

jaunisse, shoh-neess, *f* jaundice.

javelot, shăhv-lo, *m* javelin.

je (j' before a vowel), sher, *pron* I.

jésuite, sheh-zweet, *m* Jesuit.

Jésus, sheh-zE, *m* Jesus.

jet, shay, *m* throw; jet; ray.

jetée, sher-teh, *f* pier; jetty.

jeter, sher-teh, *v* to throw; to fling.

jeton, sher-tong, *m* chip;

token.

jeu, sher, *m* play; sport; gambling; set; acting; game.

jeudi, sher-de, *m* Thursday.

jeun (à), ăh-sh**u**ng, *adv* fasting; on an empty stomach.

jeûne, shern, *m* fast; fasting.

jeune, shern, *a* young; junior; youthful.

jeûner, sher-neh, *v* to fast.

jeunesse, sher-ness, *f* youth; young people.

joaillerie, sho'ah'e-ree, *f* jewelry; jeweler's trade.

joie, sho'ă̆h, *f* joy; delight; gladness.

joignant, sho'ă̆hn-yahng, *pres part* & *a* adjoining; near to.

joindre, sho'ang-dr, *v* to join; to adjoin; to clasp; to get in touch.

joint, e, sho'ang, *a* joined; united; **ci-joint,** se-sh**o'** ang, herewith; annexed.

joli, e, sholl-e, *a* pretty.

joliment, sholl-e-mahng, *adv* nicely; (*fam*) very; terribly.

jonc, shong, *m* rush; cane.

joncher, shong-sheh, *v* to strew; to scatter.

jonction, shongk-se-ong, *f* junction.

jongler, shong-gleh, *v* to juggle.

joue, shoo, *f* cheek.

jouer, shoo-eh, *v* to play; to gamble; to stake; to act; to deceive.

jouet, shoo-ay, *m* toy.

joueu-r, se, shoo-er, *mf* player; gambler.

joug, shoogh, *m* yoke.

jouir, shoo-eer, *v* to enjoy; to possess; to use.

jouissance, shoo-iss-ahngss, *f* enjoyment; possession; use; joy.

joujou, shoo-shoo, *m* plaything; toy.

jour, shoohr, *m* day; daylight; gap.

journal, shoohr-nă̆hl, *m* newspaper; journal; diary; record.

journali-er, ère, shoohr-nă̆h-le-eh, *a* daily.

journée, shoohr-neh, *f* daytime; day's work.

journellement, shoohr-nell-mahng, *adv* daily.

jovial, e,* shov-e-ă̆hl, *a* jovial.

joyau, sho'ă̆h-yoh, *m* jewel.

joyeu-x, se,* sho'ă̆h-yer, *a* cheerful; merry; joyful.

jubilation, shE-be-lă̆h-se-ong, *f* rejoicing; jubilation.

jucher (se), ser sh**E**-sheh,

v to roost; to perch.

judiciaire,* shE-de-se-air, *a* judicial; legal.

judicieu-x, se,* shE-de-se-er, *a* judicious.

juge, shEEsh, *m* judge; magistrate.

jugement, shEEsh-mahng, *m* judgment; trial; sentence; opinion.

juger, shEE-sheh, *v* to judge; to try; to sentence; to believe.

jui-f, ve, shweef, *mf* & *a* Jew; Jewish.

juillet, shwe-yay, *m* July.

juin, shwang, *m* June.

juke-box, dshook-boks *m* juke box.

jumeau, jumelle, shE-moh, sh**E**-mell, *mf* & *a* twin.

jumelles, shE-mell, *fpl* binoculars.

jument, shE-mahng, *f* mare.

jupe, shEEp, *f* skirt.

jupon, shE-pong, *m* petticoat.

juré, shE-reh, *m* juror.

jurer, shE-reh, *v* to swear; to clash (colors, etc).

juridique,* shE-re-deeck, *a* judicial.

juron, shE-rong, *m* curse.

jury, shE-re, *m* jury.

jus, shE, *m* juice; gravy.

jusque, shEEs-ker, *prep* to;

A
B
C
D
E
F
G
H
I
J
K
L
M
N
O
P
Q
R
S
T
U
V
W
X
Y
Z

as far as; until; up to; down to; even.

juste, shEEst, *m* upright man; virtuous man; *a* just; correct; fair; tight.

juste, shEEst, *adv* just; right; exactly.

justement, shEEs-ter-mah*n*g, *adv* just so; exactly.

justesse, shEEs-tess, *f* accuracy; precision.

justice, shEEs-teess, *f* justice; fairness; law.

justifier, shEEs-te-fe-eh, *v* to justify; to prove.

jute, shEEt, *m* jute.

juteu-x, se, shEE-ter, *a* juicy.

juvénile, shE-veh-neel, *a* youthful.

juxtaposer, shEEx-tăh-po-zeh, *v* to place side by side.

kaolin, kăh-oll-a*ng*, *m* clay (for china); kaolin.

képi, keh-pe, *m* military cap.

kermesse, kair-mess, *f* bazaar; charity fête.

kilo(gramme), ke-loh-grăhm; *m* kilo(gram).

kilomètre, ke-loh-met-tr, *m* kilometer.

kiosque, ke-osk, *m* kiosk; newsstand.

klaxon, klacks-o*ng*, *m* horn.

klaxonner, klacks-on-eh, *v* to hoot.

krach, krăhck, *m* financial disaster.

kyste, kee-st, *m* cyst.

a
b
c
d
e
f
g
h
i
j
k
l
m
n
o
p
q
r
s
t
u
v
w
x
y
z

la, lăh, *f* art the; *pron* her; it; *m* (music) A.

là, lăh, *adv* there; then.

labeur, lăh-ber, *m* labor; toil; work.

laborieu-x, se,* lăh-bor-e-er, *a* laborious.

labourer, lăh-boo-reh, *v* to till; to plow.

laboureur, lăh-boo-rer, *m* plowman.

lac, lăhck, *m* lake.

lacer, lăh-seh, *v* to lace.

lacet, lăh-say, *m* lace; snare.

lâche, lahsh, *m* coward; *a** loose; cowardly.

lâcher, lah-sheh, *v* to slacken; to loosen; to release.

lâcheté, lahsh-teh, *f* cowardice; meanness.

laconique,* lăh-konn-eeck, *a* laconic.

lacs, lah, *m* snares.

lacté, e, lăhck-teh, *a* milky; **voie –e,** vo'ăh –, Milky Way.

lacune, lăh-kEEn, *f* gap; blank.

lagune, lăh-ghEEn, *f* lagoon.

laid, e,* lay, *a* ugly; plain; unbecoming.

laideron, layd-rong, *mf* ugly creature.

laideur, lay-der, *f* ugliness.

lainage, lay-năhsh, *m* woolen goods; woolly garment.

laine, layn, *f* wool.

laisse, layss, *f* leash.

laisser, layss-eh, *v* to leave; to bequeath; to allow; to give up.

laissez-passer, layss-eh-păhss-eh, *m* pass.

lait, lay, *m* milk.

laitage, lay-tăhsh, *m* milk; dairy produce.

laitance, lay-tahngss, *f* soft roe.

laiterie, lay-tree, *f* dairy.

laiteu-x, se, lay-ter, *a* milky.

laiti-er, ère, lay-te-eh, *m* milkman; **produits –s,** prod-wee –, dairy produce.

laiton, lay-tong, *m* brass.

laitue, lay-tE, *f* lettuce.

lambeau, lahng-boh, *m* rag; shred; scrap; bit.

lambris, lahng-bre, *m* wainscot; paneling; ceiling.

lame, lăhm, *f* plate; blade; wave.

lamentable,* lăh-mahng-tăh-bl, *a* woeful; mournful; deplorable.

lamentation, lăh-mahng-tăh-se-ong, *f* lament; bewailing.

lampadaire, lahng-păh-dair, *m* floor lamp.

lampe, lahngp, *f* lamp.

lampion, lahng-pe-ong, *m* chinese lantern.

lance, lahngss, *f* lance; spear.

lancer, lahng-seh, *v* to throw; to fling; to issue; to launch; to set someone on his feet.

lancinant, e, lahng-se-nahng, *a* shooting (pain).

landau, aus, lahng-do, *m* baby carriage.

lande, lahngd, *f* barren land.

langage, lahng-gähsh, *m* language; speech; expression.

lange, lahngsh, *f* diaper; swaddling cloth.

langoureu-x, se,* lahng-ghoo-rer, *a* pining; melancholy.

langouste, lahng-ghoost, *f* crayfish.

langue, lahng-gh, *f* tongue; language; narrow strip (land).

languette, lahng-ghett, *f* small tongue (of wood, land, etc.); tab.

langueur, lahng-gher, *f* languor; weakness.

languir, lahng-gheer, *v* to languish; to pine away.

languissamment, lahng-ghiss-äh-mahng, *adv* languishingly.

lanière, läh-ne-air, *f* thong; lash; thin strap.

lanterne, lahng-tairn, *f* lantern; lamp.

lapider, läh-pe-deh, *v* to stone to death.

lapin, läh-pang, *m* rabbit.

laps, lähps, *m* lapse (of time).

laquais, läh-kay, *m* valet.

laque, lähck, *m* lacquer.

laquelle, läh-kell, *pron f* who; whom; which; that.

larcin, lähr-sang, *m* larceny.

lard, lähr, *m* bacon; lard.

larder, lähr-deh, *v* to lard.

lardon, lähr-dong, *m* piece of bacon; (*fig*) jibe.

large, lährsh, *m* breadth; width; open sea; *a* broad; generous.

largeur, lähr-sher, *f* breadth; width.

larme, lährm, *f* tear; drop.

larmoyer, lähr-mo'äh-yeh, *v* to weep; to whine.

larron, läh-rong, *m* thief.

larve, lährv, *f* larva; grub.

laryngite, läh-rang- sheet, *f* laryngitis.

la-s, sse, lah, *a* tired; weary.

lasci-f, ve,* lähss-eef, *a* lascivious; lewd.

lasser, lahss-eh, *v* to tire; to be weary; to fatigue.

latent, e, läh-tahng, *a* latent; concealed.

latte, läht, *f* lath.

lauréat, te, lor-eh-äh, *mf* laureate.

laurier, lor-e-eh, *m* laurel; bay.

lavabo, läh-väh-bo, *m* wash-bowl; lavatory; sink.

lavage, läh-vähsh, *m* washing; wash.

lavande, läh-vahngd, *f* lavender.

lavement, lähv-mahng, *m* enema.

laver, läh-veh, *v* to wash.

lave-vaisselle, lähv-vayss-ell, *m* dishwasher.

lavoir, läh-vo'ähr, *m* washing place.

layette, lay-yett, *f* baby clothes; layette.

le, ler, *m art* the; *m pron* him; it.

lécher, leh-sheh, *v* to lick.

leçon, ler-song, *f* lesson; lecture.

lec-teur, trice, leck-ter, *mf* reader; assistant.

lecture, leck-tEEr, *f* reading.

ledit, ler-de, *a* the aforementioned; *f* **ladite,** läh-deet.

légal, e,* leh-gähl, *a* legal; lawful.

légaliser, leh-gäh-le-zeh, *v* to legalize.

légataire, leh-gäh-tair, *mf* legatee.

légation, leh-gäh-se-ong, *f* legateship; legation.

légende, leh-shahngd, *f* legend; caption.

A
B
C
D
E
F
G
H
I
J
K
L
M
N
O
P
Q
R
S
T
U
V
W
X
Y
Z

lég-er, ère,* leh-**sheh**, *a* light; faint; fickle.

légèreté, leh-**shair**-teh, *f* lightness; fickleness.

légion, leh-**she**-*ong*, *f* legion.

législation, leh-**shees**-lăh-se-*ong*, *f* legislation; set of laws.

légiste, leh-**sheesst**, *m* lawyer.

légitime,* leh-**she**-teem, *a* legitimate; lawful.

legs, leh, *m* legacy.

léguer, leh-**gheh**, *v* to bequeath.

légume, leh-**ghEEm**, *m* vegetable; greens.

lendemain, lah*ng*d-mang, *m* next day; morrow.

lent, e,* lah*ng*, *a* slow; sluggish.

lenteur, lah*ng*-ter, *f* slowness; delay.

lentille, lah*ng*-tee-ye, *f* lentil; lens; *pl* contacts.

léopard, leh-op-ăhr, *m* leopard.

lèpre, laypr, *f* leprosy.

lépreu-x, se, leh-prer, *mf* & *a* leper; leprous.

lequel, ler-kell, *m pron* who; whom; which; that.

lesdits, lay-de, *a mpl* the aforementioned; *f* **lesdites,** lay-deet.

léser, leh-zeh, *v* to wrong; to injure.

lésion, leh-ze-ong, *f* lesion; injury; wrong.

lesquels, lay-kell, *mpl* of **lequel;** *f* **lesquelles,** lay-kell who; whom; which; that.

lessive, layss-eev, *f* washing (of clothes); wash; laundry; detergent.

lest, lesst, *m* ballast.

leste,* lesst, *a* nimble.

lettre, lay-tr, *f* letter; note; *pl* literature; letters.

lettré, e, lay-treh, *a* learned; literary.

leur, ler, *pers pron* to them.

leur, leurs, ler, *poss a* their.

leurrer, ler-reh, *v* to lure; to decoy.

levain, ler-va*ng*, *m* yeast.

levant, ler-vah*ng*, *m* East; *a* rising.

levée, ler-veh, *f* raising; removal; levy; collection of mail.

lever, ler-veh, *v* to raise; to collect; **se–,** to stand up; to get up; *m* rising.

levier, ler-ve-eh, *m* lever; crowbar.

lèvre, lay-vr, *f* lip.

lévrier, leh-vre-eh, *m* greyhound.

levure, ler-vEEr, *f* yeast.

lézard, leh-zăhr, *m* lizard.

lézarde, leh-zăhrd, *f* crevice; crack.

liaison, lee-ay-zong, *f* joining; junction; affair.

liant, e, lee-ahng, *a* pliant; affable; sociable.

liasse, lee-ăhss, *f* bundle; wad; file (of papers).

libellé, lee-bel-leh, *m* wording.

libellule, lee-bel-lEEl, *f* dragonfly.

libérer, lee-beh-reh, *v* to liberate; to discharge.

liberté, lee-bair-teh, *f* liberty; freedom; ease.

libraire, lee-brair, *m* bookseller.

librairie, lee-bray-ree, *f* bookstore.

libre,* lee-br, *a* free; bold; disengaged.

libre-échange, leebr-eh-shahngsh, *m* free trade.

licence, lee-sahngss, *f* license; degree; licentiousness.

licencier, lee-sahng-se-eh, *v* to disband; to fire.

licencieu-x, se,* lee-sahng-se-er, *a* licentious.

licite,* lee-seett, *a* lawful; licit.

lie, lee, *f* dregs; (*fig*) scum.

liège, lee-aysh, *m* cork.

lien, lee-ang, *m* bond.

lier, lee-eh, *v* to bind; to

tie; to join; to thicken.
lierre, lee-air, *m* ivy.
lieu, lee-er, *m* place; spot.
lieutenant, lee-ert-nahng, *m* lieutenant.
lièvre, lee-ay-vr, *m* hare.
ligne, leen-yer, *f* line; row; rank.
ligoter, lee-got-eh, *v* to bind; to tie up.
ligue, leegh, *f* league.
lilas, lee-lăh, *m* lilac; *a* lilac-colored.
limace, lee-măhss, *f* slug.
limaçon, lee-măh-song, *m* snail.
limande, lee-mahngd, *f* lemon sole.
lime, leem, *f* file.
limer, lee-meh, *v* to file; to polish.
limier, lee-me-eh, *m* bloodhound; detective.
limite, lee-meet, *f* limit; boundary; landmark.
limitrophe, lee-me-trof, *a* bordering; adjacent.
limon, lee-mong, *m* slime; mud.
limonade, lee-monn-ăhd, *f* lemonade.
lin, lang, *m* flax; linen.
linceul, lang-serl, *m* shroud.
linge, langsh, *m* household linen; cloth; rag.
lingerie, langsh-ree, *f* lingerie; linen closet.

lingot, lang-go, *m* ingot.
linon, lee-nong, *m* lawn (fine linen).
linotte, lee-nott, *f* linnet; **tête de –,** tayt der –, scatterbrained person.
lion, ne, lee-ong, *mf* lion; lioness.
liqueur, lee-ker, *f* liqueur.
liquidation, lee-ke-dăh-se-ong, *f* liquidation; clearance.
liquide, lee-keed, *a & m* liquid.
lire, leer, *v* to read.
lis, leess, *m* lily.
lis-eur, euse, lee-zer, *mf* reader; *f* book cover.
lisible,* lee-zee-bl, *a* legible.
lisière, lee-ze-air, *f* selvage; border.
lisse, leess, *a* smooth; sleek; glossy.
liste, leest, *f* list; roll; schedule; catalog.
lit, lee, *m* bed; layer; channel.
litanie, lee-tăh-nee, *f* long story; *pl* litany.
literie, leet-ree, *f* bedding.
litière, lee-te-air, *f* litter (stable).
litige, lee-teesh, *m* litigation.
littéraire, lee-teh-rair, *a* literary.
littéral, e,* lee-teh-răhl, *a*

literal.
littérateur, lee-teh-răh-ter, *m* man of letters.
littérature, lee-teh-răh-tEEr, *f* literature.
littoral, lee-tor-ăhl, *m* coast-line; *a* of the seacoast.
livide, lee-veed, *a* livid.
livraison, lee-vray-zong, *f* delivery.
livrée, lee-vreh, *f* livery; servants.
livrer, lee-vreh, *v* to deliver; to betray.
livret, lee-vray, *m* booklet; handbook; bank book.
livreur, lee-vrer, *m* delivery man.
local, lock-ăhl, *m* place; premises.
local, e,* lock-ăhl, *a* local.
locataire, lock-ăh-tair, *m* tenant; lodger.
location, lock-ăh-se-ong, *f* hiring; renting.
location de voitures, loh-kăh-se-ong-der-vo'ăh-tEEr *f* car rental.
locomo-teur, trice, lock-omm-ot-er, *a* locomotive.
locomotive, lock-omm-ot-eev, *f* locomotive; engine.
locution, lock-E-ong, *f* locution; expression.
loge, losh, *f* lodge; hut;

A B C D E F G H I J K **L** M N O P Q R S T U V W X Y Z

box.

logement, losh-mah*ng*, *m* lodging; accommodation; quarters.

loger, losh-eh, *v* to lodge; to house; to dwell.

logique, losh-eeck, *f* logic; *a** logical.

logis, losh-e, *m* dwelling; house; home.

loi, lo'ăh, *f* law; act.

loin, lo'ang, *adv* far; distant.

lointain, e, lo'ang-tang, *a* remote; far off.

loisir, lo'ăh-zeer, *m* leisure; time.

long, ue,* long, *a* long.

longer, long- sheh, *v* to pass along; to walk along; to coast.

longtemps, long-tah*ng*, *adv* long; a long while.

longueur, long-gher, *f* length.

longue-vue, long-gh-vE, *f* field-glass; telescope.

lopin, lop-ang, *m* patch of ground.

loque, lock, *f* rag; tatter.

loquet, lock-ay, *m* latch.

lorgner, lorn-yeh, *v* to ogle; to have an eye on.

lorgnette, lorn-yett, *f* opera-glasses; lorgnette.

lorgnon, lorn-yong, *m* lorgnette; pince-nez.

lors, lor, *adv* then; at the time; **dès** –, day –, ever since.

lorsque, lors-ker, *conj* when.

losange, loz-ah*ng*sh, *m* lozenge; diamond.

lot, lo, *m* portion; share; prize.

loterie, lot-ree, *f* raffle; lottery.

lotir, lot-eer, *v* to allot; to portion.

louable,* loo-ăh-bl, *a* laudable; praiseworthy.

louage, loo-ăhsh, *m* hire; renting.

louange, loo-ah*ng*sh, *f* praise.

louche, loosh, *f* soup-ladle; *a* squint-eyed; suspicious.

louer, loo-eh, *v* to rent; to hire; to praise.

loup, loo, *m* wolf.

loup-garou, loo-găh-roo, *m* werewolf.

loupe, loop, *f* magnifying glass; loupe.

lourd, e,* loor, *a* heavy; lumpish; clumsy.

lourdaud, loor-doh, *m* oaf; *a* clumsy; awkward.

lourdeur, loor-der, *f* heaviness; weight.

louve, loov, *f* female wolf.

loyal, e,* lo'ăh-yăhl, *a* honest; true; faithful.

loyauté, lo'ăh-yoh-teh, *f* honesty; fairness.

loyer, lo'ăh-yeh, *m* hire; rent.

lubie, lE-bee, *f* whim; fad.

lubrifiant, lE-bre-fe-ah*ng*, *m* lubricant; *a* lubricating.

lubrifier, lE-bre-fe-eh, *v* to lubricate.

lucarne, lE-kăhrn, *f* skylight.

lucide,* lE-seedd, *a* lucid; clear.

lucrati-f, ve,* lE-krăh-teeff, *a* lucrative.

lueur, lE- er, *f* glimmer; gleam.

lugubre,* lE-ghE-br, *a* lugubrious.

lui, lwe, *pers pron* he; him; to him; her; to her; it; to it.

luire, lweer, *v* to shine; to glitter.

luisant, e, lwe-zah*ng*, *a* shining; glossy.

lumière, lE-me-air, *f* light; *pl* knowledge.

lumineu-x, se,* lE-me-ner, *a* luminous.

lunaire, lE-nair, *a* lunar.

lundi, lung-de, *m* Monday.

lune, lEEn, *f* moon; **–de miel,** – der me-ell, honeymoon.

lunette, lE-nayt, *f* telescope; *pl* glasses.

lustre, lEEs-tr, *m* luster;
gloss; chandelier.

luth, lEEt, *m* lute.

lutin, lE-tang, *m* goblin;
imp (of child).

lutiner, lE-te-neh, *v* to
tease.

lutte, lEEt, *f* wrestling;
struggle; contest; strife.

lutter, lE-teh, *v* to wrestle;
to struggle.

luxe, lEEks, *m* luxury.

luxer, lEEk-seh, *v* to
dislocate.

luxueu-x, se,* lEEk-sE- er,
a luxurious.

luxure, lEEk-sEEr, *f* lust.

lycée, lee-seh, *m*
secondary school; high
school.

lyre, leer, *f* lyre.

lyrique, lee-reeck, *a*
lyrical.

lyrisme, lee-reessm, *m*
lyricism.

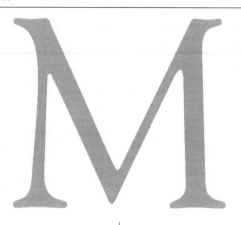

ma, măh, *poss af* my.

macabre, măh-kah-br, *a* macabre.

macédoine, măh-seh-do'ăhn, *f* mixed dish (of vegetables or fruit).

mâcher, mah-sheh, *v* to chew.

machinal, e,* măh-she-năhl, *a* mechanical.

machine, măh-sheen, *f* machine; engine; implement.

machiner, măh-she-neh, *v* to plot; to contrive.

mâchoire, mah-sho'ăhr, *f* jaw; jawbone.

mâchonner, mah-shonn-eh, *v* to munch.

maçon, măh-song, *m* mason; bricklayer; freemason.

madame, măh-dăhm, *f* madam; Mrs.

mademoiselle, măhd-mo'ăh-zell, *f* Miss; the young lady.

madone, măh-donn, *f* madonna.

madré, e, măh-dreh, *a* speckled; cunning.

magasin, măh-găh-zang, *m* shop; warehouse; stock store.

magasinage, măh-găh-ze-năhsh, *m* warehousing.

magazine, măh-găh-zeen, *m* magazine.

magie, măh-shee, *f* magic.

magique,* măh-sheeck, *a* magical.

magistral, e,* măh-shees-trăhl, *a* masterly; authoritative.

magistrat, măh-shees-trăh, *m* magistrate.

magistrature, măh-shees-trăh-tEEr, *f* prosecuting attorneys.

magnanime,* măhn-yăh-neem, *a* magnanimous.

magnétique, măhn-yeh-teeck, *a* magnetic.

magnétophone, măhn-yeh-toh-fonn, *m* tape recorder.

magnifique,* măhn-yee-feeck, *a* magnificent.

magot, mah-go, *m* baboon; grotesque figure; hoard

mai, may, *m* May; maypole.

maigre,* may-gr, *a* lean; thin; scanty; barren.

maigrir, may-greer, *v* to become thin; to lose weight.

maille, mah'e, *f* mesh; stitch; mail (chain).

maillot, mah'e-yo, *m* shirt; swimsuit (sports).

main, mang, *f* hand.

main-d'œuvre, mang-der-vr, *f* workmanship; labor.

main-forte, mang-fort, *f* assistance; help.

maint, e, mang, *a* many; several.

maintenant, mangt-nahng, *adv* now.

maintenir, mangt-neer, *v* to maintain; to keep up.

maintien, mang-te-ang, *m*
maintenance;
deportment;
countenance.

maire, mair, *m* mayor.

mairie, may-ree, *f* town
hall.

mais, may, *conj* but; **–oui,**
– we, "why, yes".

maïs, măh-eess, *m* maize.

maison, may-zong, *f*
house; home; firm.

maisonnette, may-zonn-
ett, *f* cottage; small
house.

maître, may-tr, *m* master;
owner; teacher.

maîtresse, may-tress, *f*
schoolmistress; mistress.

maîtrise, may-treez, *f*
mastery; self-control.

maîtriser, may-tre-zeh, *v*
to master; to keep under
control.

majesté, măh-shess-teh, *f*
majesty.

majestueu-x, se,* măh-
shess-tE-er, *a* majestic.

majeur, e, măh-sher, *a*
greater; major; **force –e,**
fors –, of necessity.

major, măh-shor, *m*
major.

majorité, măh-shor-e-teh,
f majority; coming of
age.

majuscule, măh-shEEs-
kEEl, *f* capital (letter).

mal, măhl, *adv* ill; badly;
amiss; on bad terms; *m*
evil; mischief;
misfortune; ache;
sickness.

malade, măh-lăhd, *mf* sick
person; patient; *a* ill;
sick.

maladie, măh-lăh-dee, *f*
illness.

maladi-f, ve,* măh-lăh-
deeff, *a* sickly.

maladresse, măh-lăh-
dress, *f* awkwardness;
blunder.

maladroit, e,* măh-lăh-
dro'ăh, *a* clumsy.

malaise, măh-layz, *m*
uneasiness; discomfort;
faintness; dizziness.

malaisé, e, măh-lay-zeh, *a*
difficult.

malappris, e, măhl-ăh-
pree, *mf* vulgar person; *a*
illbred.

malavisé, e, măhl-ăh-ve-
zeh, *a* ill-advised.

malaxer, măhl-acks-seh, *v*
to knead; to mix.

mâle, mahl, *m* male; *a*
male; manly; virile.

malchance, măhl-
shahngss, *f* bad luck.

maléfice, măh-leh-feess, *m*
witchcraft.

malencontreu-x, se,*
măh-lahng-kong-trer *a*
unlucky; unfortunate.

malentendu, măh-lahng-
tahng-dE, *m*
misunderstanding.

malfaisant, e, măhl-fer-
zahng, *a* mischievous;
noxious.

malfai-teur, trice, măhl-
fay-ter, *mf* criminal;
gangster; thief.

malgré, măhl-greh, *prep* in
spite of.

malhabile,* măhl-ăh-beel,
a unskillful.

malheur, măh-ler, *m*
unhappiness;
misfortune; bad luck.

malheureu-x, se,* măhl-
er-rer, *mf* & *a* unhappy;
wretched.

malhonnête,* măhl-onn-
ayt, *a* dishonest.

malice, măh-leess, *f*
malice; spite.

malicieu-x, se,* măh-le-
se-er, *a* spiteful;
mischievous.

malin, maligne,* măh-
lang, măh-leen-yer *a*
malignant; malicious;
mischievous; sly;
cunning.

malle, măhl, *f* trunk.

mallette, măh-lett, *f* small
suitcase.

malmener, măhl-mer-neh,
v to handle roughly; to
abuse.

malotru, e, măhl-ot-rE, *mf*

A
B
C
D
E
F
G
H
I
J
K
L
M
N
O
P
Q
R
S
T
U
V
W
X
Y
Z

ill-bred person; boor.

malpropre,* măhl-propr, *a* slovenly; dirty.

malsain, e, măhl-sang, *a* unwholesome (things); unhealthy (persons).

malséant, e, măhl-seh-ahng, *a* unbecoming.

malsonnant, e, măhl-sonn-ahng, *a* ill-sounding; offensive.

maltraiter, măhl-tray-teh, *v* to maltreat.

malveillant, e, măhl-vay'e-ahng, *a* malevolent.

maman, măh-mahng, *f* mummy.

mamelle, măh-mell, *f* breast; udder.

mamelon, măh-mer-long, *m* nipple; teat.

mammifère, măh-me-fair, *m* mammal.

manche, mahngsh, *m* handle; *f* sleeve.

manchette, mahng-shett, *f* cuff.

manchon, mahng-shong, *m* muff.

manchot, e, mahng-sho, *a* & *mf* one-armed.

mandat, mahng-dăh, *m* mandate; money order; warrant.

mandataire, mahng-dăh-tair, *m* proxy; agent.

mander, mahng-deh, *v* to

send word; to send for.

manège, măh-naish, *m* riding school; roundabout; (*fam*) trick.

manette, măh-nett, *f* small handle.

mangeable, mahng-shăh-bl, *a* edible.

mangeaille, mahng-shăh'e, *f* feed; (*fam*) grub.

manger, mahng-sheh, *v* to eat; to squander; *m* food.

maniable, măh-ne-ăh-bl, *a* easy to handle.

maniaque, măh-ne-ăhck, *m* maniac; *a* eccentric.

manie, măh-nee, *f* mania; craze.

maniement, măh-ne-mahng, *m* handling; management.

manier, măh-ne-eh, *v* to handle; to manage; to govern.

manière, măh-ne-air, *f* manner; style; *pl* manners; airs.

maniéré, e, măh-ne-eh-reh, *a* affected.

manifestation, măh-ne-fes-tah-se-ong, *f* manifestation; political demonstration.

manifeste, măh-ne-fest, *m* manifesto; manifest; *a** manifest; evident.

manifester, măh-ne-fess-teh, *v* to manifest; to

demonstrate.

manipuler, măh-ne-pE-leh, *v* to manipulate; to handle.

manivelle, măh-ne-vell, *f* handle; crank.

mannequin, măhn-kang, *m* dummy; fashion model; mannequin.

manœuvre, măh-ner-vr, *m* laborer; *f* move; drill.

manœuvrer, măh-ner-vreh, *v* to handle; to work; to maneuver.

manoir, măh-no'ăhr, *m* manor; mansion.

manque, mahngk, *m* lack; deficiency; failure.

manqué, é, mahng-keh, *a* missed; defective; failed.

manquement, mahngk-mahng, *m* omission; failure; oversight.

manquer, mahng-keh, *v* to fail; to want; to miss; to be very near to (doing something).

mansarde, mahng-săhrd, *f* attic.

manteau, mahng-toh, *m* mantle.

manuel, măh-nE-ell, *m* manual; textbook.

manuel, le,* măh-nE-ell, *a* manual.

manufacture, măh-nE-făhck-tEEr, *f* factory; manufacture.

manuscrit, măh-nEEs-kree, *m* manuscript.

maquereau, măhck-roh, *m* mackerel.

maquette, măhck-ett, *f* model; dummy (book); mock-up

maquillage, măh-kee-yăhsh, *m* makeup.

maquiller, măh-kee-yeh, *v* to make up (face); to disguise.

maraîch-er, ère, măh-ray-sheh, *a* & *m* truck farming; market-gardener.

marais, măh-ray, *m* marsh; swamp; bog.

marâtre, măh-rah-tr, *f* cruel stepmother.

marauder, măh-roh-deh, *v* to maraud; to plunder.

marbre, măhr-br, *m* marble; marble slab.

marchand, e, măhr-shahng, *mf* merchant; storekeeper; dealer; *a* salable; commercial.

marchandage, măhr-shahng-dăhsh, *m* bargaining.

marchandise, măhr-shahng-deez, *f* goods; wares.

marche, măhrsh, *f* stair; walking; march; progress; running (trains, etc).

marché, măhr-sheh, *m* market; bargain; purchase; contract; **bon –, bong –,** cheap; **meilleur –,** may-yer – cheaper.

marchepied, măhr-sher-pe-eh, *m* footstool; step.

marcher, măhr-sheh, *v* to walk; to tread; to work; to move

mardi, măhr-de, *m* Tuesday.

mare, măhr, *f* pool; pond.

marécage, măh-reh-kăhsh, *m* marsh; bog; swamp.

maréchal, măh-reh-shăhl, *m* marshal; **–ferrant, –** feh-rahng, blacksmith.

marée, măh-reh, *f* tide; fish (fresh).

margarine, măhr-ghăh-reen, *f* margarine.

marge, măhrsh, *f* margin; border; time.

marguerite, măhr-gher-reet, *f* daisy; marguerite.

mari, măh-re, *m* husband.

mariage, măh-re-ăhsh, *m* marriage; wedding; union.

marié, e, măh-re-eh, *mf* bridegroom; bride.

marier, măh-re-eh, *v* to marry; to unite; **se –,** to get married.

marin, măh-rang, *m* sailor; seaman.

marin, e, măh-rang, *a* marine; seagoing.

marinade, măh-re-năhd, *f* pickle; marinade.

marine, măh-reen, *f* navy; **bleu –,** bler –, navy blue.

marionnette, măh-re-onn-ett, *f* puppet; *pl* puppet show.

marmaille, măhr-mah'e, *f* crowd of kids.

marmite, măhr-meet, *f* pot (cooking).

marmot, măhr-mo, *m* brat; child.

marmotter, măhr-mot-eh, *v* to mutter.

maroquin, măh-rock-ang, *m* morocco leather.

marquant, e, măhr-kahng, *a* striking.

marque, măhrk, *f* mark; stamp; brand; token.

marquer, măhr–keh, *v* to mark.

marqueterie, măhr-kert-ree, *f* inlaid work.

marquis, e, măhr-ke, *mf* marquess; marchioness; marquee.

marraine, măh-rain, *f* godmother.

marrant, măh-rahng, *a* (*fam*) funny; amusing.

marron, măh-rong, *m* chestnut; *a* chestnut-

A B C D E F G H I J K L **M** N O P Q R S T U V W X Y Z

colored; brown.

marronnier, măh-ronn-e-eh, *m* chestnut tree.

mars, măhrs, *m* March; Mars.

marseillaise, măhr-say'e-ayz, *f* Marseillaise.

marsouin, măhr-soo-ang *m* porpoise.

marteau, măhr-toh, *m* hammer; door knocker.

marteler, măhr-ter-leh, *v* to hammer.

martial, e,* măhr-se-ăhl, *a* martial.

martinet, măhr-te-nay, *m* swift; whip.

martre, măhr-tr, *f* martin (bird); sable.

martyre, măhr-teer, *m* martyrdom.

masculin, e, măhss-kE-lang, *a* & *m* masculine; male.

masque, măhsk, *m* mask; pretense.

masquer, măhss-keh, *v* to mask; to disguise; to hide.

massacrer, măhss-ăh-kreh, *v* to slaughter; to bungle.

masse, măhss, *f* mass; heap; bulk; lot; pool.

massif, măhss-eef, *m* thicket; clump of shrubs; chain of mountains.

massi-f, ve,* măhss-eef, *a*

massive; heavy; solid.

massue, măhss-E, *f* club.

mastic, măhss-teeck, *m* putty.

mastiquer, măhss-te-keh, *v* to cement; to masticate.

mat, măht, *m* mate (chess).

mat, e, măht, *a* mat; unpolished; dull; heavy.

mât, mah, *m* mast; pole.

matelas, măht-lăh, *m* mattress.

matelot, măht-lo, *m* sailor; seaman.

mater, măh-teh, *v* to checkmate; to mat; (*fam*) to curb; to subdue.

matériaux, măh-te-re-oh, *mpl* materials.

matériel, măh-teh-re-ell, *m* stock; plant.

matériel, le,* măh-teh-re-ell, *a* material.

maternel, le,* măh-tair-nell, *a* motherly; maternal; *f* nursery school.

maternité, măh-tair-ne-teh, *f* maternity; maternity ward.

mathématiques, măh-teh-măh-teeck, *fpl* mathematics.

matière, măh-te-air, *f* matter; material; subject; cause.

matin, măh-tang, *m* morning.

matinal, e, măh-te-năhl, *a* early.

matinée, măh-te-neh, *f* morning; matinee.

matois, e, măh-to´ăh, *mf* sly person; *a* cunning.

matrice, măh-treess, *f* matrix; womb.

matricule, măh-tre-kEEl, *f* registration; roll.

maturité, măh-tE-re-teh, *f* maturity; ripeness.

maudire, moh-deer, *v* to curse.

maudit, e, moh-de, *a* cursed.

maugréer, moh-greh-eh, *v* to grumble.

maussade,* moh-săhd, *a* sulky.

mauvais, e, moh-vay, *a* evil; bad; ill; wrong.

mauve, mohv, *a* & *m* mauve.

me, mer, *pron* me; to me; at me.

mécanicien, meh-kăh-ne-se-ang, *m* mechanic; engineer.

mécanique, meh-kăh-neeck, *f* mechanics; machinery; *a** mechanical.

mécanisme, meh-kăh-nissm, *m* mechanism; machinery.

méchamment, meh-shăh-mahng, *adv* wickedly; unkindly.

méchanceté, meh-shahngss-teh, *f* wickedness; unkindness.

méchant, e, meh-shahng, *mf* wicked person; naughty child; *a* wicked; ill-natured; naughty.

mèche, maysh, *f* wick; match; lock (of hair).

mécompte, meh-kongt, *m* miscalculation; disappointment.

méconnaissable, meh-konn-ess-ăh-bl, *a* unrecognizable.

méconnu, e, meh-konn-E, *pp* & *a* unacknowledged; unappreciated.

mécontent, e, meh-kong-tahng, *a* discontented; unhappy.

mécréant, meh-kreh-ahng, *m* unbeliever.

médaille, meh-dah´e, *f* medal.

médaillon, meh-dah´e-yong, *m* medallion; locket.

médecin, mehd-sang, *m* physician; doctor.

médecine, mehd-seen, *f* medicine (art of).

médiat, e, meh-de-ăh, *a* mediate.

média-teur, trice, meh-de-ăh-**ter**, *mf* mediator.

médicament, meh-de-kăh-mahng, *m* medicine.

médiocre, * meh-de-ockr, *a* mediocre.

médire, meh-deer, *v* to slander.

médisance, meh-de-zahngss, *f* slander.

méditer, meh-de-teh, *v* to meditate; to plan.

méduse, meh-dEEz, *f* jellyfish.

méfait, meh-fay, *m* misdeed.

méfiance, meh-fe-ahngss, *f* mistrust; caution.

méfiant, e, meh-fe-ahng, *a* mistrustful; suspicious.

méfier (se), ser meh-fe-eh, *v* to mistrust (**de**); to beware of.

mégarde (par), păhr meh-găhrd, *adv* inadvertently.

mégère, meh-**shair**, *f* shrew (of woman).

meilleur, e, may'e-er, *a* & *mf* better; best.

mélancolique, * meh-lahng-koll-eeck, *a* melancholy; gloomy.

mélange, meh-lahngsh, *m* mixture; blending; medley.

mélanger, meh-lahng-sheh, *v* to mix; to blend.

mêlée, may-leh, *f* fray; scuffle; free-for-all.

mêler, may-leh, *v* to mix; to blend; to entangle.

mélodieu-x, se, * meh-lod-e-er, *a* melodious.

melon mer-long, *m* melon.

membrane, mahng-brăhn, *f* membrane; film.

membre, mahng-br, *f* member; limb; penis.

même, maym, *a* same; even; very same; self.

mémoire, meh-mo'ăhr, *m* memorandum; bill; *pl* memoirs; *f* memory; fame.

menaçant, e, mer-năh-sahng, *a* threatening.

menace, mer-năhss, *f* menace; threat.

menacer, mer-năhss-eh, *v* to threaten.

ménage, meh-năhsh, *m* housekeeping; household; housecleaning; married couple.

ménagement, meh-năhsh-mahng, *m* regard; caution; tact.

ménager, meh-năh-sheh, *v* to treat with care.

ménag-er, ère, meh-năh-sheh, *a* domestic; of the household.

ménagère, meh-năh-**shair**, *f* housewife.

mendiant, e, mahng-de-

A B C D E F G H I J K L **M** N O P Q R S T U V W X Y Z

ahng, *mf* & *a* beggar; begging.

mendicité, mahng-de-se-teh, *f* begging.

mendier, mahng-de-eh, *v* to beg.

menées, mer-neh, *fpl* intrigues.

mener, mer-neh, *v* to lead; to head; to convey.

meneur, mer-ner, *m* leader; ringleader.

méningite, meh-nang-sheet, *f* meningitis.

menotte, mer-not, *f* little hand; *pl* handcuffs.

mensonge, mahngss-ongsh, *m* lie.

mensuel, le,* mahng-sE-ell, *a* monthly.

mental, e,* mahng-tăhl, *a* mental.

mentalité, mahng-tăh-le-teh, *f* frame of mind; mentality.

menteu-r, se, mahng-ter, *mf* liar; *a* lying.

menthe, mahngt, *f* mint.

mentionner, mahng-se-onn-eh, *v* to mention.

mentir, mahng-teer, *v* to lie; to fib.

menton, mahng-tong, *m* chin.

menu, mer-nE, *m* menu.

menu e, mer-nE, *a* thin; slender; fine.

menuisier, mer-nwee-ze-

eh, *m* carpenter.

méprendre (se), ser meh-prahng-dr, *v* to be mistaken.

mépris, meh-pree, *m* contempt; scorn.

méprisable, meh-pre-zăh-bl, *a* contemptible; despicable.

méprise, meh-preez, *f* mistake.

mépriser, meh-pre-zeh, *v* to despise; to scorn.

mer, mair, *f* sea; **mal de –,** măhl der –, seasickness.

mercernaire, mair-ser-nair, *m* & *a* mercenary.

mercerie, mair-ser-ree, *f* notions store.

merci, mair-se, *m* thanks; thank you; *f* mercy.

merci-er, ère, mair-se-eh, *mf* notions dealer.

mercredi, mair-krer-de, *m* Wednesday.

mère, mair, *f* mother; *a* principal.

méridien, ne, meh-re-de-ang, *a* meridian.

méridional, e, meh-re-de-onn-ăhl, *a* & *mf* southern; southerner.

mérite, meh-reet, *m* merit; worth; talent.

mériter, meh-re-teh, *v* to deserve; to be worth; to require.

méritoire,* meh-re-to'ăhr,

a meritorious.

merlan, mair-lahng, *m* whiting.

merle, mairl, *m* blackbird.

merveille, mair-vay'e, *f* marvel; wonder; *adv phr* à –, ăh –, excellently.

merveilleu-x, se,* mair-vay'e-er, *a* wonderful.

mes, may, *poss a pl* my.

mésallier (se), ser meh-zăh-le-eh, *v* to marry beneath oneself.

mésange, meh-zahngsh, *f* titmouse (bird).

mésaventure, meh-zăh-vahng-tEEr, *f* mischance; mishap.

mésestimer, meh-zess-te-meh, *v* to undervalue.

mesquin, e,* mess-kang, *a* mean; petty; stingy.

mesquinerie, mess-keen-ree, *f* meanness; pettiness.

message, mess-ăhsh, *m* message; errand.

messag-er, ère, mess-ăh-sheh, *mf* messenger.

messagerie, mess-ăhsh-ree, *f* mail service; shipping service.

messe, mayss, *f* mass.

mesure, mer-zEEr, *f* measure; measurement; proportion; step; propriety; bar (music); time.

mesuré, e, mer-zE-reh, *a* regular; guarded.

mesurer, mer-zE-reh, *v* to measure; to consider; to proportion.

mésuser, meh-zE-zeh, *v* to misuse.

métal, meh-tăhl, *m* metal.

métamorphose, meh-tăh-mor-fohz, *f* metamorphosis; transformation.

météore, meh-teh-or, *m* meteor.

météorologique, meh-teh-o-ro-lo-**sheeck,** *a* meteorological.

méthode, meh-tod, *f* method; way; system.

méthodique,* meh-tod-eeck, *a* methodical.

méticuleu-x, se,* meh-te-kE-ler, *a* meticulous; particular.

métier, meh-te-eh, *m* trade; profession; handicraft; loom.

métis, se, meh-tee, *mf & a* person of mixed race; of mixed race.

métrage, meh-trăhsh, *m* measuring; metric length; length of film.

mètre, met-tr, *m* meter; rule.

métrique, meh-treeck, *a* metric.

métropole, meh-trop-ol, *f* metropolis; mother country.

métropolitain, meh-trop-oll-e-tang, *a* metropolitan; **le métro,** lermeh-tro, *m* subway.

mets, may, *m* food; dish.

mettre, met-tr, *v* to put; to set; to wear.

meuble, mer-bl, *m* piece of furniture; *pl* furniture; *a* movable.

meubler, mer-bleh, *v* to furnish; to stock.

meule, merl, *f* grindstone; millstone.

meuni-er, ère, mer-ne-eh, *mf* miller.

meurtre, mer-tr, *m* murder.

meurtri-er, ère, mer-tre-eh, *mf* murderer; murderess; *a* deadly.

meurtrir, mer-treer, *v* to bruise.

meurtrissure, mer-triss-EEr, *f* bruise.

meute, mert, *f* pack; *(fam)* mob.

mi, me, *m* Mi (music); E.

mi, me, half; mid; semi-.

miasme, me-ăhssm, *m* miasma.

miauler, me-ohl-eh, *v* to mew.

microbe, me-krob, *m* microbe; *(fam)* germ.

microfilm, me-kroh-feelm, *m* microfilm.

microphone, me-krof-onn, *m* microphone.

microsillon, me-croh-se-yong, *m* long-playing record.

midi, me-de, *m* midday; noon; south (of France).

mie, me, *f* crumb (inside of a loaf).

miel, me-ell, *m* honey.

mielleu-x, se,* me-ell-er, *a* honeyed; bland; soft-spoken.

mien, ne, me-ang, *poss pron* mine.

miette, me-ett, *f* crumb; bit.

mieux, me-er, *adv* better; best; more; *m* best thing; *a* better.

mignon, ne, meen-yong, *a* cute.

migraine, me-grain, *f* migraine; headache.

mijaurée, me-shohr-eh, *f* affected woman.

mijoter, me-shot-eh, *v* to simmer.

milieu, me-le-er, *m* middle; circle; environment; social class.

militaire, me-le-tair, *m* soldier; *a* military.

mille, mill, *m* one thousand; *a* thousand.

milliard, mill-e-ăhr, *m*

one thousand millions.

millième, mill-e-aim, *m* & *a* thousandth.

million, mill-e-*ong*, *m* million.

millionième, mill-e-onn-e-emm, *m* & *a* millionth.

mime, meem, *m* mime.

minable, me-năh-bl, *a* shabby; pitiable.

minauder, me-nohd-eh, *v* to simper.

mince, ma*ng*ss, *a* slender; slim; scanty.

mine, meen, *f* appearance; look; mine; lead (of pencil).

miner, me-neh, *v* to undermine; to wear away.

minerai, meen-ray, *m* ore.

minéral, e, me-neh-răhl, *a* mineral.

mineur, me-ner, *m* miner; *a* minor (music); minor.

mineur, e, me-ner, *a* minor; underage.

miniature, me-ne-ăh-tEEr, *f* miniature.

mini-er, ère, me-ne-eh, *a* mining.

minime, me-neem, *a* very small; trifling.

ministère, me-niss-tair, *m* ministry; services.

ministre, me-neestr, *m* minister; secretary of

state; clergyman.

minois, me-no'ăh, *m* (*fam*) pretty face.

minuit, me-nwe, *m* midnight.

minuscule, me-nEEs-kEEl, *f* small letter; *a* minute.

minute, me-nEEt, *f* minute; instant.

minutieu-x, se,* me-nEE-se-er, *a* particular; detailed.

miracle, me-răh-kl, *m* miracle; wonder.

miraculeu-x, se,* me-răh-kE-ler, *a* miraculous; wonderful.

mirage, me-răhsh, *m* mirage; delusion.

mirer, me-reh, *v* to aim at; **se–,** ser, to look at (oneself).

miroir, me-ro'ăhr, *m* mirror.

miroiter, me-ro'ăh-teh, *v* to flash; to glisten; **faire–,** fehr–, to promise.

mise, meez, *f* placing; dress; stake.

misérable, me-zeh-răh-bl, *mf* wretch.

misère, me-zair, *f* misery; poverty; trifle.

miséricorde, me-zeh-re-kord, *f* mercy.

mission, miss-e-o*ng*, *f* mission.

missionnaire, miss-e-onn-air, *n* missionary.

mitaine, me-tain, *f* mitten.

mite, meet, *f* clothes moth; mite.

mi-temps, me-tah*ng*, *f* halftime; interval; part time.

mitiger, me-te-sheh, *v* to mitigate.

mitraille, me-trah'e, *f* grapeshot.

mitrailleuse, me-trah'e-erz, *f* machine gun.

mixte, meekst, *a* mixed; **école –,** eh-kol –, coed school.

mixtion, meeks-te-o*ng*, *f* mixture; compounding; blending.

mobile, mob-eel, *m* moving body; motive; mobile; *a* movable; changing.

mobilier, mob-e-le-eh, *m* furniture.

mobili-er, ère, mob-e-le-eh, *a* movable; personal.

mobiliser, mob-e-le-zeh, *v* to mobilize.

mobilité, mob-e-le-teh, *f* mobility; instability.

mode, mod, *m* mood; mode; method.

mode, mod, *f* fashion; way; *pl* millinery.

modèle, mod-ell, *m*

model; pattern.

modeler, mod-leh, *v* to model; to shape; to mold.

modération, mod-eh-răh-se-ong, *f* moderation.

modérer, mod-eh-reh, *v* to moderate.

moderne, mod-airn, *mf* & *a* modern style; modern.

modeste, * mod-est, *a* modest; unassuming.

modestie, mod-ess-tee, *f* modesty.

modifier, mod-e-fe-eh, *v* to modify.

modique, * mod-eeck, *a* moderate; small.

modiste, mod-eest, *f* milliner.

moelle, mwăhl, *f* marrow (bone); pith.

moelleu-x, se, * mwăhller, *a* marrowy; soft; mellow.

mœurs, mers, *fpl* manners; customs; morals.

moi, mwăh, *pers pron* I; me; to me; *m* self; ego.

moindre, * mwang-dr, *a* less; **le –,** ler –, the least.

moine, mwăhn, *m* monk.

moineau, mwăh-noh, *m* sparrow.

moins, mwang, *adv* less; fewer; least; *prep* minus.

mois, mwăh, *m* month.

moisir, mwăh-zeer, *v* to go

moldy;(*fam*) to vegetate.

moisson, mwăhss-ong, *f* harvest; crop.

moite, mwăht, *a* moist; damp; clammy.

moiteur, mwăh-ter, *f* moistness; dampness.

moitié, mwăh-te-eh, *f* half; *adv* half; partly.

mol, le, (* see **mou**).

molaire, moll-air, *f* molar tooth.

môle, mohl, *m* mole; pier.

molester, moll-ess-teh, *v* to molest; to annoy.

mollasse, moll-ăhss, *a* flabby; spineless.

mollesse, moll-ess, *f* softness; indolence.

mollet, moll-ay, *m* calf (of leg).

molletonné, moll-tonn-eh, *a* lined with fleece; with raised nap.

mollir, moll-eer, *v* to soften; to slacken; to give way.

moment, mom-ahng, *m* moment; time; occasion.

momentané,* e, mom-ahng-tăh-neh, *a* momentary.

momie, mom-ee, *f* mummy.

mon, mong, *poss a m* my; *f* **ma,** măh, *pl* **mes,** may.

monarchie, monn-ăhr-

shee, *f* monarchy.

monarque, monn-ăhrk, *m* monarch.

monastère, monn-ăhss-tair, *m* monastery.

monceau, mong,soh, *m* heap.

mondain, e, * mong-dang, *a* worldly; mundane; fashionable.

monde, mongd, *m* world; mankind; people; society.

mondial, e, mong-de-ăhl, *a* worldwide.

monétaire, monn-eh-tair, *a* monetary.

moniteur, monn-e-ter, *m* monitor; instructor; gazette.

monnaie, monn-ay, *f* money; coin; change; mint.

monocle, monn-ockl, *m* monocle.

monopole, monn-op-ol, *m* monopoly.

monotone, monn-ot-onn, *a* monotonous.

monseigneur, mong-sehn-yer, *m* Your Grace; Your Royal Highness.

monsieur, mer-se-er, *m* gentleman; Mr.; master; sir.

monstre, mongss-tr, *m* monster.

monstrueu-x, se, *

a
b
c
d
e
f
g
h
i
j
k
l
m
n
o
p
q
r
s
t
u
v
w
x
y
z

mongss-trE-er, *a* monstrous; shocking.

mont, mong, *m* mount; mountain.

montage, mong-tăhsh, *m* raising; putting up.

montagnard, e, mong-tăhn-yăhr, *mf* mountaineer.

montagne, mong-tăhn-yer, *f* mountain.

montant, mong-tahng, *m* upright; rise; amount.

montant, e, mong-tahng, *a* rising; uphill; high-necked.

montée, mong-teh, *f* rise; ascent; step.

monter, mong-teh, *v* to ascend; to rise; to ride; to set up; to mount (jewel); **se –,** to amount.

monticule, mong-te-kEEl, *m* hillock.

montre, mong-tr, *f* watch; show; display window.

montrer, mong-treh, *v* to show; to teach.

monture, mong-tEEr, *f* mount; frame; setting.

monument, monn-E-mahng, *m* monument.

moquer (se), ser mock-eh, *v* to mock; to make fun of.

moquerie, mock-ree, *f* mockery; derision.

moquette, mock-ett, *f* carpet.

moqueu-r, se, mock-er, *mf* mocker; *a* mocking.

moral, mor-ăhl, *m* state of mind; morale; spirits.

moral, e, * mor-ăhl, *a* moral; mental.

morale, mor-ăhl, *f* morals; reprimand; moral (of story).

morceau, mor-soh, *m* piece; bit; morsel; extract.

morceler, mor-ser-leh, *v* to cut up into small pieces; to parcel out.

mordant, e, mor-dahng, *a* biting; sarcastic.

mordicus, mor-de-kEEss, *adv* stubbornly; doggedly.

mordre, mor-dr, *v* to bite; to gnaw; to eat away.

morfondre (se), ser mor-fong-dr, *v* to be chilled; to be bored stiff waiting.

morgue, morgh, *f* mortuary; arrogance.

moribond, e, mor-e-bong, *mf & a* dying person; dying.

morne, morn, *a* gloomy; sad; dull.

morose, mor-ohz, *a* morose.

morphine, mor-feen, *f* morphine.

mors, mor, *m* bit; **prendre le –aux dents, prahng-dr ler – oh dahng,** to bolt.

morsure, mor-sEEr, *f* bite; sting.

mort, mor, *f* death.

mort, e, mor, *mf* dead person; *a* dead; stagnant; spent.

mortalité, mor-tăh-le-teh, *f* mortality; death rate.

mortel, le, * mor-tell, *a* mortal; deadly; tedious.

mortier, mor-te-eh, *m* mortar.

mortifier, mor-te-fe-eh, *v* to mortify; to hang (game).

morue, mor-EE, *f* codfish.

morveu-x, se, mor-ver, *mf* dirty child; brat; *a* snotty-nosed.

mot, moh, *m* word; saying; hint.

moteur, mot-er, *m* motor; engine.

mo-teur, trice, mot-er, *a* motive; moving.

motif, mot-eeff, *m* motive; reason.

motion, mo-se-ong, *f* motion; proposal.

motiver, mot-e-veh, *v* to state reason for; to motivate.

motocyclette, mot-oss-e-klett, *f* motorcycle.

motocycliste, mot-oss-e-kleesst, *m* motorcyclist.

motte, mot, *f* clod; pat (of butter).

mou (mol before a word beginning with a vowel or **"h"** mute); *f* **molle,** moo, mol; *a* soft; indolent; muggy (weather).

mouchard, moo-shǎhr, *m* (*fam*) sneak; informer.

mouche, moosh, *f* fly; beauty-spot; bull's eye.

moucher, moo-sheh, *v* to wipe the nose of; **se –,** to blow one's nose.

moucheron, moosh-rong, *m* gnat; snuff (candle).

mouchoir, moo-sho'ǎhr, *m* handkerchief.

moudre, moodr, *v* to grind.

moue, moo, *f* pout.

mouette, moo-ett, *f* seagull.

mouillé, e, moo'e-yeh, *a* wet; soaked; anchored.

mouiller, moo'e-yeh, *v* to wet; to soak; to anchor.

moule, moo, *m* mold; cast; form; *f* mussel.

mouler, moo-leh, *v* to mold; to cast; to shape.

moulin, moo-lang, *m* mill; windmill; **– à paroles, –** ǎh pǎh-rol, chatterbox.

moulu, e, moo-lE, *pp* & *a* ground.

mourant, e, moo-rahng,

mf & *a* dying person; dying.

mourir, moo-reer, *v* to die; to die away; to go out (fire, light).

mousquetaire, mooss-ker-tair, *m* musketeer.

mousse, mooss, *m* ship's-boy; *f* moss; froth; lather.

mousseline, mooss-leen, *f* muslin; chiffon.

mousser, mooss-eh, *v* to foam; to lather; to sparkle; **faire –,** fair **–,** to froth.

mousseu-x, se, mooss-*er*, *a* frothy.

moustache, mooss-tǎhsh, *f* moustache; whiskers (animals).

moustiquaire, mooss-te-kair, *m* mosquito net.

moustique, mooss-teeck, *m* mosquito.

moutarde, moo-tǎhrd, *f* mustard.

mouton, moo-tong, *m* sheep; sheepskin.

mouvant, e, moo-vahng, *a* moving; shifting.

mouvement, moov-mahng, *m* movement; motion; disturbance.

mouvementé, e, moov-mahng-teh, *a* agitated; lively; eventful; fluctuating.

mouvoir, moo-vo'ǎhr, *v* to move; to stir; to start.

moyen, mo'ǎh-yang, *m* means; medium; power.

moyen, ne, mo'ǎh-yang, *a* middle; mean; average.

moyennant, mo'ǎh-yay-nahng *prep* on condition that; for a consideration.

moyenne, moǎh-yain, *f* average; mean.

muer, mE-eh, *v* to molt; to break (voice).

muet, te, mE-ay, *mf* dumb person; *a* dumb; taciturn.

mufle, mEE-fl, *m* muzzle; (*fam*) face; bore.

mugir, mE-sheer, *v* to moo; to bellow; to roar.

mugissement, mE-shiss-mahng, *m* mooing; bellowing; roaring.

muguet, mE-ghay, *m* lily of the valley.

mule, mEEl, *f* female-mule; slipper.

mulet, mE-lay, *m* mule; mullet.

multiplier, mEEl-te-ple-eh, *v* to multiply.

multitude, mEEl-te-tEEd, *f* multitude.

municipalité, mE-ne-se-pǎh-le-teh, *f* municipality; town hall.

munificence, mE-ne-fe-sahngss, *f* munificence.

munir, mE-neer, *v* to provide; to supply; to arm (**de,** with).

munitions, mE-ne-se-ong, *fpl* ammunition; stores.

mur, mEEr, *m* wall; **au pied du –,** oh pe-eh dE –, in a corner.

mûr, e, * mEEr, *a* ripe; mature; mellow.

muraille, mE-rah'e, *f* wall; rampart.

mûre, mEEr, *f* mulberry; blackberry.

mûrir, mEE-reer, *v* to ripen; to mature.

murmure, mEEr-mEEr, *m* murmur; babbling; whisper.

murmurer, mEEr-me-reh, *v* to murmur; to grumble; to whisper.

muscade, mEEss-kăhd, *f* nutmeg.

muscat, mEEss-kăh, *m* muscatel.

muscle, mEEss-kl, *m* muscle.

musculeu-x, se, mEEss-kE-ler, *a* muscular.

museau, mE-zoh, *m* snout; muzzle; (*fam*) face.

musée, mE-zeh, *m* museum.

museler, mEEz-leh, *v* to muzzle.

muser, mE-zeh, *v* to loiter; to dawdle.

musicien, ne, mE-ze-se-ang, *mf* musician; *a* musical.

musique, mE-zeeck, *f* music; band.

mutation, mE-tăh-se-ong, *f* change; transfer.

mutiler, mE-te-leh, *v* to mutilate; to maim; to deface.

mutin, e, mE-tang, *mf* & *a* mutinous; unruly.

mutinerie, mE-teen-ree, *f* mutiny.

mutisme, mE-tissm, *m* muteness.

mutuel, le, * mE-tE-ell, *a* mutual.

myope, me-op, *a* myopic.

myosotis, me-oz-ot-iss, *m* forget-me-not.

myrte, meert, *m* myrtle.

mystère, miss-tair, *m* mystery.

mystérieu-x, se, * miss-teh-re-er, *a* mysterious.

mystifier, miss-te-fe-eh, *v* to mystify; to fool.

mystique, * miss-teeck, *mf* & *a* mystic; mystical.

myth, meth, *m* myth.

mythique, me-teek, *a* mythical.

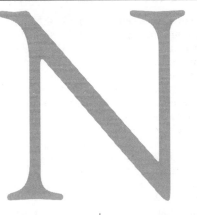

nacelle, năh-sell, *f* small boat; basket (of balloon).

nacre, năh-kr, *f* mother-of-pearl.

nage, năhsh, *f* swimming.

nageoire, năh-sho'ăhr, *f* fin.

nager, năh-sheh, *v* to swim; to float.

nageu-r, se, năh-sher, *mf* swimmer.

naguère, năh-ghair, *adv* not long ago.

na-ïf, ïve,* năh-eeff, *a* gullible; naive.

nain, e, nang, *mf* dwarf; *a* dwarfish.

naissance, ness-ahngss, *f* birth; descent; rise.

naissant, e, ness-ahng, *a* newborn; rising; budding.

naître, nay-tr, *v* to be born; to spring; to dawn.

naïveté, năh-eev-teh, *f* naïveté; gullibility.

nantir, nahng-teer, *v* to provide; to secure.

nantissement, nahng-tiss-mahng, *m* security; pledge.

nappe, năhpp, *f* tablecloth; sheet (of water).

narcisse, năhr-seess, *m* narcissus; daffodil.

narcotique, năhr-ko-teeck, *m & a* narcotic.

narguer, năhr-gheh, *v* to flout; to scoff at.

narine, năh-reen, *f* nostril.

narration, năh-răh-se-ong, *f* narrative.

nasal, e,* năh-zăhl, *a* nasal.

nasiller, năh-zee-yeh, *v* to speak through the nose.

natal, e, năh-tàhl, *a* natal; native.

natalité, năh-tăh-le-teh, *f* birthrate.

natation, năh-tăh-se-ong, *f* swimming.

nati-f, ve, năh-teeff, *a* native.

nation, năh-se-ong, *f* nation.

national, e, năh-se-onn-ăhl, *a* national.

nationalité, năh-se-onn-ăh-le-teh, *f* nationality.

nationaux, năh-se-onn-oh, *mpl* nationals.

natte, năht, *f* mat; matting; plait.

naturaliser, năh-tE-răh-le-zeh, *v* to naturalize.

naturaliste, năh-tE-răh-leesst, *m* naturalist; taxidermist.

nature, năh-tEEr, *f* nature; kind; constitution; *a* plain (of cooking).

naturel, năh-tE-rell, *m* nature; character; native.

naturel, le,* năh-tE-rell, *a* natural; unaffected; illegitimate.

naufrage, noh-frăhsh, *m* shipwreck.

nauséabond, e, noh-zeh-ăh-bong, *a* nauseous.

nausée, noh-zeh, *f* nausea; disgust.

nautique, noh-tecck, *a* nautical; aquatic.

naval, e, năh-văhl, *a* naval.

navet, năh-vay, *m* turnip; (*fam*) bad film.

navette, năh-vett, *f* shuttle; **faire la –,** fair lăh –, to go to and fro.

navigable, năh-ve-ghăh-bl, *a* navigable; seaworthy.

naviguer, năh-ve-gheh, *v* to navigate; to sail.

navire, năh-veer, *m* ship; vessel.

navrant, e, năh-vrahng, *a* heartrending; distressing.

navrer, năh-vreh, *v* to break the heart of; to distress.

ne (n'), ner, *adv* not.

né, e, neh, *pp* & *a* born.

néanmoins, neh-ahng-mo'ang, *adv* nevertheless; for all that; however.

néant, neh-ahng, *m* naught; nothingness; worthlessness.

nébuleuse, neh-bE-lerz, *f* nebula.

nébuleu-x, se, neh-bE-ler, *a* nebulous; cloudy; obscure.

nécessaire, neh-sess-air, *m* the needful; necessaries; outfit; *a** necessary; needful.

nécessité, neh-sess-e-teh, *f* necessity; need; *pl* necessaries.

nécessiter, neh-sess-e-teh, *v* to necessitate; to compel.

nécessiteu-x, se, neh-sess-e-ter, *a* needy.

nef, neff, *f* nave.

néfaste, neh-făhsst, *a* ill-omened; unlucky; disastrous.

négati-f, ve,* neh-ghăh-teeff, *a* negative; *m* negative (photo).

négligé, neh-gle-sheh, *m* negligee.

négligé, e, neh-gle-sheh, *pp* & *a* neglected; careless; slovenly.

négligeable, neh-gle-shăh-bl, *a* negligible.

négligemment, neh-gle-shăh-mahng, *adv* carelessly.

négligence, neh-gle-shahngss, *f* neglect; needlessness; oversight.

négligent, e, neh-gle-shahng, *a* negligent; careless.

négliger, neh-gle-sheh, *v* to neglect; to omit; to overlook; to disregard.

négoce, neh-goss, *m* trade; business; trafficking.

négociable, neh-goss-e-ăh-bl, *a* negotiable.

négociant, neh-goss-e-ahng, *m* merchant.

négocier, neh-goss-e-eh, *v* to negotiate; to deal; to trade.

nègre, négresse, nay-gr, neh-gress, *mf* Negro; Negress.

négrillon, ne, neh-gree-yong, *mf* Negro boy, girl.

neige, naysh, *f* snow.

neiger, nay-sheh, *v* to snow.

neigeu-x, se, nay-sher, *a* snowy.

nénuphar, neh-nE-făhr, *m* water lily.

nerf, nair, *m* nerve; sinew; energy.

ne rien connaître à, ner-re-ang-konn-ay-trăh *v* to be ignorant of something.

nerveu-x, se,* nair-ver, *a* nervous; vigorous; highly strung.

nervure, nair-vEEr, *f* nerve; cording; rib.

net, nett, *m* fair copy; *adv* plainly; entirely; at once; flatly.

net, te,* nett, *a* neat; clean; clear; net (price); sharp.

netteté, nett-teh, *f* cleanness; clearness; distinctness.

nettoiement, nay-to'ăh-mahng, *m* cleaning; clearing.

nettoyage, nay- to'ăh-yăhsh, *m* cleaning (at dry cleaners).

nettoyer, nay-to'ăh-yeh, *v* to clean; to wipe; to rid of; to clear.

neuf, nerf, *a* nine; ninth.

neu-f, ve, nerf, *a* new; fresh; raw; inexperienced.

neutre, ner-tr, *m* & *a* neuter; neutral.

neuvième, ner-ve-aym, *m* & *a* ninth.

neveu, ner-ver, *m* nephew.

névralgie, neh-vrăhl-**shee**, *f* neuralgia.

névrose, neh-vrohz, *f* neurosis.

névrosé, neh-vro-zeh, *a* neurotic.

nez, neh, *m* nose; face; scent; **–à –, – ăh –,** face to face.

ni, ne, *conj* neither; nor; either; or.

niable, ne-ăh-bl, *a* deniable.

niais, e,* ne-ay, *mf* & *a* silly person; simpleton; stupid.

niaiser, ne-ay-zeh, *v* to play the fool; to trifle.

niaiserie, ne-ayz-ree, *f* silliness; foolery.

niche, neesh, *f* nook; kennel; trick.

nichée, ne-sheh, *f* nestful; brood; lot.

nicher, ne-sheh, *v* to build a nest; to lodge; **se –,** to nestle.

nickelé, e, neek-leh, *pp* & *a* nickeled; nickel-plated.

nid, ne, *m* nest.

nièce, ne-ess, *f* niece.

nier, ne-eh, *v* to deny.

nigaud, e, ne-ghoh, *mf* & *a* simpleton; silly; foolish.

nimbe, nangb, *m* nimbus; halo.

nipper, ne-peh, *v* (*fam*) to rig out.

nitouche (sainte), sangt ne-toosh, *f* (*fam*) little hypocrite.

niveau, ne-voh, *m* level; standard.

niveler, neev-leh, *v* to level.

nivellement, ne-vell-mahng, *m* leveling.

noble, nobl, *mf* & *a* nobleman; noble; high.

noblesse, nob-less, *f* nobility.

noce, noss, *f* wedding; wedding party; *pl* usually: **voyage de –s,** vo'ăh-yăhsh der –, honeymoon.

noci-f, ve, noss-eeff, *a* harmful.

nocturne, nock-tEErn, *m* (music) nocturne; *a* nocturnal; nightly.

Noël, no-ell, *m* Christmas.

nœud, ner, *m* knot; bow.

noir, no'ăr, *m* black; Negro.

noir, e, no'ăhr, *a* black; swarthy; dark; gloomy; wicked.

noirâtre, no'ăh-rah-tr, *a* blackish.

noiraud, e, no'ăh-roh, *mf* & *a* swarthy-looking person; swarthy.

noirceur, no'ăhr-ser, *f* blackness; atrocity.

noircir, no'ăhr-seer, *v* to blacken.

noisette, no'ăh-zett, *f* hazelnut; *a inv* nut-brown.

noix, no'ăh, *f* walnut; nut; kernel.

nom, nong, *m* name; fame; noun; **–de famille,** – der făh-mee-ye, last name.

nomade, nomm-ăhd, *mf* & *a* nomad; nomadic.

nombre, nong-br, *m* number; quantity.

nombreu-x, se, nong-brer,

a
b
c
d
e
f
g
h
i
j
k
l
m
n
o
p
q
r
s
t
u
v
w
x
y
z

A B C D E F G H I J K L M N O P Q R S T U V W X Y Z

a numerous; many.

nombril, nong-bre, *m* navel.

nomenclature, nomm-ahng-klăh-tEEr, *f* nomenclature.

nominal, e,* nomm-e-năhl, *a* nominal.

nominatif, nomm-e-năh-teeff, *m* nominative case.

nominati-f, ve, nomm-e-năh-teeff, *a* nominative; registered; personal.

nomination, nomm-e-năh-se-ong, *f* nomination; appointment.

nommément, nomm-eh-mahng, *adv* by name; particularly.

nommer, nomm-eh, *v* to call; to mention; to appoint; **se –,** to give one's name; to be called.

non, nong, *adv* no; not.

nonchalamment, nong-shăh-lăh-mahng, *adv* non- chalantly.

nonchalance, nong-shăh-lahngss, *f* nonchalance.

nonne, nonn, *f* nun.

nonpareil, le, nong-păh-ray'e, *a* nonpareil; matchless.

non-sens, nong-sahngss, *m* absurd sentence.

nord, nor, *m* north; north

wind; *a* north.

nord-est, nor-esst, *m* northeast.

nord-ouest, nor-wesst, *m* northwest.

normal, e,* nor-măhl, *a* normal; standard.

nos, noh, *poss a mfpl* our.

nostalgie, noss-tahl-shee, *f* nostalgia; homesickness.

notable,* not-ăh-bl, *a* notable; considerable; eminent.

notaire, not-air, *m* notary.

notamment, not-ăh-mahng, *adv* particularly.

note, not, *f* note; mark; bill; memorandum.

noter, not-eh, *v* to note; to notice; to bear in mind.

notice, not-eess, *f* notice; account; instructions.

notifier, not-e-fe-eh, *v* to notify.

notion, noss-e-ong, *f* notion; idea.

notoire,* not-o'ăhr, *a* well-known; notorious.

notoriété, not-or-e-eh-teh, *f* notoriety.

notre, notr, *poss a m & f* our.

nôtre, noh-tr, *poss pron,* ours.

nouer, noo-eh, *v* to tie; to knot; to engage in.

noueu-x, se, noo-er, *a* knotty; knotted.

nougat, noo-găh, *m* nougat.

nourri, e, noo-re, *pp & a* fed; full; rich.

nourrice, noo-reess, *f* nurse; wet-nurse.

nourrir, noo-rEEr, *v* to feed; to nurse; to entertain (**de,** on; with).

nourrissant, e, noo-riss-ahng, *a* nourishing; nutritious.

nourrisson, noo-riss-ong, *m* newborn.

nourriture, noo-re-tEEr, *f* food; diet; sustenance.

nous, noo, *pers pron* we; us; to us; at us; ourselves; each other.

nouveau, noo-voh, *m* new thing; new person; *adv* newly.

nouveau (nouvel before a word beginning with a vowel or **h** mute), *f* **nouvelle,*** noo-voh, noo-vell, *a* new; novel; recent; fresh; additional; another.

nouveau-né, e, noo-voh-neh, *a* newborn.

nouveauté, noo-voh-teh, *f* newness; novelty; *pl* fancy articles.

nouvelle, noov-ell, *f* short story.

nova-teur, trice, nov-ăh-ter, *a* innovative.

novembre, nov-ahng-br, *m* November.

novice, nov-eess, *mf* novice; *a* inexperienced.

noyade, no'ăh-yăhd, *f* drowning.

noyau, no'ăh-yoh, *m* stone; kernel; nucleus; core.

noyer, no'ăh-yeh, *v* to drown; to swamp; to inundate; *m* walnut tree.

nu, nE, *m* bare part; nude; **à –, ăh –,** bare.

nu, e, nE, *a* bare; plain.

nuage, nE-ăhsh, *m* cloud; mist; gloom.

nuageu-x, se, nE-ăh-sher, *a* cloudy.

nuance, nE-ahngss, *f* shade; tint; very small difference.

nuancer, nE-ahngss-eh, *v* to shade; to vary.

nubile, nE-beel, *a* nubile; marriageable.

nucléaire, nEE-cleh-air, *a* nuclear.

nudité, nE-de-teh, *f* nakedness; *pl* naked figures.

nuée, nE-eh, *f* cloud; swarm; shower (of objects).

nuire (à), nweer ăh, *v* to hurt; to prejudice; to hinder.

nuisible,* nwee-zee-bl, *a* harmful; detrimental.

nuit, nwee, *f* night; darkness; **–blanche, –** blahngsh, sleepless night.

nul, le, nEEl, *a* no; not any; of no force; void; worth less; *pron* nobody; no one.

nullement, nEEl-mahng, *adv* by no means.

nullité, nEEl-le-teh, *f* nullity; incapacity; nonentity.

numérateur, nE-meh-răh-ter, *m* numerator.

numérique,* nE-meh-reeck, *a* numerical.

numéro, nE-meh-ro, *m* number; ticket; item (on program); issue (of magazines, etc).

numéroter, nE-meh-rot-eh, *v* to number.

nuptial, e, nEEp-se-ăhl, *a* nuptial.

nuque, nEEk, *f* nape of the neck.

nutriti-f, ve, nE-tre-teeff, *a* nourishing.

nylon, nee-long, *m* nylon.

nymphe, nangf, *f* nymph.

A
B
C
D
E
F
G
H
I
J
K
L
M
N
O
P
Q
R
S
T
U
V
W
X
Y
Z

ô! o, *interj* oh!

obéir, ob-eh-eer, *v* to obey; to submit.

obéissance, ob-eh-iss-ahngss, *f* obedience; allegiance.

obéissant, e, ob-eh-iss-ahng, *a* obedient; dutiful.

obèse, ob-ayz, *a* obese; corpulent.

obésité, ob-eh-ze-teh, *f* obesity; corpulence.

objecter, ob-sheck-teh, *v* to object; to allege against.

objectif, ob-sheck-teeff, *m* lens; aim; target.

objecti-f, ive,* ob-sheck-teeff, *a* objective.

objection, ob-sheck-se-ong, *f* objection.

objet, ob-shay, *m* object; subject; matter; thing.

oblation, ob-lǎh-se-ong, *f* offering.

obligataire, ob-le-gǎh-tair, *m* debenture holder.

obligation, ob-le-gǎh-se-ong, *f* obligation; duty; debenture; *v* to bond.

obligatoire,* ob-le-gǎh-to'ǎhr, *a* obligatory; compulsory.

obligeamment, ob-le-shǎh-mahng, *adv* obligingly.

obligeance, ob-le-shahngss, *f* obligingness; kindness.

obligeant, e, ob-le-shahng, *a* obliging; kind.

obliger, ob-le-sheh, *v* to oblige; to compel; to bind; to gratify.

oblique,* ob-leeck, *a* oblique; slanting; underhand.

obliquité, ob-le-kwe-teh, *f* obliquity; insincerity.

oblitérer, ob-le-teh-reh, *v* to obliterate; to cancel.

obscène, ob-sain, *a* obscene.

obscur, e, ob-skEEr, *a* dark; obscure; hidden; mysterious.

obscurcir, ob-skEEr-seer, *v* to obscure; to cloud; to darken.

obscurément, ob-skE-reh-mahng, *adv* obscurely.

obscurité, ob-skE-re-teh, *f* darkness; obscurity; mysteriousness.

obséder, ob-seh-deh, *v* to obsess.

obsèques, ob-sayk, *fpl* funeral.

obséquieu-x, se,* ob-seh-kee-er, *a* obsequious.

observa-teur, trice, ob-sair-vǎh-ter, *mf* & *a* observer; observant.

observation, ob-sair-vǎh-se-ong, *f* observation; observance; remark; reprimand.

observatoire, ob-sair-vǎh-to'ǎhr, *m* observatory.

observer, ob-sair-veh, *v* to observe; to comply with.

obsession, ob-seh-se-ong, *f* obsession.

obstacle, obs-tăh-kl, *m* obstacle, hindrance.

obstination, obs-te-năh-se-*ong*, *f* obstinacy; stubbornness.

obstiné, e, obs-te-neh, *mf* & *a* obstinate person; obstinate; stubborn.

obstinément, obs-te-neh-mah*ng*, *adv* obstinately.

obstiner (s'), obs-te-neh, *v* to be obstinate; to persist (**à,** in).

obstruer, obs-trE-eh, *v* to obstruct.

obtempérer (à), ob-tah*ng*-peh-reh, *v* to obey (a summons, etc); to comply with.

obtenir, ob-ter-neer, *v* to obtain; to get; to procure.

obtus, e, ob-tE, *a* obtuse; dull.

obus, ob-EEz, or ob-E, *m* shell (artillery).

occasion, ock-ăh-ze-ong, *f* occasion; opportunity; bargain; **d'–,** secondhand.

occasionnel, le,* ock-ăh-ze-onn-ell, *a* occasional.

occasionner, ock-ăh-ze-onn-eh, *v* to occasion; to cause.

occident, ock-se-dah*ng*, *m* West.

occidental, e, ock-se-

dah*ng*-tăhl, *a* western.

occulte, ock-EElt, *a* occult; secret.

occupant, e, ock-E-pang, *mf* & *a* occupier; occupying.

occupation, ock-E-păh-se-ong, *f* occupation; work; profession; capture (of a place).

occupé, e, ock-E-peh, *pp* & *a* occupied; engaged; busy; inhabited.

occuper, ock-E-peh, *v* to occupy; to employ; to inhabit.

occurrence, ock-E-rah*ng*ss, *f* occurrence.

océan, oss-eh-ah*ng*, *m* ocean; sea.

océanique, oss-eh-ăh-neeck, *a* oceanic.

ocre, ockr, *f* ochre.

octobre, ock-tobr, *m* October.

octogénaire, ock-tosh-eh-nair, *mf* & *a* octogenarian.

octogone, ock-to-gonn, *m* octagon.

octroyer, ock-tro'ăh-yeh, *v* to grant.

oculaire,* ock-E-lair, *a* ocular.

oculiste, ock-E-lisst, *m* oculist.

odeur, od-er, *f* odor; smell; fragrance; repute.

odieu-x, se,* od-e-er, *a* odious; hateful; obnoxious.

odorant, e, od-or-ah*ng*, *a* odorous; fragrant.

odorat, od-or-ăh, *m* sense of smell.

œil, er-ye, *m* eye; look; bud; *pl* **yeux,** yer.

œillade, er'e-yăhd, *f* glance; ogle; leer.

œillet, er'e-yay, *m* eyelet; pink; carnation.

œuf, erf, *m* egg; *pl* **œufs,** er.

œuvre, er-vr, *f* work; society; works.

offensant, e, off-ah*ng*-sah*ng*, *a* offensive.

offense, off-ah*ng*ss, *f* offense; trespass; contempt.

offensé, e, off-ah*ng*-seh, *mf* & *a* offended party.

offenser, off-ah*ng*-seh, *v* to offend; to injure; to shock.

offenseur, off-ah*ng*-ser, *m* offender.

offensi-f, ve,* off-ah*ng*ss-eef, *a* offensive.

office, off-eess, *m* office; duty; worship; service; *f* pantry.

officiel, le,* off-eess-e-ell, *a* official.

officier, off-eess-e-eh, *v* to officiate; *m* officer.

a
b
c
d
e
f
g
h
i
j
k
l
m
n
o
p
q
r
s
t
u
v
w
x
y
z

A
B
C
D
E
F
G
H
I
J
K
L
M
N
O
P
Q
R
S
T
U
V
W
X
Y
Z

officieu-x, se,* off-eess-e-er, *a* officious; semiofficial.

offrande, off-rahngd, *f* offering.

offre, ofr, *f* offer; tender; bidding.

offrir, off-reer, *v* to propose; to present; to bid.

offusquer, off-EEss-keh, *v* to obscure; to offend.

oh! o, *interj* oh!

oie, wăh, *f* goose.

oignon, onn-yong, *m* onion; bulb.

oindre, wang-dr, *v* to anoint.

oiseau, wăh-zoh, *m* bird.

oiseu-x, se,* wăh-zer, *a* idle; trifling; useless.

oisi-f, ve,* wăh-zeeff, *a* idle; unoccupied.

oisiveté, wăh-zeev-teh, *f* idleness.

oison, wăh-zong, *m* gosling; (*fig & fam*) simpleton.

olive, oll-eev, *f* olive; *a inv* olive-green.

olivier, oll-e-ve-eh, *m* olive tree.

olympique, oll-ang-peeck, *a* Olympic.

ombrage, ong-brăhsh, *m* shade; umbrage.

ombrageu-x, se,* ong-brăh-**sher,** *a* prickly; touchy.

ombre, ong-br, *f* shade; shadow; ghost.

ombrelle, ong-brell, *f* parasol.

ombreu-x, se, ong-brer, *a* shady.

omelette, omm-lett, *f* omelet.

omettre, omm-et-tr, *v* to omit; to leave out.

omission, omm-iss-e-ong, *f* omission.

omnibus, omm-ne-bEEss, *m* omnibus.

omoplate, omm-op-lăht, *f* shoulder blade.

on, ong *indefinite pron m sing* one; someone; anyone; people; we, you; they.

once, ongss, *f* ounce; grain; bit.

oncle, ong-kl, *m* uncle.

onction, ongk-se-ong, *f* unction.

onctueu-x, se,* ongk-tE-er, *a* unctuous; oily.

onde, ongd, *f* wave; surge; water; sea.

ondée, ong-deh, *f* shower.

ondoyant, e, ong-do'ăh-yahng, *a* undulating; flowing.

ondoyer, ong-do'ăh-yeh, *v* to undulate; to baptize privately.

onduler, ong-dE-leh, *v* to undulate; to wave (hair).

onéreu-x, se,* onn-eh-rer, *a* onerous.

ongle, ong-gl, *m* nail; claw.

onglée, ong-gleh, *f* numbness in the end of fingers (caused by cold).

onguent, ong-ghahng, *m* ointment; salve.

onze, ongz, *m & a* eleven.

onzième, ong-ze-aym, *m & a* eleventh.

opacité, op-ăh-se-teh, *f* opacity.

opaque, op-ăhck, *a* opaque.

opéra-teur, trice, op-eh-răh-ter, *mf* operator.

opération, op-eh-răh-se-ong, *f* operation; transaction.

opératoire, op-eh-răh-to'ăhr, *a* operative.

opérer, op-eh-reh, *v* to operate; to operate on; to work.

opiner, op-e-neh, *v* to give one's opinion.

opiniâtre, op-e-ne-ah-tr, *a* stubborn.

opiniâtrément, op-e-ne-ah-treh-mahng, *adv* stubbornly.

opiniâtrer (s'), sop-e-ne-ah-treh, *v* to be obstinate.

opinion, op-e-ne-ong, *f*

opinion.

opportun, e, op-or-tung, *a*
opportune; timely;
seasonable.

opportunité, op-or-tE-ne-
teh, *f* opportuneness;
seasonableness;
opportunity.

opposant, e, op-o-zahng,
mf opponent; *a* adverse.

opposé, op-oz-eh, *m*
opposite; reverse.

opposé, e, op-oz-eh, *a*
opposite; contrary; *pp*
opposed.

opposer, op-oz-eh, *v* to
oppose; s'–, to be
opposed; to object (à,
to).

opposition, op-oz-e-se-
ong, *f* opposition;
contrast.

oppresser, op-ress-eh, *v* to
oppress.

oppression, op-ress-e-ong,
f oppression.

opprimer, op-re-meh, *v* to
oppress; to crush.

opprobre, op-robr, *m*
disgrace; shame;
opprobrium.

opter, op-teh, *v* to choose;
to decide.

opticien, op-tiss-e-ang, *m*
optician.

optimisme, op-te-mism, *m*
optimism.

option, op-se-ong, *f*

option.

optique, op-teeck, *f*
optics; *a* optical; optic.

opulence, op-E-lahngss, *f*
opulence; wealth.

opulent, e, op-E-lahng, *a*
opulent; wealthy.

or, or, *conj* now; well.

or, or, *m* gold.

oracle, or-ăh-kl, *m* oracle.

orage, or-ăhsh, *m* storm;
(*fig*) tumult.

orageu-x, se,* or-ăh-sher,
a stormy.

oraison, or-ay-zong, *f*
oration; orison.

oral, e,* or-ăhl, *a* oral;
verbal; *m* oral
examination.

orange, or-ahngsh, *f*
orange; *a inv* orange-
colored.

orangeade, or-ahng-
shăhd, *f* orangeade.

oranger, or-ahng- sheh, *m*
orange tree.

orateur, or-ăh-ter, *m*
speaker; orator.

orbite, or-beet, *f* orbit;
socket.

orchestre, or-kestr, *m*
orchestra; band.

orchidée, or-ke-deh, *f*
orchids.

ordinaire, or-de-nair, *m*
the ordinary custom; *a**
ordinary; common;
vulgar.

ordinateur, or-de-năh-ter,
m computer.

ordonnance, or-donn-
ahngss, *f* prescription.

ordonna-teur, trice, or-
donn-ăh-ter, *mf*
organizer; manager; *a*
directing.

ordonné, or-donn-eh, *a*
orderly; tidy.

ordonner, or-donn-eh, *v*
to order; to prescribe; to
ordain.

ordre, or-dr, *m* order;
discipline; warrant;
decoration.

ordure, or-dEEr, *f* filth;
filthy thing; *pl* rubbish.

orée, or-eh, *f* border; edge
(of a wood, etc).

oreille, or-ay'e, *f* ear.

oreiller, or-ay'e-yeh, *m*
pillow.

oreillons, or-ay'e-yong,
mpl mumps.

orfèvre, or-fay-vr, *m*
goldsmith; silversmith.

organe, or-ghăhn, *m*
organ; voice; agent;
spokesman.

organique,* or-ghăh-
neeck, *a* organic.

organisa-teur, trice, or-
ghăh-ne-zăh-ter, *mf* & *a*
organizer.

organisation, or-ghăh-ne-
zah-se-ong, *f*
organization.

A
B
C
D
E
F
G
H
I
J
K
L
M
N
O
P
Q
R
S
T
U
V
W
X
Y
Z

organiser, or-ghăh-ne-zeh,
  v to organize; to get up.
organisme, or-ghăh-nism,
  m organism; structure.
organiste, or-ghăh-neesst,
  m organist.
orge, orsh, *f* barley.
orgelet, oar-je-lè, *m* sty
  (of eye).
orgie, or-shee, *f* revel;
  drinking bout; orgy.
orgue, orgh, *m* organ.
orgueil, or-gher'e, *m*
  pride; haughtiness.
orgueilleu-x, se,* or-
  gher'e-yer, *a* proud;
  haughty.
orient, or-e-ahng, *m*
  Orient; East.
oriental, e, or-e-ahng-tăhl,
  a Eastern; oriental.
orienter, or-e-ahng-teh, *v*
  to point; to guide.
orifice, or-e-feess, *m*
  orifice; aperture.
originaire,* or-e-she-nair,
  a native; originating.
original, e, or-e-she-năhl,
  mf eccentric person;
  original; *a** original;
  novel; odd.
originalité, or-e-she-năh-
  le-teh, *f* originality;
  eccentricity.
origine, or-e-sheen, *f*
  origin; beginning;
  source; extraction.
orme, orm, *m* elm.

ornement, or-ner-mahng,
  m ornament.
orner, or-neh, *v* to adorn;
  to decorate; to deck.
ornière, or-ne-air, *f* rut;
  beaten track; groove.
orphelin, e, or-fer-lang, *mf*
  & *a* orphan.
orphelinat, or-fer-le-năh,
  m orphanage.
orteil, or-tay'e, *m* toe;
  gros–, grohz–, big toe.
orthographe, or-tog-răhf,
  f spelling.
ortie, or-tee, *f* nettle.
os, oss, *m* bone; *pl* **os,** oh.
osciller, oss-sil-leh, *v* to
  oscillate; (*fam*) to waver.
osé, e, o-zeh, *a* daring;
  bold; cheeky; *pp*
  attempted.
oseille, oz-ay'e, *f* sorrel.
oser, o-zeh, *v* to dare; to
  venture.
osier, o-ze-eh, *m* wicker;
  osier.
osselet, oss-lay, *m* small
  bone.
osseu-x, se, oss-er, *a* bony.
ostensible,* oss-tahng-see-
  bl, *a* ostensible.
otage, ot-ăhsh, *m* hostage.
ôter, oht-eh, *v* to take
  away; to relieve; to pull
  off.
ou, oo, *conj* or; either;
  else.
où, oo, *adv* where;

whither; when; through
  which; at which; in
  which; to which.
ouate, oo-ăht, *f* cotton-
  wool; wadding; padding.
oubli, oo-ble, *m*
  forgetfulness; oblivion.
oublier, oo-blee-yeh, *v* to
  forget; to neglect.
ouest, west, *m* West; *a inv*
  westerly; western.
oui, wee, *adv* yes.
ouï-dire, oo-e-deer, *m inv*
  hearsay.
ouïe, oo-ee, *f* hearing; *pl*
  gills.
ouïr, oo-eer, *v* to hear
  (not used very often).
ouragan, oo-răh-ghahng,
  m hurricane.
ourdir, oor-deer, *v* to
  warp; (*fig*) to plot.
ourlet, oor-lay, *m* hem.
ours, oors, *m* bear.
ourse, oors, *f* female bear.
outil, oo-te, *m* tool;
  implement.
outillage, oo-tee-yăhsh, *m*
  tools; implements;
  plant.
outrage, oo-trăhsh, *m*
  outrage; insult.
outrager, oo-trăh-sheh, *v*
  to insult; to outrage.
outrageu-x, se,* oo-trăh-
  sher, *a* outrageous.
outrance, oo-trahngss, *f*
  excess; **à –,** ăh –, to the

utmost.

outre, oo-tr, *f* goatskin bottle.

outre, oo-tr, *prep* beyond; besides; *adv* beyond.

outré, e, oo-treh, *pp* & *a* exaggerated; extravagant; indignant.

outremer, oo-trer-mair, *m* ultramarine; overseas.

outrepasser, oo-trer-păhss-eh, *v* to go beyond; to exceed.

outrer, oo-treh, *v* to overdo; to exasperate.

ouvert, e,* oo-vair, *pp* & *a* opened; open; bare; frank.

ouverture, oo-vair-tEEr, *f* opening; overture; inauguration; *pl* proposals.

ouvrable, oo-vrăh-bl, *a* workable; **jour** –,**shoor** –, working day.

ouvrage, oo-vrăhsh, *m* work; workmanship; piece of work.

ouvré, e, oo-vreh, *a* diapered; wrought; worked.

ouvre-boîtes, oo-vr-bo'ăht, *m inv* can opener.

ouvri-er, ère, oo-vre-yeh, *mf* workman; work woman; laborer.

ouvrir, oo-vreer, *v* to open; to begin; to sharpen (appetite).

ovale, o-văhl, *a* & *m* oval.

ovation, o-văh-se-ong, *f* ovation.

ovipare, o-ve-păhr, *a* oviparous.

ovulation, o-vEE-lăh-se-ong, *f* ovulation.

oxyde, ox-eed, *m* oxide.

oxygène, ox-e-**shenn**, *m* oxygen.

ozone, oz-onn, *m* ozone.

a
b
c
d
e
f
g
h
i
j
k
l
m
n
o
p
q
r
s
t
u
v
w
x
y
z

A
B
C
D
E
F
G
H
I
J
K
L
M
N
O
P
Q
R
S
T
U
V
W
X
Y
Z

P

pacifique, * păh-se-feeck, *a* peaceful; pacific.

pacte, păckt, *m* pact; compact; covenant.

pagaie, păh-gay, *f* paddle.

page, păhsh, *m* page (boy); *f* page (book).

paie, pay, *f* pay; wages.

paiement, pay-mahng, *m* payment.

païen, ne, păh-e-ang, *mf* & *a* pagan; heathen.

paillasse, pah'e-yăhss, *f* straw mattress.

paillasson, pah'e-yăhss-ong, *m* doormat.

paille, pah'e, *f* straw; chaff; flaw; mote; *a* straw-colored.

pain, pang, *m* bread; loaf; livelihood; **petit –,** per-te –, roll.

pain complet, pang (kong-play) *a* wholewheat bread.

pair, e, pair, *a* even; equal.

paire, pair, *f* pair; couple; brace.

pairie, pay-ree, *f* peerage.

paisible, * pay-zee-bl, *a* peaceful; quiet; still.

paître, pay-tr, *v* to graze; to feed on; to pasture.

paix, pay, *f* peace; quiet; rest.

palais, păh-lay, *m* palace; palate.

pâle, pahl, *a* pale; wan; white.

palefrenier, păhl-frer-ne-eh, *m* groom; stable boy.

pâleur, pah-ler, *f* paleness.

palier, păh-le-eh, *m* landing (of stairs); floor.

pâlir, pah-leer, *v* to turn pale; (*fig*) to wane.

palissade, păh-liss-ăhd, *f* paling; fence.

pallier, păhl-le-eh, *v* to palliate.

palme, păhlm, *f* palm; triumph.

palmier, păhl-me-eh, *m* palm tree.

pâlot, te, pah-loh, *a* palish; peaky.

palper, păhl-peh, *v* to feel; to finger.

palpiter, păhl-pe-teh, *v* to throb; to pant.

paludisme, păh-lEE-dism, *m* malaria.

pâmer (se), ser pah-meh, *v* to swoon; nearly to die (**de,** with).

pamplemousse, pang-pl-mooss, *m* grapefruit.

pan, pahng, *m* part of a wall; side; lappet; flap.

panache, păh-năhsh, *m* plume; tuft; (*fam*) flourish.

panaché, e, păh-năh-sheh, *a* variegated; mixed.

panaris, păh-năh-re, *m* whitlow.

pancarte, pahng-kăhrt, *f* placard; sign; notice.

pané, e, păh-neh, *a* covered with breadcrumbs.

panier, păh-ne-eh, *m* basket; hamper.

panique, păh-neeck, *f*

panic.

panne, păhn, *f*
breakdown; failure;
plush; lard.

panneau, păh-noh, *m*
panel; board; trap; snare;
sign.

panse, pahngss, *f* (*fam*)
paunch; belly.

panser, pahngss-eh, *v* to
dress (wound); to
groom.

pantalon, pahng-tăh-long,
m trousers; pants.

pantin, pahng-tang, *m*
puppet.

pantoufle, pahng-too-fl, *f*
slipper.

paon, ne, pahng, *mf*
peacock; peahen.

papa, păh-păh, *m* daddy;
dad.

papauté, păh-poh-teh, *f*
papacy.

pape, păhp, *m* Pope.

paperasse, păhp-răhss, *f*
old paper; wastepaper.

papier hygiénique, păh-
pee-eh-e-**she**-eh-neeck
m toilet paper.

papeterie, păhp-tree, *f*
papermill; paper trade;
stationery; stationer.

papetier, păhp-te-eh, *m*
stationer.

papier, păh-pe-eh, *m*
paper; **–à lettres,** – ăh
let-tr, stationery.

papier d'emballage, păh-
pe-eh-dahng-băh-lăhsh
m wrapping paper.

papillon, păh-pee-yong, *m*
butterfly; **–de nuit,** – der
nwee, moth.

papillote, păh-pee-yot, *f*
curlpaper.

paquebot, păhck-boh, *m*
liner; steamer; ship.

pâquerette, pahck-rett, *f*
daisy.

Pâques, pahk, *m* Easter.

paquet, păh-kay, *m* parcel;
packet.

par, păhr, *prep* by;
through; out of; per;
about; for; with; in; into.

parachute, păh-răh-shEEt,
m parachute.

parade, păh-răhd, *f*
parade; display; show;
parrying (fencing).

parader, păh-răh-deh, *v* to
parade; to show off.

paradis, păh-răh-de, *m*
Paradise; heaven; the
gods (theater).

parafe, paraphe, păh-răhf,
m flourish; initials.

parage, păh-răhsh, *m*
extraction; birth; *pl*
regions; latitudes.

paragraphe, păh-răh-grăf,
m paragraph.

paraître, păh-ray-tr, *v* to
appear; to look; to come
out; to show; **vient de –,**

ve-ang der –, just out.

paralyser, păh-răh-le-zeh,
v to paralyze.

paralysie, păh-răh-le-zee, *f*
paralysis.

parapet, păh-răh-pay, *m*
parapet.

parapluie, păh-răh-plwee,
m umbrella.

parasite, păh-răh-zeet, *m*
parasite; *a* parasitic.

paratonnerre, păh-răh-
tonn-air, *m* lightning
conductor.

paravent, păh-răh-vahng,
m screen; folding screen.

parc, păhrk, *m* park;
enclosure; playpen.

parcelle, păhr-sell, *f* small
part; particle; plot.

parce que, păhr-ser ker,
conj because.

parchemin, păhr-sher-
mang, *m* parchment; *pl*
diplomas.

parcimonieu-x, se,* păhr-
se-monn-e-er, *a*
parsimonious.

parcourir, păhr-koo-reer,
v to travel over; to go
through; to glance at.

parcours, păhr-koohr, *m*
distance; line; journey;
route.

pardessus, păhr-der-sE, *m*
overcoat.

pardon, păhr-dong, *m*
forgiveness; pardon.

a
b
c
d
e
f
g
h
i
j
k
l
m
n
o
p
q
r
s
t
u
v
w
x
y
z

A
B
C
D
E
F
G
H
I
J
K
L
M
N
O
P
Q
R
S
T
U
V
W
X
Y
Z

pardonner, păhr-donn-eh, *v* to forgive; to excuse.

pare-brise, păhr-breez, *m* *inv* in *pl* windshield.

pare-chocs, păhr-shock, *m* *inv* in *pl* bumper.

pareil, le,* păh-ray'e, *a* like; similar; such; to match.

pareille, păh-ray'e, *f* the like; the same.

parent, e, păh-rahng, *mf* relative; kinsman; kinswoman; parents (father and mother); relatives; folks.

parenté, păh-rahng-teh, *f* relationship; consanguinity; kith and kin; family.

parer, păh-reh, *v* to adorn; to dress; to ward off; to provide for.

paresse, păh-ress, *f* idleness; sluggishness; indolence.

paresseu-x, se, păh-ress-er, *mf* idler; *a** idle; lazy; slothful.

parfaire, păhr-fair, *v* to perfect; to complete.

parfait, e,* păhr-fay, *a* perfect; faultless.

parfois, păhr-fo'ăh, *adv* sometimes; now and then.

parfum, păhr-fung, *m* perfume; scent.

parfumer, păhr-fE-meh, *v* to perfume; to scent.

pari, păh-ree, *m* bet; wager; stake.

parier, păh-re-eh, *v* to bet; to wager; to stake.

parité, păh-re-teh, *f* parity; equality.

parjure, păhr-shEEr, *m* perjury; perjurer.

parjurer (se), ser păhr-shE-reh, *v* to perjure oneself.

parlant, e, păhr-lahng, *a* speaking; talking.

parlement, păhr-ler-mahng, *m* Parliament.

parlementer, păhr-ler-mahng-teh, *v* to parley; to argue.

parler, păhr-leh, *v* to speak; *m* way of speaking.

parleu-r, se, păhr-ler, *mf* talker.

parmi, păhr-me, *prep* among; amongst; amid; amidst.

parodie, păh-rod-ee, *f* parody.

paroi, păh-ro'ăh, *f* wall; side; partition; coat.

paroisse, păh-ro'ăhss, *f* parish; parishioners.

paroissien, ne, păh-ro'ăhss-e-ang, *mf* parishioner.

parole, păh-rol, *f* word; speech; saying right to speak; promise.

parquer, păhr-keh, *v* to pen up.

parquet, păhr-kay, *m* inlaid floor; flooring.

parrain, păh-rang, *m* godfather; sponsor.

parricide, păh-re-seed, *mf* parricide.

parsemer, păhr-ser-meh, *v* to strew (**de,** with).

part, păhr, *f* share; portion; participation.

partage, păhr-tăhsh, *m* sharing.

partance, păhr-tahngss, *f* departure; **en –,** ahng –, about to sail; bound (for).

partant, păhr-tahng, *adv* consequently.

partenaire, păhr-ter-nair, *mf* partner (at cards or dancing).

parterre, păhr-tair, *m* flower-bed; pit (theater).

parti, păhr-tee, *m* party; side; decision; profit.

partial, e,* păhr-se-ăhl, *a* partial; biased.

participation, păhr-te-se-păh-se-ong, *f* participation; share.

participe, păhr-te-seep, *m* participle.

participer, păhr-te-se-peh,

v to share (à, in).

particuli-er, ère, păhr-te-kE-le-eh *a* specific.

particularité, păhr-te-kE-lăh-re-teh, *f* peculiarity.

particule, păhr-te-kEEl, *f* particle.

particuli-er, ère, păhr-te-kE-le-eh, *mf* private person; individual; *a** particular; peculiar; odd.

partie, păhr-tee, *f* part; party; match; business; field; subject; (law) opponent.

partiel, le,* păhr-se-ell, *a* partial.

partir, păhr-teer, *v* to set out; to leave; to go off.

partition, păhr-te-se-*ong*, *f* partition; score (music).

partout, păhr-too, *adv* everywhere.

parure, păh-rEEr, *f* ornament; dress.

parvenir, păhr-ver-neer, *v* to reach; to succeed.

parvenu, e, păhr-ver-nE, *mf* upstart; self-made person.

parvis, păhr-ve, *m* parvis.

pas, pah, *m* step; gait; threshold; precedence.

pas, pah, *adv* not; not any; **–du tout,** – dE too, not at all.

passable,* păhss-ăh-bl, *a* passable; tolerable.

passag-er, ère, păhss-ăh-sheh, *mf* passenger; **a*** transitory.

passant, e, păhss-ah*ng*, *mf* passer-by.

passe, păhss, *f* pass; spell; situation; channel.

passé, păhss-eh, *prep* after; *m* the past.

passé, e, păhss-eh, *pp & a* past; last; faded.

passer, păhss-eh, *v* to pass; to omit; to allow; to pass away; to fade; to cease; to spend (time).

passereau, păhss-roh, *m* sparrow.

passerelle, păhss-rell, *f* footbridge.

passible, păhss-ee-bl, *a* liable (**de,** to).

passif, păhss-eeff, *m* liabilities. **passi-f, ve*** păhss-eeff, *a* passive.

passion, păhss-e-*ong*, *f* passion.

passionnant, păhss-e-onn-ah*ng*, *a* thrilling; fascinating.

passionné, e, păhss-e-onn-eh, *a* passionate; passionately fond (**de, pour,** of).

passionnément, păhss-e-onn-eh-mah*ng*, *adv* passionately.

passoire, păhss-o'ăhr, *f* strainer; colander.

pastèque, păhss-teck, *f* watermelon.

pasteurisé, e, păhs-ter-e-zeh *a* pasteurized.

pastille, păhss-tee-ye, *f* pastille; lozenge.

patauger, păh-toh-**sheh,** *v* to dabble; to flounder; to make a mess of.

pâte, paht, *f* paste; dough; *pl* pasta.

pâté, pah-teh, *m* pie; pâté; blot of ink; block (of houses).

pâte d'amandes, păht-dăh-mah*ng*d *f* marzipan .

patelin, păht-lang, *m* (*fam*) small village.

patente, păh-tah*ng*t, *f* license; patent.

patère, păh-tair, *f* peg; curtain hook.

paternel, le,* păh-tair-nell, *a* fatherly; on the father's side.

pâteu-x, se,* pah-ter, *a* pasty; sticky; heavy (style, voice); dull.

patiemment, păh-se-ăh-mah*ng*, *adv* patiently.

patience, păh-se-ah*ng*ss, *f* patience; puzzle.

patient, e, păh-se-ah*ng*, *mf* patient; sufferer; *a* patient.

patienter, păh-se-ah*ng*-teh, *v* to wait.

patinage (sur glace), păh-

a
b
c
d
e
f
g
h
i
j
k
l
m
n
o
p
q
r
s
t
u
v
w
x
y
z

A
B
C
D
E
F
G
H
I
J
K
L
M
N
O
P
Q
R
S
T
U
V
W
X
Y
Z

te-năhsh (sEEr-glăhss) *f* ice skating.

patiner, păh-te-neh, *v* to skate.

patinoire, păh-te-noăhr *f* ice rink.

patio, păh-te-oh *m* patio.

pâtisserie, pah-tiss-ree, *f* pastry; bakery.

patois, păh-to'ăh, *m* dialect.

pâtre, pah-tr, *m* herdsman; shepherd.

patrie, păh-tree, *f* native country; fatherland; home.

patrimoine, păh-tre-mo'ăhn, *m* patrimony.

patriote, păh-tre-ot, *m* patriot; *a* patriotic.

patron, ne, păh-trong, *mf* employer; patroness; boss; skipper; pattern.

patronner, păh-tronn-eh, *v* to patronize; to stencil.

patrouille, păh-troo'ye, *f* patrol.

patte, păht, *f* paw; foot; leg; strap; flap.

pâturage, pah-tE-răhsh, *m* pasture; grazing.

paume, pohm, *f* palm (of the hands); tennis.

paupière, poh-pe-air, *f* eyelid.

pause, pohz, *f* pause; stop; rest.

pauvre, poh-vr, *m* poor man; *a** poor; wretched.

pauvresse, poh-vress, *f* beggar woman.

pauvreté, poh-vrer-teh, *f* poverty; wretchedness.

pavaner (se), ser păh-văh-neh, *v* to strut.

pavé, păh-veh, *m* paving stone; pavement.

pavillon, păh-vee-yong, *m* pavilion; flag.

pavoiser, păh-vo'ăh-zeh, *v* to deck with flags.

pavot, păh-voh, *m* poppy.

payant, e, pay-yahng, *mf* payer; *a* paying; charged for.

paye, see **paie.**

payement, see **paiement.**

payer, pay-yeh, *v* to pay; to stand; to treat.

pays, pay-ee, *m* country; home; place.

paysage, pay-ee-zăhsh, *m* landscape; scenery.

paysan, ne, pay-ee-zahng, *mf* peasant; *a* rustic.

péage, peh-ăhsh, *m* toll.

peau, poh, *f* skin; hide; peel; life.

pêche, paysh, *f* fishing; fishery; angling; peach.

péché, peh-sheh, *m* sin.

pécher, peh-sheh, *v* to sin; to err.

pêcher, pay-sheh, *v* to fish; to angle; *m* peach

tree.

pêcheu-r, se, pay-sher, *mf* fisherman; fisherwoman.

péch-eur, eresse, peh-sher, pehsh-ress, *mf* sinner.

pécuniaire,* peh-kE-ne-air, *a* pecuniary.

pédaler, peh-dăh-leh, *v* to pedal; to cycle.

pédant, e, peh-dahng, *mf* pedant; *a* pedantic.

pédestre,* peh-dess-tr, *a* pedestrian.

pédicure, peh-de-kEEr, *mf* chiropodist; pedicure.

pedigree, peh-de-greh, *m* pedigree.

peigne, payn-yer, *m* comb.

peigner, payn-yeh, *v* to comb; se –, to comb one's hair.

peignoir, payn-yo'ăhr, *m* dressing gown; bathrobe.

peindre, pang-dr, *v* to paint; to depict; to represent.

peine, payn, *f* pain; punishment; difficulty; sorrow.

peiner, pay-neh, *v* to grieve; to labor; to toil.

peintre, pang-tr, *m* painter.

peinture, pang-tEEr, *f* painting; picture; description; paint.

péjorati-f, ve, peh-sho-răh-teef, *a* derogatory.

pêle-mêle, payl-mayl, *adv* pell-mell; *m* jumble.

peler, per-leh, *v* to peel; to pare.

pèlerin, payl-ra*ng*, *m* pilgrim.

pèlerinage, payl-re-năhsh, *m* pilgrimage.

pèlerine, payl-reen, *f* cape.

pelle, payl, *f* shovel; spade.

pelleterie, payl-tree, *f* fur trade; *pl* furs.

pellicule, payl-le-kEEl, *f* dandruff; film; roll (film).

pelote, plot, *f* pincushion; ball (of wool, etc).

pelouse, plooz, *f* lawn; grass plot.

peluche, plEEsh, *f* plush.

pelure, plEEr, *f* paring; peel; rind.

pénalité, peh-năh-le-teh, *f* penal system; penalty.

penaud, e, per-noh, *a* abashed; shamefaced.

penchant, pah*ng*-shah*ng*, *m* declivity; inclination; partiality.

pencher, pah*ng*-sheh, *v* to incline; to lean.

pendaison, pah*ng*-day-zo*ng*, *f* hanging.

pendant, pah*ng*-dah*ng*, *prep* during; *m* counterpart; earring.

(pendant) la nuit, (pah*ng*-dah*ng*) lăh-nwee *adv* overnight.

pendre, pah*ng*-dr, *v* to hang; to hang up.

pendule, pah*ng*-dEEl, *m* pendulum; *f* clock.

pêne, payn, *m* bolt (of a lock).

pénétrant, e, peh-neh-trah*ng*, *a* penetrating; piercing; keen.

pénétrer, peh-neh-treh, *v* to penetrate; to enter.

pénible,* peh-nee-bl, *a* painful; laborious.

péniche, peh-neesh, *f* barge.

pénicilline, peh-ne-se-leen *f* penicillin.

pénitence, peh-ne-tah*ng*ss, *f* penance; penitence; repentance; disgrace.

pénitent, e, peh-ne-tah*ng*, *mf* penitent; *a* penitent.

pénombre, peh-no*ng*-br, *f* semidarkness; dim light.

pensant, e, pah*ng*-sah*ng*, *a* thinking.

pensée, pah*ng*-seh, *f* thought; opinion; pansy.

penser, pah*ng*-seh, *v* to think; to deem.

penseu-r, se, pah*ng*-ser, *mf* thinker.

pensi-f, ve,* pah*ng*-seeff, *a* pensive; thoughtful.

pension, pah*ng*-se-o*ng*, *f* pension; boardinghouse; boarding school.

pensionnaire, pah*ng*-se-onn-air, *mf* boarder; pensioner.

pente, pah*ng*t, *f* slope; gradient; bent.

pentecôte, pah*ng*t-koht, *f* Pentecost.

pénurie, peh-nEE-ree, *f* scarcity; dearth; poverty.

pépier, peh-pe-eh, *v* to chirp.

pépin, peh-pa*ng*, *m* pip; kernel; hitch.

pépinière, peh-pe-ne-air, *f* nursery (tree).

percale, pair-kăhl, *f* cotton cambric.

perçant, e, pair-sah*ng*, *a* piercing; sharp; shrill.

percé, e, pair-seh, *pp* & *a* pierced; in holes.

percepteur, pair-sep-ter, *m* tax collector.

percer, pair-seh, *v* to pierce; to bore.

percevoir, pair-ser-vo'ăhr, *v* to collect (taxes, etc); to perceive.

perche, pairsh, *f* pole; perch.

percher (se), pair-sheh, *v* to roost; to perch.

perdant, e, pair-dah*ng*, *mf* loser; *a* losing.

perdre, pair-dr, *v* to lose;

to waste; to ruin; to corrupt.

perdrix, pair-dree, *f* partridge.

perdu, e, pair-dE, *pp* & *a* lost; ruined; done for; spoilt.

père, pair, *m* father.

perfectionnement, pair-feck-se-onn-mahng, *m* improvement; perfecting.

perfectionner, pair-feck-se-onn-eh, *v* to improve; to perfect.

perfide, pair-feed, *mf* perfidious person; *a** perfidious.

perforer, pair-for-eh, *v* to bore; to punch.

péricliter, peh-re-kle-teh, *v* to be in jeopardy.

péril, peh-reel, *m* peril; danger.

périlleu-x, se,* peh-ree-yer, *a* perilous.

périmé, e, peh-re-meh, *a* out of date; lapsed.

période, peh-re-od, *f* period.

périodique, peh-re-od-eeck, *a* periodical; *m* periodical (publication).

péripétie, peh-re-peh-see, *f* ups and downs; *pl* vicissitudes.

périr, peh-reer, *v* to perish; to die; to be lost.

périssable, peh-riss-ăh-bl, *a* perishable.

perle, pair, *f* pearl; bead.

permanent, e, pair-măh-nahng, *a* permanent; license; *f* permanent wave.

permanente, pair-măh-nahngt *f hair* perm.

permettre, pair-met-tr, *v* to allow; to enable.

permis, pair-mee, *m* permit; licence; pass.

permis, e, pair-mee, *pp* & *a* allowed; allowable.

permis de conduire, pair-me-der-kong-dweer *m* drivers license.

permission, pair-miss-e-ong, *f* permission; leave.

pernicieu-x, se,* pair-ne-se-er, *a* pernicious; hurtful.

perpétuel, le,* pair-peh-tE-ell, *a* perpetual.

perpétuer, pair-peh-tE-eh, *v* to perpetuate.

perpétuité, pair-peh-twe-teh, *f* endlessness; à –, ăh –, for life.

perplexe, pair-plex, *a* perplexed.

perron, pay-rong, *m* flight of steps to house door.

perroquet, payr-ock-ay, *m* parrot.

perruche, pay-rEEsh, *f* parakeet.

perruque, pay-rEEk, *f* wig.

persécuter, pair-seh-kE-teh, *v* to persecute; to importune.

persévérance, pair-seh-veh-rahngss, *f* perseverance.

persévérer, pair-seh-veh-reh, *v* to persevere; to persist.

persienne, pair-se-ain, *f* shutter.

persil, pair-see, *m* parsley.

persistant, e, pair-siss-tahng, *a* persistent.

persister, pair-siss-teh, *v* to persist (**à, dans,** in).

personnage, pair-sonn-ăhsh, *m* personage; somebody; character.

personnalité, pair-sonn-ăh-le-teh, *f* personality; person.

personne, pair-sonn, *pron* anybody; (with a negation) nobody; *f* person; individual.

(ne) personne, (ner) pair-sonn *pron* no one.

personnel, pair-sonn-ell, *m* staff.

personnel, le,* pair-sonn-ell, *a* personal.

personnifier, pair-sonn-e-fe-eh, *v* to personify; to impersonate.

perspective, pairs-peck-teev, *f* perspective;

prospect.

perspicace, pairs-pe-kăhss, *a* perspicacious.

persuader, pair-sE-ăh-deh, *v* to persuade; to convince; to prevail on.

persuasion, pair-sE-ăh-ze-ong, *f* persuasion.

perte, pairt, *f* loss; waste; ruin; death.

pertinemment, pair-te-năh-mahng, *adv* pertinently.

perturba-teur, trice, pair-tEEr-băh-ter, *mf* disturber; *a* disturbing.

perturbation, pair-tEEr-băh-se-ong, *f* disturbance.

perturber, pair-tEEr-beh, *v* to disrupt (disturb, break up).

pervers, e, pair-vair, *mf* evildoer; pervert; *a* perverse.

perversion, pair-vair-se-ong, *f* perversion.

pervertir, pair-vair, *v* to pervert; to corrupt.

pesamment, per-zăh-mahng, *adv* heavily.

pesant, e, per-zahng, *a* weighty; ponderous.

pesanteur, per-zahng-ter, *f* weight; gravity; dullness.

peser, per-zeh, *v* to weigh; to ponder; to be a burden.

peste, pesst, *f* plague; (*fam*) pest; bore.

pester, pess-teh, *v* to rave (**contre,** at).

pétillant, e, peh-tee-yahng, *a* sparkling; crackling.

pétiller, peh-tee-yeh, *v* to crackle; to sparkle.

petit, e, per-te, *mf* young child; young animal; *a** little; small.

petite-fille, per-teet-fee-ye, *f* granddaughter.

petit-fils, per-te-feess, *m* grandson.

pétition, peh-te-se-ong, *f* petition.

pétitionnaire, peh-te-se-onn-air, *mf* petitioner.

petits-enfants, per-te-zahng-fahng, *mpl* grandchildren.

pétri, e, peh-tre, *pp* & *a* kneaded.

pétrin, peh-trang, *m* kneading trough; (*fam*) **dans le –,** dahng ler –, in a mess.

pétrir, peh-treer, *v* to knead; to mold.

pétulant, e, peh-tE-lahng, *a* lively; full of spirits.

peu, per, *adv* little; not much; *m* little; few; bit.

peuplade, per-plăhd, *f* tribe.

peuple, per-pl, *m* people; nation; the masses.

peupler, per-pleh, *v* to populate (**de,** with); to throng.

peuplier, per-ple-eh, *m* poplar.

peur, per, *f* fear; fright; dread.

peureu-x, se,* per-rer, *a* timid; fearful.

peut-être, per-t'ay-tr, *adv* perhaps; maybe.

phare, făhr, *m* lighthouse; beacon; headlight.

pharmacie, făhr-măh-see, *f* pharmacy; drugstore.

pharmacien, făhr-măh-se-ang, *m* chemist.

phase, fahz, *f* phase; stage; turn.

phénomène, feh-nomm-ain, *m* phenomenon; (*fam*) freak.

philatéliste, fe-lăh-teh-leesst, *m* stamp collector.

philosophe, fe-loz-off, *m* philosopher; *a* philosophical.

philosophie, fe-loz-off-ee, *f* philosophy.

philtre, feel-tr, *m* philter; love potion.

phonographe, fonn-og-răhf, *m* phonograph.

phoque, fock, *m* seal.

phosphore, foss-for, *m* phosphorous.

A
B
C
D
E
F
G
H
I
J
K
L
M
N
O
P
Q
R
S
T
U
V
W
X
Y
Z

photocopie, fot-o-ko-pee, *f* photocopy.

photographe, fot-og-răhf, *m* photographer.

photographie, fot-og-răh-fee, *f* photograph; photography.

phrase, frahz, *f* sentence.

physicien, fe-ze-se-ang, *m* physicist.

physiologie, fe-ze-oll-osh-ee, *f* physiology.

physionomie, fe-ze-onn-omm-ee, *f* physiognomy; look; expression.

physique, fe-zeeck, *m* constitution; *f* physics; *a** physical.

piaffer, pe-ăh-feh, *v* to paw the ground.

piailler, pe-ah'e-yeh, *v* to squall.

piano, pe-ăh-no, *adv* softly; *m* pianoforte.

pic, peek, *m* pickax; peak; woodpecker; **à –,** ăh –, perpendicularly.

picoter, pe-kot-eh, *v* to prick; to tease; to peck.

pie, pee, *f* magpie.

pièce, pe-ess, *f* piece; bit; play; room; document.

pied, pe-eh, *m* foot; footing; leg; stalk.

piédestal, pe-eh-dess-tăhl, *m* pedestal.

piège, pe-aysh, *m* snare; trap.

pierre, pe-ayr, *f* stone; flint; gem.

pierreries, pe-ay-rer-ree, *fpl* gems; precious stones.

pierreu-x, se, pe-ay-rer, *a* stony.

piété, pe-eh-teh, *f* piety.

piétiner, pe-eh-te-neh, *v* to trample; to mark time.

piéton, pe-eh-tong, *m* pedestrian.

piètre,* pe-ay-tr, *a* paltry; wretched; worthless.

pieu, pe-er, *m* stake.

pieuvre, pe-ervr *f* octopus.

pieu-x, se,* pe-er, *a* pious; godly.

pigeon, pe-shong, *m* pigeon; dove.

pigeonnier, pe-shonn-e-eh, *m* pigeon house; dovecote.

pigment, peeg-mahng, *m* pigment.

pignon, peen-yong, *m* gable.

pile, peel, *f* heap; pier; battery; reverse (of coin); (*fam*) thrashing.

piler, pe-leh, *v* to pound; to crush.

pilier, pe-le-eh, *m* pillar; post.

pillage, pee-yăhsh, *m* plundering; pillage.

piller, pee-yeh, *v* to

plunder; to pillage; to ransack; to pilfer.

pilon, pe-long, *m* pestle; pounder; drumstick.

pilori, pe-lor-e, *m* pillory.

pilote, pe-lot, *m* pilot.

pilule, pe-lEEl, *f* pill.

pimbêche, pang-baish, *f* minx.

piment, pe-mahng, *m* pimento.

pimpant, e, pang-pahng, *a* spruce; smart.

pin, pang, *m* pine; pine tree.

pince, pangss, *f* pincers; pliers; crowbar; tongs;

pincé, e, pang-seh, *a* affected; stiff-necked.

pinceau, pang-soh, *m* brush.

pincée, pang-seh, *f* pinch (of salt, etc).

pince-nez, pangss-neh, *m* pince-nez.

pincer, pang-seh, *v* to pluck (harp, guitar, etc.); to play; to catch in the act.

pince-sans-rire, pangss-sahng-reer, *m* person of dry humor.

pincettes, pang-sett, *fpl* tongs; tweezers.

ping-pong, pe-ng-pongg *f* table tennis.

pintade, pang-tăhd, *f* guinea fowl.

piocher, pe-osh-eh, *v* to dig; to work hard.

pion, pe-ong, *m* pawn.

pioncer, pe-ong-seh, *v* (*pop*) to snooze.

pionnier, pe-onn-e-eh, *m* pioneer.

pipe, peep, *f* tobacco pipe; pipe.

piquant, e, pe-kah*ng*, *a* pricking; pungent; stinging; sharp.

pique, peek, *m* spade (cards).

pique-nique, peek-neek, *m* picnic.

piquer, pe-keh, *v* to prick; to sting; to bite; to goad; to spur; to rouse; to offend; to be pungent; –à la machine, – ăh lăh măh-sheen, to machine sew.

piquet, pe-kay, *m* stake; peg.

piqûre, pe-kEEr, *f* sting; bite; injection.

pirate, pe-răht, *m* pirate.

pire, peer, *a* worse; *m* le –, ler –, the worst.

pirouetter, pe-roo-ett-eh, *v* to whirl round.

pis, pee, *adv* worse; *m* udder.

pis-aller, pe-z'ăh-leh, *m* makeshift.

piscine, peess-seen, *f* swimming pool.

pissenlit, peess-ahng-lee, *m* dandelion.

piste, peesst, *f* track; trail; trace; scent; runway.

piste de ski, peest-der-ske *f* ski slope.

pistolet, peesst-toll-ay, *m* pistol.

piston, peess-tong, *m* piston; sucker; (*fam*) influence.

piteu-x, se,* pe-ter, *a* piteous; pitiable.

pitié, pe-te-eh, *f* pity; compassion.

pitoyable,* pe-to'ăh-yăh-bl, *a* pitiful; pitiable; wretched.

pittoresque,* pit-tor-esk, *a* picturesque; graphic.

pivot, pe-voh, *m* pivot; (*fig*) basis; support.

placard, plăh-kăhr, *m* cupboard; poster; bill.

place, plăhss, *f* place; spot; square; space; seat; situation; fortress.

placement, plăhss-mahng, *m* placing; sale; investment.

placer, plăhss-eh, *v* to place; to sell; to invest.

placide,* plăhss-eed, *a* placid.

plafond, plăh-fong, *m* ceiling.

plage, plăhsh, *f* beach; shore.

plagiaire, plăh-she-air, *m* plagiarist.

plaider, play-deh, *v* to plead; to argue; to intercede.

plaideu-r, se, play-der, *mf* litigant.

plaidoirie, play-do'ăh-ree, *f* pleading; address.

plaie, play, *f* wound; sore; plague.

plaignant, e, playn-yahng, *mf* plaintiff.

plaindre, plang-dr, *v* to pity; **se –,** to complain.

plaine, plain, *f* plain; flat open country.

plainte, plangt, *f* lamentation; complaint; charge.

plainti-f, ve,* plang-teeff, *a* plaintive; mournful.

plaire, plair, *v* to please; to be agreeable; to suit; **s'il vous plaît,** sill voo play, (if you) please.

plaisamment, play-zăh-mahng, *adv* pleasantly; humorously.

plaisant, e, play-zahng, *a* pleasing; funny; droll.

plaisanter, play-zahng-teh, *v* to joke; to jest; to trifle (**avec,** with).

plaisanterie, play-zahngt-ree, *f* joke; jest; fun; humor; mockery.

plaisir, play-zeer, *m*

A
B
C
D
E
F
G
H
I
J
K
L
M
N
O
P
Q
R
S
T
U
V
W
X
Y
Z

pleasure; recreation.

plan, plah*ng*, *m* plan; model; map; scheme.

plan, e, plah*ng*, *a* level; even; flat.

planche, plah*ng*sh, *f* plank; board; shelf; plate; garden bed.

planche de surf, plah*ng*sh-der-sErf *f* surfboard.

plancher, plah*ng*-sheh, floor.

planer, plăh-neh, *v* to soar; to hover; to smooth.

planeur, plăh-ner, *m* glider.

plante, plah*ng*t, *f* plant; sole of the foot.

planté, e, plah*ng*-teh, *pp* & *a* planted; situated; **bien –,** be-a*ng* –, firmly set.

planter, plah*ng*-teh, *v* to plant; to set; to fix.

planton, plah*ng*-to*ng*, *m* orderly.

plaque, plăhck, *f* plate; slab; badge; (license) plate.

plastique, plăhss-teeck, *m* plastic.

plastron, plăhss-tro*ng*, *m* breastplate; shirt front.

plat, e,* plăh, *a* flat; level; dull; straight (hair); *m* dish; course.

platane, plăh-tăhn, *m* plane tree.

plateau, plăh-toh, *m* tray; disk; plateau.

plâtrage, plah-trăhsh, *m* plastering; plasterwork.

plâtras, plah-trăh, *m* rubbish (plaster).

plâtre, plah-tr, *m* plaster; plastercast.

plâtrer, plah-treh, *v* to plaster; to patch up.

plausible,* ploh-zee-bl, *a* plausible.

plèbe, playb, *f* mob.

plein, e,* pla*ng*, *a* full; whole; broad; with young (animal).

plénière, pleh-ne-air, *af* plenary; full.

plénitude, pleh-ne-tEEd, *f* plenitude; fullness.

pleurer, pler-reh, *v* to weep; to cry; to mourn.

pleureu-r, se, pler-rer, *a* weeping; *mf* mourner.

pleurnicher, pler-ne-sheh, *v* to whimper; to snivel.

pleurs, pler, *mpl* tears; weeping; lament.

pleuvoir, pler-vo'ăhr, *v* to rain.

pli, ple, *m* fold; pleat; wrinkle; crease; bend; letter.

pliable, ple-ăh-bl, *a* flexible; docile.

pliant, ple-ah*ng*, *m* folding

chair; *a* flexible; folding.

plier, plee-eh, *v* to fold; to bend; to give way.

plissé, e, pliss-eh, *pp* & *a* pleated; tucked.

plisser, pliss-eh, *v* to pleat; to crease; to corrugate.

plomb, plo*ng*, *m* lead; shot; sinker; plumb line; seal; fuse.

plombage, plo*ng*-băhsh, *m* leadwork; plumbing; sealing; filling (teeth).

plombier, plo*ng*-be-eh, *m* plumber.

plonger, plo*ng*- sheh, *v* to dive.

pluie, plwee, *f* rain.

plume, plEEm, *f* feather; nib; quill.

plupart (la), lăh plE-păhr, *f* most; the greatest part; most people.

pluriel, le, plE-re-ell, *m* & *a* plural.

plus, plE, *adv* more; **le –,** ler –, the most.

plusieurs, plE-ze-er, *pron* & *a* several.

plus-que-parfait, plEEs-ker-păhr-fay, *m* pluperfect.

plutôt, plE-toh, *adv* rather; sooner.

pluvieu-x, se, plE-ve-er, *a* rainy.

pneu, pner, *m* tire.

pneumatique, pner-măh-teeck, *m* express letter sent by a tube (in Paris).

poche, posh, *f* pocket; bag; pouch; net.

pocher, posh-eh, *v* to poach (egg); to bruise (eye).

pochette, posh-ett, *f* small pocket; kit.

poêle, po'ăhl, *m* stove; pall; *f* frying pan.

poème, po-emm, *m* poem.

poésie, po-eh-zee, *f* poetry; poems.

poète, po-ett, *m* poet.

poétique, po-eh-teeck, *f* poetics; *a** poetical.

poids, po'ăh, *m* weight; burden.

poignant, e, po'ăhn-yahng, *a* poignant.

poignard, po'ăhn-yăhr, *m* dagger.

poigne, po'ăhn-yer, *f* grip; will; energy.

poignée, po'ăhn-yeh, *f* handful; handle.

poignet, po'ăhn-yay, *m* wrist; wristband; cuff.

poil, po'ăhl, *m* hair (animal); hair (on human body); bristle; (*fam*) mood; **au –,** super.

poilu, e, po'ăh-lE, *a* hairy; shaggy.

poinçon, po'ang-song, *m* bodkin; awl; punch; stamp; die.

poinçonner, po'ang-sonn-eh, *v* to punch (ticket, etc); to stamp.

poindre, po'ang-dr, *v* to dawn.

poing, po'ang, *m* fist; hand.

point, po'ang, *adv* no; not; none; never.

point, po'ang, *m* point; stop; stitch; dot; mark; full stop; degree.

pointe, po'angt, *f* point; tip; touch; dawn.

pointer, po'ang-teh, *v* to point; to prick; to aim; to soar.

pointillé, po'ang-tee-yeh, *m* stippling; dotted line.

pointilleu-x, se, po'ang-tee-yer, *a* captious; caviling.

pointu, e, po'ang-tE, *a* pointed; sharp.

pointure, po'ang-tEEr, *f* size (shoes, gloves, etc).

poire, po'ăhr, *f* pear; (*slang*) gullible person.

poireau, po'ăh-roh, *m* leek; wart.

poirier, po'ăh-re-eh, *m* pear tree.

pois, po'ăh, *m* pea; **petits –,** per-te –, green peas.

poison, po'ăh-zong, *m* poison.

poisseu-x, se, po'ăhss-er, *a* sticky.

poisson, po'ăhss-ong, *m* fish.

poissonnerie, po'ăhss-onn-ree, *f* fishmarket or shop.

poitrine, po'ăh-treen, *f* chest; breast; lungs; bosom; brisket.

poivre, po'ăh-vr, *m* pepper.

poivrier, po'ăh-vree-eh, *f* pepperpot.

poivron po'ăh-vrong, *m* green or red sweet pepper.

poix, po'ăh, *f* pitch; shoemaker's wax.

pôle, pohl, *m* pole.

polémique, poll-eh-meeck, *f* polemics; controversy; *a* polemical.

poli, e, poll-ee, *a* polished; polite; civil; refined.

police, poll-eess, *f* police; **agent de –,** ăh-shahng der –, policeman.

polichinelle, poll-e-she-nell, *m* buffoon.

polici-er, ère, poll-iss-e-eh, *a* of the police; *m* policeman.

poliment, poll-e-mahng, *adv* politely.

polir, poll-eer, *v* to polish; to brighten; to improve.

polisson, ne, poll-iss-ong, *mf* mischievous child;

scamp.

politesse, poll-e-tess, *f* politeness; civility; good breeding.

politique, poll-e-teeck, *f* policy; politics; *a** political; prudent; politic.

pollen, poll-a*ng* m pollen.

polluer, poll-lE-eh, *v* to pollute.

pollution, poll-lE-se-o*ng* f pollution.

poltron, ne, poll-tro*ng*, *mf* coward; *a* cowardly.

polythène, poll-e-tayn m polythene.

pommade, pomm-ăhd, *f* lip-salve; ointment.

pomme, pomm, *f* apple; **–de terre,** – de*r* tair, potato.

pommé, e, pomm-eh, *a* rounded; (*fam*) downright.

pommelé, e, pomm-leh, *a* dappled; mottled.

pommette, pomm-ett, *f* cheekbone.

pommier, pomm-e-eh, *m* apple tree.

pompe, po*ng*p, *f* pomp; pump.

pompe à essence, po*ng*p-ăh-eh-sa*ng*ss *f* gas pump.

pomper, po*ng*-peh, *v* to pump up; to imbibe.

pompeu-x, se, * po*ng*-per,

a pompous; stately.

pompier, po*ng*-pe-eh, *m* fireman.

pomponner, po*ng*-ponn-eh, *v* to adorn; **se –,** to smarten oneself.

ponce (pierre), pe-ay*r* po*ng*ss, *f* pumice stone.

ponctuation, po*ng*k-tE-ah-se-o*ng*, *f* punctuation.

ponctuel, le, * po*ng*k-tE-ell, *a* punctual.

pondre, po*ng*dr, *v* to lay eggs.

pont, po*ng*, *m* bridge; deck.

pontage, po*ng*-tăsh, *m* *med* bypass.

populace, pop-E-lăhss, *f* the masses.

populaire, * pop-E-lair, *a* popular.

population, pop-E-lăh-se-o*ng*, *f* population.

populeu-x, se, pop-E-ler, *a* populous.

porc, por, *m* pig; swine; hog; pork.

porcelaine, por-ser-lain, *f* porcelain; chinaware.

porc-épic, por-keh-peeck, *m* porcupine.

porche, porsh, *m* porch.

pore, por, *m* pore.

poreu-x, se, por-er, *a* porous.

pornographie, por-nog-răhf-ee, *f* pornography.

port, por, *m* port; harbor; carriage; postage; deportment.

portable, por-tăh-bl, *a* wearable.

portail, por-tah'e, *m* portal.

portant, e, por-tah*ng*, *a* bearing; **bien –,** be-a*ng* –, in good health; **mal –,** măhl –, in bad health.

portati-f, ve, por-tăh-teeff, *a* portable.

porte, port, *f* door; gate; doorway; threshold; pass.

porte-bagages, por-ter-băh-găhsh, *m* luggage rack.

porte-clefs, por-ter-kleh, *m inv* key ring.

portefeuille, por-ter-fer'e, *m* portfolio; wallet.

porte-monnaie, por-ter-monn-ay, *m* purse.

porte-parapluies, por-ter-păh-răh-plwee, *m* umbrella stand.

porte-plume, por-ter-plEEm, *m* penholder.

porter, por-teh, *v* to bear; to carry; to wear; to induce; to tell; **comment vous portez-vous?** komm-ah*ng* voo por-teh voo? how are you?

porteu-r, se, por-ter, *mf* porter; carrier; holder.

porti-er, ère, por-te-eh, *mf* doorkeeper.

portière, por-te-air, *f* door (of car, train, etc).

portion, por-se-ong, *f* portion; allowance.

portrait, por-tray, *m* portrait; likeness.

pose, pohz, *f* putting; pose; affectation.

posé, e, poh-zeh, *pp & a* placed; sedate.

posément, poh-zeh-mahng, *adv* sedately; slowly.

poser, poh-zeh, *v* to place; to pose.

poseu-r, se, poh-zer, *mf* affected person.

positi-f, ve,* poh-ze-teeff, *a* positive; matter-of-fact.

position, poh-ze-se-ong, *f* position; status; posture.

possédé, e, poss-eh-deh, *mf* mad; *a* possessed.

posséder, poss-eh-deh, *v* to possess; to enjoy.

possesseur, poss-ess-er, *m* owner.

possession, poss-ess-e-ong, *f* ownership; right; possession.

possibilité, poss-e-be-le-teh, *f* possibility.

possible, poss-ee-bl, *m* utmost; *a* possible.

postal, e, poss-tăhl, *a* postal.

poste, post, *m* post; station; position; *f* post office.

poste de télévision, post-der-teh-leh-ve-se-ong *m* television set.

poster, poss-teh, *v* to post; to station.

postérieur, e,* poss-teh-re-er, *a* subsequent; later; hind.

postérité, poss-teh-re-teh, *f* posterity; issue.

post-scriptum, post-skrip-tom, *m* postscript.

postuler, poss-tE-leh, *v* to apply for.

posture, poss-tEEr, *f* posture; position.

pot, po, *m* pot; jug; tankard; jar; crock; carton (of yogurt).

potable, pot-ăh-bl, *a* drinkable.

potage, pot-ăhsh, *m* soup; **pour tout –,** poohr too –, *(fam)* in all.

potager, pot-ăh-sheh, *m* kitchen garden.

potasse, pot-ăhss, *f* potash.

poteau, pot-oh, *m* post; stake.

potelé, e, pot-leh, *a* plump; fat.

potence, pot-ahngss, *f* gallows; gibbet.

poterie, pot-ree, *f* earthenware; pottery.

potier, pot-e-eh, *m* potter.

potin, pot-ang, *m* (*fam*) gossip; clatter.

pou, poo, *m* louse.

pouce, pooss, *m* thumb; big toe; inch.

poudre, poo-dr, *f* powder; dust; gunpowder.

poudrier, poo-dre-eh, *m* powder compact.

pouffer, poo-feh, *v* **–de rire,** – der reer, to burst out laughing.

poulailler, poo-lah'e-yeh, *m* henhouse; (peanut gallery) the gods.

poulain, poo-lang, *m* foal; colt.

poule, pool, *f* hen.

poulet, poo-lay, *m* chicken; (*fam*) detective.

poulie, poo-lee, *f* pulley; block.

pouls, poo, *m* pulse.

poumon, poo-mong, *m* lung.

poupe, poop, *f* stern.

poupée, poo-peh, *f* doll; puppet.

pour, poohr, *prep* for; towards; to; in order to; as to.

pourboire, poohr-bo'ăhr, *m* gratuity; tip.

pourceau, poohr-soh, *m*

a
b
c
d
e
f
g
h
i
j
k
l
m
n
o
p
q
r
s
t
u
v
w
x
y
z

hog; pig; swine.

pourcentage, poohr-sahng-tăhsh, *m* percentage.

pour étouffer une affaire, poo-reh-too-feh-E-năh-fair, *v* to cover-up.

pourparler, poohr-păhr-leh, *m* usually; *pl* parley; conference; negotiations.

pourpre, poohr-pr, *m & a* crimson; *f* purple dye.

pourquoi, poohr-kwăh, *adv & conj* why; wherefore; what ... for.

pourrir, poo-reer, *v* to rot.

pourriture, poo-re-tEEr, *f* decay; rot.

poursuite, poohr-sweet, *f* pursuit; *pl* proceedings.

poursuivre, poohr-swee-vr, *v* to pursue; to proceed against.

pourtant, poohr-tahng, *adv* yet; still; however.

pourtour, poohr-toohr, *m* circumference.

pour une personne, poohr-En-pair-sonn *f* single room.

pourvoi, poohr-vo'ăh, *m* appeal.

pourvoir, poohr-vo'ăhr, *v* to provide; to supply; to endow (**à,** for; **de,** with).

pourvu que, poohr-vE, ker, *conj* provided that.

pousser, pooss-eh, *v* to push; to thrust; to urge on; to utter; to grow.

poussette, pooss-ett, *f* stroller.

poussière, pooss-e-air, *f* dust; powder; spray.

poussin, pooss-ang, *m* chick.

poutre, pootr, *f* beam; rafter; girder.

pouvoir, poo-vo'ăhr, *v* to be able; to be allowed.

pouvoir, poo-vo'ăhr, *m* power; authority; power of attorney.

prairie, pray-ree, *f* meadow; prairie.

praline, prăh-leen, *f* praline.

praticable, prăh-te-kăh-bl, *a* practicable; feasible.

praticien, ne, prăh-te-se-ang, *mf* practitioner.

pratique, prăh-teek, *f* practice; experience; *a** practical; useful.

pratiquer, prăh-te-keh, *v* to practice; to use;t o make; to associate with.

pré, preh, *m* meadow.

préalable, * preh-ăh-lăh-bl, *a* previous; *adv phr* **au –,** first of all.

préavis, preh-ah-ve, *m* previous notice.

précaire, * preh-kair, *a* precarious.

précaution, preh-koh-se-ong, *f* precaution; caution.

précédemment, preh-seh-dăh-mahng, *adv* previously.

précédent, e, preh-seh-dahng, *a* preceding; *m* precedent.

précéder, preh-seh-deh, *v* to precede.

précepteur, preh-sep-ter, *m* tutor.

prêcher, pray-sheh, *v* to preach; to lecture.

précieu-x, se, * preh-se-er, *a* precious; valuable; affected.

précipice, preh-se-peess, *m* precipice.

précipitamment, preh-se-pe-tăh-mahng, *adv* hurriedly; headlong.

précipiter, preh-se-pe-teh, *v* to precipitate; to hurl headlong; to hasten.

précis, preh-se, *m* summary; précis.

précis, e, preh-se, *a* precise; exact; specific.

précisément, preh-se-zeh-mahng, *adv* precisely; just so.

préciser, preh-se-zeh, *v* to state precisely; to specify.

précité, e, preh-se-teh, *a* aforesaid.

précoce, preh-koss, *a* precocious; early.

préconiser, preh-konn-e-zeh, *v* to extol; to advocate.

prédicateur, preh-de-kăh-ter, *m* preacher.

prédire, preh-deer, *v* to predict; to foretell.

préface, preh-făhss, *f* preface.

préférable,* preh-feh-răh-bl, *a* preferable; advisable.

préférer, preh-feh-reh, *v* to prefer; to like better.

préfet, preh-fay, *m* prefect; administrator (of French county).

préjudice, preh-shE-deess, *m* prejudice; wrong.

préjudiciable, preh-shE-de-se-ăh-bl, *a* prejudicial.

préjugé, preh-shE-sheh, *m* prejudice; preconception.

prélasser (se), ser preh-lăhss-eh, *v* to strut; to take one's ease.

prélever, prehl-veh, *v* to deduct beforehand; to levy.

préliminaire, preh-le-me-nair, *a* preliminary.

prélude, preh-lEEd, *m* prelude.

prématuré,* e, preh-măh-tE-reh, *a* premature.

premier, prer-me-eh, *m* chief; leader; first.

premi-er, ère,* prer-me-eh, *a* first; former; early; next; leading.

prémunir, preh-mE-neer, *v* to forewarn; to caution.

prendre, prahngdr, *v* to take; to seize; to assume; to congeal; to set; to catch on.

prendre un bain de soleil, prahngdr-ung-bang-der-soll-a'ye *v* sunbathe.

preneu-r, se, prer-ner, *mf* taker; buyer.

prénom, preh-nong, *m* first name.

préoccuper, preh-ock-E-peh, *v* to preoccupy; to engross the mind; to disturb.

préparatif, preh-păh-răh-teeff, *m* preparation (used almost exclusively in the plural).

préparer, preh-păh-reh, *v* to prepare; to get ready.

prépondérance, preh-pong-deh-rahngss, *f* preponderance; sway.

préposé, preh-poh-zeh, *m* official in charge.

près, pray, *adv* & *prep* near; close by; **–de,** about to.

présage, preh-zăhsh, *m* presage; omen.

présager, preh-zăh-sheh, *v* to forebode.

pré-salé, preh-săh-leh, *m* salt-meadow sheep.

presbyte, prez-beet, *mf* & *a* farsighted.

presbytère, prez-be-tair, *m* vicarage.

prescience, preh-se-ahngss, *f* prescience.

prescrire, press-kreer, *v* to order; to prescribe.

préséance, preh-seh-ahngss, *f* precedence.

présence, preh-zahngss, *f* presence.

présent, e, preh-zahng, *a* present.

présenter, preh-zahng-teh, *v* to present; to offer; to introduce.

présenta-teur, trice, preh-zahng-tah-tez, *mf* anchorman (new); anchorwoman (news).

préservati-f, ve, preh-zair-văh-teeff, *a* protective; *m* condom.

préserver, preh-zair-veh, *v* to preserve (**de,** from).

président, preh-ze-dahng, *m* president; chairman.

présider, preh-ze-deh, *v* to preside.

présomption, preh-zongp-se-ong, *f* presumption;

a b c d e f g h i j k l m n o p q r s t u v w x y z

self-assurance.

présomptueu-x, se,* preh-zongp-tE- er, *a* presumptuous.

presque, press-ker, *adv* almost; nearly.

presqu'île, press-keel, *f* peninsula.

pressant, e, press-ahng, *a* pressing; urgent.

presse, press, *f* press; crowd; urgency; squeezer.

pressé, e, press-eh, *a* in a hurry; urgent.

pressentiment, press-ahng-te-mahng, *m* presentiment.

pressentir, press-ahng-teer, *v* to have a presentiment of.

presser, press-eh, *v* to press; to crowd; to urge.

pression, press-e-ong, *f* pressure.

prestance, press-tahngss, *f* fine presence.

preste,* presst, *a* quick; nimble.

prestidigitateur, press-te-de-**she-tăh-ter,** *m* conjuror.

prestige, press-teesh, *m* prestige.

prestigieu-x, se, press-te-**she-er** *a* glamorous (job).

présumer, preh-zE-meh, *v*

to presume.

prêt, pray, *m* loan.

prêt, e, pray, *a* ready; prepared; willing.

prétendant, e, preh-tahng-dahng, *mf* claimant; pretender; suitor.

prétendre, preh-tahng-dr, *v* to claim; to intend; to maintain.

prétendu, e, preh-tahng-dE, *mf* intended (husband or wife); *a* so-called.

prête-nom, prayt-nong, *m* figurehead.

prétentieu-x, se,* preh-tahng-se-er, *a* pretentious; conceited.

prétention, preh-tahng-se-ong, *f* pretension; affectation.

prêter, pray-teh, *v* to lend; to ascribe; to give rise.

prêteu-r, se, pray-ter, *mf* lender.

prétexte, preh-text, *m* pretext; pretense.

prêtre, pray-tr, *m* priest.

preuve, prerv, *f* proof; evidence; token.

prévaloir, preh-văh-lo'ăhr, *v* to prevail.

prévenance, prehv-nahngss, *f* kind attention.

prévenant, prehv-nahng, *a* obliging; prepossessing.

prévenir, prehv-neer, *v* to advise; to inform.

prévention, preh-vahng-se-ong, *f* imprisonment on suspicion; prevention.

prévenu, e, prehv-nE, *mf* accused; *a* prejudiced.

prévision, prehv-ve-ze-ong, *f* forecast; anticipation.

prévoir, preh-vo'ăhr, *v* to foresee; to provide for or against.

prévoyance, preh-vo'ăh-yahngss, *f* foresight; forethought.

prier, pre-eh, *v* to pray; to entreat; to invite.

prière, pre-air, *f* prayer; entreaty; request.

primaire, pre-mair, *a* primary; elementary.

prime, preem, *f* premium; bonus; option.

primé, e, pre-meh, given a prize.

primer, pre-meh, *v* to surpass; to award a prize to.

primeur, pre-mer, *f* early fruit or vegetable; freshness.

primevère, preem-vair, *f* primrose.

primiti-f, ve,* pre-me-teeff, *a* primitive.

prince, sse, prangss, *mf* prince; princess.

princi-er, ère,* prang-se-eh, *a* princely.

principal, prang-se-păhl, *m* chief thing; main point; *a* principal; main.

principauté, prang-se-poh-te, *f* principality.

principe, prang-seep, *m* principle.

printani-er, ère, prang-tăh-ne-eh, *a* springlike.

printemps, prang-tahng, *m* spring; springtime.

priorité, pre-or-e-teh, *f* priority; right of way.

pris, e, pre, *pp* & *a* taken; occupied; busy.

prise, preez, *f* taking; hold; quarrel; catch.

priser, pre-zeh, *v* to value; to take snuff.

priseu-r, se, pre-zer, *mf* snuff-taker; appraiser.

prison, pre-zong, *f* prison.

prisonni-er, ère, pre-zonn-e-eh, *mf* & *a* prisoner.

privation, pre-văh-se-ong, *f* privation; loss.

privauté, pre-voh-teh, *f* familiarity.

privé, e, pre-veh, *a* private.

priver, pre-veh, *v* to deprive.

privilège, pre-ve-laysh, *m* privilege.

prix, pre, *m* price; value; reward; prize; – de revient, de rer-ve-ang, *m* cost.

probabilité, prob-ăh-be-le-teh, *f* probability.

probable,* prob-ăh-bl, *a* probable; likely.

probant, e, prob-ahng, *a* conclusive; convincing.

probe, prob, *a* honest; upright.

probité, prob-e-teh, *f* honesty; uprightness.

problème, prob-laym, *m* problem.

procédé, pross-eh-deh, *m* process; behavior; method.

procéder, pross-eh-deh, *v* to proceed; to behave; to prosecute (**contre,** against).

procédure, pross-eh-dEEr, *f* proceedings; practice.

procès, pross-ay, *m* lawsuit; trial; litigation.

procès-verbal, pross-ay-vair-băhl, *m* report; minutes; record.

prochain, prosh-ang, *m* neighbor; fellow.

prochain, e, prosh-ang, *a* next; nearest.

prochainement, prosh-ain-mahng, *adv* shortly.

proche, prosh, *a* close; *mpl* relations; *adv* near.

proclamer, prock-lăh-meh, *v* to proclaim.

procuration, prock-E-răh-se-ong, *f* proxy.

procurer, prock-E-reh, *v* to procure.

procureur, prock-E-rer, *m* state prosecutor/general; attorney.

prodigalité, prod-e-găh-le-teh, *f* prodigality; extravagance.

prodige, prod-eesh, *m* prodigy; wonder.

prodigieu-x, se,* prod-e-she-er, *a* prodigious; wonderful.

prodigue, prod-eeg, *m* spendthrift; *a* prodigal.

prodiguer, prod-e-gheh, *v* to lavish; to squander.

produc-teur, trice, prod-EEk-ter, *mf* producer; *a* productive.

production, prod-EEk-se-ong, *f* production; product; output.

produire, prod-weer, *v* to produce; to yield; to show.

produit, prod-wee, *m* produce; product; proceeds.

produit pour la vaisselle, prod-wee-poohr-lăh-vayss-ell *m* dishwashing liquid.

profane, prof-ăhn, *mf* & *a* outsider; profane; lay.

profaner, prof-ăh-neh, *v* to profane.

proférer, prof-eh-reh, *v* to utter.

professer, prof-ess-eh, *v* to profess; to teach.

professeur, prof-ess-er, *m* professor; teacher.

profession, prof-ess-e-ong, *f* profession; business.

profil, prof-eel, *m* profile; section.

profit, prof-e, *m* profit; gain; utility.

profiter, prof-e-teh, *v* to profit (**de,** by); to take advantage (**de,** of).

profond, e, prof-ong, *a* deep; profound; sound.

profondément, prof-ong-deh-mahng, *adv* deeply.

profondeur, prof-ong-der, *f* depth; profoundness.

programme, prog-răhm, *m* program; bill; platform.

progrès, prog-ray, *m* progress; improvement.

prohiber, pro-e-beh, *v* to prohibit.

proie, prwăh, *f* prey.

projecteur, pro-sheck-ter, *m* projector; headlight.

projectile, pro-sheck-teel, *m & a* missile.

projection, prosh-eck-se-ong, *f* projection.

projet, prosh-ay, *m* project; scheme; rough draft.

projeter, prosh-teh, *v* to project; to plan.

prolétaire, proll-eh-tair, *m & a* proletarian.

prolonger, proll-ong-sheh, *v* to prolong; to protract; to lengthen.

promenade, promm-năhd, *f* walk; drive; ride; excursion.

promener, promm-neh, *v* to take about; to walk; **se –,** to take a walk.

promeneu-r, se, promm-ner, *mf* walker.

promesse, promm-ayss, *f* promise.

promettre, promm-ay-tr, *v* to promise; to look promising.

promontoire, promm-ong-to'ăhr, *m* promontory.

promouvoir, promm-oo-vo'ăhr, *v* to promote.

prompt, e,* prong, *a* prompt; sudden; hasty.

promptitude, prong-te-tEEd, *f* quickness.

promulguer, promm-EEl-gheh, *v* to promulgate.

pronom, pron-ong, *m* pronoun.

prononcé, e, pron-ong-seh, *pp & a* pronounced; decided.

prononcer, pron-ong-seh, *v* to pronounce; to utter.

propagande, prop-ăh-gahngd, *f* propaganda.

propager, prop-ăh-sheh, *v* to propagate; **se –,** to spread.

propension, prop-ahng-se-ong, *f* propensity.

prophétie, prof-eh-see, *f* prophecy.

propice, prop-eess, *a* propitious; favorable.

proportionnel, le,* prop-or-se-onn-ell, *a* proportional; commensurate.

propos, prop-oh, *m* purpose; talk.

proposer, prop-oh-zeh, *v* to propose; to move; **se –,** to intend; to mean.

proposition, prop-oh-ze-se-ong, *f* proposal; proposition; clause.

propre, propr, *m* own characteristic; *a** own; proper; clean.

propreté, prop-rer-teh, *f* neatness; cleanliness.

propriétaire, prop-re-eh-tair, *mf* proprietor; landlord.

propriété, prop-re-eh-teh, *f* property; ownership; propriety.

propulsion, prop-EEl-se-ong, *f* propelling.

prorata, pro-răh-tăh, *m* proportion.

prorogation, pror-ogh-ăh-se-*ong*, *f* prorogation; adjournment.

proroger, pror-osh-eh, *v* to extend; to adjourn.

prosaïque, pro-zăh-eek, *a* prosaic.

prosateur, pro-zăh-ter, *m* prosewriter.

proscrire, pross-kreer, *v* to proscribe; to banish.

proscrit, e, pross-kre, *mf* exile; outlaw.

prose, prohz, *f* prose.

prospère, pross-pair, *a* prosperous.

prospérer, pross-peh-reh, *v* to prosper; to thrive.

prosterner (se), ser pross-tair-neh, *v* to prostrate oneself.

prostituée, pross-te-tE-eh, *f* prostitute.

protec-teur, trice, prot-eck-ter, *mf* & *a* protector; protective.

protectorat, prot-eck-tor-ăh, *m* protectorate.

protégé, e, prot-eh-**sheh**, *mf* protégé; dependent.

protéger, prot-eh-**sheh**, *v* to protect; to shield.

protestant, e, prot-ess-tahng, *mf* & *a* Protestant.

protester, prot-ess-teh, *v* to protest.

prouesse, proo-ess, *f* prowess; exploit.

prouver, proo-veh, *v* to prove; to show.

provenance, prov-nahngss, *f* origin; source.

provenir, prov-neer, *v* to proceed; to originate.

proverbe, prov-airb, *m* proverb.

proverbial, e,* prov-air-be-ăhl, *a* proverbial.

providence, prov-e-dahngss, *f* Providence.

province, prov-angss, *f* province; the country.

provincial, e, prov-ang-se-ăhl, *mf* & *a* provincial.

proviseur, prov-e-zer, *m* principal.

provision, prov-e-ze-*ong*, *f* provision; supply; retainer.

provisoire,* prov-e-zo'ăhr, *a* provisional.

provocant, e, prov-ock-ahng, *a* provoking; alluring.

provoca-teur, trice, prov-ock-ăh-ter, *mf* aggressor; agitator.

provoquer, prov-ock-eh, *v* to provoke; to challenge; to cause.

prudemment, prE-dăh-mahng, *adv* prudently.

prudence, prE-dahngss, *f* prudence.

pruderie, prEEd-ree, *f* prudishness.

prune, prEEn, *f* plum.

pruneau, prE-noh, *m* prune.

prunelle, prE-nell, *f* sloe; pupil (eye).

prunier, prE-ne-eh, *m* plum tree.

psaume, psohm, *m* psalm.

pseudonyme, pser-donn-eem, *m* pseudonym.

psychanalyste, pse-kăh-năh-leest *mf* psychoanalyst.

psychiatre, pse-ke-ah-tr, *m* psychiatrist.

psychologique, pse-koll-o-sheeck *a* psychological.

psychologue, pse-koll-og, *m* psychologist.

psychopathe, pse-ko-paht *mf* psychopath.

puant, e, pE-ahng, *a* stinking.

puanteur, pE-ahng-ter, *f* stench.

pubère, pE-bair, *a* pubescent.

public, pE-bleeck, *m* public.

publi-c, que,* pE-bleeck, *a* public; common.

publication, pE-bli-cah-se-*ong*, *f* publication; publishing.

publicité, pE-ble-se-teh, *f* publicity; advertisement.

a
b
c
d
e
f
g
h
i
j
k
l
m
n
o
p
q
r
s
t
u
v
w
x
y
z

A
B
C
D
E
F
G
H
I
J
K
L
M
N
O
P
Q
R
S
T
U
V
W
X
Y
Z

publier, pE-ble-eh, *v* to publish.

puce, pEEss, *f* flea.

pucelle, pE-sell, *f* virgin.

pudeur, pE-der, *f* bashfulness; modesty; reserve.

pudique,* pE-deeck, *a* chaste; modest.

puer, pE-eh, *v* to stink; to smell strongly of.

puéril, e,* pE-eh-reel, *a* childish.

pugilat, pE- she-lăh, *m* boxing.

puis, pwee, *adv* then; afterwards; next; besides.

puiser, pwee-zeh, *v* to draw (water); to derive.

puisque, pweess-ker, *conj* since.

puissamment, pweess-ăh-mahng, *adv* powerfully; mightily.

puissance, pweess-ahngss, *f* power; force; influence.

puissant, e, pweess-ahng, *a* powerful; mighty; (*fam*) stout.

puits, pwee, *m* well; shaft; pit.

pull (-over), pEl (lo-vair) *m* pullover.

pulluler, pEEl-lE-leh, *v* to swarm.

pulsation, pEEl-săh-se-ong,

f beating; throbbing.

pulvériser, pEEl-veh-re-zeh, *v* to pulverize.

punaise, pE-nayz, *f* bedbug; thumbtack.

punir, pE-neer, *v* to punish.

punition, pE-niss-e-ong, *f* punishment.

pupille, pE-peell, *mf* ward; *f* pupil (of eye).

pupitre, pE-pee-tr, *m* desk; music stand.

pur, e,* pEEr, *a* pure; genuine; clean; mere.

purée, pE-reh, *f* mash; purée; mashed potatoes.

pureté, pEEr-teh, *f* purity; chastity.

purgati-f, ve, pEEr-găh-teeff, *a* purgative.

purgatoire, pEEr-găh-to'ăhr, *m* purgatory.

purge, pEErsh, *f* purge; cleansing.

purger, pEEr-sheh, *v* to purge; to cleanse; to serve (jail).

purifier, pE-re-fe-eh, *v* to purify.

pus, pE, *m* pus; matter.

pusillanime, pE-zill-lăh-neemm, *a* fainthearted.

pustule, pEEs-tEEl, *f* pimple.

putréfier, pE-treh-fe-eh, *v* to putrefy; to rot.

puzzle, pEEzl *m* jigsaw.

pyramide, pe-răh-meedd, *f* pyramid.

quadragénaire, kwăh-drăh-**sheh**-nair, *mf* & *a* forty year old.

quadrillé, e, kăh-dree-yeh, *a* checkered.

quadruple, kwăh-drEE-pl, *m* & *a* quadruple.

quai, kay, *m* quay; wharf; platform.

qualification, kăh-le-fe-kăh-se-ong, *f* title.

qualifier, kăh-le-fe-eh, *v* to qualify; to call.

qualité, kăh-le-teh, *f* quality; property; rank; qualification.

quand, kahng, *adv* when (at what moment); *conj* when (at the time).

quant à, kahng t'ăh, *prep* as to; as for.

quantième, kahng-te-aym, *m* day of the month.

quantité, kahng-te-teh, *f* quantity.

quarantaine, kăh-rahng-tain, *f* about forty; quarantine.

quarante, kăh-rahngt, *m* & *a* forty.

quarantième, kăh-rahng-te-aym, *m* & *a* fortieth.

quart, kăhr, *m* quarter; (*nau*) watch; point (of compass).

quartier, kăhr-te-eh, *m* quarter; piece; neighborhood; district.

quartier des prostituées, kăhr-te-eh-deh-pross-te-tE-eh *m* red-light district.

quartiers défavorisés, kăhr-te-eh-deh-făh-vor-e-zeh *mpl* inner city.

quasi, kăh-ze, *adv* quasi; all but; almost.

quatorze, kăh-torz, *m* & *a* fourteen.

quatorzième, kăh-tor-ze-aym, *m* & *a* fourteenth.

quatre, kăh-tr, *m* & *a* four.

quatre-vingt-dix, kăh-trer-vang-deess, *m* & *a* ninety.

quatre-vingts, kăh-trer-vang, *a* eighty.

quatrième, kăh-tre-aym, *m* & *a* fourth.

quatuor, kwăh-tE-or, *m* quartet.

que, ker, *pron* whom; that; which; what.

que, ker, *adv* how; how much; how many; why.

que, ker, *conj* that; if; when; as; until; while; whether; lest; **ne...–,** ner...–, only.

quel, le, kell, *a* what; what a; which.

quelconque, kell-kongk, *a* whatever; any; (*fam*) commonplace.

quelque, kell-ker, *adv* some; about; *a* some;

a
b
c
d
e
f
g
h
i
j
k
l
m
n
o
p
q
r
s
t
u
v
w
x
y
z

any; a few.

quelquefois, kell-ker-fo'ăh, *adv* sometimes.

quelqu'un, e, kell-kung, *pron* somebody; one; *pl* **quelques-uns, unes,** kell-ker-z'ung, some; a few; any.

querelle, ker-rell, *f* quarrel; row.

question, kess-te-ong, *f* question; matter.

questionnaire, kess-te-onn-air, *m* set of questions; questionnaire.

quête, kayt, *f* quest; collection.

quêter, kay-teh, *v* to search; to make a collection.

queue, ker, *f* tail; train; cue; tailpiece.

qui, ke, *pron* who; whom; which; that; whoever; what.

quiconque, ke-kongk, *pron* whoever.

qui continue à évoluer, ke-kong-te-nE-ăh-eh-voll-E-eh *a* ongoing.

quille, kee-ye, *f* keel; skittle.

quincaillerie, kang-kah'e-ree, *f* hardware store.

quinquagénaire, kang-kwăh-sheh-nair, *mf & a* to be fifty.

quinte, kangt, *f* coughing fit; fifth.

quintuple, kwang-tEE-pl, *m & a* fivefold.

quinzaine, kang-zain, *f* about fifteen; two weeks.

quinze, kangz, *m & a* fifteen; fifteenth.

quinzième, kang-ze-aym, *m & a* fifteenth.

quittance, ke-tahngss, *f* receipt; discharge.

quitte, keet, *a* clear; quit; –à, – ăh, at the risk of.

quitter, ke-teh, *v* to leave; to forsake; to depart.

qui-vive, ke-veev, *m* to be on the alert.

quoi, kwăh, *pron* what; which, that; (exclamation) what!

quoique, kwăh-ker, *conj* although.

quolibet, koll-e-bay, *m* gibe; jeer.

quota, kot-ăh, *m* quota.

quote-part, kot-păhr, *f* share.

quotidien, ne, kot-e-de-ang, *a* daily.

quotient, ko-sseahng, *m* quotient: I.Q.

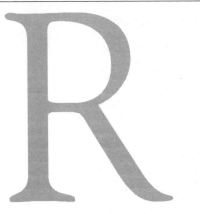

rabâcher, răh-bah-sheh, *v* to repeat over and over again.

rabais, răh-bay, *m* abatement; rebate.

rabaisser, răh-bess-eh, *v* to lower; to humble.

rabattre, răh-băh-tr, *v* to lower; to bring down; to deduct.

rabbin, răh-bang, *m* rabbi.

râblé, e, rah-bleh, *a* broad-backed; stocky.

raboter, răh-bot-eh, *v* to plane.

raboteu-x, se, răh-bot-er, *a* rugged; harsh; jagged.

rabougri, e, răh-boo-gre, *a* stunted.

raccommoder, răh-komm-od-eh, *v* to mend; to patch; to darn; to reconcile.

raccorder, răh-kor-deh, *v* to join; to unite.

raccourcir, răh-koohr-seer, *v* to shorten; to curtail.

raccrocher, răh-krosh-eh, *v* to hang up; **se –,** to clutch.

race, răhss, *f* race; stock; breed; family.

rachat, răh-shăh, *m* repurchase; atonement; redemption.

racheter, răhsh-teh, *v* to buy back; to atone for.

rachitique, răh-she-teeck, *a* rickety.

racine, răh-seen, *f* root; origin.

racisme, răh-sism *m* racism.

raciste, răh-seest *a* & *mf* racist.

raclée, rah-kleh, *f* (*pop*) thrashing; licking.

racler, rah-kleh, *v* to scrape.

racoler, răh-koll-eh, *v* to recruit; to pick up.

racontar, răh-kong-tăhr, *m* gossip.

raconter, răh-kong-teh, *v* to relate; to tell.

rade, răhd, *f* harbor.

radeau, răh-doh, *m* raft.

radiateur, răh-de-ăh-ter, *m* radiator.

radieu-x, se,* răh-de-er, *a* radiant.

radio, răh-de-o, *f* radio.

radioactif, răh-de-oh-ăhk-teef *a* radioactive.

radiodiffusion, răh-de-o-diff-E-ze-ong, *f* broadcasting.

radiographie, răh-de-o-grăh-fe, *f* X-ray photography; X-ray.

radis, răh-de, *m* radish.

radoter, răh-dot-eh, *v* to rave; to drivel.

radoucir, răh-doo-seer, *v* to soften; to calm.

rafale, răh-făhl, *f* squall.

raffermir, răh-fair-meer, *v* to strengthen; to make firm.

raffiné, e, răh-fe-neh, *a* refined; delicate.

raffinerie, răh-feen-ree, *f* sugar refinery.

a
b
c
d
e
f
g
h
i
j
k
l
m
n
o
p
q
r
s
t
u
v
w
x
y
z

A
B
C
D
E
F
G
H
I
J
K
L
M
N
O
P
Q
R
S
T
U
V
W
X
Y
Z

raffoler, răh-foll-eh, *v* to dote (**de,** on); (*fam*) to be mad about.

rafler, rah-fleh, *v* to sweep off.

rafraîchir, răh-fray-sheer, *v* to cool; to brighten up.

rafraîchissement, răh-fray-shiss-mahng, *m* cooling; refreshing; *pl* refreshments.

rage, răhsh, *f* rabies; rage; violent pain.

rager, răh-sheh, *v* to fume; to be in a rage.

ragoût, răh-goo, *m* stew; relish.

ragoût (en cocotte), răh-goo, (ahng-kock-ot) *m* casserole (food).

raide, rayd, *adv* quickly; sharply; outright; *a* stiff; tight; steep; stubborn.

raideur, ray-der, *f* stiffness; tightness; sternness.

raidir, ray-deer, *v* to stiffen; to tighten.

raie, ray, *f* streak; stroke; parting (hair); skate (fish).

rail, rah'e, *m* rail (railroad).

railler, rah'e-yeh, *v* to scoff at; to mock.

raillerie, rah'e-ree, *f* mocking; banter; jeer.

rainure, ray-nEEr, *f* groove.

raisin, ray-zang, *m* grapes.

raison, ray-zong, *f* reason; cause; satisfaction; right; ratio.

raisonnable,* ray-zonn-ăh-bl, *a* reasonable; sensible.

raisonnement, ray-zonn-mahng, *m* reasoning; argument.

raisonner, ray-zonn-eh, *v* to reason.

rajeunir, răh-sher-neer, *v* to rejuvenate.

rajouter, răh-shoo-teh, *v* to add.

rajuster, răh-shEs-teh, *v* to readjust; to repair.

ralentir, răh-lahng-teer, *v* to slacken; to slow down.

râler, rah-leh, *v* to rattle (in one's throat); (*fam*) to fume.

rallier, răh-le-eh, *v* to rally; to rejoin.

rallonger, rah-long-sheh, *v* to lengthen; to let down.

ramage, răh-măhsh, *m* warbling; floral design.

ramas, răh-mah, *m* heap; set.

ramasser, răh-măhss-eh, *v* to gather; to pick up.

rame, răhm, *f* oar; ream

(paper); prop.

rameau, răh-moh, *m* bough; branch.

ramener, răhm-neh, *v* to bring back; to restore.

ramer, răh-meh, *v* to row; to stake (peas).

ramifier (se), ser răh-me-fe-eh, *v* to branch out.

ramollir, răh-moll-eer, *v* to soften; to weaken.

ramoner, răh-monn-eh, *v* to sweep (chimneys).

ramoneur, răh-monn-er, *m* chimneysweep.

rampant, e, rahng-pahng, *a* creeping; servile.

rampe, rahngp, *f* handrail; slope; footlights.

ramper, rahng-peh, *v* to crawl; to cringe.

rance, rahngss, *a* rancid.

rançon, rahng-song, *f* ransom.

rançonner, rahng-sonn-eh, *v* to ransom; (*fam*) to fleece.

rancune, rahng-kEEn, *f* rancor; grudge.

rang, rahng, *m* row; line; rank; range; rate.

rangée, rahng-sheh, *f* row; line; tier.

ranger, rahng-sheh, *v* to arrange; to tidy.

ranimer, răh-ne-meh, *v* to revive.

rapace, răh-păhss, *m* bird

of prey; *a* rapacious.

rapatrier, răh-păh-tre-eh, *v* to repatriate.

râpé, e, rah-peh, *pp* & *a* grated; threadbare.

râper, rah-peh, *v* to grate.

rapetisser, răhp-tiss-eh, *v* to shorten; to shrink.

rapide, răh-peed, *m* fast train; *a** fast.

rapidité, răh-pe-de-teh, *f* swiftness; speed.

rappel, răh-pell, *m* recall; call to arms; repeal.

rappeler, răhp-leh, *v* to call again; to remind; **se –,** to remember.

rapport, răh-por, *m* report; tale; relation; bearing.

rapporter, răh-por-teh, *v* to bring back; to report; to yield; to tell tales; **se –à,** to relate to.

rapporteur, răh-por-ter, *m* sneak; reporter; protractor.

rapprocher, răh-prosh-eh, *v* to bring near; to reconcile; to compare.

raquette, răh-kett, *f* racket.

raquette de tennis, răh-kett-der-teh-neess *f* tennis racket.

rare,* răhr, *a* rare; scarce; uncommon.

rareté, răhr-teh, *f* scarcity; rare object.

ras, e, rah, *a* shorn; flat; smooth.

rasade, răh-zăhd, *f* glassful.

raser, rah-zeh, *v* to shave; to graze; to skim; (*fam*) to bore.

rasoir, rah-zo'ăhr, *m* razor.

rassasier, răhss-ăh-ze-eh, *v* to satiate; to satisfy (hunger, etc).

rassemblement, răhss-ahng-bler-mahng, *m* gathering; crowd.

rassembler, răhss-ahng-bleh, *v* to reassemble; to gather; **se –,** to meet.

rasseoir, răhss-o'ăhr, *v* to reseat; to settle.

rasséréner, răhss-eh-reh-neh, *v* to clear up; to calm.

rassis, e, răhss-e, *a* stale; sedate.

rassurer, răhss-E-reh, *v* to reassure.

rat, răh, *m* rat.

ratatiné, e, răh-tăh-te-neh, *pp* & *a* shriveled up.

rate, răht, *f* spleen.

râteau, rah-toh, *m* rake.

râtelier, rah-ter-le-eh, *m* rack; (*fam*) denture.

rater, răh-teh, *v* to misfire; to fail.

ratifier, răh-te-fe-eh, *v* to ratify.

ration, răh-se-ong, *f* ration; share; allowance.

rationnel, le,* răh-se-onn-ell, *a* rational.

ratisser, răh-tiss-eh, *v* to scrape; to rake.

rattacher, răh-tăh-sheh, *v* to fasten; **se –,** to be connected (**à,** with).

rattraper, răh-trăh-peh, *v* to catch up; to recover; **se –,** to recoup oneself.

rature, răh-tEEr, *f* erasure.

rauque, rohk, *a* hoarse.

ravage, răh-văhsh, *m* ravage; devastation; havoc.

ravaler, răh-văh-leh, *v* to swallow again; to disparage.

ravi, răh-vee, *a* entranced; delighted.

ravin, răh-vang, *m* ravine.

ravir, răh-veer, *v* to rob; to carry off; to enrapture.

raviser (se), ser răh-ve-zeh, *v* to change one's mind.

ravissant, e, răh-viss-ahng, *a* ravishing; charming.

ravissement, răh-viss-mahng, *m* ravishment; rapture.

ravoir, răh-vo'ăhr, *v* to get back (only in *inf*).

A
B
C
D
E
F
G
H
I
J
K
L
M
N
O
P
Q
R
S
T
U
V
W
X
Y
Z

rayer, ray-yeh, *v* to erase; to scratch; to strip.

rayon, ray-yong, *m* ray; bookshelf; radius; spoke; department.

rayonnement, ray-ongn-mahng *m* radiation.

rayonner, ray-yonn-eh, *v* to radiate.

rayure, ray-yEEr, *f* stripe.

réaction, reh-ăhck-se-ong, *f* reaction.

réagir, reh-ăh-**sheer**, *v* to react.

réaliser, reh-ăh-le-zeh, *v* to realize; to produce (film); to achieve.

réalité, reh-ăh-le-teh, *f* reality.

rébarbati-f, ve, reh-băhr-băh-teeff, *a* gruff; repulsive.

rebattu, e, rer-băh-tE, *a* trite; hackneyed.

rebelle, rer-bell, *mf* rebel; *a* rebellious.

rebondi, e, rer-bong-de, *a* plump; chubby.

rebondir, rer-bong-deer, *v* to rebound; to bounce.

rebord, rer-bor, *m* edge; brim.

rebours, rer-boohr, *m* wrong way; reverse.

rebrousse-poil (à), ăh rer-brooss-po'ăhl, *adv* the wrong way.

rebrousser, rer-brooss-eh, *v* to brush up; **–chemin,** – sher-mang, to retrace one's steps.

rebut, rer-bE, *m* rejection; scum; outcast.

rebuter, rer-bE-teh, *v* to repulse; to dishearten.

récalcitrant, e, reh-kăhl-se-trahng, *a* refractory.

recaler, rer-kăhl-eh, *v* to fail an exam.

recéler, rer-seh-leh, *v* to receive (stolen goods); to harbor.

récemment, reh-săh-mahng, *adv* recently.

recensement, rer-sahngss-mahng, *m* census.

récent, e, reh-sahng, *a* recent.

récépissé, reh-seh-piss-eh, *m* acknowledgment of receipt.

réception, reh-sep-se-ong, *f* reception; receipt; catching (sports).

recette, rer-sett, *f* receipt; returns; recipe.

receveu-r, se, rer-ser-ver, *mf* receiver; collector; conductor (bus, etc).

recevoir, rer-ser-vo'ăhr, *v* to receive; to admit.

rechange, rer-shahng-sh, *m* replacement; **de –,** spare.

réchaud, reh-shoh, *m* chafing dish; small stove.

réchauffer, reh-shoh-feh, *v* to reheat; to stir up.

recherche, rer-shairsh, *f* search; refinement; research.

recherché, e, rer-shair-sheh, *a* in great request; farfetched; choice.

rechercher, rer-shair-sheh, *v* to search; to seek.

rechute, rer-shEEt, *f* relapse.

récidive, reh-se-deev, *f* second offense.

récif, reh-seeff, *m* reef.

récipient, reh-se-pe-ahng, *m* container.

réciproque,* reh-se-prock, *a* reciprocal.

récit, reh-se, *m* account; narration.

réciter, reh-se-teh, *v* to recite; to relate.

réclamation, reh-klăh-măh-se-ong, *f* claim; complaint.

réclame, reh-klăhm, *f* advertisement.

réclamer, reh-klăh-meh, *v* to claim; to protest; to implore; to need.

reclus, e, rer-klE, *mf* recluse.

recoin, rer-ko'ang, *m* corner; nook.

récolte, reh-kollt, *f*
harvest; crop.

recommandable, rer-
komm-ahng-dăh-bl, *a*
commendable;
advisable.

recommandation, rer-
komm-ahng-dăh-se-*ong*,
f recommendation;
advice.

recommander, rer-komm-
ahng-deh, *v* to
recommend; to advise;
to register (letter).

recommencer, rer-komm-
ahngss-eh, *v* to begin
again; to do it again.

récompense, reh-kong-
pahngss, *f* reward.

récompenser, reh-kong-
pahngss-eh, *v* to reward.

réconcilier, reh-kong-se-
le-eh, *v* to reconcile.

reconduire, rer-kong-
dweer, *v* to lead back; to
escort; to renew
(document).

réconforter, reh-kong-for-
teh, *v* to strengthen; to
cheer up.

reconnaissance, rer-konn-
ess-ahngss, *f* recognition;
gratitude.

reconnaissant, e, rer-
konn-ess-ahng, *a*
grateful.

reconnaître, rer-konn-ay-
tr, *v* to recognize; to

acknowledge.

recourir, rer-koo-reer, *v* to
have recourse.

recours, rer-koohr, *m*
recourse; resource;
appeal.

recouvrement, rer-koo-
vrer-mahng, *m* recovery;
collection (debts);
covering.

recouvrer, rer-koo-vreh, *v*
to regain; to collect.

recouvrir, rer-koo-vreer, *v*
to recover; to cover.

récréation, reh-kreh-ăh-
se-*ong*, *f* recreation;
playtime.

recréer, rer-kreh-eh, *v* to
create again.

récrier (se), ser reh-kre-
eh, *v* to exclaim; to
protest.

recrue, rer-krE, *f* recruit.

recruter, rer-krE-teh, *v* to
recruit.

recteur, reck-ter, *m* rector.

rectifier, reck-te-fe-eh, *v*
to rectify.

recto, reck-to, *m* right-
hand page.

reçu, rer-sE, *m* receipt.

recueil, rer-ker'e, *m*
collection.

recueillement, rer-ker'e-
mahng, *m* meditation;
composure; quietude.

recueillir, rer-ker'e-eer, *v*
to gather; to collect; to

reap;
se –, to collect one's
thoughts.

recul, rer-kEEl, *m* retreat;
retirement; room to
move back.

reculé, e, rer-kE-leh, *a*
distant; remote.

reculer, rer-kE-leh, *v* to
move back; to defer.

reculons (à), ăh rer-kE-
long, *adv* backwards.

récupérer, reh-kE-peh-
reh, *v* to retrieve; to
recover.

récurer, reh-kE-reh, *v* to
scour; to clean.

récuser, reh-kE-seh, *v* to
challenge; to object; **se
–,** to decline.

rédac-teur, trice, reh-
dăhck-ter, *mf* writer;
editor.

rédaction, reh-dăhck-se-
ong, *f* wording; editing;
editorial staff; editorial
office.

rédemption, reh-dahngp-
se-*ong*, *f* redemption;
redeeming.

redescendre, rer-deh-
sahng-dr, *v* to come
down again; to take
down again.

redevable, rerd-văh-bl, *a*
indebted.

redevance, rerd-vahngss, *f*
rent; royalty; due.

A
B
C
D
E
F
G
H
I
J
K
L
M
N
O
P
Q
R
S
T
U
V
W
X
Y
Z

rédiger, reh-de-**sheh**, v to draw up; to edit.

redire, rer-**deer**, v to say again; to find fault (**à,** with).

redite, rer-**deet**, f repetition.

redoubler, rer-doo-**bleh**, v to redouble; to increase; to repeat a year (in school).

redoutable, rer-doo-tǎh-bl, a formidable.

redouter, rer-doo-teh, v to dread.

redresser, rer-dress-eh, v to straighten; to correct.

réduction, reh-dEEk-se-ong, f reduction; discount.

réduire, reh-dweer, v to reduce; to subdue; to compel.

réduit, reh-dwe, m nook; cubbyhole.

réel, le,* reh-ayl, a real.

réfectoire, reh-fehck-to'ǎhr, m refectory.

référendum, reh-feh-rahng-dom m referendum.

référer, reh-feh-reh, v to refer.

réfléchir, reh-fleh-sheer, v to reflect; to ponder.

reflet, rer-flay, m reflection.

refléter, rer-fleh-teh, v to reflect.

réflexion, reh-fleck-se-ong, f reflection; (fam) remark.

refluer, rer-flE-eh, v to flow back.

reflux, rer-flE, m ebbing; ebb.

réforme, reh-form, f reform; reformation.

réformer, reh-for-meh, v to reform; to discharge.

refouler, rer-foo-leh, v to drive back; to repress (instinct, etc).

réfractaire, reh-frǎhck-tair, a refractory.

refrain, rer-frang, m refrain (song); chorus.

refréner, rer-freh-neh, v to restrain.

réfrigérateur, reh-fre-sheh-rǎh-ter, m refrigerator.

refroidir, rer-fro'ǎh-deer, v to cool; to chill.

refuge, rer-fEE sh, m refuge; shelter.

réfugié, e, reh-fE-she-eh, mf & a refugee.

réfugier (se), ser reh-fE-she-eh, v to take shelter.

refus, rer-fE, m refusal; denial.

refuser, rer-fE-zeh, v to refuse; to decline.

réfuter, reh-fE-teh, v to refute; to disprove.

régal, reh-gǎhl, m feast; relish; pleasure.

régaler, reh-gǎh-leh, v to entertain; **se –,** to enjoy oneself.

regard, rer-gǎhr, m look; glance.

regarder, rer-gǎhr-deh, v to look at; to concern.

régate, reh-gǎht, f boat race; regatta.

régénérer, reh-sheh-neh-reh, v to regenerate.

régie, reh-shee, f administration; excise.

régime, reh-sheem, m rule; diet.

région, reh-she-ong, f region.

régir, reh-sheer, v to govern; to rule.

régisseur, reh-shiss-er, m manager; steward.

registre, rer-shees-tr, m register; account.

règle, ray-gl, f ruler; rule; discipline; pl periods (menstrual).

réglé, e, reh-gleh, pp & a regular; steady.

règlement, ray-gler-mahng, m regulation; regulations; rules; settlement.

régler, reh-gleh, v to regulate; to rule; to adjust.

réglisse, reh-gleess, f

licorice.

règne, rayn-yer, *m* reign; prevalence.

régner, rehn-yeh, *v* to reign; to rule; to prevail.

regorger, rer-gor-sheh, *v* to overflow; to abound.

regret, rer-gray, *m* regret; sorrow.

regretter, rer-gray-teh, *v* to regret; to be sorry.

régularité, reh-ghE-läh-reteh, *f* regularity.

régula-teur, trice, rehghE-läh-ter, *a* regulating; standard.

réguli-er, ère,* reh-ghEle-eh, *a* regular.

réhabituer (se), ser rehäh-be-tE-eh, *v* to become reaccustomed (**à,** to).

rehausser, rer-ohss-eh, *v* to raise; to enhance.

réimpression, reh-angpress-e-ong, *f* reprint.

rein, rang, *m* kidney; *pl* loins; back.

reine, rayn, *f* queen; **–claude,** – klohd, greengage; plum.

réinstaller, reh-angs-tähleh, *v* to reinstall; **se –,** to settle down again.

réintégrer, reh-ang-tehgreh, *v* to reinstate.

réitérer, reh-e-teh-reh, *v* to reiterate.

rejet, rer-**sh**ay, *m* rejection.

rejeter, rer **sh**-teh, *v* to throw back; to reject.

rejeton, rer **sh**-tong, *m* shoot; offspring.

rejoindre, rer-**sh**o'ang-dr, *v* to rejoin; to join; to overtake; **se –,** to meet.

réjoui, e, reh-**sh**oo'e, *pp* & *a* delighted; jolly.

réjouir, reh-**sh**oo-eer, *v* to rejoice; to delight; **se –,** to be delighted (**de,** at, with).

réjouissance, reh-**sh**ooiss-ahngss, *f* rejoicing.

relâche, rer-lahsh, *f* respite; no performance (theater) ; port of call.

relâche, e, rer-lah-sheh, *a* slack; lax.

relâcher, rer-lah-sheh, *v* to loosen; to abate; to release.

relais, rer-lay, *m* relay; stage.

relater, rer-läh-teh, *v* to relate.

relati-f, ve,* rer-läh-teeff, *a* relative.

relation, rer-läh-se-ong, *f* relation; connection; *pl* intercourse; dealings.

relayer, rer-lay-yeh, *v* to relieve; to relay.

relevé, rerl-veh, *m* statement; abstract.

relevé, e, rerl-veh, *a* raised; high; noble; highly seasoned.

relever, rerl-veh, *v* to raise up again; to relieve; to notice; to dismiss.

relief, rer-le-eff, *m* relief; raised.

relier, rer-le-eh, *v* to bind again; to connect; (books) to bind.

relieur, rer-le-er, *m* bookbinder.

religieu-x, se, rer-le-sheer, *mf* monk; nun; *a** religious.

religion, rer-le-she-ong, *f* religion.

reliquaire, rer-le-kair, *m* reliquary; shrine.

relire, rer-leer, *v* to read again.

reliure, rer-le-Er, *f* bookbinding; binding.

reluire, rer-lweer, *v* to shine; to glitter.

remanier, rer-mäh-ne-eh, *v* to handle again; to alter.

remarquable,* rer-mährkäh-bl, *a* remarkable.

remarque, rer-mährk, *f* remark; observation.

remarquer, rer-mähr-keh, *v* to remark; to observe.

remblai, rahng-blay, *m* embankment.

rembourrer, rahng-boo-

a
b
c
d
e
f
g
h
i
j
k
l
m
n
o
p
q
r
s
t
u
v
w
x
y
z

reh, *v* to stuff.

rembourser, rahng-boohr-seh, *v* to reimburse; to refund.

rembrunir, rahng-brE-neer, *v* to darken; to make sad.

remède, rer-mayd, *m* remedy.

remédier, rer-meh-de-eh, *v* to remedy (**à**).

remerciement, rer-mair-se-mahng, *m* thanks.

remercier, rer-mair-se-eh, *v* to thank (**de,** for).

remettre, rer-met-tr, *v* to put back again; to put off; to deliver; to restore; to hand; to recollect.

remise, rer-meez, *f* putting back; delivery; remittance; discount; putting off; shed.

rémission, reh-miss-e-ong, *f* forgiveness; remission.

remonte-pente, rer-mongt-pahngt *m* ski lift.

remonter, rer-mong-teh, *v* to go up again; to go back to; to wind up; to restock.

remontoir, rer-mong-to'åhr, *m* winder (of watch).

remontrer, rer-mong-treh, *v* to show again; to remonstrate.

remords, rer-mor, *m*

remorse.

remorque, rer-mork, *f* trailer

remorquer, rer-mor-keh, *v* to tow.

rémouleur, reh-moo-ler, *m* grinder.

remous, rer-moo, *m* eddy; stir.

rempailler, rahng-pah-yeh, *v* to restuff with straw.

rempart, rahng-påhr, *m* rampart.

remplaçant, e, rahng-plåhss-ahng, *mf* substitute.

remplacer, rahng-plåhss-eh, *v* to replace; to succeed.

remplir, rahng-pleer, *v* to fill up; to fulfill.

remporter, rahng-por-teh, *v* to take back; to carry away; to win.

remue-ménage, rer-mE-meh-nåhsh, *m* bustle; confusion.

remuer, rer-mE-eh, *v* to move; to stir; to wag.

rémunéra-teur, trice, reh-mE-neh-råh-ter, *mf* remunerator; *a* remunerative.

rémunérer, reh-mE-neh-reh, *v* to reward; to pay.

renaissance, rer-ness-ahngss, *f* rebirth; revival.

renaître, rer-nay-tr, *v* to

be born again; to revive.

renard, rer-nåhr, *m* fox.

renchérir, rahng-sheh-reer, *v* to raise the price of; to become more expensive.

rencontre, rahng-kong-tr, *f* meeting; encounter.

rencontrer, rahng-kong-treh, *v* to meet; to come across; to hit upon.

rendement, rahngd-mahng, *m* yield; output.

rendez-vous, rahng-deh-voo, *m* appointment; meeting place.

rendre, rahng-dr, *v* to give back; to render; to yield; to surrender; to make; to express.

rêne, rayn, *f* usually *pl* rein.

renégat, rer-neh-gåh, *m* renegade.

renfermé, rahng-fair-meh, *m* musty smell; withdrawn person.

renfermer, rahng-fair-meh, *v* to shut up; to contain.

renflement, rahng-fler-mahng, *m* swelling.

renfoncement, rahng-fongss-mahng, *m* hollow; recess.

renforcer, rahng-for-seh, *v* to strengthen; to reinforce.

renfort, rah*n*g-for, *m* reinforcement; help.

renfrogné, e, rah*n*g-fronn-yeh, *a* sullen; frowning.

rengaine, rah*n*g-gain, *f* (*fam*) old story.

rengorger (se), s*er* rah*n*g-gor-sheh, *v* to swagger.

reniement, r*er*-ne-mah*n*g, *m* denial; disowning.

renier, r*er*-ne-eh, *v* to deny; to disown.

renifler, r*er*-ne-fleh, *v* to sniff; to snivel.

renne, renn, *m* reindeer.

renom, r*er*-no*n*g, *m* renown.

renommé, e, r*er*-nomm-eh, *a* renowned.

renommée, r*er*-nomm-eh, *f* fame.

renoncer, r*er*-no*n*gss-eh, *v* to renounce; to give up.

renouer, r*er*-noo-eh, *v* to tie again; to renew.

renouveler, r*er*-noov-leh, *v* to renew; to revive.

renouvellement, r*er*-noo-vell-mah*n*g, *m* renewal; renovation; increase.

renseignement, rah*n*g-sain-yer-mah*n*g, *m* information; inquiry.

renseigner, rah*n*g-sain-yeh, *v* to inform; **se –,** to inquire.

rente, rah*n*gt, *f* yearly income; annuity; funds.

renti-er, ère, rah*n*g-te-eh, *mf* person of independent means.

rentrée, rah*n*g-treh, *f* return; reopening; payment.

rentrer, rah*n*g-treh, *v* to enter again; to return; to gather in; to go home; to be included in.

renversant, e, rah*n*g-vair-sah*n*g, *a* stunning.

renverser, rah*n*g-vair-seh, *v* to upset; to reverse.

renvoi, rah*n*g-vo'ăh, *m* sending back; dismissal; adjournment; reference.

renvoyer, rah*n*g-vo'ăh-yeh, *v* to send back; to dismiss; to postpone; to fire someone.

repaire, r*er*-pair, *m* den; lair.

répandre, reh-pah*n*g-dr, *v* to spill; to spread; **se –** to spread about.

répandu, reh-pah*n*g-dE, *a* widespread; widely known.

reparaître, r*er*-păh-ray-tr, *v* to reappear.

répara-teur, trice, reh-păh-răh-ter, *a* refreshing; restorative.

réparation, reh-păh-răh-se-ong, *f* repair; atonement.

réparer, reh-păh-reh, *v* to repair; to atone for.

repartie, r*er*-păhr-tee, *f* retort; repartee.

repartir, r*er*-păhr-teer, *v* to set out again; to retort.

répartir, reh-păhr-teer, *v* to deal out; to distribute.

repas, r*er*-pah, *m* meal; repast.

repas froid, r*er*-păh-fro'ăhd *m* packed lunch.

repasser, r*er*-pahss-eh, *v* to pass again; to iron; to grind; to think over.

repêcher, r*er*-pay-sheh, *v* to fish up; (*fam*) to help out.

repentir (se), s*er* r*er*-pah*n*g-teer, *v* to repent.

repentir, r*er*-pah*n*g-teer, *m* repentance.

répercuter, reh-pair-kE-teh, *v* to reverberate.

repère, r*er*-pair, *m* reference; **point de –,** po'a*n*g der –, landmark.

repérer, r*er*-peh-reh, *v* to mark; to locate; **se –,** to take one's bearings.

répertoire, reh-pair-to'ăhr, *m* repertoire; repertory.

répéter, reh-peh-teh, *v* to repeat; to rehearse.

répétition, reh-peh-te-se-ong, *f* repetition;

rehearsal.

répit, reh-pe, *m* respite.

repl-et, ète, rer-play, *a* fat, plump.

repli, rer-ple, *m* fold; winding; coil; retreat.

replier, rer-ple-eh, *v* to fold again; to coil.

réplique, reh-pleek, *f* rejoinder; cue; replica.

répliquer, reh-ple-keh, *v* to reply; to rejoin.

répondant, reh-pong-dahng, *m* surety; bail.

répondeur automatique or **téléphonique,** reh-pong-der-oh-toh-măh-teeck, *m* answering machine.

répondre, reh-pong-dr, *v* to answer; to reply; to be security for.

réponse, reh-pongss, *f* answer; reply.

report, rer-por, *m* amount brought forward.

reportage, rer-por-tăhsh, *m* coverage; report (newspaper); running commentary; scoop.

reporter, rer-por-teh, *v* to carry over; **se** –, to refer; *m* news reporter; journalist.

repos, rer-poh, *m* rest.

reposer, rer-poh-zeh, *v* to put back; to rest; **se** –, to rest; to rely.

repoussant, e, rer-pooss-ahng, *a* repulsive.

repousser, rer-pooss-eh, *v* to push back; to repel; to shoot out again.

reprendre, rer-prahng-dr, *v* to take back; to return; to resume.

représaille, rer-preh-zah'e, *fpl* reprisals; retaliation.

représentant, rer-preh-zahng-tahng, *m* representative.

représentation, rer-preh-zahng-tăh-se-ong, *f* representation; performance.

représenter, rer-preh-zahng-teh, *v* to represent; to point out; to perform; to show well.

réprimande, reh-pre-mahngd, *f* rebuke.

réprimander, reh-pre-mahng-deh, *v* to rebuke

réprimer, reh-pre-meh, *v* to repress; to curb.

reprise, rer-preez, *f* resumption; repetition; darning.

repriser, rer-pree-zeh, *v* to mend; to darn.

reproche, rer-prosh, *m* reproach.

reprocher, rer-prosh-eh, *v* to reproach.

reproduire, rer-prod-weer, *v* to reproduce; **se** –, to happen again.

réprouver, reh-proo-veh, *v* to reprobate; to disallow.

reptile, rehp-teel, *m* reptile.

repu, e, rer-pE, *a* satiated.

république, reh-pE-bleeck, *f* republic.

répudier, reh-pE-de-eh, *v* to repudiate.

répugnant, e, reh-pEEn-yahng, *a* repugnant.

répulsi-f, ve, reh-pEEl-siff, *a* repulsive.

réputation, reh-pE-tăh-se-ong, *f* reputation; character.

réputer, reh-pE-teh, *v* to repute; to deem.

requérant, e, rer-keh-rahng, *m a* applicant; plaintiff.

requérir, rer-keh-reer, *v* to require; to demand.

requête, rer-kayt, *f* request; petition.

requin, rerkang, *m* shark.

requis, erer-ke, *a* necessary; requisite.

réseau, reh-zoh, *m* net; network; system.

réserve, reh-zairv, *f* reservation; reserve; store.

réserver, reh-zair-veh, *v* to reserve.

réservoir, reh-zair-vo'ăhr, *m* reservoir; tank; pond.

résidence, reh-ze-dah*ng*ss, *f* residence; abode.

résider, reh-ze-deh, *v* to reside.

résidu, reh-ze-dE, *m* residue.

résignation, reh-zeen-yăh-se-o*ng*, *f* resignation.

résigner, reh-zeen-yeh, *v* to resign.

résine, reh-zeen, *f* resin; rosin.

résistant, e, reh-ziss-tah*ng*, *a* resistant; tough.

résister, reh-ziss-teh, *v* to resist.

résolu,* e, reh-zoll-E, *a* resolute.

résolution, reh-zoll-E-se-o*ng*, *f* resolution.

résonner, reh-zonn-eh, *v* to resound.

résoudre, reh-zoo-dr, *v* to resolve; to dissolve.

respect, ress-pay, *m* respect; regard.

respectueu-x, se,* ress-payk-tE-er, *a* respectful.

respirer, ress-pe-reh, *v* to breathe; to inhale.

resplendir, ress-plahng-deer *v* to be resplendent.

resplendissant, e, ress-plahng-diss-ahng, *a* resplendent.

responsabilité, ress-pong-săh-be-le-teh, *f* responsibility.

responsable, ress-pongss-ăh-bl, *a* responsible; answerable.

ressaisir, rer-say-zeer, *v* to seize again; **se–,** to recover oneself.

ressembler, rer-sahng-bleh, *v* to resemble.

ressemeler, rer-serm-leh, *v* to resole.

ressentiment, rer-sahng-te-mahng, *m* resentment.

ressentir, rer-sahng-teer *v* to feel; to resent.

resserrer, rer-say-reh, *v* to tighten.

ressort, rer-sor, *m* spring; jurisdiction; department.

ressortir, rer-sor-teer, *v* to get out again; to stand out; to result from (**de**); to be in the jurisdiction of.

ressource, rer-soohrss, *f* resource.

ressusciter, reh-sE-se-teh, *v* to resuscitate.

restant, ress-tahng, *m* remainder.

restaurant, ress-toh-rahng, *m* restaurant.

restauration rapide, ress-toh-răh-se-ong-răh-peed, *f* fast food.

restaurer, ress-toh-reh, *v* to restore; to refresh.

reste, resst, *m* remainder; *pl* remnants; scraps; **du–,** dE–, besides.

rester, ress-teh, *v* to remain; to be left; to stay.

restituer, ress-te-tE-eh, *v* to refund; to restore.

restreindre, ress-trang-dr, *v* to restrict.

résultat, reh-zEEl-tăh, *m* result.

résulter, reh-zEEl-teh, *v* to result.

résumé, reh-zE-meh, *m* summary; resume.

résumer, reh-zE-meh, *v* to sum up; to summarize.

rétablir, reh-tăh-bleer, *v* to restore; to reestablish; **se–,** to recover.

rétablissement, reh-tăh-bliss-mahng, *m* restoration; recovery.

retard, rer-tăhr, *m* delay; **enahng–,** late.

retardataire, rer-tăhr-dăh-tair, *mf* & *a* straggler; in arrears.

retarder, rer-tăhr-deh, *v* to delay; to postpone; to be too slow.

retenir, rert-neer, *v* to detain; to withhold; to book.

retentir, rer-tahng-teer, *v*

to resound.

retentissant, e, rer-tahng-tiss-ahng, *a* resounding; noisy.

retentissement, rer-tahng-tiss-mahng, *m* resounding.

retenue, rert-nE, *f* modesty; reserve; stoppage; detention.

réti-f,ve, reh-teeff, *a* restive.

retiré, e, rer-te-reh, *pp* & *a* withdrawn; secluded; retired.

retirer, rer-te-reh, *v* to draw again; to withdraw; to retract.

retombée, rer-tong-beh, *f* fallout (radioactive).

retomber, rer-tong-beh, *v* to fall again; to fall back; to hang down.

rétorquer, reh-tor-keh, *v* to retort.

retoucher, rer-too-sheh, *v* to touch up.

retour, rer-toohr, *m* return; recurrence; reciprocity.

retourner, rer-toohr-neh, *v* to turn; to return.

retracer, rer-trǎhss-eh, *v* to retrace; to recall.

rétracter, reh-trǎhck-teh, *v* to retract; to recant.

retrai-te, rer-trayt, *f* retreat; retirement;;

shelter.

retraiter, rer-tray-teh, *v* to pension off.

rétrécir, reh-treh-seer, *v* to narrow; to shrink.

rétribuer, reh-tre-bE-eh, *v* to remunerate.

rétribution, reh-tre-bE-se-ong, *f* reward; salary.

rétrograder, reh-trog-rǎh-deh, *v* to move back; to demote.

retrousser, rer-trooss-eh, *v* to tuck up; to turn up.

retrouver, rer-troo-veh, *v* to find again.

rétroviseur, reh-tro-ve-zer, *m* side-view mirror (auto).

réunion, reh-E-ne-ong, *f* reunion; meeting; gathering.

réunir, reh-E-neer, *v* to reunite; to gather; **se –,** to meet.

réussir, reh-EEss-eer, *v* to succeed; to thrive.

réussite, reh-EEss-eet, *f* success.

revanche, rer-vahngsh, *f* retaliation; revenge; return (games); **en –,** ahng –, in return.

rêve, rayv, *m* dream.

revêche, rer-vaysh, *a* peevish, cantankerous.

réveil, reh-vay'e, *m* awakening; alarm clock.

réveiller, reh-vay'e-yeh, *v* to awake; to rouse; to revive;

se –, to wake up.

réveillon, reh-vay'e-yong, *m* midnight supper (New Year's and Christmas).

révéler, reh-veh-leh, *v* to reveal; to disclose.

revenant, rerv-nahng, *m* ghost.

revendeu-r, se, rer-vahng-der, *mf* retailer.

revendication, rer-vahng-de-kǎh-se-ong, *f* claim.

revendiquer, rer-vahng-de-keh, *v* to claim.

revendre, rer-vahng-dr, *v* to sell again.

revenir, rerv-neer, *v* to come back; to recur; to grow again; to amount; to please; to cost.

revenu, rerv-nE, *m* income; revenue.

rêver, ray-veh, *v* to dream; to muse.

reverbère, reh-vair-bair, *m* streetlight.

révérence, reh-veh-rahngss, *f* reverence; curtsy.

révérer, reh-veh-reh, *v* to revere.

rêverie, rayv-ree, *f* musing; dreaming.

revers, rer-vair, *m* back;

reverse; facing (coat).

revêtir, re*r*-vay-teer, *v* to clothe.

rêveu-r, se, ray-ver, *mf* dreamer; *a** dreaming; pensive.

revirement, re*r*-veer-mah*ng*, *m* sudden change; transfer.

reviser, réviser, re*r*-ve-zeh, reh-ve-zeh, *v* to revise.

revivre, re*r*-vee-vr, *v* to live again.

révocation, reh-vock-ăh-se-*ong*, *f* repeal; dismissal.

revoir, re*r*-vo'ăhr, *v* to see again; **au –,** oh –, goodbye.

révolte, reh-vollt, *f* revolt.

révolter, reh-voll-teh, *v* to rouse; to shock.

révolu, e, reh-voll-E, *a* in days gone by; past.

révolution, reh-voll-E-se-*ong*, *f* revolution.

revue, re*r*-vE, *f* review; survey; magazine.

rez-de-chaussée, reh-der-shohss-eh, *m* first floor.

rhabiller (se), se*r* răh-bee-yeh, *v* to get dressed again.

rhum, romm, *m* rum.

rhumatisme, rE-măh-tissm, *m* rheumatism.

rhume, rEEm, *m* cold.

riant, e, re-ahng, *a* smiling; pleasant.

ricaner, re-kăh-neh, *v* to sneer; to laugh unpleasantly.

riche, reesh, *a** rich; copious; fertile; *mf* wealthy person.

richesse, re-shess, *f* riches; wealth; fertility.

ricin, re-sang, *m* castor-oil plant.

ricochet, re-kosh-ay, *m* rebound.

ride, reed, *f* wrinkle; ripple.

rideau, re-doh, *m* curtain; screen.

rider, re-deh, *v* to wrinkle; to ripple.

ridicule, re-de-kEEl, *m* ridiculousness; *a** ridiculous.

ridiculiser, re-de-kE-le-zeh, *v* to ridicule.

rien, re-ang, *m* nothing; anything; trifle; **–que, –**ker, only; **cela ne fait –,** slăh n'fay –, that does not matter.

rieu-r, se, re-er, *n* & *a* laughter; laughing.

rigide, re-sheed, *a* rigid; stern; strict.

rigole, re-gol, *f* trench; drain; gutter.

rigoler, re-goll-eh, *v* (*pop*) to laugh; to giggle.

rigolo,–ote, re-goll-o, *a* (*pop*) jolly; funny.

rigoureu-x, se, re-goo-re*r*, *a* rigorous.

rigueur, re-gher, *f* rigor; **de –, der –,** indispensable.

rime, reem, *f* rhyme.

rincer, rang-seh, *v* to rinse.

ripaille, re-pah'e, *f* (*fam*) feasting.

riposte, re-post, *f* parry and thrust; repartee.

rire, reer, *v* to laugh; to scoff at; to joke; *m* laughter.

ris, re, *m* sweetbread.

risée, re-zeh, *f* laughingstock.

risible, re-zee-bl, *a* laughable; ludicrous.

risqué, e, riss-keh, *a* hazardous; improper.

risquer, riss-keh, *v* to risk; to venture.

rivage, re-văhsh, *m* shore; bank.

rival, e, re-văhl, *a* rival.

rivaliser, re-văh-le-zeh, *v* to rival; to vie; to compete.

rive, reev, *f* bank; shore; border.

river, re-veh, *v* to rivet.

rivière, re-ve-air, *f* river; stream.

riz, re, *m* rice.

robe, rob, *f* robe; gown; dress; **–de chambre, –**

a
b
c
d
e
f
g
h
i
j
k
l
m
n
o
p
q
r
s
t
u
v
w
x
y
z

der shah*ng*-br, bathrobe.

robinet, rob-e-nay, *m* faucet.

robuste, rob-EEst, *a* robust; sturdy; stalwart.

roc, rock, *m* rock.

rocailleu-x, se, rock-ah'e-er, *a* stony; rugged.

roche, rosh, *f* rock; boulder.

rocher, rosh-eh, *m* rock (mass of).

rock and roll, rock-eh-roll *m* rock and roll.

rôder, rohd-eh, *v* to prowl; to roam.

rogner, ronn-yeh, *v* to cut; to pare; to clip.

rognon, ronn-yong, *m* kidney (of edible animals).

roi, ro'ăh, *m* king.

rôle, rohl, *m* roll; list; part; character.

roman, romm-ah*ng*, *m* novel.

romance, romm-ah*ng*ss, *f* sentimental song.

romanci-er, ère, romm-ah*ng*ss-e-eh, *mf* novelist.

romanesque, romm-ăhn-esk, *a* romantic.

romantique, romm-ah*ng*-teeck *a* romantic.

romarin, romm-ăh-ra*ng*, *m* rosemary.

rompre, ro*ng*-pr, *v* to break; to snap; to break

in.

ronce, rong*ss*, *f* blackberry bush.

rond, e,* ro*ng*, *a* round; plump; full; (*fam*) drunk.

rond, ro*ng*, *m* round; circle.

ronde, rongd, *f* patrol; semibreve (music).

rondelle, ro*ng*-dell, *f* washer; slice.

rondeur, ro*ng*-der, *f* roundness; plumpness; frankness.

ronflant, e, ro*ng*-flah*ng*, *a* snoring; bombastic.

ronfler, ro*ng*-fleh, *v* to snore; to roar.

ronger, ro*ng*-sheh, *v* to nibble; to corrode; to erode.

ronron, ro*ng*-rong, *m* purr.

rosaire, roz-air, *m* rosary.

rosbif, ross-beeff, *m* roast beef.

rose, rohz, *f* rose; *a* rose; rosy; pink; *m* pink (color).

roseau, roz-oh, *m* reed.

rosée, roh-zeh, *f* dew.

rosier, roh-ze-eh, *m* rosebush.

rosser, ross-eh, *v* (*fam*) to thrash.

rossignol, ross-een-yol, *m* nightingale; (*fam*) picklock; unsaleable

article.

rot, roh, *m* (*fam*) belch.

rôti, roh-te, *m* roast meat; joint.

rôtir, roh-teer, *v* to roast.

rotule, rot-EEl, *f* kneecap.

rouage, roo-ăhsh, *m* wheel-work; machinery.

roucouler, roo-koo-leh, *v* to coo.

roue, roo, *f* wheel; **faire la –,** fair lăh –, to strut; to turn cartwheels.

roué, e, roo-eh, *mf* rake; *a* sly; artful.

rouet, roo-ay, *m* spinning wheel.

rouge, roosh, *m* red color; red paint; *a* red.

rougeaud, e, roo-shoh, *a* (*fam*) red-faced.

rouge-gorge, roosh-gorsh, *m* robin.

rougeole, roo-shol, *f* measles.

rougeur, roo-sher, *f* redness.

rougir, roo-sheer, *v* to redden; to blush.

rouille, roo'e-ye, *f* rusty; blight.

rouillé, roo'e-yeh, *a* rust; rusted.

rouleau, roo-loh, *m* roll; roller.

roulement, rool-mah*ng*, *m* rolling; rumbling; rotation.

rouler, roo-leh, *v* to roll; to wheel; to revolve.

roulette, roo-lett, *f* castor; roulette.

roulis, roo-le, *m* rolling.

roulotte, roo-lot, *f* caravan.

rouspéter, rooss-peh-teh, *v* (*pop*) to protest; to complain.

rousseur, rooss-**er**, *f* redness; **tache de** –, tăhsh der –, freckle.

roussir, rooss-eer, *v* to redden; to singe; to scorch.

route, root, *f* road; route; course; journey.

routine, roo-teen, *f* routine; rote.

rou-x, sse, roo, *a* reddish; red-haired; russet.

royal, e,* ro'ăh-yăhl, *a* royal; regal.

royaume, ro'ăh-yohm, *m* kingdom.

royauté, ro'ăh-yoh-teh, *f* kingship; royalty.

ruade, rE-ăhd, *f* kick (horse's).

ruban, rE-bahng, *m* ribbon.

rubéole, rE-beh-oll, *f* German measles.

rubis, rE-be, *m* ruby.

ruche, rEEsh, *f* beehive.

rude,* rEEd, *a* harsh; severe; uneven; rough.

rudesse, rE-dess, *f* harshness; roughness; severity;

rudoyer, rE-do'ăh-yeh, *v* to treat roughly; to bully.

rue, rE, *f* street; road; thoroughfare.

ruelle, rE-ell, *f* lane; alley.

ruer, rE-eh, *v* to kick(horse's); **se** –, to rush.

rugby, rEg-be *m* rugby.

rugir, rE-**sheer**, *v* to roar.

rugissement, rE-**shiss**-mahng, *m* roaring; howling.

rugueu-x, se, rE-gher, *a* rough; rugged.

ruine, rween, *f* ruin; decay; downfall.

ruineu-x, se,* rwee-ner, *a* ruinous.

ruisseau, rweess-oh, *m* stream; brook; gutter.

ruisseler, rweess-leh, *v* to stream; to trickle down.

rumeur, rE-mer, *f* rumor; noise; report.

ruminant, e, rE-me-nahng, *m* & *a* ruminant; ruminating.

rupture, rEEp-tEEr, *f* rupture; breaking.

rural, e, rE-răhl, *a* rural.

ruse, rEEz, *f* cunning; artfulness; dodge.

rusé, e, rEE-zeh, *a* cunning; sly; wily; artful.

ruser, rEE-zeh, *v* to use cunning; to dodge.

rustaud, e, rEEss-toh, *a* boorish.

rustique, rEEss-teeck, *a* rural; rough.

rustre, rEEss-tr, *m* & *a* boor; boorish.

rut, rEEt, *m* rut.

rythme, reetm, *m* rhythm.

a
b
c
d
e
f
g
h
i
j
k
l
m
n
o
p
q
r
s
t
u
v
w
x
y
z

sa, săh, *poss af* his; her; its.

sabbat, săh-băh, *m* Sabbath.

sable, săh-bl, *m* sand; gravel.

sablonneu-x, se, săh-blonn-er, *a* sandy.

sabot, săh-bo, *m* wooden clog; hoof.

sabotage, săh-bot-ăhsh, *m* sabotage.

saboter, săh-bot-eh, *v* to bungle.

sabre, săh-br, *m* saber; broadsword.

sac, săhck, *m* sack; bag; knapsack.

sac à dos, săhk-ăh-doh *m* rucksack; backpack.

saccade, săh-kăhd, *f* jerk.

saccager, săh-kăh-**sh**eh, *v* to ransack; to upset.

sac de couchage, săhk-der-koo-shăsh *m* sleeping bag.

sacerdoce, săh-sair-doss, *m* priesthood.

sachet, săh-sheh *m* sachet; teabag.

sacoche, săh-kosh, *f* bag; saddlebag.

sacre, săh-kr, *m* consecration; coronation.

sacrement, săh-krer-mahng, *m* sacrament.

sacrer, săh-kreh, *v* to consecrate; to crown; to curse.

sacrifier, săh-kre-fe-eh, *v* to sacrifice.

sacrilège, săh-kre-laysh, *m* & *a* sacrilege; sacrilegious.

sacristain, săh-kriss-tang, *m* sexton.

sacristie, săh-kriss-tee, *f* vestry.

sagace,* săh-găhss, *a* sagacious; shrewd.

sage, săhsh, *a** wise; discreet; well-behaved.

sage-femme, săhsh-făhm, *f* midwife.

sagesse, săh-shess, *f* wisdom; prudence; good behavior.

saignant, e, sayn-yahng, *a* bleeding; underdone (meat); rare.

saigner, sayn-yeh, *v* to bleed.

saillie, sah'e-yee, *f* projection; spurt; (*fam*) outburst.

saillir, sah'e-yeer, *v* to jut out; to stand out.

sain, e,* sang, *a* sound; healthy; wholesome.

saindoux, sang-doo, *m* lard.

saint, e, sang, *mf* & *a** saint; holy; sacred.

sainteté, sang-ter-teh, *f* saintliness; holiness; sanctity.

saisie, say-zee, *f* seizure; distraint.

saisir, say-zeer, *v* to seize; to startle; to understand; to distrain.

saisissant, e, say-ziss-ahng, *a* startling; thrilling.

saisissement, say-zissmahng, *m* shock; chill.

saison, say-zong, *f* season; time.

salade, săh-lăhd, *f* salad.

saladier, săh-lăh-de-eh, *m* salad bowl.

salaire, săh-lair, *m* wages; salary; (*fig*) reward.

salarié, e, săh-lăh-re-eh, *pp* & *a* paid.

sale,* săhl, *a* dirty; messy.

salé, e, săh-leh, *pp* & *a* salted; salt; spicy (story).

saler, săh-leh, *v* to salt; (*fig*) to fleece.

saleté, săhl-teh, *f* dirtiness; nastiness; obscenity; dirty trick.

salière, săh-le-air, *f* saltbox.

salir, săh-leer, *v* to soil; to dirty; to taint.

salissant, săh-le-sahng, *a* soiling; messy; easily soiled.

salive, săh-leev, *f* saliva; spittle.

salle, săhl, *f* hall; large room; –**à manger,** – ăh mahng-sheh, dining room; –**d'attente,** – dăh-tahngt, waitingroom.

salon, săh-long, *m* living room; exhibition.

salopette, săh-lo-pet, *f* overalls; dungarees (jeans).

salubre, săhl-EE-br, *a*

healthy; salubrious.

saluer, săh-lE-eh, *v* to salute; to bow; to greet.

salut, săh-lE, *m* salute; greeting; safety; salvation.

salutaire,* săh-lE-tair, *a* salutary; beneficial.

salutation, săh-lE-tăh-se-ong, *f* salutation; greetings.

samedi, săhm-de, *m* Saturday.

sanction, sahngk-se-ong, *f* sanction; penalty; approval.

sanctuaire, sahngk-tE-air, *m* sanctuary.

sandale, sahng-dăhl, *f* sandal.

sang, sahng, *m* blood; race; parentage.

sang-froid, sahng-fro'ăh, *m* coolness.

sanglant, e, sahng-glahng, *a* bloody; outrageous.

sangler, sahng-gleh, *v* to strap; to gird.

sanglier, sahng-gle-eh, *m* wild boar.

sangloter, sahng-glot-eh, *v* to sob.

sangsue, sahng-sE, fleech; (*fig*) extortioner.

sanguinaire, sahng-ghe-nair, *a* bloodthirsty.

sanitaire, săh-ne-tair, *a* sanitary.

sans, sahng, *prep* without; but for; …less.

sans-façon, sahng-făh-song, *m* straightforwardness.

sans-gêne, sahng-shayn, *m* inconsiderateness.

sans plomb, sahng-plong *a* unleaded (gas, fuel).

santé, sahng-teh, *f* health.

saper, săh-peh, *v* to undermine.

sapeur, săh-per, –**pompier,** – pong-pe-eh, fireman.

sapin, săh-pang, *m* fir tree.

sarcasme, săhr-kăhssm, *m* sarcasm.

sarcler, săhr-kleh, *v* to weed.

sardine, săhr-deen, *f* sardine.

sarrau, săh-roh, *m* smock.

satané, e, săh-tăh-neh, *a* confounded.

satellite, săh-teh-leet, *m* satellite.

satiné, e, săh-te-neh, *a* satin-like; glazed; smooth.

satire, săh-teer, *f* satire.

satisfaction, săh-tiss-făhck-se-ong, *f* satisfaction.

satisfaire, săh-tiss-fair, *v* to satisfy; to meet.

satisfaisant, e, săh-tiss-fer-zahng, *a* satisfactory.

a
b
c
d
e
f
g
h
i
j
k
l
m
n
o
p
q
r
s
t
u
v
w
x
y
z

A
B
C
D
E
F
G
H
I
J
K
L
M
N
O
P
Q
R
S
T
U
V
W
X
Y
Z

satisfait, e, săh-tiss-fay, *a* satisfied.

saturer, săh-tE-reh, *v* to saturate (**de,** with).

sauce, sohss, *f* sauce; gravy.

saucer, sohss-eh, *v* to sop; (*fam*) to drench; to reprimand.

saucière, sohss-e-air, *f* gravy-boat.

saucisse, sohss-eess, *f* sausage.

saucisson, sohss-iss-*ong*, *m* big, dry sausage.

sauf, sohff, *prep* save; except; but; subject to.

sau-f, ve, sohff, *a* safe; secure.

sauf-conduit, sohf-kong-dwee, *m* safe conduct.

sauge, sohsh, *f* sage.

saugrenu, e, soh-grer-nE, *a* absurd; preposterous.

saule, sohl, *m* willow; **–pleureur,** – pler-rer, weeping willow.

saumâtre, soh-mah-tr, *a* brackish; briny.

saumon, soh-mong, *m* salmon.

sauna, soh-năh *m* sauna.

saupoudrer, soh-poo-dreh, *v* to sprinkle (**de,** with).

saur, sor, *a* salted and smoked.

saut, soh, *m* leap; jump.

sauter, soh-teh, *v* to leap; to jump; to blow up; to skip; to fry quickly.

sauterelle, soht-rell, *f* grasshopper.

sauteu-r, se, soh-ter, *mf* & *a* leaper; leaping.

sautiller, soh-tee-yeh, *v* to hop; to skip.

sauvage, soh-văhsh, *m* savage; *a** wild; untamed; shy; unsociable.

sauvagerie, soh-văhsh-ree, *f* savagery; unsociability.

sauvegarde, sohv-găhrd, *f* safeguard.

sauve-qui-peut, sohv-ke-per, *m* stampede.

sauver, soh-veh, *v* to save; to rescue; **se –,** to escape; to run away.

sauvetage, sohv-tăhsh, *m* lifesaving; rescue; salvage.

sauveur, soh-ver, *m* saver; deliverer.

savamment, săh-văh-mahng, *adv* skillfully; knowingly.

savant, e, săh-vahng, *m* scientist; scholar; *a* learned; skillful.

savate, săh-văht, *f* shoe.

saveur, săh-ver, *f* taste; savor; relish; flavor.

savoir, săh-vo'ăhr, *v* to know; to understand; to be able to; *m* learning.

savoir-faire, săh-vo'ăhr-fair, *m* skill; ability.

savoir-vivre, săh-vo'ăhr-vee-vr, *m* good breeding.

savon, săh-vong, *m* soap.

savonner, săh-vonn-eh, *v* to soap; to lather.

savonnette, săh-vonn-ett, *f* bar of soap.

savourer, săh-voo-reh, *v* to relish.

scabreu-x, se, skăh-brer, *a* rugged; dangerous; ticklish.

scandaleu-x, se,* skahng-dăh-ler, *a* scandalous.

scarlatine, skăhr-lăh-teen, *f* scarlet fever.

sceau, soh, *m* seal.

scélérat, e, seh-leh-răh, *mf* & *a* scoundrel; villainous.

sceller, sell-eh, *v* to seal.

scénario, seh-năh-re-o, *m* scenario; screenplay.

scène, sayn, *f* scene; stage; row.

scepticisme, sehp-tiss-eessm, *m* skepticism.

sceptre, sayp-tr, *m* scepter.

schéma, sheh-măh, *m* diagram; schema.

scie, se, *f* saw.

sciemment, se-ăh-mahng, *adv* knowingly.

science, se-ahngss, *f* science; learning.

scientifique,* se-ahng-te-feeck, *a* scientific.

scier, se-eh, *v* to saw.

scierie, se-ree, *f* sawmill.

scintiller, sang-tee-yeh, *v* to twinkle (of star); to sparkle.

scission, siss-e-ong, *f* division; secession.

sciure, se-EEr, *f* sawdust.

scolaire, skoll-air, *a* scholastic; school.

scorbut, skor-bE, *m* scurvy.

scrupule, skrE-pEEl, *m* scruple; scrupulousness.

scrupuleu-x, se,* skrE-pE-ler, *a* scrupulous; precise.

scruter, skrE-teh, *v* to scrutinize.

scrutin, skrE-tang, *m* ballot; poll.

sculpter, skEEl-teh, *v* to sculpt; to carve.

se, ser, *pers pron* oneself; himself; herself; itself; themselves; each other; one another.

séance, seh-ahngss, *f* sitting; meeting; performance.

seau, soh, *m* bucket; pail.

sec, sayk, **sèche,*** saysh, *a* dry; harsh; barren.

sécher, seh-sheh, *v* to dry.

sécheresse, sehsh-ress, *f* dryness; drought;

barrenness.

second, ser-gong, *m* assistant; second floor.

second, e,* ser-gong, *a* second.

seconde, ser-gongd, *f* second (time).

seconder, ser-gong-deh, *v* to support; to further.

secouer, ser-koo-eh, *v* to shake; to shock; to stir up.

secourable, ser-koo-răh-bl, *a* helpful.

secourir, ser-koo-reer, *v* to help; to relieve.

secours, ser-koohr, *m* help; relief.

secousse, ser-kooss, *f* shake; jolt; blow; shock.

secret, ser-kray, *m* secret; secrecy.

secr-et, ète,* ser-kray, *a* secret; private.

secrétaire, ser-kreh-tair, *mf* secretary; writing desk.

secrétariat, ser-kreh-tăh-re-ăh, *m* secretaryship; secretariat.

sécréter, ser-kreh-teh, *v* to secrete.

sectaire, seck-tair, *mf & a* sectarian.

secte, seckt, *f* sect.

secteur, seckt-er, *m* sector; district area (served by electricity, etc).

section, seck-se-ong, *f* section; fare zone.

séculaire, seh-kE-lair, *a* age-old; time-honored.

séculi-er, ère, seh-kE-le-eh, *a* secular.

sécurité, seh-kE-re-teh, *f* security.

sédentaire, seh-dahng-tair, *a* sedentary.

séditieu-x, se,* seh-de-se-er, *a* seditious.

séduc-teur, trice, seh-dEEk-ter, *mf & a* seducer; fascinating; seductive.

séduire, seh-dweer, *v* to seduce; to delude; to captivate.

séduisant, e, seh-dwee-zahng, *a* captivating; enticing; glamorous (person).

seigle, say-gl, *m* rye.

seigneur, sehn-yer, *m* lord.

sein, sang, *m* breast; bosom; (*fig*) womb; midst.

seize, sayz, *m & a* sixteen.

seizième, say-ze-aym, *m & a* sixteenth.

séjour, seh-shoohr, *m* stay; sojourn; living room.

séjourner, seh-shoohr-neh, *v* to stay; to dwell.

sel, sell, *m* salt; (*fam*) wit.

a
b
c
d
e
f
g
h
i
j
k
l
m
n
o
p
q
r
s
t
u
v
w
x
y
z

self-service, self-sair-veess *a* self-service.

selle, sell, *f* saddle, stool.

seller, sell-eh, *v* to saddle.

selon, ser-long, *prep* according to; **–que,** –ker, according as.

semailles, ser-mah'e, *fpl* sowing; sowing time.

semaine, ser-main, *f* week; week's wages.

semblable, sahng-blăh-bl, *m* fellow-man; *a** alike; similar.

semblant, sahng-blahng, *m* appearance; show; **faire** –, fair –, to pretend.

sembler, sahng-bleh, *v* to seem; to appear.

semelle, ser-mell, *f* sole (boots, shoes).

semence, ser-mahngss, *f* seed.

semer, ser-meh, *v* to sow; to scatter.

semestre, ser-mays-tr, *m* half-year.

semeu-r, se, ser-mer, *mf* sower.

semi, ser-me, *prefix* semi; half.

séminaire, seh-me-nair, *m* seminary.

semonce, ser-mongss, *f* lecture; reprimand; rebuke.

semoule, ser-mool, *f* semolina.

sénat, seh-năh, *m* senate.

senilité, seh-ne-le-teh, *f* senility.

sens, sahngss, *m* sense; senses; opinion; direction.

sensation, sahng-săh-se-ong, *f* sensation; excitement.

sensé, e, sahng-seh, *a* sensible; judicious.

sensibilité, sahng-se-be-le-teh, *f* sensibility; sensitivity.

sensible, sahng-see-bl, *a* sensitive; obvious; sore (of flesh, etc.).

sensiblement, sahng-se-bler-mahng, *adv* perceptibly; greatly.

sensuel, le,* sahng-sE-ell, *a* sensual.

sentence, sahng-tahngss, *f* sentence; maxim; judgment.

senteur, sahng-ter, *f* scent; fragrance.

senti, e, sahng-te, *a* felt; vividly expressed.

sentier, sahng-te-eh, *m* path.

sentiment, sahng-te-mahng, *m* sentiment; sense; feeling.

sentimental, e, sahng-te-mahng-tăhl *a* romantic.

sentinelle, sahng-te-nell, *f* sentry.

sentir, sahng-teer, *v* to feel; to smell; to taste of; to see; to foresee.

séparation, seh-păh-răh-se-ong, *f* separation.

séparer, seh-păh-reh, *v* to separate; to divide.

sept, sett, *m* & *a* seven.

septembre, sayp-tahng-br, *m* September.

septentrional, e, sayp-tahng-tre-onn-ăhl, *a* northern.

septième, say-te-aym, *m* & *a* seventh.

septuple, sayp-tE-pl, *m* & *a* septuple; sevenfold.

sépulture, seh-pEEl-tEEr, *f* tomb; burial.

séquestre, seh-kayss-tr, *m* sequestration; sequestrator.

serein, ser-rang, *m* evening dew.

sérénade, seh-reh-năhd, *f* serenade.

sérénité, seh-reh-ne-teh, *f* serenity.

sergent, sair-**shahng**, *m* sergeant.

série, seh-re, *f* series; set.

sérieu-x, se, * seh-re-er, *a* serious; earnest; grave.

serin, ser-rang, *m* canary; (*pop*) simpleton.

seringue, ser-rang-gh, *f* syringe.

serment, sair-mahng, *m*

oath.

sermon, sair-mo*ng*, *m*
sermon; lecture.

sermonner, sair-monn-eh,
v to lecture.

serpe, sairp, *f* billhook.

serpent, sair-pah*ng*, *m*
serpent; snake.

serpenter, sair-pah*ng*-teh,
v to meander.

serpette, sair-pett, *f*
pruning knife.

serpillière, sair-pe-yair, *f*
dishcloth.

serre, sair, *f* greenhouse;
pressing; talon.

serré, e, say-reh, *a* close;
compact; precise; tight.

serrer, say-reh, *v* to
squeeze; to tighten.

serrure, say-rEEr, *f* lock.

serrurier, say-rE-re-eh, *m*
locksmith.

servant, sair-vah*ng*, *m*
gunner; *a* serving.

servante, sair-vah*ng*t, *f*
servant.

serviable, sair-ve-ăh-bl, *a*
obliging.

service, sair-veess, *m*
service; attendance;
duty; set; divine service.

service des chambres,
sair-veess-deh-cha*ng*-br
m room service.

service de réanimation,
sair-veess-der-reh-ăh-
ne-măh-se-o*ng* *m*

intensive care.

serviette, sair-ve-ett, *f*
napkin; towel; briefcase.

servile,* sair-veell, *a*
servile.

servir, sair-veer, *v* to
serve; to wait upon; **se**
–de, to use.

serviteur, sair-ve-ter, *m*
servant.

ses, say, *poss a pl* his; her;
its; one's.

session, sess-e-o*ng*, *f*
session; sitting; term
(law).

seuil, ser'e, *m* threshold;
sill; doorstep; beginning.

seul, e,* serl, *a* only; sole;
alone; mere; single.

sève, sayv, *f* sap; (*fig*)
vigor.

sévère,* seh-vair, *a*
severe; stern; harsh.

sévir, seh-veer, *v* to
punish severely; to rage.

sevrer, ser-vreh, *v* to
wean.

sexagénaire, secks-ăh-
sheh-nair, *mf* & *a* sixty
year old.

sexe, secks, *m* sex.

sexiste, secks-eest *a* sexist.

sextuple, secks-tEE-pl, *m*
& *a* sixfold.

sexuel, le, secks-E-ell, *a*
sexual.

sexy, seck-se *a* sexy.

si, se, *adv* so; however;

yes; *conj* if; whether.

SIDA; sida; Sida, see-
dăh, *m* AIDS.

siècle, se-ay-kl, *m* century;
time; age.

siège, se-ay*sh*, *m* seat; see;
siege.

siéger, se-eh-sheh, *v* to sit;
to hold sittings.

sien, ne (le, la), ler se-
a*ng*, lăh se-enn, *poss*
pron his; hers; its.

sieste, se-esst, *f* siesta;
afternoon nap.

siffler, se-fleh, *v* to
whistle; to hiss.

sifflet, se-flay, *m* whistle;
hiss.

signal, seen-yăhl, *m*
signal.

signalé, e, seen-yăh-leh, *a*
signal.

signalement, seen-yăhl-
mah*ng*, *m* description.

signaler, seen-yăh-leh, *v*
to signal; to point out.

signataire, seen-yăh-tair,
m signer.

signature, seen-yăh-tEEr, *f*
signature.

signe, seen-yer, *m* sign;
mark; token.

signer, seen-yeh, *v* to sign;
se –, to cross oneself.

signifier, seen-yee-fee-eh,
v to mean; to notify.

silence, se-lah*ng*ss, *m*
silence; stillness.

A
B
C
D
E
F
G
H
I
J
K
L
M
N
O
P
Q
R
S
T
U
V
W
X
Y
Z

silencieu-x, se,* se-lah*ng*-se-*er*, *a* silent; still.

sillon, see-yo*ng*, *m* furrow; trail; groove (record).

sillonner, see-yonn-eh, *v* to furrow; to plough.

simagrée, se-măh-greh, *f* grimace; *pl* fuss.

similaire, se-me-lair, *a* similar.

simple, sa*ng*-pl, *m* simpleton; *a** simple; single; plain; **(billet)** –, bee-yeh- sa*ng* pl, *a* one-way (ticket).

simplicité, sa*ng*-ple-se-teh, *f* simplicity.

simulacre, se-m*E*-lăh-kr, *m* image; sham.

simuler, se-m*E*-leh, *v* to simulate; to feign.

simultané, e, se-m*EE*l-tăh-neh, *a* simultaneous.

simultanément, se-m*EE*l-tăh-neh-mah*ng*, *adv* simultaneously.

sincère,* sa*ng*-sair, *a* sincere; candid; true.

sincérité, sa*ng*-seh-re-teh, *f* sincerity; honesty.

singe, sa*ng*sh, *m* ape; monkey.

singer, sa*ng*-sheh, *v* to mimic.

singularité, sa*ng*-gh*E*-lăh-re-teh, *f* singularity.

singuli-er, ère,* sa*ng*-gh*E*-le-eh, *a* singular;

peculiar; odd.

sinistre, se-neess-tr, *m* disaster; *a** sinister; gloomy.

sinon, se-no*ng*, *conj* if not; otherwise; else; except.

sinueu-x, se, se-n*E*-*er*, *a* winding.

sirène, se-rain, *f* mermaid; siren.

sirop, se-roh, *m* syrup.

sis, e, se, *a* situated.

site, seet, *m* site; landscape; scenery.

sitôt, se-toh, *adv* as soon; **–que,** – ker, as soon as.

situation, se-t*E*-ăh-se-o*ng*, *f* situation; position.

situé, e, se-t*E*-eh, *a* situated.

six, seess (before a consonant, see), *m & a* six.

sixième, se-ze-aym, *m & a* sixth.

skateboard, sket-bor *m* skateboard.

ski, ske, *m* ski; skiing.

skier, ske-eh, *v* to ski.

ski nautique, ske-noh-teeck *m* waterskiing.

sobre,* sobr, *a* sober; temperate; sparing.

sobriété, sob-re-eh-teh, *f* sobriety.

sobriquet, sob-re-kay, *m* nickname.

soc, sock, *m* plowshare.

sociable, soss-e-ăh-bl, *a* sociable.

social, e,* soss-e-ăhl, *a* social.

socialisme, soss-e-ăh-leessm, *m* socialism.

sociétaire, soss-e-eh-tair, *mf & a* member; partner.

société, soss-e-eh-teh, *f* society; party; partnership; company.

sociologue, soss-e-o-log, *m* sociologist.

socle, soc-kl, *m* pedestal.

sœur, ser, *f* sister; nun.

sofa, soh-făh *m* sofa.

software, soft-wair *m* (*comput*) software.

soi, so'ăh, *pron* oneself; itself; self; himself; herself.

soi-disant, so'ăh-de-zah*ng*, *a* would-be; so-called; *adv* supposedly.

soie, so'ăh, *f* silk; bristle.

soierie, so'ăh-ree, *f* silk; silk trade.

soif, so'ăhf, *f* thirst; **avoir** –, ăh-vo'ăhr –, to be thirsty.

soigné, e, so'ăhn-yeh, *a* done with care; well-groomed.

soigner, so'ăhn-yeh, *v* to take care of; to nurse.

soigneu-x, se,* so'ăhn-yer, *a* careful.

soin, so'ăng, *m* care; *pl*

attentions.

soir, so'ăhr, *m* evening; night.

soirée, so'ăh-reh, *f* evening (duration of); evening party.

soit, so'ăh, *conj* either; whether; or.

soit! so'ăh, *interj* so be it! well and good!

soixantaine, so'ăhss-ahng-tain, *f* about sixty.

soixante, so'ăhss-ahngt, *m* & *a* sixty; **-dix,** – dess, seventy.

soixantième, so'ăhss-ahng-te-aym, *m* & *a* sixtieth.

sol, sol, *m* soil; ground; the note G.

solaire, soll-air, *a* solar.

soldat, soll-dăh, *m* soldier.

solde, solld, *m* balance; sale (of remnants); *f* soldiers' pay.

solder, soll-deh, *v* to settle; to sell off; to disount

sole, sol, *f* sole (fish).

soleil, soll-ay'e, *m* sun; sunshine.

solennel, le,* soll-ăh-nell, *a* solemn.

solennité, soll-ăh-ne-teh, *f* solemnity.

solidaire,* soll-e-dair, *a* jointly liable; interdependent.

solide,* soll-eed, *a* solid;

strong; firm; sound.

solitaire,* soll-e-tair, *a* solitary; lonely.

solitude, soll-e-tEEd, *f* solitude; loneliness.

solive, soll-eev, *f* joist; rafter.

solliciter, soll-e-se-teh, *v* to solicit; to urge; to petition.

soluble, soll-E-bl, *a* soluble; solvable.

solution, soll-E-se-ong, *f* solution; break.

solvable, soll-văh-bl, *a* solvent.

sombre, song-br, *a* dark; gloomy; dismal; dull.

sombrer, song-breh, *v* to sink; to founder.

sommaire, somm-air, *m* & *a** summary; abstract.

sommation, somm-ăh-se-ong, *f* summons.

somme, somm, *m* nap; *f* sum; **en –,** ahng –, on the whole; in short.

sommeil, somm-ay'e, *m* sleep.

sommeiller, somm-ay'e-yeh, *v* to doze.

sommelier, somm-er-le-eh, *m* sommelier.

sommer, somm-eh, *v* to summon; to call upon.

sommet, somm-ay, *m* summit; top; acme.

sommier, somm-e-eh, *m*

bedspring.

somnifère, somm-ne-fair, *m* sleeping pill; soporific (sleep-inducing).

somnolent, e, somm-noll-ahng, *a* sleepy, drowsy.

somnoler, somm-no-leh, *v* to drowse; to doze.

somptueu-x, se,* songp-tE-er, *a* sumptuous.

son, song, *poss a m* his; her; its; one's.

son, song, *m* sound; bran.

sonate, sonn-ăht, *f* sonata.

sondage, song-dăhsh, *m* poll; sounding; boring.

sonde, songd, *f* sounding line; probe.

sonder, song-deh, *v* to sound; to fathom; to probe.

songe, songsh, *m* dream.

songer, song-sheh, *v* to dream; to think; to muse.

songerie, songsh-ree, *f* dreaming.

songeu-r, se, song-**sher,** *mf* & *a* dreamer; thoughtful.

sonnant, e, sonn-ahng, *a* sounding; striking.

sonner, sonn-eh, *v* to sound; to ring; to strike (the hour).

sonnerie, sonn-ree, *f* ringing; bells.

sonnette, sonn-ett, *f* small

a
b
c
d
e
f
g
h
i
j
k
l
m
n
o
p
q
r
s
t
u
v
w
x
y
z

bell; doorbell; buzzer.

sonore, sonn-or, *a* sonorous.

sorbet, sor-bay, *m* sherbert; sorbet.

sorcellerie, sor-sell-ree, *f* witchcraft; sorcery.

sorci-er, ère, sor-se-eh, *mf* & *a* sorcerer; wizard; witch.

sordide,* sor-deed, *a* sordid; disgusting; mean.

sornettes, sor-nett, *fpl* idle talk.

sort, sor, *m* fate; lot; spell.

sorte, sort, *f* sort; kind; manner.

sortie, sor-tee, *f* going out; way out; outburst.

sortir, sor-teer, *v* to go out; to emerge; to take out.

sosie, soz-ee, *m* doppelganger; double.

sot, te,* soh, sott, *a* silly; stupid; fool.

sottise, sot-eez, *f* silliness; foolishness; abuse (language); *pl* insults.

sou, soo, *m* old French coin; (*fam*) penny.

soubresaut, soo-brer-soh, *m* sudden start.

souche, soosh, *f* stump; stem; counterfoil; (*fig*) blockhead.

souci, sooss-e, *m* worry; concern; anxiety; marigold.

soucier (se), ser sooss-e-eh, *v* to care (**de,** about; for); to mind; to be concerned; to worry.

soucieu-x, se,* sooss-e-er, *a* anxious; careworn.

soucoupe, soo-koop, *f* saucer.

soudain, e,* soo-dang, *a* sudden; unexpected; *fig* overnight; **soudain,** *adv* suddenly.

soudaineté, soo-dain-teh, *f* suddenness.

soude, sood, *f* soda.

souder, soo-deh, *v* to solder; to weld.

soudure, soo-dEEr, *f* solder; soldering.

souffle, soo-fl, *m* breath; puff.

souffler, soo-fleh, *v* to blow; to breathe; to whisper; to prompt.

soufflet, soo-flay, *m* bellows; (*fam*) slap in the face; insult.

souffleter, soo-fler-teh, *v* to slap in the face; (*fig*) to insult.

souffrance, soo-frahngss, *f* suffering; pain; **en –,** ahng –, unsettled; in suspense.

souffrant, e, soo-frahng, *a* suffering; poorly.

souffrir, soo-freer, *v* to suffer; to allow; to be injured.

soufre, soo-fr, *m* sulfur.

souhait, soo-ay, *m* wish.

souhaiter, soo-ay-teh, *v* to wish; to desire.

souiller, soo'e-yeh, *v* to dirty; to soil.

soûl, soo, *m* (*fam*) fill.

soûl, e, soo, *a* drunk.

soulagement, soo-lăhsh-mahng, *m* relief; alleviation.

soulager, soo-lăh-sheh, *v* to relieve; to soothe.

soûler (se), ser soo-leh, *v* (*pop*) to get drunk.

soulèvement, soo-layv-mahng, *m* rising; upheaval; insurrection.

soulever, sool-veh, *v* to raise; to lift; to stir up; **se–,** to rise; to revolt.

soulier, soo-le-eh, *m* shoe.

souligner, soo-leen-yeh, *v* to underline; to emphasize.

soumettre, soo-met-tr, *v* to subdue; to submit; to lay before.

soumis, e, soo-me, *a* submissive.

soumission, soo-miss-e-ong, *f* submission; compliance.

soupape, soo-păhp, *f* valve.

soupçon, soop-song, *m*

suspicion; surmise; (*fig*) touch.

soupçonner, soop-sonn-eh, *v* to suspect.

soupe, soop, *f* soup.

souper, soo-peh, *v* to have supper.

soupeser, soo-per-zeh, *v* to weigh by hand.

soupière, soo-pe-air, *f* soup tureen.

soupir, soo-peer, *m* sigh.

soupirail, soo-pe-rah'e, *m* ventilator; basement window.

soupirer, soo-pe-reh, *v* to sigh.

souple,* soo-pl, *a* supple; flexible; compliant.

source, soohrss, *f* source; spring; authority.

sourcil, soohr-se, *m* eyebrow.

sourciller, soohr-see-yeh, *v* to frown.

sourd, e, soohr, *mf* & *a** deaf person; deaf; dull; secret; mute.

sourdine, soohr-deen, *f* damper; **à la–,** ăh lăh–, secretly.

souriant, e, soo-re-ahng, *a* smiling.

souricière, soo-riss-e-air, *f* mousetrap.

sourire, soo-reer, *v* to smile. *m* smile.

souris, soo-ree, *f* mouse.

sournois, e,* soohr-no'ăh, *a* sly; cunning; artful.

sous, soo, *prep* under; beneath; below.

souscripteur, sooss-krip-ter, *m* subscriber.

souscrire, sooss-kreer, *v* to subscribe; to sign.

sous-entendre, soo-z'ahng-tahng-dr, *v* to imply.

sous-entendu, soo-z'ahng-tahng-dE, *m* implication.

sous-marin, soo-măh-rang, *m* submarine. *a* underwater.

soussigné, e, sooss-een-yeh, *mf* & *a* the undersigned; undersigned.

sous-sol, sooss-ol, *m* basement.

sous-titre, soo-tee-tr, *m* subtitle.

soustraction, sooss-trăhck-se-ong, *f* subtraction.

soustraire, sooss-trair, *v* to subtract; to shelter; **se –,** to get away (**à,** from).

soutien-gorge, soo-te-ang-gorsh, *m* bra.

soutane, soo-tăhn, *f* cassock.

souteneur, soot-ner, *m* upholder.

soutenir, soot-neer, *v* to sustain; to support; to

assert; to stand.

soutenu, soot-nE, *pp* & *a* sustained; lofty.

souterrain, soo-tay-rang, *m* underground.

souterrain, e, soo-tay-rang, *a* underground; underhand.

soutien, soo-te-ang, *m* support; prop; supporter.

soutien-gorge, soo-te-ang-gorsh, *m a* bra(ssiere).

soutirer, soo-te-reh, *v* to draw off; (*fig*) to extract.

souvenir (se), ser soov-neer, *v* to remember (**de**).

souvenir, soov-neer, *m* remembrance; keepsake.

souvent, soo-vahng, *adv* often.

souverain, e, soov-rang, *mf* & *a** sovereign.

souveraineté, soov-rain-teh, *f* sovereignty; dominion.

soyeu-x, se, so'ah'e-er, *a* silky.

spacieu-x, se,* spăh-se-er, *a* roomy; spacious.

sparadrap, spăh-răh-drăp, *m* bandage.

spécial, e,* speh-se-ăhl, *a* special; particular.

spécialité, speh-se-ăhl-e-teh, *f* speciality; line of business; proprietary article.

A
B
C
D
E
F
G
H
I
J
K
L
M
N
O
P
Q
R
S
T
U
V
W
X
Y
Z

spécifier, speh-se-fe-eh, *v* to specify.

spectacle, speck-răh-kl, *m* spectacle; show; play.

specta-teur, trice, speck-tăh-ter, *mf* spectator; *pl* audience.

spectre, speck-tr, *m* specter; ghost.

spéculer, speh-kE-leh, *v* to speculate.

sperme, spairm, *m* sperm; semen.

sphère, sfair, *f* sphere; globe.

spirale, spe-răhl, *f* spiral; *a* spiral.

spirituel, le,* spe-re-tE-ell, *a* spiritual; witty.

spiritueu-x, se, spe-re-tE-er, *a* alcoholic.

splendeur, splahng-der, *f* splendor; magnificence.

splendide,* splahng-deed, *a* splendid; magnificent.

spongieu-x, se, spong-she-er, *a* spongy.

spontané, e, spong-tăh-neh, *a* spontaneous.

spontanément, spong-tăh-neh-mahng, *adv* spontaneously.

sport, spor, *m* sport; *a* casual (clothes).

sports d'hiver, spor-de-vair *mpl* winter sports.

squelette, sker-lett, *m* skeleton.

stable, stăh-bl, *a* stable; steady; durable.

stade, stăhd *m* stadium.

stage, stăhsh, *m* period of probation, course.

stagnant, e, stăhgh-nahng, *a* stagnant; still.

stalle, stăhl, *f* stall.

stance, stahngss, *f* stanza.

station, stăh-se-ong, *f* standing; subway stop; stand; station; taxi stand.

station de radio, stăh-se-ong-der-răh-de-oh *f* radio station.

stationner, stăh-se-onn-eh, *v* to stop; to park.

stationnement, stăh-se-onn-mahng, *m* parking.

station-service, stăh-se-ong-sair-veess *f* gas station.

statistique, stăh-tiss-teeck, *f* statistics. *a* statistical.

statue, stăh-tE, *f* statue.

statuer, stăh-tE-eh, *v* to decree; to rule.

stature, stăh-tEEr, *f* stature; height.

statut, stăh-tE, *m* statute; regulation; status.

sténodactylo(graphe), steh-no-dăhck-te-log-răhf, *mf* shorthand typist.

sténographe, steh-nog-

răhf, *mf* stenographer.

sténographie, steh-nog-răh-fe, *f* shorthand.

stéréo, steh-rch-oh *f* stereo.

stéréophonique, steh-reh-o-fo-neeck, *a* stereophonic.

stérile,* steh-reel, *a* sterile; barren.

stérilité, steh-re-le-teh, *f* barrenness.

stigmate, stigg-măht, *m* stigma; brand; stain.

stigmatiser, stigg-măh-te-zeh, *v* to stigmatize; to denounce.

stimulant, e, ste-mE-lahng, *a* stimulating; *m* stimulant.

stimuler, ste-mE-leh, *v* to stimulate; to urge on.

stipuler, ste-pE-leh, *v* to stipulate.

stoïque,* sto-eeck, *a* stoical.

stomacal, e, stomm-ăh-kăhl, *a* stomach.

stoppage, stop-ăhsh, *m* invisible mending.

store, stor, *m* blind.

strapontin, străh-pong-tang, *m* jumpseat.

stratégie, străh-teh-she *f* strategy.

strict, e,* strikt; *a* strict; severe; precise.

strident, e, stre-dahng, *a*

shrill.

strié, e, stre-eh, *a* striated; streaked; scored.

structure, strEEk-tEEr, *f* structure; frame; build.

studieu-x, se,* stE-de-er, *a* studious.

stupéfait, e, stE-peh-fay, *a* stupefied; amazed; flabbergasted.

stupéfier, stE-peh-fe-eh, *v* to stupefy; to amaze.

stupeur, stE-per, *f* stupor.

stupide,* stE-peed, *a* stupid.

stupidité, stE-pe-de-teh, *f* stupidity.

style, steel, *m* style.

stylo, stee-lo, *m* fountain pen; –à **bille,** – ăh bee-ye, ballpoint pen.

suaire, sE-air, *m* shroud.

suave,* sE-ăhv, *a* sweet; soft; suave.

subdiviser, sEEb-de-ve-zeh, *v* to subdivide.

subir, sE-beer, *v* to undergo; to suffer; to endure; to submit.

subit, e,* sE-bee, *a* sudden.

subjecti-f, ve,* sEEb-sheck-teeff, *a* subjective.

subjonctif, sEEb-shongk-teeff, *a* subjunctive.

subjuguer, sEEb-shE-gheh, *v* to subjugate.

sublime,* sEEb-leem, *a*

sublime.

submerger, sEEb-mair-sheh, *v* to submerge, to swamp.

subordonner, sE-bor-donn-eh, *v* to subordinate.

subséquemment, sEEb-seh-kăh-mahng, *adv* subsequently.

subséquent, e, sEEb-seh-kahng, *a* subsequent.

subside, sEEb-seed, *m* subsidy.

subsister, sEEb-ziss-teh, *v* to subsist; to stand.

substance, sEEbs-tahngss, *f* substance.

substantiel, le,* sEEbs-tahngs-e-ell, *a* substantial.

substituer, sEEbs-te-tE-eh, *v* to substitute (à, for).

substitut, sEEbs-te-tE, *m* substitute; deputy.

subterfuge, sEEb-tair-fEEsh, *m* subterfuge.

subtil, e,* sEEb-teel, *a* subtle; sharp; acute; keen.

subtilité, sEEb-te-le-teh, *f* subtlety, acuteness.

subvenir, sEEb-ver-neer, *v* to provide (à, for); to help; to relieve.

subventionner, sEEb-vahng-se-onn-eh, *v* to subsidize.

subversi-f, ve,* sEEb-vair-seeff, *a* subversive.

suc, sEEk, *m* juice; essence; (*fig*) substance.

succéder, sEEk-seh-deh, *v* to succeed; to follow after.

succès, sEEk-say, *m* success.

successi-f, ve,* sEEk-sess-eeff, *a* successive.

succession, sEEk-sess-e-ong, *f* succession; inheritance.

succinct, e,* sEEk-sang, *a* succinct; concise.

succomber, sEE-kong-beh, *v* to succumb; to sink; to yield; to die.

succion, sEEk-se-ong, *f* suction.

succulent, e, sE-kE-lahng, *a* juicy, savory.

succursale, sE-kEEr-săhl, *f* branch (of store, etc).

sucer, sEEss-eh, *v* to suck; to suck in; to drain.

sucre, sEE-kr, *m* sugar.

sucre glace, sE-kr-glăhss *m* sugar.

sucrer, sE-kreh, *v* to sweeten; to sugar.

sucrerie, sE-krer-ree, *f* sugar refinery; *pl* sweets.

sucrier, sE-kre-eh, *m* sugar bowl.

sud, sEEd, *m* South; *a* south, southern.

A
B
C
D
E
F
G
H
I
J
K
L
M
N
O
P
Q
R
S
T
U
V
W
X
Y
Z

suer, sE-eh, *v* to sweat; (*fig*) to toil.

sueur, sF-er, *f* sweat, perspiration; (*fig*) toil.

suffire, sE-feer, *v* to suffice; to do; **cela suffit,** ser-lăh sE-fe, that will do.

suffisamment, sE-fe-zăh-mahng, *adv* sufficiently.

suffisance, sE-fe-zahngss, *f* sufficiency; conceit.

suffisant, e, sE-fe-zahng, *a* sufficient; conceited.

suffocant, e, sE-fock-ahng, *a* stifling.

suffoquer, sE-fock-eh, *v* to suffocate; to stifle.

suffrage, sE-frăhsh, *m* suffrage; approbation.

suggérer, sEEgh-sheh-reh, *v* to suggest; to hint.

suicide, swee-seed, *m* suicide.

suicider (se), ser swee-see-deh, *v* to commit suicide.

suie, swee, *f* soot.

suif, sweef, *m* tallow.

suinter, swang-teh, *v* to ooze out; to leak.

suite, sweet, *f* suite; consequence; attendants; series; sequence; sequel; continuation; **tout de –,** too der –, at once.

suivant, swee-vahng, *prep* according to; **–que, –ker,** according as.

suivant, e, swee-vahng, *mf* attendant; *a* following, next.

suivi, e, swee-ve, *pp & a* followed; consistent; sought after.

suivre, swee-vr, *v* to follow; to result; to study; **faire –,** fair –, to forward.

sujet, sE-shay, *m* subject; person; cause; topic.

sujet, te, sE-shay, *a* subject; liable; inclined.

sujétion, sE-sheh-se-ong, *f* subjection; constraint.

superbe,* sE-pairb, *a* superb; majestic; proud.

supercherie, sE-pair-sher-ree, *f* deceit; cheat; fraud.

superficie, sE-pair-feess-ee, *f* surface; area.

superficiel, le,* sE-pair-fe-se-ell, *a* superficial; shallow.

superflu, e, sE-pair-flE, *a* superfluous.

supérieur, e,* sE-peh-re-er, *a* upper; superior.

supermarché, soo-pair-măhr-sheh *m* supermarket.

superstitieu-x, se,* sE-pair-ste-se-er, *a* superstitious.

supplanter, sE-plahng-teh, *v* to oust.

suppléant, e, sE-pleh-ahng, *mf & a* substitute; deputy.

suppléer, sE-pleh-eh, *v* to make good; **–à,** to make up for.

supplément, sE-pleh-mahng, *m* supplement; extra charge.

supplémentaire, sE-pleh-mahng-tair, *a* additional.

suppliant, e, sE-ple-ahng, *mf & a* supplicant.

supplication, sE-ple-kăh-se-ong, *f* entreaty.

supplice, sE-pleess, *m* torture; (*fig*) torment.

supplier, sE-ple-eh, *v* to entreat; to beseech.

supplique, sE-pleek, *f* petition.

support, sE-por, *m* support; stand.

supportable, sE-por-tăh-bl, *a* bearable.

supporter, sE-por-teh, *v* to support; to bear.

supposer, sE-poh-zeh, *v* to suppose; (*jur*) to substitute.

supposition, sE-poh-ze-se-ong, *f* supposition; (*jur*) substitution; forgery.

supprimer, sE-pre-meh, *v* to suppress; to abolish.

supputer, sE-pE-teh, *v* to reckon; to calculate.

suprématie, sE-preh-măhss-ee, *f* supremacy.

suprême,* sE-praym, *a* supreme; crowning; last.

sur, sEEr, *prep* on; upon; over; above; by; out of; towards; concerning.

sur, e, sEEr, *a* sour.

sûr, e,* sEEr, *a* sure; safe; trustworthy.

surcroît, sEEr-kro'ăh, *m* increase.

surdité, sEEr-de-teh, *f* deafness.

sûreté, sEEr-teh, *f* safety; security.

surexciter, sEEr-eck-se-teh, *v* to overexcite.

surf, sErf *m* surfing.

surface, sEEr-făhss, *f* surface; outside; area.

surfaire, sEEr-fair, *v* to overcharge; to overrate.

surfin, sEEr-fang, *a* superfine.

surgeler, sEEr-sher-leh, *v* to deep-freeze.

surgir, sEEr-sheer, *v* to arise; to appear suddenly.

surhumain, e, sEE -E-mang, *a* superhuman.

surintendant, sEEr-ang-tahng-dahng, *m* superintendent.

surlendemain, sEEr-lahngd-mang, *m* second day after.

surmener, sEEr-mer-neh, *v* to overwork.

surmonter, sEEr-mong-teh, *v* to overcome; to rise above (of fluids, etc.).

surnager, sEEr-năh-sheh, *v* to float; (*fig*) to survive.

surnaturel, le,* sEEr-năh-tE-rell, *a* supernatural.

surnom, sEEr-nong, *m* nickname.

surnuméraire, sEEr-nE-meh-rair, *m & a* supernumerary.

surpasser, sEEr-păhss-eh, *v* to exceed; to excel.

surplomber, sEEr-plong-beh, *v* to overhang.

surplus, sEEr-plE, *m* surplus; **au –,** oh –, moreover.

surprenant, e, sEEr-prer-nahng, *a* surprising.

surprendre, sEEr-prahng-dr, *v* to surprise.

surprise, sEEr-preez, *f* surprise.

sursaut, sEEr-soh, *m* start; jump.

sursauter, sEEr-soh-teh, *v* to start; to give a jump; to be startled.

surseoir, sEEr-so'ăhr, *v* to put off (à).

sursis, sEEr-see, *m* delay; suspension; reprieve.

surtaxe, sEEr-tăhcks, *f* extra tax; surcharge.

surtout, sEEr-too, *adv* above all; particularly.

surveillance, sEEr-vay'e-ahngss, *f* superintendence; supervision.

surveiller, sEEr-vay'e-yeh, *v* to supervise; to keep an eye on.

survenir, sEEr-ver-neer, *v* to come unexpectedly.

survie, sEEr-vee, *f* survival.

survivance, sEEr-ve-vahngss, *f* relic.

survivre, sEEr-vee-vr, *v* to survive (à); to outlive.

sus, sEEss, *prep* on; **en –de,** ahng – der, over and above.

susceptibilité, sEEss-ep-te-be-le-teh, *f* touchiness.

susciter, sEEss-e-teh, *v* to raise up; to create.

susdit, e, sEEss-de, *a* aforesaid.

suspect, e, sEEss-paykt, *m & a* suspect.

suspecter, sEEss-payk-teh, *v* to suspect.

suspendre, sEEss-pahng-dr, *v* to suspend; to hang up.

suspens (en), ahng sEEss-pahng, *adv* in abeyance.

suture, sEE-tEEr, *f* suture;

a
b
c
d
e
f
g
h
i
j
k
l
m
n
o
p
q
r
s
t
u
v
w
x
y
z

point de –, po'a*ng* der –, stitch.

svelte, svaylt, *a* slender; slim.

syllabe, seell-lǎhb, *f* syllable.

sylvestre, sill-vays-tr, *a* sylvan.

symbole, sa*ng*-bol, *m* symbol.

symétrique,* se-meh-treeck, *a* symmetrical.

sympathique,* sa*ng*-pǎh-teeck, *a* sympathetic; likable.

symptôme, sa*ng*p-tohm, *m* symptom.

syncope, sa*ng*-kop, *f* fainting fit; blackout.

syndicat, sa*ng*-de-kah, *m* syndicate; **–d'initiative,** – de-ne-se-ah-teev, tourists' information office.

syndicat d'initiative, sa*ng*-de-kǎh-de-ne-se-ǎh-teev *m* tourist office.

système, siss-taym, *m* system.

T

ta, tăh, *poss a f sing*
familiar form of 'your.'

tabac, tăh-băh, *m* tobacco;
snuff.

tabatière, tăh-băh-te-air, *f*
snuffbox.

table, tăh-bl, *f* table;
board; index.

tableau, tăh-bloh, *m*
picture; painting;
blackboard; list

tablette, tăh-blett, *f* shelf;
lozenge; slab.

tablier, tăh-blee-eh, *m*
apron; workcoat.

tabouret, tăh-boo-ray, *m*
stool.

tache, tăhsh, *f* spot; stain;
blemish.

tâche, tahsh, *f* task; job.

tâcher, tah-sheh, *v* to
endeavor; to strive.

tacheté, e, tăhsh-teh, *a*
spotted; speckled.

tacite,* tăh-seet, *a*
implied; tacit.

taciturne, tăh-se-tEErn, *a*
taciturn; quiet.

tact, tăhckt, *m* touch; (*fig*)
tact; discretion.

taie, tay, *f* pillowcase.

taie d'oreiller, tay-dor-
ay'e-yeh *f* pillowcase.

taille, tah'e, *f* cut; waist;
height; pruning.

tailler, tah'e-yeh, *v* to cut;
to prune; to sharpen.

tailleur, tah'e-yer, *m*
tailor.

taillis, tah'e-ye, *m* copse;
thicket.

taire, tair, *v* to conceal; **se
–,** to be silent.

talc, tăhlk *m* talcum
powder.

talent, tăh-lahng, *m*

talent; (*fig*) ability.

talon, tăh-long, *m* heel;
voucher.

talonner, tăh-lonn-eh, *v*
to urge; to follow
closely.

talus, tăh-lE, *m* slope;
embankment.

tambour, tahng-boohr, *m*
drum; barrel.

tamis, tăh-mee, *m* sieve.

tampon, tahng-pong, *m*
plug; tampon; buffer.

tampon hygiénique,
tahng-pong-e-**she**-eh-
neeck *m* tampon.

tamponner, tahng-ponn-
eh, *v* to stop up; to
collide.

tancer, tahngss-eh, *v* to
scold.

tandis que, tahng-de ker,
conj while; whereas.

tangage, tahng-găhsh, *m*
pitching (of ship).

tanière, tăh-ne-air, *f* den;
lair.

tanner, tăh-neh, *v* to tan.

tant, tahng, *adv* so much;
as much; so many; as
many; **–mieux,** – me-er,
so much the better;
–pis, – pee, so much the
worse.

tante, tahngt, *f* aunt.

tantôt, tahng-toh, *adv*
presently; shortly; now
… now.

A B C D E F G H I J K L M N O P Q R S **T** U V W X Y Z

tapage, tăh-păhsh, *m* uproar; row.

tape, tăhp, *f* slap; pat; thump.

taper, tăh-peh, *v* to tap; to pat; to strike.

tapir (se), ser tăh-peer, *v* to squat; to crouch.

tapis, tăh-pe, *m* carpet; rug; cover.

tapisserie, tăh-piss-ree, *f* tapestry.

tapissier, tăh-piss-e-eh, *m* upholsterer.

tapoter, tăhp-ot-eh, *v* to tap; to strum.

taquiner, tăh-ke-neh, *v* to tease.

tard, tăhr, *adv* late.

tarder, tăhr-deh, *v* to delay; to be long.

tardi-f, ve,* tăhr-deeff, *a* late; tardy; backward.

tare, tăhr, *f* (*fam*) blemish; (*fam*) defect; tare.

taré, e, tăh-reh, *a* damaged; spoiled.

tarif, tăh-reeff, *m* tariff; price list; rate; scale of prices.

tarir, tăh-reer, *v* to dry up.

tarte, tăhrt, *f* tart; pie.

tartine, tăhr-teen, *f* slice of bread with butter and jam.

tas, tah, *m* heap; pile; (*fig*) lot.

tasse, tahss, *f* cup.

tasser, tahss-eh, *v* to heap up; to press down; **se –,** to settle.

tâter, tah-teh, *v* to feel; to try; to taste.

tâtillon, ne, tah-tee-*yon*g, *mf & a* meddler; meddlesome.

tâtonner, tah-tonn-eh, *v* to grope; to feel one's way.

tâtons (à), ăh tah-to*n*g, *adv* gropingly.

taudis, toh-dee, *m* hovel.

taupe, tohp, *f* mole.

taupinière, toh-pinn-e-air, *f* molehill.

taureau, toh-roh, *m* bull.

taux, toh, *m* rate.

taverne, tăh-vairn, *f* tavern.

taxer, tăhx-eh, *v* to tax; to assess; to accuse.

te, ter, *pers pron mf sing* (familiar form) you; to you; yourself.

technique, teck-neeck, *a* technical. *f* technique.

tee-shirt, tee-shert *m* T-shirt.

teigne, tayn-yer, *f* moth; ringworm.

teindre, ta*n*g-dr, *v* to dye; to tint.

teint, ta*n*g, *m* complexion; dye; color.

teinte, ta*n*gt, *f* tint; shade; tinge.

teinture, ta*n*g-tEEr, *f* dye; dyeing; tincture.

tel, le, tell, *a* such; like; **–que,** – ker, similar to; such as.

télé, teh-leh *abbr f* TV.

télécopie teh-leh-ko-pee *f* fax.

télégramme, teh-leh-grăhm, *m* telegram.

télégraphier, teh-leh-grăh-fe-eh, *v* to wire.

téléphone, teh-leh-fon, *m* telephone.

téléphone de voiture, teh-leh-fon-der-vo'ăh-tEEr, *m* car phone.

téléphone public, teh-leh-fonn-pE-bleeck *f* payphone.

téléphonique, teh-leh-fonn-eeck, *a* telephonic; **cabine –,** kăh-been –, phone booth.

télescope, teh-less-kop, *m* telescope.

télévision, teh-leh-ve-ze-o*n*g, *f* television.

télévision par câble, teh-leh-ve-se-o*n*g-păhr-kah-bl, *f* cable television.

tellement, tell-mah*n*g, *adv* so; so much; **–que, –** ker, so that.

téméraire,* teh-meh-rair, *a* rash; foolhardy.

témoignage, teh-mo'ăhn-yăhsh, *m* testimony;

evidence.

témoigner, teh-mo'ăhn-yeh, *v* to show; to testify.

témoin, teh-mo-ang, *m* witness.

tempe, tahngp, *f* temple.

tempérament, tahng-peh-răh-mahng, *m* temperament; constitution.

tempérant, e, tahng-peh-rahng, *a* temperate.

température, tahng-peh-răh-tEEr, *f* temperature.

tempérer, tahng-peh-reh, *v* to moderate; to allay.

tempête, tahng-payt, *f* tempest; storm.

tempêter, tahng-pay-teh, *v* to storm; to fume.

temple, tahng-pl, *m* temple.

temporaire,* tahng-por-air, *a* temporary.

temporel, le,* tahng-por-ell, *a* temporal.

temps, tahng, *m* time; while; period; season; weather; tense; beat.

tenace, ter-năhss, *a* tenacious.

tenailles, ter-nah'e, *fpl* pincers.

tendance, tahng-dahngss, *f* tendency; leaning.

tendon, tahng-dong, *m* sinew.

tendre, tahng-dr, *v* to

stretch; to strain; to hold out; to tend.

tendre,* tahng-dr, *a* tender; affectionate; new.

tendresse, tahng-dress, *f* tenderness.

tendu, e, tahng-dE, *a* tight; stretched; tense.

ténèbres, teh-nay-br, *fpl* darkness; gloom.

teneur, ter-ner, *f* tenor; purport.

tenir, ter-neer, *v* to hold; to keep; to last; to deem; to depend on; **–à, –** ăh, to value; to care about.

tension, tahng-se-ong, *f* tension.

tension artérielle, tahng-se-ong-ăhr-teh-re-ell, *f* blood pressure.

tentant, e, tahng-tahng, *a* tempting.

tentation, tahng-tăh-se-ong, *f* temptation.

tentative, tahng-tăh-teev, *f* attempt; endeavor.

tente, tahngt, *f* tent.

tenter, tahng-teh, *v* to attempt; to tempt.

tenture, tahng-tEEr, *f* hangings; wallpaper.

ténu, e, teh-nE, *a* slender; thin.

tenue, ter-nEE, *f* holding; behavior; attitude; dress.

térébenthine, teh-reh-

bahng-teen, *f* turpentine.

terme, tairm, *m* term; limit; *pl* condition.

terminaison, tair-me-nay-zong, *f* ending.

terminal, tair-me-năhl *m* terminal (computer, oil).

terminale, tair-me-năhl *a* terminal.

terminer, tair-me-neh, *v* to finish; to conclude.

terminus, tair-me-nEs *m* terminal (*rail*).

terne, tairn, *a* dull; colorless.

ternir, tair-neer, *v* to tarnish; to dim.

terrain, tay-rang, *m* ground; soil; piece of land.

terrasse, tay-răhss, *f* terrace.

terrasser, tay-răhss-eh, *v* to bank up; to throw on the ground.

terre, tair, *f* earth; ground; land; estate; the world.

terrestre, tay-ress-tr, *a* terrestrial.

terreur, tay-rer, *f* terror; dread; awe.

terrible,* tay-ree-bl, *a* terrible; dreadful; frightful.

terrifier, tay-re-fe-eh, *v* to terrify.

A B C D E F G H I J K L M N O P Q R S **T** U V W X Y Z

terrine, tay-reen, *f* earthen dish; pâté.

territoire, tay-re-to'ăhr, *m* territory.

terroriste, teh-ro-rest *mf* terrorist.

tertre, tair-tr, *m* hillock.

tes, tay, *poss a mf pl* (familiar form) your.

test, tayst *m* quiz.

testament, tess-tăh-mahng, *m* testament; will.

têtard, teh-tahr, *m* tadpole.

tête, tayt, *f* head; top; wits; (*fig*) presence of mind.

téter, teh-teh, *v* to suck (at the breast).

tétine, teh-teen, *f* teat.

têtu, e, tay-tE, *a* stubborn; headstrong.

texte, text, *m* text; subject.

textile, tex-teell, *m* textile; material; *a* textile.

textuel, le,* tex-tE-ell, *a* textual.

thé, teh, *m* tea; tea party.

théâtral, e, teh-ah-trăhl, *a* theatrical.

théâtre, teh-ah-tr, *m* theater; stage; plays; **coup de –,** koo der–, unexpected event.

théière, teh-yair, *f* teapot.

thème, taym, *m* topic; theme; exercise (in school).

théorie, teh-or-ee, *f* theory; procession.

théorique,* teh-or-eeck, *a* theoretical.

thérapie, teh-rah-pee, *f* therapy.

thermomètre, tair-momm-ay-tr, *m* thermometer.

thèse, tayz, *f* thesis; argument.

thon, tong, *m* tuna fish.

thorax, to-racks, *m* thorax; chest.

thrombose coronarienne, trong-bohz-kor-oh-năh-re-en, *f* coronary.

thym, tang, *m* thyme.

tibia, te-be-ăh, *m* shinbone.

tic, teek, *m* tic; habit.

ticket, te-kay, *m* ticket (bus, etc).

tiède,* te-aid, *a* lukewarm; tepid; indifferent.

tiédir, te-eh-deer, *v* to grow lukewarm.

tien, ne, te-ang, *poss pron mf* (familiar form) yours.

tier-s, ce, te-air, *mf* third person; *a* third.

tige, teesh, *f* stem; stalk; trunk; rod; shaft.

tigre, tigresse, tee-gr, tee-gress, *mf* tiger; tigress.

tilleul, tee-yerl, *m* lime tree; lime blossom.

timbale, tang-băhl, *f* kettledrum; metal cup.

timbre, tang-br, *m* bell; (*fig*) tone; stamp.

timbré, e, tang-breh, *a* stamped; sonorous; (*fam*) mad.

timide,* te-meed, *a* timid; shy; bashful.

timoré, e, te-mor-eh, *a* timorous.

tintamarre, tang-tăh-măhr, *m* uproar; hubbub; clatter.

tinter, tang-teh, *v* to ring; to tinkle; to toll.

tir, teer, *m* shooting; firing; rifle range.

tirage, te-răhsh, *m* drawing; draft; printing; circulation (newspapers).

tiraillement, te-rah'e-mahng, *m* pulling; pain.

tire-bouchon, teer-boo-shong, *m* corkscrew.

tiré, e, te-reh, *a* drawn (face); worn out.

tirelire, teer-leer, *f* piggybank.

tirer, te-reh, *v* to draw; to pull; to drag; to verge on; to shoot.

tiret, te-reh, *m* hyphen; dash.

tiroir, te-ro'ăhr, *m* drawer;

slide.

tisane, te-zähn, *f* infusion.

tison, te-zong, *m* fire brand.

tisonnier, te-zonn-e-eh, *m* poker.

tisser, teess-eh, *v* to weave.

tissu, teess-E, *m* material; fabric.

titre, tee-tr, *m* title; right; certificate.

tituber, tee-tE-beh, *v* to stagger; to lurch.

titulaire, tee-tE-lair, *mf* holder; titular.

tocsin, tock-sang, *m* alarm bell.

tohu-bohu, toh-E-boh-E, *m* confusion; chaos.

toi, to'äh, *pers pron mf sing* (familiar form) you (subject or object).

toile, to'ähl, *f* cloth; linen; canvas; picture.

toilette, to'äh-lett, *f* wash; dress; toilet; dressing table.

toiser, to'äh-zeh, *v* to measure; (*fig*) to eye (someone).

toison, to'äh-zong, *f* fleece; (*fam*) mop of hair.

toit, to'äh, *m* roof; (*fam*) home.

tôle, tohl, *f* sheet.

tolérable, toll-eh-räh-bl, *a* tolerable.

tolérance, toll-eh-rahngss, *f* toleration.

tolérer, toll-eh-reh, *v* to tolerate.

tomate, tomm-äht, *f* tomato.

tombant, e, tong-bahng, *a* falling.

tombe, tongb, *f* tomb; grave.

tombeau, tong-boh, *m* tomb; grave; tombstone.

tomber, tong-beh, *v* to fall; to abate; **–sur,** to come across.

tome, tohm, *m* tome; volume.

ton, tong, *poss a m sing* (familiar form) your; *m* tone; style; shade.

tondeuse, tong-derz, *f* lawnmower; shears.

tondre, tong-dr, *v* to shear; to mow; to clip.

tonne, tonn, *f* ton.

tonneau, tonn-oh, *m* cask; barrel.

tonner, tonn-eh, *v* to thunder.

tonnerre, tonn-air, *m* thunder.

toque, took, *f* cap.

toqué, e, tock-eh, *a* (*fam*) crazy.

torche, torsh, *f* torch.

torchon, tor-shong, *m* dishcloth; duster.

tordre, tor-dr, *v* to wring; to twist; **se –,** to writhe.

torpeur, tor-per, *f* torpor; numbness.

torpille, tor-pee-ye, *f* torpedo.

torpilleur, tor-pee-yer, *m* torpedo boat.

torréfier, tor-reh-fe-eh, *v* to roast.

torrent, tor-rahng, *m* torrent.

torrentiel, le, tor-rahng-se-ell, *a* torrential.

torse, torss, *m* torso; trunk; chest.

tort, tor, *m* wrong; harm; injury; **avoir –,** äh-vo'ähr –, to be wrong.

tortiller, tor-tee-yeh, *v* to twist; to shuffle; **se –,** to wriggle

tortue, tor-tE, *f* tortoise; turtle.

tortueu-x, se,* tor-tE- er, *a* winding; crooked.

torture, tor-tEEr, *f* torture.

tôt, toh, *adv* soon; early.

total, tot-ähl, *m* total.

total, e,* tot-ähl, *a* total; whole.

touchant, too-shahng, *prep* concerning; regarding.

touchant, e, too-shahng, *a* touching; affecting.

touche, toosh, *f* touch; stroke; key.

a
b
c
d
e
f
g
h
i
j
k
l
m
n
o
p
q
r
s
t
u
v
w
x
y
z

toucher, too-sheh, *v* to touch; to cash; to hit; to affect; to be contiguous to.

toucher, too-sheh, *m* touch; feeling.

touffe, toof, *f* tuft; bunch; clump.

touffu, e, too-fE, *a* tufted; bushy; thick.

toujours, too-shoohr, *adv* always; ever; nevertheless.

toupet, too-pay, *m* tuft; (*fam*) impudence; cheek.

toupie, too-pee, *f* top (spinning).

tour, toohr, *m* turn; revolution; circumference; trick; trip; lathe.

tour, toohr, *f* tower.

tourbe, toohrb, *f* peat; turf; mob.

tourbillon, toohr-bee-yong, *m* whirlwind.

tourelle, too-rell, *f* turret.

touriste, too-risst, *mf* tourist; tripper.

tourment, toohr-mahng, *m* torment; anguish.

tourmente, toohr-mahngt, *f* tempest; (*fig*) turmoil.

tourmenté, e, toohr-mahng-teh, *a* stormy; worried.

tourmenter, toohr-mahng-teh, *v* to torment.

tournant, toohr-nahng, *m* turning; bend; corner.

tournée, toohr-neh, *f* round; walk.

tourner, toohr-neh, *v* to turn; to change.

tourneur, toohr-ner, *m* turner.

tournevis, toohr-ner-veess, *m* screwdriver.

tournoi, toohr-no'ăh, *m* tournament.

tournoyer, toohr-no'ăh-yeh, *v* to whirl round.

tournure, toohr-nEEr, *f* figure; appearance; turn; course.

tourte, toohrt, *f* tart; fruitpie.

tourterelle, toohr-ter-rell, *f* turtledove.

toussaint (la), lăh-tooss-ang, *f* All Saints' Day.

tousser, tooss-eh, *v* to cough.

tout, too, *adv* wholly; quite. *m* all; the whole; chief point.

tout, e, too, *a* all; whole.

tout, too, *pron* all; everything.

tout-à-l'égout, toot-ăh-leh-ghoo, *m* main sewer.

toutefois, toot-fo'ăh, *adv* yet; however.

toute-puissance, toot-pweess-ahngss, *f* omnipotence.

tout(e) petit(e) enfant, too-per-te-ahng-fahng *mf* toddler.

tout-puissant, too-pweess-ahng, *m* Almighty; *a* all-powerful.

toux, too, *f* cough; coughing.

toxique, tox-eeck, *m* poison. *a* poisonous; toxic.

trac, trăhck, *m* (*fam*) fright; stage fright.

tracas, trăh-kah, *m* bother; anxiety; worries.

tracasser, trăh-kăhss-eh, *v* to worry; to plague.

trace, trăhss, *f* trace; track; footstep.

tracé, trăhss-eh, *m* outline; planning; line.

tracer, trăhss-eh, *v* to trace; to draw out; to lay down.

tracteur, trăhk-ter *m* tractor.

traduc-teur, trice, *mf* translator.

traduction, trăh-dEEk-se-ong, *f* translation; translating.

traduire, trăh-dweer, *v* to translate.

trafic, trăh-feek, *m* traffic; trade.

trafiquer, trăh-fe-keh, *v* to

trade; to traffic.

tragique,* trăh-**sheeck**, *a* tragic(al).

trahir, trăh-**eer**, *v* to betray; to deceive.

trahison, trăh-e-*zong*, *f* treachery; betrayal; treason.

train, trang, *m* train; pace; rate; speed; way; style.

traînard, tray-năhr, *m* straggler; slowpoke.

traîneau, tray-noh, *m* sled.

traînée, tray-neh, *f* train; trail.

traîner, tray-neh, *v* to drag; to drawl; to lag behind; to lie about.

traire, trayr, *v* to milk.

trait, tray, *m* dart; arrow; stroke; dash (of the pen, etc.); touch; draft (of liquor); act; feature.

traitable, tray-tăh-bl, *a* tractable.

traite, trayt, *f* journey; draft; trading (on the African coast).

traité, tray-teh, *m* treatise; treaty.

traitement, trayt-mahng, *m* treatment; salary.

traiter, tray-teh, *v* to treat; to handle; to negotiate.

traître, sse, tray-tr, *mf & a* traitor; traitress; treacherous.

traîtreusement, tray-trerz-mahng, *adv* treacherously.

traîtrise, tray-treez, *f* treachery; betrayal.

trajet, trăh-**shay**, *m* journey; passage; distance.

trame, trăhm, *f* woof; weft; web; plot; framework.

tramer, trăh-meh, *v* to weave; to plot.

tranchant, trahng-shahng, *m* edge.

tranchant, e, trahng-shahng, *a* sharp; cutting; peremptory.

tranche, trahngsh, *f* slice.

tranchée, trahng-sheh, *f* trench; *pl* gripes.

trancher, trahng-sheh, *v* to cut off; to decide; to solve; to contrast (*sur*, with).

tranquilisant, trahng-ke-le-zahng *m* tranquilizer.

tranquille,* trahng-keel, *a* quiet; peaceful; easy.

tranquilliser, trahng-ke-le-zeh, *v* to calm.

tranquillité, trahng-ke-le-teh, *f* calm; stillness.

transatlantique, trahngss-ăht-lahng-teeck, *m* transatlantic liner. *a* transatlantic.

transborder, trahngss-bor-deh, *v* to transship.

transcrire, trahngss-kreer, *v* to transcribe.

transe, trahngss, *f* fright; apprehension; trance.

transférer, trahngss-feh-reh, *v* to transfer.

transfert, trahngss-fair, *m* transfer.

transformer, trahngss-for-meh, *v* to transform; to change into.

transfusion, trahngss-fe-ze-ong, *f* transfusion.

transi, e, trahng-ze, *pp & a* chilled; benumbed.

transiger, trahng-ze-**sheh**, *v* to compromise.

transitoire,* trahng-ze-to'ăhr, *a* transitory.

transmettre, trahngss-met-tr, *v* to transmit; to broadcast.

transparence, trahngss-păh-rahngss, *f* transparency.

transparent, trahngss-păh-rahng, *a* transparent.

transpiration, trahngss-pe-răh-se-ong, *f* perspiration.

transpirer, trahngss-pe-reh, *v* to perspire; to transpire; to sweat.

transport, trahngss-por, *m* carriage; conveyance; rapture.

transporter, trahngss-por-teh, *v* to convey; to

a
b
c
d
e
f
g
h
i
j
k
l
m
n
o
p
q
r
s
t
u
v
w
x
y
z

A B C D E F G H I J K L M N O P Q R S T U V W X Y Z

enrapture.

transvaser, trahngss-vah-zeh, *v* to decant.

trappe, trăhp, *f* trapdoor; trap; pitfall.

trapu, e, trăh-pE, *a* thickset; dumpy.

traquenard, trăhck-năhr, *m* (*fig*) snare; trap.

traquer, trăh-keh, *v* to hunt out; to surround.

travail, trăh-vah'e, *m* work; labor; toil.

travailler, trăh-vah'e-yeh, *v* to work; too work on; to ferment (of wines).

travers, trăh-vair, *m* breadth; defect; oddity; à –, ăh –, across.

traversée, trăh-vair-seh, *f* passage; crossing.

traverser, trăh-vair-seh, *v* to cross; to travel over; to thwart.

traversin, trăh-vair-sang, *m* bolster.

travestir, trăh-vess-teer, *v* to disguise; to travesty.

trébucher, treh-bE-sheh, *v* to stumble.

trèfle, tray-fl, *m* clover; clubs (cards).

treillage, tray'e-yăhsh, *m* latticework.

treille, tray'e, *f* climbing vine.

treize, trayz, *m* & *a* thirteen.

treizième, tray-ze-aym, *m* & *a* thirteenth.

tréma, treh-mah, *m* diaeresis.

tremblement, trahng-bler-mahng, *m* shake; tremor; –de terre, – der tair, earthquake.

trembler, trahng-bleh, *v* to tremble; to quake; to shake; to quaver; to fear.

trémousser (se), ser treh-mooss-eh, *v* to bestir oneself.

tremper, trahng-peh, *v* to dip; to soak; to temper (steel).

trentaine, trahng-tenn, *f* about thirty.

trente, trahngt, *m* & *a* thirty.

trentième, trahng-te-aym, *m* & *a* thirtieth.

trépasser, treh-pahss-eh, *v* to die.

trépied, treh-pe-eh, *m* tripod.

trépigner, treh-peen-yeh, *v* to stamp.

très, tray, *adv* very; very much; most.

trésor, treh-zor, *m* treasure; treasury.

trésori-er, ère, treh-zor-e-eh, *mf* treasurer.

tressaillir, tress-sah'e-yeer, *v* to start; to thrill; to shudder.

tresse, trayss, *f* plait.

tréteau, treh-toh, *m* trestle; *pl* stage.

treuil, trer-e, *m* windlass.

trêve, trayv, *f* truce; –de, – der, no more.

tri, triage, tre, tre-ăhsh, *m* sorting; picking.

tribu, tre-bE, *f* tribe.

tribunal, tre-bE-năhl, *m* tribunal; bench; courthouse.

tribune, tre-bEEn, *f* tribune; (*fig*) platform; (*fig*) grandstand.

tribut, tre-bE, *m* tribute.

tricher, tre-sheh, *v* to cheat.

tricot, tre-ko, *m* knitting; sweater.

tricoter, tre-ko-teh, *v* to knit.

tricycle, tre-see-kl, *m* tricycle.

trier, tre-eh, *v* to sort; to pick; to choose.

trimbaler, trang-băh-leh, *v* (*fam*) to carry about; to trail (children) about.

trimestre, tre-mess-tr, *m* quarter; term.

tringle, trang-gl, *f* rod; curtain rod.

trinquer, trang-keh, *v* to touch glasses; (*fam*) to drink together.

triompher, tre-ong-feh, *v* to triumph.

tripe, treep, *f* tripe; (*fam*)
pl guts.

triple, * tre-pl, *a* treble;
triple.

tripoter, tre-pot-eh, *v* to
mess about.

triste, * trisst, *a* sad;
gloomy; dreary.

tristesse, triss-tess, *f*
sadness; gloom;
melancholy.

triturer, tre-tE-reh, *v* to
grind; to masticate.

troc, trock, *m* barter;
exchange in kind.

trognon, tronn-yong, *m*
core (of a pear); stump
(of a cabbage).

trois, tro'ăh, *m* & *a* three.

troisième, tro'ăh-ze-aym,
m & *a* third.

trombe, trongb, *f*
waterspout.

trombone, trong-bonn, *f*
trombone; paper clip.

trompe, trongp, *f* horn;
trunk (of elephants,
etc.); proboscis.

tromper, trong-peh, *v* to
deceive; to cheat; **se –,**
to make a mistake.

trompette, trong-pett, *f*
trumpet.

trompeu-r, se, trong-per,
mf & *a* * deceiver;
betrayer; deceitful.

tronc, trong, *m* trunk;
collection box.

tronçon, trong-song, *m*
stump.

trône, trohn, *m* throne.

tronquer, trong-keh, *v* to
mutilate; to cut off.

trop, tro, *adv* too; too
much; too many.

troquer, trock-eh, *v* to
barter; to exchange.

trotter, trot-eh, *v* to trot;
to run.

trottinette, trot-e-nett, *f*
child's scooter.

trottoir, trot-o'ăhr, *m*
pavement.

trou, troo, *m* hole; gap;
mouth.

trouble, troo-bl, *m*
disturbance; perplexity;
a muddy; dull; confused.

troubler, troo-bleh, *v* to
disturb; to make muddy;
to put about.

trouer, troo-eh, *v* to hole;
to pierce.

troupe, troop, *f* troupe;
gang; set; crew; *pl*
troops.

troupeau, troo-poh, *m*
flock; herd.

troupier, troo-pe-eh, *m*
soldier; trooper.

trousse, trooss, *f* truss;
bundle; case; kit.

trousseau, trooss-oh, *m*
bunch of (keys);
trousseau.

trouvaille, troo-vah'e, *f*
discovery.

trouver, troo-veh, *v* to
find; to think; to
consider.

truc, trEEk, *m* (*fam*) trick;
thing.

truffe, trEEf, *f* truffle.

truie, trwee, *f* sow.

truite, trweet, *f* trout.

truquer, trE-keh, *v* to fake.

tu, tE, *pers pron sing*
(familiar form) you.

tuba, tEEb-ăh *m* snorkel.

tube, tEEb, *m* tube; pipe.

tuer, tE-eh, *v* to kill; to
slaughter.

tuerie, tE-ree, *f* slaughter.

tue-tête (à), ăh tE-tayt,
adv at the top of one's
voice.

tuile, tweel, *f* tile.

tumeur, tE-mer, *f* tumor;
growth.

tumulte, tE-mEElt, *m*
tumult; turmoil.

turbot, tEEr-bo, *m* turbot.

turbulence, tEEr-bE-
lahngss *m* turbulence.

turbulent, tEEr-bE-lahng, *a*
turbulent; boisterous.

tutelle, tE-tell, *f* tutelage;
protection;
guardianship.

tu-teur, trice, tE-ter, *mf*
guardian.

tutoyer, tE-to'ăh-yeh, *v* to
address as **tu**; to be on
familiar terms with.

A
B
C
D
E
F
G
H
I
J
K
L
M
N
O
P
Q
R
S
T
U
V
W
X
Y
Z

tuyau, twee-yoh, *m* pipe; tube; funnel; (*fam*) tip.

type, teep, *m* type; symbol; (*pop*) man; guy.

typhon, te-fong, *m* typhoon.

typique, te-peeck, *a* typical.

tyran, te-rahng, *m* tyrant.

tyrannie, te-răhn-nee, *f* tyranny.

tzigane, tse-găhn, *mf* & *a* gypsy.

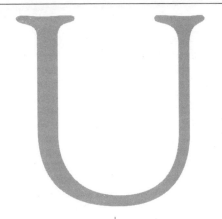

ulcère, EEl-sair, m ulcer.

ulcéré, EEl-seh-reh, pp & a
ulcerated; (fig)
embittered.

ultérieur, e,* EEl-teh-re-
er, a subsequent;
ulterior.

un, e, ung, a & n one;
unit; first.

un, e, ung, indef art & pron
an; one; any.

unanime,* E-năh-neem, a
unanimous.

uni, e, E-ne, a united;
smooth; even; level;
plain.

unième, E-ne-aym, a first
(used only in
compounds: vingt et
unième, twenty-first,
etc).

unifier, E-ne-fe-eh, v to
unify.

uniforme, E-ne-form, a &
m uniform.

uniformément, E-ne-for-
meh-mahng, adv
uniformly.

union, E-ne-ong, f union;
marriage; harmony.

unique,* E-neeck, a only;
sole; unique; matchless.

unir, E-neer, v to unite; to
smooth.

unisson, E-niss-ong, m
unison.

unité, E-ne-teh, f unity;
unit.

univers, E-ne-vair, m
universe.

universel, le,* E-ne-vair-
sell, a universal.

universitaire, E-ne-vair-
se-tair, mf & a member
of the university;
belonging to the
university.

université, E-ne-vair-se-
teh, f university.

urbain, e, EEr-bang, a
urban.

urbanité, EEr-băh-ne-teh,
f urbanity.

urgence, EEr-shahngss, f
urgency; emergency.

urgent, e, EEr-shahng, a
urgent.

urine, E-reen, f urine.

uriner, E-reen-eh, v to
urinate.

urinoir, E-re-no'ăhr, m
urinal.

urne, EE rn, f urn.

usage, E-zăhsh, m use;
custom; habit; wear.

usagé, e, E-zăh-sheh, a
that has been used.

usé, e, E-zeh, pp & a
worn-out; stale;
hackneyed.

user, E-zeh, v to wear; to
spend; –de, to make use
of

usine, E-zeen, f factory;
plant.

usité, e, E-ze-teh, a in use;
customary.

ustensile, EEss-tahng-seel,
m utensil.

usuel, le,* E-zE-ell, a
usual.

usure, E-zEEr, f wear;
usury.

usurpa-teur, trice, E-zEEr-

A
B
C
D
E
F
G
H
I
J
K
L
M
N
O
P
Q
R
S
T
U
V
W
X
Y
Z

păh-**ter**, *mf* & *a* usurper; usurping.

usurper, E-zEEr-peh, *v* to usurp.

ut, EEt, *m* C (of music).

utérus, E-teh-rEss, *m* uterus; womb.

utile, E-teel, *m* & *a** utility; useful; serviceable.

utiliser, E-te-le-zeh, *v* to utilize; to make use of.

utilité, E-te-le-teh, *f* utility; usefulness.

utopique, E-top-eeck, *a* utopian.

V

vacance, văh-kahngss, *f*
vacancy; *pl* vacation;
holiday.

vacant, e, văh-kahng, *a*
vacant; unoccupied.

vacarme, văh-kăhrm, *m*
hubbub; uproar; din.

vaccination, văhck-seen-
ăh-se-ong, *f* vaccination.

vacciner, văhck-seen-eh,
v to vaccinate.

vache, văhsh, *f* cow;
cowhide.

vaciller, văh-sill-leh or
văh-see-yeh, *v* to waver;
to wobble.

va-et-vient, văh-eh-ve-
ang, *m* coming and
going.

vagabond, e, văh-găh-
bong, *a* & *mf* vagabond;
vagrant.

vague, văhg, *m* vagueness;
empty space; *a** vague;
indistinct; vacant; waste
(land).

vague, văhg, *f* wave;
billow; generation.

vague de chaleur, văhg-
der-shăh-ler *f* heat
wave.

vaillamment, vah'e-yăh-
mahng, *adv* valiantly.

vaillance, vah'e-yahngss, *f*
valor; bravery.

vaillant, e, vah'e-yahng, *a*
valiant; brave; gallant.

vain, e,* vang, *a* vain;
fruitless; vainglorious.

vaincre, vang-kr, *v* to
vanquish; to conquer; to
defeat.

vaincu, vang-kE, *m* & *a*
conquered; vanquished.

vainqueur, vang-ker, *m*
victor; prizewinner; *a*

victorious.

vaisseau, vayss-oh, *m*
vessel; ship; structure.

vaisselle, vayss-ell, *f*
dishes; washing up.

val, văhl, *m* vale; valley;
dale.

valable,* văh-lăh-bl, *a*
valid.

valet, văh-lay, *m* footman;
knave (cards).

valeur, văh-ler, *f* value;
worth; courage; *pl*
securities.

valeureu-x, se,* văh-ler-
rer, *a* valiant; brave.

valide,* văh-leed, *a* valid.

validité, văh-le-de-teh, *f*
validity.

valise, văh-leez, *f* suitcase.

vallée, văh-leh, *f* valley;
vale; dale.

vallon, văh-long, *m* dale;
small valley.

valoir, văh-lo'ăhr, *v* to be
worth; to yield.

valse, văhls, *f* waltz.

valve, văhlv, *f* valve.

vanille, văh-nee-ye, *f*
vanilla.

vanité, văh-ne-teh, *f*
vanity.

vaniteu-x, se,* văh-ne-
ter, *a* vain; vainglorious.

vanne, văhn, *f* sluice;
watergate.

vanner, văh-neh, *v* to
winnow.

vannerie, văhn-ner-ree, *f* basketwork.

vantard, e, vahng-tăhr, *mf* & *a* boaster; boastful; boasting.

vanter, vahng-teh, *v* to praise; to extol; **se –,** to boast.

vapeur, văh-per, *m* steamer; *f* vapor; steam.

vaporeu-x, se,* văh-por-er, *a* vaporous; hazy.

vaporiser, văh-por-e-zeh, *v* to vaporize; to spray.

vaquer, văh-keh, *v* to be vacant; **–à, –** ăh, to attend to.

vareuse, văh-rerz, *f* pea jacket.

variable,* văh-re-ăh-bl, *a* variable; changeable.

variation, văh-re-ăh-se-ong, *f* variation.

varice, văh-reess, *f* varicose vein.

varicelle, văh-re-sell, *f* chicken pox.

varier, văh-re-eh, *v* to vary; to differ.

variété, văh-re-eh-teh, *f* variety.

variole, văh-re-ol, *f* smallpox.

vase, vahz, *m* vase; urn; vessel; *f* mud; slime.

vaseu-x, se, vah-zer, *a* muddy; miry.

vaste,* văhsst, *a* vast; spacious; wide; great.

va-tout, văh-too, *m* last stake.

vaurien, ne, voh-re-ang, *mf* worthless person.

vautour, voh-toohr, *m* vulture.

vautrer (se), ser voh-treh, *v* to wallow; to sprawl.

veau, voh, *m* calf; calf's leather; veal.

vedette, ver-dett, *f* motorboat; star (film).

végétal, e, veh-sheh-tăhl, *a* vegetable.

véhément, e,* veh-eh-mahng, *a* vehement.

véhicule, veh-e-kEEl, *m* vehicle.

veille, vay'e, *f* wakefulness; watch; eve.

veillée, vay'e-yeh, *f* sitting up; vigil.

veiller, vay'e-yeh, *v* to sit up; to watch; to be awake; **–(á)** to see to.

veilleuse, vay'e-yerz, *f* night-light; pilot light.

veine, vayn, *f* vein; (*fam*) luck.

velléité, veh-leh-e-teh, *f* slight desire.

vélo, veh-lo, *m* (*fam*) bicycle.

vélodrome, veh-lod-rohm, *m* cycling track.

vélo tout terrain, (veh-lo) too-tay-rang *m* mountain bike.

velours, ver-loohr, *m* velvet.

velouté, e, ver-loo-teh, *a* velvety; soft; rich (soup, etc).

velu, e, ver-lE, *a* hairy; shaggy.

venaison, ver-nay-zong, *f* venison.

venant, e, ver-nahng, *a* coming; thriving; **á tout –,** ăh-too–, to all and sundry.

vendable, vahng-dăh-bl, *a* marketable.

vendange, vahng-dahng sh, *f* vintage; grape harvest.

vendeu-r, se, vahng-der, *mf* seller; salesman (-woman).

vendre, vahng-dr, *v* to sell; to betray.

vendredi, vahng-drer-de, *m* Friday.

véneneu-x, se, veh-neh-ner, *a* poisonous.

vénérer, veh-neh-reh, *v* to venerate.

vénérien, ne, veh-neh-re-ang, *a* venereal.

vengeance, vahng-shahngss, *f* revenge.

venger, vahng- sheh, *v* to avenge; to revenge.

veng-eur, eresse, vahng-sher, *mf* & *a* avenger.

véniel, le, veh-ne-ell, *a* venial.

venimeu-x, se, ver-ne-mer, *a* venomous.

venin, ver-nang, *m* venom; (*fig*) spite; (*fig*) rancor.

venir, ver-neer, *v* to come; to arrive; to happen; to grow; **–de,**–der, to have just...

vent, vahng, *m* wind; scent; (*fig*) emptiness.

venter, vahngt, *f* sale.

vente, vahng-teh, *v* to be windy.

ventilateur, vahng-te-lăh-ter, *m* ventilator; fan.

ventouse, vahng-tooz, *f* suction cup.

ventre, vahng-tr, *m* abdomen; belly; stomach.

ventru, e, vahng-trE, *a* corpulent; big-bellied.

venu, e, ver-nE, *mf* comer.

venue, ver-nE, *f* coming; arrival; growth.

vêpres, vay-pr, *fpl* vespers.

ver, vair, *m* worm; maggot.

verbal, e,* vair-băhl, *a* verbal.

verbe, vairb, *m* verb.

verbeu-x, se, vair-ber, *a* verbose.

verbiage, vair-be-ăhsh, *m* verbiage; mere talk.

verdâtre, vair-dah-tr, *a* greenish.

verdeur, vair-der, *f* greenness; tartness.

verdir, vair-deer, *v* to grow green; to make green.

verdoyant, e, vair-do'aăh-yahng, *a* verdant.

verdure, vair-dEEr, *f* greenness; verdure; foliage.

véreu-x, se, veh-rer, *a* worm-eaten; (*fam*) suspicious; dishonest.

verge, vairsh, *m f* penis; *pl* birch rod.

verger, vair-sheh, *m* orchard.

verglas, vair-glah, *m* black ice.

vergogne (sans), sahng vair-gonn-yer, *f* shameless.

véridique,* veh-re-deeck, *a* veracious; truthful.

vérifier, veh-re-fe-eh, *v* to verify; to check.

véritable,* veh-re-tăh-bl, *a* true; genuine; downright.

vérité, veh-re-teh, *f* truth.

vermeil, vair-may'e, *m* vermeil .

vermeil, le, vair-may'e, *a* ruby; rosy; vermilion.

vermine, vair-meen, *f* vermin.

vermisseau, vair-miss-oh, *m* small worm.

vermoulu, e, vair-moo-lE, *a* worm-eaten.

vernir, vair-neer, *v* to varnish.

vernis, vair-ne, *m* varnish; japan (japonaiserie); French polish.

vérole (petite), per-teet veh-rol, *f* smallpox.

verre, vair, *m* glass.

verrerie, vay-rer-ree, *f* glassworks.

verrou, vay-roo, *m* bolt.

verrouiller, vay-roo'e-yeh, *v* to bolt.

verrue, vay-rE, *f* wart.

vers, vair, *prep* towards; about.

vers, vair, *m* verse; line.

versant, vair-sahng, *m* slope; bank.

verse (à), ăh vairss, *adv* in torrents (rain).

versé, e, vair-seh, *a* well-versed; well up (**dans, en,** in).

versement, vair-ser-mahng, *m* payment; partial installment.

verser, vair-seh, *v* to pour; to shed; to lodge; to pay in; to overturn.

verset, vair-say, *m* verse (Bible, etc.).

verso, vair-so, *m* back; reverse (of paper, etc).

a
b
c
d
e
f
g
h
i
j
k
l
m
n
o
p
q
r
s
t
u
v
w
x
y
z

vert, e, vair, *a* green;
unripe; sharp; *m* color
green.

vertement, vair-ter-
mah*n*g, *adv* sharply;
severely.

vertical, e,* vair-te-kăhl,
a vertical.

vertige, vair-teesh, *m*
giddiness; vertigo.

vertigineu-x, se, vair-te-
she-ner, *a* giddy; dizzy.

vertu, vair-tE, *f* virtue;
chastity; power;
property.

vertueu-x, se,* vair-tE-
er, *a* virtuous.

verve, vairv, *f* animation;
zest; spirits.

vessie, vayss-ee, *f* bladder.

veste, vaysst, *f* jacket.

vestiaire, vayss-te-air, *m*
cloakroom; locker room;
changing room (sport).

vestibule, vayss-te-bEEl, *m*
vestibule.

vestige, vayss-teesh, *m*
vestige; remains; track.

veston, vayss-tong, *m*
jacket.

vêtement, vaytt-mahng, *m*
garment; *pl* clothes.

vétérinaire, veh-teh-re-
nair, *m & a*
veterinarian; veterinary.

vêtir, vay-teer, *v* to
clothe; to dress; to array.

veu-f, ve, verf, *mf & a*
widower; widow;
widowed.

veule, verl, *a* weak; soft.

veuvage, ver-văhsh, *m*
widowhood.

vexatoire, veck-săh-
to'ăhr, *a* vexatious.

vexer, veck-seh, *v* to vex;
to annoy.

viable, ve-ăh-bl, *a* viable.

viag-er, ère, ve-ăh-**sh**eh, *a*
for life.

viande, ve-ahngd, *f* meat;
flesh.

vibrant, e, ve-brahng, *a*
vibrating.

vibrer, ve-breh, *v* to
vibrate.

vicaire, ve-kair, *m* curate.

vice, veess, *m* vice; defect;
blemish; flaw.

vice versa, vess-vair-săh
adv vice versa.

vicié, e, veess-e-eh, *a*
vitiated; corrupt.

vicier, veess-e-eh, *v* to
vitiate; to corrupt.

vicieu-x, se,* veess-e-er, *a*
vicious; faulty;
depraved.

vicomte, ve-kongt, *m*
viscount.

vicomtesse, ve-kong-tess, *f*
viscountess.

victime, vick-teem, *f*
victim.

victoire, vick-to'ăhr, *f*
victory.

victorieu-x, se,* vick-tor-
e-er, *a* victorious.

victuaille, vick-tE-ah'e, *f*
victuals; *pl* provisions.

vidange, ve-dahng sh, *f*
clearing out; draining.

vide, veed, *m* empty space;
vacuum; *a* empty.

vidéo, ve-deh-oh *f* video
(film).

vidéocassette, vee-deh-
oh-kăh-sett *f* video
cassette.

vider, vee-deh, *v* to
empty; to drain; to
settle.

vie, vee, *f* life; living;
existence.

vieillard, ve-ay'e-ăhr, *m*
old man.

vieille, ve-ay'e, *f* old
woman.

vieillerie, ve-ay'e-ree, *f*
old things.

vieillesse, ve-ay'e-ess, *f*
old age.

vieillir, ve-ay'e-eer, *v* to
grow old; to age.

vierge, ve-airsh, *f* virgin.

vieux, ve-er, *m* old man;
pl old folk.

vieux (before a vowel or **h**
mute: **vieil**), *f* **vieille,**
ve-er, ve-ay'e, *a* old.

vi-f, ve,* veef, *a* alive;
sharp; quick-tempered;
bright (of colors);
strong; running.

vif-argent, veef-ăhr-shahng, *m* quicksilver (mercury).

vigie, ve-shee, *f* lookout.

vigilamment, ve-she-lăh-mahng, *adv* vigilantly.

vigilance, ve-she-lahngss, *f* vigilance.

vigilant, e, ve-she-lăhng, *a* vigilant.

vigne, veen-yer, *f* vine; vineyard.

vigneron, veen-yer-rong, *m* winegrower.

vignoble, veen-yo-bl, *m* vineyard.

vigoureu-x, se,* ve-goo-rer, *a* vigorous; sturdy; energetic.

vigueur, ve-gher, *f* vigor; strength.

vil, e,* veel, *a* vile; base; mean; despicable.

vilain, e,* ve-lang, *a* ugly; nasty; naughty (child).

vilenie, ve-ler-nee, *f* meanness; dirty trick; *pl* abuse.

village, ve-lăhsh, *m* village.

villageois, e, ve-lăh-sho'ăh, *mf* & *a* villager; rustic.

ville, veel, *f* town; city.

vin, vang, *m* wine.

vinaigre, ve-nay-gr, *m* vinegar.

vinaigrette, ve-nay-grett, *f* oil and vinegar dressing; vinagrette.

vindicati-f, ve, vang-de-kăh-teeff, *a* revengeful.

vingt, vang, *m* & *a* twenty; twentieth.

vingtaine, vang-tain, *f* about twenty.

vingtième, vang-te-aym, *m* & *a* twentieth.

viol, ve-ol, *m* rape.

violation, ve-oll-ăh-se-ong, *f* violation; infringement.

violemment, ve-oll-ăh-mahng, *adv* violently.

violence, ve-oll-ahngss, *f* violence.

violent, e, ve-oll-ahng, *a* violent.

violer, ve-oll-eh, *v* to violate; to infringe; to rape.

violet, te, ve-oll-ay, *a* violet-colored; *m* color violet.

violette, ve-oll-ett, *f* violet.

violon, ve-oll-ong, *m* violin; violinist; (*pop*) prison.

vipère, ve-pair, *f* viper; adder.

virage, ve-răhsh, *m* turning; bend; toning (photography); changing (of color).

virement, veer-mahng, *m* transfer (finance).

virer, ve-reh, *v* to turn; to take a bend; (*naut*) to tack.

virgule, veer-ghEEl, *f* comma.

viril, e,* ve-reel, *a* manly; virile.

virilité, ve-re-le-teh, *m* manhood; virility; vigor.

virtuel, le,* veer-tE-ell, *a* virtual.

virulence, ve-rE-lahngss, *f* virulence.

virus, ve-rEEss, *m* virus.

vis, veess, *f* screw.

visa, ve-zăh, *m* signature; visa.

visage, ve-zăhsh, *m* face; visage; look.

vis-à-vis, ve-zăh-ve, *adv* in relation to.

viscère, veess-sair, *m* viscus; entrails.

visée, ve-zeh, *f* aim; design; end.

viser, ve-zeh, *v* to aim at; to aspire to; to endorse.

visible,* ve-zee-bl, *a* visible.

visière, ve-ze-air, *f* visor (of a helmet); peak (of caps, etc.).

vision, ve-ze-ong, *f* vision; sight; phantom.

visionnaire, ve-ze-onn-air, *a* visionary.

visite, ve-zeet, *f* visit;

search; medical examination.

visiter, ve-ze-teh, *v* to visit; to inspect; to search.

visqueu-x, se, veess-ker, *a* viscous; sticky.

visser, veess-eh, *v* to screw on.

visuel, le, * ve-zE-ell, *a* visual.

vital, e, ve-tăhl, *a* vital.

vitalité, ve-tăh-le-teh, *f* vitality.

vitamine, ve-tăh-meen *f* vitamin.

vite, veet, *adv* quickly; fast; *a* quick; swift.

vitesse, ve-tess, *f* quickness; speed.

vitesse maximale permise, ve-tess-măhks-e-măhl *f* speed limit.

viticulture, ve-te-kEEl-tEEr, *f* wine-growing.

vitrail, ve-trah'e, *m* stained glass window.

vitre, vee-tr, *f* pane; windowpane.

vitrier, ve-tre-eh, *m* glazier.

vitrine, ve-treen, *f* store window; display cabinet.

vivace, ve-văhss, *a* long-lived; deep-rooted.

vivacité, ve-văhss-e-teh, *f* vivacity; hastiness (of temper).

vivant, ve-vahng, *m* living person; lifetime.

vivant, e, ve-vahng, *a* living; alive; lively.

vivier, ve-ve-eh, *m* fish pond; breeding ground.

vivre, vee-vr, *v* to live; to board.

vivres, vee-vr, *mpl* food; provisions.

vocable, vock-ăh-bl, *m* word; term.

vocabulaire, vock-ăh-bE-lair, *m* vocabulary; word list.

vocal, e, vock-ăhl, *a* vocal.

vocatif, vock-ăh-teeff, *m* vocative case.

vocation, vock-ăh-se-ong, *f* vocation; calling.

vociférer, voss-e-feh-reh, *v* to bawl; to cry out.

vœu, ver, *m* vow; wish.

vogue, vogh, *f* vogue; fashion.

voguer, vogh-eh, *v* to sail.

voici, vo'ăh-se, *adv* here is; here are.

voie, vo'ăh, *f* way; road; track; (*fig*) gauge; means.

voilà, vo'ăh-lăh, *adv* there is; there are.

voile, vo'ăhl, *m* veil; voile; *f* sail.

voiler, vo'ăh-leh, *v* to veil; to cloak; to conceal.

voilier, vo'ăh-le-eh, *m* sail-maker; sailboat.

voir, vo'ăhr, *v* to see; to behold; to inspect; to visit; to meet.

voire, vo'ăhr, *adv* indeed; nay; even.

voisin, e, vo'ăh-zang, *mf* neighbor; *a* adjoining.

voisinage, vo'ăh-ze-năhsh, *m* neighborhood.

voiture, vo'ăh-tEEr, *f* automobile; cart; carriage.

voix, vo'ăh, *f* voice; tone; vote.

vol, vol, *m* flight; theft.

volage, voll-ăhsh, *a* fickle.

volaille, voll-ah'e, *f* poultry.

volant, voll-ahng, *m* shuttlecock; steering wheel.

vol à l'étalalge, voll-ăh-leh-tăh-lăhsh *m* shoplifting.

volant, e, voll-ahng, *a* flying; loose.

volcan, voll-kahng, *m* volcano.

volée, voll-eh, *f* flight (of birds); flock; volley (of guns); shower (of blows); peal (of bells).

voler, voll-eh, *v* to fly; to soar; to steal; **il ne l'a pas volé,** ill ner lăh păh voll-eh, it serves him right.

volet, voll-ay, *m* shutter.

voleu-r, se, voll-**er**, *mf* thief; robber.

voliére, voll-e-air, *f* aviary.

vol libre, voll-lee-br *m* hang-gliding.

volontaire, voll-*ong*-tair, *m* volunteer; *a** voluntary; headstrong.

volonté, voll-*ong*-teh, *f* will; *pl* whims; caprices.

volontiers, voll-*ong*-te-eh, *adv* willingly.

voltage, voll-tăh**sh,** *m* voltage.

volte-face, voll-ter-făhss, *f* turning round; about-face.

voltiger, voll-te-**sheh,** *v* to flutter; to perform on rope, trapeze, etc.

voltigeur, voll-te-**sher,** *m* performer on rope, trapeze, etc.

volubilité, voll-E-be-le-teh, *f* volubility.

volume, voll-EEm, *m* volume; bulk; mass; size.

volumineu-x, se, voll-E-me-ner, *a* voluminous.

volupté, voll-EEp-teh, *f* voluptuousness; luxury.

vomir, vomm-eer, *v* to vomit; to throw up.

vomissement, vomm-iss-mah*ng*, *m* vomiting.

vomitif, vomm-e-teeff, *m* emetic.

vorace,* vor-ăhss, *a* voracious; ravenous.

voracité, vor-ăhss-e-teh, *f* voracity; ravenousness.

vote, vot, *m* vote; suffrage; poll; division.

voter, vot-eh, *v* to vote.

votre, votr, *poss a* your; *pl* **vos,** voh.

vôtre (le, la, les), ler, lăh, leh voh-tr, *poss pron* yours.

vouer, voo-eh, *v* to devote; to vow; to dedicate.

vouloir, voo-lo'ăh**r,** *v* to be willing; to want; to require; to order; to consent.

vouloir, voo-lo'ăh**r,** *m* will.

voulu, e, voo-lE, *pp* & *a* wanted; required; intentional.

vous, voo, *pers pron* you.

voûte, voot, *f* vault.

vouvoyer, voo-vo'ăh-yeh, *v* to address as **vous.**

voyage, vo'ăh-yăh**sh,** *m* travel; journey; trip.

voyager, vo'ăh-yăh-**sheh,** *v* to travel; to journey.

voyageu-r, se, vo'ăh-yăh-**sher,** *mf* & *a* traveler; passenger; traveling.

voyant, e, vo'ăh-yah*ng*, *mf* fortune-teller; *a* showy; gaudy.

voyelle, vo'ăh-yell, *f* vowel.

voyou, vo'ăh-yoo, *m* hooligan; ruffian.

vrac (en), ah*ng* vrăhck, *adv* in bulk.

vrai, vray, *m* truth.

vrai, e, vray, *a* true; genuine; regular; errant.

vraiment, vray-mah*ng*, *adv* truly; indeed.

vraisemblable,* vray-sah*ng*-blăh-bl, *a* likely.

vraisemblance, vray-sah*ng*-blah*ng*ss, *f* likelihood.

vrille, vree-ye, *f* gimlet.

vu, vE, *prep* seeing; considering; *m* sight; examination.

vu, e, vE, *pp* & *a* seen; examined.

vue, vE, *f* sight; view; prospect; design; purpose.

vulgaire, vEEl-ghair, *m* the common people; *a** vulgar; coarse.

a
b
c
d
e
f
g
h
i
j
k
l
m
n
o
p
q
r
s
t
u
v
w
x
y
z

A B C D E F G H I J K L M N O P Q R S T U V **W** X Y Z

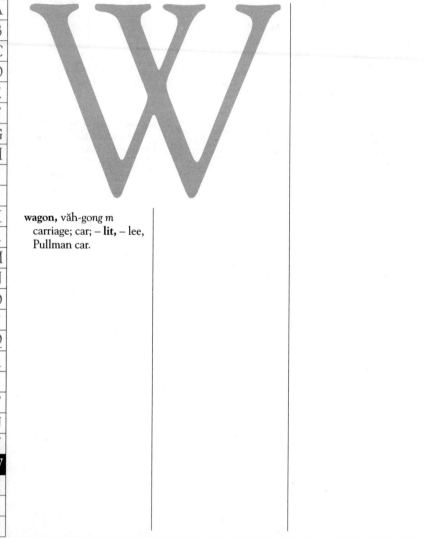

wagon, vǎh-*gong* m
   carriage; car; – **lit,** – lee,
   Pullman car.

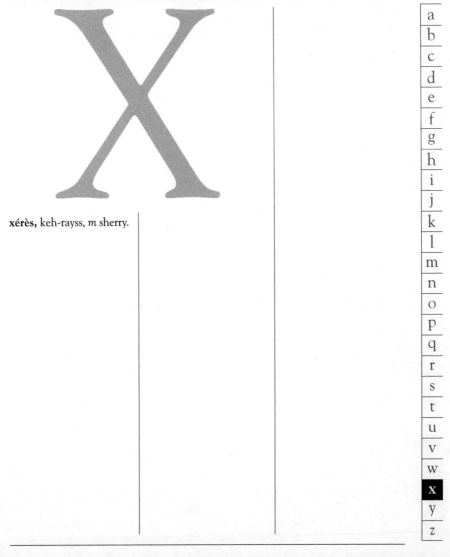

xérès, keh-rayss, *m* sherry.

a
b
c
d
e
f
g
h
i
j
k
l
m
n
o
p
q
r
s
t
u
v
w
x
y
z

y, e, *pron* to it; at it; by it; for it; to them; at them, etc.

y, e, *adv* there; within; – **compris,** – ko*ng*-pree, including.

yaourt, yah-oort, *m* yogurt.

yacht, e-ăhck, *m* yacht.

yeux, e-er, *mpl* eyes.

youyou, yoo-yoo, *m* dinghy.

a
b
c
d
e
f
g
h
i
j
k
l
m
n
o
p
q
r
s
t
u
v
w
x
y
z

zèbre, zay-br, *m* zebra.

zébré, e, zeh-breh, *a* striped.

zéla-teur, trice, zeh-lăh-ter, *mf* zealot.

zèle, zayl, *m* zeal; ardor; earnestness.

zénith, zeh-neet, *m* zenith.

zéphir, zeh-feer, *m* zephyr; gentle breeze.

zeppelin, zehp-lang, *m* zeppelin.

zéro, zeh-ro, *m* zero; (*fig*) cipher; (*fig*) nobody.

zeste, zaysst, *m* zest; peel; zeal.

zézaiement, zeh-zay-mahng, *m* lisping; limp.

zézayer, zeh-zay-yeh, *v* to lisp.

zibeline, zeeb-leen, *f* sable.

zigzaguer, zeeg-zăh-gheh, *v* to stagger; to zigzag.

zinc, zangk, *m* zinc.

zingueur, zang-gher, *m* zinc worker.

zizanie, zze-zah-nee, *f* ill-feeling.

zodiaque, zod-e-ăhck, *m* zodiac.

zona, zoh-năh, *m* shingles.

zone, zohn, *f* zone.

zoo, zoh, *m* (*fam*) zoo.

zoologie, zo-oll-osh-ee, *f* zoology.

zoophyte, zo-off-eet, *m* zoophyte.

zut! zEEt, *interj* (*fam*) nuts!

ENGLISH · FRENCH
ANGLAIS · FRANÇAIS

Pour l'explication de la
prononciation figurée,
lire avec soin la page 5.

A

a, é, *art* un, une.

abandon, *a*-bănn´-d'n, *v* abandonner; **–ed,** *a* abandonné; (morally) dissolu.

abase, *a*-béce´, *v* abaisser; humilier.

abash, *a*-băche´, *v* déconcerter.

abate, *a*-béte´, *v* diminuer.

abbey, ăb´ei, *n* abbay *f*.

abbot, ăb´-otte, *n* abbé *m*.

abbreviate, *a*b-bri´-vi-éte, *v* abréger.

abdicate, ăb´-di-quéte, *v* abdiquer.

abdomen, ăb-dau´-menn, *n* abdomen *m*.

abduction, ăb-doc´-ch'n, *n* enlèvement *m*.

abeyance, *a*-bé´-annce, *n* suspension *f*.

abide, *a*-bâïde´, *v* demeurer; **–by,** s'en tenir à.

ability, *a*-bil´-i-ti, *n* habileté *f*; capacité *f*.

ablaze, *a*-bléze´, *a* en flammes; enflammé.

able, é´-b'l, *a* capable; habile; **to be –,** pouvoir.

abnormal*, ăb-nôr´-m'l, *a* anormal.

aboard, *a*-bôrde´, *adv* à bord.

abode, *a*-bôde´, *n* demeure *f*.

abolish, *a*-bol´-iche, *v* abolir.

abominable, *a*-bomm´-inn-*a*-b'l, *a* abominable.

aboriginal, ab-ŏr-idj´-inn-'l, *a* aborigène.

abortion, *a*-bôr´-ch'n, *n* avortement *m*.

abound, *a*-bâ´´ounnde, *v* abonder.

about, *a*-bâoute´, *adv* environ; à peu près; autour. *prep* auprès de; autour de; au sujet de.

above, *a*-bove´, *adv* en haut; au-dessus; ci-dessus. *prep* au-dessus de; plus de; sur.

abrasion, *a*-bré´-j'n, *n* écorchure *f*.

abreast, *a*-breste´, *adv* de front.

abroad, *a*-brôde´, *adv* à l'étranger.

abrupt*, *a*-bropte´, *a* brusque; (steep) escarpé.

abscess, ăb´-sesse, *n* abcès *m*.

abscond, ăb-skonnde´, *v* s'enfuir; se cacher.

absence, ăb´-sennce, *n* absence *f*.

absent, ăb´-sennte, *a* absent. *v* (– oneself) s'absenter; **–ee,** *n* absent *m* absente *f*; **–minded,** *a* distrait.

absolute*, ăb´-sŏ-lioute, *a* absolu.

absolve, ăb-zolve´, *v* absoudre.

absorb, ăb-sorb´, *v* absorber.

abstain, *a*b-sténe´, *v* s'abstenir de.

abstainer, *a*b-sténe´-'r, *n* abstinent *m*.

a
b
c
d
e
f
g
h
i
j
k
l
m
n
o
p
q
r
s
t
u
v
w
x
y
z

A
B
C
D
E
F
G
H
I
J
K
L
M
N
O
P
Q
R
S
T
U
V
W
X
Y
Z

abstemious*, *ab*-sti´-mi-*euce*, *a* sobre.

abstinence, ăb´-sti-nennce, *n* abstinence *f.*

abstract, ăb-străcte´, *v* abstraire; résumer.

abstract, ăb´-străcte, *n* résumé *m. a* abstrait.

absurd*, ăb-seurde´, *a* absurde.

abundant, *a*-bonne´d'nt, *a* abondant.

abuse, *a*-biouze´, *v* abuser de; injurier.

abuse, *a*-biouce´, *n* abus *m*; injures *fpl.*

abusive*, *a*-biou´-cive, *a* injurieux; abusif.

abyss, *a*-bisse´, *n* abîme *m.*

academy, *a*-kăd´-é-mi, *n* académie *f.*

accede, ăx-îde´, *v* accéder; monter (sur).

accelerate, ăx-el´-é-réte, *v* accélérer.

accent, ăx-ennte´, *v* accentuer.

accent, ăx´-ennte, *n* accent *m.*

accentuate, ăx-ennte´-iou-éte, *v* accentuer.

accept, ăx-epte´, *v* accepter; **–ance,** *n* acceptation *f.*

access, ăx´-esse, *n* accès *m.*

accession, ăx-ech'n, *n* avènement *m.*

accessory, ăx´-ess-ŏ-ri, *n* complice *m*; accessoire *m.*

accident, ăx´-i-dennte, *n* accident *m.*

accidental*, ăx-i-denn´-t'l, *a* accidentel; accessoire.

acclaim, ac-cléme´, *v* acclamer.

accommodate, ac-comm´-mŏ-déte, *v* accommoder; loger; fournir.

accommodation, ac-comm-mŏ-dé´-ch'n, *n* logement *m*; arrangement *m*; aménagement *m.*

accompaniment, ac-comm´-pa-ni-m'nt, *n* accompagnement *m.*

accompanist, ac-comm´-pa-nisste, *n* accompagnateur *m*; accompagnatrice *f.*

accompany, ac-comm´-pa-ni, *v* accompagner.

accomplice, ac-comm´-plisse, *n* complice *m.*

accomplish, ac-comm´-pliche, *v* accomplir.

accomplishment, ac-comm´-pliche-m'nt, *n* accomplissement *m*; **–s,** talents *mpl.*

accord, ac-côrde´, *v* accorder. *n* accord *m*; **of one's own –,** de plein

gré; **in –ance with,** d'accord avec; **–ing to,** *prep* selon, d'après; **–ingly,** *adv* en conséquence

accordion, ac-côr´-di'n, *n* accordéon *m.*

accost, ac-coste´, *v* accoster; aborder.

account, *a*-câ"ounnte´, *n* (bill) compte *m*; **on –,** (payment) en acompte; **–able,** *a* responsable; **–ant,** *n* comptable *m.*

accrue, ac-croue´, *v* provenir (de); s'accumuler.

accumulate, ac-kiou´-miou-léte, *v* (s')accumuler.

accuracy, ă´-kiou-ra-ci, *n* exactitude *f*; précision *f.*

accurate*, ă´-kiou-réte, *a* exact; correct; juste.

accursed, *a*-keur´-st, *a* maudit.

accusation, ac-kiou-zé´-ch'n, *n* accusation *f.*

accuse, *a*-kiouze´, *v* accuser.

accustom, *a*-coss´-t'm, *v* accoutumer; habituer.

ace, éce, *n* (cards) as *m.*

ache, éque, *n* douleur *f*; mal *m. v* faire mal.

achieve, *a*-tchîve´, *v* accomplir; **–ment,** *n* accomplissement *m*;

exploit *m.*

acid, ă´-side, *n & a* acide *m.*

acidity, *a*-side´-i-ti, *n* acidité *f*; (*med*) aigreurs *fpl.*

acknowledge, ăc-nol´-èdje, *v* reconnaître; accuser réception de.

acorn, é´-côrne, *n* gland *m.*

acoustics, *a*-couss´-tiks, *npl* acoustique *f.*

acquaint, *a*-couénnte´, *v* informer; **–ance,** *n* connaissance *f.*

acquiesce, ă-coui-esse´, *v* acquiescer (à).

acquire, *a*-couâïre´, *v* acquérir; apprendre.

acquisition, *a*-coui-zi´-ch'n, *n* acquisition *f.*

acquit, *a*-couitte´, *v* acquitter.

acquittal, *a*-coui´-t'l, *n* acquittement *m.*

acre, é´-*keur, n* acre *m.*

acrid, ăc´-ridde, *a* âcre.

across, *a*-crosse´, *adv* à travers; de l'autre côté. *prep* au travers de.

act, ăcte, *n* action *f*; (deed) acte *m*; (of a play) acte *m*; (law) loi *f. v* agir; (in theater) jouer; **–or,** *n* acteur *m*; **–ress,** actrice *f.*

action, ăk´-ch'n, *n* action

f; procès *m*; combat *m.*

active*, ăc´-tive, *a* actif; alerte; agile.

actual*, ăc´-tiou-*al, a* réel; actuel.

actuate, ăc´-tiou-éte, *v* mettre en action; animer; faire agir.

acumen, *a*-kiou´-mène, *n* perspicacité *f.*

acute, *a*-kioute´, *a* aigu.

acuteness, *a*-kioute´-nesse, *n* acuité *f*; finesse *f.*

adamant, ăd´-*a*-mannte, *a* inflexible.

adapt, *a*-dăpt´, *v* adapter; **–oneself,** s'adapter.

adaptation, *a*-dăpp-té´-ch'n, *n* adaptation *f.*

add, ădde, *v* additionner; **–to,** ajouter à; **–ition,** *n* addition *f*; **–itional,** *a* supplémentaire.

adder, ăd´-*eur, n* (snake) vipère *f.*

addict, ăd´-icte´, *n* personne adonnée (à) *f*; **–ed,** *a* adonné (à).

address, ad-dresse´, *n* adresse *f*; (speech) discours *m*; *v* (letters, etc.) adresser; (a meeting) prendre la parole; **–ee,** *n* destinataire *m & f.*

adequate, ăd´-i-couéte, *a* proportionnel; suffisant.

adhere, ăd-hîre´, *v* adhérer; s'en tenir à; **–nt,** *a & n,* adhérent *m*; partisan *m.*

adhesive, ăd-hî´-cive, *n* colle *f. a* adhésif.

adjacent, *ȧ*d-jé´-sennte, *a* adjacent (à); avoisinant.

adjourn, ad-jeurne´, *v* ajourner; remettre. *n* remise *f.*

adjournment, ad-jeurne´-m'nt, *n* ajournement *m.*

adjunct, ăd´-jonn-kt, *n* accessoire *m. a* adjoint.

adjust, ad-joste´, *v* ajuster; régler.

adjustment, ad-joste´-m'nt, *n* ajustement *m.*

adjutant, ăd´-djou-t'nt, *n* adjudant-major *m.*

administer, ad-minn´-isse-*teur, v* administrer.

admirable, ăd´-mi-ra-b'l, *a* admirable.

admiral, ăd´-mi-ral, *n* amiral *m*; **–ty,** amirauté *f.*

admire, ad-mâïre´, *v* admirer.

admission, ad-mi´-ch'n, *n* admission *f*; entrée *f.*

admit, ad-mitte´, *v* admettre; laisser entrer.

admittance, ad-mit´-t'nce, *n* entrée *f*; aveu *m.*

admonish, ad-monn´-iche, *v* exhorter.

A
B
C
D
E
F
G
H
I
J
K
L
M
N
O
P
Q
R
S
T
U
V
W
X
Y
Z

adopt, *a*-dopte´, *v* adopter.

adore, *a*-daure´, *v* adorer.

adorn, *a*-dôrne´, *v* parer; **–ment,** *n* parure *f*.

adrift, *a*-drifte´, *adv* (*naut*) à la dérive.

adroit*, *a*-drô'ïte´, *a* adroit; habile.

adult, *a*-dolte´, *n* adulte *m* & *f*. *a* adulte.

adulterate, *a*-dol´-té-réte, *v* falsifier; corrompre.

adultery, *a*-dol´-té-ri, *n* adultère *m*.

advance, ăd-vânnce´, *v* avancer; (price) hausser; faire avancer. *n* (progress) progrès *m*; (money) avance *f*; (prices) hausse *f*; **in –,** d'avance; **–ment,** *n* avancement *m*; progrès *m*.

advantage, ăd-vănn´-tèdje, *n* avantage *m*.

advantageous*, ăd-vann-té´-djeusse, *a* avantageux.

advent, ăd´-vennte, *n* venue *f*; (*eccl*) Avent *m*.

adventure, ad-venn´-tioure, *n* aventure *f*.

adventurer, ad-venn´-tiou-r'r, *n* aventurier *m*.

adventurous, ad-venn´-tiou-*reuce*, *a* aventureux.

adversary, ăd´-veur-sa-ri,

n adversaire *m* & f.

adverse*, ăd´-veursse, *a* défavorable; adverse; opposé.

advertise, ăd´-veur-tâïze, *v* annoncer; faire de la réclame.

advertisement, ad-veur´-tize-m'nt, *n* annonce *f*; réclame *f*.

advertising, ăd-veur-tăï´-zinng, *n* publicité *f*.

advice, ad-văïsse´, *n* conseil *m*.

advisable, ad-vâï´-za-b'l, *a* prudent; préférable.

advise, ad-vâïze´, *v* conseiller; aviser.

adviser, ad-vâï´-z'r, *n* conseiller *m*.

advocate, ăd´-vŏ-kéte, *n* avocat *m*. *v* soutenir.

aerial, é-i´-ri-*al*, *n* antenne *f*. *a* aérien.

afar, a-fare´, *adv* loin; de loin; au loin.

affable, ăf´-fa-b'l, *a* affable.

affair, a-faire´, *n* affaire *f*; (love) aventure *f*; liaison *f*.

affect, a-fecte´, *v* affecter; émouvoir; prétendre; **–ed,** *a* (manners, style) maniéré; (moved) affecté, ému; **–ing,** touchant; **–ion,** *n* affection *f*; tendresse *f*.

affectionate*, a-féque´-chŏ-néte, *a* affectueux.

affidavit, ă-fi-dé´-vitte, *n* déposition sous serment *f*.

affiliate, a-fil´-i-éte, *v* affilier.

affinity, a-fine´-i-ti, *n* affinité *f*.

affirm, a-feurme´, *v* affirmer; **–ative*,** *a* affirmatif.

affirmation, ă-feur-mê´-ch'n, *n* affirmation *f*.

affix, a-fixe´, *v* apposer; attacher.

afflict, a-flicte´, *v* affliger; **–ion,** *n* affliction *f*.

affluence, ă-flou-ennce, *n* affluence *f*; opulence *f*.

afford, a-faurde´, *v* avoir les moyens de.

affray, a-fré´, *n* échauffourée *f*; rixe *f*.

affront, a-fronnte´, *n* affront *m*. *v* affronter; insulter.

aflame, a-fléme´, *adv* & *a* enflammé; en flammes.

afloat, a-flôte´, *adv* à flot.

afraid, a-fréde´, **to be –,** *v* avoir peur; être effrayé.

afresh, a-fréche´, *adv* de nouveau.

aft, ăfte, *adv* (*naut*) à l'arrière.

after, âf´-t'r, *adv* après; suivant. *prep* après;

–noon, n après-midi m & f; **–wards,** adv ensuite.

again, a-guénne´, adv encore; de nouveau.

against, a-gué´-n'ste, prep contre.

age, é´-dje, n âge m; (period) siècle m. **to be of –,** v être majeur; **–d,** a âgé; vieux.

agency, é´-djenn-ci, n agence f; entremise f; bureau m.

agenda, ă-djenn´-d'r, n ordre du jour m.

agent, é´-dj'nt, n agent m; représentant m.

aggravate, ăg´-gra-véte, v aggraver; empirer; (fam) agacer.

aggregate, ăg´-gri-guette, v rassembler. n total m.

aggression, a-grè´-ch'n, n agression f; attaque f.

aggressive*, a-gresse´-ive, a agressif.

aggrieve, a-grîve´, v chagriner.

aghast, a-gâsste´, a consterné; bouche bée.

agile, ă-djâil, a agile.

agitate, ă-dji-téte, v agiter.

agitation, a-dji-té´-ch'n, n agitation f.

ago, a-gau´, adv passé; **long –,** il y a longtemps.

agonize, ăg´-o-nâïze, v agoniser; torturer.

agony, ăg´-o-ni, n agonie f; (mental) angoisse f.

agree, a-grî´, v s'accorder; être d'accord; consentir; **–able,** a agréable; **–ment,** n accord m; contrat m.

agricultural, ăg-gri-kol´-tiou-r'l, a agricole.

agriculture, ăg´-gri-kol-tioure, n agriculture f.

aground, a-grâ'ounnde´, adv (naut) échoué.

ahead, a-hêdde´, adv en avant; devant.

aid, éde, n aide f; secours m; v aider.

aids, éds, n sida m.

ail, éle, v avoir mal; **–ing,** a souffrant.

ailment, éle´-m'nt, n maladie f; mal m.

aim, éme, v viser. n but m; visée f; **–less,** a sans but.

air, aire, v aérer; n air m; **–-conditioned,** a climatisé; **–-hostess,** hôtesse de l'air f; **–-plane,** avion m; **–-port,** aéroport m; **–-tight,** a hermétique.

aisle, âïle, n nef f; allée f.

ajar, a-djârre´, a entrouvert.

akin, a-quinne´, a apparenté; de même nature.

alabaster, ăl´-a-băss-t'r, n albâtre m.

alarm, a-lârme´, n alarme f; **–clock,** réveil m.

alarming*, a-lârme´-ing, a alarmant.

album, ăl´-bomme, n album m.

alcohol, ăl-koh-holl, n alcool m.

alert, a-leurte´, a éveillé; **on the –,** sur ses gardes; **–ness,** n vigilance f; vivacité f.

alias, é-li-ăsse, adv autrement dit. n nom supposé m.

alibi, ăl´-i-bâï, n alibi m.

alien, é´-lienne, n étranger m. a étranger.

alight, a-lâïte´, v descendre de; se poser sur; (aero) atterrir. a allumé; en flammes.

alike, a-lâïke´, adv également. a semblable.

alive, a-lâïve´, a vivant; éveillé.

all, oale, adv entièrement. a tout; **–right,** adv très bien; **not at –,** pas du tout.

allay, a-lé´, v adoucir; calmer.

allege, a-lèdje´, v alléguer; **–d,** a présumé.

allegiance, a-li´-dji-annce, n allégeance f.

A B C D E F G H I J K L M N O P Q R S T U V W X Y Z

allergic, *a-leur´-*djique, *a* allergique.

alleviate, *a-*li´-vi-éte, *v* adoucir; soulager.

alley, ăl´-lie, *n* ruelle *f*; allée *f*; **blind –,** impasse *f*.

alliance, *a-*lâï´-*a*nnce, *n* alliance *f*.

allied, ăl´-lâïde, *a* allié.

allot, *a-*lotte´, *v* assigner; **–ment,** *n* part *f*.

allow, *a-*lâ'ou´, *v* allouer; permettre; admettre

allowance, *a-*lâ'ou´-*a*nnce, *n* concession *f*; (monetary) allocation *f*; (rebate) remisé *f*; argent de poche.

alloy, *a-*lôïe´, *n* alliage *m*. *v* allier.

allude, *a-*lioude´, *v* faire allusion (à).

allure, *a-*lioure´, *v* attirer; séduire.

alluring, *a-*liou´-rinng, *a* alléchant.

allusion, *a-*liou´-j'n, *n* allusion *f*.

ally, *a-*lâï´, *n* allié *m*. *v* allier.

Almighty, oal-mâï´-ti, *n* Tout-Puissant *m*.

almond, â´-mŏnnde, *n* amande *f*.

almost, oale´-mauste, *adv* presque.

aloft, *a-*lofte´, *adv* en l'air.

alone, *a-*laune´, *a* seul; solitaire.

along, *a-*lonng´, *prep* le long de.

aloof, *a-*loufe´, *adv* & *a* distant; réservé.

aloud, *a-*lâ'oude´, *adv* à haute voix; tout haut.

already, oal-redd´-i, *adv* déjà.

also, oal´-sau, *adv* aussi; également.

altar, oal´-t'r, *n* autel *m*.

alter, oal´-t'r, *v* changer; modifier.

alteration, oal-teur-é´-ch'n, *n* modification *f*.

alternate*, oal-teur´-néte, *a* alternatif.

alternating, oal-teur-né´-tinng, *a* alternant.

alternative, oal-teur´-né-tive, *n* alternative *f*.

although, oal-dʒau´, *conj* quoique; bien que.

altitude, ăl´-ti-tioude, *n* altitude *f*; élévation *f*.

altogether, oal-tou-gué´-dʒeur, *adv* tout à fait.

aluminium, *a-*lioue-mine´-i-omme, *n* aluminium *m*.

always, oal´-ouèze, *adv* toujours.

amass, *a-*măsse´, *v* amasser.

amateur, ămm´-*a-*tioure, *n* amateur *m*.

amaze, *a-*méze´, *v* étonner; stupéfier; ébahir.

amazement, *a-*méze´-m'nt, *n* stupéfaction *f*.

ambassador, am-băss´-*a-*deur, *n* ambassadeur *m*.

amber, ămm´-b'r, *n* ambre *m*.

ambiguous*, ămm-bi´-ghiou-*e*usse, *a* ambigu.

ambition, amm-bi-ch'n, *n* ambition *f*.

ambitious*, amm-bi´-cheusse, *a* ambitieux.

ambulance, ămm´-biou-l'nse, *n* ambulance *f*.

ambush, ămm´-bouche, *n* embuscade *f*.

ameliorate, *a-*mill´-ior-éte, *v* améliorer.

amenable, *a-*mî´-na-b'l, *a* disposé à; justiciable de.

amend, *a-*mennde´, *v* modifier; corriger; réformer; **–ment,** *n* modification *m*; **make –s,** *v* dédommager (de).

amenity, *a-*mî-nit-ti, *n* agrément *m*; commodité *f*.

amethyst, ămm´-î-*ts*ist, *n* améthyste *f*.

amiable, é´-mi-*a*-b'l, *a* aimable.

amicable, ămm´-i-ca-b'l, *a* amical.

amid, amidst, *a-*midde´, *a-*midste´, *prep* au milieu

de; –**ships,** *adv* par le travers.

amiss, *a*-mice´, *a* de travers. *adv* mal; **take –,** prendre en mauvaise part.

ammonia, *a*-mau´-ni-*a*, *n* ammoniaque *f.*

ammunition, ămm-ioue-ni´-ch'n, *n* munitions *fpl.*

amnesty, ămm´-nesse-ti, *n* amnistie *f.*

among(st), *a*-monng´(ste), *prep* parmi.

amorous*, ămm´-o-*re*uce, *a* amoureux.

amount, *a*-mâ´´ounnte, *n* montant *m*; quantité *f*; *v* s'élever à.

ample, ămm´-p'l, *a* ample; abondant.

amplify, ămm´-pli-fâï, *v* amplifier.

amputate, amm´-pioue-téte, *v* amputer.

amuse, *a*-miouze´, *v* amuser.

amusement, *a*-miouze´-m'nt, *n* amusement *m.*

an, ănne, *art* un; une.

analogous, *a*-năl´-o-gue*u*sse, *a* analogue.

analysis, *a*-nă´-li-sice, *n* analyse *f.*

analyze, ănn´-*a*-lâïze, *v* analyser.

anarchy, ănn´-ar-ki, *n* anarchie *f.*

ancestor, ănn´-cèsse-*te*ur, *n* ancêtre *m* & *f.*

anchor, ain´-n'g-*ke*ur, *n* ancre *f. v* ancrer.

anchorage, ain´-n'g-*ke*ur-édje, *n* mouillage *m*; ancrage *m*

anchovy, ănn-tchô´-vi, *n* anchois *m.*

ancient*, énn´-tchi-ennte, *a* ancien; âgé.

and, ănnde, *conj* et.

anesthetize, *a*-nîce-*tz*-eur-tâïze, *v* anesthésier.

angel, énne´-dj'l, *n* ange *m.*

anger, ain´-n'g*he*ur, *n* colère *f. v* mettre en colère.

angina, ănn-djâï´-n*a*, *n* angine *f*; – pectoris; anginede poitrine.

angle, ain´-n'gl, *n* angle *m. v* (fish) pêcher à la ligne; **–r,** *n* pêcheur à la ligne *m.*

angling, ain´-n'glinng, *n* pêche à la ligne *f.*

angry, ain´-n'gri, *a* en colère; (vexed) irrité.

anguish, ain´-n'gouiche, *n* angoisse *f.*

animal, ă´-ni-m*a*l, *n* & *a* animal *m.*

animate, ănn´-i-méte, *v* animer; **–d,** *a* animé.

animosity, *a*-ni-mo´-zi-ti,

n animosité *f.*

aniseed, ănn´-i-sîde, *n* anis *m.*

ankle, ain´-n'kl, *n* cheville *f.*

annals, ănn´-*a*lz, *npl* annales *fpl.*

annex, *a*-nex´, *v* annexer; *n* annexe *f.*

annihilate, *a*-nâï´-hi-léte, *v* anéantir; annihiler.

anniversary, *a*-ni-veur´-*se*u-ri, *n* anniversaire de mariage *m.*

annotate, ănn´-nau-téte, *v* annoter.

announce, *a*-nâ´´ounnce, *v* annoncer.

annoy, *a*-noa'ï´, *v* ennuyer.

annoyance, *a*-noa'ï-n'se, *n* désagrément *m.*

annual, ă´-niou-*e*ul, *n* annuaire *m. a** annuel.

annuity, *a*-niou´-i-ti, *n* rente annuelle *f.*

annul, *a*-nol´, *v* annuler; **–ment,** *n* annulation *f.*

anoint, *a*-nô'ïnnte´, *v* oindre.

anomalous, *a*-nom´-*a*-le*u*ce, *a* abnormal.

anonymous*, *a*-no´-ni-m*eu*ce, *a* anonyme.

another, *a*-nod*z*r´, *a* un(e) autre.

answer, ănn´-s'r, *v* répondre; résoudre. *n* réponse *f.*

a
b
c
d
e
f
g
h
i
j
k
l
m
n
o
p
q
r
s
t
u
v
w
x
y
z

A
B C D E F G H I J K L M N O P Q R S T U V W X Y Z

ant, ănnte, n fourmi f.

antagonist, ănn-tăgue´-au-nist, n antagoniste m.

antecedent, ănn-ti-ci´-dennte, n & a antécédent m.

antedate, ănn´-ti-déte, v antidater; avancer.

antelope, ănn´-ti-laupe, n antilope f.

anterior, ănn-ti´-ri-eur, a antérieur.

anteroom, ănn´-ti-roume, n antichambre f.

anthem, ănn´-tzème, n hymne national m.

anticipate, ănn-ti´-ci-péte, v anticiper; s'attendre à.

anticipation, ănn-tice-i-pé´-ch'n, n anticipation f; attente f.

antics, ănn´-tikss, npl gambades fpl; singeries fpl.

antidote, ănn´-ti-daute, n antidote m.

antifreeze, ănn´ti-frîze, n anti-gel m inv.

antipathy, ănn-ti´-pa-tsi, n antipathie f.

antipodes, ănn-ti´-pŏ-dize, npl antipodes mpl.

antiquarian, ănn-ti-coué´-ri-anne, n antiquaire m.

antiquated, ănn´-ti-coué-tedde, a vieilli; suranné.

antique, ănn-tique´, n antiquité f. a ancien.

antiseptic, ănn-ti-sepp´-tique, n & a antiseptique m.

antler, ănn´-t'leur, n (stag, etc) bois mpl.

anvil, ănn´-vil, n enclume f.

anxiety, aingue-zâï´-é-ti, n inquiétude f; anxiété.

anxious, aink´-chieuce, a inquiet; désireux.

any, ènn´-i, a quelque; l'un ou l'autre; –**body,** pron quelqu'un; –**how,** adv de toute façon; n'importe comment; –**one,** pron n'importe lequel; –**where,** n'importe où.

apart, a-pârte´, adv à part; en dehors.

apartment, a-pârte´-m'nt, n appartement m.

apathy, ă´-pa-tsi, n apathie f.

ape, épe, n singe sans queue m.

aperture, ă´-peur-tioure, n ouverture f; orifice m.

apologize, a-pol´-ŏ-djâïze, v faire des excuses.

apology, a-pol´-ŏ-dji, n excuses fpl.

apostle, a-po´-s'l, n apôtre m.

appall, a-poal´, v épouvanter; –**ling,** a épouvantable.

apparatus, ăp-pa-ré´-teuce, n appareil m.

apparent*, a-pă´-rennte, a évident; apparent.

apparition, ăp-pa-ri´-ch'n, n apparition f.

appeal, a-pîle, v faire appel; attirer. n appel m.

appear, a-pîre´, v paraître; sembler; (law) comparaître.

appearance, a-pî´-r'ns, n apparence f.

appease, a-pîze´, v apaiser; –**ment,** n apaisement m.

append, a-pennde´, v apposer; annexer; attacher.

appendix, ăp-penne´-dikse, n appendice m; annexe f.

appetite, ăp´-pi-tâïte, n appétit m.

appetizing, ăp´-pi-tâï-zing, a appétissant.

applaud, a-ploade´, v applaudir.

applause, a-ploaze´, n applaudissement m.

apple, ăpp´-'l, n pomme f; –**tree,** pommier m.

appliance, a-plâï´-annce, n appareil m, instrument m; electro ménager m.

applicant, ă´-pli-k'nt, n candidat m.

application, ăp-pli-ké´-ch'n, n demande f;

application.

apply, *a*-plâï´, *v* appliquer; solliciter; **–to,** s'adresser à; **–for a job,** poser sa candidature.

appoint, *a*-pô'ïnnte´, *v* nommer; **–ment,** *n* rendez vous *m*; nomination *f*; situation *f*.

apportion, *a*-pôr´-ch'n, *v* répartir.

appraise, *a*-préze´, *v* évaluer; **–r,** *n* commissaire priseur *m*; **appraisal,** évaluation *f*.

appreciable, ăp-pri´-chi-*a*-b'l, *a* appréciable.

appreciate, *a*-pri´-chi-éte, *v* apprécier.

appreciation, ăp-pri-chi-é´-ch'n, *n* appréciation *f*.

apprehend, ăp-pri-hennde´, *v* saisir; craindre.

apprehension, ăp-pri-henn´-ch'n, *n* crainte *f*; arrestation *f*.

apprehensive*, ăp-pri-henn´-cive, *a* craintif.

apprentice, *a*-prenn´-tice, *v* mettre en apprentissage. *n* apprenti *m*; **–ship,** apprentissage *m*.

approach, *a*-prautche´, *v* (s')approcher (de).

appropriate*, *a*-prau´-pri-

éte, *a* convenable.

approval, *a*-prou´-v'l, *n* approbation *f*.

approve, *a*-prouve´, *v* approuver.

approximate*, *a*-prox´-i-méte, *a* approximatif.

apricot, é´-pri-cotte, *n* abricot *m*.

April, é´prile, *n* avril *m*.

apron, é´-preune, *n* tablier *m*.

apt, ăpte, *a* apte; propre à; enclin à.

aptitude, ăp´-ti-tioude, *n* aptitude *f*; disposition *f*.

aqueduct, ă´-coui-dokte, *n* aqueduc *m*.

aqueous, ă´-coui-*eu*ce, *a* aqueux.

aquiline, ă´-coui-linne, *a* aquilin.

arable, ăr´-*a*-b'l, *a* labourable.

arbitrary, ăr´-bi-tra-ri, *a* arbitraire.

arbitrate, âr´-bi-tréte, *v* arbitrer; juger.

arbitration, ăr´-bi-tré-ch'n, *n* arbitrage *m*.

arbitrator, âr´-bi-tré-*teu*r, *n* arbitre *m*.

arbor, âr-*beu*r, *n* tonnelle *f*.

arc, ărc, *n* arc *m*; **–-lamp,** lampe à arc *f*.

arcade, ăr-kéde´, *n* arcade *f*, galerie *f*.

arch, ârtche, *n* arche *f*; **–way,** vôute *f*.

arch, ărtche, *a* archi–;
–bishop, *n* archevêque *m*; **–deacon,** archidiacre *m*; **–duke,** archiduc *m*.

archer, ărtch´-*eu*r, *n* archer *m*; **–y,** tir à l'arc *m*.

architect, ăr´-ki-tecte, *n* architecte *m*.

archives, âr´-kâïvz, *npl* archives *fpl*.

arctic, ărc´-tik, *a* arctique.

ardent, âr´-d'nt, *a* ardent; véhément.

ardor, âr´-*deu*r, *n* ardeur *f*; zèle *m*.

arduous*, âr´-diou-*eu*ce, *a* ardu; difficile.

area, ai´-ri-*a*, *n* surface *f*; zone *f*; région *f*.

arena, *a*-ri´-na, *n* arène *f*.

argue, âr´-ghiou, *v* raisonner; discuter; se disputer.

argument, âr´-ghiou-m'nt, *n* argument *m*; discussion *f*.

arise, *a*-râîze´, *v* s'élever; provenir de.

aristocracy, ă-rice-to´-cra-ci, *n* aristocratie *f*.

aristocratic, ă-rice´-to-cra´-tik, *a* aristocratique.

arithmetic, *a*-rits´-mé-tique, *n* arithmétique *f*.

ark, ărque, *n* arche *f*;

a
b
c
d
e
f
g
h
i
j
k
l
m
n
o
p
q
r
s
t
u
v
w
x
y
z

Noah's –, arche de Noé *f.*

arm, ărme, *n* bras *m*; **– chair,** fauteuil *m*; **–ful,** brassée *f*; **–let,** brassard *m*; **–pit,** aisselle *f*.

arm, ârme, *v* armer; **–ament,** *n* armement *m*; **–or,** armure *f*; blindage *m*; **–ored,** *a* blindé; **–ory,** *n* armurerie *f*; **–s,** (*mil*) armes *fpl*; (heraldry) armoiries *fpl*; **–y,** armée *f*.

aromatic, *a*-rau-mă´-tik, *a* aromatique *n*; aromate *m*.

around, *a*-ră'ounnde´, *prep* autour de. *adv* à l'entour.

arouse, *a*-râ'ouze´, *v* exciter; (awake) éveiller.

arrange, *a*-réne´-dje, *v* arranger; disposer.

array, *a*-ré´, *v* ranger; revêtir. *n* ordre *m*.

arrears, *a*-rirze´, *npl* arrérages *mpl*; **to be in –** être en retard; âvoir de l'arriéré.

arrest, *a*-reste´, *v* arrêter. *n* arrestation *f*.

arrival, *a*-râï´-v'l, *n* arrivée *f*; (com) arrivage *m*.

arrive, *a*-râïve´, *v* arriver.

arrogant, ăr´-ro-gannte, *a* arrogant.

arrow, ăr´-rau, *n* flèche *f*.

arsenal, âr´-s'n-'l, *n* arsenal *m*.

arson, âr´-s'n, *n* incendie par malveillance *m*.

art, ărte, *n* art *m*; habileté *f*.

artery, âr´-*teur*-i, *n* artère *f*.

artful, ârte´-foull, *a* (sly) rusé.

artichoke, âr´-ti-tchauke, *n* artichaut *m*; **Jerusalem–,** *n* topinambour *m*.

article, âr´-ti-k'l, *n* article *m*; clause *f*.

articulate, ăr-ti´-kiou-léte, *v* articuler. *a* articulé.

artifice, âr´-ti-fisse, *n* artifice *m*; ruse *f*.

artificial*, âr-ti-fi´-ch'l, *a* artificiel.

artillery, âr-til´-*eur*-i, *n* artillerie *f*.

artisan, âr´-ti-zănne, *n* artisan *m*.

artist, âr´-tisste, *n* artiste *m & f*.

artless*, ârte´-lesse, *a* simple; naïf.

as, ăze, *conj* comme; car; aussi; que; à mesure que; puisque; **–for, –to,** quant à; **–soon –,** aussitôt que; **–well,** aussi.

asbestos, ass-bess´-teuce, *n* amiante *m*.

ascend, *a*-cennde´, *v* monter.

ascendancy, *a*-cenn´-denn-ci, *n* ascendant *m*.

ascent, *a*-cennte´, *n* ascension *f*; montée *f*.

ascertain, *a-seur*-téne´, *v* s'assurer de; constater.

ascribe, ass-crâïbe´, *v* attribuer; imputer.

ash, ăche, *n* cendre *f*; (tree) frêne *m*; **–tray,** cendrier *m*.

ashamed, *a*-chémmde´, *a* honteux.

ashore, *a*-chaure´, *adv* à terre; (naut) échoué.

aside, *a*-sâïde, *adv* de côté; à l'écart; à part.

ask, ăske, *v* demander; inviter.

askew, ass-kiou´, *adv* de travers.

asleep, *a*-slîpe´, *a* endormi; **fall –,** *v* s'endormir.

asp, ăspe, *n* (snake) aspic *m*.

asparagus, ass-păr´-*a*-gheuce, *n* asperge *f*.

aspect, ăss´-pecte, *n* aspect.

aspen, ăss´-p'n, *n* tremble *m*.

asphyxia, ass-fik´-si-a, *n* asphyxie *f*.

aspirate, ăss´-pi-réte, *v* aspirer. *a* aspiré.

aspire, ass-pâïre´, *v*

aspirer (à).

assail, *a*-céle´, *v* assaillir; **–ant,** *n* assaillant *m*.

assassinate, *a*-săss´-i-néte, *v* assassiner.

assault, *a*-soalte´, *v* attaquer. *n* attaque *f*.

assay, *a*-cé´, *v* (metals) essayer. *n* essai *m*.

assemble, *a*-cemm´-b'l, *v* assembler; se réunir.

assembly, *a*-cemm´-bli, *n* assemblée *f*; montage *m*.

assent, *a*-cennte´, *n* assentiment *m*. *v* consentir à.

assert, *a*-seurte´, *v* affirmer; revendiquer; **–ion,** *n* assertion *f*; revendication *f*.

assess, *a*-cesse´, *v* taxer; évaluer.

assessment, *a*-cesse´-m'nt, *n* évaluation *f*.

asset, ăs´-sèt, *n* avoir *m*.

assets, ăs-sètse, *npl* actif *m*.

assiduous, *a*-ci´-diou-euce, *a* appliqué; assidu.

assign, *a*-sâïne´, *v* assigner à; (law) transférer; **–ee,** *n* cessionnaire *m*; **–ment,** transfert *m*.

assist, *a*-ciste´, *v* aider; secourir.

assistant, *a*-ciss´-t'nt, *n* aide *m*; commis *m*. *a* auxiliaire.

associate, *a*-sau´-chi-éte, *v* associer. *n* associé *m*.

assort, *a*-sôrte´, *v* assortir.

assortment, *a*-sôrte´-m'nt, *n* assortiment *m*.

assuage, *a*-souédje, *v* calmer; adoucir.

assume, *a*-sioume´, *v* supposer; prendre sur soi.

assuming, *a*-siou´-minng, *a* prétentieux; arrogant.

assumption, *a*-sommp´-ch'n, *n* présomption *f*.

assurance, *a*-chou´-r'ns, *n* assurance *f*.

assure, *a*-choure´, *v* assurer.

asterisk, ăss´-teu-risque, *n* astérisque *f*.

astern, *a*-steurne´, *adv* (naut) à l'arrière.

asthma, ăss´-ma, *n* asthme *m*.

astir, *a*-steur´, *a* en mouvement; (up) debout.

astonish, ass-tonn´-iche, *v* étonner.

astound, ass-tâ'ounnde´, *v* stupéfier; ébahir.

astray, ass-tré´, *a* égaré.

astride, ass-trăïde´, *adv* à califourchon.

astronaut, ass´-tro-nôt, *n* astronaute *m*.

astute*, ass-tioute´, *a* fin; avisé.

asylum, *a*-sâï´-leume, *n* asile *m*.

at, ătte, *prep* à; chez.

athlete, ă´-*ts*lite, *n* athlète *m*.

atmosphere, atte´-moss-fire, *n* atmosphère *f*; (*fam*) ambiance *f*.

atom, ă´-tŏme, *n* atome *m*.

atomizer, ă´-to-mâï-z'r, *n* vaporisateur *m*; atomiseur *m*.

atone, *a*-taune´, *v* expier; **–ment,** *n* expiation *f*.

atrocious*, *a*-trau´-cheuce, *a* atroce.

atrophy, ât´-rau-fi, *n* atrophie *f*. *v* atrophier.

attach, *a*-tătche´, *v* attacher; joindre; (law) saisir.

attachment, *a*-tătch´-m'nt, *n* attachement *m*.

attack, *a*-tăque´, *v* attaquer. *n* attaque *f*.

attain, *a*-téne´, *v* atteindre; **–ment,** *n* talent *m*.

attempt, *a*-temmpte´, *v* tenter; essayer. *n* tentative *f*; essai *m*; (crime) attentat *m*.

attend, *a*-ntende´, *v* assister à; **–to,** s'occuper de.

attendance, *a*-tenn´d'ns, *n* service *m*; auditoire *m*; présence *f*.

a
b
c
d
e
f
g
h
i
j
k
l
m
n
o
p
q
r
s
t
u
v
w
x
y
z

A
B
C
D
E
F
G
H
I
J
K
L
M
N
O
P
Q
R
S
T
U
V
W
X
Y
Z

attendant, *a*-tenn´-d'nt, *n* ouvreuse *f.*

attention, *a*-tenn´-ch'n, *n* attention *f.*

attest, *a*-teste´, *v* attester.

attic, ăt´-tique, *n* grenier *m;* mansarde *f.*

attire, *a*-tâïre´, *v* vêtir; parer. *n* vêtements *mpl.*

attitude, ăt´-ti-tioude, *n* attitude *f;* pose *f.*

attorney, *a*-teur´-ni, *n* avoué *m;* **power of** –,procuration *f.*

attract, *a*-trăcte´, *v* attirer; –**ion,** *n* attraction *f;* (personal) attrait *m;* –**ive,** *a* attirant; sédûisant.

attribute, *a*-tri´-bioute, *v* attribuer. *n* attribut *m.*

auburn, ô´-beurne, *a* auburn.

auction, ôque´-ch'n, *n* vente aux enchères *f.*

auctioneer, ôque´-ch'n-îre, *n* commissaire-priseur *m.*

audacious*, ô-dé´-cheuce, *a* audacieux.

audacity, ô-dăss´-i-ti, *n* audace *f.*

audible, ô´-di-b'l, *a* distinct; intelligible.

audience, ô´-di-ennce, *n* (assembly) auditoire *m;* spectateurs *mpl.*

audit, ô´-ditte, *v* apurer; vérifer; –**or,** *cn* censeur *m;* vérificateur *m.*

augment, ôgue-mennte´, *v* augmenter.

augur, ô´-gueur, *v* augurer. *n* augure *m.*

August, ô´-gueusste, *n* août *m.*

august, ô-gueusste´, *a* auguste.

aunt, ânnte, *n* tante *f.*

auspicious*, ôss-pi´-cheuce, *a* propice.

austere, ô-stîre´, *a* austère.

authentic, ô-tsenn´-tique, *a* authentique.

author, ô´-tseur, *n* auteur *m.*

authoritative, ô-tsor´-i-ta-tive, *a* autoritaire.

authority, ô-tsor´-i-ti, *n* autorité *f.*

authorize, ô-tsŏr-âï´ze, *v* autoriser.

automatic, ô-tŏ-mătt´-ique, *a* automatique.

autumn, ô´-teumme, *n* automne *m.*

auxiliary, ôg-zil´-i-a-ri, *a* auxiliaire.

avail, *a*-véle´, *n* avantage *m;* utilité *f.* *v* servir à; –**oneself of,** profiter de.

available, *a*-véle´-a-b'l, *a* valable; disponible.

avalanche, ă´-va-lanche, *n* avalanche *f.*

avarice, ă´-va-risse, *n* avarice *f.*

avaricious*, a-va-ri´-cheuce, *a* avare.

avenge, *a*-venndje´, *v* venger.

avenue, ă´-vi-ni'ou, *n* avenue *f.*

average, ă´-veu-rédje, *n* moyenne *f.* *a* moyen.

aversion, *a*-veur´-ch'n, *n* aversion *f;* répugnance *f.*

avert, *a*-veurte´, *v* détourner; écarter.

aviary, é´-vi-a-ri, *n* volière *f.*

aviation, é-vi-é´-ch'n, *n* aviation *f.*

avidity, *a*-vid´-i-ti, *n* avidité *f.*

avoid, *a*-vô´ïde´, *v* éviter.

await, *a*-ouéte´, *v* attendre.

awake, *a*-ouéque´, *v* s'éveiller; réveiller.

awakening, *a*-ouéque´-ninng, *n* réveil *m.*

award, *a*-ouôrde´, *v* adjuger; accorder; (prize) décerner. *n* récompense *f;* prix *m.*

aware, *a*-ouère´, **to be** –,*v* savoir; être au courant.

away, *a*-oué´, *adv* absent; loin; **far** –, au loin.

awe, oa, *n* crainte *f;* admiration *f;* **to be held in awe by someone,** en imposer à quelqu'un; **to**

stand in awe of someone, avoir une crainte respectueuse de quelqu'un.

awful, oa´-foull, *a* terrible; imposant.

awhile, *a*-ou'âïle´, *adv* pour un instant.

awkward, oa´-koue*u*rde, *a* gêné; (clumsy) gauche; **–ness,** *n* gaucherie *f.*

awning, oann´-inng, *n* banne *f.*

awry, *a*-râï´, *adv* de travers.

ax, ăx, *n* hache *f.*

axis, ăk´-siss, *n* axe *m.*

axle, ăk´-s'l, *n* essieu *m.*

azure, ă´-jioure, *n* azur *m.*

a
b
c
d
e
f
g
h
i
j
k
l
m
n
o
p
q
r
s
t
u
v
w
x
y
z

babble, băb´-b'l, *n* babil *m*. *v* babiller.

baby, bé´-bi, *n* bébé *m*.

bachelor, bătch´-eul-eur, *n* célibataire *m*; bachelier *m*.

back, băque, *n* dos *m*; arrière *m*. *v* (support) soutenir; (car) aller en arrière. *adv* (behind) en arrière; (return) de retour; **–bone,** *n* épine dorsale *f*; **–ground,** fond *m*; **–ward,** *adv* en arrière. *a* (mentally) arriéré.

bacon, bé´-k'n, *n* lard *m*.

bad, bădde, *a* mauvais; méchant; **–ly,** *adv* mal; gravement.

badge, bàdje, *n* insigne *m*.

badger, băd´-jeur, *n* blaireau *m*. *v* harceler.

baffle, băf´-f'l, *v* déjouer; confondre, déconcerter.

bag, băgue, *n* sac *m*. *v* mettre en sac.

baggage, băgg´-idje, *n* bagage *m*.

bail, béle, *v* cautionner. *n* caution *f*; **out on –,** sous caution.

bailiff, bé´-liff, *n* huissier *m*.

bait, béte, *n* appât *m*. *v* amorcer; (molest) tourmenter.

bake, béque, *v* cuire au four; **–r,** *n* boulanger *m*; **–ry,** boulangerie *f*.

balaclava, *n* băla´-kla-vas, *n* passe-montagne *m*.

balance, băl´-n'ce, *v* équilibrer; balancer. *n* équilibre *m*; (com.) solde *m*; **–sheet,** bilan *m*.

balcony, băl´-kau-ni, *n* balcon *m*.

bald, boalde, *a* chauve; **–ness,** *n* calvitie *f*.

bale, béle, *n* balle *f*; ballot *m*. *v* emballer; (*naut*) écoper.

balk, boak, *v* frustrer; contrarier.

ball, boale, *n* balle *f*; (hard) boule *f*; (foot) ballon *m*; (dance) bal *m*.

ballast, băl´-aste, *n* lest *m*. *v* (weight) lester.

ballet, băl´-lay, *n* ballet *m*.

balloon, bal-loune´, *n* ballon *m*.

ballot, băl´-lŏtte, *v* voter. *n* scrutin *m*.

ballpoint, boale poa´´innte, *n* stylo à bille *m*.

balm, bâ´me, *n* baume *m*.

bamboo, bămm-bou´, *n* bambou *m*.

ban, bănne, *n* ban *m*; interdiction *f*. *v* interdir.

banana, ba-na´-na, *n* banane *f*.

band, bănnde, *n* bande *f*; (brass) fanfare *f*; (string) orchestre *m*; (ribbon) bandeau *m*; (gang) bande *f*. *v* se liguer; **–age,** *n* bandage *m*; **–leader,** chef de musique *m*.

bandy, bănn´-di, *a* bancal.

bang, bain-nng, *v* claquer (door); frapper; cogner. *n* détonation *f*; claquement *m*.

banish, bănn´-iche, *v* bannir.

banister, bănn´-iss-t'r, *n* rampe *f*.

bank, bain´-nk, *n* banque *f*; (river) rive *f*; (mound) talus *m*. *v* (money) déposer dans une banque; **–er,** *n* banquier *m*; **–ing- account,** compte en banque *m*; **–- note,** billet de banque *m*; **–rupt,** *a* insolvable; en banque route; **–ruptcy,** *n* faillite *f*.

banner, bann´-eur, *n* bannière *f*; étendard *m*.

banquet, bănn´-couette, *n* banquet *m*; festin *m*.

banter, bănn´-teur, *n* raillerie *f*. *v* railler.

baptism, băp´-tizme, *n* baptême *m*.

bar, bâre, *n* bar *m*, (metal) barre *f*; (law) barreau *m*. *v* barrer; defendre.

barb, bârbe, *n* barbe *f*; **–ed,** *a* barbelé.

barbarian, bâre-bé´-ri-ann, *n* & *a* barbare *mf*.

barbarity, bâre-băr´-i-ti, *n* barbarie *f*.

barber, bâre-beur, *n* barbier *m*; coiffeur *m*.

bare, bère, *v* mettre à nu. *a* nu; **–-faced,** effronté; **–-footed,** nu-pieds; **–ly,** *adv* à peine; **–ness,** *n* nudité *f*; dénuement *m*.

bargain, bâre´-guinne, *v* marchander. *n* occasion *f*; bonne affaire *f*.

barge, bârdje, *n* chaland *m*; péniche *f*.

bark, bârque, *v* aboyer. *n* aboiement *m*; (tree) écorce *f*.

barley, bâre´-li, *n* orge *f*.

barn, bâre-'n, *n* grange *f*.

barometer, ba-ro´-mi-teur, *n* baromètre *m*.

baron, bă´-reune, *n* baron *m*; **–ess,** baronne *f*.

barracks, băr´-axe, *npl* caserne *f*.

barrel, băr´-el, *n* tonneau *m*; (gun) canon de fusil *m*.

barren, băr´-enne, *a* stérile; (land) aride.

barrier, băr´-i-eur, *n* barrière *f*.

barrow, bâr´-au, *n* brouette *f*.

barter, bâre´-teur, *v* échanger. *n* échange *m*.

base, béce, *v* baser. *n* base *f*. *a** vil; **–less,** sans fondement; **–ment,** *n* sous-sol *m*; **–ness,** bassesse *f*.

bash, băch, *v* cogner; *n* coup *m*.

bashful*, bâche´-foull, *a* timide.

bashfulness, bâche´-foull-nesse, *n* timidité *f*.

basin, bé´-s'n, *n* (bowl) bol *m*; (wash) lavabo *m*.

basis, bé´-cisse, *n* base *f*; fondement *m*.

bask, bâsque, *v* se chauffer au soleil.

basket, bâsse´-kett, *n* panier *m*; corbeille *f*.

bass, béce, *n* basse *f*; (fish) bar *m*.

bassoon, băss´oun, *n* basson *m*.

baste, béste, *v* (cooking) arroser de graisse; (sewing) bâtir; faufiler.

bat, bătte, *n* bat *m*; (animal) chauve-souris *f*.

batch, bătche, *n* fournée *f*; (articles, etc.) tas *m*.

bath, bâ*t*s, *n* bain *m*; (tub) baignoire *f*; **–room,** salle de bain *f*.

bathe, bé-*dz*e, *v* se baigner; **–r,** *n* baigneur *m*; baigneuse *f*; **bathing suit,** *n* maillot de bain *m*.

batter, bătt´-eur, *n* pâte à friture *f*. *v* démolir.

battery, băt´-trî, *n* pile *f*; batterie *f*.

battle, bătt´-'l, *n* bataille *f*;

–ship, cuirassé *m.*

bawl, boal, *v* brailler.

bay, bé, *n* (*geog*) baie *f. a* (color) bai. *v* aboyer (à); **at –,** aux abois; **–tree,** *n* laurier *m.*

bayonet, bé´-onn-ette, *n* baïonnette *f.*

be, bî, *v* être.

beach, bîtche, *n* plage *f;* rivage *m;* grève *f.*

beacon, bi´-k'n, *n* phare *m;* (*naut*) balise *f.*

bead, bîde, *n* perle *f;* (drop) goutte *f.*

beak, bîke, *n* bec *m.*

beam, bîme, *n* rayon *m;* (wood) poutre *f.*

bean, bîne, *n* haricot *m;* (broad) fève *f.*

bear, bère, *n* ours *m. v* donner naissance à; porter; endurer; **–able,** *a* supportable.

beard, birde, *n* barbe *f;* **–ed,** *a* barbu; **–less,** *a* imberbe.

beast, bîste, *n* bête *f;* **wild –,** fauve *m.*

beat, bîte, *v* battre. *n* coup *m;* (pulse, etc) battement *m;* secteur *m.*

beautiful*, bioue´-ti-foull, *a* beau; magnifique.

beautify, bioue´-ti-fâï, *v* embellir.

beauty, bioue´-ti, *n* beauté *f;* **–spot,** grain de beauté *m.*

beaver, bî´-veur, *n* castor *m.*

becalm, bi-câme´, *v* calmer; (*naut*) abriter du vent.

because, bi-coaze´e, *conj* parce que; **–of,** à cause de.

beckon, bekk´'n, *v* faire signe.

become, bi-komme´, *v* devenir.

becoming, bi-komm´-inng, *a* convenable; (conduct) bienséant; (dress) qui va bien; seyant.

bed, bedde, *n* lit *m;* **flower- –,** plate-bande *f;* **–ding,** literie *f;* **–-pan,** bassin de lit *m;* **–ridden,** *a* alité; **–room,** *n* chambre à coucher *f.*

bedeck, bi-dèque´, *v* parer; orner.

bee, bî, *n* abeille *f;* **–hive,** ruche *f.*

beech, bîtche, *n* hêtre *m.*

beef, bîfe, *n* boeuf *m;* **–-steak,** bifteck *m.*

beer, bîre, *n* bière *f.*

beet, bîte´, *n* betterave *f.*

beetle, bî´-t'l, *n* coléoptère *m;* **black –,** cafard *m.*

befitting, bi-fitt´-inng, *a* convenable à.

before, bi-foare´, *adv &*
prep (time) avant; (place) devant; **–hand,** *adv* d'avance; à l'avance.

befriend, bi-frennde´, *v* traiter en ami; aider.

beg, bègue, *v* (alms) mendier; (request, etc) prier; **–gar,** *n* mendiant *m;* **–ging,** mendicité *f.*

begin, bi-guinne´, *v* commencer; **–ner,** *n* débutant *m;* **–ning,** commencement *m.*

begrudge, bi-grodge´, *v* donner à contre-cœur.

beguile, bi-gâïle´, *v* tromper; séduire.

behalf, bi-hâfe´, **on –of,** en faveur de; au nom de; de la part de.

behave, bi-héve´, *v* se conduire; se comporter.

behavior, bi-hé´-vieur, *n* conduite *f;* tenue *f.*

behead, bi-hédde´, *v* décapiter.

behind, bi-hâïnnde´, *adv* en arrière. *prep* derrière; en retard de; *n* derrière *m.*

behold, bi-haulde´, *v* voir. *interj* regardez!

being, bî´-inng, *n* existence *f;* (human) être *m.*

belch, beltche, *v* (pop) roter. (pop) rot *m.*

belfry, bel´-fri, *n* beffroi *m;*

clocher *m.*

belie, bi-lâï´, *v* démentir.

belief, bi-lîfe´, *n* croyance *f*; foi *f*.

believable, bi-lîve´-a-b'l, *a* croyable.

believe, bi-lîve, *v* croire; —**r,** *n* croyant *m.*

bell, belle, *n* cloche *f*; sonnette *f*; grelot *m.*

belligerent, bel-lidj´-eur-'nt, *a* & *n* belligérant *m.*

bellow, bél´-lô, *v* beugler; mugir.

bellows, bél´-lôze, *npl* soufflet *m.*

belly, bél´-li, *n* ventre *m.*

belong, bi-lonng´, *v* appartenir.

belongings, bi-lonng´-inngze, *npl* affaires *fpl.*

beloved, bi-lo´-vèdde, *n* & *a* bien-aimé *m.*

below, bi-lau´, *adv* & *prep* au-dessous; en bas.

belt, bellte, *n* ceinture *f*; (*mech*) courroie *f.*

bemoan, bi-maune´, *v* gémir sur; se lamenter.

bench, benntche, *n* banc *m*; tribunal *m*; établi *m.*

bend, bennde, *v* courber; plier. *n* courbure *f*; (road, etc) coude *m*; tournant *m*; virage *m.*

beneath, bi-nîts´, *adv* & *prep* sous; au-dessous.

benediction, benn-i-dic´-

ch'n, *n* bénédiction *f.*

benefactor, benn-i-fâque´-teur, *n* bienfaiteur *m.*

beneficial*, benn-i-fi´-cheul, *a* salutaire; avantageux.

beneficiary, benn-i-fi´-chi-*eur*-i, *n* bénéficiaire *mf.*

benefit, benn´-i-fite, *v* profiter. *n* bénéfice *m.*

benevolence, bi-nèv´-ŏ-lennce, *n* bienveillance *f.*

benevolent, bi-nèv´-ŏ-lennte, *a* bienveillant; charitable.

benign, bi-nâïne´, *a* bénin; doux.

bent, bennte, *pp* courbé; résolu. *n* (*fig*) penchant *m.*

bequeath, bi-kouîds´, *v* léguer.

bequest, bi-koueste´, *n* legs *m.*

bereave, bi-rîve´, *v* priver de; —**ment,** *n* perte *f.*

berry, bê´-ri, *n* baie *f.*

berth, beurts, *n* couchette *f.*

beseech, bi-cîtche´, *v* supplier; implorer.

beside, bi-sâïde´, *prep* à côté de; hors de.

besides, bi-sâïdze, *adv* en outre; d'ailleurs. *prep* en plus; excepté.

besiege, bi-cîdje, *v* assiéger.

besotted, bi-sotte´-èdde, *a* abruti.

best, besste, *adv* le mieux. *a* & *n* le meilleur.

bestial, bess´-ti'l, *a* bestial.

bestir, bi-steur´, *v* —**oneself,** se remuer.

bestow, bi-stau´, *v* accorder; conférer; —**al,** *n* don *m.*

bet, bette, *v* parier. *n* pari *m.*

betoken, bi-tau´-k'n, *v* indiquer; dénoter.

betray, bi-tré, *v* trahir; —**al,** *n* trahison *f.*

betroth, bi-traud*z*´, *v* fiancer.

betrothal, bi-traud*z*´-'l, *n* fiançailles *fpl.*

better, bett´r, *v* améliorer. *adv* mieux. *a* meilleur.

betterment, bett´-eur-m'nt, *n* amélioration *f.*

between, bi-touîne´, *prep* entre.

bevel, bév´l, *v* tailler en biseau; **beveled,** *a* de biais; en biseau.

beverage, bèv´-eur-idj, *n* boisson *f*; breuvage *m.*

bewail, bi-ouéle´, *v* déplorer.

beware, bi-ouère´, *v* se méfier de; prendre garde à.

a
b
c
d
e
f
g
h
i
j
k
l
m
n
o
p
q
r
s
t
u
v
w
x
y
z

A
B
C
D
E
F
G
H
I
J
K
L
M
N
O
P
Q
R
S
T
U
V
W
X
Y
Z

bewilder, bi-ouile´-*deur, v* ahurir; déconcerter.

bewilderment, bi-ouile´-*deur*-m'nt, *n* ahurissement *m.*

bewitch, bi-ouitche´, *v* ensorceler; enchanter.

beyond, bi-ionnde´, *adv* au delà; là-bas. *prep* au delà de.

bias, bâï´-*asse, n* biais *m;* préjugé *m;* **biased,** *a* partial.

Bible, bâï´-b'l, *n* bible *f.*

bicker, bik´eur, *v* se quereller; se chamailler.

bicycle, bâï´-ci-k'l, *n* bicyclette *f.*

bid, bide, *v* commander; prier; (auction) faire une offre; *n* offre *f;* enchère *f;* **–ding,** commandement *m;* enchère *f.*

bide, bâïde, *v* attendre; endurer.

bier, bîre, *n* corbillard *m,* bière *f.*

big, bigue, *a* gros; grand; vaste.

bigot, bigg-*eute, n* bigot *m;* **–ed,** *a* bigot.

bilberry, bil´-bê-ri, *n* airêlle *f.*

bile, bâïle, *n* bile *f.*

bilingual, bâï-linn´-guou'l, *a* bilingue.

bilious, bi´-li-*euce, a* bilieux.

bill, bil, *n* note *f;* compte *m,* facture *f;* (restaurant) addition *f;* (bird) bec *m;* (poster) affiche *f;* **–of exchange,** lettre de change *f;* **–of fare,** menu *m;* **–of lading** connaissement *m.*

billet, bil´-ette, *v* loger. *n* (mil) logement *m.*

billiards, bil´-lieurdze, *npl* billard *m.*

bin, bine, *n* huche *f;* (wine) porte-bouteilles *m;* poubelle *f.*

bind, bâïnnde, *v* lier; obliger; (books) relier; **–ing** *n* reliure *f. a* obligatoire; **–up,** *v* bander.

binocular(s), bi-nok´-ioue-*leur*(ze), *n* jumelle *f.*

biography, bâï-o´-grã-fi, *n* biographie *f.*

birch, beurtche, *n* (tree) bouleau *m;* (punitive) verges *fpl.*

bird, beurde, *n* oiseau *m.*

birth, beurts, *n* naissance *f;* **–day,** anniversaire *m;* **–mark,** tache de naissance *f;* **–place,** lieu natal *m;* **–rate,** natalité *f.*

biscuit, biss´-kitte, *n* biscuit *m.*

bishop, bich´-*eup, n* évêque *m.*

bit, bitte, *n* morceau *m;* (horse) mors *m.*

bite, bâïte, *v* mordre, *n* morsure *f;* piqûre *f.*

biting, bâït´-inng, *a* mordant.

bitter*, bitt´-*eur, a* amer; **–ness,** *n* amertume *f.*

black, blăque, *v* (shoes) cirer; noircir. *a* noir. *n* noir *m;* **–berry,** *n* mûre *f;* **–bird,** merle *m;* **–currant,** cassis *m;* **–en,** *v* noircir; **–mail,** chantage *m. v* faire chanter; **–mailer,** *n* maître chanteur *m;* **–smith,** forgeron *m.*

bladder, blăd´-*eur, n* vessie *f.*

blade, bléde, *n* lame *f;* (grass) brin *m;* (oar) plat *m.*

blame, bléme, *v* blâmer. *n* blâme *m;* faute *f.*

blameless*, bléme´-lesse, *a* irréprochable.

blanch, blânntche, *v* blanchir; pâlir.

bland, blănnde, *a* doux; **–ishment,** *n* flatterie *f.*

blank, blain-n'k, *n* blanc *m. a* blanc; (mind) vide.

blanket, blaing´-kette, *n* couverture *f.*

blare, blére, *v* retentir.

blaspheme, blass-fîme´, *v* blasphémer.

blasphemy, blass´-fé-mi, *n* blasphème *m*.

blast, blâsste, *v* (explode) faire sauter; (blight) flétrir. *n* (trumpet) son *m*; coup *m*.

blatant, blé´-t'nt, *a* bruyant.

blaze, bléze, *v* flamber. *n* flamme *f*; éclat *m*.

bleach, blîtche, *v* blanchir; décolorer.

bleak, blîque, *a* froid; exposé aux vents; morne.

bleat, blîte, *v* bêler. *n* bêlement *m*.

bleed, blîde, *v* saigner; –**ing,** *n* saignement *m*.

blemish, blèm´-iche, *n* tache *f*. *v* tacher.

blend, blennde, *v* mélanger. *n* mélange *m*.

bless, bless, *v* bénir; –**ed,** *a* béni.

blessing, bless´-inng, *n* bénédiction *f*.

blight, blâïte, *n* nielle *f*; rouille *f*; (*fam*) influence néfaste.

blind, blâïnnde, *n* (window) store *m*; (venetian) jalousie *f*. *n* & *a* (sight) aveugle *m* & *f*. *v* aveugler. –**fold,** bander les yeux; –**ness,** *n* aveuglement *m*; cécité *f*.

blink, blinng-k, *v* clignoter; *n* battement (*m*) de paupière; –**er,** *n* œillère *f*.

bliss, blisse, *n* félicité *m*; béatitude *f*.

blissful, bliss´-foull, *a* bienheureux.

blister, bliss´-t'r, *n* ampoule *f*; cloque *f*.

blithe*, blâï*dz*, *a* gai; joyeux.

blizzard, bliz´-*eu*rde, *n* tempête de neige *f*.

bloated, blau´-tedde, *a* boursouflé; bouffi; **bloater,** *n* hareng fumé *m*.

block, bloque, *v* bloquer. *n* bloc *m*; billot *m*; obstacle *m*; (of houses) pâté de maisons *m*; –**ade** blocus *m*; –**head,** *n* imbécile *m* & *f*.

blood, blodde, *n* sang *m*; –**hound,** limier *m*; –**shot,** *a* injecté de sang; –**thirsty,** sanguinaire; –**y,** sanglant.

blossom, bloss-*eu*me, *v* fleurir. *n* fleur *f*.

blot, blotte, *v* tacher; (dry) sécher. *n* tache *f*; (ink) pâté *m*; –**ting paper,** papier buvard *m*.

blotch, blotche, *n* tache *f*.

blouse, blâ´-ouze, *n* blouse *f*; (woman's shirt) chemisier *m*.

blow, blau, *n* coup *m*. *v* souffler; (trumpet) sonner; (nose) se moucher.

blubber, blob´-*eu*r, *n* (whale) graisse de baleine *f*.

bludgeon, blod´-jeune, *n* matraque *f*.

blue, bloue, *a* & *n* bleu; –**bell,** *n* jacinthe des bois *f*; clochette *f*.

bluff, bloffe, *n* bluff *m*. *v* bluffer.

bluish, bloue´-iche, *a* bleuâtre.

blunder, blonne´-*d*eur, *n* maladresse *f*. *v* commettre une maladresse.

blunt, blonnt, *v* émousser. *a** brusque; émoussé.

blur, bleure, *v* brouiller. *n* tache *f*.

blush, bloche, *v* rougir. *m* rougeur *f*.

bluster, bloce´-teur, *v* faire du vacarme. *n* fanfaronnade *f*; –**er,** fanfaron *m*; –**ing,** *a* tapageur; (wind) violent.

boar, baure, *n* (wild) sanglier *m*.

board, baurde, *n* planche

a
b
c
d
e
f
g
h
i
j
k
l
m
n
o
p
q
r
s
t
u
v
w
x
y
z

f; (directors) conseil d'administration m; (food) pension f. v garnir de planches; **bulletin–,** n tableau d'annonces m; **–er,** pensionnaire m & f; **–ing house,** pension f; **–ing school,** pensionnat m; pension f.

boast, bauste, v se vanter.

boaster, baus´-t'r, n vantard m.

boat, baute, n bateau m; (row) bateau à rames m; **motor–,** canot à moteur m; **steam–,** vapeur m; **–hook,** gaffe f.

bob, bobbe, v ballotter; osciller; s'agiter.

bobbin, bob´-ine, n bobine f.

bodice, bod´-ice, n corsage m.

bodkin, bode´-kinne, n passe-lacet m; poinçon m.

body, bod´-i, n corps m; (vehicle) carrosserie f.

bog, bogue, n marécage m; **–gy,** a marécageux.

bogeyman, bau´-gui-mănne, n croquemitaine m.

boil, boa'île, v faire bouillir; bouillir. n (med) furoncle m.

boiler, boa'îl´-eur, n

chaudière f.

boisterous*, bo'ïce´-teur-euce, a bruyant; turbulent.

bold*, bôlde, a hardi; audacieux; effronté.

boldness, bôlde´-nesse, n hardiesse f; effronterie f.

bolster, bôle´-steur, n traversin m. v (fig) soutenir.

bolt, bôlte, v verrouiller; décamper. n verrou m.

bomb, bomme, n bombe f; **–ard,** v bombarder.

bond, bonnde, n (tie) lien m; (word) engagement m; bon m.

bondage, bonnd´-idj, n esclavage m; servitude f.

bone, baune, n os m; (fish) arête f.

bonfire, bonn´-fâïre, n feu de joie m.

bonnet, bonn´-ette, n chapeau m; bonnet.

bonus, bau´-neuce, n prime f.

bony, bau´-ni, a osseux.

boob, boub, n (pop) gaffe f. v faire une gaffe.

book, bouk, n livre m. v inscrire; réserver; **–binder,** n relieur m; **–case,** bibliothèque f; **–ing office,** guichet m; **–keeper,** comptable m; **–seller,** libraire m;

–shop, librairie f.

boom, boume, n (com) boom m; (noise) grondement m; (spar) bout-dehors m. v gronder; (com) faire hausser; être à la hausse.

boon, boune, n bienfait m.

boor, boure, n rustre m; **–ish,** a grossier.

boot, boute, n botte f; — **maker,** bottier m.

booth, boudz, n cabine f.

booty, boue´-ti, n butin m.

border, bôre´-d'r, n frontière f; bord m; bordure f; **–ing,** a (adjacent) contigu à; touchant.

bore, bôre, v percer; (ground) forer; (weary) ennuyer. n calibre m; (person) raseur m; raseuse f; barbe f.

born, bôrne, pp né.

borrow, bor´-au, v emprunter.

bosom, bou´-zeume, n sein m.

boss, bosse, n (fam) patron m. v diriger.

botanist, bott´-a-niste, n botaniste mf.

botany, bott´-a-ni, n botanique f.

both, bôts, a les deux; ensemble.

bother, bô-dz'r, v

tracasser. *n* ennui *m*.

bottle, bott´-'l, *v* mettre en bouteilles. *n* bouteille *f*.

bottom, bott´-*eume*, *n* fond *m*; bas *m*; derrière *n*:.

bottomless, bott´-*eume*-lesse, *a* sans fond.

boudoir, bou´-do'ar, *n* boudoir *m*.

bough, bâ'ou, *n* rameau *m*; branche *f*.

bounce, bâ'ounnce, *v* rebondir.

bound, bâ'ounn´-de, *v* borner; (jump) bondir. *n* (jump) bond *m*; **–ary,** borne *f* limites *fpl*; **–for,** à destination de.

bountiful*, bâ'ounn´-ti-foull, *a* généreux.

bounty, bâ'ounn´-ti, *n* libéralité *f*; prime *f*.

bouquet, bou-kay, *n* bouquet *m*.

bout, bâ'oute, *n* accès *m*.

bow, bâ'ou, *v* saluer; s'incliner. *n* salut *m*; révérence *f*; (ship) avant *m*.

bow, bau, *n* (archery) arc *m*; (tie; knot) nœud *m*; (violin) archet *m*.

bowels, bâ'ou´-elze, *n* boyaux *mpl*; intestins *mpl*.

bowl, baule, *n* bol *m*;

(ball) boule *f*. *v* jouer aux boules; (cricket) lancer la balle.

box, boxe, *v* boxer. *n* boîte *f*; (theater) loge *f*; (on the ears) gifle *f*; **–ing,** boxe *f*.

boy, boa'ï, *n* garçon *m*; **–cott,** *v* boycotter. *n* boycottage *m*; **–hood,** enfance *f*.

brace, bréce, *v* lier; fortifier. *n* (*mech*) vilebrequin *m*; (two) couple *m*; **–s,** bretelles *fpl*; appareil dentaire *m*.

bracelet, bréce´-lette, *n* bracelet *m*.

bracing, bréce´-inng, *a* fortifiant; tonique.

bracken, brăk´-'n, *n* fougère *f*.

bracket, brăk´-ette, *n* console *f*; parenthèse *f*.

brackish, brăk´-iche, *a* saumâtre.

brag, brăgue, *v* se vanter; **–gart,** *n* vantard *m*.

braid, bréde, *v* tresser. *n* tresse *f*; (dress) galon *m*.

brain, bréne, *n* (substance) cervelle *f*; (mind) cerveau *m*; brainy. *a* (*fam*) intelligent.

braise, bréze, *v* braiser.

brake, bréque, *n* frein *m*. *v* freiner.

bramble, brămm´-b'l, *n* ronce *f*.

bran, brănne, *n* son *m*.

branch, brănntche, *n* branche *f*; (*com*) succursale *f*.

brand, brănnde, *n* marque *f*; (fire) brandon *m*. *v* marquer; stigmatiser; **–ish,** brandir.

brandy, brănn´-di, *n* eau de vie *f*.

brass, brăce, *n* laiton *m*, cuivre jaune *m*.

brasserie (*fam* **bra**), brăssiaire (bră), *n* soutiengorge *f*.

bravado, bra-vâ´-dô, *n* bravade *f*.

brave*, bréve, *a* brave; courageux. *v* braver; **–ry,** *n* bravoure *f*.

brawl, broale, *v* se chamailler.

brawn, broanne, *n* fromage de tête *m*; muscles *mpl*; **–y,** *a* musclé.

bray, bré, *v* braire.

brazen, bré´-z'n, *a* de laiton; (insolent) effronté.

Brazil nut, bra-zile´-notte, *n* noix du Brésil *f*.

breach, brîtche, *n* fracture *f*; violation *f*; rupture *f*.

bread, brède, *n* pain *m*; (*pop*) argent.

a
b
c
d
e
f
g
h
i
j
k
l
m
n
o
p
q
r
s
t
u
v
w
x
y
z

breadth, brèdt*s*, *n* largeur *f*.

break, bréque, *v* casser; (amity, etc) rompre; (law) violer; (smash) briser. *n* brisure *f*; (pause) pause *f*; (school) récréation; **–age,** casse *f*; **–down,** rupture *f*; écroulement *m*; dépression *f*; (*mech*) panne *f*; **–er,** (*naut*) grosse vague *f*; **–water,** brise-lames *m*.

breakfast, brèque´-fâste, *n* petit-déjeuner *m*.

bream, brîmme, *n* brème *f*.

breast, breste, *n* sein *m*; poitrine *f*.

breath, brè-*ts*, *n* haleine *f*; souffle *m*; **–less,** *a* essoufflé.

breathe, brî-*dz*, *v* respirer.

breech, brîtche, *n* (firearms) culasse *f*.

breed, brîde, *v* élever; procréer; se reproduire; *n* race *f*; espèce *f*; **–er,** éleveur *m*; **–ing,** élevage *m*; éducation *f*.

breeze, brîze, *n* brise *f*.

brevity, brèv´-i-ti, *n* brièveté *f*.

brew, broue, *v* brasser; faire infuser; **–er,** *n* brasseur *m*.

brewery, broue´-eur-i, *n* brasserie *f*.

briar, brâï´-*eur*, *n* (bramble) ronce *f*; églantier *m*.

bribe, brâïbe, *v* corrompre; (*fam*) graisser la pâte. *n* paiement illicite *m*.

bribery, brâï´-beur-i, *n* corruption *f*.

brick, brique, *n* brique *f*; **–layer,** macon *m*.

bridal, brâï´-d'l, *a* nuptial.

bride, brâïde, *n* mariée *f*; **–groom,** marié *m*; **–smaid,** demoiselle d'honneur *f*.

bridge, bridje, *n* pont *m*; (*naut*) passerelle *f*; bridge *m*.

bridle, brâï´-d'l, *n* bride *f*. *v* brider.

brief, brîfe, *n* dossier *m*. *a** bref; **–case,** *n* serviette *f*; **–ing,** instruction *f*; directives *f*.

brigade, bri-guéde´, *n* brigade *f*.

bright*, brâïte, *a* luisant; lumineux; intelligent; **–en,** *v* faire briller; (enliven) égayer; (weather) s'éclaircir; **–ness,** *n* éclat *m*; vivacité *f*.

brilliancy, bril´-iann-ci, *n* éclat *m*; lustre *m*.

brilliant, bril´-iannte, *a* brillant; éclatant.

brim, brime, *n* bord *m*; **–over,** *v* déborder.

brimstone, brime´-staune, *n* soufre *m*.

brine, brâïne, *n* saumure *f*.

bring, brinng, *v* apporter; conduire; **–forward,** (*com*) reporter; **–in,** (*com*) rapporter; **–up,** élever.

brink, brinng-k, *n* bord *m*.

brisk, brisque, *a* vif; animé; **–ness,** *n* vivacité *f*.

brisket, briss´-quette, *n* poitrine de bœuf *f*.

bristle, briss´-'l, *n* poil raide *m*; soie *f*. *v* se hérisser.

bristly, briss´-li, *a* poilu; hérissé.

brittle, britt´-'l, *a* fragile; cassant.

broad, broad, *a* large; (accent) prononcé.

broadcast, broade´-câste, *v* radiodiffuser.

broadcasting, broade´-câste-inng, *n* émission *f*.

brocade, brô-quéde´, *n* brocart *m*.

broccoli, broque´-o-li, *n* brocoli *m*.

brogue, braugue, *n* patois *m*; chaussure *f*.

broil, broa´ïle, *v* griller.

broker, brau´-keur, *n* courtier *m*; **stock–,** agent de change *m*; **–age,**

courtage *m.*

bronchitis, bronng-kâï´-tice, *n* bronchite *f.*

bronze, bronnze, *n* bronze *m. v* bronzer.

brooch, brautche, *n* broche *f.*

brood, broude, *v* couver; (*fam*) remâcher; ruminer (une idée). *n* couvée *f.*

brook, brouque, *n* ruisseau *m.*

broom, broume, *n* balai *m;* (plant) genêt *m.*

broth, brot*s, n* bouillon *m.*

brother, bro*dz´-eur, n* frère *m* **–hood,** fraternité *f;* (*eccl*) confrérie *f;* **–in-law,** beau-frère *m;* **–ly,** *a* fraternel.

brow, brâ'ou, *n* front *m;* sourcil *m;* **–beat,** *v* intimider.

brown, brâ'oune, *v* brunir. *a* brun; marron; **–ish,** brunâtre.

browse, brâ'ouze, *v* brouter; regarder sans acheter.

bruise, brouze, *n* contusion *f;* bleu *m. v* meurtrir.

brunette, brou-nette´, *n* brunette *f.*

brunt, bronnte, *n* choc *m;* violence *f.*

brush, broche, *n* brosse *f. v* brosser; (sweep) balayer.

brushwood, broche´-ou'oude, *n* broussailles *fpl.*

brusque, br*euske, a* brusque.

brussels sprouts, bross´-lze-spr'outse, *npl* choux de Bruxelles *mpl.*

brutal*, brou*e´-*t'l, *a* brutal; **–ity,** *n* brutalité *f.*

brutalize, brou*e´-*t'l-âïze, *v* abrutir; brutaliser.

brute, brout*e, n* brute *f.*

bubble, bo´-b'l, *n* bulle *f. v* bouillonner; (wine) pétiller.

buck, bo*que, a* mâle. *n* (deer) daim *m.*

bucket, bok´-ette, *n* seau *m;* baquet *m.*

buckle, bo´-k'l, *n* boucle *f. v* boucler; attacher.

bud, bo*dde, n* bourgeon *m;* (flower) bouton *m. v* bourgeonner; fleurir.

budge, bo*dje, v* bouger.

budget, bodj´-ette, *n* budget *m.*

buff, boffe, *a* couleur chamois. *v* polir.

buffalo, boff´-*a*-lau, *n* buffle *m.*

buffer, boff´-*eur, n* tampon (de choc) *m.*

buffet, boff´-ette, *n* (bar) buffet *m. v* battre.

buffoon, b*euf*-foune´, *n*

bouffon *m.*

bug, bogue, *n* punaise *f;* insecte *m;* **–bear,** (*fam*) bête noire *f.*

bugle, bioue´-g'l, *n* (*mil*) clairon *m.*

build, bilde, *v* bâtir. *n* forme *f;* **–er,** constructeur *m;* **–ing,** bâtiment *m.*

bulb, b*olbe, n* bulbe *m;* (lamp) ampoule électrique *f.*

bulge, bol-dj, *v* bomber; gonfler.

bulk, b*olke, n* volume *m;* **in –,** en gros.

bulky, boll´-ki, *a* volumineux; encombrant.

bull, boull, *n* taureau *m;* (stock exchange) haussier *m;* **–-dog,** bouledogue *m;* **–finch,** bouvreuil *m;* **–'s eye,** (target) mouche *f.*

bullet, boull´-ette, *n* balle *f.*

bulletin, boull´-i-tinne, *n* bulletin *m.*

bullion, boull´-i*eune, n* or en barres *m.*

bully, boull´-i, *v* malmener. *n* tyran *m;* brute *f.*

bulrush, boull´-roche, *n* jonc *m.*

bulwark, boull´-

a b c d e f g h i j k l m n o p q r s t u v w x y z

A
B
C
D
E
F
G
H
I
J
K
L
M
N
O
P
Q
R
S
T
U
V
W
X
Y
Z

ou'e*ur*que. n rempart m;
(*naut*) pavois m.

bumblebee, bomm´-b'l-bî,
n bourdon m.

bump, bommpe, n coup m;
secousse f; (swelling)
bosse f. v heurter;
cogner.

bumper, bomm´-peur, n
(glass) rasade f (of car)
pare-chocs m.

bumptious, bommpe´-
che*u*ce, a arrogant.

bunch, bonntche, v
grouper; se tasser. n
(vegetables) botte f;
(flowers) bouquet m;
(grapes) grappe de raisin
f; (keys) trousseau de
clefs m; groupe m.

bundle, bonn´-d'l, n
paquet m; ballot m; (of
wood) fagot m.

bung, bonng, n bondon m;
–hole, bonde f.

bungalow, bonng´-ga-lau,
n bungalow m.

bungle, bonng´-g'l, v
gâcher; **–r,** n gâcheur m.

bunion, bonn´-ieune, n
oignon aux pieds m.

bunker, bonng´-keur, n
(coal) soute à charbon f.

bunting, bonn´-tinng, n
étamine f; (flags)
drapeaux mpl.

buoy, bôa´ï, n bouée f;
–ancy, légèreté f; (fam)

entrain m; **–ant,** a
flottable; (fam) plein
d'entrain.

burden, beur´-d'n, v
charger; accabler. n
fardeau m; charge f;
–some, a lourd.

bureau, biou´-rau, n
(furniture) bureau m;
secrétaire m; (office)
bureau m; office m.

bureaucracy, biou-rau-
cra-si, n bureaucratie f.

burglar, beur´-gleur, n
cambrioleur m.

burglary, beur´-gleur-i, n
cambriolage m.

burial, bè´-ri-al, n
enterrement m.

burial ground, bè´-ri-al-
grâ'ounnde, n cimetière
m.

burlesque, beur-lesque´, n
& a burlesque m.

burly, beur´-li, a
corpulent.

burn, beurne, v brûler;
(arson) incendier. n
brûlure f; **–er,** (gas;
lamp) bec m.

burr, beurre, n (botanical)
carde f.

burrow, beurr´-au, v
terrer. n terrier m.

bursar, beurr´-sar, n
(school) économe m.

burst, beurste, v éclater;
(crack) crever; sauter.

bury, bèr-i, v enterrer.

bus, boss, n autobus m.

bush, bouche, n buisson
m; fourré m; **–y,** a touffu.

business, biz´-nesse, n
affaires fpl; occupation f.

bust, bosste, n buste m;
poitrine f.

bustle, boss´´l, v se remuer.
n mouvement m; remue-
ménage m.

bustling, boss´-linng, a
affairé.

busy, biz´-i, a occupé;
affairé.

but, botte, conj mais. adv
seulement.

butcher, boutt´-cheur, n
boucher m. v massacrer.

butler, bott´-leur, n maître
d'hôtel m.

butt, bott, n bout m; (gun)
crosse f; (cask) tonneau
m. v buter.

butter, bott´-eur, v beurrer.
n beurre m; **–cup,**
bouton d'or m; **–dish,**
beurrier m; **–fly,**
papillon m.

buttock, bott´-ŏque, n
fesse f; culotte de bœuf f.

button, bott´-'n, n bouton
m. v boutonner; **–hole,**
n boutonnière f.

buxom, box´-eume, a
(woman) bien en chair;
grassouillette.

buy, bâï, v acheter; **–er,** n

acheteur *m*; acheteuse *f*.
buzz, bozze, *v* bourdonner.
buzzard, bozz´-*eu*rde, *n*
   buse *f*.
by, bâï, *prep* par; près de;
   –gone, *a* passé; **–-**
   stander, *n* spectateur *m*;
   –-word, dicton *m*.
bylaw, bâï´-loa, *n*
   réglement *m*; arrêté *m*.
bypass, bâï´-pâsse, *v*
   contourner, éviter.

a
b
c
d
e
f
g
h
i
j
k
l
m
n
o
p
q
r
s
t
u
v
w
x
y
z

A B **C** D E F G H I J K L M N O P Q R S T U V W X Y Z

C

cab, căbbe, n taxi m.

cabbage, căb´-ădj, n chou m.

cabin, căb´-inn, n cabine f; (hut) cabane f.

cabinet, căb´-inn-ett, n cabinet m; meuble m; vitrine f; classeur m; **– maker,** ébéniste m.

cable, ké´-b'l, n câble m. v câbler.

cablegram, ké´-b'l-grămme, n câblogramme m.

cackle, căk´-'l, v caqueter. n caquet m.

cage, kédje, n cage f. v mettre en cage.

cajole, ca-djaule´, v cajoler.

cake, kéque, n gâteau m. v se coaguler.

calabash, căl´-a-băche, n calebasse f.

calamitous, ca-lămm´-i-teuce, a désastreux.

calamity, ca-lămm´-i-ti, n calamité f.

calculate, căl´-kiou-léte, v calculer.

calculator, căl´-kiou-lă-teur, n calculette m.

calendar, căl´-ènn-deur, n calendrier m.

calf, câfe, n veau m; (leg) mollet m.

calico, căl´-i-kô, n calicot m.

call, coal, v appeler; (name) nommer; (visit) visiter; passer chez. n appel m; visite f.

callous, căl´-euce, a (unfeeling) insensible; endurci.

calm, câme, v calmer. n &

a* calme m.

calorie, călor´-ri, n calorie f

cambric, kéme´-brique, n batiste f.

camel, cămm´-'l, n chameau m.

cameo, cămm´-î-ô, n camée m.

camera, cămm´-eur-a, n appareil photographique m; **in –,** à huis clos; **cameraman,** n cameraman m.

camomile, cămm´-ô-mâïle, n camomille f.

camp, cămmpe, v camper. n camp m; **–cot,** lit de camp m; **to go camping,** faire du camping.

campaign, cămm-péne´, n campagne f.

camphor, cămm´-feur, n camphre m.

can, cănne, n bidon m; (of food) boîte. v (preserve) conserver en boîte.

can, cănne, v pouvoir; savoir.

canal, cănn-ăl´, n canal m.

canary, că-né´-ri, n canari m, serin m.

cancel, cănn´-s'l, v annuler.

cancer, cănn´-ceur, n cancer m.

candid*, cănn´-dide, a candide; franc.

candidate, cănn´-di-déte, *n* candidat *m.*

candle, cănn´-d'l, *n* bougie *f*; chandelle *f*; –**stick,** bougeoir *m*; chandelier *m.*

candor, cănn´-deur, *n* candeur *f*; franchise *f.*

candy, cănn´-di, *n* bonbons *mpl. v* cristalliser.

cane, quéne, *n* canne *f.*

canine, că-nâïnne´, *a* canin. *n* (tooth) canine *f.*

canister, cănn´-iss-teur, *n* boîte en fer blanc *f.*

canker, caing´-k'r, *n* chancre *m.*

canned, cănn-'d, *a* en boîte; en conserve.

cannibal, cănn´-i-b'l, *n* & *a* cannibale *m* & *f.*

cannon, cănn´-eune, *n* canon *m.*

canoe, ca-noue´, *n* périssoire *f*; (native) pirogue *f*; canoe *m.*

canon, cănn´-eune, *n* (title) chanoine *m*; (law) canon *m.*

can opener, cănn´-ôp-neur, *n* ouvre-boîte(s) *m.*

canopy, cănn´-ŏ-pi, *n* baldaquin *m.*

cant, cănnte, *n* hypocrisie *f.*

cantankerous, cănn-taing´-keur-euce, *a* revêche.

canteen, cănn-tîne, *n* cantine *f.*

canter, cănn´-teur, *v* aller au petit galop.

canvas, cănn´-vasse, *n* toile *f*; (sail) voile *f.*

canvass, cănn´-vasse, *v* solliciter.

cap, căppe, *n* casquette *f*; (of bottle) capsule *f*; (pen) capuchon *m.*

capable, qué´-pa-b'l, *a* capable; competent.

capacity, ca-păsse´-i-ti, *n* capacité *f.*

cape, quépe, *n* (*geog*) cap *m*; (cover) cape *f.*

caper, qué´-peur, *n* cambriole; gambade *f*; (cooking) câpre *f.*

capital, căp´-i-t'l, *n* (city) capitale *f*; (money) capital *m*; (letter) majuscule *f.*

capitulate, ca-pitte´-ioue-léte, *v* capituler.

capricious*, ca-prich´-euce, *a* capricieux.

capsize, căp-sâîze´, *v* chavirer.

capstan, căp´-stănne, *n* cabestan *m.*

capsule, căp´-sioulle, *n* capsule *f.*

captain, căp´-t'n, *n* capitaine *m*; (sport) chef d'équipe *m.*

caption, căp´-ch'n, *n* légende *f.*

captive, căp´-tive, *n* & *a* captif *m*; captive *f.*

captivity, căp-tive´-i-ti, *n* captivité *f.*

capture, căp´-tioure, *v* capturer. *n* prise *f.*

car, câre, *n* automobile *f*; voiture *f*; (*aero*) nacelle *f.*

caramel, căr´-a-m'l, *n* caramel *m.*

carat, căr´-atte, *n* carat *m.*

caravan, căr´-a-vănne, *n* caravane *f*; roulotte *f.*

caraway, căr´-a-oué, *n* (seed) carvi *m.*

carbide, căr´-bâïde, *n* carbure *m.*

carbolic, căr-bol´-ique, *a* phénique; –**acid,** *n* phénol *m.*

carbon, căr´-b'n, *n* carbone *m*; –**copy,** *n* double *m*; –**paper,** *n* papier carbone *m.*

carbuncle, căr´-bonng-k'l, *n* (*med*) anthrax *m.*

carburetor, căr-bi'oue-rett´-'r, *n* carburateur *m.*

carcass, căr´-casse, *n* carcasse *f.*

card, cârde, *v* carder. *n* carte *f*; –**board,** carton *m.*

cardinal, că'r-di-n'l, n cardinal m. a cardinal.

care, quére, n soin m; attention f; inquiétude f. v se soucier de; **take –!** interj attention!; **take –of,** v faire attention à; **–for,** aimer; **–ful*,** a soigneux; prudent; **–less,** négligent; sans soin; **–lessness,** n négligence f; **c/o,** chez; aux bons soins de; **–taker,** n gardien m; concierge m & f.

career, ca-rîre', n carrière f.

caress, ca-resse', v caresser. n caresse f.

cargo, că'r-gau, n cargaison f.

caricature, că'r-i-ca-tioure', n caricature f.

carmine, câ'r-mine, n carmin m.

carnage, câ'r-nidj, n carnage m.

carnal*, câ'r-n'l, a charnel.

carnation, câr-né'-ch'n, n œillet m.

carnival, câr-ni-v'l, n carnaval m.

carol, că'r-ŏl, n cantique de Noël m.

carp, câ'rpe, n (fish) carpe f. v chicaner sur.

carpenter, că'r-penn-teur,

n charpentier m.

carpet, câ'r-pette, n tapis m; moquette f.

carriage, că'r-idj, n voiture f; (freight) port m; (deportment) maintien m; (rail) wagon m.

carrier, că'r-i-eur, n entrepreneur de transports m; (on car, cycle, etc) porte-bagages m; **–pigeon,** pigeon voyageur m.

carrion, că'r-ri-eune, n charogne f.

carrot, câr'-ŏtte, n carotte f.

carry, că'r-i, v porter; transporter.

cart, cârte, v transporter; (fam) trimbaler. n charette f; **–age,** camionnage m.

cartoon, câr-toune', n caricature f; dessin animé m.

cartridge, câr'-tridj, n cartouche f.

carve, cârve, v (wood) sculpter; (meat) découper.

carving, câr'-vinng, n sculpture f; découpage m.

cascade, căsse-quéde', n cascade f.

case, quéce, n (box) caisse

f; (cigarette etc) étui m; (jewel) écrin m; cas m; affaire f; **in –,** au cas où.

casement, quéce'-m'nt, n croisée f; fenêtre f.

cash, căche, n argent m; argent liquide m. v encaisser; **–book,** n livre de caisse m.

cashier, căche-îre', n caissier m; caissière f.

cashmere, căche'-mîre, n cachemire m.

cask, câsque, n tonneau m, baril m; fût m.

casket, câsse'-quette, n cassette f; écrin m; cercueil m.

cassock, căss'-ŏque, n soutane f.

cast, câste, n (throw) coup m; (theater) distribution des rôles f; (metal) moule m. v (throw) jeter; lancer; (metal) couler; **–iron,** n fonte f.

castanet, căsse'-ta-nette, n castagnette f.

caste, câste, n caste f.

castigate, căsse'-ti-guéte, v châtier.

castle, câ'-s'l, n château m.

castor, câsse'-tŏr, n (wheel) roulette f.

castor oil, câsse'-tŏr-oa'ile, n huile de ricin f.

casual, căj'-iou-eul, a

fortuit; indifférent; détaché.

casualty, căj´iou-*eul*-ti, *n* accidenté *m*; (*mil*) perte *f*.

cat, cătte, *n* chat *m*.

catalog, căt´-*a*-logue, *n* catalogue *m*.

catarrh, c*a*-târre´, *n* catarrhe *m*.

catastrophe, c*a*-tăce´-trŏ-fi, *n* catastrophe *f*.

catch, cătche, *n* prise *f*. *v* attraper; **–ing,** *a* contagieux; **–up,** *v* rattraper.

category, căt´-i-gŏr-i, *n* catégorie *f*.

cater, qué´-*teur*, *v* approvisionner; **–er,** *n* traiteur *m*.

caterpillar, căt´-*eur*-pil-*eur*, *n* chenille *f*.

cathedral, c*a*-tsi´-dralle, *n* cathédrale *f*.

catholic, că´-tsŏ-lique, *n* & *a* catholique *m* & *f*.

cattle, căt´-t'l, *n* bétail *m*.

cauldron, côl-t'-dr*o*nne, *n* chaudron *m*; chaudière *f*.

cauliflower, col´-i-flâ´ou-*eur*, *n* chou-fleur *m*.

caulk, côke, *v* calfater.

cause, côze, *n* cause *f*. *v* causer; occasionner.

caustic, côce´-tique, *n* & *a* caustique *m*.

cauterize, cô´-*teur*-âïze, *v* cautériser.

caution, cô´-ch'n, *n* prudence *f*; (warning) avis *m*. *v* avertir.

cautious, cô´-cheuce, *a* prudent.

cavalier, căv-*a*-lîre´, *n* cavalier *m*.

cavalry, căv´-*al*-ri, *n* cavalerie *f*.

cave, quéve, *n* caverne *f*; (animals') antre *m*.

cavil, căv´-il, *v* chicaner.

cavity, căv´-i-ti, *n* cavité *f*; carie *f*.

cease, sîce, *v* cesser; **–less,** *a* incessant.

cedar, sî-d*eur*, *n* cèdre *m*.

cede, sîde, *v* céder.

ceiling, sîl´-inng, *n* plafond *m*.

celebrate, sell´-i-bréte, *v* célébrer; **–d,** *a* célèbre.

celery, sell´-*eur*-i, *n* céleri *m*.

celestial, si-lesse´-ti-'l, *a* céleste.

celibacy, sell´-i-b*a*-ci, *n* célibat *m*.

cell, selle, *n* cellule *f*.

cellar, sell´-*eur*, *n* cave *f*.

celluloid, sell´-ioue-lo-ide, *n* celluloïde *m*.

cement, sé-mennte´, *n* ciment *m*. *v* cimenter.

cemetery, sém´-i-t*eur*-i, *n* cimetière *m*.

cenotaph, senn´-ô-tă?e, *n* cénotaphe *m*.

censor, senn´-*seur*, *n* censeur *m*; **–ship,** censure *f*.

censure, senn´-chioure, *v* censurer. *n* censure *f*.

census, senn´-ceusse, *n* recensement *m*.

cent, sennte, *n* sou *m*; centime *m*; **per –,** pour cent; **–enary,** *a* centenaire; **–ury,** *n* siècle *m*.

center, senn´-t'r, *n* centre *m*. *v* placer au centre.

central, senn´-tr'l, *a* central; **–heating,** *n* chauffage central *m*; **–ize,** *v* centraliser.

cereal, sî´-rî-'l, *n* céréale *f*.

ceremonious*, sair-i-mau´-ni-euce, *a* cérémonieux.

ceremony, sair´-i-mau-ni, *n* cérémonie *f*.

certain*, seur´-t'n, *a* certain.

certificate, s*eur*-tif´-i-quéte, *n* certificat *m*; acte *m*.

certify, seur´-ti-fâï, *v* certifier; (law) attester.

cessation, saiss-sé´-ch'n, *n* cessation *f*; suspension *f*.

cesspool, saiss´-poule, *n* fosse d'aisances *f*.

chafe, tchéfe, *v* irriter;

a
b
c
d
e
f
g
h
i
j
k
l
m
n
o
p
q
r
s
t
u
v
w
x
y
z

écorcher.

chaff, tchâffe, *v* taquiner.
n (husk) menue paille *f.*

chaffinch, tchăf´-finntche, *n* pinson *m.*

chain, tchéne, *n* chaîne *f;* **–up,** *v* enchaîner.

chair, tchaire, *n* chaise *f;* **–man,** président *m.*

chalice, tchăl´-isse, *n* calice *m.*

chalk, tchôque, *n* craie *f;* **–y,** *a* crayeux.

challenge, tchăl´-inndje, *v* défier. *n* défi *m.*

chamber, tchéme´-b'r, *n* chambre *f;* **–lain,** chambellan *m;* **–-maid,** femme de chambre *f;* **–-pot,** pot de chambre *m.*

chamois, tchăme´oï, *n* chamois *m.*

champion, tchăme´-pi-eune, *n* champion *m. v* soutenir.

chance, tchânnce, *n* hasard *m;* (opportunity) occasion *f. a* fortuit. *v* risquer.

chancel, tchânn´-s'l, *n* sanctuaire *m.*

chancellor, tchânn´-seul-eur, *n* chancelier *m.*

chancery, tchânn´-ceu-ri, *n* chancellerie *f.*

chandelier, chănn-di-lîre´, *n* lustre *m.*

change, tchéne´-dje, *v* changer. *n* changement *m;* (cash) monnaie *f;* **–able,** *a* variable; **–less,** immuable.

channel, tchănn´-'l, *v* creuser. *n* canal *m;* voie *f;* (TV) chaîne *f;* **the English –,**La Manche *f.*

chant, tchânnte, *v* chanter. *n* chant *m;* plain-chant *m.*

chaos, qué´-oce, *n* chaos *m.*

chap, tchăpe, (hands, lips, etc.) *v* gercer. *n* gerçure *f;* (person) type *m.*

chapel, tchăp´-'l, *n* chapelle *f.*

chaperon, tchăpe´-eur-aune, *v* chaperonner. *n* chaperon *m.*

chaplain, tchăp´-l'n, *n* aumônier *m;* chapelain *m.*

chapter, tchăp´-teur, *n* chapitre *m.*

char, tchâre, *v* carboniser; (clean) faire le ménage; **–woman,** *n* femme de ménage *f.*

character, căr´-ac-teur, *n* caractère *m;* genre *m;* personnage *m.*

charcoal, tchâr´-caule, *n* charbon de bois *m;* (*art*) fusain *m.*

charge, tchârdje, *n* attaque *f;* accusation *f;* (load) chargement *m;* (price) prix *m. v* attaquer; accuser; charger; (price) demander; **to take –,** se charger de.

chariot, tchăr´-i-otte, *n* char *m.*

charitable, tchăr´-i-ta-b'l, *a* charitable.

charity, tchăr´-i-ti, *n* charité *f.*

charm, tchârme, *v* charmer. *n* charme *m.*

charming, tchărm´-inng, *a* charmant.

chart, tchârte, *n* carte *f;* carte marine *f;* graphique *m;* tableau *m.*

charter, tchâr´-teur, *n* charte *f. v* (hire) affréter.

chary, tché´-ri, *a* circonspect; économe.

chase, tchéce, *v* chasser. *n* chasse *f.*

chasm, căz'm, *n* abîme *m.*

chaste*, tchéste, *a* chaste; **–n,** *v* châtier; purifier.

chastise, tchàss-tâïze´, *v* châtier.

chat, tchătte, *v* bavarder. *n* causerie *f;* **–ter,** caquet *m. v* jaser; (teeth) claquer; **–terbox,** *n* moulin à paroles *m.*

chattel, tchătt´-'l, *n* mobilier *m;* effets *mpl.*

chauffeur, chau´-*feur*, *n* chauffeur *m*.

cheap*, tchîpe, *a* & *adv* bon marché; **–en,** *v* baisser les prix; discréditer (réputation); **–er,** *a* meilleur marché; **–ness,** *n* bon marché *m*; médiocrité *f*.

cheat, tchîte, *v* tricher. *n* tricheur *m*; tricheuse *f*.

cheating, tchîte´-inng, *n* tricherie *f*.

check, tchéque, *n* chèque *m*; (restraint; chess) échec *m*; (verification) contrôle *m*; (pattern) à carreaux *mpl*. *v* (stop) arrêter; (repress) réprimer; (verify) vérifier; **–mate,** *n* échec et mat *m*. *v* mater; **–book,** carnet de chèques *m*.

checkered, tchèque´*curde*, *a* varié; mouvementé.

cheek, tchîque, *n* joue *f*; (*fam*) toupet *m*.

cheer, tchîre, *n* gaieté *f*; (applause) acclamation *f*. *v* acclamer; (brighten) égayer; **to –** (someone) **up,** remonter le moral (de quelqu'un); **–ful,** *a* joyeux; gai; **–less,** triste; sombre.

cheese, tchîze, *n* fromage *m*.

chemical, quèm´-i-k'l, *a* chimique.

chemist, quèm´-isste, *n* pharmacien,-ne *m* & *f*; chimiste *m*; (shop) pharmacie *f*; **–ry,** chimie *f*.

cherish, tchèr´-iche, *v* chérir.

cherry, tchèr´-i, *n* cerise *f*; **–tree,** cerisier *m*.

cherub, tchèr´-*eub*, *n* chérubin *m*.

chess, tchèss, *n* échecs *mpl*.

chest, tchèste, *n* coffre *m*; boîte *f*; (box) caisse *f*; (human) poitrine *f*; **–of drawers,** commode *f*.

chestnut, tchèste´-*notte*, *n* marron *m*; châtaigne *f*; (tree) châtaignier *m*. *a* châtain; **horse –,** *n* marron d'Inde *m*; (tree) marronnier *m*.

chew, tchiou, *v* mâcher.

chicken, tchik´-enne, *n* poulet *m*; **–pox,** varicelle *f*.

chide, tchâïde, *v* réprimander.

chief, tchîfe, *n* chef *m*; (*fam*) patron *m*. *a** principal.

chilblain, tchil´-bléne, *n* engelure *f*.

child, tchâïlde, *n* enfant *m* & *f*; **–hood,** enfance *f*;

–ish, *a* enfantin.

chill, tchill, *n* coup de froid *m*. *v* refroidir; réfrigérer.

chilly, tchil´-i, *a* un peu froid; frais.

chime, tchâïme, *v* carillonner. *n* carillon *m*.

chimney, tchime´-ni, *n* cheminée *f*.

chimneysweep, tchime´-ni-souîpe, *n* ramoneur *m*.

chin, tchine, *n* menton *m*.

china, tchâï-*na*, *n* porcelaine *f*.

chintz, tchine'tse, *n* perse *f*.

chip, tchipe, *v* tailler par éclats; ébrécher. *n* fragment *m*; éclat *m*; pomme frite *f*.

chiropodist, câï-rop´-o-diste, *n* pédicure *m*.

chirp, tcheurpe, *v* gazouiller.

chisel, tchiz´-'l, *n* ciseau *m*. *v* ciseler.

chivalrous, chiv´-*al*-*reusse*, *a* courtois; chevaleresque.

chives, tchâïvze, *npl* ciboulette *f*.

chloride, clau´-râïde, *n* chlorure *m*.

chlorine, clau´-rine, *n* chlore *m*.

chloroform, clau´-roforme, *n* chloroforme *m*.

chocolate, tchok´-ŏ-léte, *n* chocolat *m*.

choice, tchoa'ïce, *n* choix *m*. *a* choisi; surfin.

choir, couaï'r, *n* chœur *m*.

choke, tchauque, *v* étouffer; (block up) boucher; (car) *n* starter *m*.

cholera, col´-eŭr-a, *n* choléra *m*.

choose, tchouze, *v* choisir; **choosy,** *a* (*fam*) difficile.

chop, tchoppe, *n* côtelette *f*. *v* hacher; **-off,** couper; **-per,** *n* hachoir *m*.

choral, co´-r'l, *a* choral.

chord, côrde, *n* (*mus*) accord *m*.

chorister, cor´-iss-teur, *n* choriste *m*.

chorus, côr´-eusse, *n* chœur *m*; refrain *m*.

Christ, craïsste, *n* le Christ.

christen, criss-'n, *v* baptiser; **-ing,** *n* baptême *m*.

Christian, criss´-ti-'n, *n* & *a* chrétien *m*; chrétienne *f*.

Christianity, criss-ti-ann´-i-ti, *n* christianisme *m*.

Christmas, criss´-meusse, *n* Noël *m*; **-tree,** arbre de Noël *m*.

chronic, cronn´-ique, *a* chronique.

chronicle, cronn´-i-k'l, *n* chronique *f*.

chrysanthemum, cri-sanne´-tsi-meumme, *n* chrysanthème *m*.

chuck, tcho´-k, *v* jeter; lancer; flanquer.

chuckle, tcho´-k'l, *v* rire tout bas; glousser. *n* gloussement *m*.

church, tcheurtche, *n* église *f*; **-yard,** cimetière *m*.

churlish, cheur´-liche, *a* revêche; maussade.

churn, tcheurne, *n* baratter. *n* baratte *f*.

cider, sâï´-d'r, *n* cidre *m*.

cigar, si-gâre´, *n* cigare *m*.

cigarette, sig-a-rette´, *n* cigarette *f*; **-butt,** (*fam*) mégot *m*.

cinder, sinn´-d'r, *n* cendre *f*.

cinema, si´-ni-ma, *n* cinéma *m*.

cinnamon, sin´-na-meune, *n* cannelle *f*.

cipher, sâï´-f'r, *v* chiffrer. *n* chiffre *m*; zéro *m*.

circle, seur´-k'l, *v* entourer; tourner autour de. *n* cercle *m*.

circuit, seur´-kitte, *n* circuit *m*; tournée *f*.

circuitous, seur-kiou´-i-teusse, *a* détourné.

circular, seur´-kiou-l'r, *n* & *a* circulaire *f*.

circulate, seur´-kiou-léte, *v* circuler; faire circuler.

circulation, seur-kiou-lé´-ch'n, *n* circulation *f*; (newspaper, etc) tirage *m*.

circumference, seur-komm´-feur-'nce, *n* circonférence *f*.

circumflex, seur´-keume-flèxe, *a* circonflexe.

circumscribe, seur´-keume-scrâïbe, *v* circonscrire.

circumspect, seur´-keume-specte, *a* circonspect.

circumstance, seur´-keume-stănnce, *n* circonstance *f*.

circumstantial, seur-keume-stănn´-ch'l, *a* circonstanciel; **-evidence,** *n* preuve indirecte *f*.

circus, seur´-keusse, *n* cirque *m*; (place) rondpoint *m*.

cistern, siss´-teurne, *n* citerne *f*; (lavatory) réservoir de chasse d'eau *m*.

cite, sâïte, *v* citer.

citizen, sit´-i-z'n, *n* citoyen *m*; **-ship,** nationalité *f*.

city, sit´-i, *n* cité *f*; grande

ville.

civil, siv´-il, *a* civil; **–ian,**
n civil *m*; **–isation,**
civilization *f*; **–ity,**
politesse *f*; civilité *f*.

claim, cléme, *n*
réclamation *f*;
(inheritance) droit *m*;
prétention *f*; demande
de remboursement *f*. *v*
réclamer; prétendre;
–ant, *n* prétendant *m*.

clammy, clă´-mi, *a*
(hands) moite;
(weather) humide.

clamor, clămm´-*eur*, *v*
vociférer. *n* clameur *f*.

clamp, clămmpe, *n*
crampon *m*. *v*
cramponner.

clan, clănne, *n* clan *m*;
tribu *f*; (*fam*) clique *f*.

clandestine, clănne-
desse´-tinne, *a*
clandestin.

clang, clainng, *n* bruit
métallique *m*;
résonnement *m*. *v*
retentir.

clap, clăppe, *v* applaudir. *n*
(thunder) coup *m*.

clapping, clăpp´-innng, *n*
applaudissement *m*.

claret, clăr´-ette, *n* vin
rouge de Bordeaux *m*.

clarify, clăr´-i-fâï, *v*
clarifier; éclaircir.

clarinet, clăr´-i-nette, *n*

clarinette *f*.

clash, clăche, *n* choc *m*;
conflit *m*; *v* (se) heurter;
(of colors) jurer.

clasp, clâsspe, *v* étreindre.
n étreinte *f*; (catch)
fermoir *m*.

class, clâss, *n* classe *f*;
(school) classe *f*; cours
m. *v* classer.

classify, clăss´-i-fâï, *v*
classifier.

clatter, clătt´-*eur*, *n* fracas
m. *v* retentir.

clause, cloaze, *n* clause *f*;
(gram) proposition *f*.

claw, cloa, *v* griffer. *n*
griffe *f*; (bird of prey)
serre *f*; (crab, etc) pince
f.

clay, clé, *n* argile *f*; **–ey,** *a*
argileux.

clean, clîne, *v* nettoyer. *a*
propre. *adv* absolument;
–ing, *n* nettoyage *m*;
–liness, propreté *f*.

cleanse, clènnz, *v* purifier.

clear, clîre, *a* clair; net. *v*
éclaircir; évacuer;
dégager; (table)
desservir; **–ness,** *n* clarté
f.

clearance, clîr´-*a*nnce, *n*
dégagement *m*;
(customs)
dédouanement *m*; (sale)
liquidation *f*.

cleave, clîve, *v* fendre;

(cling) s'attacher à.

cleft, clefte, *n* fente *f*.

clemency, clémm´-enn-ci,
n clémence *f*.

clench, clentche, *v* serrer.

clergy, cleur´-dji, *n* clergé
m; **–man,** pasteur *m*;
prêtre *m*.

clerical, clé´-ri-k'l, *a*
clérical; de bureau;
–error, *n* erreur de
plume *f*; faute decopiste
f.

clerk, clărque, *n* employé
m; (law) clerc *m*.

clever*, clèv´-*eur*, *a*
habile; intelligent;
–ness, *n* habileté *f*.

click, clique, *n* déclic *m*.

client, clâï´-ennte, *n*
client, -ente *m* & *f*; **–ele,**
clientèle *f*.

cliff, cliffe, *n* falaise *f*.

climate, clâï´-méte, *n*
climat *m*.

climax, clâï´-măxe, *n*
comble *m*; point
culminant *m*; apogée *f*.

climb, clâïmme, *v* monter;
grimper; (mountain,
etc) gravir.

clinch, *v* conclure.

cling, clinng, *v* se
cramponner; adhérer.

clinic, clinn´-ik, *n*
clinique *f*; **–al,** *a*
clinique.

clink, clinnque, *v* tinter;

A
B
C
D
E
F
G
H
I
J
K
L
M
N
O
P
Q
R
S
T
U
V
W
X
Y
Z

(glasses) trinquer.

clip, clippe, v (cut) tondre; couper; agrafer; rogner.

cloak, clauque, n manteau m; cape f. v (fig) voiler; **—room,** vestiaire m; (station) consigne f.

clock, cloque, n horloge f; pendule f; **—maker,** horloger m; **—work,** mouvement d'horlogerie m.

clod, clodde, n motte de terre f.

clog, clogue, n entrave f; (shoe) sabot m. v obstruer.

cloister, cloa'ïss´-t'r, n cloître m.

close, clauze, n fin f. v fermer; terminer. a (weather) lourd; proche. adv (near) près de.

closet, cloz´-ette, n cabinet m; placard m.

closure, clau´-jeure, n fermeture f; résolution f.

clot, clotte, v cailler. n caillot m.

cloth, clots, n drap m; tissu m; **table- —,** nappe f.

clothe, claudz, v habiller; vêtir.

clothes, claudz-z, npl vêtements mpl; **—brush,** brosse à habits f.

clothing, claudz´-inng, n vêtements mpl.

cloud, clâ'oude, n nuage m. v obscurcir; **—y,** a nuageux.

clout, clâ'oute, n claque f; gifle f; influence f.

clove, clauve, n clou de girofle m.

clover, clauv´-'r, n trèfle m; **to be in —,** être comme coq en pâte.

clown, clâ'oune, n clown m.

club, clobbe, n club m; (cards) trèfle m; (stick) massue f; **golf —,** club m; **—foot,** pied bot m.

cluck, cloque, v glousser. n gloussement m.

clue, cloue, n indice m.

clump, clommpe, n (trees) bosquet m; (flowers) massif m; touffe f.

clumsiness, clomme´-zi-nesse, n maladresse f.

clumsy, clomme´-zi, a maladroit; gauche.

cluster, closs´-teur, n groupe m; (fruit) grappe f; (trees) bosquet m. v se grouper.

clutch, clotche, n griffe f; (motor) embrayage m. v saisir.

coach, cautche, n (motor) car m; (rail) wagon m; (tutor) répétiteur m. v donner des leçons

particulières; (sport) entraîner.

coagulate, cau-ăgue´-ioue-léte, v coaguler.

coal, caule, n houille f, charbon de terre m; **—mine,** mine f.

coalition, cau-ă-li´-ch'n, n coalition f.

coarse*, caurse, a grossier; gros; **—ness,** n grossièreté f; rudesse f.

coast, causste, n côte f; littoral m. v côtoyer.

coast guard, causste´-gârde, n garde-côte m.

coat, caute, n manteau m; pardessus m; (animal) manteau m, pelage m; (paint) couche f.

coax, cauxe, v enjôler; encourager.

cob, cobbe, n (horse) cob m; (swan) cygne mâle m; (nut) noisette f; (corn) épi de mais m.

cobbler, cob´-bleur, n cordonnier m.

cobweb, cob´-ouèbbe, n toile d'araignée f.

cochineal, cotch´-i-nîl, n cochenille f.

cock, coque, n (bird) coq m; (gun) chien m; (turn valve) robinet m; **—ade,** cocarde f; **—erel,** cochet m; **—roach,** blatte f; cafard m.

cockle, coque´-'l, n coque f.

cocoa, cau´-cau, n cacao m.

coconut, cau´-cau-notte, n noix de coco f.

cocoon, co-coune´, n cocon m.

cod, codde, n morue f; –– liver oil, huile de foie de morue f.

coddle, cod´-d'l, v choyer; dorloter.

code, caude, n code m.

codicil, codd´-i-sile, n codicille m.

coeducation, cau-èd-iou-ké´-ch'n, n coéducation f; enseignement mixte m.

coerce, cau-eurce´, v contraindre.

coffee, cof´-i, n café m; –– pot, cafetière f.

coffer, cof´-eur, n coffre m; caisse f.

coffin, cof´-inne, n cercueil m.

cog, cogue, n dent de roue f; ––wheel, roue dentée f.

coherent*, cau-hî´-r'nt, a cohérent.

cohesion, cau-hî´-j'n, n cohésion f.

coil, coa´ile, n rouleau m; (electric) bobine f. v en-rouler; (reptile) s'enrouler.

coin, coa'inne, n pièce de monnaie f.

coincide, cau-inn-çâïde´, v coïncider.

coincidence, cau-inn´-si-d'ns, n coïncidence f.

coke, cauque, n coke m.

cold, caulde, n froid m; (med) rhume m. a* froid.

colic, col´-ique, n colique f.

collaborate, cŏl-la´-bo-réte, v collaborer.

collaborator, col-la´-bo-ra-t'r, n collaborateur m.

collapse, cŏl-lăpse´, v s'affaisser. n effondrement m.

collar, col´-eur, n col m; (dog) collier m; ––bone, clavicule f.

collate, col-léte´, v collationner; assembler.

colleague, col´-ligue, n collègue m.

collect, cŏl-lècte´, v rassembler; (stamps, etc) collectionner; (money) encaisser; (charity) quêter; –ion, n collection f; (charity) quête f; (postal) levée f; –ive*, a collectif; –or, n collectionneur m; (tax) percepteur m.

college, col´-idj, n collège m; école f.

collide, cŏl-lâïde´, v se heurter; se tamponner.

collier, col´-i-eur, n mineur m; –y, houillère f.

collision, cŏl-li´-j'n, n collision f; rencontre f; (railroad) tamponnement m; (ships) abordage m.

colloquial*, cŏl-lau´-coui-al, a familier.

collusion, cŏl-lioue´-j'n, n collusion f.

colon, cau´-l'n, n deux points mpl; (anat) côlon m.

colonel, queur´-n'l, n colonel m.

colonist, col´-ŏnn-iste, n colon m.

colonnade, col-ŏnn-éde´, n colonnade f.

colony, col´-ŏ-ni, n colonie f.

color, col´-eur, n couleur f. v colorier.

coloring, col´-eur-inng, n coloris m; teint m.

colossal, cau-loss´-'l, a colossal.

colt, caulte, n poulain m.

column, col´-eume, n colonne f.

coma, cau´-mă, n (med) coma m.

comb, caume, n peigne m;

(bird) crête f. v peigner.

combat, comm´-batte, n combat m. v combattre; **–ant,** n combattant m; **–ive,** a batailleur.

combination, comm-bi-né´-ch'n, n combinaison f.

combine, cŏmm-bâïne´, v combiner.

combustion, cŏmm´-bosse´-tch'n, n combustion f.

come, comme, v venir; arriver; **–down,** descendre; **–in,** entrer; **–off,** se détacher; **–out,** sortir; **–up,** monter.

comedian, cŏ-mi´-di-anne, n comédien m.

comedy, comm´-i-di, n comédie f.

comet, comm´-ette, n comète f.

comfort, comm´-feurte, n confort m; consolation f; (relief) soulagement m. v consoler.

comfortable, comm´-feurta-b'l, a confortable.

comic, comm´-ique, a comique.

coming, comm´-inng, a proche; futur. n venue f.

comma, comm´-ma, n virgule f.

command, cŏmm-ânnde´, v commander; dominer.

n ordre m; (knowledge) facilité f; **–er,** commandant m; **–ment(s),** commandement(s) m (pl).

commence, cŏmm-ennce´, v commencer; **–ment,** n commencement m.

commend, cŏmm-ennde´, v recommander; (praise) louer; **–ation,** n éloge m; louange f.

comment, comm´-ennte, n commentaire m; observation f. v commenter; **commentary,** n commentaire m.

commerce, comm´-eurce, n commerce m.

commercial, cŏmm-eur´-ch'l, a commercial.

commiserate, cŏmm-iz´-eur-été, v plaindre.

commission, cŏmm-ich´-'n, v charger de. n commission f; (mil) brevet m.

commit, cŏmm-itte´, v commettre; envoyer en prison; (bind) engager.

commitment, cŏmm-it´-ment, n engagement m; responsabilité f.

committee, cŏmm-it´-ti, n comité m.

commodious, cŏmm-aud´-

i-euce, a spacieux.

commodity, cŏmm-od´-i-ti, n produit m; marchandise f.

common, comm´-'n, a commun; ordinaire; **–place,** banal.

commotion, cŏmm-au´-ch'n, n commotion f.

commune, cŏmm-ioune´, n commune f. v converser.

communicate, cŏmm-ioue´-ni-quéte, v communiquer.

communication, cŏmm-ioue´-ni-qué´-ch'n, n communication f.

communion, cŏmm-ioue´-nieune, n communion f.

communism, cŏmm´-ioue-niz'm, n communisme m.

communist, comm´-ioue-nisste, a & n communiste mf.

community, cŏmm-ioue´-ni-ti, n communauté f.

commute, cŏmm-moute´, v (é)changer; commuer.

compact, comm´-păcte, n pacte m; (powder) poudrier m. a compact.

companion, cŏmm-pănn´-ieune, n compagnon m; **–ship,** n camaraderie f.

company, comm´-pa-ni, n compagnie f.

comparative*, cŏmm-păr´-*a*-tive, *a* comparatif.

compare, cŏmm-père´, *v* comparer.

comparison, cŏmm-păr´-i-s'n, *n* comparaison *f.*

compartment, cŏmm-parte´-m'nt, *n* compartiment *m*; case *f.*

compass, comm´-*passe*, *n* (magnetic) boussole *f*; (a pair of) –**es**, *pl* compas *m.*

compassionate, cŏmm-păch´-*eune*-éte, *a* compatissant.

compel, cŏmm-pel´, *v* contraindre; forcer.

compensate, comm´-penn-séte, *v* compenser.

compensation, cŏmm-penn-sé´-ch'n, *n* compensation *f.*

compete, cŏmm-pîte´, *v* concourir.

competence, comm´-pi-t'nce, *n* compétence *f.*

competent*, *a* capable; compétent.

competition, cŏmm-pi-ti´-ch'n, *n* (*com*) concurrence *f*; (games, sport) concours *m.*

competitor, cŏmm-pett´-i-*teur*, *n* (*com*) concurrent *m*; (sport, etc) compétiteur *m.*

compile, cŏmm-pâîle´, *v* compiler; composer.

complacent, cŏmm-plé´-cennte, *a* content de soirmême.

complain, cŏmm-pléne´, *v* se plaindre.

complaint, cŏmm-plénnte´, *n* plainte *f*; maladie *f.*

complement, comm´-plî-m'nt, *n* effectif *m*; complément.

complete, cŏmm-plîte´, *v* achever. *a** complet.

completion, cŏmm-plî-ch'n, *n* achèvement *m.*

complex, comm´-plexe, *a* compliqué; complexe. *n* complexe *m.*

complexion, cŏmm-plèque´-ch'n, *n* (face) teint *m.*

compliance, cŏmm-plâî´-'nt, *n* conformité *f.*

compliant, cŏmm-plâî´-'nt, *a* complaisant; soumis.

complicate, comm´-pli-quéte, *v* compliquer.

compliment, comm´-pli-m'nt, *n* compliment *m. v* faire des compliments; –**s**, *npl* compliments *mpl.*

comply, cŏmm-plâî´, *v* –**with**, se conformer à.

component, cŏmm-pau´-n'nt, *n* composant *m.*

compose, cŏmm-pauze´, *v* composer; calmer.

composer, cŏmm-pau´-*zeur*, *n* compositeur *m.*

composition, cŏmm-pau-si´-ch'n, *n* composition *f.*

compositor, cŏmm-po´-zi-t'r, *n* compositeur *m.*

composure, cŏmm-pau´-*jeure*, *n* calme *m*; sang-froid *m.*

compound, comm´-pâ'ounnde, *v* composer. *n* espace clos *m. a* composé; –**interest**, intérêt composé *m.*

comprehend, cŏmm-pri-hennde´, *v* comprendre.

comprehension, cŏmm-pri-henn´-ch'n, *n* compréhension *f.*

compress, cŏmm-presse´, *v* comprimer. *n* compresse *f.*

comprise, cŏmm-prâîze´, *v* contenir; comprendre.

compromise, comm´-prŏmâîze, *n* compromis *m. v* compromettre.

compulsion, cŏmm-pol´-ch'n, *n* contrainte *f.*

compulsory, cŏmm-pol´-sŏr-i, *a* obligatoire.

compunction, cŏmm-ponnk´-ch'n, *n* remords *m.*

computation, cŏmm-piou-

te-ch'n, *n* calcul *m*;
computation *f*.

compute, cŏmm-pioute´, *v*
estimer; calculer.

computer, cŏmm-piou´-t'r,
n ordinateur *m*.

comrade, comm´-réde, *n*
camarade *m* & *f*;
compagnon *m*.

concave, cŏnn´-quéve, *a*
concave.

conceal, cŏnn-cîle´, *v*
cacher.

concede, cŏnn-cîde´, *v*
concéder.

conceit, cŏnn-cîte´, *n*
vanité *f*; prétention *f*;
–ed, *a* prétentieux.

conceive, cŏnn-cîve´, *v*
concevoir; (s') imaginer.

concentrate, cŏnn´-seune-
tréte, *v* concentrer.

conception, cŏnn-seppe´-
ch'n, *n* conception *f*.

concern, cŏnn-seurne´, *n*
affaire *f*; (disquiet) souci
m. *v* concerner; **to be
–ed,** s'inquiéter.

concert, cŏnn´-seurte, *n*
concert *m*.

concession, cŏnn-sèch´-
eune, *n* concession *f*.

conciliate, cŏnn-cil´-i-éte,
v concilier.

concise, cŏnn-sâïce´, *a*
concis.

conclude, cŏnn-cloude´, *v*
conclure.

conclusion, cŏnn-cloue´-
j'n, *n* conclusion *f*.

conclusive, cŏnn-cloue´-
cive, *a* concluant.

concoct, cŏnn-cocte´, *v*
élaborer; préparer;
combiner.

concord, cŏnn´-côrde, *n*
concorde *f*; accord *m*.

concrete, cŏnn´-crîte, *n*
béton *m*. *a* concret.

concur, cŏnn-queur´, *v*
concourir; être d'accord.

concussion, cŏnn-coch´-
'n, *n* choc *m*; (*med*)
commotion *f*.

condemn, cŏnn-demme´,
v condamner.

condense, cŏnn-dennce´,
v condenser.

condescend, cŏnn-di-
cennde´, *v*
condescendre.

condescension, cŏnn-di-
cenn´-ch'n, *n*
condescendance *f*.

condition, cŏnn-di´-ch'n,
n condition *f*.

conditional*, cŏnn-dich´-
eun-'l, *a* conditionnel.

condole, cŏnn-daule´, *v*
exprimer ses
condoléances.

condolence, cŏnn-daul´-
'ns, *n* condoléance *f*.

condone, cŏnn-daune´, *v*
pardonner; fermer les
yeux sur.

conducive, cŏnn-dioue´-
cive, *a* contribuant à.

conduct, cŏnn-docte´, *v*
conduire; (*mus*) diriger.
n conduite *f*.

conductor, cŏnn-doct´-'r,
n conducteur *m*; chef
d'orchestre *m*.

cone, caune, *n* cône *m*;
(ice cream) cornet *m*.

confectioner, cŏnn-
féque´-cheunn-*eur*, *n*
confiseur *m*; (shop)
confiserie *f*; **–y,** bonbons
mpl; confiserie *f*.

confederate, cŏnn-féd´-
eur-éte, *n* & *a* confédéré
m; complice *m*.

confederation, cŏnn-féd´-
eur-é´-ch'n, *n*
confédération *f*.

confer, cŏnn-feur´, *v*
conférer; accorder.

conference, cŏnn´-feur-
ennce, *n* conférence *f*;
congrès *m*.

confess, cŏnn-fesse´, *v*
avouer; (*eccl*) confesser.

confession, cŏnn-fé´-ch'n,
n aveu *m*; (*eccl*)
confession *f*.

confide, cŏnn-fâïde´, *v*
confier; se confier à.

confidence, cŏnn´-fi-d'ns,
n confidence *f*; (faith)
confiance *f*.

confident, cŏnn´-fi-
dennte, *a* confiant;

assuré.

confidential*, cŏnn-fi-
denn´-ch'l, *a*
confidentiel.

confine, cŏnn-fâïne´, *v*
limiter; enfermer;
–ment, *n*
emprisonnement *m*;
(birth) accouchement
m.

confirm, cŏnn-feurme´, *v*
confirmer.

confirmation, cŏnn-feur-
mé´-ch'n, *n*
confirmation *f*.

confiscate, cŏnn´-fisse-
quéte, *v* confisquer.

conflagration, cŏnn-fla-
gré´-ch'n, *n* incendie *m*;
conflagration *f*.

conflict, conn´-flicte, *n*
conflit *m*; (combat)
lutte *f*. *v* être en conflit.

conflicting, cŏnn-flique´-
tinng, *a* contradictorie.

conform, cŏnn-foarme´, *v*
se conformer.

confound, cŏnn-
fâ'ounnde´, *v* confondre.

confront, cŏnn-fronnte´, *v*
confronter; affronter.

confuse, cŏnn-fiouze´, *v*
déconcerter;
embrouiller.

confusion, cŏnn-fioue´-
j'n, *n* confusion *f*.

congeal, cŏnn-djîle´, *v*
congeler; se congeler.

congenial, cônn-djî´-ni-*al*,
a sympathique.

congenital, cŏnn-djenn´-
i-t'l, *a* (*med*) congénital.

congest, cŏnn-djeste´, *v*
entasser; congestionner;
–ion, *n* (traffic)
embouteillage *m*; (*med*)
congestion *f*.

congratulate, cŏnn-grăt´-
iou-léte, *v* féliciter.

congratulation, cŏnn-
grăt-iou-lé´-ch'n, *n*
félicitation *f*.

congregate, conng´-gri-
guéte, *v* se rassembler.

congregation, cŏnng-gri-
gué´-ch'n, *n* assemblée *f*;
congrégation *f*.

congress, conng´-gresse, *n*
congrès *m*.

conjecture, cŏnn-djéque´-
tioure, *n* conjecture *f*. *v*
conjecturer.

conjugal, cŏnn´-djoue-g'l,
a conjugal.

conjunction, cŏnn-
djonngk´-ch'n, *n*
conjonction *f*.

conjurer, conn´-djeur-*eur*,
n prestidigitateur *m*.

connect, cŏnn-necte´, *v*
unir; relier à.

connection, cŏnn-nec´-
ch'n, *n* rapport *m*; lien
m; (train, etc)
correspondance *f*.

connoisseur, cŏnn-oss-

eur´, *n* connaisseur *m*.

conquer, conng´-queur, *v*
conquérir; vaincre.

conqueror, cónng´-queur-
eur, *n* conquérant *m*.

conquest, conng´-coueste,
n conquête *f*.

conscience, conn´-
chennce, *n* conscience *f*.

conscientious*, cŏnn-
chienn´-*cheuce*, *a*
consciencieux.

conscious, conn´-*cheuce*,
a conscient; **–ness,** *n*
conscience *f*; (*med*)
connaissance *f*.

conscript, conn´-scripte, *n*
conscrit *m*.

consecrate, conn´-ci-
créte, *v* consacrer; bénir.

consecutive*, cŏnn-sèk´-
iou-tive, *a* consécutif.

consent, cŏnn-cennte´, *v*
consentir. *n*
consentement *m*.

consequence, conn´-ci-
couènnce, *n*
conséquence *f*.

consequently, conn´-ci-
couènn-tli, *adv* par
conséquent.

conservative, cŏnn-seur´-
va-tive, *n* & *a*
conservateur, -trice *m* &
f.

conservatory, cŏnn-seur´-
va-teur-i, *n* serre *f*;
conservatoire *f*.

a
b
c
d
e
f
g
h
i
j
k
l
m
n
o
p
q
r
s
t
u
v
w
x
y
z

A
B
C
D
E
F
G
H
I
J
K
L
M
N
O
P
Q
R
S
T
U
V
W
X
Y
Z

conserve, cŏnn-seurve´, v conserver.

consider, cŏnn-cid´-eur, v considérer; **–able,** a considérable; **–ate,** attentionné; **–ation,** n considération f; **–ing,** prep vu; étant donné.

consign, cŏnn-sâïne´, v livrer; consigner; confier à; **–ee,** n destinataire m; **–ment,** envoi m; **–or,** expéditeur m.

consist, cŏnn-cisste´, v consister; **–ency,** n consistance f; **–ent,** a compatible; conforme; logique; stable.

consolation, cŏnn-saule-é´-ch'n, n consolation f.

console, cŏnn-saule´, v consoler.

consonant, conn´-so-nennte, n consonne f.

conspicuous, cŏnn-spik´-iou-euce, a apparent; en évidence; **to make oneself –,** se faire remarquer.

conspiracy, cŏnn-spir´-a-ci, n complot m.

conspirator, cŏnn-spir´-é-teur, n conspirateur m.

conspire, cŏnn-spâïre´, v conspirer.

constable, conn´-sta-b'l, n agent de police m.

constabulary, cŏnn-stăb´-iou-la-ri, n gendarmerie f; police f.

constancy, conn´-stann-ci, n constance f.

constant, conn´-stannte, a constant; continuel.

constipation, cŏnn-sti-pé´-ch'n, n constipation f.

constituency, cŏnn-sti´-tiou-enn-ci, n circonscription électorale f; électeurs mpl.

constituent, cŏnn-sti´-tiou-'nt, n électeur m.

constitute, conn´-sti-tioute, v constituer.

constitution, cŏnn-sti-tiou´-ch'n, n constitution f.

constrain, cŏnn-stréne´, v contraindre.

constraint, cŏnn-strénnte´, n contrainte f.

constriction, cŏnn-stric´-ch'n, n rétrécissement m; resserrement m.

construct, cŏnn-strocte´, v construire.

construction, cŏnn-stroc´-ch'n, n construction f.

construe, conn´-stroue, v construire; interpréter.

consul, conn´-seul, n consul m; **–ate,** consulat m.

consult, cŏnn-solte´, v consulter; **–ation,** n consultation f.

consume, cŏnn-sioume´, v consumer; (food) consommer.

consumer, cŏnn-sioue´-meur, n consommateur m.

consummate, conn´-somm-éte, v consommer; a âchevé.

consummation, cŏnn-somm-mé´-ch'n, n consommation f; accomplissement m.

consumption, cŏnn-sommp´-ch'n, n (use) consommation f; (med) comsomption pulmonaire f.

consumptive, cŏnn-sommp´-tive, a & n tuberculeux.

contact, conn´-tăcte, n contact m; **–lens,** verre de contact m.

contagious, cŏnn-té´-djeuce, a contagieux.

contain, cŏnn-téne´, v contenir; retenir.

contaminate, cŏnn-tămm´-i-néte, v contaminer.

contemplate, cŏnn´-temm-pléte, v contempler; projeter.

contemporary, cŏnn-temm´-pŏ-ra-ri, n & a

contemporain, -aine.

contempt, cŏnn-temmp´- 't, n mépris m; – of court, refus de comparaître.

contemptible, cŏnn- temmp´-ti-b'l, a méprisable.

contend, cŏnn-tennde´, v contester; (maintain) soutenir.

content, cŏnn-tennte´, v contenter. a satisfait; **–ment,** n contentement m.

content, cŏnn´-tennte, n contenu m.

contention, cŏnn-tenn´- ch'n, n prétention f.

contentious, cŏnn-tenn´- cheuce, a discutable.

contents, conn´-tenn-ts, npl contenu m.

contest, cŏnn-tesste´, v contester. n concours m; match m.

contiguous, cŏnn-tigue´- iou-euce, a contigu.

continent, conn´-ti- nennte, n continent m.

contingency, cŏnn-tinn´- djenn-ci, n éventualité f.

contingent, cŏnn-tinn´- djennte, a éventuel; contingent.

continual*, cŏnn-tinn´- iou'l, a continuel.

continuation, cŏnn-tinn´-

iou-é´-ch'n, n continuation f.

continue, cŏnn-tinn´- ioue, v continuer.

continuous*, cŏnn-tinn´- iou-euce, a continu.

contortion, cŏnn-toar´- ch'n, n contorsion f.

contraband, conn´-tra- bănnde, n contrebande f.

contract, conn´-trăcte, n contrat m. v contracter; **–ion,** n contraction f; **–or,** fournisseur m; (builder) entrepreneur m.

contradict, cŏnn-tra- dicte´, v contredire; **–ion,** n contradiction f.

contrary, conn´-tra-ri, n & a contraire m.

contrast, conn´-traste, n contraste m.

contrast, cŏnn-traste´, v contraster.

contravene, cŏnn-tra- vîne´, v enfreindre.

contravention, cŏnn-tra- venn´-ch'n, n contravention f.

contribute, cŏnn-trib´- ioute, v contribuer.

contribution, cŏnn-trib- iou´-ch'n, n contribution f; (literary) article m.

contrite, conn´-trăïte, a

contrit.

contrivance, cŏnn-trâï´- v'nce, n invention f; dispositif m; (fam) manigance f.

contrive, cŏnn-trâïve´, v inventer; trouver moyen; (fam) machiner.

control, cŏnn-traule´, v contrôler; (feelings) (se) maîtriser. n contrôle m; (feelings) maîtrise f; (authority) direction f; **–ler,** contrôleur m.

controversial, cŏnn-trŏ- veur´-ch'l, a polémique.

controversy, conn´-trŏ- veur-ci, n controverse f.

convalescence, cŏnn-va- less-ennce, convalescence f.

convalescent, cŏnn-va- less´-'nt, a & n convalescent.

convenience, cŏnn-vî´- ennce, n convenance f; commodité f.

convenient, cŏnn-vî´-ni- ennte, a commode.

convent, conn´-vennte, n couvent m.

convention, cŏnn-venn´- ch'n, n convention f.

converge, cŏnn-veurdje´, v converger.

conversant, conn-veur´- s'nt, a au courant de.

conversation, cŏnn-veur-

a b **c** d e f g h i j k l m n o p q r s t u v w x y z

cé´-ch'n, n conversation f.

converse, cŏnn-veurse´, v s'entretenir.

conversion, cŏnn-veur´-ch'n, n conversion f.

convert, cŏnn-veurte´, v convertir. n converti m.

convex, conn´-vexe, a convexe.

convey, cŏnn-vé´, v transporter; transmettre; présenter; **–ance,** n transport m; (law) transfert m.

convict, cŏnn-victe´, v condamner; **–ion,** n condamnation f; (belief) conviction f.

convict, conn´-victe, n forçat m; bagnard m.

convince, cŏnn-vinnce´, v convaincre.

convivial, cŏnn-viv´-ial, a jovial; sociable; digne de bons convives.

convoy, cŏnn-voa'i´, v convoyer; escorter. n convoi m.

convulse, cŏnn-vol´, v convulser.

convulsion, cŏnn-vol´-ch'n, n convulsion f.

coo, cou, v roucouler.

cook, couk, v faire cuire; faire la cuisine; cuire. n cuisinier, -ère m & f.

cookery, couk´-eur-i, n cuisine f.

cool, coule, v refroidir. a frais; froid; **–ness,** n fraîcheur f; (nerve) sang-froid m.

coop, coupe, n cage à poulets f.

cooperate, cau-op´-eur-éte, v coopérer.

cope, caupe, v **–with,** se débrouiller de.

copious*, cau´-pi-euce, a copieux.

copper, cop´-eur, n cuivre m. a de cuivre.

coppice, copse, cop´-ice, copce, n taillis m.

copy, cop´-i, v copier. n copie f; (of book) exemplaire m; (newspaper, etc) numéro m; **–right,** droits d'auteur m.

coquetry, coque´-éte-ri, n coquetterie f.

coral, cor´-al, n corail m.

cord, côrde, v corder. n corde f.

cordial, côr´-di-al, a cordial.

corduroy, coar´-diou-roa'ï, n velours côtelé m.

core, caure, n cœur m; trognon m.

cork, corque, v boucher. n liège m; (stopper) bouchon m; **–screw,** tire-bouchon m.

corn, côrne, n blé m; (foot, etc) cor m.

corner, côr´-n'r, n coin m; (road bend) tournant m; virage m, accaparer; acculer.

cornflower, côrne´-flâ'ou-eur, n bluet m.

cornice, cor´-nice, n corniche f.

coronation, cor-ŏ-né´-ch'n, n couronnement m.

coroner, cor´-o-neur, n magistrat enquêteur m.

coronet, cor´-o-nette, n couronne f.

corporal, coar´-pŏ-r'l, n caporal m; (artillery and cavalry) brigadier m. a corporel.

corporation, coar´-pŏ-ré´-ch'n, n corporation f.

corps, core, n corps m.

corpse, coarpse, n cadavre m.

corpulence, cor´-piou-lenn-ce, n corpulence f.

corpulent, cor´-piou-l'nt, a corpulent.

corpuscle, cor´-peuss-'l, n corpuscule m.

correct*, cŏr-recte´, a correct. v corriger; **–ive,** a correctif; **–ness,** n exactitude f.

correspond, cŏr-i-sponnde´, v

correspondre; **–ence,** *n* correspondance *f*.

corridor, cŏr´-i-doar, *n* corridor *m*; couloir *m*.

corroborate, cŏr-rôb´-ŏ-réte, *v* corroborer.

corroboration, cŏr-rôb´-ŏ-ré´-ch'n, *n* corroboration *f*.

corrode, cŏr-raude´, *v* corroder.

corrosive, cŏr-rau´-sive, *n* & *a* corrosif *m*.

corrugated, cor´-rou-gué-tedde, **–paper,** *n* papier ondulé *m*; **–iron,** tôle ondulée *f*.

corrupt, cŏr-ropte´, *v* corrompre. *a* corrompu.

corruption, cŏr-rope´-ch'n, *n* corruption *f*.

corset, cor´-cette, *n* corset *m*.

cortege, cŏr-téje´, *n* cortège *m*.

cost, coste, *n* prix *m*; (expense) frais *mpl*. *v* coûter; **–ly,** *a* coûteux; **–s,** *npl* (law) dépens *mpl*.

costume, cosse´-tioume, *n* costume *m*.

cot, cotte, *n* lit d'enfant *m*.

cottage, cot´-idj, *n* (thatched) chaumière *f*; cottage *m*.

cotton, cot´-t'n, *n* coton *m*; **–wool,** ouate *f*;

(*med*) coton hydrophile *m*.

couch, câ'outche, *n* canapé *m*; divan *m*.

cough, coaf, *v* tousser. *n* toux *f*.

council, câ'ounn´-cil, *n* conseil *m*; **–lor,** conseiller *m*.

counsel, câ'ounn´-s'l, *n* avocat conseil *m*. *v* conseiller; **–or,** *n* conseiller *m*; (law) conseil *m*.

count, câ'ounnte, *v* compter. *n* compte *m*; **–inghouse,** la comptabilité *f*; **–less,** *a* innombrable.

count, câ'ounnte, *n* (title) comte *m*; **–ess,** comtesse *f*.

countenance, câ'ounn´-teu-nannce, *v* approuver. *n* contenance *f*.

counter, câ'ounn´-teur, *n* comptoir *m*; (games) jeton *m*. *adv* contre; **–act,** *v* contrarier; neutraliser; (frustrate) déjouer; **–balance,** contrebalancer; **–feit,** *v* contrefaire. *a* faux. *n* faux *m*; **–foil,** talon *m*; **–mand,** *v* contremander. *n* contre-ordre *m*; **–pane,** couvre-lit *m*;

–part, contre-partie *f*; **–sign,** *v* contresigner. *n* mot d'ordre *m*.

country, conn´-tri, *n* (state) pays *m*; (rural) campagne *f*.

county, câ'ounn´-ti, *n* comté *m*.

couple, cop´-p'l, *v* accoupler. *n* couple *m*.

courage, cor´-idj, *n* courage *m*.

courageous*, keur-é´-djeuce, *a* courageux.

course, corse, *n* (river, tuition) cours *m*; (direction) route *f*; (race) champ de courses *m*; (meals) plat *m*; **of –**,*adv* naturellement.

court, côrte, *n* (royal) cour *f*; (law) tribunal *m*; (tennis) court *m*. *v* faire la cour à; **–ier,** *n* courtisan *m*; **– martial,** conseil de guerre *m*; **–ship,** cour *f*; **–yard,** cour *f*.

courteous*, keur-ti-*eu*ce, *a* courtois.

courtesy, keur-ti-ci, *n* courtoisie *f*.

cousin, co´-z'n, *n* cousin *m*; cousine *f*.

cove, cauve, *n* (*geog*) anse *f*; petite baie *f*.

covenant, cov´-nannte, *n* pacte *m*; contrat *m*. *v*

A
B
C
D
E
F
G
H
I
J
K
L
M
N
O
P
Q
R
S
T
U
V
W
X
Y
Z

stipuler.

cover, cov´-*eur,* n
couverture f; (lid)
couvercle m; (shelter)
abri m. v couvrir.

covet, cov´-ette, v
convoiter.

cow, câ´ou, n vache f. v
intimider: **–slip,** n
coucou m.

coward, câ´ou´-*eur*de, n
lâche m & f; **–ice,**
lâcheté f.

cower, câ´ou´-*eur,* v se
tapir.

cowl, câ´oule, n (hood,
chimney) capuchon m.

coy, côa´ï, a réservé;
timide.

cozy, cauz´-i, a
confortable; à l'aise.

crab, crăbbe, n crabe m; **–
apple,** pomme sauvage f.

crack, crăque, n (small)
craquelure f; fente f;
(glass) fêlure f; (noise)
craquement m; (whip)
claquement m. v
craqueler; fendre; fêler;
craquer; claquer; (nuts)
casser; **–er,** n (firework)
pétard m; (nut)
cassenoisette m; **–le,** v
craquer; (fire) pétiller.

cradle, cré´-d'l, n (crib)
berceau m.

craft, crâfte, n (trade)
métier m; (naut)

embarcation f;
(cunning) ruse f; **–sman,**
artisan m; **–y,** a rusé.

crag, crăgue, n rocher à
pic m.

cram, crămme, v bourrer.

cramp, crămmpe, n
crampe f.

cranberry, crănne´-bê-ri,
n airelle f.

crane, créne, n grue f.

crank, crain-ngk, n (mech)
manivelle f.

crash, crăche, v (break)
briser; (aero) s'écraser;
(car) se tamponner. n
(car, train) accident m;
(noise) fracas m.

crate, créte, n caisse f,
cageot m.

crater, cré-*teur,* n cratère
m.

crave, créve v implorer;
désirer ardemment.

craving, créve´-inng, n
désir ardent m.

crawl, croal, v ramper.

crayfish, cré´-fiche, n
écrevisse f; (sea)
langouste f.

crayon, cré´-onn, n pastel
m.

craze, créze, n (mode)
manie f; engouement m.

crazy, cré´-zi, a toqué; fou.

creak, crîque, v grincer. n
craquement m.

cream, crîme, n crème f;

–y, a crémeux.

crease, crîce, n (press) pli
m; (crush) faux pli m. v
se froisser.

create, cri-éte´, v créer;
produire.

creature, crî´-tioure, n
créature f.

credentials, cri-denn´-
ch'lz, npl lettres de
créance fpl; papiers
d'identité mpl.

credible, crèd´-i-b'l, a
croyable.

credit, crèd´-itte, n crédit
m. v créditer; **–able,** a
estimable; honorable;
–or, n créancier m.

credulous, crèd´-iou-
leuce, a crédule.

creed, crîde, n croyance f.

creek, crîque, n crique f.

creep, crîpe, v se traîner;
(silently) se glisser;
(plants, animals, etc)
ramper.

creeper, crî´-*peur,* n plante
grimpante f.

cremate, cri-méte´, v
incinérer.

cremation, cri-mé´-ch'n, n
crémation f.

creole, crî´-ôle, n & a
créole m & f.

crescent, cress-´'nt, n
croissant m.

cress, cresse, n cresson m.

crest, cresste, n (heraldry)

armes *fpl*; (seal, etc) écusson; *m* (hill, bird's) crête *f*; **–fallen,** *a* penaud; abattu.

crevice, crév´-ice, *n* crevasse *f*.

crew, croue, *n* (*naut*) équipage *m*.

crick, crique, *n* crampe *f*; (neck) torticolis *m*.

cricket, cri´-quette, *n* grillon *m*; (game) cricket *m*.

crime, crâïme, *n* crime *m*.

criminal, crimm´-i-n'l, *n* & *a* criminel *m* & *f*.

crimson, crimm´-z'n, *n* & *a* cramoisi *m*.

cringe, crinn´-dje, *v* faire des courbettes; se blottir.

crinkle, crinn´-k'l, *v* froisser. *n* froissement *m*.

cripple, crip´-p'l, *n* estropié *m*. *v* estropier.

crisis, crâï´-cisse, *n* crise *f*.

crisp, crispe, *a* (food) croustillant.

criterion, crâï-ti´-ri-*eu*ne, *n* critère *m*.

critic, cri´-tique, *n* critique *m*; **–al*,** *a* critique.

criticism, crit´-i-ci-z'm, *n* critique *f*.

criticize, crit´-i-sâïze, *v* critiquer.

croak, crauque, *v* (bird) croasser; (frog) coasser.

n croassement *m*; coassement *m*.

crochet, cro´-ché, *n* crochet *m*. *v* faire du crochet.

crockery, crok´-*eu*-ri, *n* vaisselle *f*.

crocodile, crok´-o-dâïle, *n* crocodile *m*.

crocus, cro´-qu*eu*ce, *n* crocus *m*.

crook, crouk, *n* (*pers*) escroc *m*.

crooked, crouk´-edde, *a* tordu; de travers; malhonnête.

crop, crope, *n* récolte *f*; (haircut) coupe *f*. *v* tondre.

cross, crosse, *n* croix *f*. *a* fâché; entravers. *v* (intersect) croiser; **–examine,** interroger; **–ing,** *n* traversée *f*; **–out,** *v* rayer; **–over,** traverser; **–road,** *n* carrefour *m*.

crotchet, crotch´-ette, *n* (music) noire *f*.

crouch, crâ'outche, *v* se tapir; s'accroupir.

crow, crau, *n* corbeau *m*. *v* (cock) chanter.

crowbar, crau´-bâre, *n* pince *f*.

crowd, crâ'oude, *n* foule *f*. *v* encombrer; (s') entasser.

crown, crâ'ounne, *n*

couronne *f*; (top) sommet *m*. *v* couronner.

crucible, croue´-ci-b'l, *n* creuset *m*.

crucifix, croue´-ci-fixe, *n* crucifix *m*.

crucify, croue´-ci-fâï, *v* crucifier.

crude*, croude, *a* (raw) cru; (vulgar) grossier.

cruel*, croue´-*eul*, *a* cruel; **–ty,** *a* cruauté *f*.

cruise, crouze, *v* faire une croisière. *n* croisière *f*.

cruiser, croue´-zeur, *n* croiseur *m*.

crumb, cromme, *n* mie *f*; (particle) miette *f*.

crumble, cromm´-b'l, *v* tomber en poussière; émietter.

crumple, cromm´-p'l, *v* chiffonner.

crunch, cronntche, *v* croquer.

crush, croche, *v* écraser; (pound) broyer. *n* cohue *f*.

crust, crosste, *n* croûte *f*; **–y,** *a* croustillant.

crutch, crotche, *n* béquille *f*.

cry, crâï, *v* crier; (weep) pleurer. *n* cri *m*.

cryptic, cripe´-tic *a* occulte.

crystal, criss´-t'l, *n* cristal *m*.

cub, cobbe, n (bear) ourson m; (lion) lionceau m.

cube, kioube, n cube m.

cuckoo, cou´-coue, n coucou m.

cucumber, kiou´-comm-b'r, n concombre m.

cud, code, n (to chew the −) ruminer.

cuddle, cod´-d'l, v caresser.

cudgel, codd´-j'l, n gourdin m.

cue, kioue, n (billiard) queue f; (acting) réplique f; avis m.

cuff, coffe, n manchette f.

culinary, kiou´-li-na-ri, a . culinaire.

culminate, col´-mi-néte, v culminer.

culpability, col-pa-bile´-i-ti, n culpabilité f.

culpable, col´-pa-b'l, a coupable.

culprit, col´-pritte, n coupable m & f.

cultivate, col´-ti-véte, v cultiver.

culture, col´-tioure, n culture f.

cumbersome, comm´-beur-somme, a encombrant.

cunning*, conn´-inng, n ruse f. a rusé

cup, coppe, n tasse f; (trophy) coupe f.

cupboard, cob´-eurde, n placard m; armoire f.

cupola, kiou´-po-la, n coupole f.

cur, keur, n cabot m; (fig) vil individu m.

curate, kiou´-réte, n vicaire m.

curb, keurbe, n frein m; rebord de trottoir m. v (fig) réprimer.

curd, keurde, n lait caillé m.

curdle, keur´-d'l, v se figer; (milk) se cailler.

cure, kioure, n traitement m; (remedy) remède m. v guérir; (meat, fish, etc) saler; fumer.

curiosity, kiou-ri-o´-si-ti, n curiosité f.

curious*, kiou´-ri-euce, a curieux.

curl, keurle, v (hair) friser. n boucle f.

currant, cor´-annte, n (dried) groseille f.

currency, cor´-enn-ci, n monnaie f; **foreign** −,n devises fpl.

current, cor´-ennte, n courant m. a courant.

curse, keurce, n malédiction f. v maudire.

cursory, keur´-so-ri, a rapide; superficiel.

curt, keurte, a bref;

brusque.

curtail, keur-télé, v abréger; −**ment,** n raccourcissement m.

curtain, keur´-t'n, n rideau m.

curtsy, keurtt´-ci, n révérence f.

curve, keurve, n courbe f. v courber.

cushion, cou´-ch'n, n coussin m.

custard, cosse´-teurde, n flan m; crème cuite f.

custody, cosse´-tŏ-di, n garde f; détention f.

custom, cosse´-teume, n coutume f; douane fpl; −**ary,** a d'usage; −**er,** n client m; −**house,** douane f; −**s-duty,** droits de douane mpl.

cut, cotte, n coupure f; (joint, etc) tranche f; coupe f. v couper; (suit diamonds, etc) trailer; −**lery,** argenterie f; −**let,** côtellete f; −**ter,** n (tailor) coupeur m.

cuticle, kiou´-ti-k'l, n cuticule f.

cuttlefish, cott´-'l-fiche, n seiche f.

cyclamen, sique´-lă-menn, n cyclamen m.

cycle, sâï´-k'l, n cycle m; (vehicle) bicyclette f. v faire de la bicyclette.

cylinder, sill´-inn-d*eu*r, *n*
  cylindre *m*.
cynical, sinn´-i-k'l, *a*
  cynique.
cypress, săï´-presse, *n*
  cyprès *m*.

a
b
c
d
e
f
g
h
i
j
k
l
m
n
o
p
q
r
s
t
u
v
w
x
y
z

D

dabble, dăbb´-l, v
s'occuper; barboter;
(shares) boursicoter.
daffodil, dăff´-o-dile, n
narcisse sauvage m;
jonquille f.
dagger, dăgg´-'r, n
poignard m.
dahlia, dél´-i-ă, n dahlia
m.
daily, dé´-li, a quotidien.
dainty, dénne´-ti, a
délicat.
dairy, dé´-ri, n laiterie f;
(shop) crèmerie f.
daisy, dé´-zi, n (field)
pâquerette f.
dale, déle, n vallon m.
dam, dăme, n digue f;
barrage m. v endiguer.
damage, dămm´-idj, n
dommage m; dégât m;
avarie f. v endommager;

abîmer.
damask, dămm´-asque, n
damas m.
damn, dămme, v damner.
interj zut!
damnation, dămm-né´-
ch'n, n damnation f.
damp, dămmpe, v
mouiller. a humide.
dampness, dămmpe´-
nesse, n humidité f;
moiteur f.
damson, dămm´-s'n, n
prune de Damas f.
dance, dânnce, v danser. n
danse f.
dancer, dânne´-ceur, n
danseur m; danseuse f.
dandelion, dănn´-di-lâï-
onn, n pissenlit m.
dandruff, dănnde´-rof, n
pellicules fpl.
danger, déne´-djeur, n

danger m; **–ous***, a
dangereux; **–ously,** adv
dangereusement.
dangle, dănn´-g'l, v
pendiller; se balancer.
dare, daire, v oser;
(challenge) défier.
daring, daire´-inng, n
audace f. a* audacieux.
dark, dârque, a sombre;
(skin) brun; **–ness,** n
obscurité f.
darling, dâre´-linng, n & a
chéri, -ie m & f.
darn, dârne, v repriser. n
reprise f.
dart, dârte, n dard m;
(game) fléchette f;
(sewing) pince f.
dash, dăche, n (short line)
trait m. v lancer; (rush)
s'élancer.
data, dé´-ta, npl données
fpl; information f.
data processing, dé´-ta-
prau´-cess-inng, n
informatique f.
date, déte, n date f; (fruit)
datte f. v dater; **–d,** a
démodé; qui date.
daughter, doa´-t'r, n fille f;
–in-law, belle-fille f.
daunt, doannt, v
décourager; intimider.
dauntless, doannte´-lesse,
a intrépide.
dawdle, doa´-d'l, v flâner;
traîner.

dawn, doanne, *n* aurore *f.*
v faire jour.

day, dé, *n* jour *m*; journée
f; **–break,** point du jour
m; aube *f.*

dazzle, dăz´-z'l, *v* éblouir.

deacon, dî´-k'n, *n* diacre
m.

dead, dède, *a* mort; **–en,** *v*
amortir; **–ly,** *a* mortel.

deaf, deffe, *a* sourd; **–en,** *v*
assourdir.

deafness, deff´-nesse, *n*
surdité *f.*

deal, dîle, *n* quantité *f*;
(business) affaire *f*; *v*
(trade) faire des affaires;
(attend to) s'occuper de;
(cards) donner.

dealer, dîl´-*eur*, *n*
négociant *m.*

dean, dîne, *n* doyen *m.*

dear*, dîre, *a* cher.

dearth, deurts, *n* manque
m; pénurie *f.*

death, dèts, *n* mort *f.*

debar, di-bâre´, *v* exclure;
priver de.

debase, di-béce´, *v* avilir;
dégrader.

debate, di-béte´, *v*
discuter. *n* débat *m.*

debauch, di-boatch´- *v*
débaucher.

debauchery, di-boatch´-
eur-i, *n* débauche *f.*

debenture, di-benn´-
tioure, *n* obligation *f.*

debility, di-bile´-i-ti, *n*
débilité *f.*

debit, dèb´-itte, *n* débit *m.*
v débiter.

debt, dette, *n* dette *f*; **–or,**
débiteur *m.*

decadence, dè´-ca-dennce,
n décadence *f.*

decant, di-cănnte´, *v*
décanter; **–er,** *n* carafe *f.*

decapitate, di-căpe´-i-téte,
v décapiter.

decay, di-qué´, *n* (decline)
décadence *f*; (rot)
délabrement *m*. *v*
détériorer; pourrir;
(teeth) carier.

decease, di-cîce´, *n* décès
m; **–d,** *a* décédé.

deceit, di-cîte´, *n*
tromperie *f*; **–ful*,** *a*
trompeur.

deceive, di-cîve´, *v*
décevoir; tromper.

December, di-semm´-b'r,
n décembre *m.*

decency, dî´-cenn-ci, *n*
(moral) décence *f.*

decent, dî´-cennte, *a*
décent; (nice)
convenable.

deception, di-cepp´-ch'n,
n tromperie *f.*

deceptive, di-cepp´-tive, *a*
trompeur.

decide, di-sâide´, *v*
décider; **–d,** * *a* décidé.

decimal, dé´-ci-m'l, *a*
décimal.

decipher, di-sâï´-f'r, *v*
déchiffrer.

decision, di-ci´-j'n, *n*
décision *f.*

decisive,* di-sâî´-cive, *a*
décisif.

deck, dèque, *n* pont *m*. *v*
orner.

declaim, di-cléme´, *v*
déclamer.

declaration, di-cla-ré´-
ch'n, *n* déclaration *f.*

declare, di-clére´, *v*
déclarer; se déclarer.

declension, di-clenn´-
ch'n, *n* déclinaison *f.*

decline, di-clâïne´, *n*
baisse *f*; (slope) pente *f*;
(decadence) déclin *m*. *v*
refuser; (grammar)
décliner.

decompose, di-cŏmm-
pauze´, *v* décomposer.

decompress, di-comm-
presse´, *v* décomprimer.

decorate, dè´-cŏ-réte, *v*
décorer.

decorous, dè-cô´-*reuce*, *a*
décent; convenable.

decoy, di-coa'ï´, *n* piège *m*;
(bird) appeau *m*; (bait)
appât *m*. *v* leurrer.

decrease, di-crîce´, *v*
décroître; (knitting)
diminuer. *n* diminution
f.

decree, di-crî´, *n* décret *m.*

A
B
C
D
E
F
G
H
I
J
K
L
M
N
O
P
Q
R
S
T
U
V
W
X
Y
Z

v décréter.

decry, di-crâï´, *v* décrier.

dedicate, dè´-di-quéte, *v* dédier.

deduce, di-diouce´, *v* déduire.

deduct, di-docte´, *v* déduire.

deduction, di-doc´-ch'n, *n* déduction *f*; (*com*) remise *f*.

deed, dîde, *n* action *f*; (heroic) exploit *m*; (law) acte *m*; titre *m*.

deem, dîme, *v* juger; estimer.

deep, dîpe, *a* profond; **–en,** *v* approfondir.

deep freeze, dîpe´-frîze, *n* congélateur *m*.

deer, dire, *n* daim *m*; (red) cerf *m*.

deface, di-féce´, *v* dégrader; mutiler.

defamation, dé-fa-mé´-ch'n, *n* diffamation *f*.

defame, di-féme´, *v* diffamer.

default, di-foalte´, *n* défaut de payement *m*; (law) contumace *f*. *v* faire défaut.

defeat, di-fîte´, *n* défaite *f*. *v* vaincre; déjouer.

defect, di-fecte´, *n* défaut *m*; **–ive,** *a* défectueux.

defend, di-fennde´, *v* défendre; **–ant,** *n*

défendeur *m*; **–er,** défenseur *m*.

defense, di-fennce´, *n* défense *f*.

defenseless, di-fennce´-lesse, *a* sans défense.

defensive, di-fenn´-cive, *n* défensive *f*. *a* défensif.

defer, di-feur´, *v* différer; ajourner; **to – someone's judgement,** en déférer à quelqu'un.

deference, dèf´-eur-ennce, *n* déférence *f*.

defiance, di-fâï´-'nce, *n* défi *m*.

deficiency, di-fich´-enn-ci, *n* manque *m*.

deficient, di-fich´-'nt, *a* défectueux; insuffisant.

deficit, dèf´-i-cite, *n* déficit *m*.

defile, di-fâïle´, *v* souiller.

define, di-fâïne´, *v* définir.

definite, dèf´-i-nitte, *a* déterminé; défini.

definition, dèf-i-ni´-ch'n, *n* définition *f*.

deflect, di-flecte´, *v* dévier.

deform, di-foarme´, *v* déformer; **–ed,** *a* difforme.

defraud, di-froade´, *v* frauder.

defray, di-fré´, *v* défrayer.

deft*, defte, *a* adroit; (clever) habile; (quick) leste.

defunct, di-fonnkt´, *a* défunt.

defy, di-fâï´, *v* défier; provoquer.

degenerate, di-djènn´-eur-éte, *v* dégénérer. *n* & *a* dégénéré *m*.

degrade, di-gréde´, *v* dégrader.

degree, di-grî´, *n* degré *m*; (university) licence *f*.

dehydrate, di´-hâï-dréte, *v* déshydrater.

deign, déne, *v* daigner.

deject, di-djèque't´, *v* décourager; déprimer.

dejection, di-djèque´-ch'n, *n* abattement *m*.

delay, di-lé´, *n* retard *m*; délai *m*. *v* tarder; différer.

delegate, dèl´-i-guéte, *n* délégué *m*.

delete, di-lîte´, *v* effacer; rayer; supprimer.

deletion, de-lîch'n, *n* effacement *m*; rature *f*.

deliberate, di-lib´-eur-éte, *v* délibérer. *a** délibéré.

delicacy, dèl´-i-ca-ci, *n* délicatesse *f*.

delicate*, dèl´-i-quéte, *a* délicat.

delicious*, di-lich´-euce, *a* délicieux.

delight, di-lâïte, *v* enchanter. *n* délices *fpl*; joie *f*.

delightful*, di-lâïte´-foull, *a* délicieux.

delineate, di-linn´-i-éte, *v* tracer.

delinquent, di-linng´-couente, *n* délinquant, -e *m* & *f*.

delirious*, di-lir´-i-*euce*, *a* en délire.

delirium, di-lir´-i-*eume*, *n* délire *m*.

deliver, di-liv´-*eur*, *v* (letters) distribuer; (goods) livrer; (set free, rid) délivrer; **–y**, *n* délivrance *f*; (letters) distribution *f*; (goods) livraison *f*.

delude, di-lioude´, *v* tromper.

delusion, di-liou´-j'n, *n* illusion *f*.

demand, di-mânnde´, *v* exiger. *n* demande *f*.

demeanor, di-mî´-*neur*, *n* conduite *f*; tenue *f*.

demented, di-menn´-tedde, *n* & *a* dément *m*.

democratic, dè-mo-crä´-tique, *a* démocratique.

demolish, di-mol´-iche, *v* démolir.

demon, dî´-mŏnne, *n* démon *m*.

demonstrate, dè´-monn-stréte, *v* démontrer; donner une démonstration.

demonstrative, di-monn´-stra-tive, *a* démonstratif; expansif.

demoralize, di-mô-rä-lâïze, *v* démoraliser.

demur, di-meure´, *v* hésiter.

demure, di-mioure´, *a* modeste.

den, dènne, *n* tanière *f*; repaire *m*; cabinet de travail *m*.

denial, di-nâï´-'l, *n* dénégation *f*.

denomination, di-nŏmm-i-né´-ch'n, *n* dénomination *f*.

denote, di-naute´, *v* dénoter.

denounce, di-nâ'ounnce´, *v* dénoncer.

dense, dènnce, *a* dense; épais; (person) stupide.

dent, dènnte, *n* marque *f*; creux *m*. *v* cabosser; bosseler.

dentist, dènn´-tiste, *n* dentiste *m*.

denude, di-nioude´, *v* dénuder.

deny, di-nâï´, *v* nier.

deodorant, di-ô´-*deur*-'nt, *n* déodorant *m*.

deodorize, di-ô´-*deur*-âïze, *v* désodoriser.

depart, di-pârte´, *v* partir; **–ment,** *n* branche *f*; service *m*; (shop) rayon *m*; **–ure,** départ *m*.

depend (upon), di-pennde´, *v* (contingent) dépendre; (trust) compter sur; **–ent,** *a* dépendant; à charge.

depict, di-picte´, *v* dépeindre.

depletion, di-plî´-ch'n, *n* épuisement *m*.

deplore, di-plaure´, *v* déplorer.

deport, di-paurte´, *v* déporter.

deportment, di-paurte´-m'nt, *n* maintien *m*.

depose, di-pauze´, *v* déposer.

deposit, di-pauz´-itte, *n* (bank, sediment) dépôt *m*; (on account) acompte *m*; arrhes *fpl*. *v* déposer; **–or,** *n* déposant *m*.

depot, depp´-au, *n* dépôt *m*.

deprave, di-préve´, *v* dépraver.

deprecate, dè´-pri-quéte, *v* désapprouver.

depreciate, di-prî´-chi-éte, *v* déprécier.

depress, di-press´, *v* déprimer; décourager; **–ion,** *n* (trade) crise *f*; (spirits) abattement *m*; dépression *f*; (hollow) affaissement *m*.

A
B
C
D
E
F
G
H
I
J
K
L
M
N
O
P
Q
R
S
T
U
V
W
X
Y
Z

deprive, di-prâïve´, *v* priver.

depth, dep*t*s, *n* profondeur *f*.

deputation, dè-piou-té´-ch'n, *n* députation *f*.

deputy, dèp´-iou-ti, *n* représentant *m*; remplacant *m*.

derailment, di-réle´-m'nt, *n* déraillement *m*.

derange, di-rénndje´, *v* déranger.

derangement, di-rénndje´-m'nt, *n* dérangement *m*.

derelict, dèr´-i-licte, *a* abandonné. *n* (ship) épave *f*.

deride, di-râïde´, *v* railler.

derision, di-rî´-jeune, *n* dérision *f*.

derisive*, di-râï´-cive, *a* dérisoire.

derive, di-râïve´, *v* dériver; provenir.

descend, di-cennde´, *v* descendre; **–ant,** *n* descendant, -ante *m* & *f*.

descent, di-cennte´, *n* descente *f*; origine *f*.

describe, diss-crâïbe´, *v* décrire.

description, diss-crippe´-ch'n, *n* description *f*.

desecrate, dess´-si-créte, *v* profaner.

desert, dèz´-*eu*rte, *n* désert *m*.

desert, diz-eurte´, *v* abandonner; (*mil*) déserter; **–er,** *n* déserteur *m*; **–ion,** désertion *f*; abandon *m*.

deserve, di-zeurve´, *v* mériter.

design, di-zâïne´, *n* (sketch) dessin *m*; (intention) dessein *m*; (pattern) modèle *m*; motif *m*. *v* dessiner; (plan) projeter; créer; **–ing,** *a* intrigant.

desirable, di-zâï´-ra-b'l, *a* désirable; souhaitable.

desire, di-zâïre´, *v* désirer. *n* désir *m*.

desirous, di-zâï´-*reu*ce, *a* désireux.

desist, di-zisst´, *v* cesser; se désister.

desk, dessque, *n* bureau *m*; (school) pupitre *m*.

desolate, dess´-ŏ-léte, *a* désolé; désert.

despair, diss-pair´, *n* désespoir *m*. *v* désespérer.

desperate*, dess´-peur-éte, *a* désespéré; forcené.

despicable, dess´-pi-ca-b'l, *a* méprisable.

despise, diss-pâïze´, *v* mépriser.

despite, diss-pâïte´, *prep* en dépit de; malgré.

despoil, diss-poa'ïle´, *v* dépouiller.

despondent, diss-ponn´-d'nt, *a* découragé; déprimé.

despot, dess´-pŏtte, *n* despote *m*.

dessert, di-zeurte´, *n* dessert *m*.

destination, dèss-ti-né´-ch'n, *n* destination *f*.

destiny, dess´-ti-ni, *n* sort *m*; destin *m*.

destitute, dess´-ti-tioute, *a* indigent; dénué.

destitution, dess-ti-tiou´-ch'n, *n* dénuement *m*.

destroy, diss-troa'ï´, *v* détruire.

destruction, diss-trok´-ch'n, *n* destruction *f*.

destructive, diss-trok´-tive, *a* destructif.

desultory, dé´-seul-to-ri, *a* irrégulier; décousu.

detach, di-tătche´, *v* détacher; **–able,** *a* détachable.

detail, di-téle´, *v* détailler. *n* détail *m*.

detain, di-téne´, *v* détenir; retenir.

detect, di-tecte´, *v* découvrir; surprendre.

detective, di-tèque´-tive, *n* détective *m*; **–novel,** roman policier *m*.

detention, di-tenn´-ch'n,

n détention *f*; (*sch*)
retenue *f*.

deter, di-teur´, *v* dissuader;
détourner; **–rent,** *n*
préventif; (nuclear, etc)
arme de dissuasion *f*.

deteriorate, di-tî´-ri-*o*-
réte, *v* détériorer.

determine, di-teur´-
minne, *v* déterminer;
décider.

detest, di-tesste´, *v*
détester.

dethrone, di-*ts*rône´, *v*
détrôner.

detonation, di-to-né´-
ch'n, *n* explosion *f*.

detour, di-tour´, *n* détour
m.

detract, di-trăcte´, *v*
enlever (à); dénigrer.

detrimental*, dèt-ri-
menn´-t'l, *a*
préjudiciable.

deuce, diouce, *n* (tennis)
égalité *f*; (cards, etc)
deux *m*.

devaluate, di-val´-iou-éte,
v dévaluer, **–tion,** *n*
dévaluation *f*.

devastate, dè´-vass-téte, *v*
dévaster.

develop, di-vèl´-ŏpe, *v*
développer.

development, di-vèl´-ope-
m'nt, *n* développement
m; fait *m*.

deviate, dî´-vi-éte, *v*

dévier.

device, di-vâïce´, *n* moyen
m; dispositif *m*; appareil
m; truc *m*.

devil, dév´-'l, *n* diable *m*;
–ry, diablerie *f*.

devise, di-vâïze´, *v*
inventer; tramer; (law)
léguer.

devoid, di-voa´ïde´, *a*
dénué; dépourvu.

devote, di-vaute´, *v*
dévouer; **–oneself to,** se
consacrer à.

devour, di-vâ'oure´, *v*
dévorer.

devout*, di-vâ'oute´, *a*
dévot; pieux.

dew, dioue, *n* rosée *f*.

dexterous*, deks´-*t*eur-
euce, *a* adroit; habile.

diabetes, dâï-*a*-bî´-tize, *n*
diabète *m*.

diabolical*, dâï-*a*-bol´-i-
k'l, *a* diabolique.

diagnose, dâï-ăgue-nauze´,
v diagnostiquer.

diagonal, dâï-ăgue´-o-n'l,
a diagonal.

diagram, dâï´-*a*-grâmme, *n*
diagramme *m*; schéma
m.

dial, dâï´-*a*l, *n* cadran *m*. *v*
composer un numéro de
téléphone.

dialect, dâï-*a*-lecte, *n*
dialecte *m*.

dialogue, dâï-*a*-logue, *n*

dialogue *m*.

diameter, dâï-ămm´-i-*t*eur,
n diamètre *m*.

diamond, dâï´-*a*-meunnde,
n diamant *m*; (cards)
carreau *m*.

diarrhea, dâï-*a*-rî´-*a*, *n*
diarrhée *f*.

diary, dâï´-*a*-ri, *n* journal
m; (pocket) agenda *m*.

dice, dâïce, *npl* dés *mpl*.

dictaphone, dic´-ta-faune,
n machine à dicter *f*.

dictate, dic-téte´, *v* dicter;
faire la loi; **dictator,**
dictateur *m*.

dictionary, dic´-chŏnn-*a*-
ri, *n* dictionnaire *m*.

die, dâï, *v* mourir.

diet, dâï´-ette, *v* (to go on
a –) faire un régime. *n*
régime *m*.

differ, dif´-*e*ur, *v* différer;
–ence, *n* différence *f*;
–ent, *a* différent.

difficult, diff´-i-keulte, *a*
difficile; **–y,** *n* difficulté
f.

diffident, diff´-i-d'nt, *a*
défiant de soi-même.

diffuse, dif-fiouze´, *v*
répandre. *a* diffus.

dig, digue, *v* (garden)
bêcher; (excavate)
creuser; (*archeol*) faire
des fouilles.

digest, di-djeste´, *v*
digérer; **–ion,** *n*

a
b
c
d
e
f
g
h
i
j
k
l
m
n
o
p
q
r
s
t
u
v
w
x
y
z

A
B
C
D
E
F
G
H
I
J
K
L
M
N
O
P
Q
R
S
T
U
V
W
X
Y
Z

digestion f.

dignified dig´-ni-fàïde, a digne.

dignitary, dig´-ni-ta-ri, n dignitaire m.

dignity, dig´-ni-ti, n dignité f.

digression, di-grèch´-eunne, n digression f.

dike, dâïke, n digue f.

dilapidated, di-lăpp´-i-dé-tedde, a délabré.

dilapidation, di-lăpp´-i-dé-ch'n, n délabrement m.

dilate, di-léte´, v dilater; se dilater.

dilatory, dil´-a-tŏ-ri, a tardif; dilatoire.

dilemma, di-lemm´-ma, n dilemme m.

diligence, dil´-i-djennce, n diligence f.

diligent*, dil´-i-djennte, a appliqué.

dilute, di-lioute´, v diluer; (wine) couper.

dim, dime, v obscurcir. a trouble; faible.

dimension, di-menn´-ch'n, n dimension f.

diminish, di-minn´-iche, v diminuer.

dimple, dime´-p'l, n fossette f.

din, dinn, n vacarme m. v assourdir.

dine, dâïne, v dîner.

dingy, dinn´-dji, a sombre; sale; défraîchi.

dining, dâï´-ninng, **–car,** n wagon-restaurant m; **–room,** salle à manger f.

dinner, dinn´-eur, n dîner m.

dip, dippe, v plonger; tremper; baisser subitement; (slope) incliner.

diphtheria, diff-tsî´-ri-a, n diphtérie f.

diplomacy, di-plau´-ma-ci, n diplomatie f.

diplomat, dippe´-lau-mătte, n diplomate m.

dire, dâïre, a cruel; terrible; affreux.

direct, di-recte´, v diriger; indiquer. a direct; **–ion,** n direction f; **–ly,** adv tout de suite; directement; **–or,** n directeur m; administrateur m; **–ory,** annuaire m.

dirt, deurte, n saleté f; ordure f.

dirty, deur´-ti, a sale. v salir.

disability, diss-a-bile´-i-ti, n incapacité f.

disable, diss-é´-b'l, v mutiler; rendre infirme; (mech) mettre hors de service.

disadvantage, diss-ăd-

vânne´-tidj, n désavantage m.

disagree, diss-a-grî´, v être en désaccord.

disagreeable, diss-a-grî´-a-b'l, a désagréable.

disallow, diss-a-la'ou´, v refuser; désapprouver; désavouer.

disappear, diss-a-pîre, v disparaître.

disappearance, diss-ap-pîr´-'nce, n disparition f.

disappoint, diss-a-poa'innte´, v décevoir; **–ment,** n déception f.

disapprove, diss-a-prouve´, v désapprouver.

disarm, diss-ârme´, v désarmer; **–ament,** désarmement m.

disaster, diz-âsse´-teur, n désastre m; accident m.

disastrous*, diz-âsse´-treuce, a désastreux.

discard, diss-cârde´, v rejeter.

discern, diz-zeurne´, v discerner.

discharge, diss-tchârdje´, n (dismissal) congé m; (gun) décharge f; (med) suppuration f; perte f. v congédier; décharger; (fulfill) remplir; (acquit) acquitter; (release) libérer.

disciple, diss-sâï´-p'l, n

disciple *m.*

discipline, diss´-si-plinne, *n* discipline *f.*

disclaim, diss-cléme´, *v* renier; répudier.

disclose, diss-clauze´, *v* révéler.

disclosure, diss-clau´-jioure, *n* révélation *f.*

discolor, diss-col´-*eur, v* décolorer.

discomfort, diss-comm´-feurte, *n* incommodité *f;* manque de confort *m;* (uneasy) malaise *m.*

disconnect, diss-cŏnn-necte´, *v* disjoindre; couper.

discontent, diss-cŏnn-tennte´, *n* mécontentement *m;* **–ed,** *a* mécontent.

discontinue, diss-cŏnn-tinn´-ioue, *v* cesser.

discord, diss´-coarde, *n* discorde *f.*

discount, diss´-câ'ounnte, *n* (*com*) remise *f;* (*fin*) escompte *m.*

discourage, diss-cor´-idj, *v* décourager.

discourse, diss-caurse´, *v* discourir. *n* discours *m.*

discourteous, diss-keur´-ti-*euce, a* discourtois.

discover, diss-cov´-*eur, v* découvrir.

discovery, diss-cov´-*eur*-i,

n découverte *f.*

discreet*, diss-crîte´, *a* discret.

discrepancy, diss-crèp´-ann-ci, *n* différence *f.*

discriminate, diss-crimm´-i-néte, *v* discerner; destinguer.

discuss, diss-cosse´, *v* discuter.

discussion, diss-coch´-'n, *n* discussion *f.*

disdain, diss-déne´, *v* dédaigner. *n* dédain *m.*

disdainful*, diss-déne´-foull, *a* dédaigneux.

disease, di-zîze´, *n* maladie *f;* **–d,** *a* malade.

disembark, diss-emm-bărke´, *v* débarquer; **–ation** *n* débarquement *m.*

disengaged, diss-enn-guédje´, *a* libre.

disentangle, diss-enn-tain´-g'l, *v* démêler.

disfigure, diss-figue´-*eur, v* défigurer.

disgrace, diss-gréce´, *n* disgrâce *f;* (shame) honte *f. v* déshonorer; **–ful,** *a* honteux.

disguise, diss-gâïze´, *v* déguiser. *n* déguisement *m.*

disgust, diss-gosse´, *v* dégoûter. *n* dégoût *m;* **–ing,** *a* dégoûtant.

dish, diche, *n* plat *m;* (food) mets *m;* **–cloth,** torchon *m;* **–up,** *v* servir.

dishearten, diss-hâre´-t'n, *v* décourager.

disheveled, di-chè´-vellde, *a* échevelé.

dishonest, diss-onn´-este, *a* malhonnête.

dishonor, diss-onn´-*eur, v* déshonorer. *n* déshonneur *m.*

dishwashing liquid, diche-ou'oache-inng-lik-ouide, *n* produit pour la vaisselle *m.*

disillusion, diss-il-lioue´-j'n, *v* désillusionner.

disinclination, diss-inn-cli-né´-ch'n, *n* aversion *f.*

disinfect, diss-inn-fecte´, *v* désinfecter; **–ant** *n* désinfectant *m.*

disinherit, diss-inn-hèr´-itte, *v* déshériter.

disintegrate, diss-inn´-teur-gréte, *v* désintégrer.

disintegration, diss-inn-teur-gré´-ch'n, *n* désintégration *m.*

disjointed, diss-djoa'inn´-tedde, *a* désarticulé.

disk, disque, *n* disque *m.*

dislike, diss-lâïque´, *v* ne pas aimer. *n* aversion *f.*

dislocate, diss´-lo-kéte, *v* disloquer.

A
B
C
D
E
F
G
H
I
J
K
L
M
N
O
P
Q
R
S
T
U
V
W
X
Y
Z

disloyal, diss-lo´-ial, *a* déloyal.

dismal*, diz´-m'l, *a* triste; lugubre; sombre.

dismay, diss-mé´, *v* consterner. *n* consternation *f*.

dismiss, diss-mice´, *v* congédier; (mentally) écarter.

dismount, diss-mâ'ounnte´, *v* descendre de.

disobedient, diss-o-bî´-di-ennte, *a* désobéissant.

disobey, diss-o-bé´, *v* désobéir.

disorder, diss-oar´-de*ur*, *n* désordre *m*.

disorganization, diss-oar-ga-nâï-zé´-ch'n, *n* désorganisation *f*.

disorganize, diss-oar´-ga-nâïze, *v* désorganiser.

disown, diz-aune´, *v* renier.

disparage, diss-pär´-idj, *v* dénigrer.

dispatch, diss-pǎtché, *v* expédier; *n* dépêche *f*; envoi *m*.

dispel, diss-pelle´, *v* chasser; dissiper.

dispensary, diss-penn´-sa-ri, *n* dispensaire *m*.

disperse, diss-peurce´, *v* disperser.

display, diss-plé´, *v* exposer. *n* (*com*) étalage *m*.

displease, diss-plîze´, *v* déplaire.

displeasure, diss-plè´-jeu*re*, *n* mécontentement *m*.

disposal, diss-pau´-z'l, *n* disposition *f*.

dispose, diss-pauze´, *v* disposer; se débarasser.

disprove, diss-prouve´, *v* réfuter.

disputable, diss-pioue´-ta-b'l, *a* contestable.

dispute, diss-piout´e, *v* se disputer; contester. *n* dispute *f*; contestation *f*.

disqualify, diss-couoll´-i-fâï, *v* disqualifier.

disquiet, diss-couâï´-ètte, *v* inquiéter. *n* inquiétude *f*.

disregard, diss-ri-gârde´, *v* négliger; ne pas observer; faire peu de cas de. *n* mépris *m*; indifférence *f*.

disrepute, diss-ri-pioute´, *n* discrédit *m*; mauvaise réputation *m*.

disrespect, diss-ri-specte´, *n* manque de respect *m*; irrévérence *f*; –**ful,** *a* irrespectueux.

dissatisfy, diss-sǎt´-is-fâï, *v* mécontenter.

dissect, diss-secte´, *v* disséquer.

dissemble, diss-semm´-b'l, *v* dissimuler.

dissent, diss-sennte´, *v* différer d'opinion.

dissimilar, diss-simm´-i-l'r, *a* dissemblable.

dissipate, diss´-si-péte, *v* dissiper.

dissociate, diss-sau´-chi-éte, *v* dissocier; se désintéresser.

dissolute, diss´-sŏ-lioute, *a* dissolu.

dissolve, diss-solv´, *v* dissoudre.

dissuade, diss-souéde´, *v* dissuader.

distance, diss´-tannce, *n* distance *f*.

distant, diss´-tannte, *a* éloigné; distant.

distasteful, diss-téste´-foull, *a* répugnant.

distemper, diss-temm´-peu*r*, *n* (paint) détrempe *f*; (veterinary) maladie des chiens *f*.

distend, diss-tennde´, *v* dilater; gonfler.

distill, diss-till´, *v* distiller.

distinct*, diss-tinng´-kt, *a* distinct; clair.

distinction, diss-tinng´-kch'n, *n* distinction *f*.

distinguish, diss-tinng´-gouiche, *v* distinguer.

distort, diss-toarte´, *v*

défigurer; (*fig*)
dénaturer; fausser.

distract, diss-trăkt´, *v*
distraire; détourner;
affoler; **–ion,** *n*
distraction *f*.

distrain, diss-tréne´, *v*
saisir.

distress, diss-tresse´, *n*
détresse *f*; (poverty)
misère *f*. *v* affliger; **–ing,**
a affligeant; pénible.

distribute, diss-trib´-ioute,
v distribuer.

distributor, diss-trib´-iou-
t'r, *n* concessionnaire *m*;
(in car, etc) distributeur
m.

district, diss´-tricte, *n*
région *f*; arrondissement
m.

distrust, diss-trosste´, *v* se
mefier de. *n* méfiance *f*.

disturb, diss-teurbe´, *v*
déranger; **–ance,** *n*
dérangement *m*; (mob)
désordre *m*.

disuse, diss-iouce´, *n*
désuétude *f*.

ditch, ditche, *n* fossé *m*.

dive, dâïve, *v* plonger.

diver, dâï´-veur, *n*
plongeur *m*; (salvage,
etc) scaphandrier *m*.

diverge, di-veurdje´, *v*
diverger.

diverse, dâï-veurse´, *a*
divers; varié.

diversion, di-veur´-ch'n, *n*
diversion *f*;
divertissement *m*.

divert, di-veurte´, *v*
détourner; distraire.

divest, di-veste´, *v*
dépouiller de; (clothes)
dévêtir.

divide, di-vâïde´, *v* diviser;
partager.

divine, di-vâïne´, *v*
deviner. *a** divin.

division, di-vi´-j'n, *n*
division *f*.

divorce, di-vaurce´, *v*
divorcer. *n* divorce *m*.

divulge, di-voldje´, *v*
divulguer.

dizzy, diz´-i, *a* étourdi;
vertigineux.

do, doue, *v* faire;
accomplir; suffire; jouer
le rôle de.

docile, do´-sâïle, *a* docile.

dock, doc, *n* bassin *m*;
(court) banc des accusés
m; **dry –,** cale sèche *f*.

doctor, doc´-t'r, *n* docteur
m.

doctrine, doc´-trine, *n*
doctrine *f*.

document, doc´-iou-m'nt,
n document *m*.

documentary, doc´-iou-
menn´-ta-ri, *n*
documentaire *m*.

dodge, dodje, *v* esquiver;
éviter. *n* truc *m*.

dog, dogue, *n* chien *m*;
–ged*, *a* tenace.

dole, daule, *v* distribuer. *n*
allocation de chômage *f*.

doleful*, daule´-foull, *a*
plaintif; triste.

doll, dolle, *n* poupée *f*.

domain, dau-méne´, *n*
domaine *m*.

dome, daume, *n* dôme *m*.

domestic, do-mess´-tique,
n & *a* domestique *m* & *f*.

domesticated, do-mess´-ti-
qué-tedde, *a* bonne
ménagère.

domicile, domm´-i-sâïle, *n*
domicile *m*.

dominate, domm´-i-néte,
v dominer.

domineer, domm-i-nîre´, *v*
régenter.

donation, dau-né´-ch'n, *n*
donation *f*.

donkey, donng´-qui, *n* âne
m; baudet *m*.

donor, dau´-neur, *n*
donateur *m*.

doom, doume, *n* (fate)
sort *m*. *v* condamner.

doomsday, doumze´-dé, *n*
jugement dernier *m*.

door, daur, *n* porte *f*;
(vehicle) portière *f*; **–
keeper,** concierge *m* & *f*;
–mat, paillasson *m*; **–
step,** pas de la porte *m*.

dormitory, dor´-mi-to-ri, *n*
dortoir *m*.

a
b
c
d
e
f
g
h
i
j
k
l
m
n
o
p
q
r
s
t
u
v
w
x
y
z

dose, dauce, n dose f. v doser.

dot, dotte, n point m. v mettre un point sur; (art) pointiller.

dote, daute, v raffoler (de).

double, dob´-'l, v doubler. n & a double m.

doubt, dâ'oute, v douter. n doute m; **–ful,** a douteux; indécis; **–less,** adv sans doute.

douche, douche, n douche f. v doucher.

dough, dau, n pâte f.

dove, dove, n colombe f; **--cote,** colombier m.

dowager, dâ'ou´-édj-eur, n douairière f.

down, dâ'ounn, adv & prep en bas. n (feathers) duvet m; **–cast,** a abattu; **–fall,** n chute f; ruine f; **–pour,** pluie torrentielle f; **–stairs,** adv en bas; **–wards,** vers le bas.

dowry, dâ'ou´-ri, n dot f.

doze, dauze, v somnoler. n somme m.

dozen, doz´-'n, n douzaine f.

drab, drăbbe, a terne.

draft, drâfte, n (money) traite f; (sketch) esquisse f; (writing) brouillon m; project m; v rédiger; n courant d'air m; (drinking) coup m; **--board,** damier m.

draftsman, drâfts´-mănne, n dessinateur m.

drag, drăgue, v traîner; (water) draguer.

dragon, drăgue´eune, n dragon m; **--fly,** libellule f.

drain, dréne, v faire égoutter; faire écouler; (land) drainer. n égout m; **–age,** système d'égouts m; **--pipe,** n gouttière f.

drake, dréke, n canard m.

drama, drâm´-a, n drame m.

dramatic, dra-ma´-tique, a dramatique.

draper, dré´-peur, n marchand de nouveautés m.

drastic, drass´-tique, a énergique; drastique; draconien.

draw, droa, n (lottery) tirage m; (game) partie nulle f. v (pull) tirer; (pull out) arracher; (attract) attirer; (sketch) dessiner; (bill) tirer; (money) retirer; **–back,** n inconvénient m; **–er,** n (furniture) tiroir m; **–ing,** (sketch) dessin m.

drawl, droal, v parler d'une voix traînante; n débit (m) traînant.

dread, drèdde, v redouter. n terreur f; **–ful*,** a terrible.

dream, drîme, n rêve m. v rêver.

dreary, drî´-ri, a triste; morne; monotone.

dredge, drèdje, v draguer; **–r,** n dragueur m.

dregs, drègze, npl lie f; sédiment m.

drench, drenntche, v tremper.

dress, dresse, n robe f; toilette f; costume m. v habiller; vêtir; (wounds) panser; **–ing,** n (med) pansement m; (culinary) assaisonnement m; **–ing gown,** robe de chambre f; peignoir m; **–ing room,** cabinet de toilette m.

dressmaker, dresse´-mék´-eur, n couturière f.

dribble, drib´-'l, v baver; (of water) dégoutter.

drift, drifte, n (naut) dérive f; (snow, etc) monceau m; (tendency) but m. v dériver; **–wood,** bois flottant m.

drill, drile, n (mil) exercice m; (tool) foret m. v exercer; forer; percer.

drink, drinnque, *n* boisson *f.* *v* boire.

drip, drippe, *v* dégoutter. *n* goutte *f.*

dripping, dripp´-inng, *n* (fat) graisse de rôti *f.*

drive, drâïve, *v* conduire. *n* (approach) allée *f;* (outing) promenade en . . . (auto, etc) *f;* (of car) conduite *f.*

driver, drâï´-veur, *n* conducteur *m;* chauffeur *m.*

drizzle, driz´-z'l, *v* pleuvasser. *n* bruine *f.*

droll, draule, *a* drôle.

drone, draune, *n* faux-bourdon *m.* *v* bourdonner.

droop, droupe, *v* languir; (plants) tomber.

drop, droppe, *n* chute *f;* (liquid) goutte *f;* (prices) baisse *f.* *v* tomber; (let fall) laisser tomber.

drought, drâ'oute, *n* sécheresse *f.*

drown, drâ'ounne, *v* noyer; se noyer.

drowsy, drâ'au´-zi, *a* somnolent.

drudge, drodje, *v* trimer; **—ry,** *n* corvée *f.*

drug, drogue, *v* droguer. *n* drogue *f.*

drum, dromme, *n* tambour *m;* **—mer,** tambour *m.*

drunk, dronnque, *a* ivre; soûl; **—ard,** ivrogne *m;* **—enness,** ivresse *f;* ivrognerie *f.*

dry, drâï, *v* sécher. *a** sec; **—-cleaning,** nettoyage à sec *m.*

dryness, drâï´-ness, *n* sécheresse *f.*

dubious*, dioue´-bi-*e*uce, *a* douteux.

duchess, dotch´-esse, *n* duchesse *f.*

duck, doque, *n* canard *m;* cane *f.* *v* plonger; se baisser.

due, dioue, *n* dû *m;* (toll, rights, etc) droits *mpl. a* (owing) dû; (bill) échu.

duel, dioue´-'l, *n* duel *m.*

duet, diou-ette´, *n* duo *m.*

duke, diouque, *n* duc *m.*

dull, dolle, *a* (weather) gris; (tedious) ennuyeux; (mind) lent; (metal) terne.

duly, dioue´-li, *adv* dûment; en temps voulu.

dumb, domme, *a* muet; (*fam*) bête; **—found,** *v* confondre.

dummy, domm´-i, *n* mannequin *m;* (sham) simulacre *m;* (cards) le mort *m.*

dump, dommpe, *v* déposer.

n dépôt *m.*

dung, donng, *n* (horse) crottin *m;* (cow) bouse de vache *f;* (manure) fumier *m.*

dungeon, donn´-djeune, *n* cachot *m.*

dupe, dioupe, *v* duper. *n* dupe *f.*

duplicate, dioue´-pli-quéte, *n* duplicata *m; a* double. *v* faire le double; tirer (des copies).

durable, dioue´-ra-b'l, *a* durable.

duration, dioue-ré´-ch'n, *n* durée *f.*

during, dioue´-rinng, *prep* pendant.

dusk, dossque, *n* crépuscule *m.*

dusky, doss´-ki, *a* sombre; (color) noirâtre.

dust, dosste, *n* poussière *f.* *v* épousseter; **—er,** *n* chiffon *m.*

dutiful*, dioue´-ti-foull, *a* obéissant; dévoué.

duty, dioue´-ti, *n* devoir *m;* (customs) droits *mpl;* (task) fonction *f.*

dwarf, douoarfe, *n & a* nain *m & f.* *v* rapetisser.

dwell, douelle, *v* demeurer; habiter; **—er,** *n* habitant *m;* **—ing,** demeure *f.*

dwindle, douinn´-d'l, *v*

diminuer; s'amoindrir.

dye, dâï, *n* teinture *f. v*
teindre.

dynamite, dâïn´-*a*-mãïte,
n dynamite *f.*

dynamo, dâï´-n*a*-mau, *n*
dynamo *f.*

dysentery, diss´-'n-tri, *n*
dysenterie *f.*

each, îtche, *pron* chacun, -une. *a* chaque; **–other,** *pron* l'un l'autre; l'une l'autre; les uns; les autres.

eager, î´-gueur, *a* avide; ardent.

eagerness, î´-gueur-nesse, *n* avidité *f*; empressement *m*.

eagle, î´-g'l, *n* aigle *m* & *f*.

ear, îre, *n* oreille *f*; (corn) épi *m*; – **-ring,** boucle d'oreille *f*; **–wig,** perce-oreille *m*.

earl, eurle, *n* comte *m*.

early, eur´-li, *adv* de bonne heure, tôt. *a* matinal; tôt.

earn, eurne, *v* gagner; mériter; **–ings,** *npl* salaire *m*.

earnest*, eur´-nesste, *a* sérieux; sincère; empressé.

earth, eurts, *n* terre *f*; monde *m*. *v* (electricity) mettre à la terre; **–enware,** *n* faïence *f*; **–ly,** *a* terrestre; **–quake,** *n* tremblement de terre *m*.

ease, îze, *n* aise *f*; repos *m*; (facility) facilité *f*. *v* soulager.

easel, î´-z'l, *n* chevalet *m*.

easily, î´-zi-li, *adv* facilement.

east, îsste, *n* est *m*; **–erly,** *a* d'est; **–ern,** oriental.

Easter, îss´-teur, *n* Pâques *m*.

easy, î´-zi, *a* facile; **–chair,** *n* fauteuil *m*.

eat, îte, *v* manger; (worm; acid) ronger; **–able,** *a* mangeable; **–ables,** *npl* comestibles *mpl*.

eavesdropper, îvz´-dropp-eur, *n* oreille indiscrète *f* (aux portes).

ebb, èbe, *v* refluer. *n* reflux *m*.

ebony, èb´-ŏ-ni, *n* èbéne *f*.

eccentric, èque-senn-´-trique, *a* excentrique.

echo, èk´-au, *n* écho *m*. *v* répéter.

eclipse, i-klipse´, *n* éclipse *f*. *v* éclipser.

economize, i-konn´-ŏ-măize, *v* économiser.

economy, i-konn´-ŏ-mi, *n* économie *f*.

ecstasy, ex´-ta-zi, *n* extase *f*.

eddy, éd´-i, *n* tourbillon *m*; remous *m*.

edge, èdje, *n* bord *m*; (blade) tranchant *m*. *v* border.

edible, èd´-i-b'l, *n* & *a* comestible *m*.

edify, èd´-i-fâï, *v* édifier.

edit, èd´-itte, *v* éditer; **–ion,** *n* édition *f*; **–or,** rédacteur *m*; **–orial,** *a* éditorial.

educate, èd´-iou-quéte, *v* instruire; éduquer.

education, èd-iou-ké´-ch'n, *n* éducation *f*; enseignement *m*; études *fpl*.

A B C D E F G H I J K L M N O P Q R S T U V W X Y Z

eel, île, *n* anguille *f.*

efface, ef-féce´, *v* effacer.

effect, ef-fecte´, *v* effectuer. *n* effet *m*; **–ive*,** *a* efficace; effectif; **–ual*,** efficace.

effeminate, ef-femm´-i-néte, *a* efféminé.

effervescent, ef-feur-vess´-'nt, *a* effervescent.

efficiency, ef-fich´-enn-ci, *n* efficacité *f*; capacité *f.*

efficient, ef-fich´-ennt, *a* (person) capable; compétent.

effort, ef´-feurte, *n* effort *m.*

effrontery, ef-fron´-teur-i, *n* effronterie *f.*

effusive, ef-fioue´-cive, *a* expansif.

egg, ègg, *n* œuf *m*; **––cup,** coquetier *m.*

egotism, ègg´-au-tizme, *n* égoïsme *m.*

eiderdown, aï´-deur-dâ'ounne, *n* édredon *m.*

eight, éte, *n & a* huit *m*; **–een,** dix-huit *m*; **–eenth,** dix-huitième *m*; **–h,** huitième *m*; **–ieth,** quatre vingtième *m*; **–y,** quatre-vingts *m.*

either, âï´-dzeur, *pron* l'un ou l'autre, *conj* ou; soit.

eject, i-djecte´, *v* expulser.

elaborate, i-lăb´-ŏ-réte, *a* soigné; raffiné; élaboré.

v élaborer.

elapse, i-lăpse´, *v* s'écouler.

elastic, i-lăss´-tique, *n & a* élastique *m.*

elate, i-léte´, *v* exalter; transporter; **–d,** *a* exalté; transporté.

elbow, el´-bau, *n* coude *m*. *v* coudoyer.

elder, el´-deur, *n & a* aîné *m & f*; (tree) sureau *m.*

elderly, el´-deur-li, *a* d'un certain âge.

eldest, el´-deste, *n & a* aîné *m & f.*

elect, i-lecte´, *v* élire; nommer. *n & a* élu *m.*

election, i-léque´-ch'n, *n* élection *f.*

electric(al)*, i-léque´-trique('l), *a* électrique.

electrician, i-léquetri´-ch'n, *n* électricien *m.*

electricity, i-léque-tri´-ci-ti, *n* électricité *f.*

electrify, i-lèque´-tri-fâï, *v* électriser; électrifier.

electron, i-lèque´-tronne, *n* électron *m*; **–ics,** électronique *f.*

electroplate, i-lèqu´-tro-pléte, *n* plaqué *m*. *v* plaquer.

elegance, el´-i-gannce, *n* élégance *f.*

elegant*, el´-i-gannte, *a* élégant.

element, el´-i-m'nt, *n* élément *m.*

elementary, i-li-menn´-ta-ri, *a* élémentaire.

elephant, el´-i-fannte, *n* éléphant *m.*

elevate, el´-i-véte, *v* élever; exalter.

elevator, el´-évé-teur, *n* ascenseur *m.*

eleven, i-lèv´-'n, *n & a* onze *m*; **–th,** onzième *m.*

elicit, i-liss´-ite, *v* faire jaillir; mettre au jour; provoquer.

eligible, el´-i-dji-b'l, *a* éligible; *n* un bon parti.

eliminate, i-lime´-i-néte, *v* éliminer.

elite, é-lîte´, *n* élite *f.*

elk, elk, *n* élan *m.*

elm, elme, *n* orme *m.*

elongate, î´-longue-éte, *v* prolonger; allonger.

elope, i-laupe´, *v* se laisser; enlever.

elopement, i-laupe´-m'nt, *n* fugue amoureuse *f*; fuite *f.*

eloquent, el´-ŏ-couennte, *a* éloquent.

else, elce, *a* autre. *adv* autrement; **–where,** ailleurs.

elucidate, i-lioue´-ci-déte, *v* éclaircir; élucider.

elude, i-lioude´, *v* éviter; éluder.

elusive, i-lioue´-sive, *a* évasif.

emaciate, i-mé´-chi-éte, *v* amaigrir.

emanate, emm´-*a*-néte, *v* émaner.

emancipate, i-mănn´-ci-péte, *v* émanciper.

embalm, emm-băme´, *v* embaumer.

embankment, emm-bainque´-m'nt, *n* terrassement *m*; (railroad) remblai *m*; (river) quai *m*.

embark, emm-bârke´, *v* embarquer.

embarrass, emm-băr´-*ass*, *v* gêner.

embarrassment, emm-băr´-*ass*-m'nt, *n* gêne *f* & *m*.

embassy, emm´-băss-i, *n* ambassade *f*.

embellish, emm-bell´-iche, *v* embellir.

ember, emm´-*beur*, *n* braise *f*.

embezzle, emm-bez´-z'l, *v* détourner.

embitter, emm-bitt´-*eur*, *v* (*fig*) aigrir.

embody, emm-bod´-i, *v* incorporer; personnifier.

embrace, emm-bréce´, *n* étreinte *f*. *v* étreindre.

embroider, emm-broa'i´-d'r, *v* broder.

embroidery, emm-broa'i´-deur-i, *n* broderie *f*.

embroil, emm-broa'il´, *v* embrouiller.

emerald, emm´-*eur*-alde, *n* émeraude *f*.

emerge, i-meurdje´, *v* surgir; émerger; **–ncy,** *n* circonstance imprévue *f*; cas d'urgence *m*.

emetic, i-mett´-ique, *n* émétique *m*.

emigrant, emm´-i-grannte, *n* émigrant, -e *m* & *f*.

emigrate, emm´-i-gréte, *v* émigrer.

eminence, emm´-i-nennce, *n* éminence *f*.

eminent, emm´-i-nennte, *a* éminent; célèbre.

emissary, emm´-is-*sa*-ri, *n* émissaire *m*.

emit, i-mitte´, *v* émettre; dégager; exhaler.

emotion, i-mau´-ch'n, *n* émotion *f*; **–al,** *a* émotif; ému.

emperor, emm´-*peu-reu* *n* empereur *m*.

emphasis, emm´-*fa*-cice, *n* insistance *f*.

emphasize, emm´-*fa*-sâïze, *v* appuyer sur; mettre en valeur.

emphatic, emm-făte´-ique, *a* emphatique.

empire, emm´-pâïre, *n* empire *m*.

employ, emm-ploa'i´, *v* employer; **–er,** *n* patron *m*; employeur *m*; **–ment,** emploi *m*.

empower, emm-pâ'ou´-*eur*, *v* autoriser; mettre à même de.

empress, emm´-presse, *n* impératrice *f*.

empty, emm´-pti, *a* vide. *v* vider.

emulate, emm´-iou-léte, *v* rivaliser avec.

enable, enn-é´-b'l, *v* permettre de.

enact, enn-ăcte´, *v* décréter.

enamel, enn-ămm´-'l, *n* émail *m*. *v* émailler.

enamored, enn-ămm´-*eur*de, *a* épris de.

encamp, enn-cămmpe´, *v* camper.

enchant, enn-tchănnte´, *v* enchanter; **–ment,** *n* enchantement *m*.

encircle, enn-seur´-k'l, *v* entourer.

enclose, enn-clauze´, *v* (field) clôturer; (in) enfermer, joindre.

enclosure, enn-clau´-jeure, *n* enclos *m*; (*com*) pièce jointe *f*.

encore, an-coare´, *v* bisser. *interj* bis!

encounter, enn-câ'ounn´-

a
b
c
d
e
f
g
h
i
j
k
l
m
n
o
p
q
r
s
t
u
v
w
x
y
z

teur, v rencontrer. *n* recontre *f.*

encourage, enn-cor´-idj, *v* encourager; **–ment,** *n* encouragement *m.*

encroach, enn-crautche´, *v* empiéter; (time, etc) abuser de; **–ment,** *n* empiètement *m;* usurpation *f.*

encumber, enn-comm´-beur, *v* encombrer.

encumbrance, enn-comm´-brannce, *n* embarras *m;* (property) charges *fpl.*

encyclopedia, en-sâï´-clau-pî´-di-*a, n* encyclopédie *f.*

end, ènnde, *n* fin *f;* bout *m. v* finir.

endanger, enn-dénn´-dj*eur, v* mettre en danger.

endear, enn-dîre´, *v* rendre cher.

endeavor, enn-dèv´-*eur, v* s'efforcer. *n* effort *m.*

endive, enn´-dive, *n* endive *f.*

endless, ènnde´-lesse, *a* sans fin.

endorse, enn-doarse´, *v* endosser; approuver; **–ment,** *n* endossement *m;* sanction *f;* approbation *f.*

endow, enn-dâ'ou´, *v*

doter; **–with,** douer de.

endurance, enn-dioue´-rannce, *n* résistance *f.*

endure, enn-dioure´, *v* endurer; supporter.

enema, enn´-i-ma, *n* lavement *m.*

enemy, enn´-i-mi, *n* ennemi *m.*

energetic, enn-*eur*-djett´-ique, *a* énergique.

energy, enn´-*eur*-dji, *n* énergie *f;* force *f.*

enervate, enn´-*eur*-véte, *v* affaiblir; énerver.

enforce, enn-faurce´, *v* faire observer; imposer.

engage, enn-guédje´, *v* engager; embaucher; **–d,** *a* fiancé; (reserved) retenu, occupé; **–ment,** *n* fiançailles *fpl;* (mil) combat *m;* (obligation) engagement *m;* (appointment) rendez-vous *m.*

engaging, enn-guédj´-inng, *a* engageant, attirant.

engender, enn-djenn´-d'r, *v* engendrer.

engine, enn´-djinne, *n* machine *f;* (rail) locomotive *f;* (car) moteur *m;* **–er,** mécanicien *m;* (profession) ingénieur *m;* **–ering,** génie *m.*

English, inng´-gliche, *n* & *a* anglais, *m* & *f;* (language) *n* anglais *m.*

engrave, enn-gréve´, *v* graver; **–r,** *n* graveur *m;* **–ing,** *n* gravure *f.*

engross, enn-grausse´, *v* absorber.

engulf, enn-golf´, *v* engouffrer.

enhance, enn-hânnce´, *v* rehausser; mettre en valeur.

enjoy, enn-djoa'ï´, *v* jouir de; **–ment,** *n* jouissance *f;* plaisir *m;* **–oneself,** s'amuser.

enlarge, enn-lârdje´, *v* agrandir; dilater.

enlargement, enn-lârdje´-m'nt, *n* agrandissement *m.*

enlighten, enn-lâï´-t'n, *v* éclairer; illuminer.

enlist, enn-lisste´, *v* enrôler; s'engager.

enliven, enn-jâï´-v'n, *v* animer; égayer.

enmity, enn´-mi-ti, *n* inimitié *f;* hostilité *f.*

enormous, i-nôr´-m*euce, a* énorme.

enough, i-noff´, *adv* & *a* assez.

enrage, enn-rédje´, *v* exaspérer, faire enrager.

enrapture, enn-râp´-tioure, *v* ravir,

transporter.

enrich, enn-ritche´, *v*
enrichir.

enrol, enn-raule´, *v*
enrôler; s'inscrire.

ensign, enn´-sâïne, *n*
(flag) enseigne *f*; (naval
flag) pavillon *m*; (rank)
enseigne *m*.

enslave, enn-sléve´, *v*
asservir; captiver.

ensnare, enn-snére´, *v*
prendre au piège.

ensue, enn-sioue´, *v*
s'ensuivre.

ensure, enn-choure´,
s'assurer de; rendre sûr.

entail, enn-téle´, *v*
entraîner; (law)
substituer.

entangle, enn-tănn´-g'l, *v*
emmêler.

enter, enn´-teur, *v* entrer;
–up, inscrire.

enterprise, enn´-teur-
prâïze, *n* entreprise *f*;
(boldness) esprit
d'entreprise *m*.

entertain, enn-teur-téne´,
v divertir; (guests)
recevoir; (consider)
admettre; **–ment,** *n*
divertissement *m*.

enthrall, enn´-tsroale *v*
captiver, séduire.

enthusiasm, enn-tsioue´-
zi-ăzme, *n* enthousiasme
m.

entice, enn-tâïce´, *v*
tenter; séduire.

entire*, enn-tâïre´, *a*
entier, complet.

entitle, enn-tâï´-t'l, *v*
intituler; donner droit à.

entomb, enn-toum´, *v*
ensevelir.

entrance, enn´-trannce, *n*
entrée *f*.

entrance, enn-trânnse´, *v*
hypnotiser; transporter;
ravir.

entreat, enn-trîte´, *v*
supplier; implorer.

entrench, enn-trenche´, *v*
se retrancher.

entrust, enn-trosste´, *v*
confier à.

entry, enn´-tri, *n* entrée *f*;
(record) écriture *f*.

entwine, enn-tou'âïne´, *v*
enrouler; enlacer.

enumerate, i-niou´-mé-
réte, *v* énumérer.

envelop, enn-vel´-ŏpe, *v*
envelopper.

envelope, enn´-vel-ôpe, *n*
enveloppe *f*.

envious*, enn´-vî-euce, *a*
envieux.

environs, enn-vâï´-
ronnze, *npl* environs
mpl.

envoy, enn´-voa'ï, *n*
envoyé *m*.

envy, enn´-vi, *n* envie *f*. *v*
envier.

epic, èp´-i-k, *a* épique.

epicure, èp´-i-kioure, *n*
gourmet *m*.

epidemic, èp-i-demm´-
ique, *n* épidémie *f*.

episode, èp´-i-saude, *n*
épisode *m*.

epistle, è-piss´-'l, *n* épître
f.

epoch, i´-poque, *n* époque
f.

equal, î´-coual, *n* & *a**
égal, -e *m* & *f*. *v* égaler;
–ity, *n* égalité *f*; **–ize,** *v*
égaliser.

equator, i-coué´teur, *n*
équateur *m*.

equilibrium, i-coui-lib´-ri-
eume, *n* équilibre *m*.

equip, i-couipe´, *v*
équiper; munir.

equitable, èk´-oui-ta-b'l, *a*
équitable.

equity, èk´-oui-ti, *n* équité
f; justice *f*.

equivalent, i-coui´-va-
lennte, *n* & *a* équivalent
m.

era, i´-ra, *n* ère *f*.

eradicate, é-răd´-i-quéte, *v*
extirper; déraciner;
exterminer.

erase, i-réze´, *v* (rub out)
effacer; (cross out) rayer.

eraser, i-ré´-zeur, *n* gomme
f; (metal) grattoir *m*.

erect, i-recte´, *v* ériger;
bâtir. *a* droit; debout.

A
B
C
D
E
F
G
H
I
J
K
L
M
N
O
P
Q
R
S
T
U
V
W
X
Y
Z

ermine, eur´-mine, *n* hermine *f.*

erosion, i-rau´-j'n, *n* érosion; usure *f.*

err, eure, *v* errer; (mistake) se tromper.

errand, èrr´-*a*nnde, *n* commission *f.*

erratic, err-răt´-tique, *a* changeant, irrégulier.

erroneous*, err-rau´-ni-euce, *a* erroné.

error, èrr´-*eur*, *n* erreur *f;* faute.

eruption, i-rope´-ch'n, *n* éruption *f.*

escape, ess-képe´, *n* fuite *f.* évasion *f. v* échapper.

escort, ess-kôrte´, *n* escorte *f;* cavalier *m. v* escorter.

especially, ess-péch´-al-li, *adv* surtout.

essay, ès´-sé, *n* essai *m;* composition *f.*

essential*, ess-senn´-ch'l, *a* essentiel.

establish, ess-tăb´-liche, *v* établir.

establishment, ess-tăb´-liche-m'nt, *n* établissement *m.*

estate, ess-téte´, *n* propriété *f;* biens *mpl;* (status) rang *m;* (possessions) succession *f.*

esteem, ess-tîme´, *v*

estimer. *n* estime *f.*

estimate, ess´-ti-méte, *n* évaluation *f;* (cost) devis *m. v* évaluer; estimer.

estrange, ess-tréne´-dje, *v* aliéner.

etch, ètch, *v* graver.

etching, ètch´-inng, *n* gravure à l'eau-forte *f.*

eternal*, i-teur´-n'l, *a* éternel.

eternity, i-teur´-ni-ti, *n* éternité *f.*

ether, î´-*tseur*, *n* éther *m.*

ethical, é´-tsi-k'l, *a* moral.

ethics, é´-tsiks, *npl* morale *f.*

evacuate, i-văk´-iou-éte, *v* évacuer.

evade, i-véde´, *v* éviter; éluder.

evaporate, i-văp´-ŏ-réte, *v* s'évaporer.

evasive*, i-vé´-cive, *a* évasif.

eve, îve, *n* veille *f.*

even, î´-v'n, *adv* même. *a* égal; pair; quitte; (smooth) uni.

evening, ive´-ninng, *n* soir *m;* soirée *f;* **–dress,** tenue de soirée *f;* robe du soir *f.*

evensong, i´-venn-sonng, *n* service du soir *m.*

event, i-vennte´, *n* évènement *m;* cas *m;*

–ful, *a* accidenté; mémorable; **–ually,** *adv* finalement.

ever, èv´-'r, *adv* toujours; (at any time) jamais.

everlasting*, èv´-eur-lâst-inng, *a* éternel.

every, év´-ri, *a* chaque; tous les; **–body,** *n* tout le monde; **–thing,** tout *m;* **–where,** *adv* partout.

evict, i-victe´, *v* expulser; **–ion,** *n* expulsion *f.*

evidence, èv´-i-dennce, *n* évidence *f;* preuve *f;* déposition *f;* **give –,***v* déposer.

evident, èv´-i-dennte, *a* évident.

evil, î´-v'l, *n* mal *m. a* mauvais; méchant; malin.

evince, i-vinnce´, *v* manifester; faire preuve de.

evoke, i-vauque´, *v* évoquer.

evolution, î´-vau-liouе-ch'n, *n* évolution *f;* développement *m.*

evolve, i-volve´, *v* émettre; évoluer.

ewe, ioue, *n* brebis *f.*

exact, egg-zăct´, *a** exact. *v* exiger; **–ing,** *a* exigeant; **–itude,** *n* exactitude *f.*

exaggerate, egg-zădj´-iréte, *v* exagérer.

exaggeration, egg-zădj-i-ré´-ch'n, *n* exagération *f.*

exalt, egg-zoalt´, *v* exalter.

examination, egg-zămm-inn-é´-ch'n, *n* examen *m;* inspection *f;* (legal) interrogatoire *m.*

examine, egg-zămm´-inne, *v* examiner.

example, egg-zămm´-p'l, *n* exemple *m.*

exasperate, egg-zăss´-peur-éte, *v* exaspérer.

excavate, ex´-ca-véte, *v* faire des fouilles.

exceed, ex-cîde´, *v* excéder; dépasser.

exceedingly, ex-cîd´-inng-li, *adv* excessivement.

excel, ex-celle´, *v* exceller; **–lent,** *a* excellent.

except, èk-cepte´, *v* excepter. *prep* sauf; excepté; **–ion,** *n* exception *f;* **take –ion,** *v* s'offenser; **–ional** *a* exceptionnel.

excerpt, èk-seurpte´, *n* extrait *m.*

excess, èk-cesse´, *n* excès *m;* (surplus) excédent *m.*

excessive, èk-cess´-ive, *a* excessif.

exchange, ex-tchéne´-dje, *n* échange *m;* (money) change *m;* (telephone) central *m. v* échanger.

excise, èk-sâïze´, *v* retrancher; supprimer; exciser.

excitable, èk-sâï´-ta-b'l, *a* excitable; nerveux.

excite, èk-sâïte´, *v* exciter; agiter.

excitement, èk-sâïte´-m'nt, *n* émotion *f;* agitation *f.*

exciting, èk-sâï´-tinng, *a* passionnant.

exclaim, ex-cléme´, *v* s'écrier.

exclamation, ex-clă-mé´-ch'n, *n* exclamation.

exclude, ex-cloude´, *v* exclure.

exclusive*, ex-cloue´-cive, *a* exclusif.

excruciating, ex-croue´-chi-éte-inng, *a* atroce.

excursion, ex-kor´-ch'n, *n* excursion *f.*

excuse, ex-kiouze´, *v* excuser. *n* excuse *f.*

execute, ex´-ci-kioute, *v* exécuter; accomplir.

executioner, ex-ci-kiou´-chŏnn-*eur*, *n* bourreau *m.*

executor, ex-cè´-kioue-*teur*, *n* exécuteur.

exempt, egg-zemmpte, *v* dispenser. *a* dispensé.

exemption, egg-zemmpte´-ch'n, *n* dispense *f.*

exercise, ex´-*eur*-sâïze, *n*

exercice *m. v* exercer.

exert, egg-zeurte´, *v* s'efforcer; **–ion,** *n* effort *m.*

exhaust, egg-zôste´, *v* épuiser. *n* (*mech*) échappement *m.*

exhaustion, egg-zôst´n, *n* epuisement *m.*

exhibit, egg-zib´-itte, *v* exposer; montrer. *n* article exposé *m.*

exhibition, egg-zi-bi´-ch'n, *n* exposition *f.*

exhilarate, egg-zil´-ă-réte, *v* réjouir.

exhilarating, egg-zil´-a-réte-inng, *a* vivifiant.

exigency, èk´-si-djenn-ci, *n* exigence *f.*

exile, èk´-sâïle, *v* exiler. *n* exil *m;* (person) exilé *m.*

exist, egg-zisste´, *v* exister; **–ence,** *n* existence *f.*

exit, èk´-citte, *n* sortie *f.*

exonerate, egg-zonn´-*eur*-éte, *v* exonérer; disculper; innocenter.

exorbitant, èk-sôre´-bi-t'nt, *a* exorbitant.

expand, ex-pănnde´, *v* dilater; **–ing,** *a* extensible.

expansion, ex-pănn´-ch'n, *n* expansion *f.*

expect, ex-pecte´, *v* attendre; s'attendre à; **–ation,** *n* attente *f.*

a
b
c
d
e
f
g
h
i
j
k
l
m
n
o
p
q
r
s
t
u
v
w
x
y
z

A
B
C
D
E
F
G
H
I
J
K
L
M
N
O
P
Q
R
S
T
U
V
W
X
Y
Z

expedient, ex-pî´-di-ennte, n expédient m. a convenable.

expedite, ex´-pi-dâïte, v accélérer; expédier.

expel, ex-pelle´, v expulser, renvoyer.

expend, ex-pennde´, v dépenser.

expenditure, ex-penn´-di-tioure, n dépense f.

expense, ex-pennse´, n dépense f, frais mpl.

expensive*, ex-penn´-cive, a coûteux, cher.

experience, ex-pi´-ri-ennce, n expérience f. v éprouver, faire l'expérience de.

experiment, ex-pair´-i-mennte, n expérience f. v expérimenter.

expert, ex-peurte´, n & a expert m.

expire, ex-pâïre´, v expirer.

explain, ex-pléne´, v expliquer.

explanation, ex-pla-né´-ch'n, n explication f.

explicit, ex-pli´-site, a explicite, clair.

explode, ex-plaude´, v faire explosion.

exploit, ex-ploa'ite´, n exploit m v exploiter.

explore, ex-plaure´, v explorer.

explorer, ex-plaur´-eur, n explorateur m.

explosion, ex-plau´-j'n, n explosion f.

export, ex-paurte´, v exporter; n exportation f; **–er,** n exportateur m.

expose, ex-pauze´, v exposer; (fraud) démasquer; (plot) dévoiler.

expostulate, ex-poss´-tiou-léte, v faire des remontrances.

exposure, ex-pau´-jeure, n exposition f; scandale m.

expound, ex-pâ'ounnde´, v exposer; expliquer.

express, ex-presse´, n express m; rapide m. a exprès. v exprimer; **–ion,** n expression f.

expulsion, ex-pol´-ch'n, n expulsion f.

exquisite*, ex´-coui-zite, a exquis.

extend, ex-tennde´, v étendre; s'étendre.

extensive, ex-tenn´-cive, a étendu; vaste.

extent, ex-tennte´, n étendue f; point m; degré m.

extenuating, ex-tenn´-iou-é´-tinng, a atténuant.

exterior, ex-ti´-ri-eur, n & a extérieur m.

exterminate, ex-teur´-mi-néte, v exterminer.

exterminator, ex-teur´-mi-na-teur, n exterminateur m.

external*, ex-teur´-n'l, a externe; extérieur.

extinct, ex-tinng´-kt, a éteint; (race, etc) disparu.

extinguish, ex-tinng´-gouiche, v éteindre.

extortion, ex-tôr´-ch'n, n extorsion f.

extort, ex-tôrte´, v extorquer.

extra, ex´-tra, a en plus. n supplément m; **–ordinary,** a extraordinaire.

extract, ex-trăcte´, v extraire. n extrait m.

extravagant, ex-tră´-va-gannte, a dépensier.

extreme, ex-trîme´, n extrême m. a* extrême.

extremity, ex-trè´-mi-ti, n extrémité f.

extricate, ex´-tri-kéte, v dégager de.

eye, âï, n œil m; trou m; **–ball,** globe m (de l'œil); **–brow,** sourcil m; **–lash,** cil m; **–let,** œillet m; **–lid,** paupière f; **–sight,** vue f; **–witness,** témoin oculaire m.

fable, fé´-b'l, n fable f.

fabric, făb´-rik, n étoffe f; tissu m; structure f; **–ation,** fabrication f; invention f.

fabulous*, făb´-iou-leuce, a fabuleux.

façade, fă-sade´, n façade f.

face, féce, n figure f; visage m; face f; (clock) cadran m; apparence f. v faire face à; **–cream,** n crème pour le visage f.

facilitate, fa-cil´-i-téte, v faciliter.

facsimile, făk-simm´-i-li, n fac-similé m.

fact, făcte, n fait m.

factor, făk´-tŏr, n facteur m; élément m.

factory, făk´-teur-i, n fabrique f; usine f.

faculty, făk´-eul-ti, n faculté f; aptitude f.

fade, féde, v se faner; (color) passer.

fail, féle, v manquer; faillir; (exam, etc) échouer; **without –,** sans faute; **–ing,** n défaut m. prep à défaut de; faute de; **–ure,** échec m; (insolvency) faillite f; (of person) raté, -ée m & f.

faint, fé-nnte, v s'évanouir. n évanouissement m. a* léger; faible.

fair, fère, a juste; équitable; assez bon; considérable; beau; (hair) blond. n foire f; **–ness,** équité f; beauté f; honnêteté f.

fairy, fé´-ri, n fée f.

faith, féts, n foi f; confiance f; **–ful*,** a fidèle.

fake, féke, n objet (m) truqué; imposteur m; feinte f (sport); a falsifié; truqué. v faire semblant.

fall, foal, n chute f; descente f; (prices) baisse f. v tomber; baisser.

fallacy, făl´-la-ci, n fausseté f; illusion f.

false*, foalse, a faux; artificiel.

falsehood, foalse´-houde, n mensonge m.

falsification, foal´-si-fi-qué´-ch'n, n falsification m.

falsify, foal´-si-făï, v falsifier.

falter, foal´-teur, v hésiter; (speech) balbutier.

fame, féme, n renommée f; **–d,** a célèbre; renommé.

familiar*, fa-mil´-i-eur, a familier, intime.

family, fămm´-i-li, n famille f.

famine, fămm´-inn, n famine f.

famish, fămm´-iche, v affamer.

famous, féme´-euce, a fameux, célèbre.

fan, fănne, n éventail m;

ventilateur *m. v* éventer.

fanatic, fă-năt´-ique, *n &
a* fanatique *m & f.*

fanaticism, fă-năt´-i-
cizme, *n* fanatisme *m.*

fancy, fănn´-ci, *n*
imagination *f;* (liking)
goût *m;* (desire) envie *f.
v* imaginer; avoir envie
de.

fang, fainng, *n* (dog) croc
m; (snake) crochet *m.*

fantastic, fănn-tăss´-tique,
a fantastique.

fantasy, fănn´-ta-zi, *n*
fantaisie *f.*

far, fâre, *adv* loin. *a*
lointain; éloigné.

farce, fărce, *n* farce *f.*

fare, fère, *n* prix du
parcours *m;* (food)
nourriture *f;* voyageur *m.*

farewell, fère-ouel´, *n*
adieu *m.*

farm, fârme, *n* ferme *f;*
–er, fermier *m.*

farther, fâre´dzeur, *adv*
plus loin. *a* plus éloigné.

fascinate, făss´-ci-néte, *v*
fasciner.

fascinating, făss´-ci-né-
tinng, *a* séduisant;
enchanteur.

fashion, făche´-eune, *n*
mode *f. v* façonner; **to
be in –,** être à la mode;
–able, *a* à la mode.

fast, fâste, *a* rapide; ferme;

(color) bon teint. *n*
jeûne *m. v* jeûner.

fasten, fâs´-s'n, *v* attacher;
fixer; (close) fermer.

fastidious*, făss-tid´-i-
euce, *a* difficile;
exigeant.

fat, fătte, *n* graisse *f;*
(meat) gras *m. a*
(person) gros; (animal)
gras; **–ten,** *v* engraisser;
–ty, *a* graisseux, gras.

fatal*, fé´-t'l, *a* fatal;
mortel.

fate, féte, *n* destin *m;* sort
m; **–d,** *a* destiné.

father, fâ´-dzeur, *n* père *m;*
–in-law, beau-père *m;*
–ly, *a* paternel.

fatigue, fa-tîgue´, *v*
fatiguer. *n* fatigue *f.*

fault, foalte, *n* faute *f;*
(defect) défaut *m;*
–less*, *a* impeccable;
faire plaisir; **–y,**
défectueux.

favor, fé´-veur, *n* faveur *f;*
grâce *f;* (com) honorée *f.
v* favoriser; **to do**
(someone) **a –,** rendre
service; **–able,** *a*
favorable; propice; **–ite,**
n & a favori, -te *m & f.*

fawn, foanne, *n* faon *m.*

fear, fîre, *v* craindre. *n*
crainte *f;* peur *f;* **–ful,** *a*
effroyable; craintif;
–less, intrépide.

feasible, fî´-zi-b'l, *a*
praticable; faisable.

feast, fîsste, *n* fête *f;* festin
m. v régaler; se régaler.

feat, fîte, *n* exploit *m;*
(skill) tour de force *m.*

feather, fè´-dzeur, *n* plume
f. v emplumer.

feature, fît´-ieure, *n* trait
m; particularité *f.*

February, fè´-brou-èr-i, *n*
février *m.*

federation, fé´-deur-é´-
ch'n, *n* fédération *f.*

fee, fî, *n* honoraires *mpl;*
prix *m.*

feeble, fî´-b'l, *a* faible;
débile.

feed, fîde, *v* nourrir;
(cattle) paître.

feel, fîle, *v* sentir; tâter. *n*
toucher *m;* **–er,** *n*
(insects) antenne *f;*
–ing, toucher *m;*
sensation *f;* sentiment
m.

feign, féne, *v* feindre,
simuler.

fell, fèle, *v* abattre;
assommer.

fellow, fèl´-au, *n* membre
m; collègue *m;* (*pop*)
garçon *m;* homme *m;*
–ship, camaraderie *f.*

felony, fèl´-au-ni, *n* crime
m.

felt, felte, *n* feutre *m.*

female, fî´-méle, *n & a*

femelle *f; a & n* féminin *m.*

feminine, fème´-i-ninn, *a & n* féminin *m.*

fence, fènnce, *n* clôture *f. v* entourer; (swordsmanship) faire de l'escrime.

fencing, fènn-cinng, *n* escrime *f.*

fender, fenn´-deur, *n* garde-feu *m;* (auto) aile *f.*

ferment, feur-mennte´, *v* fermenter. *n* ferment *m.*

fern, feurne, *n* fougère *f.*

ferocious*, fi-rau´-cheuce, *a* féroce.

ferret, fèr´-ette, *n* furet *m. v* fureter.

ferry, fèr´-i, *n* bac *m. v* passer en bac.

fertile, feur´-tâïle, *a* fertile.

fertilize, feur´-ti-lâïze, *v* fertiliser.

fervent, feur´-vennte, *a* fervent; ardent.

fester, fess´-teur, *v* s'envenimer.

festival, fess´-ti-v'l, *n* fête *f;* festival *m. a* de fête.

festive, fess´-tive, *a* joyeux; de fête.

festoon, fess-toune´, *n* feston *m. v* festonner.

fetch, fètche, *v* aller chercher.

fetter, fèt´-teur, *v* enchaîner; –s, *npl* fers *mpl.*

fetus, fî´-teuce, *n* embryon *m;* foetus *m.*

feud, fioude, *n* inimitié *f;* –al, *a* féodal.

fever, fî´-veur, *n* fièvre *f;* –ish, *a* fiévreux.

few, fioue, *a* peu de; **a –,** quelques.

fiber, fâï´-beur, *n* fibre *f.*

fickle, fik´-'l, *a* volage; inconstant.

fiction, fique´-ch'n, *n* fiction *f;* roman *m.*

fictitious*, fique-tich´-euce, *a* fictif; faux.

fidelity, fi-dél´-i-ti, *n* fidélité *f.*

fidget, fid´-jette, *v* remuer; –y, *a* remuant; agité.

field, fîlde, *n* champ *m;* pré *m;* (games) terrain *m.*

fiend, fînnde, *n* démon *m;* –ish, *a* diabolique.

fierce*, fîrce, *a* féroce; farouche; furieux.

fiery, fâï´-eu-ri, *a* ardent; fougueux.

fifteen, fiff´-tîne, *n & a* quinze *m;* –th, *n & a* quinzième *m & f.*

fifth, fifts, *n & a* cinquième *m & f.*

fiftieth, fiff´-ti-its, *n & a* cinquantième *m & f.*

fifty, fiff´-ti, *n & a* cinquante *m.*

fig, figue, *n* figue *f;* –tree, figuier *m.*

fight, fâïte, *v* se battre; combattre. *n* combat *m.*

figure, figue´-ioure, *n* figure *f;* forme *f;* ligne; (number) chiffre *m;* tournure.

file, fâïle, *n* (tool) lime *f;* (office) classeur *m;* dossier *m;* (mil) file *f. v* limer; classer.

filigree, fil´-i-grî, *n* filigrane *m.*

fill, file, *v* remplir. *n* suffisance *f.*

filly, fil´-i, *n* pouliche *f.*

film, filme, *n* voile *m;* (snapshots, etc) pellicule *f;* (cinema) film *m. v* filmer.

filter, fil´-teur, *v* filtrer. *n* filtre *m.*

filth, filts, *n* saleté *f;* –y, *a* sale.

fin, fine, *n* nageoire *f.*

final*, fâï´-n'l, *a* final; décisif.

finance, fi-nănnce´, *n* finance *f. v* commanditer.

financial*, fi-nănn´-ch'l, *a* financier.

finch, finntche, *n* pinson *m.*

find, fâïnnde, *v* trouver.

a
b
c
d
e
f
g
h
i
j
k
l
m
n
o
p
q
r
s
t
u
v
w
x
y
z

fine, fâïnne, *v* mettre à l'amende. *n* amende *f. a* fin; délicat; beau; subtil; excellent.

finery, fâï´-*neur*-i, *n* parure *f.*

finger, finng´-*gueur*, *n* doigt *m. v* toucher.

finish, finn´-iche, *v* finir; terminer. *n* fin *f.*

fir, feur, *n* sapin *m.*

fire, fâïre, *n* feu *m*; (conflagration) incendie *m. v* incendier; (gun, etc) tirer; **–alarm,** *n* avertisseur d'incendie *m*; **–-department,** corps de pompiers *m*; **–-engine,** pompe à incendie *f*; **–escape,** échelle de sauvetage *f*; **–man,** pompier *m*; **–place,** foyer *m*; cheminée *f*; **–proof,** *a* ininflammable; **–works,** *npl* feu d'artifice *m.*

firm, feurme, *n* maison (de commerce) *f. a** solide; ferme.

first, feurste, *n* & *a** premier, -ère *m* & *f.*

fish, fiche, *n* poisson *m. v* pêcher; **–bone,** *n* arête *f*; **–erman,** pêcheur *m*; **–-hook,** hameçon *m.*

fishing, fich´-inng, *n* pêche *f*; **–rod,** canne à pêche *f.*

fissure, fich´-ioure, *n* fissure *f*; fente *f.*

fist, fiste, *n* poing *m.*

fistula, fiss´-tioue-la, *n* fistule *f.*

fit, fite, *v* ajuster; (clothes) aller; correspondre; poser; adapter. *n* (*med*) attaque *f. a* convenable; propre à; en forme.

fittings, fitt´-inngs, *npl* garnitures *fpl*; accessoires *mpl.*

five, fâïve, *n* & *a* cinq *m.*

fix, fixe, *v* fixer; arranger; préparer. *n* position *f*; combine *f.*

fixture, fixe´-tioure, *n* objet fixé à demeure *m.*

fizzy, fiz´-i, *a* gazeux.

flabby, flåb´-i, *a* flasque; mollasse.

flag, flågue, *n* drapeau *m*; (*naut*) pavillon *m*; **–ship,** vaisseau amiral *m*; **–staff,** hampe de drapeau *f.*

flagon, flåg´-ŏnn, *n* flacon *m.*

flagrant, flé´-grannte, *a* flagrant.

flake, fléke, *n* (metal) lame *f*; (snow, etc) flocon *m.*

flaky, flé´-ki, *a* (pastry) feuilleté.

flame, fléme, *n* flamme *f. v* flamber.

flange, flånndje, *n* rebord *m*; (wheel) boudin *m.*

flank, flain´-ngk, *v* flanquer; border. *n* flanc *m.*

flannel, flånn´-'l, *n* flanelle *f.*

flap, flåppe, *n* battant *m*; (pocket) patte *f*; (wings) coup d'aile *m. v* battre.

flare, flère, *n* vive clarté *f*; flamme *f. v* flamboyer; (trousers, etc) évaser.

flash, flåche, *n* éclat *m*; (lightning) éclair *m*; (guns, etc) feu *m.*

flask, flåsske, *n* flacon *m.*

flat, flåtte, *n* appartement *m*; (*mus*) bémol *m. a* plat.

flatten, flått´-'n, *v* aplatir.

flatter, flått´-*eur*, *v* flatter; **–ing*,** *a* flatteur; **–y,** *n* flatterie *f.*

flavor, flé´-*veur*, *n* saveur *f*; goût *m*; (wine) bouquet *m. v* assaisonner.

flaw, floa, *n* défaut *m.*

flax, flåxe, *n* lin *m.*

flea, flî, *n* puce *f.*

flee, flî, *v* fuir; s'enfuir.

fleece, flîce, *n* toison *f. v* tondre; (rob) écorcher.

fleet, flîte, *n* flotte *f. a** rapide; léger.

flesh, flèche, *n* chair *f.*

flexible, flè´-xi-b'l, *a* flexible; souple.

flicker, flik´-*eur*, *v* vaciller;

clignoter. *n* battement *m*.

flight, flâïte, *n* (fleeing) fuite *f*; (birds, planes) vol *m*; (stairs) escalier *m*.

flight attendant, flâite atten´d'nt, *n* hotesse de l'air *f*.

flimsy, flimm´-zi, *a* léger; fragile; (paper) papier pelure *m*.

flinch, flinntche, *v* broncher; fléchir.

fling, flinng, *v* lancer.

flint, flinnte, *n* silex *m*; (lighter) pierre *f* (à briquet).

flippant*, flipp´-annte, *a* léger; (*pers*) désinvolte.

flirt, fleurte, *v* flirter. *n* flirt *m* & *f*.

float, flaute, *n* (angler's) flotteur *m*. *v* flotter; (on back) faire la planche; (a company) lancer.

flock, floque, *n* troupeau *m*; (birds) vol *m*. *v* s'attrouper.

flog, flogue, *v* fouetter.

flood, flodde, *v* inonder. *n* inondation *f*; (tide) marée *f*.

floor, flaure, *n* plancher *m*; (story) étage *m*.

florid, flor´-ide, *a* fleuri; flamboyant.

florist, flor´-isste, *n*

fleuriste *m* & *f*.

floss, flosse, *n* bourre de soie *f*; fil dentaire *m*.

flounce, flâ´ounnce, *n* (dress) volant *m*. *v* se démener.

flour, flâ´oueur, *n* farine *f*.

flourish, flor´-iche, *n* brandissement *m*; (*mus*) fanfare *f*. *v* prospérer; (brandish) brandir.

flout, flâ´oute, *v* se moquer de.

flow, flau, *n* écoulement *m*; (river) cours *m*. *v* couler.

flower, flâ´ou´-*eur*, *n* fleur *f*. *v* fleurir.

fluctuate, floc´-tiou-éte, *v* fluctuer.

flue, floue, *n* tuyau de cheminée *m*.

fluency, floue´-enn-ci, *n* facilité *f*.

fluent, floue´-ennte, *a* facile; coulant.

fluff, floff, *n* duvet *m*; peluches *fpl*; –**y,** *a* pelucheux; duveteux.

fluid, floue´-idd, *n* & *a* fluide *m*.

fluke, flouque, *n* (chance) coup de hasard *m*.

flurry, flor´-i, *n* émoi *m*. *v* agiter; troubler.

flush, floche, *v* (redden) rougir; (rinse) laver à grande eau. *n* rougeur *f*.

a (level) au niveau de.

fluster, floce´-teur, *v* déconcerter. *n* agitation *f*.

flute, floute, *n* flûte *f*; –**d,** *a* cannelé.

flutter, flott´-*eur*, *v* palpiter; battre des ailes.

fly, flâï, *n* mouche *f*; (trouser) *n* braguette *f*. *v* voler; (flag) flotter.

foal, faule, *n* poulain *m*. *v* pouliner.

foam, faume, *n* écume *f*. *v* écumer.

focus, fau´-*keuce*, *v* mettre au point; régler. *n* foyer *m*.

fodder, fod´'r, *n* fourrage *m*.

foe, fau, *n* ennemi *m*.

fog, fogue, *n* brouillard *m*;–**gy,** *a* brumeux; — **horn,** *n* sirène *f*; trompede brume.

foil, foa'ile, *n* (fencing) fleuret *m*; (metal) feuille *f*. *v* déjouer.

foist, foa'iste, *v* imposer; introduire; fourrer.

fold, faulde, *n* (clothes, etc) pli *m*; (sheep) bercail *m*. *v* plier; (arms) croiser.

foliage, fau´-li-édje, *n* feuillage *m*.

folk, fauke, *n* gens *mpl* & *fpl*.

A B C D E F G H I J K L M N O P Q R S T U V W X Y Z

follow, foll´-au, *v* suivre; (*fig*) s'ensuivre.

follower, foll´-au'r, *n* partisan *m*; disciple *m*.

folly, foll´-i, *m* folie *f*; (stupidity) sottise *f*.

foment, fo-mennte´, *v* fomenter.

fond, fonnde, *a* affectueux; **to be –of,** aimer.

fondle, fonn´-d'l, *v* choyer; caresser.

font, fonnte, *n* fonts baptismaux *mpl*.

food, foude, *n* nourriture *f*; (a food) aliment *m*.

fool, foull, *n* imbécile *m* & *f*. *v* duper; **–hardy,** *a* téméraire; **–ish,** sot; imprudent.

foot, foutt, *n* pied *m*; **–ball,** football *m*; **–path,** sentier *m*; (pavement) trottoir *m*; **–print,** trace de pas *f*; **–step,** pas *m*.

for, fôr, *prep* pour; pendant. *conj* car.

forage, for´-idj, *n* fourrage *m*. *v* fourrager.

forbear, fôr-bére´, *v* supporter; s'abstenir.

forbearance, fôr-bèr´-annce, *n* indulgence *f*.

forbid, fôr-bide´, *v* défendre; **–ding,** *a* repoussant.

force, fôrce, *v* forcer. *n*

force *f*; **–ful,** *a* vigoureux.

forceps, for´-seppse, *n* pince *f*; forceps *m*.

forcible, fôr´-ci-b'l, *a* énergique; par force.

ford, fôrde, *v* passer à gué. *n* gué *m*.

fore, fore, *n* avant *m*. *a* antérieur; **–arm,** *n* avant-bras *m*; **–bode,** *v* présager; **–boding,** *n* présage *m*; **–cast,** prévision *f*. *v* prévoir; **–close,** *v* (law) forclore; **–fathers,** *n* aïeux *mpl*; **–finger,** index *m*; **–going,** *a* précédent; **–gone,** préconçu; **–ground,** *n* premier plan *m*; **–head,** front *m*; **–man,** contremaître *m*; **–most,** *a* le plus avancé; principal; **–runner,** *n* précurseur *m*; **–see,** *v* prévoir; **–sight,** *n* prévoyance *f*; **–stall,** *v* devancer; **–taste,** *n* avant-goût *m*; **–tell,** *v* prédire; **–thought,** *n* préméditation *f*; **–warn,** *v* avertir.

foreign, for´-ine, *a* étranger; **–er,** *n* étranger, -éren *m* & *f*.

forest, for´-este, *n* forêt *f*.

forfeit, for´-fite, *n* gage *m*; (law) dédit *m*. *v* perdre;

renoncer.

forge, fordje, *v* forger; (falsify) contrefaire. *n* forge *f*; **–ry,** contrefaçon *f*; faux *m*.

forget, fŏr-guètte´, *v* oublier; **–ful,** *a* oublieux; négligent; **–fulness,** *n* oubli *m*; **––me-not,** (flower) myosotis *m*.

forgive, fŏr-guive´, *v* pardonner.

forgiveness, fŏr-guive´-nesse, *n* pardon *m*.

forgo, fore-gau´, *v* renoncer à; s'abstenir de.

fork, forque, *n* fourchette *f*; (tool) fourche *f*; (road) bifurcation *f*. *v* bifurquer.

forlorn, fŏr-lôrne´, *a* abandonné; désespéré.

form, fôrme, *n* forme *f*; (a form to fill up) formule *f*; (seat) banc *m*; (class) classe *f*. *v* former; **–al*,** *a* de forme; formel; officiel; **–ality,** *n* formalité *f*; **–ation,** *n* formation *f*; **–er,** *a* précédent; ancien; **–erly,** *adv* autrefois.

forsake, fôr-céque´, *v* délaisser; abandonner.

fort, fôrte, *n* fort *m*; **–ification,** fortification *f*; **–ify,** *v* fortifier; **–ress,**

n forteresse *f.*

forth, fôr*ts, adv* en avant; désormais; **–coming,** *a* prochain; **–with,** *adv* sur-le-champ.

fortieth, fôr´-ti-*its, n & a* quarantième *m & f.*

fortitude, fôr´-ti-tioude, *n* courage *m.*

fortnight, forte´-nâïte, *n* quinzaine *f;* quinze jours.

fortunate*, fôr´-tiou-néte, *a* heureux; fortuné.

fortune, fôr´-tioune, *n* fortune *f;* (fate) sort *m.*

forty, fôr´-ti, *n & a* quarante *m.*

forward, fôr´-ouarde, *v* expédier; faire suivre. *adv* en avant. *a* avancé; effronté; **–ness,** effronterie *f.*

fossil, foss´-il, *n & a* fossile *m*

foster, fosse´-t'r, *v* élever; encourager; **–parents,** *npl* parents nourriciers *mpl.*

foul, fâ'oule, *v* souiller. *a** sale; impur; obscène; (unfair) déloyal.

foul play, fâ´oule-plé, *n* quelque chose de louche *m.*

found, fâ'ounnde, *v* fonder; (metal) fondre; **–ation,** *n* fondation *f;* (*fig*) fondement *m;* **–er,**

v sombrer. *n* fondateur *m;* **–ling,** enfant trouvé *m;* **–ry,** fonderie *f.*

fountain, fâ'ounn´-tinne, *n* fontaine *f;* **–pen,** stylo *m.*

four, fôr, *n & a* quatre *m;* **–fold,** *a* quadruple; **–teen,** *n & a* quatorze *m;* **–teenth,** *n & a* quartozième *m;* **–th,** quatrième *m & f.*

fowl, fâ'oule, *n* volaille *f.*

fox, foxe, *n* renard *m;* **–terrier,** fox-terrier *m.*

fraction, frăck´-ch'n, *n* fraction *f.*

fracture, frăck´-tioure, *v* fracturer. *n* fracture *f.*

fragile, frăd´-jile, *a* fragile.

fragment, frăgue´-m'nt, *n* fragment *m.*

fragrance, fré´-grannce, *n* perfum *m.*

fragrant, fré´-grannt, *a* parfumé.

frail, fréle, *a* frêle; **–ty,** *n* fragilité *f.*

frame, fréme, *n* forme *f;* cadre *m;* (car) chassis *m. v* former; (picture, etc) encadrer; **–s,** (glasses) *n* monture *f.*

franchise, frănn´-tchâïze, *n* franchise *f.*

frank*, frain-ngk, *a* franc; **–ness,** *n* franchise *f.*

frantic, frănn´-tique, *a*

frénétique; furieux.

fraud, froade, *n* fraude *f;* imposteur *m;* **–ulent*,** *a* frauduleux.

fray, fré, *n* (scuffle) bagarre *f. v* (material) s'effiler.

freak, frîque, *n* phénomène *m;* monstre *m;* **–ish,** *a* bizarre.

freckle, frèk´-'l, *n* tache de rousseur *f.*

free, frî, *v* libérer; délivrer. *a* libre; gratuit; **–dom,** *n* liberté *f;* **–trade,** libre-échange *m.*

freeze, frîze, *v* geler; glacer; congeler.

freezing, frîz´-inng, *n* congélation *f. a* glacial.

freight, fréte, *n* fret *m;* cargaison *f. v* affréter.

frenzy, frenn´-zi, *n* frénésie *f.*

frequency, fri´-couenn-ci, *n* fréquence *f.*

frequent, fri´-couennte, *a* fréquent. *v* fréquenter.

fresh*, frèche, *a* frais; **–ness,** *n* fraîcheur *f.*

fret, frette, *v* se tourmenter; **–ful,** *a* irritable; **—saw,** *n* scie à découper *f;* **–work,** découpage *m.*

friar, frâï´-'r, *n* moine *m;* **–y,** monastère *m.*

friction, frique´-ch'n, *n*

friction *f*; frottement *m*.

Friday, frâï´-dé, *n*
vendredi *m*; **Good –,**
vendredi saint *m*.

friend, frennde, *n* ami *m*;
–liness, bienveillance *f*;
a amical; **–ship,** *n* amitié
f.

fright, frâïte, *n* frayeur *f*;
peur *f*; **–en,** *v* effrayer;
–ful, *a* effroyable;
épouvantable.

frigid, fridj´-ide, *a* glacial;
frigide.

frill, frile, *n* volant *m*,
ruche *f*.

fringe, frinndje, *n* frange *f*;
bord *m*. *v* border.

frisk, frisk, *v* gambader;
fouiller.

frisky, frisk´-i, *a* frétillant;
animé.

fritter, fritt´-´r, *n* beignet
m. *v* morceler; **–away,**
dissiper; gaspiller.

frivolous*, friv´-ŏ-leuce, *a*
frivole.

frock, froque, *n* (dress)
robe *f*.

frog, frogue, *n* grenouille *f*.

frolic, frol´-ique, *v*
folâtrer. *n* espièglerie *f*.

from, fromme, *prep* de;
depuis; de la part de;
d'après.

front, fronnte, *n* devant
m; (*mil*) front *m*; *a* de
face; **–age,** *n* façade *f*.

frontier, fronnt´-i-*eur*, *n* &
a frontière *f*.

frost, froste, *v* glacer. *n*
gelée *f*; (hoar) givre *m*;
—bitten, *a* gelé; **–y,**
glacé.

froth, frôts, *n* écume *f*;
mousse *f*. *v* écumer;
mousser.

frown, frâ'oune, *v* froncer
les sourcils. *n*
froncement de sourcils
m.

frugal*, froue´-g'l, *a*
frugal.

fruit, froute, *n* fruit *m*;
–ful, *a* fructueux; **–less,**
stérile.

frustrate, fross-tréte´, *v*
frustrer.

fry, frâï, *v* frire; faire frire.

fuchsia, fioue´-chi-*a*, *n*
fuchsia *m*.

fuel, fioue´-*eul*, *n*
combustible *m*.

fugitive, fioue´-dji-tive, *n*
& *a* fugitif, –ive *m* & *f*.

fugue, fiougue, *n* fugue *f*.

fulcrum, feul´-creum, *n*
point d'appui *m*.

fulfill, foull-fill´, *v*
accomplir; réaliser;
satisfaire; **–ment,** *n*
accomplissement *m*;
réalisation *f*.

full, foull, *a* plein;
complet.

fullness, foull´-nesse, *n*

plénitude *f*; abondance
f.

fulsome, foull´-*seu*mme, *a*
vil; écœurant.

fume, fioume, *n* vapeur *f*.
v (rage) rager.

fun, fonne, *n* amusement
m; (joke) plaisanterie *f*;
–ny, *a* drôle; amusant.

function, fonnk´-ch'n, *n*
fonction *f*. *v*
fonctionner.

fund, fonnde, *n* fonds *mpl*;
caisse *f*.

fundamental*, fonn-da-
menn´-t'l, *a*
fondamental *f*.

funeral, fioue´-*neur*-'l, *n*
enterrement *m*;
funérailles *fpl*.

funnel, fonn´-'l, *n*
entonnoir *m*; (smoke)
cheminée.

fur, feure, *n* fourrure *f*;
(boiler) tartre *m*. *v*
incruster; **–rier,** *n*
fourreur *m*.

furious*, fioue´-ri-*eu*ce, *a*
furieux.

furnace, feur´-nisse, *n* four
m; fourneau *m*; (ship,
etc) foyer *m*.

furnish, feur´-niche, *v*
meubler; fournir.

furniture, feur´-ni-tioure,
n meubles *mpl*.

furrow, for´-au, *v*
sillonner. *n* sillon *m*.

further, feur´dzeur, *adv* en plus; plus loin. *a* supplémentaire. *v* avancer; seconder.

furtive*, feur´-tive, *a* furtif.

fury, fioue´-ri, *n* furie *f*.

fuse, fiouze, *n* (time) fusée *f*; (electric) plomb *m*; fusible *m*; *v* fuser; sauter.

fuss, foce, *n* embarras *m*; cérémonies *fpl*; (*fam*) des histoires *fpl*.

futile, fioue´-tâïle, *a* futile; frivole.

future, fioue´-tioure, *n* avenir *m*. *a* futur.

a
b
c
d
e
f
g
h
i
j
k
l
m
n
o
p
q
r
s
t
u
v
w
x
y
z

gable, gué´-b'l, n pignon m.

gaff, găffe, n gaffe f.

gag, găgue, v bâillonner. n bâillon m; (fam) blague f.

gaiety, gué-i-ti, n gaieté f.

gaily, gué-li, adv gaiement.

gain, guéne, n gain m. v gagner; atteindre.

gait, guéte, n démarche f; (horse) allure f.

gaiter, gué-t'r, n guêtre f.

galaxy, găl´-ak-ci, n galaxie f.

gale, guéle, n tempête f; coup de vent m.

gall, goal, n bile f. v irriter; **–stone,** n calcul biliaire m; **–bladder,** n vésicule biliaire f.

gallant, găl´-'nt, a brave; galant.

gallantry, găl´-ann-tri, n bravoure f; galanterie f.

gallery, găl´-eur-i, n galerie f.

gallop, găl´-pe, v galoper. n galop m.

gallows, găl´-auze, n potence f; gibet m.

galvanism, găl´-vann-izme, n galvanisme m.

galvanize, găl´-vann-âïze, v galvaniser.

gamble, gămm´-b'l, v jouer de l'argent; miser; **–r,** n joueur m.

game, guéme, n jeu m; partie f; (birds, etc) gibier m; **–keeper,** garde-chasse m.

gander, gănn´-d'r, n jars m.

gang, gain´-ng, n équipe f; bande f; **–way,** passage m; (ship) passerelle f.

gap, găppe, n brèche f; ouverture f; trou m; écart m.

gape, guépe, v regarder bouche bée; s'ouvrir.

garage, ga-râdge´, n garage m.

garb, gârbe, n costume m; habit m.

garbage, gâr´-bidj, n ordures fpl.

garden, găr´-d'n, n jardin m; (kitchen) (jardin) potager m; **–er,** jardinier m; **–ing,** jardinage m.

gargle, găr´-g'l, v se gargariser. n gargarisme m.

garland, gâr´-lannde, n guirlande f. v orner de guirlandes.

garlic, gâr´-lique, n ail m.

garment, gâr´-m'nt, n vêtement m.

garnish, gâr´-niche, v garnir. n garniture f.

garret, găr´-ette, n mansarde f.

garrison, găr´-i-s'n, n garnison f.

garrulous, găr´-ou-leuce, a bavard.

garter, gâr´-t'r, n jarretière f.

gas, găce, n gaz m; **–eous,** a gazeux; **–works,** usine à gaz f.

gash, găche, *v* balafrer. *n* balafre *f*; coupure *f*.

gasp, găsspe, *v* haleter. *n* soupir convulsif *m*.

gastric, găss´-trique, *a* gastrique.

gate, guéte, *n* porte *f*; (iron) grille *f*; (wooden) barrière *f*.

gather, gădz´-eur, *v* rassembler; (pluck) cueillir; (conclude) comprendre; **–ing,** *n* réunion *f*; (med) abcès *m*.

gaudy, goa´-di, *a* voyant; criard.

gauge, guédje, *n* indicateur *m*. *n* (tool) calibre *m*; (railroad) entre-rail *m*; (size) mesure *f*. *v* mesurer; estimer.

gaunt, goannte, *a* maigre; décharné.

gauze, goaze, *n* gaze *f*; (wire) toile métallique *f*.

gawky, goa´-ki, *a* dégingandé; gauche.

gay, gué, *a* gai; joyeux; dissolu; homosexuel.

gaze, guéze, *v* regarder fixement. *n* regard fixe *m*.

gazelle, ga-zelle´, *n* gazelle *f*.

gazette, ga-zette´, *n* gazette *f*.

gear, guîeur, *n* équipment; (car) boîte de vitesse *f*.

gelatin, djell´-a-tinn, *n* gélatine *f*.

gelding, guêl´-dinng, *n* cheval hongre *m*.

gem, djème, *n* pierre précieuse *f*.

gender, djenn´-d'r, *n* genre *m*.

general, djenn´-eu-ral, *n* général *m*. *a** général.

generalize, djenn´-eu-ra-lâïze, *v* généraliser.

generate, djenn´-eur-éte, *v* produire; engendrer.

generation, djenn-eur-é´-ch'n, *n* génération *f*.

generosity, djenn-eur-o´-si-ti, *n* générosité *f*.

generous*, djenn´-eur-euce, *a* généreux.

genial, dji´-ni-al, *a* doux; cordial.

genitive, djenn´-i-tive, *n* & *a* génitif *m*.

genius, dji´-ni-euce, *n* génie *m*.

genteel, djenn-tîle´, *a* comme il faut.

gentle, djenn´-t'l, *a* doux; **–man,** *n* homme bien élevé *m*; monsieur *m*; **–ness,** douceur *f*.

gently, djenn´-tli, *adv* doucement.

genuine*, djenn´-iou-ine, *a* authentique; sincère;

–ness, *n* authenticité *f*; sincérité *f*.

geography, dji-og´-ră-fi, *n* géographie *f*.

geology, dji-ol´-o-dji, *n* géologie *f*.

geometry, dji-omm´-e-tri, *n* géométrie *f*.

geranium, dji-ré´-ni-omm, *n* géranium *m*.

germ, djeurme, *n* germe *m*; microbe *m*.

germinate, djeur´-mi-néte, *v* germer.

gesticulate, djesse-tik´-ioue-léte, *v* gesticuler.

gesture, djesse´-tioure, *n* geste *m*.

get, guette, *v* obtenir; (earn) gagner; (fetch) aller chercher; (attain) arriver; **–back,** recouvrer; **–down,** descendre; **–off,** descendre; **–on,** progresser; monter; s'entendre; **–out,** sortir; **–up,** se lever.

geyser, gui´-zeur, *n* geyser *m*; chauffe-bain *m*.

ghastly, gâce´-tli, *a* blême; (awful) épouvantable.

gherkin, gueur´-quine, *n* cornichon *m*.

ghost, gôsste, *n* revenant *m*; fantôme *m*.

giant, djâï´-'nte, *n* géant *m*; **–ess,** géante *f*.

A
B
C
D
E
F
G
H
I
J
K
L
M
N
O
P
Q
R
S
T
U
V
W
X
Y
Z

gibberish, guib´-*eur*-iche, *n* baragouin *m*.

gibbet, djib´-ette, *n* gibet *m*; potence *f*.

gibe, djâïbe, *v* se moquer de. *n* raillerie *f*.

giblets, djib´-letce, *npl* abatis *mpl*.

giddiness, guid´-i-ness, *n* vertige *m*.

giddy, guid´-i, *a* étourdi; vertigineux; qui donne le vertige.

gift, guifte, *n* don *m*; cadeau *m*; talent *m*.

gifted, guif´-tédde, *a* doué.

gigantic, djâï-gănne´-tique, *a* gigantesque.

giggle, guig-'l, *v* rire nerveusement.

gild, guilde, *v* dorer.

gilding, gilt, guild´-inng, guilte, *n* dorure *f*.

gills, guilze, *npl* branchies *fpl*.

gimlet, guime´-lette, *n* vrille *f*.

gin, djine, *n* gin *m*.

ginger, djinn´-djeur, *n* gingembre *m*.

giraffe, dji-raffe´, *n* girafe *f*.

girder, gueur´-d'r, *n* poutre *f*; traverse *f*.

girdle, gueur´-d'l, *n* gaine *f*. *v* ceindre.

girl, gueurle, *n* fille *f*; jeune fille *f*; –**hood,** jeunesse *f*.

girth, gueurts, *n* contour *m*; (horse) sangle *f*.

gist, djisste, *n* substance *f*; essentiel *m*.

give, guive, *v* donner; remettre; –**in,** céder; –**up,** renoncer à.

gizzard, guiz´-*eur*de, *n* gésier *m*.

glacier, glé´-ci-*eur*, *n* glacier *m*.

glad, glădde, *a* heureux; content; –**den,** *v* réjouir; –**ness,** *n* joie *f*; plaisir *m*.

glade, gléde, *n* clairière *f*; percée *f*.

glance, glânnce, *n* coup d'œil *m*. *v* jeter un coup d'oeil; –**off,** dévier; ricocher.

gland, glănnde, *n* glande *f*.

glare, glère, *n* clarté *f*; (stare) regard fixe *m*. *v* éblouir; regarder fixement.

glaring, glèr´-inng, *a* éblouissant; voyant; (of fact, etc) manifeste.

glass, glâce, *n* verre *m*; miroir *m*; (pane) vitre *f*; –**es,** (spectacles) *n* lunettes *fpl*; –**ware,** verrerie *f*; –**y,** *a* vitreux.

glaze, gléze, *v* vitrer; (cake, etc) glacer; (pottery) émailler. *n* (luster) lustre *m*; émail *m*.

glazier, glé´-jeur, *n* vitrier *m*.

gleam, glîme, *n* lueur *f*; (ray) rayon *m*. *v* luire; briller.

glean, glîne, *v* glaner; –**er,** *n* glaneur, -euse *m* & *f*.

glee, glî, *n* joie *f*.

glen, glène, *n* vallon *m*.

glib, glibbe, *a* (of the tongue) bien déliée.

glide, glâïde, *v* glisser; planer; –**r,** *n* (aircraft) planeur *m*.

glimmer, glimm´-'r, *v* luire faiblement. *n* lueur *f*.

glimpse, glimmpse, *n* coup d'œil *m*; aperçu *m*.

glint, glinnte, *n* trait de lumière *m*. *v* luire.

glisten, gliss´-'n, *v* étinceler; reluire.

glitter, glitt´'r, *v* briller; étinceler. *n* éclat *m*.

gloat, glaute, *v* se réjouir de; couver des yeux.

globe, glaube, *n* globe *m*; sphère *f*.

globular, globb´-iou-l'r, *a* sphérique.

gloom, gloume, *n* obscurité *f*; (dismal) tristesse *f*.

gloomy, gloumm´-i, *a* obscur; (dismal) triste.

glorify, glau´-ri-fâï, *v* glorifier.

glorious*, glau´-ri-*euce*, *a* glorieux; superbe.

glory, glau´-ri, *n* gloire *f*. *v* –**in**, se glorifier de.

gloss, glsse, *n* lustre *m*; –**y**, *a* luisant, brillant.

glove, glove, *n* gant *m*.

glow, glau, *n* éclat *m*; rougeur *f*. *v* luire; rougir.

glue, gloue, *n* colle *f*. *v* coller.

glum, gleumme, *a* morose.

glut, glotte, *v* (market) inonder; (of food) (se) gorger. *n* excès *m*.

glutton, glott´-'n, *n* glouton, -onne *m* & *f*.

gnarled, nârlde, *a* noueux.

gnash, năche, *v* grincer; –**ing**, *n* grincement *m*.

gnat, nătte, *n* cousin *m*; moucheron *m*.

gnaw, noa, *v* ronger.

go, gau, *v* aller; partir; (*mech*) marcher; –**away**, s'en aller; partir; –**back**, retourner; –**down**, descendre; –**out**, sortir; –**up**, monter; –**without**, se passer de.

goad, gaude, *n* aiguillon *m*. *v* aiguillonner; inciter.

goal, gaule, *n* but *m*.

goat, gaute, *n* chèvre *f*; **male** –, bouc *m*.

gobble, gob´-'l, *v* avaler avidement; dévorer.

goblin, gob´-linne, *n* lutin

m; farfadet *m*.

god, godde, *m*, Dieu *m*; dieu *m*; –**child**, filleul, -e *m* & *f*; –**dess**, déesse *f*; –**father**, parrain *m*; –**liness**, *n* piété *f*; –**ly**, *a* pieux; –**mother**, *n* marraine *f*.

goggles, gog´-g'lze, *npl* grosses lunettes *fpl*.

goiter, go'i´-*teur*, *n* goître *m*.

gold, gaulde, *n* or *m*; –**en**, *a* d'or; –**finch**, *n* chardonneret *m*; –**fish**, poisson rouge *m*; –**leaf**, or en feuille *m*; –**smith**, orfèvre *m*.

golf, golf, *n* golf *m*; –**course**, terrain de golf *m*.

gong, gon-ng, *n* gong *m*.

good, goudd, *n* bien *m*; avantage *m*. *a* bon; sage; –**bye!** *interj* adieu! au revoir! –**morning**, –**afternoon**, –**day**, bonjour; –**night**, bonsoir.

good-natured, goudd-nét´-tiour'd, *a* d'un bon naturel.

goodness, goudd´-nesse, *n* bonté *f*.

goods, goudd´-ze, *npl* marchandises *fpl*; effets *mpl*.

goodwill, goudd-ouil´, *n*

bienveillance *f*.

goose, goûce, *n* oie *f*.

gooseberry, goûce´-*beur*-i, *n* groseille à maquereau *f*.

gore, gôre, *n* (blood) sang *m*. *v* encorner.

gorge, gôrdje, *n* gorge *f*. *v* se gorger de.

gorgeous*, gôr´-djeuce, *a* sompteux; splendide.

gorilla, go-ril´-la, *n* gorille *m*.

gorse, gôrse, *n* ajonc *m*.

gosling, goz´-linng, *n* oison *m*.

gospel, goss´-p'l, *n* évangile *m*.

gossip, goss´-ippe, *v* bavarder; papoter. *n* potin *m*; cancans *mpl*; (person) commère *f*.

gouge, gâ'oudje, *n* gouge *f*. *v* gouger; arracher.

gout, gâ'oute, *n* goutte *f*.

govern, gov´-*eurne*, *v* gouverner; –**ess**, *n* gouvernante *f*; –**ment**, gouvernement *m*; –**or**, gouverneur *m*; (*mech*) régulateur *m*.

gown, gâ'oune, *n* robe *f*.

grab, grăbe, *v* empoigner; saisir. *n* (*mech*) benne preneuse *f*.

grace, gréce, *n* grâce *f*; –**ful***, *a* gracieux.

gracious*, gré´-cheuce, *a*

gracieux.

grade, gréde, *n* grade *m*; degré *m*; rang *m*. *v* classer; graduer.

gradient, gré´-di-ennte, *n* pente *f*; rampe *f*.

gradual*, grăd´-iou-*eul*, *a* progressif.

graduate, grăd´-iou-éte, *n* diplômé, -e *m* & *f*. *v* graduer; obtenir des diplômes.

graft, grâfte, *n* greffe *f*; (*fig*) corruption *f*. *v* greffer.

grain, gréne, *n* grain *m*. *v* (paint) veiner.

grammar, grămm´-'r, *n* grammaire *f*.

granary, grănn´-*a*-ri, *n* grenier *m*.

grand*, grănnde, *a* grandiose; magnifique; –**daughter,** *n* petite-fille *f*; –**father,** grand-père *m*; –**mother,** grand-mère *f*; –**son,** petit-fils *m*.

grant, grânnte, *v* accorder. *n* subvention *f*; bourse *f*.

grape, grépe, *n* raisin *m*.

grapefruit, grépe´-froute, *n* pamplemousse *m*.

grapple, grăp´-p'l, *n* (hook) grappin *m*. *v* lutter.

grasp, grâsspe, *v* empoigner; (understand)

comprendre. *n* étreinte *f*; –**ing,** *a* avide.

grass, grâsse, *n* herbe *f*; (lawn) gazon *m*; –**hopper,** sauterelle *f*; –**y,** *a* herbeux.

grate, gréte, *n* (fire) grille *f*. *v* grincer; (cookery, etc) râper.

grateful, gréte´-foull, *a* reconnaissant.

gratification, gră-ti-fi-qué´-ch'n, *n* satisfaction *f*.

gratify, gră´-ti-fâï, *v* satisfaire; –**ing,** *a* agréable.

grating, gré´-tinng, *n* grillage *m*. *a* grinçant.

gratis, gré´-tisse, *adv* gratis.

gratitude, gră´-ti-tioude, *n* reconnaissance *f*.

gratuitous*, gra-tiou´-i-*teuce*, *a* gratuit.

gratuity, gra-tiou´-i-ti, *n* pourboire *m*.

grave, gréve, *n* tombe *f*. *a** grave; –**stone,** pierre tombale *f*; –**yard,** cimetière *m*.

gravel, grăv´-'l, *n* gravier *m*.

gravitate, grăv´-i-téte, *v* graviter.

gravity, grăv´-i-ti, *n* gravité *f*.

gravy, gré´-vi, *n* jus *m*;

sauce *f*.

gray, gré, *a* gris; (complexion) blême.

graze, gréze, *n* écorchure *f*. *v* effleurer; érafler; (feed) paître.

grease, grîce, *n* graisse *f*. *v* graisser.

greasy, grî´-zi, *a* graisseux.

great*, gréte, *a* grand; –**ness,** *n* grandeur *f*.

greed, grîde, *n* gourmandise *f*; avidité *f*; –**ily,** *adv* goulûment; –**y,** *a* gourmand; avide.

green, grîne, *n* & *a* vert *m*; –**gage,** *n* Reine-claude *f*; –**house,** serre *f*; –**ish,** *a* verdâtre.

greet, grîte, *v* saluer; –**ing,** *n* salutation *f*.

grenade, gre-néde´, *n* grenade *f*.

greyhound, gré´-hâ'ounnde, *n* lévrier *m*.

grief, grîfe, *n* chagrin *m*; douleur *f*.

grievance, grî-v'nce, *n* grief *m*; doléance *f*.

grieve, grîve, *v* s'affliger; chagriner.

grievous, grî´-veuce, *a* grave; accablant.

grill, grile, *v* griller. *n* gril *m*.

grim*, grime, *a* sinistre; menaçant.

grimace, gri-méce´, *n*

grimace *f.*

grime, grâïme, *n* saleté *f;* (dirt) crasse *f.*

grin, grinne, *v* grimacer; sourire à belles dents. *n* large sourire *m.*

grind, grâïnnde, *v* moudre; (sharpen) aiguiser.

grinder, grâïnn´-*deur, n* rémouleur *m;* broyeur *m;* (coffee, etc) moulin *m.*

grip, grippe, *n* (action) étreinte *f;* (handle) poignée *f;* prise *f. v* empoigner; saisir.

gripe, grâïpe, *v* (bowels) donner la colique.

grisly, grize´-li, *a* affreux; horrible.

grit, gritte, *n* gravier *m;* sable *m;* **–ty,** *a* graveleux.

groan, graune, *v* gémir. *n* gémissement *m.*

grocer, grau´-*ceur, n* épicier *m;* **–y,** épicerie *f.*

grog, grgue, *n* grog *m.*

groin, grô'ine, *n* aine *f;* (*arch*) arête *f.*

groom, groume, *n* palefrenier *m.*

groove, grouve, *v* rainer; creuser. *n* rainure *f.*

grope, graupe, *v* tâtonner.

gross, grauce, *n* (12 dozen) grosse *f; a* (coarse) grossier; (obvious) flagrant;

–weight, *n* poids brut *m.*

ground, grâ'ounnde, *v* (*naut*) échouer. *n* terrain *m;* terre *f;* (reason) motif *m;* base *f;* **–-floor,** rez-de- chaussée *m;* **–less,** *a* sans fondement; **–work,** *n* base *f.*

group, groupe, *n* groupe *m. v* grouper.

grouse, grâ'ouce, *n* coq de bruyère *m. v* grogner; se plaindre.

grove, grauve, *n* bocage *m;* bosquet *m.*

grovel, grov´-'l, *v* (*fig*) ramper.

grow, grau, *v* pousser; croître; grandir; cultiver; **–er,** *n* cultivateur *m;* **–n up,** adulte *m* & *f;* **–th,** croissance *f.*

growl, grâ'oule, *n* grognement *m. v* grogner.

grub, grobbe, *n* larve *f;* asticot *m;* maugeaille.

grudge, grodje, *n* rancune *f. v* donner à regret; envier à.

gruel, groue´-'l, *n* gruau *m.*

gruesome, groue´-somme, *a* affreux; macabre.

gruff*, groffe, *a* brusque; rude.

grumble, gromm´-b'l, *v* grommeler; se plaindre; **–r,** *n* grognon *m.*

grunt, gronnte, *v* grogner. *n* grognement *m.*

guarantee, ga-rann-tî´, *v* garantir. *n* garantie *f.*

guard, gârde, *n* garde *f. v* garder; **–ed,** *a* circonspect.

guardian, găr´-di-anne, *n* gardien *m;* (trustee) tuteur *m.*

guess, guesse, *v* deviner.

guest, guesste, *n* invité -ée *m* & *f;* (hotel) client -e *m* & *f.*

guidance, gâï´-d'nce, *n* direction *f;* conduite *f;* orientation *f.*

guide, gâïde, *v* guider. *n* guide *m.*

guild, guilde, *n* corps de métier *m;* corporation *f.*

guile, gâïle, *n* astuce *f;* artifice *m;* **–less,** *a* ingénu.

guilt, guilte, *n* culpabilité *f;* **–y,** *a* coupable.

guinea, gui´-ni, *n* guinée *f;* **–fowl,** pintade *f;* **–pig,** cochon d'Inde *m.*

guise, guâïze, *n* façon *f;* apparence *f.*

guitar, gui-târe´, *n* guitare *f.*

gulf, golfe, *n* (*geog*) golfe *m;* (abyss) gouffre *m.*

gull, golle, *n* mouette *f. v* duper.

gullet, goll´-ette, *n*

gosier *m.*

gulp, golpe, *v* avaler. *n* gorgée *f.*

gum, gomme, *n* gomme *f*; (teeth) gencive *f.*

gun, gonne, *n* fusil *m*; (artillery) canon *m*; **–ner,** canonnier *m*; **–powder,** poudre à canon *f*; **–smith,** armurier *m.*

gurgle, gueur´-g'l, *v* gargouiller. *n* gargouillement *m.*

gush, goche, *v* jaillir. *n* jaillissement *m.*

gust, gosste, *n* coup de vent *m*; rafale *f.*

gut, gotte, *n* boyau *m. v* vider.

gutter, gott´-'r, *n* gouttière *f*; (street) ruisseau *m.*

guy, gaille, *n* type *m*; individu *m.*

gymnasium, djimm-né´-zi-mme, *n* gymnase *m.*

gymnastics, djimm-năss´-tikse, *npl* gymnastique *f.*

gypsy, djip´-ci, *n* bohémien *m*; tzigane *m.*

N.B. La lettre H doit toujours s'aspirer distinctement sauf dans les quelques mots marqués §

haberdashery, hăb´-*eur*dăch-'ri, *n* mercerie *f.*

habit, hăb´-itte, *n* habitude *f.*; coutume *f.*

habitable, hăb´-i-t*a*-b'l, *a* habitable.

habitual*, h*a*-bit´-iou-*eul*, *a* habituel.

hack, hăque, *v* écharper; hacher; couper.

hackneyed, hăque´-nidde, *a* rebattu; banal.

haddock, hăd´-*o*que, *n* aiglefin fumé *m*; haddock *m.*

hag, hăgue, *n* mégère *f*; **–gard,** *a* hagard.

haggle, hăgg´-'l, *v* marchander.

hail, héle, *n* grêle *f. v* grêler; (greet) saluer.

hair, hère, *n* poil *m*; (of head only) cheveu *m*; (horse) crin *m*; **–brush,** brosse à cheveux *f*; **–dresser,** coiffeur, -euse *m* & *f*; **–pin,** épingle à cheveux *f*; **–y,** *a* poilu; chevelu.

hake, héke, *n* merluche *f.*

half, hâfe, *n* moitié *f*; demi, -e *m* & *f. a* demi. *adv* à moitié.

halibut, hăl´-i-botte, *n* flétan *m.*

hall, hoal, *n* vestibule *m*; entrée *f*; salle *f*; **––mark,** poinçon de contrôle *m.*

hallow, hal´-lau, *v* sanctifier.

hallucination, h*a*l-liou-ci-né´-ch'n, *n* hallucination *f.*

halo, hé´-lau, *n* auréole *m*; (astronomy) halo *m.*

halt, hoalte, *n* arrêt *m. v* arrêter. *interj* halte!

halter, hoal´-t'r, *n* licou *m.*

halve, hâve, *v* partager en deux.

ham, hămme, *n* jambon *m.*

hamlet, hămm´-lette, *n* hameau *m.*

hammer, hămm´-'r, *n* marteau *m. v* marteler.

hammock, hămm´-*o*que, *n* hamac *m.*

hamper, hămm´-p'r, *n* panier *m*; bourriche *f. v* gêner.

hand, hănnde, *n* main *f*; (clock) aiguille *f. v* passer; donner; **––bag,** *n* sac à main *m*; **–book,** manuel *m*; **–cuffs,** menottes *fpl*; **–ful,** poignée *f*; **–kerchief,** mouchoir *m*; **–le,** manche *m*; (door) bouton *m. v* manier; **––made,** *a* fait à la main; **–rail,** *n* rampe *f*; **–y,** *a* utile; commode; à portée.

handsome*, hănn´-somme, *a* beau; généreux.

hang, hain-ng, *v* pendre;

–up, v accrocher.

hangar, hain´-gueur, n hangar m.

hanger, hain´-gueur, n cintre m.

hanker, hain´-nkeur, v désirer ardemment.

happen, hăp´-p'n, v arriver; se passer.

happily, hăpp´-i-li, adv heureusement.

happiness, hăpp´-i-nesse, n bonheur m.

happy, hăpp´-i, a heureux.

harangue, hă-raingue, n harangue f. v haranguer.

harass, hăr´-ăce, v harceler.

harassment, hăz´-acemennt, n harcélement m; tracasseries f.

harbor, hâr´-b'r, n port m. v héberger.

hard, hârde, a dur; difficile; **–en,** v durcir; (refl) s'endurcir; **–ly,** adv à peine; durement; **–ness,** n dureté f; **–ship,** peine f; privation f; **–ware,** quincaillerie f; **–y,** a robuste.

hare, hère, n lièvre m; –͟ **lip,** bec de lièvre m.

harm, hârm, n mal m; tort m. v faire du mal; **–ful,** a nuisible; **–less,** inoffensif.

harmonious*, hâr-mô´-ni-euce, a harmonieux.

harmonize, hăr´-mŏnn-âïze, v harmoniser.

harness, hăr´-nesse, n équipment m; (horse) harnais m. v harnacher; (to a cart) atteler; (forces) utiliser.

harp, hârpe, n harpe f. v rabâcher.

harpoon, hâr-poune´, n harpon m.

harrow, hăr´-au, n herse f. v (fig) tourmenter.

harsh, hârche, a (sound) discordant; (severe) dur; (color) criard.

harvest, hăr´-veste, n moisson f; récolte f. v moissonner; récolter.

hash, hăche, n hachis m; (fig) gâchis m. v hacher.

hassock, hăs´-soque, coussin m.

haste, héste, n hâte f; **–n,** v hâter; se hâter.

hastily, héce´-ti-li, adv à la hâte.

hat, hătte, n chapeau m.

hatch, hătche, n trappe f; (naut) écoutille f. v (eggs) couver; (plot) tramer.

hatchet, hătch´-ette, n hachette f.

hate, héte, n haine f. v haïr; **–ful*,** a odieux.

hatred, hé´-tredde, n haine f.

haughtiness, hoa´-ti-nesse, n hauteur f; arrogance f.

haughty, hoa´-ti, a hautain; altier.

haul, hoale, n tirage m; (catch) coup de filet m. v tirer; (boat) haler; (drag) traîner.

haunch, hoanntche, n hanche f; arrière-train m.

haunt, hoannte, v hanter; (fig) fréquenter. n rendez-vous m; (animals) repaire m.

have, hâve, v avoir; posséder.

haversack, hăve´-eur-săque, n havresac m.

havoc, hăv´-ŏque, n dégât m; ravage m.

hawk, hoaque, n épervier m. v colporter.

hawker, hoak´-'r, n colporteur m.

hawthorn, hoa´-tsôrne, n aubépine f.

hay, hé, n foin m; **–fever,** rhume des foins m; –͟ **loft,** grange f; –͟**making,** fenaison f.

hazard, hăz´-arde, n hasard m. v hasarder.

hazardous, hăz´-ar-deuce, a hasardeux.

haze, héze, *n* brume *f.*

hazel, hé´-z'l, *n* noisetier *m;* **--nut,** noisette *f.*

hazy, hé´-zi, *a* brumeux

he, hî, *pron* il; lui.

head, hedde, *n* tête *f;* chef *m;* principal *m;* directeur *m;* **--ache,** mal de tête *m;* **--ing,** en tête *m;* titre *m;* **--land,** promontoire *m;* **--light,** phare *m;* **--long,** *adv* tête baissée; aveuglément; **--master,** *n* directeur *m;* **--quarters,** quartier général *m;* **--strong,** *a* entêté; opiniâtre; **--way,** progrès *m.*

heady, hedd´-i, *a* capiteux.

heal, hîle, *v* guérir; cicatriser; **--ing,** *n* guérison *f. a* curatif.

health, hêl*t*s, *n* santé *f.*

healthy, hêl*t*s´-i, *a* sain; (climate) salubre.

heap, hîpe, *n* tas *m. v* entasser; amonceler.

hear, hîre, *v* entendre; **--ing,** *n* (sense) ouïe *f;* (judicial) audience *f;* **--say,** ouï-dire *m.*

hearse, heurce, *n* corbillard *m.*

heart, hârte, *n* cœur *m;* courage *m;* **--attack,** *n* crise cardiaque *f;* **--broken,** *a* brisé de douleur; **--burn,** *n*

aigreurs d'estomac *fpl;* **--ily,** *adv* cordialement; **--less,** *a* sans cœur.

hearth, hâr*t*s, *n* foyer *m.*

heat, hîte, *n* chaleur *f. v* chauffer; **--er,** *n* réchaud *m;* radiateur *m;* **--ing,** chauffage *m.*

heath, hî*t*s, *n* lande *f;* bruyère *f.*

heathen, hî´-*dz*'n, *n & a* païen, -enne *m & f.*

heather, hè*dz*´-eur, *n* bruyère *f.*

heave, hîve, *v* hisser; (sigh) pousser un soupir.

heaven, hèv´-'n, *n* ciel *m;* **--ly,** *a* céleste.

heaviness, hêv´-i-nesse, *n* poids *m;* pesanteur *f;* lourdeur.

heavy, hêv´-i, *a* lourd; pesant.

hectic, hèk´-tik, *a* agité; mouvementé.

hedge, hêdje, *n* haie *f;* **--hog,** hérisson *m.*

heed, hîde, *v* tenir compte de. *n* attention *f;* **--ful*,** *a* attentif; **--less,** inattentif; étourdi.

heel, hîle, *n* talon *m.*

heifer, hèf´-'r, *n* génisse *f.*

height, hâïte, *n* hauteur *f;* (person) taille *f.*

heighten, hâï´-t'n, *v* rehausser; augmenter.

heinous*, hé´-neuce, *a*

atroce; abominable.

§heir, aire, *n* héritier *m;* **--ess,** héritière *f.*

helicopter, he´-li-cop-t'r, *n* hélicoptère.

hell, hêle, *n* enfer *m;* **--ish,** *a* infernal.

helm, hêlme, *n* barre *f;* (wheel) gouvernail *m.*

helmet, hêle´-mette, *n* casque *m.*

helmsman, hêlmze´-männe, *n* timonnier *m.*

help, helpe, *n* aide *f;* (in distress) secours *m. interj* au secours! *v* aider; secourir; **--er,** *n* aide *m;* **--ful,** *a* utile; serviable; **--less,** impuissant.

hem, hemme, *n* ourlet *m. v* faire un ourlet; **--in,** cerner.

hemisphere, hemm´-i-sfire, *n* hémisphère *m.*

hemlock, hemm´-loque, *n* cigüe *f.*

hemorrhage, hém´ridje, *n* hémorragie *f.*

hemp, hemmpe, *n* chanvre *m.*

hen, henne, *n* poule *f.*

hence, hennce, *adv* d'ici; **--forth,** désormais.

her, heur, *pron* elle, la. *poss a* son; sa; ses.

herb, heurbe, *n* herbe *f;* **--alist,** herboriste *m.*

herd, heurde, *n* troupe *f;*

a
b
c
d
e
f
g
h
i
j
k
l
m
n
o
p
q
r
s
t
u
v
w
x
y
z

troupeau *m. v*
s'attrouper; **–sman,** *n*
pâtre *m.*

here, hîre, *adv* ici; **–about,**
près d'ici; **–after,** ci-
après; dorénavant; **–by,**
par ceci; **–in,** là-dedans;
ci-inclus; **–of,** de ceci;
–upon, là-dessus; **–with,**
avec ceci; ci-joint.

hereditary, he-redd´-i-ta-
ri, *a* héréditaire.

heresy, hèr´-i-ci, *n* hérésie
f.

heretic, hêr´-i-tique, *n*
hérétique *m* & *f.*

hermit, heur´-mitte, *n*
ermite *m;* **–age,** ermitage
m.

hernia, hêr´-ni-*a, n* hernie
f.

hero, hi´rau, *n* héros *m.*

heroic, hi-rau´-ique, *a*
héroïque.

heroine, hêr´-o-inn, *n*
héroïne *f.*

heroism, hêr´-o-izme, *n*
héroïsme *m.*

herring, hair´-inng, *n*
hareng *m.*

hers, heurze, *poss pron* le
sien, la sienne; les siens,
les siennes.

herself, heur-self´, *pron*
elle-même.

hesitate, hêz´-i-téte, *v*
hésiter.

hesitation, hêz-i-té´-ch'n,

n hésitation *f.*

hew, hioue, *v* couper;
(stone) tailler.

hiccup, hik´-*eu*pe, *n*
hoquet *m. v* avoir le
hoquet.

hide, hâïde, *v* cacher. *n*
peau *f;* cuir *m.*

hideous*, hid´-i-*eu*ce, *a*
hideux.

hiding, hâï´-dinng *n (fig)*
raclée *f.*

hiding place, hâï´-dinng-
pléce, *n* cachette *f.*

high, hâï, *a* haut; élevé;
(game) faisandé; **–est,** le
plus élevé; le plus haut;
–fidelity, haute fidélité;
–way, grand-route *f.*

hilarity, hil-ăr´-i-ti, *n*
hilarité *f.*

hill, hile, *n* colline *f;*
(road) côte *f.*

hilly, hil´-i, *a* accidenté; à
pentes; montagneux.

hilt, hilte, *n* garde *f;*
(handle) poignée *f.*

him, himme, *pron* le, lui;
–self, lui-même.

hind, hâïnnde, *n* biche *f. a*
de derrière.

hinder, hinn´-d'r, *v*
empêcher; gêner.

hindmost, hâïnnd´-
mauste, *a* dernier.

hindrance, hinn´-
drannce, *n*
empêchement *m;*

obstacle *m.*

hinge, hinndje, *n*
charnière *f;* (door) gond
m.

hint, hinnte, *n*
insinuation *f. v* insinuer.

hip, hippe, *n* hanche *f.*

hire, hâïre, *v* louer. *n*
location *f.*

his, hize, *poss pron* le sien,
la sienne; les siens, les
siennes. *poss a* son, sa,
ses.

hiss, hice, *v* siffler. *n*
sifflement *m.*

historian, hice-to´-ri-
anne, *n* historien *m.*

historical, hice-to´-ri-k'l,
a historique.

history, hice´-tŏr-i, *n*
histoire *f.*

hit, hitte, *v* frapper;
(target, etc) toucher. *n*
coup *m.*

hitch, hitch, *n* (obstacle)
anicroche *f;* (naut)
amarre *f. v* (pull up)
remonter; (hook on)
attacher; **–hike,** *v* faire
de l'auto-stop.

hither, hidz´-'r, *adv* ici; par
ici; **–to,** *adv* jusqu'ici.

hive, hâïve, *n* ruche *f.*

hoard, haurde, *v* amasser;
(food, etc) accaparer; *n*
amas *m.*

hoarding, haurd´-inng, *n*
palissade *f;*

accumulation *f.*

hoarse, haurse, *a* rauque; enroué.

hoax, hauxe, *n* mystification *f*; tour *m. v* mystifier; jouer un tour.

hobble, hobb´-'l, *v* clopiner; boitiller.

hobby, hobb´-i, *n* passe-temps favori *m.*

hock, hoque, *n* vin du Rhin *m*; (leg) jarret *m.*

hoe, hau, *n* binette *f*; houe *f. v* biner.

hog, hogue, *n* cochon *m*; porc *m.*

hogshead, hogz´-hédde, *n* tonneau *m.*

hoist, hoa'isste, *v* hisser.

hold, haulde, *v* tenir; contenir. *n* prise *f*; (ship) cale *f*; **–back,** *v* retenir; **–er,** *n* possesseur *m*, détenteur *m*; (shares, etc) actionnaire *m* & *f*; **–ing,** possession *f*; (com) participation *f*; **–on,** *v* tenir ferme; **–over,** ajourner.

hole, haule, *n* trou *m.*

holiday, holl´-i-dé, *n* jour de fête *m*; (leave) congé *m.*

holidays, holl´-i-dêze, *npl* vacances *fpl.*

holiness, hau´-li-nesse, *n* sainteté *f.*

hollow, holl´-au, *n* cavité *f. a* creux. *v* creuser.

holly, holl´-i, *n* houx *m.*

holy, hau´-li, *a* saint, sacré; **–water,** *n* eau bénite *f*; **–week,** semaine sainte *f.*

homage, home´-idj, *n* hommage *m.*

home, hôme, *n* maison *f*; (circle) foyer *m*; chez soi *m*; (homeland) patrie *f*; **at –,** chez soi; **–less, a** sans abri; **–ly,** intime; (to be) **–sick,** (avoir) le mal du pays; **–work,** *n* devoirs *mpl.*

§honest*, onn´-este, *a* honnête; **–y,** *n* honnêteté *f.*

honey, honn´-i, *n* miel *m*; **–moon,** lune de miel *f*; **–suckle,** chèvrefeuille *m.*

§honor, onn´-eur, *n* honneur *m. v* honorer.

§honorable, onn´-eur-a-b'l, *a* honorable.

§honorary, onn´-eur-a-ri, *a* honoraire.

hood, houdd, *n* capuchon *m*; (vehicle) capote *f.*

hoodwink, houdd´-ouinnque, *v* tromper.

hoof, houff, *n* sabot *m.*

hook, houk, *n* crochet *m*; (large) croc *m*; (naut) gaffe *f*; (fish) hameçon *m. v* accrocher; **–and eye,** *n* agrafe *f.*

hoop, houpp, *n* cercle *m*; (toy) cerceau *m.*

hoot, houte, *n* (owl) hululement *m*; (derision) huée *f*; (motor) coup de klaxon *m. v* hululer; huer; (motor) klaxonner; **–er,** *n* klaxon *m.*

hop, hoppe, *v* sautiller. *n* saut *m*; (plant) houblon.

hope, hôpe, *v* espérer. *n* espoir *m*; **–ful,** *a* encourageant; plein d'espoir; **–less,** sans espoir; inutile.

horizon, ho-râï´-zonne, *n* horizon *m.*

horizontal, hor-i-zonn´-t'l, *a* horizontal.

horn, hoarne, *n* corne *f*; (motor) klaxon *m*; (hunt) cor de chasse *m.*

hornet, hoar´-nette *n* frelon *m.*

horrible, hor´-i-b'l, *a* horrible.

horrid*, hor´-ride, *a* horrible; affreux.

horrify, hor´-ri-fâï, *v* épouvanter; horrifier.

horror, hor´-rŏr, *n* horreur *f.*

horse, horce, *n* cheval *m*; **–back (on),** *adv* à cheval; **–hair,** *n* crin *m*; **–power,** puissance (*f*)

a
b
c
d
e
f
g
h
i
j
k
l
m
n
o
p
q
r
s
t
u
v
w
x
y
z

A
B
C
D
E
F
G
H
I
J
K
L
M
N
O
P
Q
R
S
T
U
V
W
X
Y
Z

en chevaux; **--radish,** n raifort m; **–shoe,** fer à cheval m.

hose, hauze, n tuyau d'arrosage m.

hospitable, hoss´-pi-ta-b'l, a hospitalier.

hospital, hoss´-pi-t'l, n hôpital m.

host, hauste, n (friend) hôte m; (army) armée f; (sacrament) hostie f; foule f; **–ess,** hôtesse f.

hostage, hoss´-tidj, n otage m.

hostel, hoss´-tell, n pension f; **youth –,** n auberge de la jeunesse f.

hostile, hoss´-tâïle a hostile.

hot, hotte, a chaud; (food, sauces, etc) épicé; fort.

hotel, hô-tel´, n hôtel m.

hothouse, hott´-hâ'ouce, n serre f.

hound, hâ'ounnde, n chien de chasse m. v chasser; traquer.

§**hour,** âour, n heure f; **–ly,** adv d'heure en heure.

house, hâ'ouce, v loger. n maison f; **–hold,** maison f; **–keeper,** femme de charge f; **–work,** ménage m.

hovel, hov´-'l, n taudis m; bouge m.

hover, hov´-'r, v voltiger;

planer; hésiter.

hovercraft, hov´'r-crâfte, n aéroglisseur m.

how, hâ'ou, adv comment; **–ever,** cependant; **–much, many?** combien?

howl, hâ'oule, v hurler. n hurlement m.

hub, hobbe, n moyeu m.

huddle, hod´-d'l, v se presser les uns contre les autres.

hue, hi'oue, n couleur f; (shade) nuance f.

hug, hogue, v étreindre. n étreinte f.

huge, hioudje, a immense; énorme; vaste.

hulk, holke, n (naut) ponton m.

hull, holle, n (naut) coque f.

hum, homme, v (insect) bourdonner; (engine) vrombir; (voice) fredonner. n bourdonnement m.

human*, hi'oue´-manne, a & n humain m.

humane, hi'oue-méné´, a humain; compatissant.

humanity, hi'oue-mă´-ni-ti, n humanité f.

humble, homm´-b'l, a humble. v humilier.

humidity, hi'oue-mid´-i-ti, n humidité f.

humiliate, hi'oue-mil´-i-éte, v humilier.

humiliation, hi'oue-mil-i-ét´-ch'n, n humiliation f.

humor, hi'oue´-meur, v complaire à. n (temper) humeur f; (wit) esprit m; humour m.

humorous*, hi'oue´-meur-euce, a comique.

hunch, honntche, n bosse f; **–back,** bossu m.

hundred, honn´-dredde, n & a cent m; **–th,** a & n centième m & f.

hunger, honng´-gueur, v avoir faim; désirer; n faim f.

hungry, honng´-gri, a affamé; **to be –,** v avoir faim.

hunt, honnte, v chasser. n chasse f.

hurdle, heur´-d'l, n claie f; (sport) obstacle m.

hurl, heurle, v lancer; précipiter.

hurricane, hor´-i-cane, n ouragan m.

hurry, hor´-i, v se dépêcher. n hâte f.

hurt, heurte, v faire mal; (feeling) blesser.

hurtful, heurte´foull, a nuisible; blessant.

husband, hoze´-bănnde, n mari m. v ménager.

hush! hoche, interj chut!

–up, v étouffer; n silence
m.

husk, hossque, n (seeds)
cosse f.

husky, hoss´-ki, a (voice)
rauque; enroué.

hustle, hoss´-'l, v se
presser; bousculer.

hut, hotte, n hutte f
baraque f.

hutch, hotche, n cabane à
lapins f; clapier m.

hyacinth, hâï´-a-sinnts, n
jacinthe f.

hydrant, hâï´-drannte, n
bouche d'incendie f.

hydraulic, hâï-drau´-lique,
a hydraulique.

hydro, hâï´-drau, **–gen,** n
hydrogène m; **–phobia,**
hydrophobie f; **–plane,**
hydravion m.

hygiene, hâï´-djeen, n
hygiène f.

hygienic, hâï-djeenn´-
ique, a hygiénique.

hymn, himme, n hymme f.

hyphen, hâï´-fenne, n
trait d'union m.

hypocrisy, hip-o´-cri-si, n
hypocrisie f.

hypocrite, hip´-ŏ-crite, n
hypocrite m & f.

hypodermic, hâï-po-
deur´-mique, a
hypodermique.

hypothetical, hâï-po-tsè´-
ti-k'l, a hypothétique;

supposé.

hysterical*, hice-tèr´-i-k'l,
a hystérique.

A B C D E F G H **I** J K L M N O P Q R S T U V W X Y Z

I, âï, *pron* je; moi.

ice, âïce, *n* glace *f*. *v* glacer; frapper; **–berg,** *n* iceberg *m*; **–cream,** *n* glace *f*.

icicle, âï´-ci-k'l, *n* glaçon *m*.

icy, âï´-ci, *a* glacial; glacé.

idea, âï-dî´-a, *n* idée *f*.

ideal, âï-dî´-*eul*, *n* & *a* idéal *m* **–ize,** *v* idéaliser.

identical*, âï-denn´-ti-k'l, *a* identique.

identify, âï-denn´-ti-fâï, *v* identifier.

identity, âï-denn´-ti-ti, *n* identité *f*.

idiom, i´-di-ŏmme, *n* idiome *m*.

idiot, i´-di-*eu*te, *n* idiot, -e *m* & *f*; **–ic,** *a* idiot.

idle, âï´-d'l, *v* flâner. *a* oisif, paresseux; **–ness,** *n*

oisiveté *f*; **–r,** flâneur *m*.

idol, âï´-dŏl, *n* idole *f*; **–ize,** *v* adorer.

if, if, *conj* si; **even –,**même si.

ignite, igue-nâïte´, *v* allumer; enflammer.

ignition, igue-ni´-ch'n, *n* (spark) allumage *m*; (car, etc) contact *m*.

ignoble, igue-nau´-b'l, *a* ignoble.

ignominious*, igue-nŏ-minn´-i-*eu*ce, *a* ignominieux.

ignominy, igue´-no-mi-ni, *n* ignominie *f*.

ignorance, igue´-nŏ-r'nce, *n* ignorance *f*.

ignorant, *a* ignorant.

ignore, igue-nore´, *v* ne pas tenir compte de; faire semblant de ne pas

voir.

ill, il, *a* malade; **–ness,** *n* maladie *f*.

illegal*, il-lî´-gal, *a* illégal.

illegible, il-lèdj´-i-b'l, *a* illisible.

illegitimate*, il-li-djitt´-i-méte, *a* illégitime.

illiterate, il-li´-*teur*-éte, *n* & *a* illettré, -e *m* & *f*.

illogical*, il-lodj´-i-k'l, *a* illogique.

illuminate, il-lioue´-mi-néte, *v* éclairer; illuminer.

illumination, il-lioue-mi-né´-ch'n, *n* illumination *f*; éclairage *m*.

illusion, il-lioue´-j'n, *n* illusion *f*.

illusory, il-lioue´-so-ri, *a* illusoire.

illustrate, il´-*leuce*-tréte, *v* illustrer; élucider.

illustration, il-*leuce*-tré´-ch'n, *n* illustration *f*.

illustrious, il-loss´-tri-*euce*, *a* illustre; célèbre.

image, imm´-idj, *n* image *f*; portrait *m*.

imagination, i-mădj-i-né´-ch'n, *n* imagination *f*.

imagine, i-mădj´-inne, *v* imaginer; s'imaginer.

imbecile, imm´-bi-sîle, *n* & *a* imbécile *m* & *f*.

imbue, imm-bioue´, *v* imprégner; pénétrer.

imitate, imm´-i-téte, v
imiter.

immaculate*, imm-
măque´-iou-léte, a
immaculé; impeccable.

immaterial, imm-ma-tî-ri-
eul, a sans importance;
indifférent.

immature, imm-ma-
tioure´, a pas mûr.

immeasurable, imm-mèj´-
iou-ra-b'l, a
incommensurable;
infini.

immediate*, imm-mî´-di-
éte, a immédiat.

immense, imm-mennce´,
a immense.

immensity, imm-menn´-
ci-ti, n immensité f.

immerge, imm-meurdje´,
v immerger; plonger.

immigrant, imm´-mi-
grannt, n & a
immigrant, -e m & f.

immigrate, imm´-mi-
gréte, v immigrer.

imminent, imm´-mi-
nennte, a imminent.

immoderate*, imm-mod´-
eur-éte, a immodéré.

immodest*, imm-mod´-
este, a immodeste.

immoral*, imm-mor´-'l, a
immoral.

immortal*, imm-mor´-t'l,
a immortel.

immortalize, imm-mor´-

tal-âïze, v immortaliser.

immovable, imm-mouv´-
a-b'l, a inébranlable.

immune, imm-miouné, a
immunisé.

immunity, imm-
mioue´,ni-ti, n
immunité f.

immunization, imm´-
mioue-nâï-zé-ch'n, n
immunisation f.

imp, immpe, n lutin m;
(fig) petit diable m.

impact, imm´-păcte, n
choc m; impact m.

impair, imm-paire´, v
détériorer; abîmer.

impale, imm-péle´ v
empaler.

impart, imm-pârte´, v
communiquer.

impartial*, imm-pâr´-ch'l,
a impartial.

impassable, imm-păss´-a-
b'l, a impraticable.

impassive*, imm-păss´-
ive, a impassible.

impatience, imm-pé´-
ch'nce, n impatience f.

impatient*, imm-pé´-
ch'nt, a impatient.

impede, imm-pîde´, v
empêcher; gêner.

impediment, imm-pèd´-i-
m'nt, n empêchement
m.

impel, imm-pelle´, v
forcer; pousser.

impending, imm-penn´-
dinng, a imminent.

imperative, imm-pair´-a-
tive, n & a impératif m.

imperfect*, imm-peur´-
fecte, n & a imparfait m.

imperfection, imm-peur-
fèque´-ch'n, n
imperfection f.

imperial, imm-pî´-ri-eul, a
impérial.

imperil, imm-pair´-il, v
mettre en danger.

imperishable, imm-pair´-
i-cha-b'l, a impérissable.

impersonal, imm-peur´-
sŏ-n'l, a impersonnel.

impersonate, imm-peur´-
sŏ-néte, v personnifier.

impertinence, imm-peur´-
ti-n'nce, n impertinence
f.

impertinent*, imm-peur´-
ti-nennte, a
impertinent.

impervious*, imm-peur´-
vi-euce, a impénétrable.

impetuous*, imm-pett´-
iou-euce, a impétueux.

impetus, imm-´pi-teuce, n
impulsion f; élan m.

implant, imm-plânnte´, v
implanter; inculquer.

implement, imm´-pli-
m'nt, n instrument m;
outil m.

implicate, imm´-pli-quéte,
v impliquer.

A
B
C
D
E
F
G
H
I
J
K
L
M
N
O
P
Q
R
S
T
U
V
W
X
Y
Z

implication, imm-pli-qué´-ch'n, *n* implication *f*; sous-entendu *m*.

implicit*, imm-pliss´-itte, *a* implicite.

implore, imm-plore´, *v* implorer.

imply, imm-plâï´, *v* impliquer; insinuer.

impolite*, imm-po-lâïte´, *a* impoli.

import, imm´-porte, *v* importer. *n* importation *f*; **–er,** importateur *m*.

importance, imm-por´-tannce, *n* importance *f*.

important, imm-por´-t'nt, *a* important.

impose, imm-pauze´, *v* imposer; **–upon,** abuser de.

imposing, imm-pauze´-inng, *a* imposant.

imposition, imm-po-zi´-ch'n, *n* abus *m*; (tax) impôt *m*.

impossibility, imm-poss´-i-bi´-li-ti, *n* impossibilité *f*.

impossible, imm-poss´-i-b'l, *a* impossible.

impostor, imm-poss´-t'r, *n* imposteur *m*.

impotent, imm´-po-tennte, *a* impuissant.

impound, imm-pâ'ounnde´, *v* (animals) mettre en fourrière; (law) déposer au greffe; saisir (des marchandises).

impoverish, imm-pov´-eur-iche, *v* appauvrir.

impracticable, imm-prăc´-ti-ca-b'l, *a* impraticable.

impregnable, imm-pregg´-na-b'l, *a* imprenable.

impregnate, imm-pregg´-néte, *v* imprégner; (fertilize) féconder.

impress, imm-presse´, *v* imprimer; (feelings) faire une impression; (make clear) faire bien comprendre; **–ion,** *n* impression *f*; (stamp) empreinte *f*; **–ive,** *a* frappant; émouvant.

imprint, imm-prinnte´, *n* marque *f*; empreinte *f*. *v* empreindre; (mind) imprimer.

imprison, imm-prize´-onn, *v* emprisonner; **–ment,** *n* emprisonnement *m*.

improbable, imm-prob´-a-b'l, *a* improbable.

improper, imm-prop´-'r, *a* inconvenant.

improve, imm-prouve´, *v* améliorer; se perfectionner; **–ment,** *n* amélioration *f*.

improvident, imm-prove´-i-dennte, *a* imprévoyant.

improvisations, imm´-pro-vâïz, *v* improviser.

improvise, imm´-prove-i-zé-ch'n, *n* improvisation *f*.

imprudent*, imm-proue´-dennte, *a* imprudent.

impudence, imm´-pioue-dennce, *n* insolence *f*.

impudent*, imm´-pioue-dennte, *a* insolent.

impulse, imm´-polse, *n* impulsion *f*; élan *m*.

impure*, imm-pioure´, *a* impur.

impurity, imm-pioue´-ri-ti, *n* impureté *f*.

impute, imm-pioute´, *v* imputer.

in, inne, *prep* dans; en; à; *adv* dedans.

inability, inn-*a*-bil´-i-ti, *n* impuissance *f*.

inaccessible, inn-ăc-sess´-i-b'l, *a* inaccessible.

inaccuracy, inn-ăc´-quiou-ra-ci, *n* inexactitude *f*.

inaccurate*, inn-ăc´-quiou-réte, *a* inexact.

inadequate, inn-ăd´-i-couéte, *a* insuffisant.

inadvertent*, inn-ăd-veur´-tennte, *a* inattentif.

inane, inn-éne´, *a* inepte.

inanimate, inn-ănn´-i-méte, *a* inanimé.

inapt, inn-ăpte´, *a* inapte;
–**itude,** *n* inaptitude *f.*

inasmuch as, inn-*a*ze-
mótche´ ăze, *conj* vu
que.

inaudible, inn-oa-di-b'l, *a*
inaudible.

inaugurate, inn-oa-
guioue-réte, *v* inaugurer.

inborn, inn´-boarne, *a*
inné.

incalculable, inn-cal´-
kiou-*l*a-b'l, *a*
incalculable.

incapable, inn-qué´-p*a*-b'l,
a incapable.

incapacitate, inn-c*a*-păss´-
i-ti´ete, *v* rendre
incapable.

incapacity, inn-c*a*-păss´-i-
ti, *n* incapacité *f.*

incarnation, inn-câr-né´-
ch'n, *n* incarnation *f.*

incautious*, inn-cô´-
che*u*ce, *a* imprudent.

incense, inn-cennse´, *n*
encens *m. v* provoquer.

incentive, inn-cenn´-tive,
n motif *m*; stimulant *m.*

incessant, inn-cess´-
annte, *a* incessant.

inch, inntche, *n* pouce
anglais *m.*

incident, inn´-ci-dennt, *n*
incident *m*; –**al,** *a*
fortuit.

incision, inn-ci´-j'n, *n*
incision *f.*

incite, inn-sâïte´, *v*
inciter.

inclination, inn-cli-né´-
ch'n, *n* inclination *f*;
(disposition) penchant
m.

incline, inn´-clâïne, *n*
(slope) pente *f. v*
incliner.

include, inn-cloude´, *v*
comprendre; renfermer.

inclusive*, inn-cooue´-
cive, *a* inclusif; compris.

incoherent*, inn-co-hî´-
rennte, *a* incohérent.

income, inn´-comme, *n*
revenu *m*; rentes *fpl*;
–**tax,** impôt sur le
revenu *m.*

incoming, inn´-comm-
inng, *a* entrant;
nouveau.

incomparable, inn-
comm´-p*a*-r*a*-b'l, *a*
incomparable.

incompatible, inn-comm-
patt´-i-b'l, *a*
incompatible.

incompetent, inn-comm´-
pi-tennte, *a*
incompétent.

incomplete*, inn-comm-
plîte´, *a* incomplet.

incomprehensible, inn-
comm´-pré-henn´-si-b'l,
a incompréhensible.

inconceivable, inn-cŏnn-
cî´-v*a*-b'l, *a*
inconcevable.

inconclusive, inn-cŏnn-
cloue´-cive, *a*
inconcluant.

incongruous*, inn-
conng´-grou-*euc*e, *a*
incongru.

inconsiderable, inn-cŏnn-
si´-*deu*r-*a*-b'l, *a*
insignifiant.

inconsiderate, inn-cŏnn-
si´-*deu*r-éte, *a* sans
égards.

inconsistent*, inn-cŏnn-
ciss´-tennte, *a* illogique.

inconsolable, inn-cŏnn-
sol´-*a*-b'l, *a*
inconsolable.

inconstant, inn-conn´-
stannte, *a* inconstant.

inconvenience, inn-cŏnn-
vî´-ni-ennce, *v*
déranger; gêner. *n*
dérangement *m*;
inconvénient *m.*

inconvenient, inn-cŏnn-
v´-ni-ennte, *a*
incommode.

incorporate, inn-kor´-po-
réte, *v* incorporer.

incorrect*, inn-cŏr-recte´,
a inexact; (behavior)
incorrect.

incorrigible, inn-cor´-i-
dji-b'l, *a* incorrigible.

increase, inn-crîce´, *v*
augmenter; accroître. *n*
augmentation *f*;

a
b
c
d
e
f
g
h
i
j
k
l
m
n
o
p
q
r
s
t
u
v
w
x
y
z

accroissement *m.*

incredible, inn-crèd´-i-b'l, *a* incroyable.

incredulous, inn-crèd´-iou-*leuce, a* incrédule.

incriminate, inn-crimm´-inn-éte, *v* incriminer.

incubate, inn´-kioue-béte, *v* couver; incuber.

incubation, inn´-kioue-bé-ch´-n, *n* incubation *f.*

incubator, inn´-kioue-bé-*teur, n* couveuse *f.*

inculcate, inn´-kol-quéte, *v* inculquer.

incur, inn-queur´, *v* encourir; (expenses) faire.

incurable, inn-kiou´-ra-b'l, *a* incurable.

indebted, inn-dett´-èdde, *a* endetté; redevable.

indecent, inn-dî´-cennte, *a* indécent.

indecision, inn-di-si´-j'n, *n* indécision *f.*

indecisive, inn-di-sâï´-cive, *a* indécis.

indeed, inn-dîde´, *adv* en effet; vraiment.

indefatigable, inn-di-fătt´-i-gă-b'l, *a* infatigable.

indefensible, inn-di-fenn´-si-b'l, *a* indéfendable.

indefinite*, inn-dèf´-i-nitte, *a* indéfini.

indelible, inn-dèl´-i-b'l, *a* indélébile; ineffaçable.

indemnify, inn-demm´-ni-făï, *v* indemniser.

indemnity, inn-demm´-ni-ti, *n* indemnité *f.*

independence, inn-di-penn´-dennce, *n* indépendance *f.*

independent*, inn-di-penn´-dennte, *a* indépendant.

indescribable, inn-di-scrâï´-ba-b'l, *a* indescriptible.

indestructible, inn-di-strok´-ti-b'l, *a* indestructible.

index, inn´-dexe, *n* table des matières *f*; index *m.*

index finger, inn´-dexe-finng´-gueur, *n* index *m.*

indicate, inn´-di-quéte, *v* indiquer.

indication, inn-di-qué´-ch'n, *n* indication *f.*

indicator, inn´-di-qué-*teur, n* indicateur *m.*

indict, inn-dâïte´, *v* poursuivre.

indifference, inn-dif´-eur-ennce, *n* indifférence *f.*

indifferent*, inn-dif´-eur-ennte, *a* indifférent.

indigestible, inn-di-djess´-ti-b'l, *a* indigeste.

indigestion, inn-di-djess´-ti-'n, *n* indigestion *f.*

indignant, inn-dig´-

nannte, *a* indigné.

indignity, inn-dig´-ni-ti, *n* indignité *f.*

indigo, inn´-di-go, *n* indigo *m.*

indirect*, inn-di-recte´, *a* indirect.

indiscreet*, inn-diss-crîte´, *a* indiscret.

indiscriminate, inn-diss-crimm´-i-néte, *a* sans discernement; –**ly,** *adv* indistinctement.

indispensable, inn-diss-penn´-sa-b'l, *a* indispensable.

indisposed, inn-diss-pauz'd´, *a* indisposé.

indisputable, inn-diss-piou´-ta-b'l, *a* incontestable.

indistinct*, inn-diss-tinng'kt´, *a* indistinct.

indistinguishable, inn-diss-tinng´-gouich-a-b'l, *a* imperceptible; indistinct.

individual*, inn-di-vid´-iou-al, *a* individuel. *n* individu *m.*

indolent, inn´-dŏ-lennte, *a* indolent.

indoor, inn-daur´, *a* d'intérieur.

indoors, inn-daurze´, *adv* à l'intérieur; à la maison.

induce, inn-diouce´, *v* provoquer; causer;

induire.

inducement, inn-diouce´-m'nt. *n* stimulant *m*; motif *m*.

indulge, inn-doldje´, *v* gâter; se livrer à; s'abandonner à.

indulgent*, inn-dol´-djennte, *a* indulgent.

industrial*, inn-doss´-tri-al, *a* industriel.

industrious*, inn-doss´-tri-*euce*, *a* laborieux.

industry, inn´-doss-tri, *n* industrie *f*.

inebriated, inn-i´-bri-é-tedde, *a* ivre.

ineffective*, inn-èf-fèque´-tive, *a* inefficace.

inefficient*, inn-èf-fich´-ennte, *a* inefficace; incapable.

inept, inn-epte´, *a* inepte; absurde.

inequality, inn-i-couol´-i-ti, *n* inégalité *f*.

inert, inn-eurte´, *a* inerte.

inestimable, inn-ess´-ti-m*a*-b'l, *a* inestimable.

inevitable, inn-èv´-i-t*a*-b'l, *a* inévitable.

inexcusable, inn-èks-kioue´-*za*-b'l, *a* inexcusable.

inexhaustible, inn-èks-hauss´-ti-b'l, *a* inépuisable.

inexpedient, inn-èks-pî´-di-ennte, *a* inopportun.

inexpensive, inn-èks-penn´-cive, *a* bon marché.

inexperienced, inn-èks-pî´-ri-enncd, *a* inexpérimenté; sans expérience.

inexplicable, inn-èks´-pli-ka-b'l, *a* inexplicable.

inexpressible, inn-èks-press´-si-b'l, *a* inexprimable.

infallible, inn-făll´-i-b'l, *a* infaillible.

infamous, inn´-fa-m*euce*, *a* infâme.

infancy, inn´-fann-ci, *n* première; enfance *f*; (law) minorité *f*.

infant, inn´-fannte, *n* enfant *m*; enbasâge; (law) mineur, -e *m* & *f*.

infantry, inn´-fann-tri, *n* infanterie *f*.

infatuation, inn-fătt-iou-é´-ch'n, *n* engouement.

infect, inn-fèkte´, *v* infecter; **–ious*,** *a* contagieux.

infer, inn-feur´, *v* inférer; déduire.

inference, inn´-*feur*-'nce, *n* déduction *f*.

inferior, inn-fî´-ri-*eur*, *n* & *a* inférieur *m*.

infernal*, inn-feur´-n'l, *a* infernal.

infest, inn-feste´, *v* infester.

infidel, inn´-fi-d'l, *n* & *a* infidèle *m* & *f*.

infiltrate, inn´-file-tréte, *v* infiltrer; imprégner.

infinite*, inn´-fi-nite, *a* infini.

infirm, inn-feurme´, *a* infirme; maladif.

infirmary, inn-feurm´-*a*-ri, *n* infirmerie *f*.

inflame, inn-fléme´, *v* enflammer.

inflammable, inn-flămm´-*a*-b'l, *a* inflammable.

inflammation, inn-fla-mé´-ch'n, *n* inflammation *f*.

inflate, inn-fléte, *v* gonfler; (prices) hausser.

inflation, inn-flé´-ch'n, *n* inflation *f*.

inflexible, inn-flèk´-si-b'l, *a* inflexible.

inflict, inn-flickte´, *v* infliger.

influence, inn´-flou-ennce, *n* influence *f*. *v* influencer.

influential, inn-flou-enn´-ch'l, *a* influent; **to be –,** avoir de l'influence.

influenza, inn-flou-enn´-za, *n* grippe *f*.

inform, inn-foarme´, *v* informer; **–al,** *a* sans cérémonie; **–ation,** *n*

a
b
c
d
e
f
g
h
i
j
k
l
m
n
o
p
q
r
s
t
u
v
w
x
y
z

A
B
C
D
E
F
G
H
I
J
K
L
M
N
O
P
Q
R
S
T
U
V
W
X
Y
Z

renseignements *mpl.*

infrequent, inn-frî´-couennte, *a* infréquent, rare.

infringe, inn-frinndje´, *v* empiéter; transgresser.

infringement, inn-frinndje´-m'nt, *n* infraction *f.*

infuriate, inn-fiou´-ri-éte, *v* rendre furieux.

infuse, inn-fiouze´, *v* verser; (tea, etc) infuser.

ingenious*, inn-djî´-ni-*euce, a* ingénieux.

ingenuity, inn-dji-niou´-i-ti, *n* ingénuité *f.*

ingot, inng´-gŏtte, *n* lingot *m.*

ingrained, inn-grénnde´, *a* enraciné; invétéré.

ingratiate, inn-gré´-chi-éte, *v* **–oneself with,** se faire bien voir de quelqu'un.

ingratitude, inn-grătt´-i-tioude, *n* ingratitude *f.*

ingredient, inn-grî´-di-ennte, *n* ingrédient *m.*

inhabit, inn-hăb´-itte, *v* habiter; **–able,** *a* habitable; **–ant,** *n* habitant *m.*

inhale, inn-héle´, *v* aspirer; (smoke) avaler.

inherent*, inn-hi´-r'nt, *a* inhérent.

inherit, inn-hér´-itte, *v*

hériter; **–ance,** *n* succession *f*; héritage *m.*

inhibit, inn-hi´-bitte, *v* empêcher; inhiber; **–ion,** *n* inhibition *f.*

inhospitable, inn-hoss´-pit-*a*-b'l, *a* inhospitalier.

inhuman*, inn-hioue´-m'n, *a* inhumain.

iniquitous, inn-ik´-oui-t*euce, a* inique.

initial, inn-i´-ch'l, *n* initiale *f. a** initial; premier.

initiate, inn-i´-chi-éte, *v* initier; commencer.

inject, inn-djecte´, *v* injecter; **–ion,** *n* injection *f*; piqûre *f.*

injudicious*, inn-djiou-dich´-*euce, a* peu judicieux.

injunction, inn-djonnk´-ch'n, *n* injonction *f.*

injure, inn´-djioure, *v* blesser; abîmer; nuire à.

injurious*, inn-djioue´-ri-*euce, a* nuisible.

injury, inn´-dj*eur*-i, *n* blessure *f*; tort *m.*

injustice, inn-djoss´-tice, *n* injustice *f.*

ink, inng´-k, *n* encre *f*; **–stand,** encrier *m.*

inlaid, inn-léde´, *a* incrusté; (wood) marqueté.

inland, inn´-lănnde, *n* & *a*

intérieur *m.*

inlet, inn´-lette, *n* entrée *f*; (*geog*) bras de mer *m.*

inmate, inn´-méte, *n* pensionnaire *m* & *f*; interné *m.*

inmost, inn´-mauste, *a* le plus profond.

inn, inne, *n* auberge *f*; **–keeper,** aubergiste *m.*

inner, inn´-'r, *a* intérieur; secret.

innocent, inn´-o-cennte, *a* innocent.

innocuous*, inn-o´-kiou-*euce, a* inoffensif.

innovation, inn-no-vé´-ch'n, *n* innovation *f.*

innumerable, inn-nioue´-meur-*a*-b'l, *a* innombrable.

inoculate, inn-o´-kiou-léte, *v* inoculer.

inoffensive, inn-o-fenn´-cive, *a* inoffensif.

inopportune, inn-opp´-or-tioune, *a* inopportun.

inquest, inn´-coueste, *n* enquête *f.*

inquire, inn-couâire, *v* demander; s'informer.

inquiry, inn-couâ'ï´-ri, *n* demande *f*; enquête *f.*

Inquisition, inn-couiz-i´-ch'n, *n* Inquisition *f.*

inquisitive*, inn-couiz´-i-tive, *a* curieux.

insane, inn-séne´, *a* fou;

dément.

insanity, inn-sann´-i-ti, *n*
folie *f*; démence *f*.

insatiable, inn-sé´-chi-*a*-b'l, *a* insatiable.

inscription, inn-scripe´-ch'n, *n* inscription *f*.

insect, inn´-secte, *n* insecte *m*.

insecure, inn-ci-kioure´, *a* peu sûr; insécurisé; incertain; peu solide.

insensible, inn-senn´-si-b'l, *a* insensible; (unconscious) sans connaissance.

inseparable, inn-sép´-a-*ra*-b'l, *a* inséparable.

insert, inn-seurte´, *v* insérer; introduire; **–ion,** *n* insertion *f*; (advertisement) annonce *f*.

inside, inn-sâïde´, *n* intérieur *m*. *a* intérieur. *adv* en dedans.

insidious*, inn-si´-di-*euce*, *a* insidieux.

insignificant, inn-sigg-nif´-i-k'nt, *a* insignifiant.

insincere*, inn-sinn-cire´, *a* faux.

insinuate, inn-sinn´-iou-éte, *v* insinuer.

insipid*, inn-sipp´-idde, *a* insipide; fade.

insist, inn-sisste´, *v* exiger;

insister.

insolence, inn´-sŏ-lennce, *n* insolence *f*.

insolent, inn´-sŏ-lennte, *a* insolent.

insolvent, inn-soll´-vennte, *a* insolvable.

inspect, inn-specte´, *v* inspecter; **–ion,** *n* inspection *f*; **–or,** inspecteur *m*.

inspiration, inn-spi-ré´-ch'n, *n* inspiration *f*.

inspire, inn-spâïre, *v* inspirer; **–d,** *a* inspiré.

install, inn-stoale´, *v* installer; (*mech*) monter; **–ation,** *n* installation *f*; montage *m*.

installment, inn-stoale´-m'nt, *n* versement partiel *m*; (of story etc.) épisode *m*; **to pay by –s,** *v* payer à tempérament.

instance, inn´-stannce, *n* exemple *m*; cas *m*.

instant, inn´-stannte, *n* instant *m*. *a* (date) courant; **–aneous*,** instantané; **–ly,** *adv* à l'instant.

instead of, inn-stedde´ ove, *adv* au lieu de.

instep, inn´-steppe, *n* cou-de-pied *m*.

instigate, inn´-sti-guéte, *v* inciter.

instill, inn-stille´, *v*

instiller.

instinct, inn´-stinng-kt, *n* instinct *m*.

institute, inn´-sti-tioute, *n* institut *m*. *v* instituer.

institution, inn-sti-tiou´-ch'n, *n* institution *f*; établissement *m*.

instruct, inn-strocte´, *v* instruire; charger de.

instruction, inn-stroc´-ch'n, *n* instruction *f*.

instrument, inn´-strou-m'nt, *n* instrument *m*.

insubordinate, inn-*seub*-oar´-din-néte, *a* insubordonné.

insufferable, inn-sof´-*feur*-a-b'l, *a* insupportable.

insufficient, inn-sof-fi´-chennte, *a* insuffisant.

insulation, inn-siou-lé´-ch'n, *n* isolation *f*; (heat, pipes, etc) calorifugeage *m*.

insult, inn-sollté, *v* insulter. *n* insulte *f*.

insurance, inn-chou´-r'nce, *n* assurance *f*.

insure, inn-choure´, *v* assurer.

insurrection, inn-*seur*-rèque´-ch'n, *n* insurrection *f*.

integrate, inn´-*teur*-gréte, *v* rendre entier; intégrer.

intellect, inn´-*teur*-lecte, *n* intelligence *f*; intellect

a
b
c
d
e
f
g
h
i
j
k
l
m
n
o
p
q
r
s
t
u
v
w
x
y
z

A
B
C
D
E
F
G
H
I
J
K
L
M
N
O
P
Q
R
S
T
U
V
W
X
Y
Z

m; **–ual,** *a* intellectuel.
intelligence, inn-tel´-li-dj'nce, *n* intelligence *f.*
intelligent*, inn-tel´-li-dj'nt, *a* intelligent.
intemperate*, inn-temm´-peur-éte, *a* immodéré.
intend, inn-tennde´, *v* se proposer; avoir l'intention de.
intense*, inn-tennce´, *a* intense; vif.
intent, inn-tennte´, *n* dessein *m. a* appliqué; **–ion,** *n* intention *f;* **–ionally,** *adv* exprès.
inter, inn-teur´, *v* enterrer; **–ment,** *n* enterrement *m.*
inter, inn´-teur, **–cept,** *v* intercepter; **–change,** échanger; **–course,** *n* commerce *m;* relations *fpl;* rapports *mpl;* **–fere,** *v* se mêler de; **–ference,** *n* intervention *f;* (radio) bruit parasite *m;* **–lude,** intermède *m;* **–mediate,** *a* intermédiaire; **–mingle,** *v* s'entremêler; **–mittent,** *a* intermittent; **–mix,** *v* entremêler; **–national,** *a* international; **–rupt,** *v* interrompre; **–val,** *n* intervalle *m;* (theater) entracte *m;* **–vene,** *v* intervenir; **–vention,** *n*

intervention *f;* **–view,** entrevue *f;* (for news) interview *f. v* interviewer.
interest, inn´-teur-reste, *n* intérêt *m. v* intéresser; **–ing,** *a* intéressant.
interior, inn-tî´-ri-eur, *n* & *a* intérieur *m.*
intern, inn-teurne´, *v* interner.
internal*, inn-teur´-n'l, *a* interne.
interpret, inn-teur´-prette, *v* interpréter.
internet, inn-teur´-naite, *n* internet *m.*
interpreter, inn-teur´-prett-'r, *n* interprète *m.*
interrogate, inn-terr´-ŏ-guéte, *v* interroger.
intestate, inn-tess´-téte, *a* intestat.
intestine, inn-tess´-tinne, *n* intestin *m.*
intimacy, inn´-ti-ma-ci. *n* intimité *f.*
intimate, inn´-ti-méte, *v* signaler; donner à entendre. *a** intime.
intimation, inn-ti-mé´-ch'n, *n* indice *m;* avis *m.*
intimidate, inn-ti´-mi-déte, *v* intimider.
into, inn´-tou, *prep* dans; en.
intolerable, inn-tol´-eur-a-b'l, *a* intolérable.

intoxicate, inn-toks´-i-quéte, *v* enivrer; griser.
intrepid*, inn-trepp´-ide, *a* intrépide.
intricate*, inn´-tri-quéte, *a* compliqué; embrouillé.
intrigue, inn-trîgue´, *n* intrigue *f. v* intriguer.
intriguing, inn-trî´-guinng, *a* intrigant.
intrinsic, inn-trinn´-sique, *a* intrinsèque.
introduce, inn-trŏ-diouce´, *v* introduire; présenter.
introductory, inn-trŏ-doc´-tŏ-ri, *a* préliminaire.
intrude, inn-troude´, *v* s'imposer; déranger; être de trop.
intuition, inn-tiou-i´-ch'n, *n* intuition *f.*
inundate, inn´-ŏnn-déte, *v* inonder.
inundation, inn-ŏnn-dé´-ch'n, *n* inondation *f.*
inure, inn-ioure´, *v* endurcir; accoutumer.
invade, inn-véde´, *v* envahir; **–r,** *n* envahisseur *m.*
invalid, inn´-va-lide, *n* malade *m & f;* infirme *m & f.*
invalid, inn-văl´-ide, *a* nul; non valable.

invaluable, inn-văl´-iou-a-b'l, *a* inestimable.

invariable, inn-vé´-ri-a-b'l, *a* invariable.

invasion, inn-vé´-j'n, *n* invasion *f.*

inveigle, inn-vî´-g'l, *v* séduire, attirer dans.

invent, inn-vennte´, *v* inventer; **–ion,** *n* invention *f.*; **–or,** inventeur *m.*

inventory, inn´-venn-to-ri, *n* inventaire *m.*

invert, inn-veurte´, *v* intervertir; renverser.

invest, inn-veste´, *v* investir; (money) placer; **–ment,** *n* placement *m.*; **–or,** épargnant *m.*

investigate, inn-vess´-ti-guéte, *v* rechercher; faire une enquête.

inveterate, inn-vett´-eur-éte, *a* invétéré.

invigorate, inn-vig´-ŏr-éte, *v* fortifier.

invincible, inn-vinn´-ci-b'l, *a* invincible.

invisible, inn-viz´-i-b'l, *a* invisible.

invitation, inn-vi-té´-ch'n, *n* invitation *f.*

invite, inn-vâïte´, *v* inviter.

invoice, inn´-voa'ice, *n* facture *f.*

invoke, inn-vauke´, *v* invoquer.

involuntary, inn-vol´-onn-ta-ri, *a* involontaire.

involve, inn-volve´, *v* impliquer; entraîner; **–d,** *a* compliqué.

inward*, inn´-oueurde, *a* intérieur.

iodine, âï´-o-dine, *n* iode *m.*

ire, âïre, *n* courroux *m*; ire *f*; colère *f.*

iris, âï´-rice, *n* iris *m.*

irksome, eurk´-somme, *a* ennuyeux; pénible.

iron, âï´-eurne, *n* fer *m*; (flat) fer à repasser *m. a* de fer. *v* repasser.

ironic, âï-ronn´-ik, *a* ironique.

irony, âï´-rŏnn-i, *n* ironie *f.*

irreconcilable, ir-rèk-ŏnn-sâï´-la-b'l, *a* irréconciliable; incompatible.

irregular*, ir-regg´-iou-l'r, *a* irrégulier.

irrelevant, ir-rèl´-i-v'nt, *a* hors de propos.

irreproachable, ir-ri-prautch´-a-b'l, *a* irréprochable.

irresistible, ir-ri-ziss´-ti-b'l, *a* irrésistible.

irrespective, ir-ress-pèk´-tive, *adv* sans tenir compte de.

irresponsible, ir-ress-ponn´-ci-b'l, *a* irresponsable.

irretrievable, ir-ri-trî´-va-b'l, *a* irréparable.

irrigate, ir´-ri-guéte, *v* irriguer; arroser.

irritable, ir´-ri-ta-b'l, *a* irritable; irascible.

irritate, ir´-ri-téte, *v* irriter; agacer.

island, âï´-lannde, *n* île *f*; **–er,** *n* insulaire *m* & *f.*

isle, âïlle, *n* île *f*; (islet) îlot *m.*

isolate, âï´-sŏ-léte, *v* isoler.

isolation, âï-sŏ-lé´-ch'n, *n* isolement *m.*

issue, i´-chiou, *n* progéniture *f*; (edition) numéro *m*; (result) issue *f*; résultat *m. v* émettre; publier; émaner; donner; délivrer.

isthmus, iss´-meuce, *n* isthme *m.*

it, itt, *pron* il, elle; le; la; lui; il; cela.

italic, i-tal´-ique, *n* & *a* (type) italique *m.*

itch, itch, *v* démanger. *n* démangeaison *f.*

item, âï´-temme, *n* article *m*; chose *f*; (news) article *m.*

its, itse, *poss pron* le sien,

la sienne; les siens, les siennes. *poss a* son; sa; ses.

itself, itt-self´, *pron* lui-même, elle-même.

ivory, âï´-*veu*r-i, *n* ivoire *m*.

ivy, âï´-vi, *n* lierre *m*.

J

jabber, jăb´-'r, *v* jacasser. *n*
baragouinage *m*.

jack, djăque, *n* (*mech*) cric
m.

jackal, djăk´-oale, *n*
chacal *m*.

jacket, djăk´-ette, *n*
veston *m*; veste *f*;
jaquette *f*.

jade, djéde, *n* (stone) jade
m.

jaded, djé´-dédde, *a*
éreinté.

jag, djăgue, *n* brèche *f*. *v*
ébrécher –**ged,** *a*
entaillé; dentelé.

jail, djéle, *n* prison *f*; –**er,**
geôlier *m*.

jam, djămme, *n*
(conserve) confiture *f*;
(traffic) embouteillage
m. *v* (lock) coincer;
(crowd) presser.

January, djănn´-iou-èr-i, *n*
janvier *m*.

jar, djârre, *n* pot *m*; bocal
m; (shock) secousse *f*. *v*
agacer.

jaundice, djoann´-dice, *n*
jaunisse *f*.

jaw, djoa, *n* mâchoire *f*.

jay, djé, *n* geai *m*.

jealous*, djèl´-*euce*, *a*
jaloux; –**y,** *n* jalousie *f*.

jeer, djire, *v* railler. *n*
raillerie *f*.

jelly, djèl´-i, *n* gelée *f*; –
fish, méduse *f*.

jeopardize, djèp´*eur*-dâïze,
v compromettre.

jeopardy, djèp´-*eur*-di, *n*
danger *m*; péril *m*.

jerk, djeurque, *v* donner
une secousse. *n* secousse
f.

jersey, djeur´-zi, *n* jersey
m; tricot *m*.

jest, djesste, *n* plaisanterie
f. *v* plaisanter.

jester, djess´-t'r, *n* farceur
m; (court) bouffon *m*.

jet, djett, *n* (mineral) jais
m; (liquid) jet *m*;
(aircraft) avion à
réaction *m*.

jettison, djett´-i-sonn, *v*
jeter à la mer.

jetty, djett´-i, *n* jetée *f*.

Jew, djioue, *n* Juif *m*; –**ish,**
a juif, -ve.

jewel, djioue-'l, *n* bijou
m; joyau *m*; –**er,**
bijoutier *m*; –**ry,**
bijouterie *f*.

jig, djigue, *n* gigue *f*.

jilt, djillte, *v* délaisser;
plaquer.

jingle, djinng´-g'l, *v* tinter.
n tintement *m*.

job, djobbe, *n* situation *f*;
emploi *m*; (task)
besogne *f*; travail *m*; job
m.

jockey, djok´-i, *n* jockey
m.

jocular, djok´-iou-l'r, *a*

a
b
c
d
e
f
g
h
i
j
k
l
m
n
o
p
q
r
s
t
u
v
w
x
y
z

jovial.

join, djoa'ine, *v* joindre; unir; (club) devenir membre; **–in,** prendre part à.

joiner, djoa'inn´-r, *n* menuisier *m*.

joint, djoa'innte, *n* joint *m*; (anatomy) articulation *f*; (meat) quartier *m*; (roast) rôti *m*. *a* uni, collectif.

jointly, djoa'innt´-li, *adv* conjointement.

joke, djauke, *n* plaisanterie *f*; blague *f*. *v* plaisanter.

joker, djauk´-'r, *n* farceur *m*.

jolly, djoll´-i, *a* gai.

jolt, djault, *n* cahot *m*; chôc. *v* cahoter; secouer.

jostle, djoss´-'l, *v* bousculer.

journal, djeur´-n'l, *n* journal *m*; **–ism,** journalisme *m*; **–ist,** journaliste *m* & *f*.

journey, djeur´-ni, *n* voyage *m*. *v* voyager.

jovial*, djau´-vi-*a*l, *a* jovial; joyeux.

joy, djoa'i, *n* joie *f*; **–ful*,** *a* joyeux.

jubilant, djoue´-bi-l'nt, *a* réjoui.

judge, djodje, *n* juge *m*; connaisseur *m*. *v* juger.

judgment, djodje´-m'nt, *n* jugement *m*. **–day,** jour du jugement.

judicial*, djoue-di´-ch'l, *a* judiciaire.

judicious*, djoue-di´-ch*eu*ce, *a* judicieux.

jug, djogue, *n* cruche *f*; pot *m*; (large) broc *m*.

juggle, djogg´-g'l, *v* jongler.

juggler, djogg´-l'r, *n* jongleur *m*.

juice, djouce, *n* jus *m*; (botanical) suc *m*.

juicy, djoue´-ci, *a* juteux; succulent.

July, djou-lâï´, *n* juillet *m*.

jumble, djomm´-b'l, *n* fouillis *m*. *v* emmêler.

jump, djommpe, *v* sauter. *n* saut *m*.

junction, djonngk´-ch'n, *n* jonction *f*; (railroad) embranchement *m*; (road) carrefour *m*.

juncture, djonngk´-tioure, *n* conjoncture *f*.

June, djoune, *n* juin *m*.

jungle, djonng´-g'l, *n* jungle *f*.

junior, djoue´-ni-*eu*r, *n* & *a* cadet *m*. *a* jeune.

juniper, djoue´-ni-p'r, *n* genièvre *m*.

jurisdiction, djoue-rice-dik´-ch'n, *n* juridiction *f*.

juror, djoue´-r*eu*r, *n* juré *m*.

jury, djoue´-ri, *n* jury *m*.

just, djosste, *a* & *adv* juste; **–ice,** *n* justice *f*; **–ification,** justification *f*; **–ify,** *v* justifier; **–ly,** *adv* justement.

jut, djotte, *v* faire saillie.

juvenile, djoue´-vi-nâïle, *a* d'enfants; jeune.

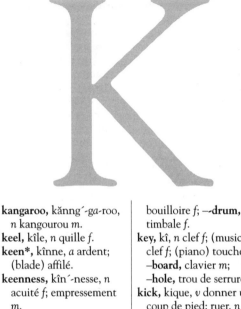

kangaroo, kănng´-ga-roo, n kangourou m.

keel, kîle, n quille f.

keen*, kînne, a ardent; (blade) affilé.

keenness, kîn´-nesse, n acuité f; empressement m.

keep, kîpe, n entretien m. v garder; maintenir; tenir; rester; **–back,** retenir; **–off,** éviter; se tenir éloigné de; **–up,** maintenir; **–er,** n gardien m; **–sake,** souvenir m.

keg, quègue, n caque f; barillet m.

kennel, quènn´-´l, n chenil m.

kernel, queur´-n'l, n noyau m; amande f.

kettle, quètt´-´l, n bouilloire f; **––drum,** timbale f.

key, kî, n clef f; (music) clef f; (piano) touche f; **–board,** clavier m; **–hole,** trou de serrure m.

kick, kique, v donner un coup de pied; ruer. n coup de pied m; (horse) ruade f.

kid, kidde, n chevreau m. fam gosse m & f.

kidnap, kidd´-năppe, v enlever; kidnapper.

kidney, kidd´-ni, n rein m; (cookery) rognon m.

kill, kille, v tuer.

kiln, kilne, n four m.

kin, kinne, n parenté f. a allié; **–dred,** de même nature.

kind, kâïnnde, n espèce f; genre m; sorte f. a* bon; aimable; **–ness,** n bonté f.

kindergarten, kinn´-d'r-gar-t'n, n jardin d'enfants m; école maternelle f.

kindle, kinn´-d'l, v allumer; (fig) enflammer.

king, kinng, n roi m; **–dom,** royaume m.

kipper, kipp´-eur, n hareng fumé m.

kiss, kisse, n baiser m. v embrasser.

kit, kitte, n équipement m; trousse f.

kitchen, kitt´-chine, n cuisine f.

kite, kâïte, n cerf-volant m; (bird) milan m.

kitten, kit´-t'n, n chaton m.

knack, năque, n don m; talent m; truc m.

knapsack, năpp´-săque, n havresac m.

knave, néve, n coquin m; (cards) valet m.

knead, nîde, v pétrir.

knee, nî, n genou m; **––cap,** rotule f.

kneel, nîle, v s'agenouiller; se mettre à genoux.

knell, nêle, n glas m.

knife, nâïfe, n couteau m; **pen–,** canif m.

A
B
C
D
E
F
G
H
I
J
K
L
M
N
O
P
Q
R
S
T
U
V
W
X
Y
Z

knight, nâïte, *n* chevalier *m*; (chess) cavalier *m*.

knit, nitte, *v* tricoter; **–ting,** *n* tricot *m*.

knob, nobbe, *n* bouton *m*; poignée.

knock, noque, *n* coup *m*. *v* frapper; **–against,** heurter; **–down,** renverser; **–er,** *n* (door)

knot, not, *n* nœud *m*. *v* nouer.

knotty, nott´-i, *a* noueux; (*fig*) embrouillé.

know, nau, *v* savoir; connaître.

knowledge, noll´-idj, *n* connaissance *f*; savoir *m*.

knuckle, nok´-'l, *n* articulation *f*; jointure *f*.

label, lé´-b'l, n étiquette f.
v mettre une étiquette.

labor, lé´-beur, v travailler;
peiner. n travail m;
labeur m; **–er,** travailleur
m; a noeuvre.

laboratory, lăb´-o-ra-to-ri,
n laboratoire m.

laborious*, la-bau´-ri-
euce, a laborieux;
pénible.

lace, léce, n dentelle f;
(shoe, etc) lacet m. v
lacer.

lacerate, lăss´-eur-éte, v
lacérer.

lack, lăque, v manquer de.
n manque m.

lacquer, lăk´-'r, n laque f.
v laquer.

lad, lădde, n garcon m;
jeune homme m.

ladder, lădd´-'r, n
échelle f.

ladle, lé´-d'l, n louche f. v
servir.

lady, lé´-di, n dame f; –-
bug, coccinelle f; (fam)
bête à bon Dieu f.

lag, lăgue, v traîner; rester
en arrière.

lagoon, la-goune´, n
lagune f.

lair, lère, n repaire m.

lake, léque, n lac m.

lamb, lămme, n agneau m;
leg of –, gigot m.

lame, léme, a boiteux. v
estropier.

lament, la-mennte´, v se
lamenter. n plainte f.

lamp, lămmpe, n lampe f;
(street lamp) réverbère
m; (electric bulb)
ampoule électrique f.

lance, lânnce, n lance f;
(med) bistouri m. v
(med) ouvrir au bistouri.

land, lănnde, n terre f;
(home) pays m. v
débarquer; (aircraft)
atterrir; **–ing,**
débarquement m; (quay)
débarcadère m; (stairs)
palier m; **–lady,**
patronne f; maîtresse;
propriétaire f; **–lord,**
propriétaire m; **–mark,**
point de repère m;
–scape, paysage m;
–slide, éboulement
deterre m.

lane, léne, n (country)
chemin m; (town) ruelle
f; (traffic) file f.

language, lănng´-gouidje,
n langage m; langue f.

languid, lănng´-gouide, a
languissant.

languish, lănng´-gouiche,
v languir.

lanky, lain´-nki, a grand
et maigre.

lantern, lănn´-teurne, n
lanterne f.

lap, lăppe, n genoux mpl;
(sport) tour m. v (drink)
laper.

lapel, lă-pèl´, n revers
d'habit m.

lapse, lăpse, v s'écouler;
retomber. n cours m;
erreur f.

larceny, lăr´-ci-ni, n

a
b
c
d
e
f
g
h
i
j
k
l
m
n
o
p
q
r
s
t
u
v
w
x
y
z

larcin *m.*

lard, lârde, *n* saindoux *m;* **–er,** garde-manger *m.*

large*, lârdje, *a* grand; gros; fort; considérable.

lark, lârque, *n* alouette *f.*

lash, lăche, *n* (whip) fouet *m;* (stroke) coup de fouet *m;* (eye) cil *m. v* fouetter; (bind) attacher.

lassitude, lăss´-i-tioude, *n* lassitude *f.*

last, lâsse, *v* durer. *a* dernier; **–ing,** durable.

latch, lătche, *n* loquet *m. v* fermer au loquet.

late, léte, *adv* tard. *a* en retard; tard; récent; tardif; (deceased) feu; **to be –,** *v* être en retard.

lately, léte-li, *adv* dernièrement.

latent, lé´-tennte, *a* caché; latent.

lathe, lédz, *n* tour *m.*

lather, lădz´-´r, *n* mousse de savon *f. v* savonner.

latitude, lăt´-i-tioude, *n* latitude *f.*

latter*, lătt´-´r, *a* dernier (des deux).

lattice, lătt´-ice, *n* treillis *m.*

laudable, loa´-da-b'l, *a* louable.

laugh, lâfe, *v* rire. *n* rire *m;* **–able,** *a* risible; **–ter,**

rires *mpl;* hilarité *f.*

launch, loanntche, *n* (boat) chaloupe *f. v* lancer; **–ing,** *n* lancement *m;* mis à l'eau.

launderette, loann´-deur-rète, *n* laverie *f.*

laundress, loann´-dresse, *n* blanchisseuse *f.*

laundry, loann´-dri, *n* blanchisserie *f.*

laundry powder, loann´-dri-pâ'ou-d'r, *n* lessive *f.*

laurel, lau´-r'l, *n* laurier *m.*

lavatory, lăv´-a-tŏ-ri, *n* lavabo *m;* toilette *f.*

lavender, lăv´-enn-d'r, *n* lavande *f.*

lavish, lăv´-iche, *a** prodigue; somptueux. *v* prodiguer.

law, loa, *n* loi *f;* (jurisprudence) droit *m;* **–ful*,** *a* légal; licite; légitime; **–suit,** *n* procès *m;* **–yer,** avocat *m;* (solicitor) avoué *m.*

lawn, loanne, *n* pelouse *f.*

lax, lăxe, *a* lâche; relâché; mou.

laxative, lăx´-a-tive, *n & a* laxatif *m.*

lay, lé, *v* coucher; placer; mettre; (hen) pondre.

layer, lé´-eur, *n* couche *f.*

layman, lé´-mănne, *n* laïque *m.*

laziness, lé´-zi-nesse, *n* paresse *f.*

lazy, lé´-zi, *a* paresseux.

lead, lèdde, *n* plomb *m;* (pencil) mine *f;* (naut) sonde *f. v* plomber.

lead, lîde, *v* conduire; guider. *n* (dog) laisse *f;* **–ing,** *a* premier; principal.

leader, lîde´-'r, *n* guide *m;* conducteur *m;* chef *m;* **–ship,** direction *f;* conduite *f.*

leaf, lîfe, *n* feuille *f;* (table) rallonge *f.*

leaflet, lîfe´-lett, *n* prospectus *m.*

league, lîgue, *n* ligue *f;* (measurement) lieue *f.*

leak, lîque, *v* fuir; (boats, etc) faire eau. *n* fuite *f.*

lean, lîne, *n & a* maigre *m;* **–against, –on,** *v* s'appuyer; **–out,** se pencher.

leap, lîpe, *v* sauter; bondir. *n* saut *m.*

leap year, lîpe´-i'îre, *n* année bissextile *f.*

learn, leurne, *v* apprendre; **–ed,** *a* savant; **–er,** *n* étudiant *m;* apprenti *m;* **–ing,** (study) étude *f;* (knowledge) savoir *m;* érudition *f.*

lease, lîce, *v* louer. *n* bail *m.*

leash, lîche, *n* laisse *f. v* tenir en laisse.

least, lîste, *adv* le moins. *a* le moindre.

leather, lè*dz*´-'r, *n* cuir *m*; (patent) cuir verni *m*.

leave, lîve, *n* permission *f. v* partir; s'en aller; quitter; abandonner; laisser; (bequeath) léguer; **–out,** omettre; exclure.

lecture, lèque´tioure, *n* conférence *f*; réprimande *f. v* faire une conférence; réprimander.

lecturer, lèque´-tiour-'r, *n* conférencier *m*.

ledge, lèdje, *n* rebord *m*.

leech, lîtche, *n* sangsue *f*.

leek, lîque, *n* poireau *m*.

leer, lîre, *v* lorgner.

left, lefte, *a* & *n* gauche *f*; **–handed,** gaucher.

leg, lègue, *n* jambe *f*; (animal) patte *f*; (mutton, lamb) gigot *m*; (fowl) cuisse *f*; (furniture) pied *m*.

legacy, lègg´-*a*-ci, *n* legs *m*; héritage.

legal,* lî´-g'l, *a* légal; licite; **–ize,** *v* légaliser.

legation, li-gé´-ch'n, *n* légation *f*.

legend, lèdj´-ennde, *n* légende *f*.

legible, lèdj´-i-b'l, *a* lisible.

legion, lî´-dj'n, *n* légion *f*.

legislate, lèdj´-iss-léte, *v* légiférer.

legislation, lèdj-iss-lé´-ch'n, *n* législation *f*.

legitimacy, lidj-itt´-i-ma-ci, *n* légitimité *f*.

legitimate*, lidj-itt´-i-méte, *a* légitime.

leisure, lè´-*jeure, *n* loisir *m*; convenance *f*.

leisurely, lè´-*jeur-li, *adv* à loisir.

lemon, lèmm´-'n, *n* citron *m*; **–ade,** limonade *f*.

lend, lennde, *v* prêter.

length, lenng´-*ts*, *n* longueur *f*; (time) durée *f*; **–en,** *v* allonger; prolonger; **–ways,** *adv* en longueur; **–y,** *a* long, prolongé.

leniency, lî´-ni-enn-ci, *n* indulgence *f*.

lenient, lî´-ni-ennte, *a* indulgent.

lens, lennze, *n* lentille *f*; verre *m*.

Lent, lennte, *n* carême *m*.

lentil, lenn´-t'l, *n* lentille *f*.

leopard, lèp´-*eur*de, *n* léopard *m*.

leper, lèp´-'r, *n* lépreux, -euse *m* & *f*.

leprosy, lèp´-rŏ-si, *n* lèpre *f*.

less, lesse, *adv* moins. *n* & *a* moindre *m*.

lessee, less-î´, *n* locataire *m*.

lessen, less´-'n, *v* diminuer; (pain) alléger.

lesson, less´-'n, *n* leçon *f*.

let, lette, *v* laisser; permettre; (lease) louer.

letter, lett´-'r, *n* lettre *f*.

lettuce, lett´-ice, *n* laitue *f*.

level, lèv´-'l, *n* niveau *m*. *a* de niveau; uni. *v* niveler; (plane) aplanir.

lever, lî´-v'r, *n* levier *m*.

levity, lèv´-i-ti, *n* légèreté *f*.

levy, lèv´-i, *v* (taxes) imposer. *n* impôt *m*; (troops) levée *f*.

lewd*, lioude, *a* impudique.

lewdness, lioude´-nesse, *n* impudicité *f*.

liabilities, lâï-*a*-bil´-i-tèze, *npl* (com) passif *m*.

liability, lâï-*a*-bil´-i-ti, *n* responsabilité *f*.

liable, lâï-*a*-b'l, *a* responsable; **–to,** exposé à; responsable de.

liar, lâï´-*eur*, *n* menteur, -euse *m* & *f*.

libel, lâï´-b'l, *n* diffamation *f. v* diffamer.

libelous, lâï´-bel-*eu*ce, *a*

A
B
C
D
E
F
G
H
I
J
K
L
M
N
O
P
Q
R
S
T
U
V
W
X
Y
Z

diffamatoire.

liberal, lib´-eur'l, *n* & *a** libéral *m.*

liberate, lib´-eur-éte, *v* délivrer; libérer.

liberty, lib´-eur-ti, *n* liberté *f.*

librarian, lâï´-brè´-ri-anne, *n* bibliothécaire *m.*

library, lâï´-bré-ri, *n* bibliothèque *f.*

license, lâï´-cennce, *n* permis *m;* autorisation *f. v* autoriser.

licentious, lâï-cenn´-cheuce, *a* licencieux; libertin.

lichen, lâï´-k'n *n* lichen *m.*

lick, lique, *v* lécher; **–up,** laper.

licorice, lik´-eur-ice, *n* réglisse *f.*

lid, lidde, *n* couvercle *m;* (eye) paupière *f.*

lie, lâï, *n* (untruth) mensonge *m. v* mentir; (in a place, situation) se trouver; **–down,** (repose) se coucher.

lieutenant, lèf-tenn´-annte, *n* lieutenant *m.*

life, lâïfe, *n* vie *f;* (vivacity) vivacité *f;* **– belt,** ceinture de sauvetage *f;* **–boat,** canot de sauvetage *m;*

–insurance, assurance sur la vie *f;* **–less,** *a* inanimé; sans vie; **–like,** naturel; **–long,** de toute la vie; **–size,** grandeur nature; **–time,** *n* cours de la vie *m.*

lift, lifte, *n* ascenseur *m. v* lever; soulever.

light, lâïte, *n* lumière *f;* clarté *f. a** léger; clair *v.* allumer; éclairer; **–en,** alléger; **–er,** *n* briquet *m;* (boat) allège *f;* **–house,** phare *m;* **–ing,** éclairage *m;* **–ness,** légèreté *f.*

lightning, lâïte´-ninng, *n* (flash) éclair *m;* (strike) foudre *f;* **– conductor,** paratonnerre *m.*

like, lâïque, *v* aimer. *a* pareil; égal; **–lihood,** *n* probabilité *f;* **–ly,** *a* probable; **–ness,** *n* ressemblance *f;* **–wise,** *adv* de même.

liking, lâïque´-innng, *n* goût *m;* penchant *m.*

lilac, lâï´-laque, *n* lilas *m.*

lily, lil´-i, *n* lis *m;* **–of the valley,** muguet *m.*

limb, limm, *n* (anatomy) membre *m.*

lime, lâïme, *n* chaux *f;* (birdlime) glu *f;* (fruit) limette *f;* citron vert; (tree) tilleul *m.*

limit, limm´-itte, *n* limite

f. v limiter.

limp, limmpe, *v* boiter. *a* (soft) mou, flasque.

limpet, limm´-pette, *n* patelle *f.*

line, lâïne, *n* ligne *f;* file *f;* queue *f;* (business) partie *f;* (rope) corde *f. v* (garment) doubler.

lineage, linn´-i-idj, *n* lignée *f.*

linen, linn´-enne, *n* toile *f;* (laundry) linge *m.*

liner, lâï´-neur, *n* paquebot *m.*

linger, linn´-gueur, *v* tarder; languir.

linguist, linn´-gouiste, *n* linguiste *m* & *f.*

lining, lâïnn´-inng, *n* doublure *f.*

link, linnque, *v* enchaîner; unir. *n* chaînon *m;* (cuff links) boutons de manchettes *mpl.*

linnet, linn´-ette, *n* linot *m.*

linseed, linn´-cîde, *n* graine de lin *f.*

lion, lâï´-eune, *n* lion *m;* **–ess,** lionne *f.*

lip, lippe, *n* lèvre *f;* **– stick,** rouge à lèvres *m.*

liquefy, lik´-oui-fâï, *v* liquéfier.

liqueur, li-kioure´, *n* liqueur *f.*

liquid, lik´-ouide, n & a liquide m.

liquidate, lik´-oui-déte, v liquider; (debts) acquitter.

liquidation, lik-oui-dé´-ch'n, n liquidation f.

liquor, lik´-eur, n alcool m.

lisp, lisspe, v zézayer. n zézaiement m.

list, lisste, n liste f; (naut) bande f. v (naut) donner de la bande.

listen, liss´-'n, v écouter.

listener, liss´-neur, n auditeur, -euse m & f.

literal*, litt´-eur-al, a littéral.

literary, litt´-eur-a-ri, a littéraire.

literature, litt´-eur-a-tioure, n littérature f.

lithograph, lits´-o-grǎfe, n lithographie f. v lithographier.

litigate, litt´i-guéte, v plaider.

litigation, litt-i-gué´-ch'n, n litige m.

litter, litt´-'r, n (stretcher, stable) litière f; (untidiness) fouillis m; (young) portée f. v (scatter) éparpiller; joncher.

little, lit´-t'l, a (quantity, time) peu de; (size) petit. adv peu.

live, live, v vivre; habiter; (dwell) demeurer.

live, lâïve, a vivant; vif; –ly, animé.

liver, liv´-eur, n foie m.

livid, liv´-ide, a livide.

living, liv´-inng, n vie f; (eccl) bénéfice m. a vivant; –room, n salle de séjour m.

lizard, liz´-eurde, n lézard m.

load, laude, v charger. n charge f.

loaf, laufe, n pain m.

loafer, lau´-feur, n (idler) fainéant m; mocassin m.

loam, laume, n terre glaise f; –y, a glaiseux.

loan, laune, n prêt m; emprunt m.

loathe, laudz, v détester; abhorrer.

loathing, laudz´-inng, n aversion f; dégoût m.

loathsome, laudze´-seume, a répugnant; odieux.

lobby, lob´-i, n antichambre f; couloir m.

lobe, laube, n lobe m.

lobster, lob´-st'r, n homard m.

local*, lau´-k'l, a local; du pays; régional; –ity, n localité f.

locate, lau´-kéte´, v situer; déterminer la position.

location, lau-ké´-ch'n, n emplacement m.

lock, loque, n serrure f; (hair) mèche f; bouche f;(canal, etc) écluse f. v fermer à clef; –et, n médaillon m; –in (or up), v enfermer; –jaw, n tétanos m; –out, v laisser dehors; –smith, n serrurier m.

locomotive, lau´-ko-mau-tive, n locomotive f.

locust, lau´-keusste, n criquet m; locuste f.

lodge, lodje, n loge f. v loger.

lodger, lodj´-'r, n locataire m & f.

lodging, lodj´-inng, n logement m.

loft, lofte, n grenier m; –y, a haut; (fig) hautain.

log, logue, n bûche f; –book,** (ship) journal de bord m.

logic, lodj´-ique, n logique f; –al*, a logique.

loin, lô'ine, n (mutton) filet m (veal) longe f.

loiter, loa'i´-t'r, v flâner; –behind, traîner.

loll, lolle, v se prélasser; (tongue) pendre la langue.

lollipop, loll´-i-poppe, n sucette f.

loneliness, laune´-li-nesse,

n solitude *f.*

lone(ly), laune´(-li), *a* solitaire; isolé.

long, lonng, *a* long. *adv* longtemps; **–for,** *v* désirer ardemment; **–ing,** *n* désir ardent *m.*

longitude, lonn´-dji-tioude, *n* longitude *f.*

look, louk, *n* regard *m. v* regarder; (seem) avoir l'air; **–after,** (take care of) s'occuper de; **–at,** regarder; **–for,** *v* chercher; **–out,** *v* regarder par. *n* (*naut*) vigie *f. interj* gare!

loom, loume, *n* métier *m. v* paraître au loin.

loop, loupe, *n* boucle *f*; **–hole,** (fort, etc) meurtrière *f*; ; échappatoire; **–the loop,** *v* boucler la boucle.

loose, louce, *a* lâche; (tooth) branlante; (morals) relâché; **–n,** *v* relâcher; desserrer.

loot, loute, *n* butin *m. v* piller.

lop, loppe, *v* (prune) élaguer; **–off,** couper.

loquacious, lo-coué´-cheuce, *a* loquace.

Lord, lôrde, *n* (Deity) le Seigneur *m*; Dieu *m.*

Lord's Prayer, lôrdze prè´-eur, *n* Pater *m.*

lose, louze, *v* perdre; (clock) retarder; **–r,** *n* perdant *m.*

loss, losse, *n* perte *f.*

lot, lotte, *n* (auction) lot *m*; (fate) sort *m*; (many) beaucoup.

lotion, lau´-ch'n, *n* lotion *f.*

lottery, lott´-*eur*-i, *n* loterie *f.*

loud*, lâ'oude, *a* fort; haut; (colors) voyant; **–speaker,** *n* (radio) haut-parleur *m.*

lounge, lâ-ounndje, *n* grand vestibule *m*; salon *m. v* flâner.

louse, lâ'ouce, *n* pou *m.*

lout, lâ'oute, *n* rustre *m*; (clumsy) lourdaud *m.*

love, love, *v* aimer. *n* amour *m*; affection *f*; **–liness,** beauté *f*; **–ly,** *a* charmant; **–r,** *n* amoureux *m*; (illicit) amant *m.*

low, lau, *v* mugir. *a* bas; vulgaire; **–er,** *v* baisser; humilier; **–land,** *n* pays plat *m*; terrain bay.

loyal*, lo´-ial, *a* loyal; fidèle; **–ty,** *n* loyauté *f.*

lozenge, loz´-enndje, *n* losange *m*; pastille *f.*

lubricate, lioue´-bri-quéte, *v* lubrifier; graisser.

lucid*, lioue´-cide, *a* lucide.

luck, loque, *n* chance *f*; fortune *f* **–y,** *a* fortuné; veinard.

ludicrous*, lioue´-di-creuce, *a* risible; ridicule.

luggage, logg´-idj, *n* bagages *mpl.*

lukewarm, liouke´-ouârme, *a* tiède.

lull, lolle, *v* endormir; (child) bercer. *n* calme *m.*

lullaby, loll´-*a*-bâï, *n* berceuse *f.*

lumbago, lomm-bé´-go, *n* lumbago *m.*

lumber, lomm´-b'r, *n* (timber) bois de charpente *m.* (old things) vieilleries *fpl.*

luminous*, loue´-minn-*eu*ce, *a* lumineux.

lump, lommpe, *n* morceau *m*; (*med*) grosseur *f*; **–y,** *a* grumeleux.

lunacy, loue´-na-ci, *n* aliénation mentale *f*; folie *f.*

lunar, loue´-n'r, *a* lunaire.

lunatic, loue´na-tique, *n* fou *m*; folle *f.*

lunch, lonntche, *n* déjeuner *m. v* déjeuner.

lung, lonng, *n* poumon *m.*

lurch, leurtche, *n* secousse *f*; (ship) coup de roulis *m;* **to leave in the –,** laisser dans l'embarras.

lure, lioure, *n* leurre *m. v* leurrer; attirer.

lurid, lioue´-ride, *a* (color) blafard.

lurk, leurque, *v* (hide) se cacher.

luscious, loch´-euce, *a* succulent.

lust, losste, *n* luxure *f;* (greed) convoitise *f. v* convoiter; **–ful,** *a* sensuel.

luster, loss´-teur, *n* lustre *m.*

lute, lioute, *n* luth *m.*

luxurious*, lok-siou´-ri-euce, *a* luxueux.

luxury, lok´-seur-i, *n* luxe *m;* somptuosité *f.*

lymph, limmfe, *n* lymphe *f.*

lynch, lintche, *v* lyncher.

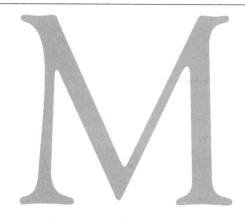

macaroon, măc-*a*-rounne´, *n* macaron *m*.

mace, méce, *n* (staff) masse *f*; massue *f*; (spice) macis; gaz incapacitant *m*.

machine, m*a*-chîne´, *n* machine *f*; **–ry,** mécanisme *m*; **–gun,** mitrailleuse *f*; **sewing,–,** machine à coudre *f*.

machinist, m*a*-chînn´-iste, *n* mécanicien *m*.

mackerel, măc´-r'l, *n* maquereau *m*.

mad, mădde, *a* fou; (dog) enragé; **–man,** *n* aliéné *m*; **–ness,** folie *f*.

madam, măd´-*a*me, *n* madame *f*.

magazine, mă-g*a*-zine´, *n* (periodical) magazine *m*; (gun) magasin *m*;

(powder) poudrière *f*.

maggot, măgg´-*eu*te, *n* ver *m*; larve *f*; asticot *m*.

magic, mădj´-ique, *n* magie *f*. *a* magique.

magistrate, mădj´-iss-tréte, *n* magistrat *m*.

magnanimity, măg´-nă-nimm´-i-ti, *n* magnanimité *f*.

magnanimous*, măg-nănn´-i-m*eu*ce, *a* magnanime.

magnet, măg´-néte, *n* aimant *m*; **–ic,** *a* magnétique. **–ism,** *n* magnétisme *m*; **–ize,** *v* magnétiser; aimanter.

magneto, măg-nî´-tau, *n* magnéto *f*.

magnificent*, măg-nif´-i-cennte, *a* magnifique.

magnify, măg´-ni-fâï, *v*

grossir; **–ing glass,** *n* loupe *f*.

magnitude, măg´-ni-tioude, *n* grandeur *f*; importance *f*.

magpie, măg´-pâï, *n* pie *f*.

mahogany, m*a*-hog´-*a*-ni, *n* acajou *m*.

maid, méde, *n* (young girl) jeune fille *f*; (servant) bonne *f*; **–en,** vierge *f*; **old –,** vieille fille *f*.

mail, méle, *n* (post) courrier *m*; (armor) cotte de mailles *f*. *v* expédier par la poste; **– bag,** *n* sac de poste *m*; **– boat,** paquebot poste *m*.

maim, méme, *v* mutiler.

main, méne, *a** principal; essentiel. *n* (pipe, cable) conduit principal *m*; **–land,** terre ferme *f*.

maintain, méne-téne´, *v* maintenir; soutenir.

maintenance, méne´-t*eu*-n*a*nnce, *n* maintien *m*; soutien *m*.

maize, méze, *n* maïs *m*.

majestic, m*a*-djess´-tique, *a* majestueux.

majesty, mădj´-ess-ti, *n* majesté *f*.

major, mé´-dj*eu*r, *n* (mil) commandant *m*. *a* majeur; **–ity,** *n* majorité *f*.

make, méque, *v* faire;

fabriquer. *n* façon *f*;
marque *f*; **--believe,** *v*
faire semblant; **-r,** *n*
fabricant *m*; **--shift,**
expédient *m*; **-up,** (face)
maquillage *m*. *v*
maquiller.

malady, măl´-*a*-di, *n*
maladie *f*.

malaria, m*a*-lé´-ri-*a*, *n*
paludisme *m*.

male, méle, *n* & *a* mâle *m*.

malediction, m*a*-lè-
dique´-ch'n, *n*
malédiction *f*.

malevolent*, m*a*-lèv´-ŏl-
ennte, *a* malveillant.

malice, măl´-ice, *n* malice
f; malveillance *f*.

malicious*, m*a*-li´-cheu*c*e,
a méchant; malveillant.

malign, m*a*-lâïne´, *v*
diffamer; calomnier.

malignant, m*a*-ligue´-
nannte, *a* malfaisant;
(*med*) malin.

malinger, m*a*-linng´-gue*u*r,
v faire le malade.

malingerer, m*a*-linng´-
gue*u*r-eur, *n* simulateur
m.

mallet, măl´-ette, *n*
maillet *m*.

mallow, măl´-au, *n* mauve
f.

malt, moalte, *n* malt *m*.

maltreat, măl-trîte´, *v*
maltraiter.

mammal, mămm´-'l, *n*
mammifère *m*.

man, mănne, *v* armer. *n*
homme *m*; **-hood,**
virilité *f*; **-kind,** genre
humain *m*; **-ly,** *a* viril;
-slaughter, homicide *m*.

manacle, mănn´-*a*-k'l, *v*
mettre les menottes.

manage, mănn´-idj, *v*
(business) diriger;
(accomplish, control)
parvenir à, arriver à;
-ment, *n* administration
f; gestion *f*; direction *f*;
-r, directeur *m*; gérant
m.

mandate, mănn´-déte, *n*
ordre *m*; (law) mandat
m.

mandolin, mănn´-dau-
linne, *n* mandoline *f*.

mane, méne, *n* (of a horse,
lion) crinière *f*.

maneuver, m*a*-noue´-v'r, *v*
manœuvrer. *n*
manœuvre *f*.

mangle, main´-ng'l, *v*
mutiler. *n* (laundry)
essoreuse *f*. *v* essorer.

mania, mé´-ni-*a*, *n* manie
f; folie *f*.

maniac, mé´-ni-ăque, *n*
fou furieux *m*.

manicure, mănn´-i-
kioure, *v* faire les ongles.

manifest, mănn´-i-feste,
a* manifeste. *v*

manifester.

manifold, mănn´-i-faulde,
a multiple; divers.

manipulate, m*a*-nipp´-
iou-léte, *v* manipuler.

manner, mănn´-'r, *n*
manière *f*; façon *f*.

manners, mănn´-eu*r*ze, *npl*
manières *fpl*.

manor, mănn´-ŏr, *n*
manoir *m*.

mansion, mănn´-ch'n, *n*
(country) château *m*.

mantelpiece, mănn´-t'l-
pîce, *n* cheminée *f*.

manual*, mănn´-iou-'l, *n*
& *a* manuel *m*.

manufacture, mănn-iou-
făc´-tioure, *v* fabriquer. *n*
fabrication *f*; **-r,**
fabricant *m*.

manure, m*a*-nioure´, *v*
fumer. *n* fumier *m*;
engrais *m*.

manuscript, mănn´-iou-
scripte, *n* manuscript *m*.

many, menn´-i, *a*
beaucoup.

map, măppe, *n* carte *f*;
(town) plan *m*.

maple, mé´-p'l, *n* érable *m*.

mar, mâre, *v* gâter;
défigurer.

marble, mâr´-b'l, *n* marbre
m; (toy) bille *f*.

march, mârtche, *v*
marcher. *n* marche *f*.

March, mârtche, *v*

mars *m.*

marchioness, mâr´-cheunn-esse, *n* marquise *f.*

mare, mère, *n* jument *f.*

margarine, mâr´-ga-rinne, *m* margarine *f.*

margin, mâr´-djinne, *n* marge *f.*

marginal*, mâr´-djinn-'l, *a* marginal.

marigold, mar´-i-gaulde, *n* souci *m.*

marine, ma-rîne´, *a* marin. *n* fusilier marin *m.*

mariner, mar´-i-neur, *n* marin *m.*

maritime, mar´-i-tâïmme, *a* maritime.

mark, mârque, *v* marquer. *n* marque *f;* **book—,** signet *m;* **trade—,** marque de fabrique *f.*

market, mâr´-kette, *n* marché *m.*

marmalade, mâr´-meu-léde, *n* confiture d'oranges *f.*

marmot, mâr´-motte, *n* marmotte *f.*

maroon, ma-rouneé, *a* (couleur) bordeaux. *v* abandonner.

marquee, mâr-ki´, *n* (tent) marquise *f.*

marquess, mâr´-couesse, *n* marquis *m.*

marriage, mâr´-idj, *n*

mariage *m.*

married, măr´-idde, *a* marié; **–couple,** *n* ménage *m;* couple *m.*

marrow, măr´-au, *n* moelle *f;* (vegetable) courge *f.*

marry, măr´-i, *v* marier; se marier; épouser.

marsh, mârche, *n* marais *m.*

marshal, mâr´-ch'l, *n* maréchal *m.*

mart, mârte, *n* marché *m;* (auction) salle de ventes *f.*

marten, mâr´-tenne, *n* martre *f.*

martial*, mâr´-ch'l, *a* martial; **court—,***n* conseil de guerre *m;* **–law,** état de siège *m.*

martyr, mâr´-teur, *n* martyr *m. v* martyriser.

martyrdom, mâr´-teur-deume, *n* martyre *m.*

marvel, mâr´-v'l, *n* merveille *f. v* s'émerveiller.

marvelous*, mâr´-veul-euce, *a* merveilleux.

masculine, măss´-kiou-line, *n & a* masculin *m.*

mash, măche, *n* purée *f;* mélange *m. v* écraser.

mask, mâssque, *n* masque *m. v* masquer.

mason, mé´-s'n, *n* maçon

m; **–ry,** *n* maçonnerie *f.*

masquerade, măss-keur-éde´, *v* se déguiser. *n* mascarade *f.*

mass, măsse, *n* masse *f;* (*eccl*) messe *f. v* masser.

massacre, măss´-a-k'r, *n* massacre *m. v* massacrer.

massage, mass-âge´, *n* massage *m. v* masser.

massive*, măss´-ive, *a* massif.

mast, mâste, *n* mât *m.*

master, mâss´-t'r, *v* maîtriser; surmonter. *n* maître *m;* patron *m;* professeur *m;* **–ful*,** impérieux; expert; **–ly,** *a* magistral; **–piece,** *n* chef-d'œuvre *m.*

masticate, măss´-ti-quéte, *v* mastiquer.

mastiff, măss´-tif, *n* mâtin *m.*

mat, mătte, *n* natte *f;* (door) paillasson *m.*

match, mătche, *n* allumette *f;* (contest) match *m. v* assortir; **–less,** *a* incomparable.

mate, méte, *n* camarade *m & f* époux *m;* épouse *f;* second maître *m. v* accoupler.

material, ma-ti´-ri-al, *n* matière *f;* (building, etc) matériaux *mpl;* (cloth) tissu *m.*

materialize, ma-ti´-ri-al-âîze, v matérialiser.

maternal*, ma-teur´-n'l, a maternel.

maternity, ma-teur´-ni-ti, n maternité f.

mathematics, mă-tsi-măt´-ikse, n mathématiques fpl.

matrimony, măt´-ri-mŏn-i, n mariage m.

matrix, mé´-trikse, n matrice f.

matron, mé´-tr'n, n infirmière en chef f.

matter, mătt´-'r, n matière f; (pus) pus m; (business, subject) affaire f. v avoir de l'importance.

matting, mătt´-inng, n natte f; (straw) paillasson m.

mattress, măt´-tress, n matelas m.

mature, ma-tioure´, v mûrir; (bill) échoir. a mûr.

maturity, ma-tiou´-ri-ti, n maturité f; échéance f.

maul, moale, v déchirer à coups de griffes.

mauve, mauve, n & a mauve m.

maxim, măx´-simm, n maxime f.

maximum, măx´-si-momm, n & a maximum m.

may, mé, v pouvoir.

May, mé, n mai m; — flower, aubépine f.

mayor, mè´-eur, n maire m.

maze, méze, n labyrinthe m.

me, mie, pron moi; me.

meadow, mèd´-au, n pré m; prairie f.

meager*, mî´-gueur, a maigre.

meal, mîle, n farine f; (repast) repas m.

mean, mîne, a avare; (action) bas. v avoir l'intention de; vouloir dire; –ing, n signification f; –ingless, a dénué de sens.

means, minn'ze, npl moyens mpl.

meanwhile, mine´-houâîle, adv en attendant.

measles, mîz´-'lz, n rougeole f.

measure, mèj´-eur, n mesure f; (tape) mètre (en ruban) m. v mesurer; –ments, n les mesures fpl.

meat, mîte, n viande f.

mechanic, mi-cănn´-ique, n ouvrier mécanicien m; –al, a mécanique; –s, n mécanique f.

mechanism, mè´-cănn-

izme, n mécanisme m.

medal, mèd´-'l, n médaille f.

meddle, mèd´-'l, v se mêler de.

mediate, mî´-di-éte, v intervenir (en faveur de).

medical*, mèd´-i-k'l, a médical.

medicine, mèd´-cine, n médecine f.

medieval, mèd-i-î´-v'l, a du moyen âge.

mediocre, mî´-di-ô-keur, a médiocre.

meditate, mèd´-i-téte, v méditer.

medium, mî´-di-ŏmme, n moyen m; (person) entremise f; (spiritualist) médium m.

meek*, mîque, a doux; humble.

meet, mîte, v rencontrer; (obligations) remplir.

meeting, mî´-tinng, n rencontre f; réunion f.

melancholy, mèl´-ann-cŏl-i, n mélancolie f.

mellow, mèl´-au, a doux; moelleux.

melodious*, mèl-au´-di-euce, a mélodieux.

melody, mèl´-o-di, n mélodie f.

melon, mèl´-eune, n melon m.

A
B
C
D
E
F
G
H
I
J
K
L
M
N
O
P
Q
R
S
T
U
V
W
X
Y
Z

melt, melte, *v* to fondre.

member, memm´-b'r, *n* membre *m;* **–ship,** sociétariat *m;* les membres dúne société; cotisation *f.*

memento, mi-menn´-to, *n* mémento *m.*

memoir*, memm´-ouâre, *n* mémoire *m.*

memorable, memm´-ŏ-ra-b'l, *a* mémorable.

memorandum, memm-ŏ-rănn´-d'm, *n* note *f;* mémorandum *m.*

memorial, mi-mau´-ri-al, *n* monument commémoratif *m.*

memory, memm´-ŏ-ri, *n* mémoire *f.*

menace, menn´-ace, *v* menacer. *n* menace *f.*

menagerie, mi-nădj´-*eur*-i, *n* ménagerie *f.*

mend, mennde, *v* réparer; (sew) raccommoder.

menial, mî´-ni-al, *a* servile. *n* domestique *m* & *f; a* inférieur; subalterne.

mental*, menn´-t'l, *a* mental.

mention, menn´-ch'n, *v* mentionner. *n* mention *f.*

menu, menn´-iou, *n* menu *m;* carte *f.*

mercantile, meur´-kann-tâïle, *a* mercantile.

merchandise, meur´-tchann-dâïze, *n* marchandise *f.*

merchant, meur´-tch'nt, *n* négociant *m;* marchand *m. a* commercial; (fleet) marchand.

merciful*, meur´-ci-foull, *a* clément; miséricordieux.

mercury, meur´-kiou-ri, *n* mercure *m.*

mercy, meur´-ci, *n* grâce *f;* indulgence *f.*

mere, mîre, *a** pur; simple; seul. *n* lac *m.*

merge, meurdje, *v* fondre; absorber; **–r,** *n* fusion *f.*

meridian, mi-ri´-di-*a*nne, *n* méridien *m. a* méridien.

merit, mair´-itte, *n* mérite *m. v* mériter.

meritorious*, mair-i-tau´-ri-*euc*e, *a* méritoire.

mermaid, meur´-méde, *n* sirène *f.*

merriment, mair´-i-m'nt, *n* gaieté *f;* joie *f.*

merry, mair´-i, *a* joveux.

mesh, maiche, *n* maille *f.*

mesmerize, mez´-*meur*-âïze, *v* hypnotiser.

mess, messe, *n* mess *m;* (dirt) saleté *f;* (spoil) gâchis *m. v* salir.

message, mess´-sédje, *n* message *m.*

messenger, mess´-enn-dj'r, *n* coursier, -ère *m* & *f;* (restaurant, hôtel, etc) chasseur *m.*

metal, mett´-'l, *n* métal *m;* **–lic,** *a* métallique.

meteor, mî´-ti-ŏre, *n* météore *m.*

meter, mî´-teur, *n* compteur *m.*

method, maits´-ŏde, *n* méthode *f.*

metropolis, mi-trop´-ŏ-lice, *n* métropole *f.*

mica, mâï´-ka, *n* mica *m.*

microscope, mâï´-cross-kaupe, *n* microscope *m.*

middle, midd´-'l, *n* centre *m;* milieu *m. a* moyen; **–aged,** *a* d'un certain âge; **–class (es),** *n* (people) classe moyenne *f;* **–man,** intermédiaire *m.*

midge, midje, *n* cousin *m;* moucheron *m.*

midget, midj´-ette, *n* nain, -e *m* & *f.*

midnight, midd´-nâïte, *n* minuit *m.*

midshipman, midd´-chipp-mănne, *n* aspirant de marine *m.*

midwife, midd´-ouâïfe, *n* sage-femme *f.*

mien, mîne, *n* mine *f;* air *m.*

might, mâïte, n force f;
puissance f.

mighty, mâï´-ti, a
puissant; fort.

migrate, mâï´-gréte, v
émigrer.

mild*, mâïlde, a doux;
léger; tempéré.

mildew, mill´-dioue, n
moisissure f.

mile, mâïle, n mille m;
–stone, borne f.

military, mil´-i-ta-ri, n &
a militaire m.

milk, milque, n lait m. v
traire; **–y,** a laiteux; **–y
way,** n voie lactée f.

mill, mill, n moulin m;
–er, meunier m.

milliner, mill´-i-n'r, n
modiste f; **–y,** modes fpl.

million, mill´ieune, n
million m.

millionaire, mill´ionn-air,
n millionnaire m.

mimic, mimm´-ique, v
mimer. n mime m.

mince, minnce, v hacher;
(words) mâcher.

mind, mâïnnde, n esprit
m; opinion f. v faire
attention à; (nurse)
soigner; **–ful,** a attentif.

mine, mâïne, poss pron le
mien, la mienne; les
miens, les miennes; à
moi.

mine, mâïne, n mine f. v

miner; **–r,** n mineur m.

mineral, minn´-eur-al, n
& a minéral m.

mingle, minng´-g'l, v
mélanger; se mêler.

miniature, minn´-i-a-
tioure, n miniature f.

minimize, minn´-i-mâïze,
v réduire; diminuer.

minister, minn´-iss-t'r, n
pasteur m.

ministry, minn´-iss-tri, n
ministère m.

mink, minque, n vison m.

minor, mâï´-neur, n
mineur, -e m & f. a
mineur.

minority, minn-or´-i-ti, n
minorité f.

minstrel, minn´-str'l, n
ménestrel m.

mint, minnte, n la
Monnaie f; (plant)
menthe f. v frapper de la
monnaie.

minuet, minn´-iou-ette, n
menuet m.

minus, mâï´-neuce, a &
adv moins. prep sans.

minute, minn´-itte, n
minute f.

minute, mâïn-ioute´, a
menu; (exact)
minutieux.

miracle, mir´-a-k'l, n
miracle m.

miraculous*, mi-răk´-iou-
leuce, a miraculeux.

mirage, mi-râge´, n mirage
m.

mire, mâïre, n fange f;
boue f; bourbe f.

mirror, mir´-eur, n miroir
m. v refléter.

mirth, meurts, n gaieté f;
hilarité f.

mis, miss, **–adventure,** n
mésaventure f;
–apprehension,
malentendu m;
–appropriate, v
détourner; **–behave,** se
conduire mal; **–carriage,**
n (med) fausse couche f;
–carry, v échouer; (med)
faire une fausse couche;
–conduct, n mauvaise
conduite f;
–construction,
mésinterprétation f;
–count, v mal compter;
–demeanor, (law) délit
m; **–direct,** v mal diriger;
–fortune, malheur m;
calamité f; **–giving,**
crainte f; **–govern,** v mal
gouverner; **–guide,**
égarer; (fig) mal
conseiller; **–hap,** n
contretemps m; accident
m; **–inform,** v mal
renseigner; **–judge,** mal
juger; **–lay,** égarer;
–lead, tromper;
–manage, mal gérer;
–place, mal placer;

a
b
c
d
e
f
g
h
i
j
k
l
m
n
o
p
q
r
s
t
u
v
w
x
y
z

–**print,** n faute d'impression f; –**pronounce,** v mal prononcer; –**represent,** fausser; –**statement,** n rapport inexact m; –**take,** v se tromper. n erreur f; –**taken,** a erroné; –**trust,** v se méfier de. n méfiance f; –**understand,** v mal comprendre; –**understanding,** n malentendu m; –**use,** v abuser de.

miscellaneous, miss-s'l-lé´-ni-euce, a varié; divers.

mischief, miss´-tchife, n mal m; dommage m; (of child) bêtise f.

mischievous*, miss´-tchi-veuce, a malicieux.

miser, mâï´-z'r, n avare m & f; –**ly,** a mesquin.

miserable, miz´-eur-a b'l, a misérable; triste.

misery, miz´-eur-i, n misère f; tourment m.

Miss, mice, n mademoiselle f.

miss, mice, v manquer; (someone's absence) regretter; –**ing,** a absent; perdu; manquant.

missile, miss´-âïl, n projectile m.

mission, mich´-eune, n mission f.

missionary, mich´-eune-ri, n (eccl) missionaire m & f.

mist, miste, n brume f, –**y,** a brumeux.

Mister, (Mr), miss´teur, n monsieur m.

mistletoe, miss´-s'l-tau, n gui m.

mistress, miss´-tresse, n madame f; (school) maîtresse f; (kept) maîtresse f.

miter, mâï´-teur, n mitre f.

mitigate, mit´-i-guéte, v adoucir; mitiger.

mix, mixe, v mêler; mélanger; (salad) tourner; –**ed,** a mixte; –**ture,** n mélange m.

moan, maune, v gémir; grogner; n gémissement m.

moat, maute, n fossé m.

mob, mobbe, n foule f; bande f. clique f; bande (f) de gangsters. v houspiller; (enthusiasm) presser par la foule.

mobile, mô´-bâïle, a & n mobile m.

mobilize, môb´-il-âïze, v mobiliser.

mock, moque, v se moquer. a simulé; faux; –**ery,** n moquerie f; –**ingly,** adv en se moquant.

mode, maude, n manière f; (fashion) mode f.

model, modd´-'l n modèle m; (fashion) mannequin m. v modeler.

moderate, modd´-eur-éte, v modérer. a* modéré; passable.

moderation, modd-eur-é´-ch'n, n modération f.

modern, modd´eurne, a moderne.

modest*, modd´este, a modeste.

modify, modd´-i-fâï, v modifier.

Mohammedan, mô-hamm´-é-danne, n & a mahométan, -e m & f.

moist, moa'isste, a moite, humide; –**en,** v humecter; –**ure,** n humidité f.

mold, maulde, v mouler. n moule m; (mildew) moisissure f; (earth) terreau m; –**er,** mouleur m; –**ing,** moulure f; –**y,** a moisi.

mole, maule, n taupe f; (mark) grain de beauté m; (jetty) môle m; –**hill,** taupinière f.

molest, mo-leste´, v molester.

mollify, moll´-i-fâï, v adoucir.

molten, maule´-t'n, *a* fondu; en fusion.

moment, mau´-m'nt, *n* moment *m*; **–ous,** *a* important; mémorable.

momentum, mau-menn´-tomme, *n* (impetus) impulsion *f*.

monarch, monn´-*eu*rque, *n* monarque *m*.

monarchy, monn´-*eu*r-ki, *n* monarchie *f*.

monastery, monn´-*a*ss-tri, *n* monastère *m*.

Monday, monn´-dé, *n* lundi *m*.

monetary, monn´-*eu*-ta-ri, *a* monétaire.

money, monn´-i, *n* argent *m*; (coin) monnaie *f*; **– lender,** prêteur d'argent *m*; **–order,** mandat-poste *m*.

mongrel, monng´-gr'l, *n* & *a* bâtard, -e *m* & *f*.

monk, monng´-k, *n* moine *m*.

monkey, monng´-ki, *n* singe *m*.

monocle, monn´-o-k'l, *n* monocle *m*.

monogram, monn´-ô-grămme, *n* monogramme *m*.

monopolize, mŏnn-op´-ŏ-lâïze, *v* monopoliser.

monopoly, mŏnn-op´-ŏ-li, *n* monopole *m*.

monotonous*, mŏnn-ot´-nŏ-n*eu*ce, *a* monotone.

monster, monn´-st'r, *n* monstre *m*.

monstrous*, monn´-stre*u*ce, *a* monstrueux.

month, monn*t*s, *n* mois *m*; **–ly,** *a* mensuel.

monument, monn´-iou-m'nt, *n* monument *m*.

mood, moude, *n* humeur *f*; (grammar) mode *m*.

moody, moud´-i, *a* d'humeur changeante.

moon, moune, *n* lune *f*; **–light,** clair de lune *m*.

Moor, mou'r, *n* Maure *m*; **–ish,** *a* mauresque.

mop, moppe, *n* balai à laver *m*. *v* éponger.

mope, maupe, *v* s'attrister; s'ennuyer.

moral, mor´*a*l, *n* morale *f*. *a** moral; **–ity,** *n* moralité *f*; **–s,** mœurs *fpl*; moralité *f*.

morale, mo-râl´, *n* moral *m*.

morass, mo-răce´, *n* marécage *m*; marais *m*.

moratorium, môr-*a*-tô´-ri-*o*mme, *n* moratorium *m*.

morbid*, môr´-bidde, *a* morbide.

more, môre, *a* & *adv* plus; plus de; davantage; encore.

moreover, môr-au´-v'r, *adv* en outre; de plus.

morning, môr´-ninng, *n* matin *m*; (period) matinée *f*; **good –,** bonjour.

morocco, mo-rok´-au, *n* (leather) maroquin *m*.

morose*, mŏ-rauce´, *a* morose.

morphine, moar´-fi-a, *n* morphine *f*.

morsel, môr´s'l, *n* morceau *m*.

mortal, môr´-t'l, *n* & *a** mortel, -elle *m* & *f*; **–ity,** mortalité *f*.

mortar, môr´-t'r, *n* mortier *m*.

mortgage, môr´-guédje, *n* hypothèque *f*. *v* hypothéquer; **–e,** *n* créancier hypothécaire *m*; **–r,** débiteur hypothécaire *m*.

mortification, môr´-ti-fi-qué´-ch'n, *n* mortification *f*.

mortify, môr´-ti-fäï, *v* mortifier.

mortuary, môr´-tiou-*a*-ri, *n* morgue *f*.

mosaic, mô-zé´-ique, *n* & *a* mosaïque *f*.

mosque, mosske, *n* mosquée *f*.

mosquito, moss-kî´-tau, *n* moustique *m*.

moss, moss, *n* mousse *f*.

A B C D E F G H I J K L **M** N O P Q R S T U V W X Y Z

most, mauste, *adv* extrêmement, le plus. *n* la plupart *f*; **–ly,** *adv* principalement.

moth, mot*z*, *n* papillon de nuit *m*; (clothes) mite *f*.

mother, m*odz´*-*eur*, *n* mère *f*; **–hood,** maternité *f*; **–in-law,** belle-mère *f*; **–of-pearl,** nacre *f*; **–ly,** *a* maternel.

motion, mau´-ch'n, *n* mouvement *m*.

motionless, mau´-ch'n-lesse, *a* immobile.

motive, mau´-tive, *n* motif *m*. *a* moteur.

motor, mau´-t'r, *n* moteur *m*; **–-car,** automobile *f*; **–-cycle,** motocyclette *f*; **–ing,** automobilisme *m*; **–ist,** automobiliste *m* & *f*.

mottled, mot´-t'ld, *a* bigarré.

motto, mot´-tau, *n* devise *f*.

mound, mâ'ounnde, *n* monticule *m*.

mount, mâ'ounnte, *n* mont *m*; (horse, jewels) monture *f*; (picture) cadre *m*. *v* monter.

mountain, mâ'ounn´-tinne, *n* montagne *f*; **–eer,** montagnard, -e *m* & *f*; **–ous,** *a* montagneux.

mourn, môrne, *v* se lamenter; pleurer; **–ful*,** *a* triste; lugubre; **–ing,** *n* deuil *m*.

mouse, mâ'ouce, *n* souris *f*; **–trap,** souricière *f*.

moustache, mousse-tache´, *n* moustache *f*.

mouth, mâ'outs, *n* bouche *f*; gueule *f*; (river) embouchure *f*; **–ful,** bouchée *f*; **–piece,** embouchure *f*; (*fig*) porte-parole *m*.

movable, moue´-va-b'l, *a* mobile.

move, mouve, *v* mouvoir; (house) déménager; (fidget) se remuer; (stir) bouger. *n* mouvement *m*; (*fig*) coup *m*.

mow, mau, *v* faucher; (lawn) tondre.

mower, mau´-*eur*, *n* tondeuse *f*.

much, motche, *adv* beaucoup; **how** –? combien?

mud, modde, *n* boue *f*; **–dy,** *a* boueux.

muddle, modd´-'l, *n* confusion *f*; fouillis *m*. *v* embrouiller.

muff, moffe, *n* manchon *m*; **–le,** *v* (sound) étouffer; (cover) emmitoufler; **–ler,** *n* écharpe *f*.

mug, mogue, *n* gobelet *m*; pot *m*.

Muhammadan, mô-hamm´-é-danne, *n* & *a* Mahometan, -e *m* & *f*.

mulberry, moll´-bèr-î, *n* mûre *f*; **–tree,** mûrier *m*.

mule, mioule, *n* mulet *m*; mule *f*.

mullet, mol´-ette, *n* mulet *m*; **red** –,rouget *m*.

multiplication, mole´-ti-pli-qué´-ch'n, *n* multiplication *f*.

multiply, moll´-ti-plaï, *v* multiplier.

multitude, moll´-ti-tioude, *n* multitude *f*.

mummy, momm´-i, *n* momie *f*.

mumps, mommpse, *npl* oreillons *mpl*.

munch, monntche, *v* mâcher; (crunch) croquer.

municipal, miou-niss´-i-p'l *a* municipal.

munition, miou-ni´-ch'n, *n* munition *f*.

murder, meur´-d'r, *v* assassiner. *n* assassinat *m*; **–er,** assassin *m*; **–ous,** *a* meurtrier.

murky, meur´-ki, *a* obscur; ténébreux.

murmur, meur´-m'r, *v* murmurer. *n*

murmure *m.*

muscle, m*o*ss´-'l, *n* muscle *m.*

muse, miouze, *v* musarder; méditer. *n* muse *f.*

museum, mioue-zî´-omme, *n* musée *m.*

mushroom, m*o*che´-roumme, *n* champignon *m.*

music, mi'oue´-zique, *n* musique *f;* –**al,** *a* musical.

musician, mi'oue-zi´-ch'n, *n* musicien, -enne *m* & *f.*

musk, m*o*ssque, *n* musc *m.*

muslin, m*o*ze´-linne, *n* mousseline *f.*

mussel, m*o*ss´-'l, *n* moule *f.*

must, m*o*ste, *v* devoir; falloir.

mustard, m*o*ss´-t'rd, *n* moutarde *f.*

muster, m*o*ss´-t'r, *v* rassembler; (*mil*) faire l'appel.

musty, m*o*ss´-ti, *a* moisi.

mute, mioute, *n* & *a* muet, -ette *m* & *f.*

mutilate, mioue´-ti-léte, *v* mutiler.

mutineer, mioue-ti-nîre´, *n* mutin *m;* révolté *m.*

mutinous, mioue´-ti-n*euce,* *a* en révolte.

mutiny, mioue´-ti-ni, *n*

mutinerie *f. v* se mutiner *m.*

mutt, meutt, *n* corniaud (chien) *m.*

mutter, m*o*tt´-'r, *v* marmotter.

mutual*, mioue´-tiou-*al,* *a* mutuel.

muzzle, m*o*zz´-'l, *n* (for dogs, etc) muselière *f;* (snout) museau *m;* (gun) bouche *f. v* museler.

my, mâï, *poss a* mon; ma; mes; –**self,** *pron* moi-même.

myrtle, meur´-t'l, *n* myrte *f.*

mysterious*, miss-tî´-ri-*euce,* *a* mystérieux.

mystery, miss´-t*eur*-i, *n* mystère *m.*

mystify, miss´-ti-fâï, *v* mystifier.

myth, mits, *n* mythe *m;* –**ology,** mythologie *f.*

a
b
c
d
e
f
g
h
i
j
k
l
m
n
o
p
q
r
s
t
u
v
w
x
y
z

N

nag, năgue, *v* gronder; harceler. *n* canasson *m.*

nail, néle, *n* (metal) clou *m;* (human) ongle *m. v* clouer; **–-brush,** *n* brosse à ongles *f;* **–-file,** lime à ongles *f.*

naive*, nâ-ive´, *a* naïf.

naked, né´-kedde, *a* nu; (trees, etc) dépouillé.

name, néme, *v* appeler; (specify) nommer. *n* nom *m;* **Christian –,**prénom *m;* **last –,** nom de famille *m;* **–less,** *a* anonyme; **–ly,** *adv* à savoir; **–sake,** *n* homonyme *m.*

nap, năppe, *n* (sleep) somme *m;* (cloth) poil *m.*

nape, népe, *n* nuque *f.*

naphtha, năph´-*ts*a, *n* naphte *m.*

napkin, năpp´-kinne, *n* serviette *f.*

narcissus, năr-siss´-*eu*ce, *n* narcisse *m.*

narcotic, nâr-cott´-ique, *n* & *a* narcotique *m.*

narrative, năr´-*ra*-tive, *n* narration *f.*

narrow, năr´-au, *v* rétrécir. *a** étroit; **–-minded,** étroit d'esprit; **–ness,** *n* étroitesse *f.*

nasal*, né´-z'l, *a* nasal.

nasturtium, n*a*ss-teur´-ch'm, *n* capucine *f.*

nasty, nâsse´-ti, *a* méchant; (*fig*) mauvais; (dirty) sale.

nation, né´-ch'n, *n* nation *f;* pays *m.*

national, năch´-*eu*nn-'l, *a* national.

nationality, năch-*eu*nn-al´-i-ti, *n* nationalité *f.*

native, né´-tive, *n* & *a* natif, -ive *m* & *f,* indigène *m* & *f. a* natal (**my native country,** mon pays natal).

natural*, năt´-tiou-r'l, *a* naturel.

naturalization, năt´-tiou-ral-âï-zé´-ch'n, *n* naturalisation *f.*

nature, nét´-tioure, *n* nature *f.*

naught, noate, *n* rien *m;* zéro *m.*

naughty, noa´-ti, *a* vilain; pas sage.

nauseous, nô´-si-*eu*ce, *a* nauséabond; écœurant.

nautical, nô´-ti-k'l, *a* nautique.

naval, né´-v'l, *a* naval; maritime; **–officer,** officier de marine *m.*

navel, né´-v'l, *n* nombril *m.*

navigate, nă´-vi-guéte, *v* naviguer.

navigation, nă-vi-gué´-ch'n, *n* navigation *f.*

navigator, năv´-i-gué-t*eu*r, *n* navigateur *m.*

navy, né´-vi, *n* marine *f;* **–blue,** *a* bleu marine.

near, nîeuz, *a* proche. *prep* près de. *adv* près. *v* s'approcher de; **–ly,** *adv* presque; **–ness,** n proximité f; **––sighted,** n & a myope m & f.

neat, nîte, a (spruce) soigné; (dainty) délicat; (tidy) rangé; (not diluted) pur.

neatness, nîte´-ness, n netteté f; (clean) propreté f.

necessarily, nèss´-ess-a-ri-li, adv nécessairement.

necessary, nèss´-ess-a-ri, a nécessaire.

necessitate, ni-sess´-i-téte, v nécessiter.

necessity, ni-sess´-i-ti, n nécessité f.

neck, nèque, n cou m; (bottle) goulot m; **–lace,** collier m; **––tie,** cravate f.

need, nîde, v avoir besoin de. n besoin m; **–ful*,** a nécessaire; **–less*,** inutile; **–y,** nécessiteux.

needle, nî´-d'l, n aiguille f.

negation, ni-gué´-ch'n, n négation f.

negative, negg´-a-tive, n négative f. a* négatif.

neglect, nig-lecte´, v négliger. n négligence f.

negligence, negg´-li-djennce, n négligence f.

negligent, negg´-li-dj'nt, a négligent.

negotiate, ni-gau´-chi-éte,

v négocier.

negotiation, ni-gau´-chi-é´-ch'n, n négociation f.

neigh, né, v hennir. n hennissement m.

neighbor, nè´-b'r, n voisin m; **–hood,** voisinage m; **–ly,** a bon voisin.

neither, nâï´-dz'r, pron & a ni l'un ni l'autre. adv non plus;**–... nor,** conj ni...ni.

nephew, név´-iou, n neveu m.

nerve, neurve, n nerf m; (fam) (pluck, etc) sang froid m; (fig) (cheek) audace f.

nervous*, neur´-veuce, a nerveux; timide; excitable.

nest, nesste, n nid m. v nicher.

nestle, ness´-'l, v se nicher; se blottir.

net, nett, n filet m. a (weight, etc) net.

nettle, nett´-'l, n ortie f.

network, nett´-oueurque, n réseau m.

neuralgia, nioue-rall´-dji-a, n névralgie f.

neuter, nioue´-teur, n & a neutre m.

neutral, nioue´-tr'l, a neutre.

never, nèv´-'r, adv (ne)...jamais; **–more,**

plus jamais; **–theless,** adv néanmoins.

new, nioue, a neuf; nouveau; frais; **–year,** n nouvel an m; **–Year's Day,** jour de l'an m.

news, niouze, npl nouvelles fpl; (radio, TV) informations fpl; **–agent,** marchand de journaux m; **–paper,** journal m.

next, nexte, a prochain (of future time); suivant (of past time); (beside) à côté, voisin. adv ensuite.

nib, nibbe, n plume f.

nibble, nib´-b'l, v grignoter; (rats, etc) ronger.

nice*, nâïce, a agréable; sympathique; (fam) aimable; (subtle) scrupuleux.

nickel, nique´-'l, n nickel m; 5 "cents".

nickname, nique´-néme, n surnom m.

nicotine, nique´-ô-tinne, n nicotine f.

niece, nîce, n nièce f.

night, nâïte, n nuit f; **––gown,** chemise de nuit f; **–fall,** tombée de la nuit f; **–ingale,** rossignol m; **–ly,** adv tous les soirs; **–mare,** n cauchemar m.

nimble, nimm´-b'l, a leste; agile; vif.

a
b
c
d
e
f
g
h
i
j
k
l
m
n
o
p
q
r
s
t
u
v
w
x
y
z

nine, nâïne, *n* & *a* neuf *m*; *m* & *a* –**teen,** dix-neuf *m*; *m* & *a* –**teenth,** dix-neuvième *m* & *f*; –**tieth,** *m* & *a* quatrevingt-dixième *m* & *f*; –**ty,** *m* & *a* quatre-vingt-dix *m*.

ninth, nâïnnts, *n* & *a* neuvième *m* & *f*.

nip, nippe, *v* pincer; filer; –**off,** couper (le bout de).

nipple, nip´-p'l, *n* mamelon *m*; têtine *f*.

nitrate, nâï´-tréte, *n* nitrate *m*.

nitrogen, nâï´-trô-dj'n, *n* azote *m*; nitrogène *m*.

no, nau, *adv* non; pas; ne ... pas. *a* aucun.

nobility, no-bil´-i-ti, *n* noblesse *f*.

noble, nau´-b'l, *n* noble *m*. *a* noble; généreux.

nobody, nau´-bŏdd-i, *n* personne sans importance *f*. *pron* personne.

nod, nodde, *v* faire un signe de tête. *n* signe de tête *m*.

noise, noa'ize, *n* bruit *m*; –**less*,** *a* silencieux.

noisily, noa'iz´-i-li, *adv* bruyamment.

noisy, noa´'-i-zi, *a* bruyant; tapageur.

nominal*, nomm´-i-n'l, *a* nominal.

nominate, nomm´-i-néte, *v* nommer; proposer.

nominee, nomm-i-nî´, *n* personne désignée *f*.

non, nonne, –-**commissioned officer,** *n* sous- officier *m*; –**plussed,** *a* confus; dérouté; –**sense,** *n* absurdité *f*; –-**stop,** *a* continu; (train, etc) direct.

nook, nouk, *n* coin *m*.

noon, noune, *n* midi *m*.

noose, nouce, *n* nœud coulant *m*.

normal*, nôr´-m'l, *a* normal.

north, nôrts, *n* nord *m*; –**erly,** *adv* au nord. *a* du nord.

nose, nauze, *n* nez *m*.

nostril, noss´-tr'l, *n* narine *f*; naseau (of a horse, etc.) *m*.

not, notte, *adv* ne ... pas; ne ... point; pas.

notable, naute´-a-b'l, *a* notable; insigne.

notary, naute´-a-ri, *n* notaire *m*.

notch, notche, *v* entailler. *n* entaille *f*; coche *f*.

note, naute, *v* noter; remarquer. *n* note *f*; (currency) billet de banque *m*; –-**book,**

carnet *m*; –**d,** *a* fameux; célèbre; –-**paper,** *n* papier à lettres *m*; –**worthy,** *a* digne de remarque.

nothing, no´-tsinng, *n* rien *m*; **for** –, *adv* en vain.

notice, nau´-tice, *v* remarquer; faire attention; observer. *n* avis *m*; affiche *f*; (to quit, to give notice) donner congé *m*; –**able,** *a* perceptible.

notify, nau´-ti-fâï, *v* notifier; signaler.

notion, nau´-ch'n, *n* notion *f*; idée *f*.

notoriety, nau-tŏ-râï´-è-ti, *n* notoriété *f*.

notorious, nau-tau´-ri-euce, *a* notoire; insigne.

notwithstanding, nott-ouidz-stănnd´-inng, *prep* & *conj* néanmoins; malgré.

noun, na'oune, *n* nom *m*; substantif *m*.

nourish, nor´-iche, *v* nourrir; –**ing,** *a* nourrissant; –**ment,** *n* nourriture *f*.

novel, nov´-'l, *n* roman *m*. *a* nouveau; –**ist,** *n* romancier *m*; –**ty,** nouveauté *f*; innovation *f*.

November, no-vemm´-b'r,

n novembre *m.*

novice, nov´-ice, *n* novice *m* & *f.*

now, nâ'ou, *adv* maintenant; **–adays,** de nos jours; **–and then,** de temps en temps.

nowhere, nau´-houère, *adv* nulle part.

noxious, noque´-che*u*ce, *a* nuisible; pernicieux.

nozzle, noz´-z'l, *n* bout *m;* lance (de tuyau) *f.*

nuclear, nioue´-kl-îr, *a* nucléaire.

nucleus, nioue´-kli-*eu*ce, *n* noyau *m.*

nude, nioude, *n* & *a* nu *m.*

nudge, nodje, *v* & *n* coup de coude *m.*

nugget, n*o*gg´-itte, *n* pépite *f.*

nuisance, nioue´-s'nce, *n* (annoyance) plaie *f;* (bother) ennui *m.*

null, n*o*lle, *a* nul; **–ify,** *v* annule.

numb, n*o*mme, *a* engourdi. *v* engourdir; **–ness,** *n* engourdissement *m.*

number, n*o*mm´-b'r, *n* nombre *m;* (of a series) numéro *m. v* numéroter; **–less,** *a* innombrable.

numerous, nioue´-me*u*r-*eu*ce, *a* nombreux.

nun, n*o*nne, *n* nonne *f;* religieuse *f.*

nuptial, n*o*pp´-ch'l, *a* nuptial; **–s,** *npl* noces *fpl.*

nurse, ne*u*rce, *n* infirmière *f;* (male) infirmier *m. v* soigner; (suckle) nourrir; **–ry school,** *n* maternelle *f;* (plants, etc) pépinière *f;* **–ry rhyme,** conte de nourrice *m.*

nurture, noitshoi, *v* élever; s'occuper de; nourire. *n* nouriture *f.*

nut, n*o*tte, *n* noix *f;* (hazel) noisette *f;* (pea) cacahuète *f;* (*mech*) écrou *m;* **–-cracker,** casse-noisettes *m;* **–meg,** muscade *f;* **–-shell,** coquille de noix *f.*

nutriment, nioue´-tri-m'nt, *n* nourriture *f.*

nutritious, nioue-tri´-che*u*ce, *a* nutritif.

nuzzle, noze*u*l, *v* fouiner; fourrer son nez.

nylon, nâï´-lonn, *n* nylon *m.*

a
b
c
d
e
f
g
h
i
j
k
l
m
n
o
p
q
r
s
t
u
v
w
x
y
z

A B C D E F G H I J K L M N **O** P Q R S T U V W X Y Z

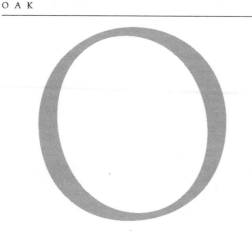

oak, auque, n chêne m.

oar, ore, n rame f; aviron m; **–sman,** rameur de pointe m.

oasis, au-é´-cisse, n oasis f.

oat, aute, n avoine f; **–meal,** farine d'avoine m.

oath, auts, n serment m; (profane) juron m.

obdurate*, ob´-diou-réte, a endurci; obstiné.

obedience, o-bî´-di-ennce, n obéissance f.

obedient*, o-bî´-di-ennte, a obéissant.

obese, au-bîce´, a obèse.

obesity, au-bîs´-i-ti, n obésité f.

obey, o-bé´, v obéir.

obituary, o-bit´-iou-a-ri, n nécrologie f. a nécrologique.

object, ob-djecte´, v protester; s'opposer à.

object, ob´-djecte, n objet m; (aim) but m; (grammar) complément m; **–ion,** objection f; **–ionable,** a répréhensible; **–ive,** n & a objectif m.

obligation, o-bli-gé´-ch'n, n obligation f.

obligatory, ob´-lî-ga-to-ri, a obligatoire.

oblige, o-blâïdje´, v obliger; (favor) rendre service.

obliging*, o-blâïdj´-inng, a obligeant.

obliterate, ob-litt´-eur-éte, v effacer.

oblivion, ob-liv´-i-eune, n oubli m.

oblivious, ob-liv´-i-euce, a oublieux.

oblong, ob´-lonng, a oblong. n rectangle m.

obnoxious*, ob-noque´-cheuce, a odieux; insupportble; repoussant.

obscene*, ob-cîne´, a obscène.

obscure, ob-skioure´, v obscurcir. a* obscur.

observant, ob-zeur´-v'nt, n & a observateur m.

observation, ob-zeur-vé´-ch'n, n observation f.

observatory, ob-zeur´-va-tŏ-ri, n observatoire m.

observe, ob-zeurve´, v observer; remarquer.

obsolete, ob´-sôlîte, a suranné; hors d'usage.

obstacle, ob´-stă-k'l, n obstacle m.

obstinacy, ob´-sti-na-ci, n obstination f; opiniâtreté f.

obstinate, ob´-sti-néte, a entêté; obstiné.

obstruct, ob-strocte´, v encombrer; (hinder) empêcher; **–ion,** n encombrement m.

obtain, ob-téne´, v obtenir; se procurer.

obtrude, ob-troude´, v s'imposer.

obtrusive*, ob-trouce´-cive, a importun.

obvious*, ob´-vi-*euce*, *a* évident; clair.

occasion, o-qué´-j'n, *n* occasion *f*; **–al,** *a* occasionnel; **–ally,** *adv* de temps en temps.

occult, ok´-kolte, *a* occulte; secret.

occupation, ok-kiou-pé´-ch'n *n* occupation *f*.

occupier, ok´-kiou-pâï-*eur*, *n* occupant *m*; (tenant) locataire *m* & *f*.

occupy, ok´-kiou-pâï, *v* de occuper; s'occuper (to be occupied in).

occur, ok-keure´, *v* (to the mind) venir à l'esprit; (happen) arriver; (opportunity) se présenter.

occurrence, ok-keur´-ennse, *n* événement *m*.

ocean, au´-ch'n, *n* océan *m*.

ocher, ô´-*keur*, *n* ocre *f*.

octagon, ok´-*ta*-gonne, *n* octogone *m*.

octagonal, ok-ta´-gonn-*al*, *a* octogonal.

octave, ok´-téve, *n* octave *f*.

October, ok-tau´-b'r, *n* octobre *m*.

octopus, ok´-tau-*peuce*, *n* pieuvre *f*; poulpe *m*.

oculist, ok´-iou-liste, *n* oculiste *m*.

odd, odde, *a* (number) impair; (single) dépareillé; (strange) étrange; **–ly,** *adv* singulièrement; **–s,** *npl* (betting) chances *fpl*; **–s and ends,** bricoles *fpl*.

odious*, au´-di-*euce*, *a* odieux; détestable.

odium, au´-di-*eume*, *n* odieux *m*; (hatred) haine *f*.

odor, o´-d'r, *n* odeur *f*; (sweet) parfum *m*.

of, ove, *prep* de; (among) parmi.

off, of, *adv* loin; à distance. *prep* de.

offal, of´-f'l, *n* abats *mpl*; (refuse) rebut *m*.

offend, of-fennde´, *v* offenser.

offense, of-fennce´, *n* offense *f*; (law) délit *m*.

offensive, of-fenn´-cive, *a** offensif. *n* offensive *f*.

offer, of´-f'r, *v* offrir. *n* offre *f*; **–ing,** offrande *f*.

office, of´-ice, *n* bureau *m*; fonctions publiques *fpl*.

officer, of´-iss-'r, *n* (mil) officier *m*.

official, of-ich´-'l, *n* fonctionnaire *m*. *a** officiel.

officious*, of-ich´-*euce*, *a* officieux.

offspring, of´-sprinng, *n* descendant *m*.

oft, often, ofte, of´-'n, *adv* souvent; fréquemment.

ogle, au´-g'l, *v* lorgner.

oil, oa'ile, *n* huile *f*. *v* lubrifier; **–cloth,** *n* toile cirée *f*.

ointment, ô'innte´-m'nt, *n* pommade *f*.

old, aulde, *a* vieux; âgé; antique; ancien.

old-fashioned, aulde-fâch´-*eun*'d, *a* démodé.

olive, ol´-ive, *n* olive *f*; **– oil,** huile d'olive *f*.

omelette, omm´-lette, *n* omelette *f*.

omen, au´-menne, *n* augure *m*; présage *m*.

ominous*, o´-mi-*neuce*, *a* de mauvais augure.

omission, o-mîch´-'n, *n* omission *f*, oubli *m*.

omit, o-mitte´, *v* omettre.

omnipotent, omm-nip´-o-tennte, *a* tout-puissant.

on, onne, *prep* en; à; sur. *adv* (upon) dessus; (onward) en avant; (date) le; **–foot,** à pied.

once, ou'onnce, *adv* une fois; (formerly) autrefois; **all at –,** tout d'un coup; **at –,** tout de suite; **–more,** encore une fois.

one, ou'onne, *n* & *a* un *m*; une *f*; *pron*

a
b
c
d
e
f
g
h
i
j
k
l
m
n
o
p
q
r
s
t
u
v
w
x
y
z

(impersonal) on.

onerous*, onn´-*eur*-*euce*, *a* onéreux.

oneself, ou'onne´-selfe, *pron* soi-même.

onion, onn´-*ieune*, *n* oignon *m*.

only, aune´-li, *adv* seulement. *a* unique; seul.

onslaught, onn´-sloate, *n* assaut *m*.

onward, onn´-oue*urde*, *adv* en avant.

onyx, onn´-ix, *n* onyx *m*.

ooze, ouze, *v* suinter; dégouliner. *n* vase *f*; fange *f*.

opal, au´-*pal*, *n* opale *f*.

opaque, ŏ-péque´, *a* opaque.

open, ôp´-'n, *v* ouvrir. *a** ouvert; **–air,** en plein air; **–er,** *n* (tool) ouvre... *m*; **–ing,** ouverture *f*; occasion *f*.

opera, op´-*eur*-*a*, *n* opéra *m*.

operate, op´-*eur*-éte, *v* faire marcher; (*med*) opérer.

operation, op-*eur*-é´-ch'n, *n* opération *f*.

operator, op´-*eur*-é-*teur*, *n* opérator *m*.

opinion, ŏ-pinn´-*ieune*, *n* opinion *f*.

opponent, ŏ-pau´-nennte, *n* adversaire *m*.

opportune, op´-ŏr-tioune, *a* opportun; à propos.

opportunity, ŏ-por-tioue´-ni-ti, *n* occasion *f*.

oppose, ŏp-auze´, *v* opposer; s'opposer.

opposite, op´-ŏ-zitte, *adv* en face de. *a* opposé. *n* opposé *m*.

opposition, ŏp-pô-zi´-ch'n, *n* opposition *f*; (*com*) concurrence *f*.

oppress, ŏp-presse´, *v* opprimer; **–ion,** *n* oppression *f*; **–ive,** *a* tyrannique; (atmosphere) accablant.

optician, ŏp-tich´-'n, *n* opticien *m*.

option, op´-ch'n, *n* option *f*; **–al,** *a* facultatif.

opulent, op´-iou-lennte, *a* opulent.

or, aur, *conj* ou; **–else,** ou bien.

oral*, au´-r'l, *a* oral.

orange, or´-inndje, *n* orange *f*.

orator, or´-*a*-t'r, *n* orateur *m*.

oratory, or´-*a*-tŏ-ri, *n* éloquence *f*.

orb, oarbe, *n* (sphere) globe *m*; orbe *m*; sphère *f*.

orbit, oar´-bitte, *n* orbite *f*.

orchard, oar´-tche*urde*, *n* verger *m*.

orchestra, oar´kess-tra, *n* orchestre *m*.

orchid, or´-kidde, *n* orchidée *f*.

ordain, oar-déne´, *v* ordonner.

ordeal, oar´-dîle, *n* épreuve *f*.

order, oar´-*deur*, *n* ordre *m*; (goods) commande *f*. *v* commander; **–ly,** *a* ordonné; (quiet) calme. *n* planton *m*.

ordinary, oar´-di-n*a*-ri, *a* ordinaire.

ordnance, oard´-nannce, *n* artillerie *f*.

ore, aure, *n* minerai *m*.

organ, oar´-guenne, *n* orgue *m*; (*med*) organe *m*.

organic, oar-gănn´-ique, *a* organique.

organization, oar´-g*a*-nâï-zé´-ch'n, *n* organisation *f*.

organize, oar´-g*a*-nâïze, *v* organiser.

orgy, oar´-dji, *n* orgie *f*.

orient, au´-ri-ennte, *n* orient *m*; **–al,** *a* oriental.

origin, or´-i-djinne, *n* origine *f*; **–al*,** *a* original.

originate, ŏr-idj´-i-néte, *v* provenir de.

ornament, oar´-na-mennte, *n* ornement *m.*

ornamental, oar´-na-menn´-t'l, *a* ornemental.

orphan, oar´-f'n, *n* orphelin, -e *m* & *f;* **–age,** orphelinat *m.*

orthodox, or´-tsŏ-dŏxe, *n* & *a* orthodoxe *m* & *f.*

orthography, oar-tsog´-ra-fi, *n* orthographe *f.*

oscillate, os´-sil-léte, *v* osciller.

ostentatious*, oss-tenn-té´-cheuce, *a* fastueux.

ostrich, oss´-tritche, *n* autruche *f.*

other, o´-dẕ'r, *a* autre; **the –one,** *pron* l'autre.

otherwise, o´-dẕ'r-ou'âïze, *adv* autrement.

otter, ot´-t'r, *n* loutre *f.*

ought, oate, *v* devoir; falloir.

our, â'our, *poss a* notres; nos *pl.*

ours, â'ourze, *poss pron* le nôtre *ms;* la nôtre *fs;* les nôtres *mfpl.*

ourselves, â'our-celves´, *pron* nous-mêmes.

out, â'oute, *adv* hors, dehors; (extinguished) éteint; (issued) paru; **–bid,** *v* surenchérir; **–break,** *n* insurrection *f;* épidémie *f;* **–burst,** explosion *f;* **–cast,**

proscrit *m;* **–cry,** clameur *f;* **–do,** *v* surpasser; **–fit,** *n* équipement *m;* confectionneur *m;* (ships) armateur *m;* **–grow,** *v* devenir trop grand pour; **–last,** survivre à; dépasser...; **–law,** *n* proscrit *m. v* proscrire; **–lay,** *n* dépenses *fpl;* **–let,** débouché *m;* issue *f;* **–line,** *v* esquisser; **–live,** survivre à; **–look,** *n* perspective *f;* aspect *m;* **–lying,** *a* éloigné; **–number,** *v* surpasser en nombre; **–post,** *n* avant-poste *m;* **–put,** rendement *m;* **–rage,** outrage *m;* **–rageous,** *a* outrageux; exorbitant; **–right,** *adv* entièrement; **–run,** *v* dépasser en vitesse; **–side,** *adv* en dehors. *n* extérieur *m;* dehors *m;* **–size,** grande taille *f;* **–skirts,** confins *mpl;* **–standing,** *a* saillant; (debts) impayé; **–ward,** *adv* à l'extérieur. *a* extérieur; **–ward bound,** (*naut*) à destination de l'étranger; **–wit,** *v* surpasser en finesse.

oval, au´-v'l, *n* & *a*

ovale *m.*

ovary, au´-va-ri, *n* ovaire *m.*

oven, o´-v'n, *n* four *m.*

over, au´-v'r, *adv* par-dessus. *prep* sur; au-dessus de; **–alls,** *n* salopette *f;* **–bearing,** *a* arrogant; **–board,** *adv* par-dessus bord; **–cast,** *a* couvert; **–charge,** *n* surcharge *f;* **–coat,** (woman) manteau *m;* (man) pardessus *m;* **–come,** *v* vaincre; triompher de; **–do,** surmener; exagérer; **–dose,** *n* dose trop forte *f;* **–draw,** *v* excéder son crédit; **–due,** *a* en retard; (debt) arriéré; **–flow,** *v* déborder; **–grow,** trop grandir; (botanical) recouvrir; **–hang,** surplomber; **–haul,** (*mech*) examiner; mettre en état; **–hear,** surprendre une conversation; **–joyed,** *pp* transporté de joie; **–land,** *adv* par voie de terre; **–lap,** *v* chevaucher; **–load,** surcharger; **–look,** avoir vue sur; (forget) oublier; (pardon) laisser passer; **–power,** (vanquish) maîtriser; (heat, fumes,

A
B
C
D
E
F
G
H
I
J
K
L
M
N
O
P
Q
R
S
T
U
V
W
X
Y
Z

etc) accabler; **–rate,**
surestimer; **–rule,** (set
aside) rejeter; **–run,**
envahir; infester; **–seas,**
a d'outremer; **–see,** *v*
surveiller; **–seer,** *n*
surveillant *m*; **–sight,**
inadvertance *f*; **–sleep,** *v*
dormir trop longtemps;
–take, rattraper; (car,
etc) doubler; **–throw,**
renverser; **–time,** *n*
(work) travail
supplémentaire *m*;
–turn, *v* renverser; se
renverser; **–weight,** *n*
excédent de poids *m*;
–whelm, *v* accabler;
écraser; **–work,** *v*
surmener. *n* surmenage
m.

owe, au, *v* devoir.
owing, au´-inng, dû; **–to,**
prep à cause de.
owl, â'oule, *n* hibou *m*.
own, aune, *v* posséder;
(admit) avouer. *a* propre
(à soi).
owner, aune´-'r, *n*
propriétaire *m*.
ox, oxe, *n* boeuf *m*.
oxygen, ok´-si-dj'n, *n*
oxygène *m*.
oyster, oa'iss´-t'r, *n* huître
f; **–-bed,** parc à huîtres
m.
ozone, ozone, *n* ozone *f*.

P

pace, péce, n pas m;
(speed) allure f. v
mesurer.

pacify, păss´-i-fâï, v
pacifier; calmer.

pack, păque, v emballer;
empaqueter; (a case)
faire les valises. n paquet
m; (load) charge f;
(cards) jeu m; (gang)
bande f; (animals)
troupeau m; (hounds)
meute f; **–age,** colis m;
–et, paquet m; **–ing,**
emballage m; (mech)
garniture f.

pact, păcte, n pacte m.

pad, pădde, v (stuff)
rembourrer. n (stamp
pad) tampon m;
(writing) bloc-notes m.

padding, pădd´-inng, n
rembourrage m.

paddle, pădd´-d'l, v pagayer;
(feet, hands) patauger. n
pagaie f; **–steamer,**
vapeur à roues m; **–
wheel,** roue à aubes f.

paddock, pădd´-ŏque, n
(meadow) enclos m.

padlock, pădd´-lŏque, n
cadenas m. v cadenasser.

pagan, pé´-ganne, n & a
païen m.

page, pédje, n page f; **–
boy,** chasseur m.

pageant, pă´-djannte, n
cortège m; spectacle;
pompeux m.

pail, péle, n seau m.

pain, péne, v faire mal. n
douleur f; **–ful,** a*
douloureux; **–less,** sans
douleur.

paint, péne-te, v peindre.
n peinture f; (art)

couleur f; **–brush,**
pinceau m; **–er,** peintre
m; **–ing,** (picture)
tableau m.

pair, père, n paire f; couple
(of married people, etc.)
m.

pajamas, pi-djâ´-maze, npl
pyjamas m.

palace, păl´-ace, n palais
m.

palatable, păl´-a-ta-b'l, a
agréable au goût.

palate, păl´-ate, n palais
m.

pale, péle, a pâle. v pâlir;
–ness, n pâleur f.

palette, păl´-ette, n palette
f.

paling, péle´-inng, n
palissade f.

palm, pâme, n (tree)
palmier m; (hand)
paume f; **–ist,**
chiromancien m; **–istry,**
chiromancie f; **–Sunday,**
dimanche des Rameaux
m.

palpitation, păl-pi-té´-
ch'n, n palpitation f.

pamper, pămm´-p'r, v
choyer.

pamphlet, pămm´-flitte, n
brochure f.

pan, pănne, n (frying)
poêle f; **–cake,** crêpe f.

pane, péne, n vitre f;
carreau m.

A
B
C
D
E
F
G
H
I
J
K
L
M
N
O
P
Q
R
S
T
U
V
W
X
Y
Z

panel, pănn´-'l, *n* panneau *m*; (persons) liste *f*.

pang, pain-ng, *n* angoisse *f*.

panic, pănn´-ique, *n* panique *f*.

pansy, pănn´-zi, *n* pensée *f*.

pant, pănnte, *v* haleter.

panther, pănn´-*tseur*, *n* panthère *f*.

pantomime, pănn´-taumâïme, *n* (Christmas) féerie *f*; pantomime *f*.

pantry, pănn´-tri, *n* (food) garde-manger *m*.

pants, pănntse, *npl* pantalon *m*.

papal, pé´-pal, *a* papal.

paper, pé´-p'r, *v* tapisser. *n* papier *m*; **news–,** journal *m*; **wall- –,** papier peint *m*.

par, pâre, *n* pair *m*; egalité *f*.

parable, păr´-*a*-b'l, *n* parabole *f*.

parachute, pă´-*ra*-choute, *n* parachute *m*.

parade, p*a*-rède´, *v* parader. *n* parade *f*.

paradise, pă´-*ra*-dâïce, *n* paradis *m*.

paraffin, pă´-*ra*-finne, *n* paraffine *f*; **–lamp,** (*colloq*) lampe à pétrole *f*.

paragraph, pă´-*ra*-grăfe, *n* paragraphe *m*.

parallel, pă´-ral-lelle, *a* parallèle; (*fig*) (similar) semblable.

paralysis, p*a*-ral´-i-sisse, *n* paralysie *f*.

paralyze, pă´-*ra*-lâïze, *v* paralyser.

parasite, pă´-*ra*-sâïte, *n* parasite *m*.

parcel, pâr´-s'l, *n* paquet *m*; colis *m*.

parched, pârtch´-'t, *a* desséché; aride.

parchment, pârtch´-m'nt, *n* parchemin *m*.

pardon, pâr´-d'n, *v* pardonner; excuser. *n* pardon *m*; (law, official) grâce *f*.

parents, pè´-renntse, *npl* parents *mpl*.

parish, păr´-iche, *n* (civil) commune *f*; (*eccl*) paroisse *f*.

park, pârque, *n* parc *m*; **–ing,** (motors) stationnement *m*; **–ing meter,** *n* parcomètre *m*.

parley, pâr´-li, *v* parlementer. *n* pourparlers *mpl*.

parliament, pâr´-limennte, *n* parlement *m*.

parlor, pâr´-l'r, *n* petit salon *m*.

parochial, p*a*-rau´-ki-al, *a* communal; paroissial.

parrot, păr´-ŏtte, *n* perroquet *m*.

parry, păr´-i, *v* parer. *n* (fenc.) parade *f*.

parsimonious*, pâr-cimau´-ni-*eu*ce, *a* parcimonieux.

parsley, pârce´-li, *n* persil *m*.

parsnip, pârce´-nippe, *n* (*bot*.) panais *m*.

parson, pâr´-s'n, *n* (Protestant) pasteur *m*; (catholic) prêtre *m*.

parsonage, pâr´-sŏnn-idj, *n* presbytère *m*.

part, pârte, *v* séparer; (hair) faire la raie; *n* (share) (actor's) rôle *m*; (district) partie *f*.

partake, pâr-téque´, *v* participer à.

partial*, pâr´-ch'l, *a* partial; **–ity,** *n* (*fig*) prédilection *f*.

participate, pâr-tiss´-ipéte, *v* participer à *or* de.

participle, pâr´-ti-ci-p'l, *n* (grammar) participe *m*.

particle, pâr´-ti-c'l, *n* particule *f*.

particular, p*a*r-tik´-iou-l'r, *a* spécial; exigeant; (exact) minutieux; **–s,** *npl* détails *mpl*.

parting, pârt´-inng, *n* séparation *f*; (hair) raie *f*.

partition, pâr-ti´-ch'n, *n* (wall) cloison *f.*

partner, pârte´n'r, *n* (business) associé *m*; (games) partenaire *m* & *f*; (dance) danseur *m.*

partnership, pârte´-n'r-chippe, *n* association *f.*

partridge, pârte´-ridje, *n* perdrix *f.*

party, pâr´-ti, *n* (political) parti *m*; féte *f*; (evening) soirée *f.*

pass, pâsse, *v* passer; (overtake) dépasser; (meet) rencontrer; (exam) réussir, (mountain) passe *f*; —book, livre de compte *m*; —port, passeport *m.*

passage, pǎss´-idj, *n* passage *m*; (house) corridor *m*; (sea) traversée *f.*

passenger, pǎss´-inn-dj'r, *a* & *n* voyageur, -euse *m* & *f*; (naut) passager, -ère *m* & *f.*

passer-by, pâsse´-'r-bâï, *n* passant, -e *m* & *f.*

passion, pǎch´-ŏnne, *n* passion *f*; (anger) colère *f.*

passionate*, pǎch´-ŏnn-éte, *a* passionné.

past, pâsst, *n* & *a* passé *m. prep* au-delà de.

paste, péste, *n* pâte *f*;

(adhesive) colle *f. v* coller (for pastry).

pastime, pâsse´-tâïme, *n* passe-temps *m.*

pastries, péss´-trize, *npl* pâtisserie *f*; gâteaux *mpl.*

pastry, péss´-tri, pâte *f.*

pasture, pâsse´-tioure, *n* pâturage *m.*

pat, pǎtte, *v* caresser de la main. *n* caresse *f.*

patch, pǎtche, *v* rapiécer. *n* pièce *f.*

patent, pé´-tennte, *v* breveter. *n* brevet d'invention *m. a* breveté; – **leather,** *n* cuir verni *m.*

paternal*, pa-teur´-n'l, *a* paternel.

path, pâts, *n* sentier *m*; (garden) allée *f.*

pathetic, pǎ-tsé´-tique, *a* pathétique.

patience, pé´-ch'nce, *n* patience *f.*

patient, pé´-ch'nt, *n* malade *m* & *f. a** patient.

patriot, pé´-tri-ŏtte, *n* patriote *m* & *f*; –ic, *a* (person) patriote; (thing) patriotique.

patrol, pa-traule´, *n* patrouille *f. v* faire une ronde.

patronize, pǎ´-trŏnn-âïse, *v* favoriser; (*fig*) faire

---

l'important.

pattern, pǎtt´-*eu*rne, *n* modèle *m*; (sample) échantillon *m*; (paper, etc) patron *m.*

paunch, poanche, *n* panse *f*, ventre *m.*

pauper, poa´-p'r, *n* pauvre *m* & *f.*

pause, poaze, *v* faire une pause; s'arrêter. *n* pause *f.*

pave, péve, *v* paver; –ment, *n* trottoir *m.*

pavilion, pǎ-vil´-*ieu*nne, *n* pavilion *m.*

paw, poa, *n* patte *f. v* (as a horse) piaffer.

pawn, poanne, *n* (*fig*) gage *m*; (chess) pion *m*; *v* mettre en gage; –broker's shop, *n* mont-de-piété *m.*

pay, pé, *v* payer. *n* (military) solde *f*; (workman's) salaire *m*; –able, *a* payable; –er, *n* payeur *m*; –ment, paiement *m.*

pea, pî, *n* pois *m*; –nut, cacahuète *f.*

peace, pîce, *n* paix *f*; –ful*, *a* paisible.

peach, pîtche, *n* pêche *f*; – tree, pêcher *m.*

peacock, pî´-coque, *n* paon *m.*

peak, pique, *n* (mountain)

---

a
b
c
d
e
f
g
h
i
j
k
l
m
n
o
p
q
r
s
t
u
v
w
x
y
z

pic *m*; (*fig*) sommet *m*.

peal, pîle, *n* (bells) carillon *m*; (thunder) coup de tonnerre *m*.

pear, père, *n* poire *f*; **– tree,** poirier *m*.

pearl, peurle, *n* perle *f*.

peasant, pèz´-'nt, *n* paysan, -anne *m* & *f*; **–ry,** les paysans *mpl*.

peat, pîte, *n* tourbe *f*.

pebble, pèb´-b'l, *n* (on sea shore) galet *m*.

peck, pèque, *v* picoter. *n* (of a bird) coup de bec *m*.

peculiar*, pi-kiou´-li-*eu*r, *a* singulier.

peculiarity, pi-kiou´-li-ăr´-i-ti, *n* singularité *f*.

pedal, pède´-'l, *n* pédale *f*. *v* pédaler.

pedantic, pé-dănn´-tique, *a* (person) pédant; (thing) pédantesque.

peddler, pèd´-l'r, *n* colporteur *m*.

pedestal, pèd´-ess-t'l, *n* piédestal *m*.

pedestrian, pi-dess´-tri-anne, *n* piéton *m*.

pedigree, pèd´-i-grî, *n* généalogie *f*; (dog) pedigree *m*.

peel, pîle, *n* pelure *f*. *v* peler; éplucher.

peep, pîpe, *v* jeter un coup

d'œil. *n* coup d'œil *m*.

peer, pîre, *n* pair *m*; **–age,** pairie *f*.

peevish*, pî´-viche, *a* grincheux; maussade.

peg, pègue, *n* cheville *f*; (for hats, etc) patère *f*; **clothes- –,** pince à linge *f*.

pellet, pel´-lite, *n* boulette *f*; (shot) grain de plomb *m*.

pelt, pelte, *n* peau *f*. *v* assaillir à coups de ...

pen, pène, *n* stylo *m*; (cattle, etc) pare *m*; **–holder,** porte-plume *m*; **–knife,** canif *m*; **–-nib,** plume *f*.

penal, pî´-n'l, *a* pénal; **–servitude,** *n* travaux forcés *mpl*.

penalty, penn´-al-ti, *n* peine *f*; (fine) amende *f*.

penance, penn´-'nce, *n* pénitence *f*.

pencil, penn´-s'l, *n* crayon *m*.

pendant, penn´-dennte, *n* (jewel) pendentif *m*.

pending, penn´-dinng, *prep* en suspens.

pendulum, penn´-diou-*leu*me, *n* pendule *m*.

penetrate, penn´-i-tréte, *v* pénétrer.

penguin, penn´-gouinne, *n* pingouin *m*.

penicillin, penn´-i-sil-inne, *n* pénicilline *f*.

peninsula, penn-inn´-siou-la, *n* péninsule *f*.

penis, pî-nisse, *n* pénis *m*.

penitent, penn´-i-tennte, *n* & *a* pénitent, -e *m* & *f*.

penniless, penn´-i-less, *a* sans le sou.

pension, penn´-ch'n *n* pension *f*. *v* mettre à la retraite; **–er,** *n* retraité, -e *m* & *f*; (of mil. or naval homes) invalide *m*.

pensive*, penn´-cive, *a* pensif.

penurious, pi-niou´-ri-*eu*ce, *a* indigent.

people, pî-p'l, *n* gens *m* & *fpl*; (community) peuple *m*.

pepper, pèp´-'r, *n* poivre *m*; **–mint,** menthe poivrée *f*.

per, peure, *prep* par; **–cent,** pour cent; **–centage,** *n* pourcentage *m*.

perceive, p*eu*r-cîve´, *v* apercevoir; (to recognize) s'apercevoir de.

perception, p*eu*r-sèpp´-ch'n, *n* perception *f*.

perch, peurtche, *n* (for fowls, etc.) perchoir *m*; (fish) perche *f*.

peremptory, pair´-emmp-tŏ-ri, *a* péremptoire.

perfect, peur´-fècte, *a** parfait. *v* perfectionner.

perfection, peur-fèque´-ch'n, *n* perfection *f.*

perfidious*, peur-fid´-i-euce, *a* perfide.

perforate, peur´-fo-réte, *v* perforer.

perform, peur-foarme´, *v* exécuter; (stage) représenter; **–ance,** *n* exécution *f*; représentation *f.*

perfume, peur´-fioume, *n* parfum *m. v* parfumer.

perhaps, peur-hăpse´, *adv* peut-être.

peril, pèr´-ile, *n* péril *m*; **–ous,** *a* périlleux.

period, pi´-ri-ode, *n* période *f*; **menstrual –s,.** règles *fpl*; **–ical,** *a* périodique.

periscope, pèr´-iss-kôpe, *n* périscope *m.*

perish, pèr´-iche, *v* périr; (spoil) avarier.

perishable, pèr´-iche-*a*-b'l, *a* périssable.

perjury, peur´-djiou-ri, *n* parjure *m.*

perm, peurme, *n* permanente *f.*

permanent*, peur´-ma-nennte, *a* permanent.

permeate, peur´-mi-éte, *v* pénétrer.

permission, peur-mich-'n, *n* permission *f.*

permit, peur´-mitte, *n* permis *m. v* permettre.

pernicious*, peur-nich´-euce, *a* pernicieux.

perpendicular, peur-penn-di´-kiou-lar, *n & a* perpendiculaire *f.*

perpetrate, peur´-pi-tréte, *v* commettre.

perpetual*, peur-pett´-iou-*al*, *a* perpétuel.

perplex, peur-plexe´, *v* embarrasser.

persecute, peur´-si-kioute, *v* persécuter.

persecution, peur-si-kiou´-ch'n, *n* persécution *f.*

perseverance, peur-si-vir´-'nce, *n* persévérance *f.*

persevere, peur-si-vire´, *v* persévérer.

persist, peur-sisste´, *v* persister.

person, peur´-s'n, *n* personne *f*; **–al,** *a** personnel; **–ality,** *n* personnalité *f.*

personify, peur-sonn´-i-făï, *v* personnifier.

personnel, peur´-sŏ-nèl, *n* personnel *m.*

perspective, peur-spèque´-tive, *n* perspective *f.*

perspicacity, peur-spi-kă´-ci-ti, *n* perspicacité *f.*

perspiration, peur-spi-ré´-ch'n, *n* transpiration *f.*

perspire, peur-spâïre´, *v* transpirer; suer.

persuade, peur-souéde´, *v* persuader.

persuasion, peur-soué´-j'n, *n* persuasion *f.*

pert, peurte, *a* éveillé; impertinent.

pertinent, peur´-ti-nennte, *a* à propos.

perturb, peur-teurbe´, *v* troubler; agiter.

perusal, peur-ouze´-'l, *n* examen *m*; lecture *f.*

peruse, peur-ouze´, *v* lire attentivement.

perverse, peur-veurce´, *a* pervers; dépravé.

pervert, peur-veurte´, *v* pervertir; dénaturer.

pest, peste, *n* peste *f.*

pester, pess´-t'r, *v* tourmenter; importuner.

pet, pette, *n* favori *m*; (child) chéri *m. v* choyer; (spoil) gâter.

petal, pett´-'l, *n* pétale *m.*

petition, pi-ti´-ch'n, *n* (law) requête *f. v* (law) présenter une requête; **–er,** *n* pétitionnaire *m &* *f.*

petrify, pett´-ri-fâï, *v* pétrifier.

petroleum, pè-trau´-li-eume, *n* pétrole *m.*

petticoat, pett´-i-caute, n jupon m.

petty, pett´-i, a mesquin; **–cash,** n argent pour menus frais m.

petulance, pett´-ioul-'nce, n pétulance f.

pew, pioue, n banc d'église m.

pewter, pioue´-t'r, n étain m.

phantom, fǎnn´-teume, n fantôme m; spectre m.

phase, féze, n phase f.

pheasant, fèz´-'nt, n faisan m.

phenomenon, fi-nomm´-i-nǒnne, n phénomène m.

philosopher, fi-loss´-ǒf-'r, n philosophe m.

phlegm, flemme, n flegme m.

phosphate, fosse´-féte, n phosphate m.

phosphorus, fosse´-fo-reuce, n phosphore m.

photograph, fau´-to-grǎfe, n photographie f.

photographer, fau-tog´-rǎf-'r, n photographe m.

phrase, fréze, n phrase f; locution f.

physical, fiz´-zi-k'l, a physique.

physician, fi-zi´-ch'n, n médecin m.

physics, fiz´-zix, npl la physique f.

piano, pi-ǎ´-nau, n piano m; **grand –,** piano à queue m.

pick, pique, n pic m; (– axe) pioche f. v choisir; (gather) cueillir; (bones) ronger; **–up,** ramasser; **–pocket,** n pickpocket m.

pickle, pik´-'l, v conserver au vinaigre.

pickles, pik´-'lze, npl conserves au vinaigre fpl; cornichon m.

picnic, pik´-nique, n pique-nique m.

picture, pik´-tioure, n tableau m; illustration f; portrait m; film m.

pie, pâï, n (meat) pâté m; (fruit-open) tourte f.

piece, pîce, n pièce f; (fragment, portion) morceau m; **–meal,** adv par morceaux; **–work,** n travail a pièce m.

pier, pire, n jetée f.

pierce, pirce, v percer.

piercing, pire´-cinng, a percant.

piety, pâï´-i-ti, n piété f.

pig, pigue, n cochon m; porc m; **–iron,** fonte en gueuse f; **–sty,** porcherie f.

pigeon, pid´-jinne, n pigeon m.

pigeonhole, pid´-jinne-haule, n (papers) case f.

pike, pâïque, n (weapon) pique f; (fish) brochet m.

pilchard, pill´-chârde, n pilchard m; sardine f.

pile, pâïle, n (building) pieu m; (heap) tas m; (carpet, etc) poil m. v empiler.

piles, pâïlze, npl (med) hémorroïdes fpl.

pilfer, pill´-f'r, v chiper.

pilgrim, pill´-grimme, n pèlerin, -e m & f.

pilgrimage, pill´-grimm-idj, n pèlerinage m.

pill, pile, n pilule f.

pillage, pill´-idj, n pillage m. v piller.

pillar, pill´-'r, n pilier m.

pillow, pill´-au, n oreiller m; **–case,** taie d'oreiller f.

pilot, pâï´-leutte, n pilote m. v piloter.

pimple, pimm´-p'l, n bouton m; pustule f.

pin, pinne, n épingle f; (safety) épingle de sûreté f. v épingler.

pinafore, pinn´-a-faure, n tablier m.

pincers, pinn´-ceurze, npl; pince fpl; tenailles fpl.

pinch, pinntche, v pincer; (press) gêner. n (salt, etc) pincée f.

pine, pâïne, *n* pin *m*; –
  apple, ananas *m*.
pinion, pinn´-ieune, *n*
  (tech) pignon *m*. *v* lier
  les bras.
pink, pinng-k, *a* rose. *n*
  œillet *m*.
pinnacle, pinn´-*a*-k'l, *n*
  pinacle *m*.
pint, pâïnnte, *n* pinte *f*.
pioneer, pâï-o-nîr', *n*
  pionnier *m*; (*mil*) sapeur
  m.
pious*, pâï´-*eu*ce, *a* pieux.
pip, pippe, *n* pépin *m*.
pipe, pâïpe, *n* tuyau *m*;
  conduit *m*; (tobacco)
  pipe *f*.
pirate, pâï´-réte, *n* pirate
  m.
pistol, piss´-t'l, *n* pistolet
  m.
piston, piss´-t'n, *n* piston
  m.
pit, pitte, *n* fosse *f*; (mine)
  mine *f*; (theater)
  parterre *m*.
pitch, pitche, *n* poix *f*;
  (*mus*) ton *m*. *v* (*naut*)
  tanguer; (throw) lancer.
pitcher, pitch´-'r, *n* (jug)
  cruche *f*.
pitchfork, pitche´-
  foarque, *n* fourche *f*.
pitfall, pit´-foale, *n* piège
  m.
pith, pits, *n* moelle *f*.
pitiful*, pitt´-i-foull, *a*

  pitoyable.
pitiless*, pitt´-i-lesse, *a*
  impitoyable.
pity, pitt´-i, *n* pitié *f*. *v*
  avoir pitié de; plaindre;
  what a –!*interj* quel
  dommage!
pivot, piv´-*eu*te, *n* pivot
  m.
placard, plă´-kârde, *n*
  affiche *f*. *v* placarder.
place, pléce, *n* place *f*;
  (locality) lieu *m*; endroit
  m. *v* mettre.
placid*, plăss´-ide, *a*
  placide; calme.
plagiarism, plé´-dji-*a*-
  rizme, *n* plagiat *m*.
plague, plégue, *n* peste *f*. *v*
  tourmenter.
plain, pléne, *n* plaine *f*. *a*
  simple; clair; évident;
  (looks, etc) ordinaire.
plaint, pléne-te, *n* plainte
  f; lamentation *f*; **–iff,**
  plaignant, -e *m* & *f*;
  –ive*, *a* plaintif.
plait, plăte, *n* natte *f*. *v*
  (hair) tresser; (fold)
  plisser.
plan, plănne, *n* plan *m*;
  projet *m*. *v* projeter.
plane, pléne, *v* raboter. *n*
  rabot *m*; –**tree,** platane
  m.
planet, plănn´-ette, *n*
  planète *f*.
plank, plain-nk, *n*

  planche *f*.
plant, plânnte, *v* planter. *n*
  plante *f*; (*mech*)
  outillage *m*; **–ation,**
  plantation *f*.
plaster, plâsse´-t'r, *v*
  plâtrer. *n* plâtre *m*;
  (*med*) emplâtre *m*.
plastic, plăsse´-tique, *n*
  plastique *m*.
plate, pléte, *v* argenter; (to
  cover with gold) dorer;
  nickeler. *n* assiette *f*;
  (silver) argenterie *f*;
  (photo) plaque *f*.
plateglass, pléte´-glâce, *n*
  glace *f*.
platform, plătt´-fôrme, *n*
  estrade *f*; (station) quai
  m.
platinum, plătt´-i-nomme,
  n platine *m*.
play, plé, *v* jouer. *n* jeu *m*;
  (theater) pièce *f*; **–er,**
  musicien, -ienne *m* & *f*;
  acteur *m*; actrice *f*;
  joueur, -euse *m* & *f*;
  –ful*, *a* enjoué;
  –ground, *n* terrain de
  jeux *m*; (school) cour *f*;
  –ing cards, cartes à
  jouer *fpl*.
plea, plî, *n* procès *m*; (law)
  prétexte *m*; défense *f*.
plead, plîde, *v* alléguer;
  (law) plaider.
pleasant*, plè´-z'nt, *a*
  plaisant; agréable.

a b c d e f g h i j k l m n o **p** q r s t u v w x y z

A
B
C
D
E
F
G
H
I
J
K
L
M
N
O
P
Q
R
S
T
U
V
W
X
Y
Z

please, plîze, *v* plaire; contenter. *interj* s'il vous plaît!

pleasing, plî´-zinng, *a* agréable; aimable.

pleasure, plè´-jeure, *n* plaisir *m*.

pleat, plîte, *n* pli *m*; –ed, *a* plissé.

pledge, plèdje, *n* gage *m*; (surety) garantie *f*. *v* (pawn) mettre en gage.

plenty, plenn´-ti, *n* abondance *f*.

pleurisy, plioue´-ri-si, *n* pleurésie *f*.

pliable, plâï´-a-b'l, *a* flexible.

pliers, plâï´-eurze, *npl* pinces *fpl*.

plight, plâïte, *n* état *m*; situation *f*.

plod, plodde, *v* (work) bûcher; –along, (walk) marcher péniblement.

plodder, plodde´-'r, *n* bûcheur, -euse *m* & *f*.

plot, plotte, *v* tramer. *n* complot *m*; (land) parcelle *f*; (story, etc) sujet *m*; –ter, conspirateur *m*.

plover, plov´-'r, *n* (*ornit*) pluvier *m*.

plow, plâ'ou, *n* charrue *f*. *v* labourer.

plowman, plâ'ou´-manne, *n* laboureur *m*.

pluck, ploque, *v* (poultry) cueillir; (flowers, fruit, etc.) plumer. *n* courage *m*.

plug, plogue, *v* boucher. *n* bouchon *m*; tampon *m*; **spark** –,bougie d'allumage *f*; **wall** –,prise de courant.

plum, plomme, *n* prune *f*; **–tree,** prunier *m*.

plumage, ploue´-midj, *n* plumage *m*.

plumb, plomme, *v* (*naut.*) sonder. *n* plomb *m*; **–ing,** plombage *m*.

plumber, plomm´-eur, *n* plombier *m*.

plump, plommpe, *a* gras; (person) potelé.

plunder, plonn´-d'r, *v* piller. *n* pillage *m*.

plunderer, plonn´-deur-eur, *n* pillard *m*.

plunge, plonndje, *v* plonger. *n* plongeon *m*.

plural, ploue´-r'l, *n* & *a* pluriel *m*.

plus, plosse, *prep* plus.

plush, ploche, *n* peluche *f*.

ply, plâï, *v* (trade) exercer; (3-ply wool) laine à trois fils *f*; **–between,** *v* faire le service entre. . . .

pneumatic, niou-mătt´-ique, *a* pneumatique.

pneumonia, niou-mau´-ni-a, *n* pneumonie *f*.

poach, pautche, *v* braconner; (eggs) pocher.

poacher, pautch´-'r, *n* braconnier *m*.

pocket, pok´-ette, *v* empocher. *n* poche *f*.

pod, pode, *n* cosse *f*; (garlic) gousse *f*.

poem, pau´-emme, *n* poème *m*.

poet, pau´-ette, *n* poète *m*; **–ry,** poésie *f*.

point, poa´'innte, *v* indiquer; (finger) montrer; (sharpen) tailler. *n* (tip) pointe *f*; (punctuation, position) point *m*; **–ed,** *a* pointu; (*fig*) direct; **–er,** *n* (rod) baguette *f*; (dog) chien d'arrêt *m*.

poise, poa´'ize, *n* équilibre *m*; (person) maintien *m*.

poison, poa'i´-z'n, *n* poison *m*. *v* empoisonner; **–ous,** *a* (of plants) vénéneux; (animal) venimeux.

poke, pauke, *v* (to push) pousser; (fire) attiser.

poker, pau´-keur, *n* tisonnier *m*; (cards) poker *m*.

pole, paule, *n* perche *f*; (arctic) pôle *m*.

police, pŏ-lîce´, *n* police *f*; **–man,** agent *m*;

—**station,** commissariat de police *m.*

policy, pol´-i-ci, *n* politique *f*; (insurance) police *f.*

polish, pol´-iche, *n* (gloss) luisant *m*; (shoes) cirage *m*; (furniture, etc) cire *f. v* polir (shoes); cirer.

polite*, pŏ-läïte´, *a* poli; —**ness,** *n* politesse *f.*

political, pŏ-lite´-i-k'l, *a* politique.

politician, pŏl-i-tiche´-ann, *n* homme politique *m.*

politics, pol´-i-tikse, *n* politique *f.*

poll, paule, *n* élection *f*; scrutin *m. v* voter.

pollute, pŏl-lioute´, *v* polluer.

pollution, pol-liou´-ch'n, *n* pollution *f.*

pomade, pau-méde´, *n* pommade *f.*

pomegranate, pomm´-gränn-éte, *n* grenade *f.*

pomp, pommpe, *n* pompe *f*; —**ous*,** *a* pompeux.

pond, ponnde, *n* étang *m.*

ponder, ponn´-d'r, *v* réfléchire; méditer.

ponderous*, ponn´-deur-euce, *a* lourd; pesant.

pony, pau´-ni, *n* poney *m.*

poodle, poue´-d'l, *n* caniche *m.*

pool, poule, *n* (water) mare *f*; (swimming) piscine *f*; (cards) cagnotte *f*; poule *f. v* mettre en commun.

poop, poue'pe, *n* poupe *f.*

poor, pou'*eur*, *a* pauvre. *n* les pauvres *mpl.*

pop, poppe, *v* sauter. *n* (of a cork) bruit d'un bouchon qui saute *m.*

Pope, paupe, *n* pape *m.*

poplar, pop´-l'r, *n* peuplier *m.*

poplin, pop´-linne, *n* popeline *f.*

poppy, pop´-i, *n* (field poppy) coquelicot *m.*

populace, pop´-iou-léce, *n* peuple *m*; foule *f.*

popular*, pop´-iou-l'r, *a* populaire.

populate, pop´-iou-léte, *v* peupler.

population, pop-iou-lé´-ch'n, *n* population *f.*

populous, pop´-iou-*leuce*, *a* populeux.

porcelain, por´-ce-linne, *n* porcelaine *f.*

porch, paurtche, *n* porche *m*; (Phil.) le Portique *m.*

porcupine, poar´-kiou-pâïne, *n* porc-épic *m.*

pore, paure, *n* pore *m*; —**over,** *v* étudier assidûment.

pork, paurque, *n* porc *m*;

—**butcher,** charcutier *m.*

porous, pau´-*reuce*, *a* poreux.

porpoise, poar´-*peuce*, *n* marsouin *m.*

porridge, por´-idj, *n* bouillie de gruau d'avoine *f.*

port, poar'te, *n* (wine) porto *m*; (harbor) port *m*; (*naut*) bâbord *m*; —**hole,** hublot *m.*

portable, paur´-ta-b'l, *a* portatif.

portend, poar-tennde´, *v* présager.

porter, paur´-t'r, *n* (luggage) porteur *m*; (door) portier *m*; —**age,** factage *m.*

portfolio, paurt-fau´-li-au, *n* serviette *f.*

portion, paur´-ch'n, *n* portion *f*; (share) part *f.*

portly, paurt´-li, *a* corpulent; d'un port majestueux.

portmanteau, paurt-männ´-tau, *n* valise *f.*

portrait, paur´-tréte, *n* portrait *m.*

portray, paur-tré´, *v* peindre; (describe) décrire.

pose, pause, *n* pose *f. v* poser; —**as,** se faire passer pour.

position, po-zi´-ch'n, *n*

a b c d e f g h i j k l m n o **p** q r s t u v w x y z

A
B
C
D
E
F
G
H
I
J
K
L
M
N
O
P
Q
R
S
T
U
V
W
X
Y
Z

position *f*; situation *f*.

positive*, poz´-i-tive, *a* positif; certain.

possess, pô-zesse´, *v* posséder; **–ion,** *n* possession *f*.

possessor, pô-zess´-*eur*, *n* possesseur *m*.

possibility, poss-i-bil´-i-ti, *n* possibilité *f*.

possible, poss´-i-b'l, *a* possible.

possibly, poss´-i-bli, *adv* peut-être.

post, pauste, *n* (*Phil*) poste *f*; courrier *m*; (wood, etc) poteau *m*; (job) emploi *m*; place *f*; *v* mettre à la poste; **–age,** *n* port *m*; **–card,** carte postale *f*; **–-date,** *v* postdater; **–er,** *n* affiche *f* **–-paid, a** franco; **–man,** *n* facteur *m*; **–master,** receveur des postes *m*; **–-mortem,** autopsie *f*; **–-office,** bureau de poste *m*; **–pone,** *v* remettre; **–script,** *n* postscriptum *m*.

posterior, poss-ti´-ri-*eur*, *n* & *a* postérieur *m*.

posterity, poss-tèr´-i-ti, *n* postérité *f*.

posture, poss´-tioure, *n* posture *f*.

pot, potte, *n* pot *m*; (cooking) marmite *f*.

potash, pot´-ăche, *n* potasse *f*.

potato, po-té´-tau, *n* pomme de terre *f*.

potent, pau´-tennte, *a* puissant; (*fig*) efficace.

potion, pau´-ch'n, *n* potion *f*.

pottery, pot´-*eur*-i, *n* poterie *f*.

pouch, pâ'outche, *n* poche *f*; (tobacco) blague *f*.

poulterer, paule´-*teur*-*eur*, *n* marchand de volailles *m*.

poultice, paule´-tice, *n* cataplasme *m*.

poultry, paule´-tri, *n* volaille *f*.

pounce, pâ'ounce, *v* (on, upon) fondre sur.

pound, pâ'ounde, *n* livre sterling *f*; (weight) livre *f*; (animals) fourrière *f*. *v* (pulverize) broyer.

pour, paure, *v* verser; (rain) pleuvoir à verse.

pour out, paure â'oute, *v* verser; (serve) servir.

pout, pâ'oute, *v* faire la moue.

poverty, pov´-*eur*-ti, *n* pauvreté *f*.

powder, pâ'ou´-d'r, *n* poudre *f*. *v* pulvériser; (face) poudrer.

power, pâ'ou´-*eur*, *n* pouvoir *m*; (*mech*) force

f; (state) puissance *f*; **–ful*,** *a* puissant; **–less,** impuissant.

pox, poxe, **small- –,**n variole *f*; **chicken- –,**varicelle *f*.

practicable, prăque´-ti-*ca*b'l, *a* praticable.

practical*, prăque´-ti-c'l, *a* pratique.

practice, prăque´-tice, *n* pratique *f*; (custom) coutume *f*; (professional) clientèle *f*; (exercise) exercise *m*; (*mus*) s'exerce; (profession) exercer.

practitioner, prăque-tiche´-onn-*eur*, *n* practicien *m*.

praise, préze, *v* louer. *n* louange *f*; éloge *m*.

praiseworthy, préze´-oueur-*dz*i, *a* louable.

pram, prămme, *n* landau *m*.

prance, prănnce, *v* se cabrer; (*fig*) se pavaner.

prank, prain-nk, *n* escapade *f*; farce *f*.

prawn, proanne, *n* bouquet *m*.

pray, pré, *v* prier.

prayer, prére, *n* prière *f*; **–book,** livre de prières *m*; **Lord's Prayer,** pater *m*.

preach, prîtche, *v* prêcher; **–er,** *n* prédicateur *m*.

precarious*, pri-ké´-ri-euce, a précaire.

precaution, pri-koa´-ch'n n précaution f.

precede, prî-cîde´, v précéder.

precedence, prè´-sid-ennce, n préséance f.

precedent, prè´-sid-ennte, n (example) précédent m.

precept, prî´-cèpte, n précepte m.

precinct, prî´-cinng-kt, n enceinte f.

precious*, prè´-cheuce, a précieux.

precipice, prèce´-i-pice, n précipice m.

precise*, pri-sâïce´, a précis; exact.

preclude, pri-cloude´, v exclure; empêcher.

precocious*, pri-kau´-cheuce, a précoce.

predecessor, pri-di-sess´-eur, n prédécesseur m.

predicament, pri-dik´-a-mennte, a mauvaise passe f; situation difficile f.

predicate, predd´-i-quéte, n (gram) attribut m.

predict, pri-dicte´, v prédire; **–ion,** n prédiction f.

predominant, pri-domm´-i-nannte, a prédominant.

preface, preff´-ace, n préface f.

prefect, pri´-fecte, n préfet m.

prefer, pri-feur´, v préférer.

preferable, preff´-eur-a-b'l, a préférable.

preference, preff´-eur-ennce, n préférence f.

prefix, prè´-fixe, n préfixe m. v mettre en tête.

pregnant, pregg´-nannte, a enceinte; (animals) pleine.

prejudice, prédj´-iou-dice, n préjugé m; préjudice m. v préjudicier; **–d,** a prévenu contre; **without –**,sans préjudice de.

prejudicial*, prédj-iou-dich´-'l, a préjudiciable.

prelate, prél´-éte, n prélat m.

preliminary, pri-limm´-i-na-ri, a préliminaire.

prelude, pré´-lioude, n prélude m.

premature*, pré´-ma-tioure, a prématuré.

premeditate, pri-medd´-i-téte, v préméditer.

premier, prî´-mi-eur, n (France) président du conseil (des ministres) m. a premier.

premises, premm´-i-cize, npl locaux mpl.

premium, prî´-mi-eume, n prime f.

preparation, prip-a-ré´-ch'n, n préparation f.

prepare, pri-pére´, v préparer.

prepossessing, pri-pŏzess´-inng, a avenant.

preposterous*, pri-poss´-teur-euce, a absurde.

prerogative, pri-rog´-a-tive, n prérogative f.

prescription, pri-skrip´-ch'n, n (med) ordonnance f.

presence, préz´-ennce, n présence f; **–of mind,** présence d'esprit f.

present, pri-zennte´, v présenter; (gift) offrir à.

present, préz´-ennte, n cadeau m. a présent; **–ation,** n présentation f; **–ly,** adv tout à l'heure.

presentiment, pri-zenn´-ti-mennte, n pressentiment m.

preservation, prèz-eur-vé´-ch'n, n protection f; (state, condition) conservation f.

preserve, pri-zeurve´, v préserver; conserver; (candied) confire; **–s,** npl conserves fpl.

preside, pri-zâïde´, v présider de.

president, préz´-i-dennte,

n président *m*.

press, presse, *n* presse *f*. *v* presser; appuyer; (clothes) repasser; **–ing,** *a* urgent.

pressure, préch´-*eur*, *n* pression *f*; urgence *f*.

presume, pri-zioume´, *v* présumer; (dare) oser.

presumption, pri-zomm´-ch'n, *n* présomption *f*.

pretend, pri-tennde´, *v* prétendre; (sham) feindre, faire semblant de.

pretense, pri-tennce´, *n* simulation *f*; prétexte *m*.

pretentious*, pri-tenn´-cheuce, *a* prétentieux.

pretext, prî´-texte, *n* prétexte *m*.

pretty, pritt´-i, *a* joli.

prevail, pri-véle, *v* prévaloir; **–upon,** persuader.

prevalent, prév´-*a*-lennte, *a* dominant; général.

prevent, pri-vennte, *v* empêcher; **–ion,** *n* prévention *f*; **–ive,** *a** préventif.

previous, prî´-vi-*euce*, *a* précédent; préalable.

prey, pré, *n* proie *f*. *v* faire sa proie de.

price, prâïce, *n* prix *m*; **–less,** *a* hors de prix.

prick, prique, *v* piquer. *n* piqûre *f*; **–le,** épine *f*; **–ly,** *a* épineux.

pride, prâïde, *n* orgueil *m*. *v* (to – oneself on) s'enorgueillir de.

priest, prîste, *n* prêtre *m*.

prim, prime, *a* collet monté; (dress) soigneux.

primary, prâï´-ma-ri, *a* primaire; fondamental.

primate, prâï´-méte, *n* primat *m*.

prime, prâïme, *n* (of life) fleur de l'âge *f*. *a* premier; de première qualité. *v* préparer; **–minister,** *n* (France) président du conseil *m*.

primer, prâï´-m*eur*, *n* (school) livre élémentaire *m*.

primitive, primm´-i-tive, *a* primitif.

primrose, primm´-rauze, *n* primevère *f*.

prince, prinnce, *n* prince *m*; **–ly,** *a* princier; **–ss,** *n* princesse *f*.

principal, prinn´-ci-p'l, *n* directeur *m*; chef *m*; (funds) principal *m*. *a** principal.

principle, prinn´-ci-p'l, *n* principe *m*.

print, prinnte, *v* imprimer. *n* impression *f*; (photo) épreuve *f*; **–er,** imprimeur *m*; **–ing,** impression *f*; **–ing-works,** imprimerie *f*.

prior, prâï´-*eur*, *n* prieur *m*. *a* antérieur. *adv* avant de; **–ity,** *n* priorité *f*; **–y,** prieuré *m*.

prism, prizme, *n* prisme *m*; **–atic,** *a* prismatique.

prison, priz´-'n, *n* prison *f*; **–er,** prisonnier, -ère *m* & *f*.

privacy, prâï´-va-ci, *n* retraite *f*; intimité *f*.

private, prâï´-véte, *a** privé; personnel; particulier. *n* (soldier) simple soldat *m*.

privation, prâï-vé´-ch'n, *n* privation *f*.

privilege, priv´-i-lidje, *n* privilège *m*. *v* privilégier.

privy, priv´-i, *a* privé; secret.

prize, prâïze, *n* prix *m*; (ship) prise *f*. *v* évaluer.

probable, prob´-*a*-b'l, *a* probable.

probate, pro´béte, *n* vérification d'un testament *f*.

probation, pro-bé´-ch'n, *n* épreuve *f*; essai *m*; **–er,** stagiaire *m* & *f*; (*eccl*) novice *m* & *f*.

probe, praube, *v* sonder; explorer. *n* sonde *f*.

problem, prob´-lemme, *n* problème *m*.

procedure, prŏ-cîd´-ioure, *n* procédé *m*; (law) procédure *f*.

proceed, prŏ-cîde´, *v* procéder; continuer; **–ings,** *npl* mesures *fpl*; (law) poursuites *fpl*.

proceeds, prau´-cîdze, *npl* produit *m*; bénéfices *mpl*.

process, prau´-cesse, *n* cours *m*; (manufacture) procédé *m*.

procession, prŏ-cé´-ch'n, *n* procession *f*.

proclaim, prŏ-cléme´, *v* proclamer; publier.

proclamation, prŏc-là-mé´-ch'n, *n* proclamation *f*.

procure, prŏ-kioure´, *v* se procurer; procurer.

prod, prŏde, *v* piquer; pousser.

prodigal*, prod´-i-g'l, *a* prodigue.

prodigious*, prŏ-di´-dj*eu*ce, *a* prodigieux.

prodigy, prod´-i-dji, *n* prodige *m*.

produce, prŏ-diouce´, *v* produire. *n* produit *m*; denrées *fpl*; **–r,** producteur, -trice *m* & *f*; (stage) metteur en scène *m*.

product, prod´-*eu*cte, *n* produit *m*; **–ion,**

production *f*; (stage) représentation *f*.

profane, prŏ-féne´, *v* profaner. *a** profane.

profess, prŏ-fesse´, *v* professer; déclarer; **–ion,** *n* profession *f*; carrière *f*; **–ional*,** *a* professionnel.

professor, prŏ-fess´-'r, *n* professeur *m*.

proficiency, prŏ-fi´-chenn-ci, *n* capacité *f*; compétence *f*.

proficient, prŏ-fi´-ch'nt, *a* avancé; versé.

profile, prau´-fâïle, *n* profil *m*.

profit, prof´-itte, *n* bénéfice *m*. *v* profiter; **–able,** *a* avantageux; **–eer,** *n* profiteur, -euse *m* & *f*.

profound*, prŏ-fâ'ounnde´, *a* profond.

profuse, prŏ-fiouce´, *a* prodigue; abondant.

program, prau´-grămme, *n* programme *m*.

progress, prau-gresse´, *v* faire des progrès; avancer.

progress, prau´-gresse, *n* progrès *m*.

prohibit, prau-hib´-itte, *v* interdire à; défendre.

project, prŏd-jecte´, *v* projeter; dépasser; déborder. *n* projet *m*;

–ile, projectile *m*; **–ion,** saillie *f*; **–or,** projecteur *m*.

proletarian, prau-lè-té´-ri-*a*nne, *n* & *a* prolétaire *m*.

prologue, prau´-logue, *n* prologue *m*.

prolong, prau-lonng´, *v* prolonger.

promenade, promm-*eu*-nâde´, *v* se promener. *n* promenade (en grande toilette) *f*.

prominent, promm´-i-nennte, *a* proéminent.

promise, promm´-iss, *n* promesse *f*. *v* promettre.

promissory note, promm´-iss-o-ri naute, *n* billet à ordre *m*.

promote, prŏ-maute´, *v* promouvoir; (business) lancer; **–r,** *n* promoteur *m*; **company –r,** lanceur d'affaires *m*.

promotion, prau-mau´-ch'n, *n* avancement *m*; promotion *f*.

prompt, prommpte, *a** prompt. *v* suggérer; (stage) souffler; **–er,** *n* souffleur *m*.

prone, praune, *a* étendu; (*fig*) enclin à; (bent) courbé.

prong, pronng, *n* dent *f*; pointe *f*.

a
b
c
d
e
f
g
h
i
j
k
l
m
n
o
p
q
r
s
t
u
v
w
x
y
z

A
B
C
D
E
F
G
H
I
J
K
L
M
N
O
P
Q
R
S
T
U
V
W
X
Y
Z

pronoun, prau´-nâ'ounne, *n* pronom *m.*

pronounce, prŏ-nâ'ounnce´, *v* prononcer.

pronunciation, prŏ-nonn-ci-é´-ch'n, *n* prononciation *f.*

proof, proufe, *n* preuve *f. a* – **against,** à l'épreuve de.

prop, proppe, *n* (*fig*) soutien *m,* support *m. v* étayer; supporter.

propaganda, prop-*a*-gănn´-da, *n* propagande *f.*

propagate, prop´-*a*-guéte, *v* propager.

propel, prŏ-pelle´, *v* faire mouvoir.

propeller, prŏ-pell´-*eur, n* hélice *f.*

proper*, prop´-'r, *a* propre; (fit) convenable.

property, prop´-*eur*-ti, *n* propriété *f;* biens *mpl.*

prophecy, prof´-i-si, *n* prophétie *f.*

prophesy, prof´-i-sâï, *v* prédire.

prophet, prof´-ette, *n* prophète *m.*

propitious*, pro-pich´-*euce, a* propice.

proportion, pro-paur´-ch'n, *n* proportion *f.*

proposal, pro-pauz´-'l, *n* proposition *f.*

propose, pro-pauze´, *v* proposer; offrir.

proposition, pro-pau-zich´-'n, *n* proposition *f.*

proprietor, pro-prâï´-è-teur, *n* propriétaire *m.*

proprietress, pro-prâï´-è-tresse, *n* propriétaire *f.*

propriety, pro-prâï´-è-ti, *n* convenances *fpl.*

prose, prauze, *n* prose *f.*

prosecute, pross´-i-kioute, *v* (law) poursuivre.

prosecution, pross-i-kioue´-ch'n, *n* poursuites *fpl.*

prosecutor, pross´-i-kioue-teur, *n* plaignant *m.*

prospect, pross´-pecte, *n* vue *f;* (future) avenir *m. v* explorer; –**ive,** *a* futur.

prospectus, pross-pec´-teuce, *n* prospectus *m.*

prosper, pross´-p'r, *v* prospérer; –**ity,** *n* prospérité *f;* –**ous*,** *a* prospère.

prostitute, pross´-ti-tioute, *n* prostituée *f.*

prostrate, pross-tréte, *v* se prosterner; (*fig*) accabler. *a* posterné; accablé; prostré; abattu.

prostration, pross-tré´-ch'n, *n* prostration *f.*

protect, pro-tecte´, *v* protéger.

protection, pro-tec´-ch'n, *n* protection *f.*

protest, pro-tesste´, *v* protester. *n* protestation *f.*

protract, pro-tracte´, *v* prolonger.

protrude, pro-troude´, *v* faire saillie; déborder.

proud*, prâ'oude, *a* fier; orgueilleux.

prove, prouve, *v* prouver; vérifier (a will, etc.).

proverb, prov´-*eu*rbe, *n* proverbe *m.*

provide, prŏ-vâide´, *v* pourvoir; fournir.

Providence, prov´-i-dennce, *n* providence *f.*

provident, prov´-i-dennte, *a* prévoyant.

province, prov´-innce, *n* province *f.*

provision, prŏ-vi´-j'n, *n* provision *f;* stipulation *f;* –**al*,** *a* provisoire; –**s,** *npl* comestibles *mpl.*

provocation, prŏv-ô-qué´-ch'n, *n* provocation *f.*

provoke, prŏ-vauke´, *v* provoquer; irriter.

prowl, prâ'oule, *v* rôder.

proximity, prok-simm´-i-ti, *n* proximité *f.*

proxy, prok´-ci, *n* fondé de pouvoir *m;* **by** –, par procuration.

prude, proude, *n* prude *f;* –**nce,** prudence *f;* –**nt*,**

a prudent; **–ry,** *n* pruderie *f*.

prudish, prou´-diche, *a* prude.

prune, proune, *n* pruneau *m*. *v* (trees, etc) tailler.

pry, prâï, *v* fureter; fourrer son nez dans . . .

psalm, sâme, *n* psaume *m*.

pseudonym, sioue´-dô-nimme, *n* pseudonyme *m*.

psychiatry, sâï-kâï´-a-tri, *n* psychiatrie *f*.

psychology, sâï-col´-ŏdj-i, *n* psychologie *f*.

public, pobb´-lique, *n* & *a* public *m*; **–an,** *n* aubergiste *m*; **–house,** auberge *f*.

publication, pobb-li-qué´-ch'n, *n* publication *f*.

publish, pobb´-liche, *v* publier; (books, etc) éditer.

publisher, pobb´-lich-*eur*, *n* éditeur *m*.

pucker, pok´-'r, *v* rider; plisser (the brows, etc.); froncer.

pudding, poudd´-inng, *n* pudding *m*.

puddle, podd´-'l, *n* flaque *f*.

puerile, pioue´-*eur*-âïl, *a* puéril.

puff, pof, *v* souffler; (swell) boursoufler. *n*

(breath) souffle *m*; (wind, etc) bouffée *f*; **powder –,** houppe à poudrer *f*; **–y,** *a* boursouflé.

pug, pogg, *n* (dog) carlin *m*; **–nacious,** *a* batailleur; **–-nosed,** qui a le nez épaté.

pugilist, pioue´-djil-ist, *n* pugiliste *m*.

pull, poull, *n* coup (d'aviron) *m*. *v* tirer; **–down,** abattre; démolir; (lower) baisser; **–out,** (draw) arracher;**–up,** remonter; hisser.

pullet, poull´ette, *n* poulette *f*.

pulley, poull´-i, *n* poulie *f*.

pulp, polpe, *n* pulpe *m*; **wood –,** pâte de bois *f*.

pulpit, poull´-pitte, *n* chaire *f*.

pulse, pollse, *n* pouls *m*.

pulverize, poll´-*veur*-âïze, *v* pulvériser.

pumice, pomm´-ice staune, *n* pierre ponce *f*.

pump, pommpe, *n* pompe *f*. *v* pomper.

pun, ponne, *n* jeu de mots *m*.

punch, ponntche, *n* (blow) coup de poing *m*; (tool) poinçon *m*; (drink) punch *m*; (to hit) *v* donner un coup

de poing à; percer.

punctilious*, ponngk-til´-i-*euce*, *a* pointilleux.

punctual*, ponngk´-tiou-*eul*, *a* ponctuel.

punctuate, ponngk´-tiou-éte, *v* ponctuer.

punctuation, ponngk-tiou-é´-ch'n, *n* ponctuation.

puncture, ponngk´tioure, *n* (*med*) ponction *f*; (tire) crevaison *f*. *v* crever.

pungency, ponn´-djenn-si, *n* âcreté *f*; aigreur *f*.

pungent, ponn´-djennte, *a* âcre; piquant.

punish, ponn´-iche, *v* punir; **–able,** *a* punissable.

punishment, ponn´-iche-mennte, *n* punition *f*.

punitive, pioue´-ni-tive, *a* punitif.

punt, ponnte, *n* bateau plat *m*.

puny, pioue´-ni, *a* chétif; faible.

pupil, pioue´-pile, *n* élève *m* & *f*; (eye) pupille *f*.

puppet, popp´-ette, *n* marionnette *f*; poupée *f*.

puppy, popp´-i, *n* jeune chien *m*.

purchase, por´-tchiss, *v* acheter. *n* achat *m*.

purchaser, por´-tché-*seur*,

A
B
C
D
E
F
G
H
I
J
K
L
M
N
O
P
Q
R
S
T
U
V
W
X
Y
Z

n acheteur, -euse *m* & *f*.
pure*, pioure, *a* pur;
   vierge.
purgative, peur´-*ga*-tive, *n*
   & *a* purgatif *m*.
purgatory, peur´-*ga*-tŏ-ri,
   n purgatoire *m*.
purge, peurdje, *v* purger. *n*
   purge *f*.
purify, pioue´-ri-fâï, *v*
   purifier.
purity, pioue´-ri-ti, *n*
   pureté *f*.
purloin, peur´-lô'ine, *v*
   dérober.
purple, peur´-p'l, *n* & *a*
   pourpre *m*.
purpose, peur´-*peu*ce, *n*
   but *m*; –**ly,** *adv* exprès.
purr, peur, *v* ronronner.
purse, peurce, *n* porte-
   monnaie *m*; (prize)
   bourse *f*.
purser, peur´-*ceu*r, *n*
   (ship's) commissaire *m*.
pursue, p*eu*r-sioue´, *v*
   poursuivre.
pursuit, p*eu*r-sioute´, *n*
   poursuite *f*.
purveyor, p*eu*r-vé´-*eu*r, *n*
   fournisseur *m*.
pus, p*o*ss, *n* pus *m*; humeur
   f.
push, pouche, *v* pousser. *n*
   poussée *f*.
pushing, pouch´-inng, *a*
   (keen) entreprenant.
put, poutt, *v* mettre;

placer; poser; –**off,**
   remettre; –**on,** mettre.
putrefy, pioue´-tri-fâï, *v* se
   putréfier; pourrir.
putrid, pioue´-tride, *a*
   putride.
putty, pott´-i, *n* mastic *m*.
puzzle, pozz-z'l, *v*
   embarrasser; intriguer. *n*
   embarras *m*; (toy) casse-
   tête *m*; puzzle *m*;
   crossword –, mots
   croisés *mpl*.
pyramid, pir´-*a*-mide, *n*
   pyramide *f*.
python, pâï´-*t*sonn, *n*
   python *m*.

quack, couăque, *v* cancaner. *n* charlatan *m*; **–ery,** charlatanisme *m*.

quadrille, couodd´rile, *n* quadrille *m*.

quadruped, couodd´-rou-pedde, *n* quadrupède *m*.

quadruple, couodd´-rou-p'l, *a* quadruple.

quagmire, couăgue´-mâïre, *n* marécage *m*.

quail, couéle, *n* caille *f*. *v* trembler.

quaint*, couénnte, *a* bizarre; étrange.

quaintness, couénnte´-nesse, *n* bizarrerie *f*.

quake, couéque, *v* trembler; **earth–,***n* tremblement de terre *m*.

Quaker, coué´-keur, *n* (sect) Quaker *m*.

qualification, couoll-i-fi-qué´-ch'n, *n* aptitude *f*.

qualified, couoll´-i-fâïd, *a* diplômé.

qualify, couoll´-i-fâï, *v* qualifier; acquérir les qualités requises.

quality, couoll´i-ti, *n* qualité *f*.

quandary, couonn´-da-ri, *n* perplexité *f*.

quantity, couonn´-ti-ti, *n* quantité *f*.

quarantine, couor´-ann-tîne, *n* quarantaine *f*.

quarrel, couor´-elle, *n* dispute *f*. *v* se disputer.

quarrelsome, couor´-ell-se*u*me, *a* querelleur.

quarry, couor´-i, *n* carrière *f*; (prey) proie *f*.

quarter, couôr´-t'r, *v* (to lodge) loger; diviser en quatre. *n* quart *m*; (period) trimestre *m*; (district) quartier *m*; **–ly,** *a* trimestriel.

quartet, couôr-tette´, *n* quatuor *m*.

quartz, couortze, *n* quartz *m*.

quash, couoche, *v* subjuguer; réprimer; (law) annuler.

quaver, coué´-v'r, *v* chevroter. *n* (*mus*) croche *f*.

quay, quî, *n* quai *m*.

queen, couîne, *n* reine *f*.

queer*, couire, *a* bizarre; étrange; drôle.

quell, couelle, *v* réprimer; dompter.

quench, couenntche, *v* éteindre; (thirst) apaiser sa soif.

querulous*, couèr´-ou-le*u*ce, *a* plaintif.

query, coui´ri, *v* mettre en doute. *n* question *f*.

quest, coueste, *n* recherche *f*; enquête *f*.

question, couess´-tie*u*ne, *v* questionner; douter. *n*

a
b
c
d
e
f
g
h
i
j
k
l
m
n
o
p
q
r
s
t
u
v
w
x
y
z

A
B
C
D
E
F
G
H
I
J
K
L
M
N
O
P
Q
R
S
T
U
V
W
X
Y
Z

question *f;* –**able,** *a*
contestable; –**mark,** *n*
point d'interrogation *m.*
queue, kioue, *n* queue *f.*
quibble, couib´-b'l, *v*
ergoter. *n* chicane *f.*
quick*, couique, *a* rapide;
(hurry) vite; (wit, etc)
vif; –**en,** *v* accélérer;
animer; –**lime,** *n* chaux
vive *f;* –**ness,** vitesse *f;*
vivacité *f;* –**sand,** sables
mouvants *mpl.*
quiet, couâï´-ette, *v*
calmer. *a** tranquille.
quill, couille, *n* (pen)
plume d'oie *f.*
quilt, couillte, *n* couvre-
pieds *m;* édredon
américain *m.*
quince, couinnce, *n* coing
m.
quinine, couinn´-âïne, *n*
quinine *f.*
quit, couitte, *v* quitter; –**s,**
adv quitte.
quite, couâïte, *adv* tout à
fait; entièrement; assez.
quiver, couiv´-'r, *n*
carquois *m. v* trembler; *n*
tremblement *m.*
quiz, couiz, *n* jeu-concours
m; devinette *f;*
interrogation *f. v*
interroger; questionner;
n test *m;* (*game*) jeu-
concours *m.*
quota, cou'au´*ta, n* quote-

part *f;* quota *m.*
quotation, cou'au-té´-
ch'n, *n* citation *f;*
(price) devis *m;* (shares,
etc) cote *f.*
quote, cou'aute, *v* citer;
coter; faire un prix.

rabbi, răb´-bâï, n rabbin m.

rabbit, răb´-itte, n lapin m.

rabble, răbb´-'l, n populace f; (riffraff) canaille f.

rabid, răb´-ide, a enragé.

rabies, ré´-bi-ize, n rage f.

race, réce, v courir; courir vite; faire la course. n (breed) race f; (contest) course f; **--course,** champ de courses m; **-- horse,** cheval de course m; **-s,** courses fpl.

racism, ré´-si-z'm, n racisme m.

racist, ré´-ssiste, a, n raciste.

rack, răque, n (torture) roue f; (luggage) filet m.

racket, răque´-ette, n (sports) raquette f.

radar, ré-dâre, n radar m.

radiant*, ré´-di-annte, a rayonnant (de); (fig) radieux.

radiate, ré´-di-éte, v rayonner (de); (heat) émettre des rayons.

radiation, ré-di-é´-ch'n, n rayonnement m.

radiator, ré´-di-é-teur, n radiateur m.

radio, ré´-di-o, n radio f.

radioactive, ré-di-o-ăc´-tive, a radioactif.

radio station, ré-di-o-stă-ch'n, n station de radio f.

radish, răd´-iche, n radis m; horse- --, raifort m.

radium, ré´-di-omme, n radium m.

radius, ré´-di-euce, n

rayon m.

raffle, ră?´-'l, n loterie f. v mettre en loterie.

raft, râfte, n radeau n.

rafter, râf´-t'r, n chevron m. poutre f.

rag, răgue, n chiffon m; --ged, a en loques.

rage, rédje, n rage f. v être furieux.

raid, réde, n incursion f; (air --) raid m; (police --) descente de police f.

rail, réle, v railler. n (railroad) rail m; (stair) barreau m; --lery, raillerie f; --road, chemin de fer m.

rain, réne, v pleuvoir. n pluie f; --bow, arc-en-ciel m; --coat, imperméable m; --fall, quantité de pluie f; -- water, eau de pluie f; --y, a pluvieux.

raise, réze, v (courage) lever; (to lift, etc.) relever; soulever; (increase) augmenter; (heighten) rehausser; (crops) cultiver.

raisin, ré´-z'n, n raisin sec m.

rake, réque, n râteau m; (person) roué m. v (mech) râtisser; (fire) secouer.

rally, răl´-i, v rallier;

rassembler; *n* rallye *m*.

ram, rămme, *n* bélier *m*. *v* enfoncer; (ship) aborder.

rampant, rămm´-pannte, *a* rampant; exubérant.

rampart, rămm´-pârte, *n* rempart *m*.

rancid, rănn´-cide, *a* rance.

rancor, rănng´-keur, *n* rancune *f*.

random, rănn´-d'm, **at –,** *adv* au hasard.

range, réne´-dje, *n* série *f*; (kitchen) fourneau *m*; (extent) étendue *f*; (mountain) chaîne *f*; (practice) champ de tir *m*; (projectile) portée *f*. *v* ranger.

ranger, réne´-djeur, *n* garde-forestier *m*.

rank, rain-nk, *a* (taste, smell) rance. *n* rang *m*; (*mil*) grade *m*; (row) rangée *f*.

ransack, rănn´-săque, *v* saccager; fouiller.

ransom, rănn´-seume, *n* rançon *f*. *v* rançonner.

rap, răppe, *n* coup *m*. *v* frapper.

rape, répe, *v* violer; enlever. *n* viol *m*.

rapid*, răp´-ide, *a* rapide; **–s,** *npl* rapides *mpl*.

rapture, răp´-tioure, *n*

ravissement *m*.

rare*, raire, *a* rare; **–fy,** *v* raréfier.

rarity, ré´-ri-ti, *n* rareté *f*.

rascal, râsse´-c'l, *n* coquin *m*; fripon *m*.

rash*, răche, *n* (skin) éruption *f*. *a** téméraire; **–er,** *n* tranche de lard *f*; **–ness,** témérité *f*.

rasp, râsspe, *n* râpe *f*; grincement *m*. *v* râper; grincer.

raspberry, râze´-beur-i, *n* framboise *f*.

rat, rătte, *n* rat *m*; **–-trap,** ratière *f*.

rate, réte, *n* proportion *f*; (tax; exchange; charge) taux *m*; (speed) vitesse *f*. *v* évaluer.

rather, râdz´-'r, *adv* plutôt; (somewhat) assez.

ratify, răt´-i-fâï, *v* ratifier.

ratio, ré´-chi-au, *n* proportion *f*.

ration, ră´-ch'n, *n* ration *f*. *v* rationner.

rational*, răch´-eunn-'l, *a* rationnel; raisonnable.

rattle, răt´-t'l, *n* (instrument) crécelle *f*; (toy) hochet *m*; (noise) tapage *m*; (death) râle de la mort *m*.

rattlesnake, răt´-t'l-snéke, *n* serpent à sonnettes *m*.

ravage, răv´-idj, *v* ravager.

n ravage *m*.

rave, réve, *v* délirer; **–about,** s'extasier sur.

raven, ré´-v'n, *n* corbeau *m*.

ravenous, răv´-'n-euce, *a* vorace.

ravine, ră-vine´, *n* ravin *m*.

raving, ré´-vinng, *a* en délire; (*fig*) furieux.

ravish, ră´-viche, *v* ravir; **–ing,** *a* ravissant.

raw, roa, *a* cru; (wound) à vif.

ray, ré, *n* rayon *m*.

raze, réze, *v* raser; abattre.

razor, ré´-z'r, *n* rasoir *m*; **safety–,**rasoir mécanique *m*; **–-blade,** lame de rasoir *f*.

reach, rîtche, *v* atteindre; (arrive) parvenir à.

react, ri-acte´, réagir; **–ion,** *n* réaction *f*.

read, rîde, *v* lire; (for exam) étudier; **–er,** *n* lecteur *m*; (print) correcteur *m*; **–ing,** lecture *f*.

readily, redd´-i-li, *adv* promptement; (willingly) volontiers.

ready, redd´-i, *a* prêt; **– made,** tout fait; (clothes) le prêt à porter.

real*, ri´-'l, *a* réel;

véritable.

reality, rî-ă´-li-tî, *n* réalité *f.*

realize, ri´-al-âïze, *v* se rendre compte de; (sell) réaliser.

realm, relme, *n* royaume *n.*

reap, rîpe, *v* moissonner; récolter; **–er,** *n* moissonneur *m*; **–ing machine,** moissonneuse *f.*

rear, rire, *v* élever; (prance) se cabrer. *n* (*mil*) arrière-garde *f*; (back) arrière *m.*

reason, rî´-z'n, *v* raisonner. *n* raison *f.*

reasonable, rî´-z'n-a-b'l, *a* raisonnable.

reassure, ri´-a-choure´, *v* rassurer.

rebate, ri-béte´, *v* rabattre.

rebel, rebb´-'l, *n & a* rebelle *m & f.*

rebel, ri-bel´, *v* se révolter; **–lion,** *n* rébellion *f.*

rebound, ri-bâ'ounnde´, *v* rebondir. *n* rebond *m*; ricochet *m*; remontee *f.*

rebuff, ri-boffe´, *v* rebuter. *n* rebuffade *f.*

rebuke, ri-biouke´, *v* réprimander. *n* réprimande *f.*

recall, ri-coale´, *v* rappeler; (retract)

retirer.

recapitulate, ri-ca-pit´-iou-léte, *v* récapituler.

recede, ri-cîde´, *v* reculer.

receipt, ri-cîte´, *n* reçu *m.* *v* acquitter.

receipts, ri-cîtse´, *npl* (*com*) recettes *fpl.*

receive, ri-cîve´, *v* recevoir; **–r,** *n* receveur *m*; (bankruptcy) syndic de faillite *m.*

recent*, rî´-cennte, *a* récent.

receptacle, ri-sèpe´-ta-k'l, *n* réceptacle *m.*

reception, ri-sèpe´-ch'n, *n* réception *f.*

recess, ri-cesse´, *n* (space) renfoncement *m*; (of a bed) alcôve *f.*

recipe, ress´-i-pi, *n* recette *f.*

reciprocate, ri-cip´-rŏ-quéte, *v* rendre la pareille.

recital, ri-sâï´-t'l, *n* récit *m*; récitation *f*; (*mus* etc) récital *m.*

recite, ri-sâïte´, *v* réciter.

reckless*, rèque´-lesse, *a* imprudent.

reckon, rèque´-'n, *v* compter; calculer.

reclaim, ri-cléme´, *v* réclamer; (land) défricher.

recline, ri-clâïne´, *v* se

pencher; s'appuyer.

recluse, ri-clouce´, *n & a* reclus, **-e** *m & f.*

recognition, rèk-ŏguen-niche´-'n, *n* reconnaissance *f.*

recognize, rèk´-ŏguen-nâïze, *v* reconnaître.

recoil, ri-coa'ile´, *v* reculer. *n* recul *m.*

recollect, rèk-ŏl-lecte´, *v* se rappeler; se souvenir de.

recollection, rèk-ŏl-lèque´-ch'n, *n* souvenir *m.*

recommence, ri-cŏmm-ennce´, *v* recommencer.

recommend, rè-cŏmm-ennde´, *v* recommander; **–ation,** *n* recommandation *f.*

recompense, rèk´-ŏmm-pennce, *v* récompenser. *n* récompense *f.*

reconcile, rèk´-ŏnn-sâïle, *v* réconcilier (avec); concilier.

reconnoiter, rèk-ŏnn-no'i´-tr, *v* faire une reconnaissance.

reconsider, ri-cŏnn-cid´-'r, *v* considérer de nouveau.

record, ri-coarde´, *v* enregistrer; (in history) mentionner.

record, rèk´-oarde, *n*

a
b
c
d
e
f
g
h
i
j
k
l
m
n
o
p
q
r
s
t
u
v
w
x
y
z

registre *m*; archives *fpl*;
(phonograph) disque *m*;
–player, *n* tourne-
disques *m*.

recoup, ri-coupe´, *v*
dédommager (de).

recourse, ri-caurse´, *n*
recours *m*.

recover, rî-cov´-'r, *v*
recouvrer; (health) se
rétablir; **–y,** *n*
recouvrement *m*;
rétablissement *m*.

recover, ri-cov´-'r, *v*
recouvrir.

recreation, rèk-ri-é´-ch'n,
n divertissement *m*.

recruit, ri-croute´, *n*
recrue *f*. *v* recruter.

rectangular, rèk-tănng´-
guiou-l'r, *a*
rectangulaire.

rectify, rèk´-ti-fâï, *v*
rectifier.

rector, rèk´-t'r, *n* recteur
m; **–y,** presbytère *m*.

recumbent, ri-comm´-
bennte, *a* étendu;
couché.

recuperate, ri-kiou´-peur-
éte, *v* se remettre.

recur, ri-keur´, *v* (to
happen again) se
reproduire; se répéter.

red, red, *n* & *a* rouge *m*;
–breast, *n* rouge-gorge
m; **–den,** *v* rougir; **–dish,**
a rougeâtre; **–hot,**

chauffé au rouge; **–ness,**
n rougeur *f*.

redeem, ri-dîme´, *v*
(promise) accomplir une
promesse; (bonds, etc)
rembourser; (pledge)
dégager; (soul) délivrer.

redemption, ri-demmp´-
ch'n, *n* (com) rachat *m*.

red-light district, rèd-lâït-
diss-tricte, *n* quartier des
prostituées *m*.

redouble, ri-dob´-'l, *v*
redoubler.

redress, ri-dresse´, *v*
réparer. *n* réparation *f*.

reduce, ri-diouce´, *v*
réduire à ou en;
(disgrace) rétrograder.

reduction, ri-doque´-ch'n,
n réduction *f*; rabais *m*.

redundant, ri-donn´-
deunt, *a* licencié;
superflu.

reed, rîde, *n* roseau *m*.

reef, rîfe, *n* récif *m*; (sail)
ris *m*. *v* prendre un ris.

reek, rîque, *v* fumer;
exhaler; empester. *n*
odeur forte *f*.

reel, rîle, *n* (cotton; film)
bobine *f*; (angling)
moulinet, *m*. *v*
chanceler.

refer, ri-feur´, *v* se référer
(à); (apply) s'adresser à;
(to a book) consulter.

referee, rèf´-eur-î´, *n*

arbitre *m*.

reference, rèf´-eur-'nce, *n*
(allusion) allusion *f*;
(testimonial) référence
f; **with –to,** concernant.

referendum, rèf-eur-èn´-
deum, *n* référendum *m*.

refine, ri-fâïne´, *v* (sugar,
etc.) raffiner; (liquids)
épurer; **–d,** *a* raffiné;
–ment, *n* raffinement *m*.

reflect, ri-flecte´, *v*
réfléchir; (lights, etc)
refléter; **–ion,** *n*
réflexion *f*; **–or,**
réflecteur *m*.

reform, ri-fôrme´, *v*
réformer; se réformer. *n*
réforme *f*; **–ation,**
réformation *f*.

refrain, ri-fréne´, *v*
s'abstenir de.

refresh, ri-frèche´, *v*
rafraîchir; se rafraîchir.

refreshment, ri-frèche´-
m'nt, *n* rafraîchissement
m.

refrigerator, ri-fridje´-eur-
é-teur, *n* frigidaire *m*.

refuge, rèf´-ioudje, *n*
refuge (contre) *m*;
(shelter) abri *m*.

refugee, rèf-iou-djî´, *n*
réfugié, -ée *m* & *f*.

refund, ri-fonnde´, *v*
rembourser. *n*
remboursement *m*.

refusal, ri-fiou´-z'l, *n*

refus *m.*

refuse, ri-fiouze, *v* refuser.

refuse, rèf´-iouce, *n* rebut *m*; (garbage) ordures *fpl.*

refute, ri-fioute´, *v* réfuter.

regain, ri-guéne´, *v* regagner; (health) récupérer.

regal*, rî´-g'l, *a* royal.

regale, ri-guéle, *v* régaler.

regard, ri-gârde´, *v* regarder; considérer. *n* regard *m*; (heed) égard (pour) *m*; **–less,** *a* sans égard; **–s,** *npl* amitiés *fpl.*

regatta, ri-găt´-ta, *n* régate *f.*

regenerate, ri-djenn´-*eur*-éte, *v* régénérer.

regent, rî´-djennte, *n* régent, -e *m* & *f.*

regiment, rèdj´-i-m'nt, *n* régiment *m.*

region, rî´-dj*eu*ne, *n* région *f.*

register, rèdje´-iss-t*eur*, *v* enregistrer; (letter) recommander. *n* registre *m.*

registrar, rèdge´-iss-trâre, *n* (births, etc) officier de l'état civil *m*; (court) greffier *m.*

registration, rèdge-iss-tré´-ch'n *n* enregistrement *m*; inscription *f.*

registry, rèdge´-iss-tri, *n*

bureau d'enregistrement *m.*

regret, ri-grette´, *v* regretter. *n* regret *m.*

regrettable, ri-grett´-*a*-b'l, *a* regrettable.

regular*, regg´-iou-l'r, *a* régulier.

regulate, regg´-iou-léte, *v* régler.

regulation, regg-iou-lé´-ch'n, *n* règlement *m.*

rehearsal, ri-heur´-s'l, *n* répétition *f.*

rehearse, ri-heurce´, *v* répéter.

reign, réne, *n* règne *m. v* régner.

reimburse, ri-imm-beurce´, *v* rembourser.

rein, réne, *n* rêne *f.*

reindeer, réne´-dire, *n* renne *m.*

reinforce, ri-inn-faurce´, *v* renforcer.

reinstate, ri-inn-stéte´, *v* réintégrer.

reject, ri-djecte´, *v* rejeter.

rejoice, ri-djoa'ice´, *v* réjouir.

rejoicings, ri-djoa'ice´-inngse, *npl* réjouissances *fpl.*

rejoin, ri-djô'ine´, *v* rejoindre.

rejuvenate, ri-djiou´-venn-éte, *v* rajeunir.

relapse, ri-lăpse´, *n*

rechute *f. v* retomber.

relate, ri-léte´, *v* raconter; **–d,** *a* apparenté à.

relation, ri-lé´-ch'n, *n* (a relative) parent, -e *m* & *f*; (com) rapport *m*; relation *f.*

relative, rèl´-*a*-tive, *n* parent, -e *m* & *f. a** relatif; *n* (person) parent *m.*

relax, ri-lăxe´, *v* se détendre; **–ation,** *n* détente; relaxation *f.*

relay, ri-lé´, *n* (radio) relais *m. v* relayer.

release, ri-lice´, *v* relâcher; libérer. *n* (an obligation) décharge *f.*

relent, ri-lennte´, *v* se laisser fléchir.

relentless*, ri-lennte´-lesse, *a* implacable.

relevant, rèl´-i-v*a*nnte, *a* applicable (à); relatif.

reliable, ri-lâï´-*a*-b'l, *a* digne de confiance; sûr.

reliance, ri-lâï´-*a*nnce, *n* confiance *f.*

relic, rèl´-ique, *n* (of a saint or martyr) relique *f*; **–s,** *pl* restes *mpl.*

relief, ri-lîfe´, *n* (anxiety; pain) soulagement *m*; (help) secours *m*; (raised) relief *m.*

relieve, ri-lîve´, *v* soulager; secourir.

a
b
c
d
e
f
g
h
i
j
k
l
m
n
o
p
q
r
s
t
u
v
w
x
y
z

religion, ri-lidj´-onn, *n*
religion *f.*

religious*, ri-lidj´-*euce*, *a*
religieux.

relinquish, ri-linng´-
couiche, *v* abandonner.

relish, rèl´-iche, *v*
savourer. *n* saveur *f.*

reluctance, ri-loque´-
t'nce, *n* répugnance *f.*

reluctant, ri-loque´-
tannte, *a* peu disposé à.

rely, ri-lâï, *v* compter sur.

remain, ri-méne´, *v* rester;
–der, *n* reste *m.*

remand, ri-mânnde. *v*
(law) renvoyer à une
autre audience.

remark, ri-mârque´, *n*
remarque *f. v* remarquer.

remarkable, ri-mâr´-ka-
b'l, *a* remarquable.

remedy, remm´-i-di, *n*
remède *m. v* remédier á.

remember, ri-memm´-b'r,
v se souvenir de.

remembrance, ri-memm´-
brannce, *n* souvenir *m.*

remind, ri-mâïnnde, *v*
rappeler.

remit, ri-mitte´, *v* (a fine,
etc.) remettre; **–tance,** *n*
remise *f.*

remnant, remm´-nannte,
n reste *m*; **–s,** *pl* (fabrics)
coupons *mpl.*

remonstrate, ri-monn´-
stréte, *v* faire des

remontrances à.

remorse, ri-moarce´, *n*
remords *m.*

remote, ri-maute´, *a*
éloigné; (of time)
reculé; lointain.

removal, ri-moue´-v'l, *n*
(of furniture)
déménagement *m.*

remove, ri-mouve´, *v*
(furniture) déménager;
(shift) déplacer.

remunerate, ri-mioue´-
neur-éte, *v* rémunérer.

remunerative, ri-mioue´-
neur-*a*-tive, *a*
rémunérateur;
avantageux.

rend, rennde, *v* déchirer;
–er, rendre; (account)
présenter; **–ering,** *n*
traduction *f.*

renegade, renn´-i-guéde, *n*
renégat, -e *m* & *f.*

renew, ri-nioue´, *v*
renouveler; **–al,** *n*
renouvellement *m.*

renounce, ri-nâ'ounce´, *v*
renoncer.

renovate, renn´-ŏ-véte, *v*
renouveler.

renown, ri-nâ'oune´, *n*
renommée *f*; renom *m.*

rent, rennte, *n* (of houses
or rooms) loyer *m*; (tear)
déchirure *f. v* louer.

renunciation, ri-nonn-
ci-é´-ch'n, *n*

renonciation *f.*

repair, ri-paire´, *v* réparer;
(sewing, clothes, etc.)
raccommoder. *n*
réparation *f.*

reparation, rèp-*a*-ré´-ch'n,
n réparation *f.*

repartee, rèp-*ar*-tî´, *n*
repartie *f.*

repay, ri-pé´, *v*
rembourser.

repeal, ri-pîle´, *v* révoquer.
n révocation *f.*

repeat, ri-pîte´, *v* répéter.

repel, ri-pelle´, *v*
repousser; **–lent,** *a*
répulsif.

repent, ri-pennte´, *v* se
repentir (de).

repetition, rèp-i-tiche´-'n,
n répétition *f.*

replace, ri-pléce´, *v* (to
substitute) remplacer;
(put back) replacer.

replenish, ri-plenn´-iche,
v remplir (de).

reply, ri-plâï´, *v* répondre.
n réponse *f.*

report, ri-paurte´, *n*
rapport *m*; compte
rendu *m*; (news)
nouvelles *fpl*; (school)
bulletin *m*; (noise)
détonation *f. v* informer;
signaler.

reporter, ri-paur´-t'r, *n*
reporter *m.*

repose, ri-pauze´, *n* repos

m. v (se) reposer.

repository, ri-poz´-i-tŏ-ri, *n* dépôt *m.*

represent, rèp-ri-zennte´, *v* représenter; **–ation,** *n* représentation *f;* **–ative,** représentant *m.*

reprieve, ri-prîve´, *v* commuer (une peine), remettre.

reprimand, rèp-ri-mânnde´, *v* réprimander.

reprimand, rép´-ri-mânnde, *n* réprimande *f.*

reprint, ri-prinnte´, *v* réimprimer. *n* réimpression *f;* nouveau tirage *m.*

reprisal, ri-prâï´-z'l, *n* représaille *f.*

reproach, ri-prautche´, *v* reprocher à. *n* reproche *m.*

reprobate, rèp´-ro-béte, *n* vaurien *m.*

reproduce, ri-prŏ-diouce´, *v* reproduire.

reproduction, ri-prŏ-dock´-ch'n, *n* reproduction *f.*

reproof, ri-proufe´, *n* réprimande *f.*

reprove, ri-prouve´, *v* blâmer; censurer.

reptile, rèp´-tâïle, *n* reptile *m.*

republic, ri-pobb´-lique, *n* république *f.*

repudiate, ri-pioue´-diéte, *v* répudier.

repugnant, ri-pog´-nannte, *a* répugnant.

repulse, ri-pollce´, *v* repousser. *n* échec *m.*

repulsive, ri-poll´-cive, *a* repoussant.

reputable, rèp´-ieu-tă-b'l, *a* de bonne réputation.

reputation, rèp´-iou-té´-ch'n, *n* réputation *f.*

repute, ri-pioute´, *n* renom *m.*

request, ri-couesste´, *n* demande *f. v* demander.

require, ri-couâïre´, *v* (to want) avoir besoin de; exiger; **–ment,** *n* besoin *m;* exigence *f.*

requisite, rèk´-oui-zitte, *a* requis; nécessaire.

rescue, ress´-kioue, *v* sauver. *n* sauvetage *m.*

research, ri-seurtche´, *n* recherche *f.*

resemble, ri-zemm´-b'l, *v* ressembler (à).

resent, ri-zennte´, *v* garder rancune; **–ful*,** *a* vindicatif; **–ment,** *n* ressentiment *m.*

reservation, rèz-eur-vé´-ch'n, *n* réservation *f;(doubt)* réserve *f.*

reserve, ri-zeurve´, *v* réserver. *n* réserve *f.*

reservoir, rèz´-eur-vo'ar, *n*

réservoir *m.*

reside, ri-zâïde´, *v* résider; habiter; demeurer.

residence, rèz´-i-dennce, *n* résidence *f;* (stay) séjour *m.*

resident, rèz´-i-dennt, *n* habitant, -e *m* & *f;* pensionnaire *m* & *f. a* résidant.

resign, ri-zâïne´, *v* abandonner; (a post) démissionner (de); (oneself to) se résigner à.

resin, rèz´-inn, *n* résine *f.*

resist, ri-zisste´, *v* résister à; **–ance,** *n* résistance *f.*

resolute*, rèz´-o-lioute, *a* résolu; déterminé.

resolution, rèz´-o-lioue´-ch'n, *n* résolution *f.*

resolve, ri-zolve´, *v* résoudre; (of deliberate bodies) décider.

resort, ri-zoarte´, **–to,** *v* recourir à.

resound, ri-zâ'ounnde´, *v* retentir; résonner.

resource, ri-soarce´, *n* ressource *f.*

respect, riss-pecte´, *v* respecter. *n* respect *m;* égard *m;* **–ability,** respectabilité *f;* **–able,** *a* respectable; **–ful*,** respectueux; **–ive*,** respectif.

A
B
C
D
E
F
G
H
I
J
K
L
M
N
O
P
Q
R
S
T
U
V
W
X
Y
Z

respite, ress´-pâïte, n répit m.

respond, riss-ponnde´, v répondre.

respondent, riss-ponn´-dennt, n (law) défendeur m.

response, riss-ponnce´, n réponse f.

responsible, riss-ponn´-ci-b'l, a responsable.

rest, reste, n repos m; (sleep) somme m; (remainder) reste m. v se reposer; –**ful,** a tranquille; –**ive,** rétif; –**less,** agité.

restaurant, ress´-to-rannte, n restaurant m; –**car,** wagon-restaurant m.

restore, ri-staure´, v restituer; (health) (to recover) rétablir.

restrain, ri-stréne´, v retenir; réprimer.

restraint, ri-strénnte, n contrainte f.

restrict, ri-stricte´, v restreindre.

restriction, ri-strick´-ch'n, n restriction f.

result, ri-zollte´, v résulter. n résultat m.

resume, ri-zioumme´, v reprendre; continuer.

resumption, ri-zomm´-ch'n, n reprise f.

resurrection, rèz-eur-rèque´-ch'n, n résurrection f.

retail, rî´-téle, v vendre au détail. n vente au détail f; –**er,** détaillant m.

retain, ri-téne´, v retenir; (keep) garder.

retaliate, ri-tăl´-i-éte, v user de représailles envers.

retard, ri-târde´, v retarder.

reticent, rètt´-i-sennte, a réservé; taciturne.

retinue, rètt´-i-nioue, n suite f; cortège m.

retire, ri-tâïre´, v se retirer; –**ment,** n retraite f.

retort, ri-toarte´, v riposter. n réplique f.

retract, ri-trăcte´, v rétracter.

retreat, ri-trîte´, v se retirer. n retraite f.

retrench, ri-trenntche´, v retrancher.

retribution, ri-tri-biu-shé-n, n châtiment m; récompense f.

retrieve, ri-trîve, v (to regain) recouvrer; (to repair) réparer.

return, ri-teurne´, v (come back) revenir; (go back) retourner; (give back) rendre. n retour m; –**s,** rendement m; –**ticket,** (fam) billet d'aller et retour m.

reveal, ri-vîle´, v révéler.

revel, rèv´-'l, v faire bombance. n réjouissances fpl.

revenge, ri-venndje´, v se venger de. n vengeance f.

revenue, rèv´-i-nioue, n revenu m; (state) fisc m.

reverse, ri-veurce´, v renverser; (engine) faire marche arrière. n revers m; contraire m. a inverse.

revert, ri-veurte´, v revenir (sur), (law) retourner à.

review, ri-vioue´, v examiner; (inspect) passer en revue; (books, etc) analyser. n revue f; (books) critique f.

revile, ri-vâïle´, v injurier.

revise, ri-vâïze´, v réviser.

revision, ri-vije´-'n, n révision f.

revive, ri-vâïve´, v ranimer; se ranimer.

revoke, ri-vauque´, v révoquer. n (cards) renonce f.

revolt, ri-volte´, n révolte f. v se révolter.

revolve, ri-volve´, v tourner.

revolver, ri-vole´-*veur*, *n*
révolver *m.*

reward, ri-ouôrde´, *n*
récompense *f. v*
récompenser.

rheumatism, roue´-mă-
tizme, *n* rhumatisme *m.*

rhinoceros, râï-noce´-i-
rŏsse, *n* rhinocéros *m.*

rhubarb, rou´-bârbe, *n*
rhubarbe *f.*

rhyme, râïme, *n* rime *f. v*
rimer.

rib, ribbe, *n* côte *f.*

ribbon, ribb´-'n, *n* ruban
m.

rice, râïce, *n* riz *m.*

rich*, ritche, *a* riche; **–es,**
n richesse *f.*

rickets, rik´-ètse, *n*
rachitisme *m.*

rickety, rik´-ett-i, *a* (*fig*)
branlant; (*med*)
rachitique.

rid, ridde, *v* débarrasser;
délivrer.

riddle, ridd´-'l, *n* énigme *f.*
v cribler de.

ride, râïde, *v* monter à
cheval; aller en auto;
aller à bicyclette. *n*
promenade à cheval *f,*
etc.

ridge, ridje, *n* (mountain)
crête *f.*

ridicule, ridd´-i-kioule, *v*
ridiculiser. *n* ridicule *m.*

ridiculous*, ri-dik´-iou-
leuce, *a* ridicule.

rifle, râï´-f'l, *v* piller. *n*
fusil *m.*

rift, rifte, *n* fente *f;* fissure
f.

rig, rigue, *v* (*fig*) (*naut*)
gréer. *n* (ship) gréement
m.

right, râïte, *n* droite *f. v*
rétablir. *a* droit; juste; en
règle.

rigid*, rid´-jide, *a* rigide;
(stiff) raide.

rigor, rigg´-eur, *n* rigueur *f.*

rigorous*, rigg´-ŏr-*euce, a*
rigoureux.

rim, rimme, *n* bord *m;*
(brim) rebord *m;*
(wheel) jante *f.*

rind, râïnnde, *n* (fruit)
pelure *f;* (bacon)
couenne *f;* (cheese)
croûte *f.*

ring, rinng, *n* anneau *m;*
(finger) bague *f;*
(wedding) alliance *f;*
(napkin) rond *m;*
(circus) arène *f;* (of bell)
coup de sonnette *m. v*
sonner; (of the ears)
tinter.

ringleader, rinng´-lî-d'r, *n*
meneur *m.*

rinse, rinnse, *v* rincer. *n*
rinçage *m.*

riot, râï´-ŏte, *n* émeute *f. v*
faire une émeute.

rip, rippe, *v* fendre;

(cloth) déchirer.

ripe, râïpe, *a* mûr; **–n,** *v*
mûrir.

ripple, rip´-p'l, *n* action de
rider *f.*

rise, râïze, *v* se lever;
(revolt) se soulever;
(river) (to ascend)
monter; (prices) hausser.
n (wages) augmentation
f.

risk, risque, *v* risquer. *n*
risque *m.*

rite, râïte, *n* rite *m.*

rival, râï´-v'l, *n* rival, -e *m*
& *f;* (*com*) concurrent, -
e *m* & *f.*

rivalry, râï´-val-ri, *n*
rivalité *f.*

river, riv´-'r, *n* fleuve *m;*
(small) rivière *f.*

rivet, riv´-ette, *v* river. *n*
rivet *m.*

road, raude, *n* chemin *m;*
route *f;* (street) rue *f.*

roam, raume, *v* rôder;
errer.

roar, raure, *v* rugir (of the
lion etc.); *n* rugissement
m.

roast, rauste, *v* rôtir. *n* & *a*
rôti *m.*

rob, robbe, *v* voler;
dépouiller; **–ber,** *n*
voleur, -euse *m* & *f.*

robbery, robb´-*eur*-i, *n* vol
m.

robe, raube, *n* robe *f;*

A
B
C
D
E
F
G
H
I
J
K
L
M
N
O
P
Q
R
S
T
U
V
W
X
Y
Z

(*eccl*) vêtements *mpl.*
robin, robb´-inn, *n* rouge-
  gorge *m.*
robust*, rọ-bọsste´, *a*
  robuste; vigoureux.
rock, roque, *n* rocher *m. v*
  (quake) secouer; (roll)
  rouler; (cradle) bercer;
  –y, *a* rocailleux; (sea)
  plein de rochers.
rock and roll, roque´-eun-
  raule´ *n* rock and roll *m.*
rocket, rok´-ette, *n* fusée *f.*
rod, rodde, *n* baguette *f;*
  (fishing) canne à pêche
  f; (curtain) triangle *f.*
roe, rau, *n* chevreuil *m;*
  biche *f;* (fish) laitance *f.*
rogue, raugue, *n* fripon *m;*
  –ry, friponnerie *f.*
roll, raule, *v* rouler; (– up)
  enrouler. *n* rouleau *m;*
  (bread, loaf) petit pain
  m; **–call,** appel *m;* **–er,**
  roulette *f;* (steam)
  rouleau *m;* **–er skate,**
  patin à roulettes *m.*
romance, rau-mănnce´, *n*
  roman dechevalerie *m;*
  (*mus*) romance *f.*
romantic, rau-mănne´-
  tique, *a* romantique;
  sentimental(e).
romp, rommpe, *v* jouer
  bruyamment.
roof, roufe, *n* toit *m;*
  (mouth) palais *m.*
rook, rouque, *n*

corneille *f.*
room, roumme, *n* pièce *f;*
  (bedroom) chambre *f;*
  living –, salon *m;* **dining**
  –, salle à manger *f;*
  bath–, salle de bains *f;*
  (public) salle *f;* (space)
  place *f;* **service–,** *n*
  service des chambres *m.*
roost, rouste, *v* percher. *n*
  perchoir *m.*
rooster, rous-teur, *n* coq
  m.
root, route, *n* racine *f. v*
  s'enraciner.
rope, raupe, *n* corde *f;*
  (*naut*) cordage *m.*
rosary, rau´-za-ri, *n* rosaire
  m.
rose, rauze, *n* rose *f;* **–**
  bush, rosier *m.*
rosemary, rauze´-mé-ri, *n*
  romarin *m.*
rosy, rauz´-i, *a* rosé;
  vermeil.
rot, rotte, *n* pourriture *f. v*
  pourrir.
rotate, rau´-téte, *v*
  tourner.
rouge, rouge, *n* rouge *m.*
rough*, roffe, *a* (manners)
  grossier; rude; (coarse)
  rugueux; rude; (sea)
  houleuse; (wind)
  tempêtueux; (bumpy)
  cahoteux.
roughness, roffe´-nesse, *n*
  rudesse *f;* grossièreté *f.*

round, râ´ounnde, *a* rond.
  v arrondir; **–about,** *a*
  détourné. *n* manège *m;*
  –ness, rondeur *f.*
rouse, râ´ouze, *v* (*fig*)
  exciter; (awaken)
  éveiller.
rout, râ´oute, *v* mettre en
  déroute. *n* déroute *f.*
route, route, *n* route *f;*
  itinéraire *m.*
routine, rou-tîne´, *n*
  routine *f.*
rove, rauve, *v* rôder; (*fig*)
  errer dans.
row, rau, *n* rangée *f;*
  (persons) file *f;*
  (boating) canotage *m. v*
  (scull) ramer.
row, râ´ou, *n* querelle *f;*
  (noise) vacarme *m.*
royal*, roa'i´-al, *a* royal;
  –ty, *n* royauté *f;*
  (payment) droits
  d'auteur *mpl.*
rub, robbe, *v* frotter; **–ber,**
  n caoutchouc *m;*
  (eraser) gomme à effacer
  f; **–off,** *v* effacer.
rubbish, robb´-iche, *n*
  ordures *fpl;* (trash)
  camelote *f.*
ruby, roue´-bi, *n* rubis *m. a*
  vermeil.
rucksack, roque´-săque, *n*
  sac à dos *m.*
rudder, rodd´-'r, *n*
  gouvernail *m.*

rude*, roude, *a* impoli; (coarse) grossier.

rudiment, roue´-di-m'nt, *n* rudiment *m*.

rue, roue, *v* déplorer; –**ful*,** *a* lamentable.

ruffian, roffe´-iane, *n* chenapan *m*.

ruffle, rof´-f'l, *v* déranger; (*fig*) troubler.

rug, rogue, *n* couverture *f*; (mat) tapis *m*.

rugby, rogg´-bî, *n* rugby *m*.

rugged, rogg´-ide, *a* (scenery) accidenté.

ruin, roue´-inne, *v* ruiner. *n* ruine *f*.

rule, roule, *v* gouverner; (lines) régler. *n* gouvernement *m*; (regulation, etc) règle *f*.

ruler, roul´-'r, *n* (drawing) règle *f*.

rum, romme, *n* rhum *m*.

rumble, romm´-b'l, *n* grondement sourd *m*.

rummage, romm´-idj, *v* fouiller. *n* fouillis *m*.

rumor, roue´-m'r, *n* rumeur *f*.

run, ronne, *v* courir; (colors) déteindre; –**away,** fuir. *n* (horse) cheval emballe *m*.

runway, ronn´-oué, *n* piste *f*.

rupture, ropp´-tioure, *n* rupture *f*; (*med*) hernie *f*.

rural, rou´-r'l, *a* champêtre; rural.

rush, roche, *n* ruée *f*; (water) torrent *m*; (reed) jonc *m*. *v* se ruer; se précipiter.

rust, rosste, *n* rouille *f*. *v* rouiller; –**y,** *a* rouillé.

rustic, ross´-tique, *a* rustique.

rustle, ross´-'l, *v* bruire. *n* bruissement *m*; (silk, of dresses) frou frou *m*.

rusty, ross´-tî, *a* rouillé(e).

rut, rotte, *n* (in a road) ornière *f*.

ruthless, rots-lèss, *a* sans pitie; cruel.

rye, râï, *n* seigle *m*.

a
b
c
d
e
f
g
h
i
j
k
l
m
n
o
p
q
r
s
t
u
v
w
x

S

sable, sé´-b'l, n (fur) zibeline f.

sachet, să´-ché, n sachet m.

sack, săque, n sac m. v piller.

sacrament, săc´-ră-m'nt, n sacrement m.

sacred, sé´-cridde, a sacré (to); consacré à.

sacrifice, săc´-ri-fâïce, n sacrifice m. v sacrifier.

sacrilege, săc´-ri-lédje, n sacrilége m.

sad*, sădde, a triste; –ness, n tristesse f.

saddle, săd´-d'l, n selle f; –r, sellier m.

afe, séfe, a sauf; sûr; n — money) coffre-fort — rd sauvegarde f. — ger; –ty, n sûreté

f.

safety pin, séf-tî-pinne, n épingle de sûreté f.

sag, săgue, v s'affaisser.

sagacious*, sa-gué´-cheuce, a sagace.

sage, sédje, n sage m; (herb) sauge f. a* sage.

sail, séle, n voile f. v naviguer.

sailor, sé´-l'r, n matelot m; marin m.

saint, sénnte, n saint, -e m & f.

sake, séque, n cause f; (for God's) égard m; (for the love of God) amour m.

salad, săl´-ade, n salade f.

salad dressing, săl-ade-drèss-inng n vinaigrette f.

salary, săl´-a-ri, n

salaire m.

sale, séle, n vente f; (shop) solde m; –able, a vendable; –sman, n vendeur m.

sales clerk, séle-s-clărque, n vendeur, -se.

salient, sé´-li-ennte, n & a (projecting) saillant m.

saliva, sa-lâï´-va, n salive f.

sallow, săl´-au, a jaunâtre.

salmon, sămm´-'n, n saumon m.

saloon, sa-loune´, n (Grand) salon m; bar m.

salt, soalte, n sel m. a salé; –-cellar, n saliére f.

salty, soal´-tî a salé.

salute, sa-lioute´, v saluer. n salut m.

salvage, săl´-védje, n sauvetage m. v sauver.

salvation, săl-vé´-ch'n, n salut m; –army, Armée du Salut f.

salver, sal´-v'r, n plateau m.

same, séme, a même.

sample, sâmme´-p'l, n échantillon m.

sanctify, sainnk´-ti-fâï, v sanctifier.

sanction, sainnk´-ch'n, v sanctionner. n sanction f.

sanctuary, sainnk´-tiou-*a*-ri, *n* sanctuaire *m.*

sand, sănnde, *n* sable *m;* **–y,** *a* sablonneux.

sandal, sănn´-d'l, *n* sandale *f.*

sandwich, sănnde´-houitche, *n* sandwich *m.*

sane, séne, *a* sain d'esprit.

sanguine, saing´-gouine, *a* sanguin; confiant.

sanitary, sănn´-i-t*a*-ri, *a* sanitaire.

sanity, sănn´-i-ti, *n* bon sens *m.*

sap, săppe, *n* sève *f. v* saper.

sapper, săpp´-*eu*r, *n* (*mil*) sapeur *m.*

sapphire, săf´-fâïre, *n* saphir *m.*

sarcasm, sâr´-căzme, *n* sarcasme *m.*

sarcastic, sâr-căs´-tique, *a* sarcastique.

sardine, sâr-dîne´, *n* sardine *f.*

sash, săche, *n* (belt) (mark of distinction) écharpe *f.*

satchel, sătt´-ch'l, *n* sacoche *f;* (school) cartable *m.*

satellite, satt´-i-lăïte, *n* satellite *m.*

satiate, sé´-chi-éte, *v* rassasier de.

satin, sătt´-inne, *n* satin *m. a* de satin.

satire, sătt´-âïre, *n* satire *f.*

satisfaction, sătt-iss-făk´-ch'n, *n* satisfaction *f.*

satisfactory, sătt-iss-făk´-t*eu*r-i, *a* satisfaisant.

satisfy, sătt´-iss-fâï, *v* satisfaire.

satsuma, săt-sou´-mă, *n* mandarine *f.*

saturate, sătt´-iou-réte, *v* saturer.

Saturday, sătt´-or-di, *n* samedi *m.*

satyr, sătt´-*eu*r, *n* satyre *m.*

sauce, soace, *n* sauce *f;* **–pan,** casserole *f.*

saucer, soa´-s*eu*r, *n* soucoupe *f.*

sauna, soa´-nă, *n* sauna *m.*

saunter, soann´-t'r, *v* marcher en flânant.

sausage, soss´-idj, *n* (to be cooked) saucisse *f;* (preserved) saucisson *m.*

savage, săv´-idj, *a** sauvage; féroce. *n* sauvage *m & f.*

save, séve, *v* (to spare) sauver; (economize) épargner (de); (keep) garder.

saving, sé´-vinng, *a* économe; frugal; (things) économique. *n* économie *f;* **–s,** épargne *f.*

savior, sé´-v'*eu*r, *n* sauveur *m.*

savor, sé´-v'r, *v* avoir le goût de; avoir l'odeur de. *n* saveur *f;* **–y,** *a* savoureux.

saw, soa, *n* scie *f. v* scier.

say, sé, *v* dire; **–ing,** *n* dicton *m.*

scabbard, scăbb´-'rd, *n* fourreau *m.*

scaffold, scăff´-ŏlde, *n* échafaud *m.*

scaffolding, scăff´-ŏldd-inng, *n* échafaudage *m.*

scald, scoalde, *v* échauder.

scale, skéle, *n* (fish) écaille *f;* (measure) échelle *f;* (*mus*) gamme *f. v* ecailler; (climb) escalader.

scales, skélze, *npl* balance *f.*

scallop, scăll´-oppe, *n* coquille Saint Jacques *f.*

scalp, scălpe, *n* cuir chevelu *m.*

scamper, scămm´-p'r, *v* déguerpir.

scan, scănne, *v* scruter; (verses) scander.

scandal, scănn´-d'l, *n* scandale *m.*

a
b
c
d
e
f
g
h
i
j
k
l
m
n
o
p
q
r
s
t
u
v
w
x
y
z

A B C D E F G H I J K L M N O P Q R **S** T U V W X Y Z

scandalous*, scănn´-dăl-euce, a scandaleux.

scanty, scănn´-ti, a insuffisant; (tight) étriqué.

scapegoat, sképe´-gaute, n bouc émissaire m.

scar, scâre, n cicatrice f. v cicatriser.

scarce*, skairce, a rare.

scarcity, skair´-ci-ti, n rareté f; (famine) disette f.

scare, skaire, n panique f. v effrayer; –**away,** épouvanter; –**crow,** n épouvantail m.

scarf, scărfe, n écharpe f; foulard m.

scarlet, scâre-lette, n & a écarlate f.

scarlet fever, scâre´-lette-fî´-veur, n scarlatine f.

scathing*, ské´-tsinng, a cinglant.

scatter, scătt´-´r, v disperser; éparpiller.

scavenger, scăv´-enn-dj'r, n boueur m.

scene, sîne, n scène f; –**ry,** (fig) vue f; paysage m; (theater) décors mpl.

scent, sennte, n parfum m; (trail) piste f. v parfumer de.

scepter, sepp´-t'r, n

sceptre m

schedule, chedd´-ioule, n inventaire m; liste f.

scheme, skîme, n plan m, projet m; v projeter.

scholar, skol´-'r, n lettré, -e m & f; (pupil) élève m & f.

scholarship, skol´-'r-chippe, n (prize) bourse f.

school, skoul, n école f; –**teacher,** maître d'école m; maîtresse d'école f.

schooner, skoue´-n'r, n goélette f.

sciatica, sâï-ătt´-i-ca, n sciatique f.

science, sâï´-ennce, n science f.

scientific, sâï-en-tiff´-ique, a scientifique.

scissors, siz´-eurze, npl ciseaux mpl.

scoff, skoffe, v se moquer de; railler.

scold, skaulde, v gronder.

scoop, skoupe, n (shovel) pelle à main f. v creuser.

scope, skaupe, n portée f; étendue f; place f.

scorch, skoartche, v roussir.

score, skaure, n (number) score m; marque f; partition f (mus); v

(win) gagner; (cut) faire des entailles; (keeping count) marquer.

scorn, skoarne, n dédain m. v dédaigner.

scornful*, skoarne´-foulle, a dédaigneux.

scoundrel, skâ'ounn´-dr'l, n coquin m; gredin m.

scour, skâ'oure, v récurer.

scourge, skeurdje, v fouetter. n fouet m; (fig) fléau m.

scout, skâ'oute, v aller en éclaireur. n éclaireur m; **boy- –,** boy-scout m.

scowl, skâ'oule, v froncer les sourcils. n regard menaçant m.

scraggy, skrăgg´-'i, a (thin) décharné.

scramble, skramm´-b'l, n (struggle) lutte f. v (climb) grimper; –**for,** se bousculer pour.

scrap, skrăppe, n fragment m; (cloth) morceau m.

scrape, skrépe, v gratter; (– mud off) (boots, etc.) décrotter.

scraper, skrépe´-'r, n grattoir m; (for shoes) décrottoir m.

scratch, skrătche, n égratignure f; (sport) ligne de départ f. v égratigner; (rub) gratter; (sports) retirer; (glass) (a smooth surface) rayer.

scream, skrîme, *v* crier; hurler. *n* cri *m*.

screen, skrîne, *n* (fire; cinema) écran *m*; (partition) paravent *m*. *v* protéger.

screw, skroue, *n* vis *f*. *v* visser.

screwdriver, skroue-drâï´-*veur*, *n* tournevis *m*.

scribble, skribb´-'l *v* griffonner. *n* griffonnage *m*.

scripture, skripp´-tioure, *n* Ecriture Sainte *f*.

scroll, skraule, *n* rouleau *m*.

scrounge, skrâ'oundje, *m* picue-assiette; que-assiette.

scrub, scrobbe, *v* laver à la brosse. *n* (bush) broussailles *fpl*.

scruple, scroue´-p'l, *n* scrupule *m*.

scrupulous*, scroue´-piou-*leuce*, *a* scrupuleux.

scrutinize, scroue´-ti-nâïze, *v* scruter.

scuffle, scoff´-'l, *n* bagarre *f*. *v* se battre.

scull, scolle, *n* godille *f*. *v* godiller.

scullery, scoll´-*eur*-i, *n* laverie *f*.

sculptor, scolp´teur, *n* sculpteur *m*.

sculpture, scolp´-tioure, *v* sculpter. *n* sculpture *f*.

scum, scomme, *v* écumer. *n* écume *f*; (*fig*) lie *f*.

scurf, skeurfe, *n* pellicules *fpl*.

scurrilous*, skorr´-i-*leuce*, *a* grossier; injurieux.

scuttle, skott´-'l, *n* (coal) seau à charbon *m*. *v* (*naut*) saborder.

scythe, sâïd*z*e, *n* faux *f*.

sea, sî, *n* mer *f*; **–man,** marin *m*; **––sickness,** mal de mer *m*; **–side,** bord de la mer *m*; **–weed,** algue *f*; **–worthy,** *a* navigable.

seal, sîle, *n* cachet *m*; (official) sceau *m*; (animal) phoque *m*. *v* cacheter; **–ingwax,** *n* cire à cacheter *f*; **–skin,** peau de phoque *f*.

seam, sîme, *n* (in sewing) couture *f*; (mine) veine *f*.

seamstress, sîme´-stresse, *n* couturière *f*.

sear, sîre, *v* (burn) brûler; (brand) marquer au fer.

search, seurtche, *v* (look for) chercher; (people; luggage) fouiller. *n* recherche *f*.

searchlight, seurtche´-lâïte, *n* projecteur *m*.

season, sî´-*z*'n, *v* assaisonner de; (timber) sécher. *m* saison *f*; **–able,** *a* de saison; **–ing,** *n* assaisonnement *m*; **–ticket,** carte d'abonnement *f*.

seat, sîte, *n* siège *m*; place *f*; (bench) banc *m*; *v* asseoir; (to place) placer.

secluded, si-cloue´-dedde, *a* retiré.

seclusion, si-cloue´-j'n, *n* retraite *f*.

second, sèk´-ŏnnde, *v* (support) seconder. *n* (time) seconde *f*; (duel) témoin *m*. *n* & *a** deuxième *m* & *f*; **–ary,** *a* secondaire; **–hand,** d'occasion.

secrecy, sî´-cri-ci, *n* secret *m*.

secret, sî´-crète, *n* secret *m*. *a** secret.

secretary, sèk´-ri-*ta*-ri, *n* secrétaire *m* & *f*.

secrete, si-crîte´, *v* cacher; (gland) sécréter.

secretion, si-crî´-ch'n, *n*

A
B
C
D
E
F
G
H
I
J
K
L
M
N
O
P
Q
R
S
T
U
V
W
X
Y
Z

sécrétion *f.*

sect, secte, *n* secte *f.*

section, sèk´-ch'n, *n* section *f;* (cross) coupe *f.*

secular, sèk´-iou-l'r, *a* (old) séculaire; (music) profane; (school) laïque.

secure, si-kioure´, *v* mettre en sûreté; (one's possession of) s'assurer (de); *a* sûr; à l'abri (de).

securities, si-kiour´-i-tize, *npl* valeurs; boursières *fpl;* titres *mpl.*

security, si-kiour´-i-ti, *n* sûreté *f;* garantie *f.*

sedate*, si-déte´, *a* posé, calme.

sedative, sedd´-a-tive, *n* & *a* sédatif *m;* calmant *m.*

sedentary, sedd´-enn-ta-ri, *a* sédentaire.

sediment, sedd´-i-mennte, *n* sédiment *m.*

sedition, si-diche´-'n, *n* sédition *f.*

seditious*, si-diche´-euce, *a* séditieux.

seduce, si-diouce´, *v* séduire.

see, sî, *v* voir; **–through,** voir à travers; (*fig*) pénétrer; **–to,** veiller à.

seed, sîde, *n* (of vegetables) graine *f;*

semence *f.*

seek, sîque, *v* chercher; (strive) s'efforcer de.

seem, sîme, *v* sembler; paraître; **–ly,** *a* convenable.

seethe, sîdz, *v* bouillonner; (*fig*) grouiller.

seize, sîze, *v* saisir; (take possession) s'emparer de.

seizure, sî´-j'r, *n* prise *f;* capture *f;* (stroke) attaque *f;* (law) saisie *f.*

seldom, sell´-d'm, *adv* rarement.

select, si-lecte´, *v* choisir. *a* choisi; d'élite.

selection, si-lec´-ch'n, *n* choix *m.*

self, selfe, **one–,**pron soi-même; se . . . ; **–ish,** *a* egoïste; **–ishness,** *n* égoïsme *m;* **—starter,** (motor) démarreur *m.*

self-catering, selfe-qué-teur-inng *a* (*Brit*) avec cuisine.

self-service, selfe-seur´-vice, *a* libre-service; self-service.

sell, selle, *v* vendre; **–er,** *n* vendeur, -euse *m* & *f.*

semblance, semm´-blannce, *n* semblant *m.*

semi, semm´-i, *prefix* semi;

demi; **–circle,** *n* demi-cercle *m;* **–colon,** point et virgule *m.*

seminary, semm´-i-na-ri, *n* séminaire *m.*

semolina, semm-ô-lî´-na, *n* semoule *f.*

senate, senn´-éte, *n* sénat *m.*

send, sennde, *v* envoyer; (goods) expédier; **–away, –back,** renvoyer; **–er,** *n* expéditeur, -trice *m* & *f;* **–for,** *v* envoyer; chercher; **–in advance,** envoyer à l'avance; **–on,** (letters, etc.) faire suivre.

senile, sî´-nâîle, *a* sénile.

senior, sî´-ni-eur, *a* aîné; (rank) plus ancien; **–partner,** *n* associé principal *m.*

sensation, senn-sé´-ch'n, *n* sensation *f.*

sense, sennce, *n* sens *m;* **–less,** *a* dénué de sens.

sensible, senn´-si-b'l, *a* sensé.

sensitive*, senn´-si-tive, *a* sensible.

sensual*, senn´-chou-'l, *a* sensuel.

sentence, senn´-t'nce, *n* phrase *f;* (law) sentence *f. v* condamner.

sentiment, senn´-ti-m'nt,
n sentiment *m.*

sentry, senn´-tri, *n*
sentinelle *f;* **–box,**
guérite *f.*

separate, sepp´-a-réte, *v*
séparer. *a** séparé.

separation, sepp-a-ré´-
ch'n, *n* séparation *f.*

September, sepp-temm´-
b'r, *n* septembre *m.*

septic, sepp´-tique, *a*
septique.

sequel, sî´-couelle, *n* suite
f; conséquence *f.*

sequence, sî´-couennce, *n*
série *f;* succession *f.*

serene*, si-rîne´, *a* calme;
serein.

serge, seurdje, *n* serge *f.*

sergeant, sâr´-dj'nt, *n*
sergent *m.*

serial, sî´-ri-al, *a* en série;
n feuilleton *m.*

series, si´-rîze, *n* série *f.*

serious*, si´-ri-euce, *a*
sérieux.

sermon, seur´-m'n, *n*
sermon *m.*

serpent, seur´-pennte, *n*
serpent *m.*

servant, seur´-vannte, *n*
domestique *m* & *f.*

serve, seurve, *v* servir.

service, seur´-vice, *n*
service *m; (eccl)*

office *m.*

serviceable, seur´-viss-a-
b'l, *a* utile (à).

servile, seur´-vâïle, *a*
servile.

servitude, seur´-vi-tioude,
n servitude *f;* (penal)
travaux forcés *mpl.*

session, sèch´-eune, *n*
session *f;* (sitting)
séance *f.*

set, sette, *v* (type)
composer; (to music)
mettre en ...; (fowls)
couver; (clock) régler;
(trap) tendre/dresser un
piege(a); (task) imposer;
(question) poser;
(example) donner;
(tools) affûter; (plants)
planter; (fracture)
réduire; (solidify)
cailler; (jewels) monter.
n collection *f;* série *f;*
(china) service *m;*
(buttons, etc) garniture
f; **–on fire,** mettre le feu
à.

settee, sett´-ie, *n* canapé
m; divan *m.*

settle, sett´-'l, *v*
(accounts) régler;
(finish) mettre fin à;
(decide) résoudre;
(assign) assigner;
(domicile) s'établir;

–ment, *n* colonie *f;*
(dowry) dot *f;*
(accounts) règlement *m;*
(agreement) solution *f;*
(foundation) tassement
m.

seven, sèv´-'n, *n* & *a* sept
m; **–teen,** dix-sept *m;*
–th, septième *m* & *f;*
–ty, soixante-dix *m.*

sever, sèv´-'r, *v* séparer;
(cut) couper net.

several, sèv´-eur-'l, *a*
plusieurs; divers.

severe*, si-vire´, *a* sévère;
(of weather) rigoureux;
(of pain) violent.

severity, si-vèr´-i-ti, *n*
sévérité *f.*

sew, sau, *v* coudre; **–ing,** *n*
couture *f;* **–ingthread,**
coton à coudre *m;* **–ing
machine,** machine à
coudre *f.*

sewage, sioue´-idj, *n* eaux
d'égout *fpl.*

sewer, sioue´-'r, *n* égout *m.*

sex, sexe, *n* sexe *m;* **–ual,** *a*
sexuel.

sexist, sexe´-iste, *a* sexiste.

sexy, sexe´-î, *a* sexy.

shabby, chăbb´-i, *a* râpé;
usé; (action) mesquin.

shackle, chăk´-'l, *n*
chaînes *fpl. v* enchaîner.

shade, chéde, *n* ombre *f;*

(color) nuance f; (lamp) abat-jour m; (eyes) visière f. v protéger; (art) ombrer.

shadow, chăd´-au, n ombre f. v (follow) filer.

shady, ché´-di, a ombragé; (fig) (dishonest) louche.

shaft, châfte, n (arrow) flèche f; (mech) arbre m; (mine) puits m; **–s,** (vehicle) brancards mpl.

shaggy, chăgg´-i, a poilu, velu.

shake, chéque, v secouer; (nerves, etc) trembler de; (sway) ébranler; **–hands,** serrer la main.

shaky, ché´-ki, a branlant; tremblotant.

shall, chăle, v aux **I s. do** je ferai. **we s. do** nous ferons.

shallow, chăl´-au, a peu profond.

sham, chămme, n feinte f. a simulé. v feindre.

shame, chéme, n honte f. v faire honte à; **–ful*,** a honteux; **–less,** éhonté.

shampoo, chămm´-poue, n shampooing m.

shamrock, chămm´-roque, n (d'Irlande) trèfle m.

shape, chépe, n forme f. v former; modeler (sur).

share, chére, n part f; (stock) action f. v partager; participer à; **–holder,** n actionnaire m & f.

shark, chârque, n requin m.

sharp, chârpe, a (blade) tranchant; (point) pointu; (edge) coupant; (taste) piquant; (mind) dégourdi. n (music) dièse m; **–en,** v aiguiser; **–ness,** n acuité f.

shatter, chătt´-'r, v briser en pièces; fracasser; renverser.

shave, chéve, v raser; se raser.

shaving, ché´-vinng, **–brush,** n blaireau m.

shavings, ché´-vinngze, npl (of wood) copeaux mpl.

shawl, choale, n châle m.

she, chî, pron elle.

sheaf, chîfe, n (corn, etc) gerbe f; (papers) liasse f.

shear, chîre, v tondre; **–s,** npl (for metal) cisailles fpl.

sheath, chîts, n (scabbard) fourreau m.

shed, chedde, n hangar m. v (tears, blood) verser; (hair, leaves, feathers)

perdre.

sheen, chîne, n lustre m.

sheep, chîpe, n mouton m.

sheer, chîre, a pur; (steep) perpendiculaire.

sheet, chîte, n drap m; (paper, metal) feuille f; **–lightning,** éclair de chaleur m.

shelf, chelfe, n planche f; (of a bookcase) rayon m; (a set) étagère f.

shell, chelle, n (hard) (empty egg) coquille f; (soft) (peas, etc.) cosse f; (projectile) (mil) obus m; v (peas, etc) écosser; (shrapnel) bombarder; **–fish** n mollusque m; crustacé m.

shelter, chel´-t'r, n abri m. v abriter; protéger.

shepherd, chepp´-eurde, n berger m; pâtre m.

sheriff, chè´-rife, n shérif m.

sherry, chèr´-i, n Xérès m.

shield, chîlde, n bouclier m. v protéger.

shift, chifte, n (working) équipe f; changement de vitesse m; v (to change place) changer de place.

shin, chine, n tibia m.

shine, châîne, v luire; briller. n lustre m;

éclat *m.*

shingle, chinng´-g'l, *n* galet *m.*

shingles, chinng´-g'lz, *n* zona *m.*

ship, chippe, *n* vaisseau *m*; navire *m*; bateau *m. v* embarquer; (goods) expédier; **–ment,** (cargo) chargement *m*; **–owner,** armateur *m*; **–wreck,** naufrage *m.*

shirk, cheurque, *v* éviter; éluder.

shirker, cheur´-ke*ur*, *n* flémard *m.*

shirt, cheurte, *n* chemise *f.*

shiver, chiv´-'r, *v* frissonner. *n* frisson *m.*

shoal, choale, *n* (multitude) foule *f*; (fish) banc *m*; (shallow) haut-fond *m.*

shock, choque, *n* (*elec*) secousse *f*; (fright) choc *m. v* (disgust) choquer; **–absorber,** *n* amortisseur *m*; **–ing,** *a* révoltant; choquant.

shoddy, chodd´-i, *a* (goods) camelote; (persons) râpé.

shoe, choue, *n* chaussure *f*; soulier *m*; (horse) fer à; cheval *m*; *v* (horse)

ferrer; **–horn,** chausse-pied *m*; **–lace,** lacet *m*; **–maker,** cordonnier *m*; **–polish,** cirage *m.*

shoot, choutte, *v* tirer; (kill) tuer d'un coup de feu; (execute) fusiller; (grow) (to push forth) pousser. *n* chasse *f*; (growth) (plant) pousse *f*; **–ing,** (of firearms) tir *m*; **–ing star,** étoile filante *f.*

shop, choppe, *n* boutique *f*; (stores) magasin *m. v* faire des achats; **–keeper,** *n* marchand, -e *m & f.*

shoplifting, choppe´-lift-inng, *n* vol à l'étalage *m.*

shore, chaure, *n* côte *f*; (beach) rivage *m*; (land) terre *f*; (support) étai *m. v* étayer.

shorn, chorne, *a* tondu.

short, choarte, *a* court; (persons) petit; (need) dénué de; **–age,** *n* insuffisance *f*; **–circuit,** courtcircuit *m*; **–en,** *v* raccourcir; abréger; **–hand,** *n* sténographie *f*; **–ly,** *adv* sous peu; **–sighted,** *a* myope.

shot, chotte, *n* (noise) coup de feu *m*; (score,

etc) coup *m*; (marksman) (shooter) tireur *m*; (pellet) plomb de chasse *m.*

should, choude, *v aux* devoir.?

shoulder, chaule´-d'r, *n* épaule *f. v* porter sur l'épaule.

shout, châ'oute, *n* cri *m. v* crier.

shovel, chov´-'l, *n* pelle *f. v* ramasser à la pelle.

show, chau, *n* spectacle *m*; (exhibition) exposition *f*; (prize –) concours *m. v* montrer; (teach) enseigner; **–room,** *n* salle d'exposition *f*; **–y,** *a* voyant.

shower, châ'ou´-e*ur*, *n* (copious) averse *f*; (bath) douche *f*; **–y,** *a* pluvieux.

shred, chredde, *n* (tatter) lambeau *m. v* déchiqueter.

shrew, chroue, *n* mégère *f.*

shrewd, chroude, *a* malin; (cunning) rusé; sagace.

shriek, chrîque, *v* pousser des cris. *n* cri perçant *m.*

shrill, chrille, *a* perçant.

shrimp, chrimmpe, *n* crevette *f.*

shrine, chrâïne, *n* châsse *f*;

A
B
C
D
E
F
G
H
I
J
K
L
M
N
O
P
Q
R
S
T
U
V
W
X
Y
Z

sanctuaire *m*.

shrink, chrinnque, *v* rétrécir; *n* psychiàtre *mf*; psychanaliste *mf*.

shrivel, chriv´-'l, *v* ratatiner.

shroud, chrâ'oude, *n* linceul *m*.

Shrove Tuesday, chrôve-tiouze´-dé, *n* mardi gras *m*.

shrub, chrobbe, *n* arbuste *m*.

shrug, chrogue, *v* hausser les épaules.

shudder, chodd´-'r, *n* frémissement *m*. *v* frémir (de).

shuffle, choff´-'l, *v* (gait) traîner les pieds; (cards) battre.

shun, chonne, *v* éviter.

shunt, chonnte, *v* changer de voie; faire la manœuvre.

shut, chotte, *v* fermer.

shutter, chott´-'r, *n* volet *m*; (camera) obturateur *m*.

shuttle, chott´-'l, *n* navette *f*.

shy, châï, *a* timide; réservé. *v* se jeter de côté.

shyness, châï´-nesse, *n* timidité *f*.

sick, sique, *a* malade; **–en,** *v* (*fig*) (to disgust) dégoûter; **–ly,** *a* maladif; **–ness,** *n* maladie *f*; **to be –,** vomir.

sickle, sik´-'l, *n* faucille *f*.

side, sâïde, *n* côté *m*; (mountain) versant *m*; (river) bord *m*; (of record) face *f*. *v* prendre parti; **–board,** *n* buffet *m*; **–car,** side-car *m*; **–ways,** *adv* de côté.

side effect, sâïd-î-fècte, *n* effet secondaire *m*.

siege, sîdje, *n* siège *m*.

sieve, sive, *n* (fine) tamis *m*; (coarse) crible *m*.

sift, sifte, *v* tamiser; cribler.

sigh, sâï, *n* soupir *m*. *v* soupirer.

sight, sâïte, *v* apercevoir. *n* (eye) vue *f*; (spectacle) spectacle *m*; (gun) guidon *m*; **at –,** *adv* à vue; **by –,** de vue.

sign, sâïne, *v* signer. *n* signe *m*; (board) enseigne *f*; **–post,** poteau indicateur *m*.

signal, sigue´-n'l, *n* signal *m*. *v* signaler.

signature, sigue´-na-tioure, *n* signature *f*.

significant*, sigue-nif´-i-

cannte, *a* significatif.

signify, sigue´-ni-fâï, *v* signifier.

silence, sâï´-lennce, *n* silence *m*. *v* faire taire.

silencer, sâï´-lenn-ceur, *n* (engine) silencieux *m*.

silent*, sâï´-lennt, *a* silencieux.

silk, silque, *n* soie *f*; **–en,** *a* de soie; **–worm,** *n* ver à soie *m*; **–y,** *a* soyeux.

sill, sile, *n* (door) seuil *m*; (window) rebord *m*.

silly, sill´-i, *a* sot, niais.

silver, sill´-v'r, *n* argent *m*. *a* d'argent. *v* argenter.

silversmith, sill´-v'r-smits, *n* orfèvre *m*.

similar*, simm´-i-l'r, *a* semblable.

similarity, simm-i-lar´-i-ti, *n* similitude *f*.

simile, simm´-i-li, *n* comparaison *f*.

simmer, simm´-'r, *v* mijoter.

simple, simm´-p'l, *a* simple; **–ton,** *n* nigaud, -e *m* & *f*.

simplicity, simm-pliss´-i-ti, *n* simplicité *f*.

simplify, simm´-pli-fâï, *v* simplifier.

simultaneous*, simm-eul-té´-ni-euce, *a* simultané.

sin, sine, *v* pécher. *n* péché *m*; **–ner,** pécheur *m*, pécheresse *f*.

since, sinnce, *prep* depuis. *adv* depuis lors. *conj* (cause) puisque; (time) depuis que.

sincere*, sinn-cire´, *a* sincère.

sinew, sinn´-ioue, *n* tendon *m*; (*fig*) nerf *m*.

sing, sinng, *v* chanter; **–er,** *n* chanteur *m*, chanteuse *f*; (star) (professional) cantatrice *f*; **–ing,** chant *m*.

singe, sinndje, (one's clothes, etc.) *v* roussir; (hair) brûler.

single, sinng´-g'l, *a* seul, (unmarried) célibataire; (ticket) simple; **– handed,** *adv* seul.

single room, sinng´-l-roumme, *n* chambre à un lit; pour une personne *f*.

singly, sinngue´-li, *adv* (individually) un à un.

singular*, sinng´-guiou-l'r, *a* singulier; unique.

sinister, sinn´-iss-teur, *a* sinistre.

sink, sinnque, *n* évier *m*. *v* enfoncer; couler; (ship) sombrer; (scuttle)

saborder; (shaft) creuser.

sip, sipe, *n* gorgée *f*. *v* boire à petites gorgées.

siphon, sâï´-f'n, *n* siphon *m*.

siren, sâï´-renn, *n* sirène *f*.

sirloin, seur´-lô'ïne, *n* aloyau *m*.

sister, siss´-t'r, *n* sœur *f*; **– in-law,** belle-sœur *f*.

sit, sitte, *v* s'asseoir; (incubate) couver; **–ting,** *a* assis. *n* séance *f*.

site, sâïte, *n* site *m*; (building) emplacement *m*.

situated, sit´-iou-é-tedde, *a* situé.

situation, sit-iou-é´-ch'n, *n* situation *f*.

six, sixe, *n* & *a* six *m*; **–teen,** seize *m*; **–teenth,** seizième *m* & *f*; **–th,** sixième *m* & *f*; **–tieth,** soixantième *m* & *f*; **–ty,** soixante *m*.

size, sâïze, *n* dimension *f*; (measure) (of gloves, shoes, etc) pointure *f*; (persons) taille *f*; (glue) colle *f*. *v* coller.

skate, skéte, *v* patiner. *n* patin *m*; (fish) raie *f*.

skateboard, skétt´-baurde, *n* skateboard *m*.

skating, skétt´-inng, *n*

patinage *m*.

skating rink, skétt-inng-rinque, *n* patinoire *m*.

skeleton, skell´-eu-t'n, *n* squelette *m*.

skeptical*, skepp´-ti-c'l, *a* sceptique.

sketch, sketche, *v* esquisser. *n* esquisse *f*, croquis *m*.

skewer, skioue´-eur, *n* brochette *f*; broche *f v* embrocher.

ski, ski, *v* skier; faire du ski; *n* ski *m*; **lift,** *n* remonte-pente *m*; **–slope,** *n* piste de ski *f*.

skid, skidde, *v* déraper. *n* dérapage *m*.

skiff, ski?e, *n* esquif *m*, skiff *m*.

skiing, skî´-inng, *n* ski *m*.

skill, skille, *n* habileté *f*, adresse *f*; (natural) talent *m*.

skillful*, skill´-foull, *a* adroit, habile.

skim, skimme, *v* (*fig*) effleurer; écrémer; (scum) écumer.

skimmed milk, skimm'd-milque, *n* lait écrémé.

skin, skinne, *n* peau *f*; (hide) cuir *m*; (peel) écorce *f*; (thin peel) pelure *f*.

skip, skippe, v sauter;
(with a rope) manquer;
sauter à la corde.

skipper, skipp´-'r, n patron
de bateau m.

skirmish, skeur´-miche, n
escarmouche f.

skirt, skeurte, n (dress)
jupe f. v border.

skull, skolle, n crâne m.

skunk, skonngk, n
canaille f; (fur) putois
m.

sky, skâï, n ciel m; –light,
châssis vitre m; –
scraper, gratte-ciel m.

slab, slăbbe, n dalle f;
plaque f.

slack, slăque, n (small
coal) menu charbon m. ¨
a (loose) lâche.

slacken, slăque´-'n, v
relâcher; (pace) (to
make slower) ralentir.

slander, slânne´-d'r, v
calomnier. n calomnie f;
(law) diffamation f; –er,
calomniateur m.

slang, slain-ngue, n argot
m.

slant, slânnte, v être en
pente; incliner; n pente
f; –ing, a oblique.

slap, slăppe, n gifle f. v
gifler.

slash, slăche, v taillader;

(gash) (the face)
balafrer.

slate, sléte, n ardoise f, v
couvrir d'ardoises.

slaughter, sloa´-t'r, v
(animals) abattre;
massacrer. n tuerie f;
–er, tueur m; –-house,
abattoir m.

slave, sléve, n esclave m &
f; –ry, esclavage m.

slay, slé, v tuer; massacrer.

sledge, slèdje, n traîneau
m; –-hammer, marteau
de forgeron m.

sleek, slîque, a lisse;
(manners) mielleux.

sleep, slîpe, v dormir. n
sommeil m; –ing car,
(railroad) wagon-lit m;
–less, a sans sommeil;
–lessness, n insomnie f;
–y, a qui a sommeil.

sleeping bag, slîp-inng-
băgue n sac de couchage
m.

sleeping pill, slîp-inng-
pile, n somnifère m.

sleet, slîte, n grésil m.

sleeve, slîve, n manche f.

sleigh, slé, n traîneau m.

sleight, slâïte, n tour
d'adresse m; –of hand,
prestidigitation f.

slender, slenn´-d'r, a
mince; (figure) svelte;

(means) modeste.

slice, slâïce, n tranche f. v
couper en tranches.

slide, slâïde, n glissade f;
toboggan m;
(microscopic) lamelle f;
(photo) diapostive f;
(lantern) verre m. v
glisser.

slight, slâïte, n marque de
mépris f. v traiter sans
égards. a* mince;
(mistake, etc) léger.

slim, slimme, a élancé. v
se faire maigrir.

slime, slâïme, n vase f;
limon m.

slimy, slâï´-mi, a vaseux;
visqueux.

sling, slinng, n (med) (for
a broken limb) écharpe
f. v (throw) lancer.

slink, slinng-k, v
s'esquiver.

slip, slippe, v glisser;
–pery, a glissant.

slipper, slipp´-'r, n
pantoufle f.

slit, slitte, v fendre. n
fente f.

sloe, slau, n (bot) prunelle
f.

slope, slaupe, v aller en
pente. n pente f.

slot, slotte, n fente f; (box;
machine) ouverture f.

sloth, slau*t*s, *n* paresse *f*; indolence *f*.

slouch, slâ'outche, *v* marcher lourdement.

slovenly, slov´-'n-li, *a* sans soin.

slow*, slau, *a* lent; **to be —,***v* (clock, etc) retarder.

slug, slogg, *n* limace *f*.

sluggish*, slogg´-iche, *a* lent; paresseux.

sluice, slouce, *n* écluse *f*; **—-way,** vanne *f*.

slum, slomme, *n* bas quartier *m*; taudis *m*.

slumber, slomm´-b'r, *v* sommeiller. *n* sommeil *m*.

slump, slommpe, *n* effondrement des cours *m*.

slur, sleur, *n* tache *f. v* tacher; déprécier.

slush, sloche, *n* boue *f*; fange *f*; neige à moitié fondue *f*.

sly, slâï, *a* sournois; rusé.

smack, smă*q*ue, *v* (hand) (to slap) donner une claque à; (lips) faire claquer. *n* claque *f*; (boat) smack *m*.

small, smoal, *a* petit; **—ness,** *n* petitesse *f*.

smallpox, smoal´-poxe, *n* petite vérole *f*.

smart, smârte, *a* vif; (clever) spirituel; habile; (spruce) pimpant; chic. *v* (pain) cuire.

smash, smă*ch*e, *n* collision *f*; (*com*) krach *m. v* **— to pieces,** briser en morceaux; briser.

smattering, smătt´-*eur*inng, *n* connaissance superficielle *f*.

smear, smire, *v* barbouiller (de); *n* barbouillage *m*.

smell, smelle, *v* sentir. *n* odeur *f*.

smelt, smelte, *v* fondre. *n* (fish) éperlan *m*.

smile, smâïle, *v* sourire. *n* sourire *m*.

smite, smâïte, *v* frapper; affliger.

smith, smi*t*s, *n* forgeron *m*; **—y,** forge *f*.

smoke, smauke, *v* fumer. *n* fumée *f*; **—less,** *a* sans fumée; **—r,** *n* fumeur *m*.

smoky, smau´-ki, *a* enfumé.

smolder, smaul´-d'r, *v* brûler sans flammes.

smooth, smoo*dz*, *a** lisse; *v* (the hair) lisser; (temper) apaiser.

smother, smo*dz*´-'r, *v* étouffer; suffoquer.

smudge, smodje, *v* tacher. *n* tache *f*.

smuggle, smo*g*´-g'l, *v* passer en contrebande.

smuggler, smo*g*´-gleur, *n* contrebandier *m*.

snack, snă*q*ue, *n* cassecroûte *m*.

snail, snéle, *n* colimaçon *m*; (edible) escargot *m*.

snake, snéque, *n* serpent *m*.

snap, snăppe, *n* (noise) (of a whip,etc.) claquement *m*; (bite) coup de dent *m. v* fermer bien; (break) briser net; (fingers) claquer les doigts; (animal) happer.

snapshot, snăppe´-chotte, *n* instantané *m*.

snare, snère, *n* piège *m. v* prendre au piège.

snarl, snârle, *v* grogner. *n* grognement *m*.

snatch, snătche, *v* saisir; **—at,** *v* chercher à saisir; **—from,** arracher à.

sneak, snîque, *n* mouchard *m. v* (steal) chiper; **—away,** *v* s'esquiver furtivement.

sneer, snire, *v* ricaner. *n* ricanement *m*.

sneeze, snîze, *v* éternuer. *n* éternuement *m*.

A
B
C
D
E
F
G
H
I
J
K
L
M
N
O
P
Q
R
S
T
U
V
W
X
Y
Z

sniff, sniffe, *v* renifler.

snip, snipe, *n* coup de ciseaux *m*. *v* couper avec des ciseaux.

snipe, snâïpe, *n* bécassine *f*; **–r,** tireur d'élite *m*.

snob, snobbe, *n* snob *m*; **–bish,** *a* poseur.

snore, snaure, *v* ronfler. *n* ronflement *m*.

snorkel, snoar´-k'l, *n* tuba *m*.

snort, snoarte, *v* renâcler. *n* renâclement *m*.

snout, snâ'oute, *n* museau *m*; (pig) groin *m*.

snow, snau, *v* neiger. *n* neige *f*; **–flake,** perceneige *m*; **–-storm,** tempête de neige *f*.

snub, snobbe, *v* dédaigner. *n* rebuffade *f*.

snuff, snoffe, *n* tabac à priser *m*; **–box,** tabatière *f*.

so, sau, *adv* (therefore) aussi; ainsi; comme cela; si.

soak, sauque, *v* tremper.

soap, saupe, *n* savon *m*.

soar, saure, *v* s'élever; – **over** planer sur.

sob, sobbe, *v* sangloter. *n* sanglot *m*.

sober*, sau´-b'r, *a* sobre; modéré.

sociable, sau´-cha-b'l, *a* sociable.

social, sau´-ch'l, *a** social; **–ism,** *n* socialisme *m*; **–ist,** socialiste *m* & *f*.

society, sŏ-sâï´-i-ti, *n* société *f*; compagnie *f*; grand monde *m*.

sock, soque, *n* chaussette *f*.

socket, sok´-ette, (eyes) orbite *f*; (teeth) alvéole *m*.

sod, sode, *n* motte de gazon *f*.

soda, sau´-da, *n* soude *f*; **–water,** eau de Seltz *f*.

sofa, sau´-fă, *n* sofa *m*; canapé *m*.

soft*, softe, *a* mou; doux; (tender) tendre; **–en,** *v* adoucir; (*fig*) attendrir; **–ness,** *n* douceur *f*.

soft drink, softe-drinnque, *n* boisson non alcoolisée *f*.

software, softe´-ouère, *n* (*comput*) logiciel *m*; software *m*.

soil, soa'ile, *v* souiller; abîmer. *n* sol *m*, (land) terre *f*.

sojourn, sô´-djeurne, *v* séjourner. *n* séjour *m*.

solace, sol´-ace, *n* consolation *f*. *v* consoler

(de).

solder, saule´-d'r, *n* soudure *f*. *v* souder.

soldier, saule´-dj'r, *n* soldat *m*.

sole, saule, *n* (shoes, etc) semelle *f*; (fish) sole *f*. *v* ressemeler. *a** seul; unique.

solemn*, sol´-emme, *a* solennel.

solicit, sŏ-liss´-itte, *v* solliciter.

solicitor, sŏ-liss´-itt-'r, *n* avoué *m*; notaire *m*.

solicitude, sol-i´-ci-tioude, *n* sollicitude *f*.

solid*, sol´-ide, *a* solide; massif; **–ify,** *v* solidifier.

solitary, sol´-i-ta-ri, *a* solitaire; seul.

solitude, sol´-i-tioude, *n* solitude *f*.

soluble, sol´-iou-b'l, *a* soluble.

solution, so-lioue´-ch'n, *n* solution *f*.

solve, solve, *v* résoudre.

solvency, sol´-venn-ci, *n* solvabilité *f*.

solvent, sol´-vennte, *a* dissolvant; (*com*) solvable.

somber, somme´-be*u*r, *a* sombre.

some, somme, *art a* & *pron*

du *m*; de la *f*; des *pl*;
quelques *pl*; en; **–body,** *n*
quelqu'un *m*; **–how,** *adv*
d'un façon ou d'une
autre; **–one,** *n* quelqu'un
m; **–thing,** quelque
chose *m*; **–times,** *adv*
quelquefois; **–what,**
quelque peu; **–where,**
quelquepart.

somersault, somm´-*eur*-
solte, *n* saut périlleux *m*;
culbute *f*.

somnambulist, somme-
nămm´-bioue-liste, *n*
somnambule *m* & *f*.

son, sonne, *n* fils *m*; **—-in-
law,** gendre *m*.

sonata, sŏ-nâ´-ta, *n* sonate
f.

song, sonng, *n* (ballad)
chanson *f*; (hymn)
chant *m*.

soon, soune, *adv* bientôt;
as –as, aussitôt que; **how
–?** quand?

soot, soute, *n* suie *f*.

soothe, soudz, *v* adoucir;
(pacify) calmer.

sophisticated, sau-fis´-tî-
qué-téde, *a* sophistiqué.

sorcerer, saur´-ceur-*eur*, *n*
sorcier *m*.

sorcery, saur´-ceur-i, *n*
sorcellerie *f*.

sordid*, sôr´-dide, *a*

sordide; vil.

sore, saure, *n* plaie *f*; mal
m. *a** mal à; douloureux.

sorrel, sorr´-'l, *n* oseille *f*.

sorrow, sor´-au, *n* chagrin
m; affliction *f*; *v*
s'affliger; **–ful,** *a*
affligeant; triste.

sorry, sor´-i, *a* fâché de;
désolé; **I am –,** je
regrette; pardon!

sort, sôrte, *n* espèce *f*;
genre *m*; sorte *f*. *v* trier.

soul, saule, *n* âme *f*.

sound, sâ'ounnde, *v*
sonner; (naut) sonder. *a*
(health) robuste;
(character) droit;
(sleep) profond. *n* son
m; (bells) son *m*;
(channel) détroit *m*;
–proof, *a* insonore;
–track, *n* bande sonore
f; **–ing,** (naut) sondage
m.

soup, soupe, *n* potage *m*;
soupe *f*.

soup tureen, soupe-tioue-
rîne´, *n* soupière *f*.

sour*, sâ'oueur, *a* sur;
aigre.

source, saurce, *n* source *f*.

south, sâ'outs, *n* sud *m*;
–of France, le midi *m*.

southerly, seudz´-eur-li, *a*
du sud; méridional.

souvenir, sou-vi-nîre´, *n*
souvenir *m*.

sovereign, sov´-eur-ine, *n*
& *a* souverain *m*.

sow, sau, *v* semer; **–er,** *n*
semeur *m*; semailles *fpl*.

sow, sâ'ou, *n* truie *f*.

soya bean, soa'ï-a-bîne, *n*
graine de soja *f*.

space, spéce, *n* espace *m*;
(time) période *f*.

spacious*, spé´-cheuce, *a*
spacieux.

spade, spéde, *n* bêche *f*;
(cards) pique *m*.

span, spănne, *n* empan *m*;
envergure *f*;
(architecture) ouverture
f; (fig) durée *f*. *v* (to
cross) traverser.

spangle, spain´-g'l, *v*
pailleter de; *n* paillette *f*.

spaniel, spănn´-ieule, *n*
épagneul *m*.

spar, spâre, *v* s'exercer à la
boxe.

spare, spére, *a* (naut) de
rechange. *v* (forbear)
épargner; **can you –this?**
pouvez-vous vous en
passer?

sparing*, spére´-inng, *a*
frugal; économe.

spark, spârke, *n* étincelle
f; *v* étinceler.

sparkle, spăr´-k'l, *v*

a
b
c
d
e
f
g
h
i
j
k
l
m
n
o
p
q
r
s
t
u
v
w
x
y
z

A B C D E F G H I J K L M N O P Q R **S** T U V W X Y Z

étinceler; (wine)
pétiller.

sparrow, spăr´-au, n
moineau m.

spasm, spăzme, n spasme
m.

spasmodic, spăz-mod´-
ique, a spasmodique.

spats, spăttse, npl guêtres
fpl.

spatter, spătt´-'r, v
éclabousser.

spawn, spoanne, v frayer.

speak, spîke, v parler; **–er,**
n orateur m.

spear, spîre, v percer d'un
coup de lance. n lance f.

special*, spè´-ch'l, a
spécial; (of
correspondence, etc.)
particulier.

speciality, spèch-i-al´-i-ti,
n spécialité f.

specie, spî´-chî, n espèces
fpl.

species, spî´-chîze, n
espèce f; (fig) sorte f.

specific, speu-si´-fique, a
précis(e);
particulier(ère); (chem
etc) spécifique.

specification, spess-i-fi-
qué´-ch'n, n description
f; (of a patent, etc,)
précise f; (schedule)
devis; descriptif m.

specify, spess´-i-fâï, v
spécifier.

specimen, spess´-i-menn,
n spécimen m; modèle
m.

specious*, spî-cheuce, a
spécieux; fallacieux.

speck, spèque, n petite
tache f.

spectacle, spèk´-ta-k'l, n
spectacle m.

spectacles, spèk´-ta-k'lse,
npl lunettes fpl.

spectator, spèk-té´-t'r, n
spectateur, -trice m & f.

specter, spèk´-t'r, n spectre
m.

speculate, spèk´-iou-léte,
v spéculer (sur); méditer
(sur).

speech, spîtche, n parole f;
(discourse) discours m;
–less, a muet; (fig)
interdit.

speed, spîde, n vitesse f;
–y, a prompt; rapide.

speed limit, spîde-limm-
itte, n limit de vitesse;
vitesse maximale
permise f.

speedometer, spî-domm´-
it'r, n indicateur de
vitesse m.

spell, spelle, v épeler. n
charme m.

spend, spennde, v

dépenser; **–thrift,** n
dépensier, -ère m & f.

sphere, sfire, n sphère f.

spice, spâïce, n épice f. v
épicer.

spicy, spâï´-ci, a épicé;
(fig) piquant.

spider, spâï´-d'r, n
araignée f.

spike, spâïke, n piquant m;
pointe f. v clouer.

spill, spille, v répandre;
renverser.

spin, spinne, v filer; faire
tourner; **–ning,** n
(process) filage m.

spinach, spinn´-idj, n
épinards mpl.

spinal, spâïne´-'l, a spinal;
vertébral.

spindle, spinn-d'l, n fuseau
m; (tech) axe m.

spine, spâïne, n épine
dorsale f.

spinster, spinn-st'r, n
femme non mariée f.

spiral, spâï´-r'l, a spiral. n
spirale f.

spire, spâïre, n flèche f.

spirit, spir´-itte, n esprit
m; (alcohol) alcool m;
(animation) entrain m;
–ed, a animé; **–ual,** n
spirituel; **–ualist,** n
(Phil) spiritualiste m.

spit, spitte, v cracher. n

crachat *m*; (roasting) broche *f*; **–toon,** crachoir *m*.

spite, spâïte, *v* dépiter. *n* dépit *m*; **–ful,** *a* vindicatif; **in –of,** *prep* malgré.

splash, splâche, *v* éclabousser; (play) patauger.

splendid*, splenn´-dide, *a* splendide.

splendor, splenn´-d'r, *n* splendeur *f*.

splint, splinnte, *n* (surgical) attelle *f*.

splinter, splinn´-t'r, *n* (in the hand) écharde *f*. *v* voler en éclats.

split, splitte, *v* fendre. *n* fente *f*.

spoil, spoa'ile, *v* gâter; (damage) abîmer.

spoke, spauke, *n* rayon d'une roue *m*.

spokesman, spaukce´-mănne, *n* porte-parole *m*.

sponge, sponndje, *n* éponge *f*. *v* éponger.

sponsor, sponn´-sor, *n* (surety) garant *m*; (baptism) parrain *m*; marraine *f*.

spontaneous*, sponn-té´-ni-*euce*, *a* spontané.

spool, spoule, *n* bobine *f*.

spoon, spoune, *n* cuiller *f*; **–ful,** cuillerée *f*.

sport, spaurte, *n* sport *m*; **–ing,** *a* sportif; **–ive,** *a* gai.

spot, spotte, *v* tacher. *n* tache *f*; (place) endroit *m*; **–less,** *a* sans tache.

spout, spâ'oute, *n* (gutter) gouttière *f*; (jug or pot) bec *m*. *v* jaillir.

sprain, spréne, *v* se fouler. *n* entorse *f*.

sprawl, sproale, *v* s'étaler; se vautrer.

spray, spré, *n* (water) embrun *m*. *v* arroser; pulvériser; atomiser.

sprayer, spré´-*eur*, *n* vaporisateur *m*; atomiseur.

spread, spredde, *v* étendre; (on bread, etc) étaler; (news) répandre; **–out,** déployer.

sprig, sprigue, *n* brin *m*; brindille *f*.

sprightly, sprâïte´-li, *a* enjoué; vif; gai.

spring, sprinng, *n* (season) printemps *m*; (leap) saut *m*; (water) source *f*; (metal) ressort *m*. *v* **– at,** sauter à la gorge de; **–y,** *a* élastique.

sprinkle, sprinng´-k'l, *v* asperger de; saupoudrer (with holy water).

sprout, sprâ'oute, *v* germer; *n* pousse *f*.

spruce, sprouce, *n* sapin *f*. *a* pimpant.

spur, speur, *n* éperon *m*. *v* éperonner.

spurious*, spiou´-ri-*euce*, *a* faux.

spurn, speurne, *v* dédaigner; (to treat with disdain) mépriser.

spy, spâï, *n* espion, -onne *m* & *f*. *v* espionner.

squabble, scouob´-b'l, *v* se chamailler; *n* dispute *f*.

squad, scouodde, *n* (*mil*) escouade *f*; **–ron,** (*mil*) escadron *m*; (naval, air) escadre *f*.

squalid*, scouoll´-ide, *a* sale; abject.

squall, scouoale, *n* (wind) rafale *f*. *v* (scream) brailler.

squalor, scouoll-*eur*, *n* abjection *f*.

squander, scouonn´-d'r, *v* dissiper; gaspiller.

square, scouère, *n* & *a* carré *m*; (public) place *f*.

squash, scouoche, *v* écraser. *n* écrasement *m*.

squat, scouotte, *v*

a
b
c
d
e
f
g
h
i
j
k
l
m
n
o
p
q
r
s
t
u
v
w
x
y
z

A B C D E F G H I J K L M N O P Q R S T U V W X Y Z

s'accroupir. *a* (*fig*) trapu.

squeak, scouîke, *v* crier; (bearings, etc) grincer.

squeeze, scouîze, *v* serrer; (cuddle) étreindre; (lemon, etc) presser.

squid, scouide, *n* calmar *m*.

squint, scouinnte, *v* loucher. *n* regard louche *m*.

squirrel, scouir´-'l, *n* écureuil *m*.

squirt, scoueurte, *n* seringue *f*. *v* seringuer; faire gicler.

stab, stǎbbe, *v* poignarder. *n* coup de poignard *m*.

stability, stǎ-bil´-i-ti, *n* stabilité *f*.

stable, sté´-b'l, *n* écurie *f*; (cattle) étable *f*. *a* (for horses) stable.

stack, stǎque, *n* pile *f*; (hay) meule *f*; (chimney) cheminée *f*. *v* empiler.

stadium, sté´-di-*e*um, *n* stade *m*.

staff, stâffe, *n* bâton *m*; (employees) personnel *m*; (*mil*) état-major *m*; **flag- –,** hampe *f*.

stag, stǎgue, *n* cerf *m*.

stage, stédje, *n* (theater) scène *f*; (hall) estrade *f*; (period) phase *f*. *v* mettre en scène.

stagger, stagg´-'r, *v* chanceler; (*fig*) renverser.

stagnate, stagg´-néte, *v* stagner; croupir.

staid*, stéde, *a* posé; sérieux.

stain, sténe, *v* (dyeing) teindre; (soil) souiller. *n* teinture *f*; (soil) tache *f*; **–less,** *a* (metal) inoxydable.

stair, stére, *n* marche *f*; **–s,** *pl* escalier *m*.

stake, stéque, *v* (to defend with stakes) garnir de pieux; (bet) parier. *n* pieu *m*; (wager) enjeu *m*; **at the –,** sur le bûcher.

stale, stéle, *a* (bread, etc) rassis; (beer, etc) éventé.

stalk, stoake, *n* tige *f*. *v* chasser à l'affût.

stall, stoale, *n* (market) étalage *m*; (cattle) box *m*. *v* (of engine) caler.

stalwart, stoal´-oueurte, *a* fort; robuste.

stamina, stǎmm´-i-n*a*, *n* force de résistance *f*.

stammer, stǎmm´-'r, *v* bégayer.

stamp, stǎmmpe, *n* (documents, letters, etc.) timbre *m*. *v* timbrer; (foot) frapper du pied.

stampede, stǎmm-pîde´, *v* (of animals) fuir en panique; *n* débandade *f*.

stand, stǎnnde, *v* être debout; (place) mettre; (endure) supporter. *n* (*fig*) tribune *f*; (platform) résistance *f*; (pedestal) support *m*; (market) étalage *m*; (exhibition) stand *m*; **–ing,** *a* permanent; *n* (rank) rang *m*; **–ingroom,** place debout *f*; **–still,** arrêt *m*.

standard, stǎnn´-d*e*urde, *n* étendard *m*. *n* & *a* (*fig*) modèle *m*; (weights, measures) étalon *m*.

staple, sté´-p'l, *n* crampon de fer à deux pointes *m*; agrafe *f*. *a* principal.

star, stârre, *n* étoile *f*; **–ry,** *a* étoilé.

starboard, stârre´-baurde, *n* tribord *m*.

starch, stârtche, *n* amidon *m*. *v* empeser.

stare, stére, *v* regarder fixement. *n* regard fixe *m*.

starling, stǎr´-linng, *n*

étourneau *m.*

start, stârte, *n* (beginning) commencement *m*; *v* (to begin) commencer; (machinery) mettre en marche; (leave) partir.

startle, stâr´-t'l, *v* (to become startled) sursauter; effrayer.

starvation, stâr-vé´-ch'n, *n* inanition *f.*

starve, stârve, *v* mourir de faim; (deprive) affamer.

state, stéte, *v* déclarer. *n* état *m*; (pomp) apparat *m*; **–ly,** *a* majestueux; **–ment,** *n* déclaration *f*; (account) relevé de compte *m.*

statesman, stéts´-mănne, *n* homme d'Etat *m.*

station, sté´-ch'n, *n* position *f*; (railroad) gare *f*; (fire, police) poste *m*. *v* poster.

stationary, sté´-chŏnn-*a*-ri, *a* stationnaire.

stationer, sté´-cheunn-*eu*r, *n* papetier *m.*

stationery, sté´-cheunn-*eu*r-i, *n* papeterie *f.*

statistics, sta-tiss´-tiks, *n* statistique *f.*

statue, stă´-tiou, *n* statue *f.*

statute, stă´-tioute, *n*

statut *m*; loi *f.*

staunch, stânnche, *v* étancher. *a* ferme.

stave, stéve, *n* portée *f* **–off,** *v* conjurer; éviter.

stay, sté, *n* séjour *m*. *v* séjourner; rester.

stays, stéze, *npl* corset *m.*

stead, stedde, *n* place *f*; **in –of,** au lieu de.

steadfast, stedd´-fâsste, *a* solide; constant.

steady, stedd´-i, *a* ferme; (reliable) sérieux; (market) ferme.

steak, stéque, *n* bifteck *m.*

steal, stîle, *v* voler; dérober.

stealth, stèl*t*s, **by –,** à la dérobée.

steam, stîme, *n* vapeur *f*; **–er,** bateau à vapeur *m.*

steel, stîle, *n* acier *m.*

steep, stîpe, *a* escarpé. *v* (soak) tremper.

steeple, stî´-p'l, *n* clocher *m.*

steer, stîre, *v* (naut) gouverner; (aero) diriger; (motor) conduire. *n* (ox) bouvillon *m.*

steerage, stîre´-idj, *n* entrepont *m.*

stem, stemme, *n* tige *f*; (glass) pied *m*; (tobacco-

pipe) tuyau *m*; (a current) *v* refouler.

stench, stenntche, *n* infection *f*; puanteur *f.*

step, steppe, *v* marcher; aller. *n* pas *m*; (stair) marche *f*; (ladder) échelon *m*; **–brother,** *n* demi-frère *m*; **–father,** beau-père *m*; **–mother,** belle-mère *f*; **–sister,** *n* demi-sœur *f*;**–ladder,** échelle double *f.*

stereo, stè´-rî-au, *n* stéréo *f.*

stereophonic, stér-io-fon´-ique, *a* stéréophonique.

sterile, stér-il, *a* stérile.

sterilize, stér´-i-lâïze, *v* stériliser.

sterling, steur´-linng, *a* sterling; pur; (fig) de bon aloi.

stern, steurne, *n* arrière *m*. *a** sévère; (cross) rébarbatif.

stew, stioue, *n* (of meat) ragoût *m*. *v* mettre en ragoût.

steward, stioue´-*eu*rde, *n* (estate) intendant *m*; (ship) garçon de cabine *m*; **–ess,** femme de chambre (de bord) *f*; *n* hôtesse (de l'air) *f*; **wine –,** sommelier *m.*

a
b
c
d
e
f
g
h
i
j
k
l
m
n
o
p
q
r
s
t
u
v
w
x
y
z

A
B
C
D
E
F
G
H
I
J
K
L
M
N
O
P
Q
R
S
T
U
V
W
X
Y
Z

stick, stique, v (affix) coller. n bâton m; (walking) canne f; **–y,** a collant.

stiff*, stife, a raide; **–en,** v raidir; (linen) empeser.

stifle, stâï´-f'l, v étouffer; suffoquer.

stigmatize, stigg´-ma-tâïze, v stigmatiser.

stile, stâïle, n barrière f; **turn –,** tourniquet m.

still, stille, n (distill) alambic m. v calmer. a tranquille; adv encore; toujours. conj (nevertheless) néanmoins.

stimulate, stimm´-iou-léte, v stimuler.

sting, stinng, v piquer. n piqûre f.

stink, stinng-k, v puer. n puanteur f.

stint, stinnte, v restreindre; rogner.

stipend, stâï´-pennde, n traitement m.

stipulate, stip´-iou-léte, v stipuler.

stipulation, stip-iou-lé-ch'n, n stipulation f.

stir, steur, v remuer; (fig) agiter; bouger. n émoi m.

stirrup, stirr´-eupe, n étrier m.

stitch, stitche, v coudre. n point m.

stock, stoque, v avoir en magasin; stocker; n (tree) tronc m; (gun) fût m; (flower) giroflée f; (goods) stock m; (live) animaux vivants mpl; (meat, etc) bouillon m; **–broker,** agent de change m; **–-exchange,** bourse f; **–s,** (securities) valeurs fpl; (pillory) pilori m; **–-taking,** inventaire m.

stocking, stok´-inng, n bas m.

stoke, stauque, v chauffer; **–r,** n chauffeur m.

stolid, stol´-id, a lourd.

stomach, stomm´-aque, n estomac m; **–-ache,** mal à l'estomac m; mal au ventre m.

stone, staune, n pierre f; (pebble) caillou m; (med) calcul m; v lapider; (fruit) enlever les noyaux.

stool, stoule, n tabouret m; (med) selle f.

stoop, stoupe, v se baisser.

stop, stoppe, n arrêt m; (interruption) pause f; (punctuation) point m; v arrêter; s'arrêter;

(payment) suspendre; (teeth) plomber; (cease) (of trains, vessels, etc.) cesser; **–up,** boucher.

stopper, stopp´-'r, n bouchon m. .

storage, staur´-idj, n magasinage m.

store, staure, n (shop) magasin m.

stores, staur´ze, npl approvisionnements mpl.

stork, stoarque, n cigogne f.

storm, stoarme, n tempête f. v donner l'assaut à.

stormy, stoar´-mi, a orageux.

story, stau´-ri, n histoire f; (untruth) mensonge m; (floor) étage m.

stout, stâ´oute, a gros; (strong) fort.

stove, stauve, n poêle m; (cooking) cuisinière f.

stow, stau, v (naut) arrimer; (away) ranger.

stowaway, stau´-a-oué, n voyageur clandestin m.

straggle, străgg´-'l, v s'écarter de; (lag) traîner.

straight, stréte, a droit; direct; **–en,** v redresser; **–forward*,** a honorable;

franc.

strain, stréne, n effort m; (music) air m; (pull) tension f. v s'efforcer; (stretch) tendre; (tendon) fouler; (liquid) filtrer.

strainer, stré´-neur, n passoire f; filtre m.

straits, strétse, npl (channel) détroit m.

strand, strǎnnde, v (naut) échouer. n plage f; (rope) brin m.

strange*, stréne'dje, a étrange; **–r,** n étranger, -ère m & f.

strangle, strain´-ng'l, v étrangler.

strap, strǎppe, v attacher avec une courroie; n courroie f.

strategy, strǎ´-ta-djî, n stratégie f.

straw, stroa, n paille f; **–berry,** fraise f.

stray, stré, v s'égarer; s'éloigner. a égaré, perdu.

streak, strîke, n raie f; rayon m. v rayer.

streaky, strîk´-i, a rayé; (meat) entrelardé.

stream, strîme, n (brook) ruisseau m; courant m. v couler; **–lined,** a

aérodynamique.

street, strîte, n rue f.

strength, strenng-ts, n force f; **–en,** v renforcer.

strenuous*, strenn´-iou-euce, a ardu.

stress, stresse, n accent m; (pressure) pression f; tension f; (urge) urgence f. v accentuer; souligner.

stretch, stretche, v (widen) élargir; (oneself) s'étirer; (pull) tirer; **–er,** n (med) brancard m.

strew, stroue, v répandre; parsemer.

strict*, stricte, a exact; strict; rigoureux.

stride, strâîde, n enjambée f. v enjamber.

strife, strâîfe, n dispute f; contestation f.

strike, strâîke, v (work) se mettre en grève; (lightning; smite) frapper; (match) allumer; n (of workmen) grève f; **–off, –out,** v effacer; (disqualify) rayer; **–r,** n gréviste m & f.

string, strinng, v (beads) enfiler. n ficelle f; (music) corde f.

stringent, strinn´-djennte,

a rigoureux.

strip, strippe, v dénuder. n bande f.

stripe, strâîpe, n raie f; (mil) galon m. v rayer.

strive, strâîve, v s'efforcer de.

stroke, strauke, n (med) attaque f; (pen) trait de plume m; (blow) coup m; (piston) course f. v caresser.

stroll, straule, v flâner; faire un tour. n tour m.

strong*, stronng, a fort; solide.

structure, strok´-tioure, n structure f.

struggle, strogg´-'l, v lutter. n lutte f.

strut, strotte, v se pavaner. n (brace) étai m.

stubborn, stobb´-eurne, a obstiné; opiniâtre.

stud, stodde, n (nail) clou à grosse tête m; (collar) bouton m; (breeding) haras m. v garnir de clous.

student, stioue´-dennte, n étudiant, -e m & f, élève m & f.

studio, stioue´-di-ô, n atelier m; studio m.

studious*, stioue´-di-euce, a studieux.

a
b
c
d
e
f
g
h
i
j
k
l
m
n
o
p
q
r
s
t
u
v
w
x
y
z

A
B
C
D
E
F
G
H
I
J
K
L
M
N
O
P
Q
R
S
T
U
V
W
X
Y
Z

study, stodd´-i, *v* étudier. *n* étude *f*; (room) cabinet de travail *m*; bureau *m*.

stuff, stoffe, *v* rembourrer; (preserve) empailler; (cookery) farcir. *n* (*fig*) matière *f*; **–ing,** (cookery) farce *f*.

stumble, stomm´-b'l, *v* trébucher.

stump, stommpe, *n* troncon *m*; (arm, leg) moignon *m*; (tooth) racine *f*.

stun, stonne, *v* étourdir.

stunning, stonn´-inng, *a* (*fig*) étourdissant.

stunt, stonnte, *n* tour de force *m*; acrobatie *f*; **–man,** cascadeur *m*.

stunted, stonn´-tedde, *a* rabougri.

stupefy, stioue´-pi-fâï, *v* stupéfier.

stupendous*, stiou-penn´-deuce, *a* prodigieux.

stupid*, stioue´-pide, *a* stupide; **–ity,** *n* stupidité *f*.

stupor, stioue´-peur, *n* stupeur *f*.

sturdy, steur´-di, *a* vigoureux; hardi.

sturgeon, steur´-dj'n, *n* esturgeon *m*.

stutter, stott´-'r, *v* bégayer; balbutier.

sty, stâï, *n* porcherie *f*; (*med*) orgelet *m*.

style, stâïle, *n* mode *f*; (manner) style *m*.

stylish, stâïl´-iche, *a* à la mode; élégant.

subdue, seub-dioue´, *v* subjuguer; (tame) dompter.

subject, sobb-djecte´, *v* assujétir; exposer à.

subject, sobb´-djecte, *n* sujet *m*.

subjection, sobb-djèque´-ch'n, *n* dépendance *f*; soumission *f*.

subjunctive, sobb-djonngk´-tive, *n* subjonctif *m*.

sublime*, seub-lâïme´, *a* sublime.

submarine, sob´-ma-rine, *n* & *a* sous-marin *m*.

submerge, seub-meurdje´, *v* submerger.

submission, seub-mich´-'n, *n* soumission *f*.

submit, seub-mitte´, *v* soumettre à; se soumettre à.

subordinate, seub-or´-di-néte, *a* subordonné.

subpœna, seub-pî´-na, *n* assignation *f*. *v* assigner.

subscribe, seub-scrâïbe´, *v* souscrire (à or pour); (papers) s'abonner; **–r,** *n* souscripteur *m*; abonné, -ée *m* & *f*.

subscription, seub-scrip´-ch'n, *n* souscription *f*; (papers, library, etc) abonnement *m*.

subsequent*, seub´-sî-couenne, *a* subséquent.

subservient, seub-seur´-vi-ennte, *a* subordonné à.

subside, seub-sâïde´, *v* (to sink) s'affaisser; (water) baisser.

subsidiary, seub-side´-i-*a*-ri, *a* subsidiaire.

subsidy, seub´-si-di, *n* (grant) subvention *f*.

subsist, seub-cisste´, *v* subsister; **–on,** vivre de.

substance, seub´-st'nce, *n* substance *f*; (meaning) fond *m*.

substantial*, seub-stănn´-cheul, *a* substantiel.

substantiate, seub-stănn´-chi-éte, *v* établir.

substantive, seub´-stănn-tive, *n* substantif *m*.

substitute, seub´-sti-tioute, *v* remplacer. *n* (proxy) remplaçant, -e *m* & *f*; **as a –,** à la place de.

subterranean, seub-tèrré´-ni-*ann*, *a* souterrain.

subtitle, sob´-tî-tl, *n*
(*cinema*) sous-titre *m*.

subtle, seutt´-'l, *a* subtil;
adroit.

subtract, seub-trăcte´, *v*
soustraire.

suburb, seub´-eurbe, *n*
banlieue *f*.

subway, seub´-ou'é, *n*
passage souterrain *m*;
métro *m*.

succeed, seuk-cîde´, *v*
succéder à; (achieve)
réussir.

success, seuk-cesse´, *n*
succès *m*; **–ful,** *a*
couronné de succés;
(person) heureux; **–ion,**
n succession *f*; **–or,**
successeur *m*.

succor, seuk´-'r, *n* secours
m. *v* secourir.

succumb, seuk-komme´, *v*
succomber.

such, sotche, *a* pareil;
semblable.

suck, soque, *v* sucer;
(baby) téter; **–le,**
allaiter.

suction, soque´-ch'n, *n*
succion *f*.

sudden*, sod´-'n, *a*
soudain; imprévu.

sue, sioue, *v* poursuivre en
justice.

suede, souéde, *n* daim *m*.

suet, sioue´-ette, *n* graisse
de rognon *f*.

suffer, so?´-'r, *v* souffrir;
supporter; **–ing,** *n*
souffrance *f*. *a* patient;
on –ance, par tolérance.

suffice, seuf-fâïce´, *v*
suffire à.

sufficient*, seuf-fî´-
chennte, *a* suffisant.

suffocate, sof´-ŏ-quéte, *v*
suffoquer.

suffrage, seuf´-frédje, *n*
suffrage *m*.

sugar, chou´-gueur, *n* sucre
m.

suggest, seudd-jeste´, *v*
suggérer; (advice)
conseiller; **–ion,** *n*
suggestion *f*; **–ive,** *a*
suggestif.

suicide, siou´-i-sâïde, *n*
suicide *m*.

suit, sioute, *v* convenir;
(dress) aller bien. *n*
complet *m*; costume *m*;
(law) procès *m*; (cards)
couleur *f*; **–able,** *a*
convenable; **–case,** *n*
valise *f*; **–or,** (wooer)
prétendant *m*.

suite, souîte, *n* (retinue)
suite *f*; (rooms)
appartement *m*;
(furniture)

ameublement *m*.

sulfur, soll´-f'r, *n* soufre *m*.

sulk, sollque, *v* bouder; **–y,**
a boudeur.

sullen*, soll´-'n, *a*
maussade; morose.

sultry, soll´-tri, *a* lourd;
accablant.

sum, somme, *n* somme *f*;
–up, *v* résumer.

summary, somm´-a-ri, *n*
résumé *m*. *a* sommaire.

summer, somm´-'r, *n* été
m.

summit, somm´-itte, *n*
sommet *m*.

summon, somm´-'n, *v*
appeler; (call)
convoquer.

summons, somm´-eunnze,
n (to surrender, etc.)
sommation *f*.

sumptuous*, sommp´-
tiou-euce, *a* somptueux.

sun, sonne, *n* soleil *m*;
–bathe, *v* prendre un
bain de soleil; **–beam,**
rayon de soleil *m*;
–burn, *n* coup de soleil
m; **–dial,** cadran solaire
m; **–glasses,** *n* lunettes
de soleil *fpl*; **–light,**
sonn´-lâïte, *n* soleil *m*;
–ny, *a* ensoleillé; **–rise,**
n lever du soleil *m*; **–set,**
coucher du soleil *m*;

a
b
c
d
e
f
g
h
i
j
k
l
m
n
o
p
q
r
s
t
u
v
w
x
y
z

A
B
C
D
E
F
G
H
I
J
K
L
M
N
O
P
Q
R
S
T
U
V
W
X
Y
Z

–**stroke,** coup de soleil *m*; insolation *m*; –**tan,** *n* bronzage *m*.

Sunday, sonn´-dé, *n* dimanche *m*.

sundries, sonn´-drize, *npl* articles divers *mpl*.

sundry, sonn´-dri, *a* divers.

sunken, sonng´-k'n, *a* enfoncé;coulé.

suntan lotion, sonn´-tanne-lau-ch'n, *a* crème solaire.

sup, soppe, *v* souper; –**per,** *n* souper *m*.

super, sioue´-p*eu*r, *n* (theatrical) figurant *m*; –**abundant,** *a* surabondant; –**annuation,** *n* retraite *f*; –**cilious,** *a* hautain; dédaigneux; –**ficial,** superficiel; –**fine,** surfin; –**intend,** *v* surveiller; –**intendent,** *n* contrôleur *m*; –**market,** *n* supermarché *m*; –**natural,** *a* surnaturel; –**sede,** *v* supplanter; –**vise,** surveiller; –**vision,** *n* surveillance *f*.

superb*, sioue-p*eu*rbe´, *a* superbe.

superfluous, sioue-p*eu*r´-flou-*eu*ce, *a* superflu.

superior, sioue-pi´-ri-*eu*r, *a* supérieur.

superlative, sioue-p*eu*r´-la-tive, *n* & *a* superlatif *m*.

superstitious*, sioue-p*eu*r-stich´-*eu*ce, *a* superstitieux.

supplant, s*eu*p-plânnte´, *v* supplanter.

supple, sopp´-'l, *a* souple.

supplement, sopp´-li-m'nt, *n* supplément *m*.

supplier, s*eu*p-plâï´-*eu*r, *n* fournisseur *m*.

supply, s*eu*p-plâï´, *v* fournir. *n* fourniture *f*.

support, s*eu*p-paurte´, *n* (prop) support *m*; (moral) appui *m*; (maintenance) entretien *m*. *v* supporter; entretenir; (morally) soutenir.

suppose, s*eu*p-pauze´, *v* supposer.

supposition, s*eu*p-pau-ziche´-'n, *n* supposition *f*.

suppress, s*eu*p-press´, *v* (to check) supprimer; (conceal) cacher.

supremacy, sioue-premm´-a-ci, *n* suprématie *f*.

supreme*, sioue-prîme´, *a* suprême.

surcharge, s*eu*r´-tchârdje, *n* surcharge *f*. *v* surcharger.

sure*, chou*eu*r, *a* sûr, certain.

surety, chou*eu*r´-ti, *n* (bail, etc) caution *f*.

surf, seurfe, *n* ressac *m*.

surface, seur´-féce, *n* surface *f*.

surfboard, seurf´-baurde, *n* planche de surf *f*.

surfing, seurf´-inng, *n* surf *m*.

surge, seurdje, *v* s'enfler. *n* houle *f*.

surgeon, seur´-dj*eu*ne, *n* chirurgien *m*.

surgery, seur´-dj*eu*r-i, *n* chirurgie *f*.

surgical, seur´-dji-c'l, *a* chirurgical.

surly, seur´-li, *a* bourru; (dog) hargneux.

surmise, s*eu*r-mâïze´, *v* conjecturer. *n* conjecture *f*.

surmount, seur-mâ'ounnte´, *v* surmonter.

surname, seur´-néme, *n* nom de famille *m*.

surpass, s*eu*r-pâsse´, *v* surpasser; l'emporter sur.

surplus, seur´-pleuce, *n* excédent *m*; surplus *m*.

surprise, s*eur*-prâïze´, *v*
surprendre. *n* surprise *f*.

surrender, s*eur*-renn´-d'r,
n (*mil*) reddition *f*. *v* se
rendre; (cede) céder.

surround, s*eur*-râ'ounnde,
v entourer; (*mil*) cerner;
–ings, *npl* environs *mpl*.

survey, s*eur*-vé´, *n* (land)
arpentage *m*; enquête *f*;
v (of land) mesurer;
(look at) inspecter; **–or,**
n (overseer) arpenteur
m; architecte *m*;
inspecteur *m*.

survival, s*eur*-vâï´-v'l, *n*
survivance *f*.

survive, s*eur*-vâïve´, *v*
survivre.

survivor, s*eur*-vâï´-v'r, *n*
survivant, -e *m* & *f*.

susceptible, s*euss*-cepp´-ti-
b'l, *a* susceptible.

suspect, s*euss*-pecte´, *v*
soupconner. *n* & *a*
suspect, -e *m* & *f*.

suspend, s*euss*-pennde´, *v*
suspendre; (defer)
ajourner; **–ers,** *npl*
bretelles *fpl*.

suspense, s*euss*-pennce´, *n*
suspens *m*; incertitude *f*.

suspension, s*euss*-penn´-
ch'n, *n* suspension *f*;
–bridge, pont suspendu
m.

suspicion, s*euss*-pich´-'n,
n soupçon *m*.

suspicious*, s*euss*-pich´-
euce, *a* méfiant; suspect.

sustain, s*euss*-téne´, *v*
soutenir; supporter.

swagger, sou'ăgg´-'r, *v* faire
le fanfaron.

swallow, sou'oll´-au, *v*
avaler. *n* (bird)
hirondelle *f*.

swamp, sou'ommpe, *n*
marécage *m*. *v*
submerger.

swan, sou'onne, *n* cygne
m.

swarm, sou'oarme, *n*
(bees, etc) essaim *m*;
(people) multitude *f*. *v*
essaimer; (crowd)
pulluler.

sway, soué, *v* (to bias)
influencer; osciller;
(totter) chanceler. *n*
influence *f*; (power)
pouvoir *m*.

swear, sou'aire, *v* jurer de;
(law) prêter serment.

sweat, sou'ète, *n* sueur *f*. *v*
suer; transpirer.

sweep, sou'îpe, *v* balayer;
(chimney) ramoner. *n*
(chimney) ramoneur *m*;
–er, balayeur *m*.

sweet, sou'îte, *a* sucré;
(*fig*) doux. *n*

(confection) bonbon *m*;
(meals) entremets *m*; **––**
bread, ris de veau ou
d'agneau *m*; **–en,** *v*
sucrer; **–heart,** *n*
amoureux, -euse *m* & *f*;
–ness, douceur *f*; **––pea,**
pois de senteur *m*.

swell, sou'elle, *v* enfler;
–ing, *n* (*med*) enflure.

swerve, sou'eurve, *v*
dévier; (skid) déraper.

swift, sou'ifte, *a** rapide. *n*
martinet *m*.

swim, sou'imme, *v* nager.
n nage *f*; **–mer,** nageur, -
euse *m* & *f*; **–ming,** *n*
natation *f*; **–ming pool,**
piscine *f*; **–ming trunks,**
n maillot de bain *m*;
–suit, *n* maillot (de
bain) *m*.

swindle, sou'inn´-d'l, *v*
escroquer; rouler; *n*
escro querie *f*; **–r,** escroc
m.

swine, sou-âïne, *n* cochon
m; porc *m*.

swing, sou'inng, *n*
oscillation *f*; (child's)
balançoire *f*. *v* osciller;
se balancer; (whirl)
tournoyer.

switch, sou'itche, *n*
(riding) cravache *f*;
(electric) commutateur

a
b
c
d
e
f
g
h
i
j
k
l
m
n
o
p
q
r
s
t
u
v
w
x
y
z

m. v (train) aiguiller;
–**off,** (light) éteindre;
–**on,** (light) allumer.

swivel, sou'ıve´-'l, *n*
tourniquet *m;* pivot *m.*

swoon, swoune, *v* se
pâmer en pâmoison *m.*

swoop, swoupe, *v* fondre
sur.

sword, saurde, *n* épée *f;*
(sabre) sabre *m.*

sworn, sou'aurne, *a* (law)
assermenté.

syllable, sil´-la-b'l, *n*
syllabe *f.*

syllabus, sil´-la-beuce, *n*
programme *m.*

symbol, simm´-b'l, *n*
symbole *m.*

symmetry, simm´-èt-ri, *n*
symétrie *f.*

sympathetic, simm´-pa-
tsèt´-ique, *a*
sympathique.

sympathize, simm´-pa-
tsâïze, *v* sympathiser.

sympathy, simm´-pa-tsi, *n*
sympathie *f.*

symptom, simmp´-t'm, *n*
symptôme *m.*

synchronize, sinn´-cronn-
âïze, *v* synchroniser.

syndicate, sinn´-di-kéte, *n*
syndicat *m.*

synonymous, si-nonn´-i-
meuce, *a* synonyme.

syringe, sir´-inndje, *n*
seringue *f. v* seringuer.

syrup, sir´-oppe, *n* sirop *m.*

system, siss´-t'm *n* système
m.

table, té-´b'l, n table f; **–cloth,** nappe f; **–land,** plateau m; **–spoon,** cuiller à bouche f.

table tennis, té-b'l-tenn-ice, n ping-pong f.

tablet, tăb´-lette, n tablette f; plaque f; comprimé m.

tack, tăque, n (nail) semence f. v clouer; (sew) faufiler; (naut) courir une bordée.

tackle, tăque´-'l, n (fishing) articles de pêche mpl; (naut) apparaux mpl; v (work, etc.) attaquer.

tact, tăkt, n tact m; **–ful,** a qui a du tact; **–ics,** n tactique f; **–less,** a sans tact.

tadpole, tăde´-pôle, n têtard m.

tail, téle, n queue f; (coat, short, etc) pan m.

tailor, té´-l'r, n tailleur m.

taint, ténnte, v souiller; infecter. n souillure f.

take, téque, v prendre; accepter; **–away,** (carry away) emporter; (clear away) enlever; (lead away) emmener; **–care of,** prendre soin de, avoir soin de; **–off,** enlever.

takings, té´-kinngse, npl recettes fpl.

talcum powder, tăl-qeum-pâ´ou-d'r, n talc m.

tale, téle, n récit m; (fairy) conte m.

talent, tăl´-ennte, n talent m.

talk, toak, v parler; causer. n conversation f.

talkative, toak´-a-tive, a bavard.

tall, toal, a (of persons) grand; (of things) haut.

tallow, tăl´-au, n suif m.

tally, tăl´-i, v concorder; correspondre.

talon, tăl´-onne, n serre f.

tame, téme, a apprivoisé; domestique. v apprivoiser; (beasts) dompter; **taming,** n apprivoisement m; **–r,** dompteur m.

tamper, tămm-´p'r, **–with,** v attérer; falsifier.

tampon, tămm´-ponne, n med tampon hygiénique m.

tan, tănne, v (leather) tanner; (sun) bronzer.

tangerine, tănn´-dje-rinne, n mandarine f.

tangible, tănn´-dji-b'l, a tangible; palpable.

tangle, tain´-ng'l, n emmêlement m. v embrouiller; emmêler.

tank, tain´-ngk, n citerne f; (mil) char d'assaut m.

tantalize, tănn´-ta-lăïze, v tenter; torturer.

tap, tăppe, n tape f; (knock at door etc.) petit coup m; (cock) robinet m; v taper; (knock) frapper; (tree)

a
b
c
d
e
f
g
h
i
j
k
l
m
n
o
p
q
r
s
t
u
v
w
x
y
z

A B C D E F G H I J K L M N O P Q R S **T** U V W X Y Z

inciser.

tape, tépe, *n* bande *f*; –**measure,** mètre en ruban *m*; –**recorder,** *n* magnétophone *m*; –**worm,** ver solitaire *m*; **red** –,(*fig*) bureaucratie *f*.

taper, tépe´-'r, *v* effiler.

tapestry, tăp´-'s-tri, *n* tapisserie *f*.

tar, târe, *n* goudron *m*. *v* goudronner.

tardy, târe´-di, *a* lent; (late) tardif.

target, târe´-guette, *n* cible *f*.

tariff, tăre´-if, *n* tarif *m*.

tarnish, târe´-niche, *v* ternir.

tarpaulin, târe-poa´-linne, *n* bâche *f*.

tart, târte, *n* tarte *f*; tourte *f*. *a** acide.

task, tâssque, *n* tâche *f*.

tassel, tăss´-'l, *n* gland *m*.

taste, téste, *v* goûter. *n* goût *m*; –**ful,** *a* de bon goût; –**less,** sans goût, insipide.

tasty, tést´-i, *a* savoureux.

tatter, tătt´-'r, *n* haillon *m*; lambeau *m*; –**ed,** *a* déguenillé.

tattle, tătt´-'l, *v* jaser. *n* bavardage *m*.

tattoo, ta-toue´, *v* (skin) tatouer. *n* tatouage *m*;

(*mil*) retraite aux flambeaux *f*.

taunt, toannte, *v* railler; persifler; *n* sarcasme *m*; raillerie *f*.

tavern, tăv´-eurne, *n* taverne *f*.

tawdry, toa´-dri, *a* clinquant.

tax, tăxe, *v* taxer. *n* impôt *m*; –**payer,** contribuable *m* & *f*.

taxi, tăk´-si, *n* taxi *m*.

tea, tî, *n* thé *m*; –**pot,** théière *f*.

teach, tîtche, *v* enseigner; –**er,** *n* professeur *m*; (primary) maître, -tresse *m* & *f*.

teaching, tîtch´-inng, *n* enseignement *m*.

team, tîme, *n* (sport) équipe *f*; (horses, etc) attelage *m*.

tear, tère, *v* (rend) déchirer. *n* déchirure *f*.

tear, tîre, *n* larme *f*.

tease, tîze, *v* taquiner; (annoy) agacer.

teat, tîte, *n* mamelon *m*; (dummy) tétine *f*.

technical*, tèque´-ni-c'l, *a* technique.

tedious*, tî´-di-euce, *a* ennuyeux; fatigant.

tedium, tî´-di-omme, *n* ennui *m*.

teem, tîme, –**with,** *v*

fourmiller de.

teenager, tîné-dje'r, *n* addescent,-e *m* & *f*.

teeny, tî-ni, *a* minuscule.

teething, tîdz´-inng, *n* dentition *f*.

teetotaler, tî-tŏ´-t'leur, *n* abstinent, -ente *m* & *f*.

telegram, tell´-i-grămme, *n* télégramme *m*.

telegraph, tell´-i-grăfe, *v* télégraphier.

telephone, tell´-i-faune, *v* téléphoner. *n* téléphone *m*.

telephone booth, tell-i-faune-boudz, *n* cabine téléphonique *f*.

telephone call, telle-i-faune-coal, *n* coup de téléphone *m*.

telephone number, telle-i-faune-nomm-b'r, *n* numéro de téléphone *m*.

telescope, tell´-i-scaupe, *n* télescope *m*; longue-vue *f*.

television, tell-i-vij´-'n, *n* télévision *f*; – **set,** *n* poste de télévision *m*.

tell, tell, *v* dire; (narrate) raconter.

temper, temm´-p'r, *n* (humor) humeur *f*; (anger) colère *f*; (steel) trempe *f*. *v* tremper; –**ance,** *n* tempérance *f*; sobriété *f*. *a* de tempérance; **–ate***, modéré; sobre; **–ature**, n température f; fièvre f.

tempest, temm´-peste, n tempête f.

temple, temm´-p'l, n temple m; (head) tempe f.

temporary, temm´-pŏ-ra-ri, a temporaire.

tempt, temmpte, v tenter; **–ing**, a tentant.

temptation, temmp-té´-ch'n, n tentation f.

ten, tenne, n & a dix m; **–th**, dixième m & f.

tenable, tenn´-a-b'l, a soutenable; (mil) tenable.

tenacious*, ti-né´-cheuce, a tenace.

tenacity, ti-năss´-i-ti, n ténacité f.

tenancy, tenn´-ann-ci, n location f.

tenant, tenn´-annte, n locataire m & f.

tend, tennde, v soigner.

tendency, tenn´-denn-ci, n tendance f.

tender, tenn´-d'r, v offrir; (contract) soumissionner pour; n offre f; soumission f. a* tendre; (painful) sensible; **–hearted**, compatissant; **–ness**, n tendresse f; sensibilité f.

tenement, tenn´-i-m'nt, n habitation f; logement m.

tennis, tenn´-ice, n tennis m; **– court**, n court de tennis m; **– racket**, n raquette de tennis f.

tenor, tenn´-'r, n (mus) ténor m; (purport) teneur f.

tense, tennce, n (grammar) temps m. a* tendu.

tension, tenn´-ch'n, n tension f.

tent, tennte, n tente f.

tentative*, tenn´-ta-tive, a expérimental.

tenure, tenn´-ioure, n jouissance f.

tepid, tepp´-idde, a tiède.

term, teurme, n terme m; (school) trimestre m; (time) durée f; **–inate**, v terminer; se terminer; **–inus**, n terminus m; **–s**, pl conditions fpl; (installments) à tempérament; **–inal**, a terminale, final; med en phase terminale; n terminal (computer, oil) m; n terminus (rail) m.

terrace, terr´-ice, n terrasse f.

terrible, terr´-i-b'l, a terrible.

terrific, terr-i´-fique, a formidable.

terrify, terr´-i-fâi, v terrifier.

territory, terr´-i-tŏr-i, n territoire m.

terror, terr´-'r, n terreur f; effroi m; **–ist**, n terroriste m/f; **–ize**, v terroriser.

terse*, teurse, a sec; net.

test, tesste, v mettre à l'épreuve; essayer; n épreuve, f, essai m; examen m; **–ify**, v attester; **–imonial**, n certificat m; (presentation) témoignage de reconnaissance m.

Testament, tess´-ta-m'nt, n Testament m.

testicle, tess´-ti-k'l, n testicule m.

testimony, tess´-ti-mo-ni, n témoignage m.

tether, tèdz´-'r, n longe f. v mettre à l'attache.

text, texte, n texte m; **–book**, manuel m

textile, tex´-tâile, a textile.

texture, tex´-tioure, n tissu m; texture f.

than, dzănne, conj que; de (between more or less and a number).

thank, tsain-ngk, v remercier; **–you!** interj

A
B
C
D
E
F
G
H
I
J
K
L
M
N
O
P
Q
R
S
T
U
V
W
X
Y
Z

merci! **–ful,** *a*
reconnaissant; **–less,**
ingrat; **–s,** *npl*
remerciements *mpl;* **–s**
to, *prep* grâce à.

thanksgiving, *t*sainngkse´-
guiv-inng, *n* actions de
grâces *fpl.*

that, d*z*ătte, *pron rel*
lequel; laquelle; lesquels;
lesquelles; cela; *a* ce;
cet; cette; *conj* que; afin
que; **–one,** *pron dem*
celui-là; celle-là.

thatch, *t*sătche, *n* chaume
m. v couvrir de chaume.

thaw, *t*s oa, *n* dégel *m. v*
dégeler.

the, d*z*e, *art* le; la; les.

theater, *t*sî´-*a*-t'r, *n* théâtre
m.

theft, *t*sefte, *n* vol *m;*
(petty) larcin *m.*

their, d*z*ère, *poss a* leur;
leurs.

theirs, d*z*èrze, *poss pron* le
leur; la leur; les leurs.

them, d*z*emme, *pron* eux;
elles; les; **to –,**leur;
–selves, eux-mêmes;
elles-mêmes; (refl.) se.

theme, *t*sîme, *n* thème *m;*
texte *m.*

then, d*z*enne, *adv* alors;
ensuite; *conj* donc.

thence, d*z*ennce, *adv* de
là; **–forth,** désormais.

theology, *t*sî-ol´-ŏdj-i, *n*

théologie *f.*

theoretical*, *t*sî-ŏ-rett´-i-
c'l, *a* thérorique.

theory, *t*sî´-ŏ-ri, *n* théorie
f.

therapy, *t*sè´-ra-pî, *n*
thérapie *f.*

there, d*z*air, *adv* là; **–by,**
adv par là; **–fore,** donc;
–upon, là-dessus; sur ce.

thermal, *t*seur´-m'l, *a*
thermal.

thermometer, *t*seur-
momm´-i-t'r, *n*
thermomètre *m.*

these, d*z*îze, *pron* ceux-ci;
celles-ci; *a* ces; ces ... -ci.

thesis, *t*sî-sisse, *n* thèse *f.*

they, d*z*é, *pron* ils; elles;
eux.

thick, *t*sique, *a** épais;
(big) gros; **–en,** *v*
épaissir; **–et,** *n* taillis *m;*
–ness, épaisseur *f.*

thief, *t*sîfe, *n* voleur, -euse
m & f.

thigh, *t*săï, *n* cuisse *f.*

thimble, *t*simm´-b'l, *n* dé à
coudre *m.*

thin, *t*sinne, *a* mince;
(lean) maigre; (sparse)
clairsemé. *v* amincir;
(trees, etc) élaguer;
–ness, *n* minceur *f;*
maigreur *f.*

thing, *t*sinng, *n* chose *f.*

think, *t*sinnque, *v* penser;
(believe) croire; **–about,**

(of), penser à, (de);
–over, réfléchir.

third, *t*seurde, *n* & *a**
troisième *m* & *f;* (one-
third) tiers *m.*

thirst, *t*seurste, *n* soif *f;* **to**
be –y, *v* avoir soif.

thirteen, *t*seur´-tîne, *n* &
a treize *m;* **–th,** treizième
m & *f.*

thirtieth, *t*seur´-ti-its, *n* &
a trentième *m* & *f.*

thirty, *t*seur´-ti, *n* & *a*
trente *m.*

this, d*z*ice, *pron* ceci; ce; *a*
ce; cet; cette.

thistle, *t*siss´-'l, *n* chardon
m.

thong, *t*sonng, *n* lanière *f.*

thorn, *t*s oarne, *n* épine *f;*
–y, *a* épineux.

thorough*, *t*sor´-ŏ, *a*
entier; (perfect) parfait;
profond; **–bred,** *n* & *a*
pur sang *m. a* (dog) de
race; **–fare,** *n* voie *f;*
(main) grande artère *f;*
no –fare, rue barrée.

those, d*z*auze, *pron* ceux-
là; celles-là. *a* ces; ces ...
-là.

though, d*z*au, *conj*
quoique; bien que.

thought, *t*s oate, *n* pensée
f; **–ful*,** *a* pensif;
attentif; **–less*,** étourdi;
inattentif.

thousand, *t*sâ'ou´-z'nd, *n*

& *a* mille *m*. *a* (date) mil.

thousandth, tsâ'ouz´-anndts, *n* & *a* millième *m* & *f*.

thrash, tsrăche, *v* battre; (flog) foutter; **–ing,** *n* raclée *f*.

thread, tsredde, *n* fil *m*. *v* enfiler; **–bare,** *a* râpé.

threat, tsrette, *n* menace *f*; **–en,** *v* menacer.

threatening*, tsrett´-ninng, *a* menaçant.

three, tsrie, *n* & *a* trois *m*.

threshold, tsrèch´-aulde, *n* seuil *m*.

thrift, tsrifte, *n* économie *f*; **–less,** *a* prodigue.

thrifty, tsrif´-ti, *a* économe.

thrill, tsrill, *v* émouvoir. *n* saisissement *m*.

thrive, tsrâïve, *v* prospérer.

throat, tsraute, *n* gorge *f*.

throb, tsrobbe, *v* vibrer; (heart) battre.

throes, tsrose, *npl* douleurs *fpl*; (fig) angoisses *fpl*.

throne, tsraune, *n* trône *m*.

throng, tsronng, *v* (together) venir en foule; *n* foule *f*.

throttle, tsrot´-t'l, *n* larynx *m*; (mech) étrangleur *m*

through, tsroue, *prep* (passage, conveyances,

etc.) par; à travers; pour cause de; **–out,** *adv* partout; **–train,** *n* train direct *m*.

throw, tsrau, *v* jeter; lancer. *n* coup *m*.

thrush, tsroche, *n* grive *f*.

thrust, tsrosste, *v* pousser; (sword) porter un coup d'épée. *n* poussée *f*; coup d'épée *m*.

thud, tsodde, *n* bruit sourd *m*.

thumb, tsomme, *n* pouce *m*.

thump, tsommpe, *v* frapper du poing. *n* coup de poing *m*.

thunder, tsonn´-d'r, *v* tonner. *n* tonnerre *m*; **–bolt,** foudre *f*; **–storm,** orage *m*.

Thursday, tseurz´-dé, *n* jeudi *m*.

thus, dzosse, *adv* ainsi.

thwart, tsouoarte, *v* (fig) contrarier; frustrer.

thyme, tâïme, *n* thym *m*.

tick, tique, *v* (clock) faire tic-tac; (check) pointer. *n* (cattle) tique *f*; (cover) toile à matelas *f*.

ticket, tik´-ette, *n* billet *m*; (price, etc) étiquette *f*; **– office,** *n* guichet *m*; **season –,** carte d'abonnement *f*.

tickle, tik´-'l, *v*

chatouiller.

ticklish, tik´-liche, *a* chatouilleux.

tidal, tâï´-d'l, *a* de marée.

tide, tâïde, *n* marée *f*; **high –,** marée haute *f*; **low –,** marée basse *f*.

tidings, tâï´-inngze, *npl* nouvelles *fpl*.

tidy, tâï´-di, *a* en ordre; (neat) rangé. *v* mettre en ordre.

tie, tâï, *n* (bow) nœud *m*; (neck) cravate *f*. *v* ficeler; (a knot) nouer; (together) attacher; (surgical) bander.

tier, tire, *n* rangée *f*; gradin *m*; rang *m*.

tiger, tâï´-gueur, *n* tigre *m*.

tight, tâïte, *a* serré; (tension) tendu; **–en,** *v* serrer; (tension) tendre; **–s,** *n* collant *m*.

tile, tâïle, *n* carreau *m*; (roof) tuile *f*; (slate) ardoise *f*. *v* carreler; couvrir de tuiles.

till, til, *n* tiroir caisse *m*. *v* (land) labourer. *conj* jusqu'à ce que. *prep* jusqu'à.

tiller, till´-eur, *n* (rudder) barre du gouvernail *f*.

tilt, tilte, *v* pencher; incliner.

timber, timm´-b'r, *n* bois de construction *m*.

a
b
c
d
e
f
g
h
i
j
k
l
m
n
o
p
q
r
s
t
u
v
w
x
y
z

A B C D E F G H I J K L M N O P Q R S T U V W X Y Z

time, tâïme, *v* contrôler; (engine) régler; *n* temps *m*; (occasion) fois *f*; (hour) heure *f*; (music) mesure *f*; (step) pas *m*; **–limit,** délai *m*; **–ly,** *a* & *adv* opportun; **–table,** *n* horaire *m*.

timid*, timm´-ide, *a* timide.

tin, tinne, *n* (sheet iron coated with tin) fer-blanc *m*; (pure metal) étain *m*; *v* étamer; **–box,** *n* boîte en fer-blanc *f*; **–foil,** feuille d'étain *f*; **–plate,** fer blanc *m*.

tincture, tinng´-ktioure, *n* teinture *f*.

tinge, tinndje, *n* teinte *f*; nuance *f*; (*fig*) soupcon *m*; *v* teinter.

tingle, tinng´-g'l, *v* picoter.

tinkle, tinng´-k'l, *v* tinter; faire tinter; *n* tintement *m*.

tinsel, tinn´-s'l, *n* clinquant *m*.

tint, tinnte, *n* teinte *f*; *v* teinter.

tiny, tâï´-ni, *a* tout petit, minuscule.

tip, tippe, *v* (give) donner un pourboire; (cart, etc) faire basculer. *n* pourboire *m*; (hint) tuyau *m*; (point) pointe

f; **on –toe,** *adv* sur la pointe des pieds.

tire, tâïeure, *v* fatiguer; se fatiguer; **–of,** se lasser de; **–some,** *a* fatigant; (*fig*) ennuyeux; *n* (auto) bande *f*; (pneumatic) pneu *m*.

tissue, ti´-chiou, *n* tissu *m*; mouchoir *m*.

tissue paper, ti´-chiou-pé´-p'r, *n* papier de soie *m*.

tithe, tâïd*z*, *n* dîme *f*.

title, tâï´-t'l, *n* titre *m*; **–deed,** titre de propriéte'e *m*; **–page,** page du titre *f*.

titter, titt´-'r, *v* ricaner. *n* ricanement *m*.

to, tou, *prep* à; (before name of countries) en; (toward) vers.

toad, taude, *n* crapaud *m*.

toast, tauste, *n* pain grillé *m*; toast *m*; *v* griller, rôtir.

toast, tauste, *n* (drink) toast *m*. *v* porter un toast à.

tobacco, to-băk´-au, *n* tabac *m*; **–nist,** marchand de tabac *m*; **–pouch,** blague à tabac *f*.

toboggan, tô-bogue´-an, *n* luge *f*.

today, tou-dé´, *adv* aujourd'hui.

toddler, tod´-l'r, *n* tout(e)

petit(e) enfant *m/f*.

toe, tau, *n* orteil *m*; doigt de pied *m*.

toffee, tof´-i, *n* caramel *m*.

together, tou-guèd*z*´-'r, *adv* ensemble.

toil, toa'ile, *v* peiner. *n* labeur *m*; **–er,** travailleur *m*

toilet, toa'il´-ette, *n* toilette *f*; toilettes *mpl*; **–paper,** *n* papier hygiénique *m*.

token, tau´-k'n, *n* marque *f*; symbole *m*; jeton *m*.

tolerable, tol´-*eu*r-a-b'l, *a* tolérable.

tolerance, tol´-*eu*r-'nce, *n* tolérance *f*.

tolerant*, tol´-*eu*r-'nt, *a* tolérant.

tolerate, tol´-*eu*r-éte, *v* tolérer.

toll, taule, *n* (knell) glas *m*; (highway) péage *m*. *v* sonner le glas.

tomato, tŏ-mâ´-tau, *n* tomate *f*.

tomb, toum, *n* tombeau *m*; **–stone,** pierre tombale *f*.

tomorrow, tou-morr´-au, *adv* demain.

tomtit, tomme´-tite, *n* mésange *f*.

ton, tonne, *n* tonne *f*; **–nage,** tonnage *m*.

tone, taune, *n* ton *m*; accent *m*; (voice)

timbre *m*.

tongs, tonngze, *npl*
pincettes *f*.

tongue, tonng *n* langue *f*.

tonic, tonn´-ique, *n* & *a*
tonique *m*. *a* fortifiant.

tonight, tou-nâïte´, *adv*
cette nuit; ce soir.

tonsil, tonn´-s'l, *n*
amygdale *f*.

tonsillitis, tonn-sil-âï´-
tice, *n* amygdalite *f*.

too, toue, *adv* trop; (also)
aussi; **–much,** trop.

tool, toule, *n* outil *m*.

tooth, touts, *n* dent *f*;
–ache, mal de dents *m*;
–brush, brosse à dents
f; **–paste,** pâte
dentifrice *f*; **–pick,** cure-
dents *m*; **–powder,**
poudre dentrifice *f*.

top, toppe, *n* (upper part)
haut *m*; (mountain)
sommet *m*; (of tree)
cime *f*; (spinning)
toupie *f*; **–hat,** chapeau
haut de forme *m*; **–less,**
a aux seins nus; **on –,***adv*
par dessus; au-dessus.

topic, top´-ique, *n* sujet *m*.

topple, topp´-'l, **–over,** *v*
culbuter; (car) verser.

topsy-turvy, topp´-ci-
teur´-vi, *adv* sens dessus
dessous.

torch, tôrtche, *n* torche *f*;
(flaming) flambeau *m*;
(electric) lampe de
poche *f*.

torment, tôr´-mennte, *n*
tourment *m*. *v*
tourmenter.

torpedo, tôr-pî´-dau, *n*
torpille *f*.

torpedo boat, tôr-pî´-dau-
baute, *n* torpilleur *m*.

torpid, tôr´-pidde, *a*
engourdi; inerte.

torpor, tôr´-peur, *n* torpeur
f.

torrent, tôr´ennte, *n*
torrent *m*.

torrid, tôr´-ride, *a* torride.

tortoise, tôr´-teuce, *n*
tortue *f*; **–shell,** écaille
f.

torture, tôr´-tioure, *v*
torturer. *n* torture *f*.

toss, tosse, *v* lancer en
l'air; (coin) tirer à pile
ou face; **–about,** s'agiter;
(*naut*) ballotter.

total, tau´-t'l, *n* total *m*; *a*
total; complet; *v*
totaliser.

totter, tott´-'r, *v*
chanceler; **–ing,** *a*
chancelant.

touch, totche, *n* contact
m; (talent) doigté *m*;
(sense) toucher *m*. *v*
toucher.

touching, totch´-innd, *a*
(emotion) touchant.

tough, toffe, *a* dur;

résistant.

tour, toueur, *n* tour *m*;
excursion *f*; **–ist,**
touriste *m* & *f*;
–nament, tournoi *m*.

tourist office, toueur-iste-
of-ice, *n* syndicat
d'initiative *m*.

tout, tâ'oute, *v* racoler. *n*
racoleur *m*.

tow, tau, *v* (haul)
remorquer. *n* (flax)
étoupe *f*; **–age,**
remorquage *m* (canal)
halage *m*; **–line,** corde
de remorque *f*.

towards, tŏ-ouôrdze´, *prep*
envers; (direction) vers.

towel, tâ'ou´-elle, *n*
serviette de toilette *f*.

tower, tâ'ou´-eur, *n* tour *f*.

town, tâ'oune, *n* ville *f*; **–
center,** tâ'oune-senn-t'r,
m centre de la ville;
centre-ville; **–hall,** hôtel
de ville *m*.

toy, toa'i, *n* jouet *m*. *v*
jouer.

trace, tréce, *n* trace *f*;
(trail) piste *f*; (harness)
trait *m*. *v* suivre; suivre
la piste; (draw) calquer;
(origin) rechercher.

tracing, tréce´-inng, *n*
calque *m*; **–paper,** papier
décalque *m*.

track, trăque, *n* trace *f*;
(race) piste *f*; (railroad)

A B C D E F G H I J K L M N O P Q R S **T** U V W X Y Z

voie *f. v* suivre la piste.
tract, trăkt, *n* étendue *f*; (religious) opuscule *m*.

traction, trăk´-ch'n, *n* traction *f*.

tractor, trăk´-t'r, *n* tracteur *m*.

trade, tréde, *v* faire le commerce. *n* commerce *m*; (craft) métier *m*; **– mark,** marque de fabrique *f*; **–sman,** fournisseur *m*; **–s union,** syndicat ouvrier *m*.

tradition, tră-dich´-*eu*nn, *n* tradition *f*.

traditional*, tră-dich´-*eu*nn-al, *a* traditionnel.

traffic, trăf´-ique, *n* (going and coming) circulation *f*; (trade) trafic *m*; **– jam,** *n* embouteillage *m*; **– lights,** tră-fique-lâïtsse, *npl* feux (de circulation) *mpl*.

tragedian, tra-djî´-di-anne, *n* tragédien *m*.

tragedy, trădj´-i-di, *n* tragédie *f*.

tragic, trădj´-ique, *a* tragique.

trail, tréle, *v* suivre à la piste; (drag) traîner; *n* piste *f*; **–er,** (van) remorque *f*.

train, tréne, *n* train *m*; (dress) traîne *f*; (retinue) suite *f. v*

instruire; éduquer; (sport; *mil*) entraîner; (animals) dresser.

training, tré´-ninng, *n* éducation *f*; entraînement *m*.

traitor, tré´-t'r, *n* traître *m*.

tram, trămme, *n* tramway *m*.

tramp, trămmpe, *n* clochard; -e *m* & *f*; *v* aller à pied.

trample, trămm´-p'l, *v* piétiner.

trance, trânnce, *n* extase *f*; (*med*) catalepsie *f*.

tranquil, trănng´-kouill, *a* tranquille; **–izer,** *n* tranquilisant *m*.

transact, trănn-săcte´, *v* traiter; faire.

transaction, trănn-săc´-ch'n, *n* affaire *f*.

transcribe, trănn-scrăïbe´, *v* transcrire.

transfer, trănnss-feur´, *v* (law) transférer; transporter; *n* transport *m*; billet de correspondance *m*; (shares) transfert *m*.

transform, trănnss-fôrme´, *v* transformer.

transgress, trănnss-grèsse´, *v* transgresser.

transit, trănn´-citte, *n* transit *m*.

translate, trănnss-léte´, *v*

traduire.

translation, trănnss-lé´-ch'n, *n* traduction *f*.

translator, trănnss-lé´-t'r, *n* traducteur, -trice *m* & *f*.

transmit, trănnss-mitte´, *v* transmettre.

transparent, trănnss-pă´-rennte, *a* transparent.

transpire, trănnss-pâïre´, *v* transpirer.

transport, trănnss-pôrte´, *v* transporter; *n* transport *m*.

transpose, trănnss-pause´, *v* transposer.

transship, trănn-chippe´, *v* transborder.

trap, trăppe, *n* piège *m*; *v* prendre au piège.

trash, trăche, *n* camelote *f*; ordure *f*; **–y,** *a* de camelote.

travel, trăv´-'l, *v* voyager; **–er,** *n* voyageur, -euse *m* & *f*; **– agent,** *n* agent de voyages *m*; **– sickness,** *n* mal de la route *m*.

traveler's check, trăv-leurz-tchèque, *n* chèque de voyage *m*.

traverse, trăv´-*eu*rse, *v* traverser.

trawler, troa´-leur, *n* chalutier *m*.

tray, tré, *n* plateau *m*; **ash-**

–, cendrier *m*.

treacherous*, trett´-cheur-*euce*, *a* trîatre; perfide.

treachery, trett´-cheur-i, *n* traîtrise *f*; perfidie *f*.

tread, tredde, *n* pas *m*; (stair) marche *f*. *v* poser le pied; (accidental) marcher sur.

treason, trî´-z'n, *n* trahison *f*.

treasure, tréj´-*eur*, *n* trésor *m*. *v* garder précieusement.

treasurer, tréj´-*eur-eur*, *n* trésorier *m*.

treasury, tréj´-*eur*-i, *n* trésor *m*.

treat, trîte, *n* (outing) partie de plaisir *f*. *v* traiter; (*fig*) régaler; (*med*) soigner; **–ment,** *n* traitement *m*.

treatise, trî´-tize, *n* traité *m*.

treaty, trî´-ti, *n* traité *m*.

treble, tréb´-'l, *v* tripler. *n* & *a* triple *m*.

tree, trî, *n* arbre *m*.

trellis, trell´-ice, *n* treillis *m*.

tremble, tremm´-b'l, *v* trembler.

tremendous*, tri-menn´-deuce, *a* prodigieux.

tremor, tremm´-'r, *n* tremblement *m*.

tremulous*, tremm´-iou-leuce, *a* (*fig*) craintif.

trench, trenntche, *n* fossé *m*; (*mil*) tranchée *f*.

trend, trennde, *n* tendance *f*.

trespass, tress´-*pass*, *v* empiéter sur.

trespasser, tress´-pass-'r, *n* intrus *m*.

trestle, tress´-'l, *n* tréteau *m*.

trial, trâï´-*al*, *n* épreuve *f*; essai *m*; (law) procès *m*.

triangle, trâï´-ănng-g'l, *n* triangle *m*.

triangular, trâï-ănng´-guiou-lar, *a* triangulaire.

tribe, trâïbe, *n* tribu *f*.

tribunal, trâï-bioue´-n'l, *n* tribunal *m*.

tributary, trib´-iou-*ta*-ri, *n* affluent *m*.

tribute, trib´-ioute, *n* tribut *m*.

trick, trique, *n* (fraud) ruse *f*; truc *m*; (dexterity) tour *m*; (cards) levée *f*; *v* duper; **–ery,** *n* duperie *f*; **–ster,** fourbe *m*.

trickle, trique´-'l, *v* dégoutter; (flow) suinter.

trifle, trâï´-f'l, *v* jouer; badiner; *n* bagatelle *f*.

trifling, trâï´-flinng, *a* insignifiant.

trigger, trigg´-'r, *n* détente *f*; gachette *f*.

trim, trime, *v* (hat, dress) garnir; (hair) tailler; égaliser; *a* soigné; **–ming,** *n* garniture *f*.

trinity, trinn´-i-ti, *n* trinité *f*.

trinket, trinng´-kitte, *n* colifichet *m*; breloque *f*.

trio, trî´-au, *n* trio *m*.

trip, trippe, *n* excursion *f*. *v* (stumble) trébucher; **–up,** *v* donner un croc-en-jambe.

tripe, trâïpe, *n* tripes *fpl*.

triple, tripp´-'l, *a* triple.

triplets, tripp´-lètse, *npl* trois triplets *mpl*.

tripod, trâï´-pode, *n* trépied *m*.

triumph, trâï´-*eummf*, *n* triomphe *m*. *v* triompher.

trivial, triv´-i-*al*, *a* trivial; insignifiant.

trolley, troll´-i, *n* chariot *m*.

trombone, tromm´-bône, *n* trombone *m*.

troop, troupe, *n* troupe *f*; **–ship,** transport *m*.

trooper, troup´-*eur*, *n* (mil) cavalier *m*.

trophy, trau´-fi, *n* trophée *m*.

tropical, tropp´-i-c'l, *a* tropical.

a
b
c
d
e
f
g
h
i
j
k
l
m
n
o
p
q
r
s
t
u
v
w
x
y
z

A
B
C
D
E
F
G
H
I
J
K
L
M
N
O
P
Q
R
S
T
U
V
W
X
Y
Z

tropics, tropp´-ikse, *npl* tropiques *mpl*.

trot, trotte, *v* trotter. *n* trot *m*; **–ter,** trotteur *m*; (pig) pied de cochon *m*.

trouble, trobb´-'l, *v* chagriner; (disturb) déranger. *n* (cares) soucis *mpl*; (inconvenience) dérangement *m*; (disturbance) trouble *m*; (difficulty) difficulté *f*; **–some,** *a* ennuyeux; difficile.

trough, troffe, *n* (kneading trough) pétrin *m*; (cattle, etc) abreuvoir *m*.

trousers, trâ'ou´-zeurce, *npl* pantalon *m*.

trout, trâ'oute, *n* truite *f*.

trowel, trâ'ou´'l, *n* (mason's) truelle *f*.

T-shirt, tî´-cheurte, *n* tee-shirt *m*.

truant, troue´-annte, **play –,***v* faire l'école buissonnière.

truce, trouce, *n* trêve *f*.

truck, troque, *n* (rail) wagon *m*; (hand) voiture à bras *f*.

truculent*, trok´-iou-lennte, *a* brutal; féroce.

trudge, trodje, *v* marcher péniblement.

true, troue, *a* vrai;

(faithful) fidèle.

truffle, troff´-'l, *n* truffe *f*.

truism, troue´-izme, *n* truisme *m*.

trump, trommpe, *n* atout *m*. *v* couper.

trumpet, trommp´-itte, *n* trompette *f*.

truncheon, tronn´-ch'n, *n* bâton *m*.

trunk, tronng-k, *n* (tree; body) tronc *m*; (elephant) trompe *f*; (traveling) malle *f*.

truss, trosse, *n* (hay, etc) botte *f*; (surgical) bandage herniaire *m*. *v* (poultry) trousser.

trust, trosste, *n* confiance *f*; (combine) trust *m*. *v* se fier à; (rely) compter sur.

trustee, tross-tî´, *n* dépositaire *m*; (public) curateur *m*; (liquidation) syndic de faillite *m*; administrateur *m*.

trustworthy, trosst´-oueurd𝓏-i, *a* digne de confiance.

truth, trou𝓉s, *n* vérité *f*; **–ful*,** *a* véridique.

try, trâï, *v* essayer; (taste) goûter; (law) juger; **–ing,** *a* pénible; **–on,** *v* essayer.

tub, tobbe, *n* baquet *m*;

(bath) baignoire *f*.

tube, tioube, *n* tube *m*; (railway) métro *m*.

tuck, toque, *n* pli *m*. *v* faire des plis; **–in,** (rug, etc) border; **–up,** retrousser.

Tuesday, tiouze´-dé, *n* mardi *m*.

tuft, tofte, *n* (grass) touffe *f*; (hair) houppe *f*.

tug, togue, *v* tirer; (boat) remorquer.

tugboat, togue´-baute, *n* remorqueur *m*.

tuition, tiou-i´-ch'n, *n* enseignement *m*; frais de scolarité *m*.

tulip, tioue´-lippe, *n* tulipe *f*.

tumble, tomm´-b'l, *v* (fall) dégringoler.

tumbler, tomm´-bl'r, *n* (glass) grand verre *m*.

tumor, tioue´-m'r, *n* tumeur *f*.

tumult, tioue´-meulte, *n* tumulte *m*; (riot) émeute *f*.

tuna, tioue´-nă, *n* thon *m*.

tune, tioune, *n* air *m*. *v* accorder.

tuneful, tioune´-foull, *a* mélodieux.

tunic, tioue´-nique, *n* tunique *f*.

tuning-fork, tioue´-ninng forque, *n* diapason *m*.

tunnel, tonn´-'l, *n* tunnel *m.* *v* percer un tunnel.

turbine, teur´-bâïne, *n* turbine *f.*

turbot, teur´-*beute,* *n* turbot *m.*

turbulence, teur´-bioul'nce, *n* turbulence *m.*

turbulent, teur´-bioulennte, *a* turbulent.

tureen, tiou-rîne´, *n* soupière *f;* (sauce) saucière *f.*

turf, teurfe, *n* (grass) gazon *m;* (peat) tourbe *f.*

turkey, teur´-ki, *n* dinde *f;* dindon *m.*

turkish, teur´-quiche, *a* turc.

turmoil, teur´-moa'ile, *n* tumulte *m;* désordre *m.*

turn, teurne, *n* tour *m.* *v* tourner; **–about,** se tourner; **–aside,** détourner; **–back,** revenir sur ses pas; **–er,** *n* (artisan) tourneur *m;* **–ing,** (corner) tournant *m;* **–ing-point,** point décisif *m;* **–into,** *v* se changer en; **–off,** fermer; **–on,** ouvrir; **–out,** (expel) renvoyer; (light) éteindre; **–over,** se retourner. *n* (com) chiffre d'affaires *m;* **–stile,** tourniquet *m;* **–to,** *v* recourir à.

turnip, teur´-nipe, *n* navet *m.*

turpentine, teur´-penntâïne, *n* térébenthine *f.*

turret, teur´-ette, *n* tourelle *f.*

turtle, teur´-t'l, *n* tortue de mer *f;* **–dove,** *n* tourterelle *f.*

tusk, tossque, *n* (long) défense *f;* (short) croc *m.*

tussle, toss´-'l, *v* lutter. *n* bagarre *f.*

tutor, tioue´-t'r, *n* précepteur *m,* professeur *m.* *v* instruire.

TV, tî-vi, *n* *abbr* télé *f.*

twang, touain-ng, *n* nasillement *m;* (sound) son *m.*

tweezers, touî´-*zeurze,* *npl* pinces *fpl.*

twelfth, tou'elf*ts,* *n & a* douzième *m & f.*

twelve, tou'elve, *n & a* douze *m.*

twentieth, tou'enn´-ti-*its,* *n & a* vingtième *m & f.*

twenty, tou'enn´-ti, *n & a* vingt *m.*

twice, tou'âïce, *adv* deux fois.

twig, tou'igue, *n* brindille *f.*

twilight, tou'âï´-lâïte, *n* crépuscule *m.*

twin, tou'inne, *n & a* jumeau *m;* jumelle *f;* **–bedded room,** *n* chambre à deux lits *f.*

twine, tou'âïne, *n* cordonnet *m.* *v* s'enrouler.

twinge, tou'inndje, *n* élancement *m;* (*fig*) tourment *m.*

twinkle, tou'inng´-k'l, *v* scintiller; (eyes) cligner.

twirl, tou'eurle, *v* tournoyer; tourner. *n* tour *m.*

twist, tou'iste, *v* tordre; tourner; contourner.

twitch, tou'itche, *v* se crisper. *n* crispation *f;* tic *m.*

twitter, tou'itt´-'r, *v* gazouiller; gazouillement *m.*

two, toue, *n & a* deux *m;* **–fold,** *a* double.

type, tâïpe, *n* type *m;* (print) caractère *m.* *v* taper à. la machine; **–writer,** *n* machine à écrire *f.*

typhoid, tâï´-fo'ide, *n* fièvre typhoïde *f.*

typhoon, tâï-foune´, *n* typhon *m.*

typical*, tip´-i-c'l, *a* typique.

typist, tâïp´-iste, *n* dactylographe *m & f.*

typography, ti-pogue´-*ra-*

a b c d e f g h i j k l m n o p q r s t u v w x y z

fi, n typographie f.

tyrannical*, ti-rănn´-i-c'l,
   a tyrannique.

tyrannize, ti´-ra-nâïze, v
   tyranniser.

tyrant, tâï´-r'nt, n tyran
   m.

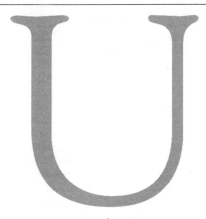

ubiquitous, ioue-bik´-oui-teuce, *a* omniprésent.

udder, odd´-'r, *n* pis *m.*

ugliness, ogg´-li-nesse, *n* laideur *f.*

ugly, ogg´-li, *a* laid; vilain.

ulcer, ol´-ceur, *n* ulcère *m;* –**ate,** *v* ulcérer.

ulterior, ol-ti´-ri-eur, *a* ultérieur.

ultimate*, ol´-ti-méte, *a* définitif; final.

ultimatum, ol-ti-mé´-tomm, *n* ultimatum *m.*

umbrella, omm-brell´-a, *n* parapluie *m;* –**stand,** porte-parapluies *m.*

umpire, omm´-pâïre, *n* arbitre *m. v* arbitrer.

unabashed, onn-a-băshte´, *a* sans honte.

unabated, onn-a-bé´-tedde, *a* continu;

soutenu.

unable, onn-é´-b'l, **to be** –,*v* être incapable de; ne pas pouvoir.

unacceptable, onn-ăx-ep´-ta-b'l, *a* inacceptable.

unaccountable, onn-a-câ'ounn´-ta-b'l, *a* inexplicable.

unacquainted, onn-a-couénn´-tedde, *a* (person) étranger à; (subject) être ignorant de.

unaffected*, onn-a-fèque´-tedde, *a* naturel; (unmoved) impassible.

unaided, onn-é´-dedde, *a* sans aide.

unalterable, onn-oal´-teur-a-b'l, *a* immuable.

unaltered, onn-oal´-teurde, *a* pas changé.

unanimous*, ioue-nănn´-i-meuce, *a* unanime.

unapproachable, onn-a-prautch´-a-b'l, *a* inabordable; inaccessible.

unarmed, onn´ârmde´, *a* sans armes.

unassailable, onn-a-cél´-a-b'l, *a* inattaquable.

unassuming, onn-a-sioue´-minng, *a* modeste.

unattainable, onn-a-tén´-a-b'l, *a* inaccessible.

unavoidable, onn-a-vô'ï´-da-b'l, *a* inévitable.

unaware, onn-a-ouère´, *a* ignorant.

unawares, onn-a-ouèrze´, *adv* à l'improviste.

unbalanced, onn-băl´-'nsste, *a* déséquilibré.

unbearable, onn-bèr´-a-b'l, *a* insupportable.

unbelievable, onn-bî-lîve´-a-b'l, *a* incroyable.

unbending, onn-benn´-dinng, *a* inflexible.

unbiased, onn-bâï´-asste, *a* impartial.

unbleached, onn-blîtchte´, *a* écru; non décoloré.

unblemished, onn-blèm´-ichte, *a* sans tache.

unbounded, onn-bâ'ounn´-dedde, *a*

A
B
C
D
E
F
G
H
I
J
K
L
M
N
O
P
Q
R
S
T
U
V
W
X
Y
Z

illimité.

unbreakable, onn-bréque´-a-b'l, a incassable.

unburden, onn-beur´-d'n, v décharger.

unbutton, onn-bot´-'n, v déboutonner.

uncalled for, onn-coalde´ fôr, a déplacé.

uncanny, onn-cănn´-i, a surnaturel; étrange.

uncared for, onn-cairde´ fôr, a négligé.

unceasing*, onn-sî´-cinng, a incessant.

uncertain*, onn-seur´-tinne, a incertain.

unchangeable, onn-tchéne´-dja-b'l, a invariable.

unclaimed, onn-clémde´, a non réclamé.

uncle, onn´-k'l, n oncle m.

unclean, onn-clîne´, a malpropre; impur.

uncomfortable, onn-comm´-feur-ta-b'l, a incommode; (not at ease) mal à l'aise.

uncommon, onn-comm´-'n, a peu commun; rare.

unconcern, onn-cŏnn-seurne´, n indifférence f.

unconditional*, onn-cŏnn-di´-ch'n-al, a sans condition.

unconscious*, onn-

conn´-cheuce, a sans connaissance; (fig) inconscient.

uncontrollable, onn-cŏnn-traul´-a-b'l, a incontrôlable.

uncork, onn-corque´, v déboucher.

uncouth*, onn-coûts, a (manners) grossier.

uncover, onn-cov´-eur, v découvrir.

uncultivated, onn-col´-ti-vé-tedde, a inculte.

undaunted, onn-doann´-tedde, a intrépide.

undeceive, onn-di-cîve´, v détromper.

undecided, onn-di-sâï´-dedde, a indécis.

undelivered, onn-di-liv´-'rde, a non livré.

undeniable, onn-di-nâï´-a-b'l, a incontestable.

under, onn´-d'r, prep sous; au-dessous de; adv dessous; **–age,** a mineur; **–done,** a peu cuit; (beef) saignant; **–estimate,** v sous-estimer; **–fed,** a mal nourri; **–go,** v endurer; **–ground,** a souterrain. n (railroad) métro m; **–hand,** a clandestin; **–line,** v souligner; **–mine,** v miner; **–neath,** adv audessous; **–rate,** v estimer trop bas; **–sell,** v

vendre à plus bas prix; **–signed,** n & a soussigné, -ée m & f; **–stand,** v comprendre; **–standing,** n entente f; compréhension f; **–study,** n doublure f; **–take,** v entreprendre; **–taker,** n entrepreneur de pompes funèbres m; **–taking,** n entreprise f; engagement m; **–tone,** adv à voix basse; **–wear,** n (men) vêtements de dessous mpl; (ladies) dessous mpl; **–writer,** n assureur m.

undeserved, onn-di-zeurvde´, a immérité.

undesirable, onn-di-zâï´-ra-b'l, a indésirable.

undignified, onn-dig´-ni-fâïde, a sans dignité.

undismayed, onn-diss-méde´, a sans peur.

undo, onn-doue´, v défaire; (untie) délier.

undoing, onn-dou´-inng, n (downfall) déchéance f.

undoubted*, onn-dâ'outt´-edde, a indubitable.

undress, onn-dresse´, v déshabiller; se déshabiller.

undulating, onn´-diou-lé-ting, a ondulé.

unduly, onn-dioue´-li, *adv*
indûment; à l'excès.

unearned, onn-eurnde´, *a*
non gagné; immérité.

unearthly, onn-eurts´-li, *a*
surnaturel.

uneasy, onn-î´-zi, *a*
inquiet; mal à l'aise.

uneducated, onn-éd´iou-
qué-tedde, *a* sans
éducation.

unemployed, onn-emm-
ploa'ide´, *a* sans travail.
n les chômeurs *mpl.*

unemployment, onn-
emm-ploa'i´-m'nt, *n*
chômage *m.*

unequal*, onn-î´-coual, *a*
inégal; –ed, sans égal.

uneven*, onn-î´-v'n, *a*
irrégulier; rugueux;
(number) impair.

unexpected*, onn-ex-
pec´-tedde, *a* inattendu.

unfailing, onn-fél´-innng, *a*
infaillible.

unfair*, onn-fère´, *a*
injuste.

unfaithful, onn-féts´-foull,
a infidèle.

unfasten, onn-fâs´-s'n, *v*
défaire; ouvrir.

unfavorable, onn-fé´-veur-
a-b'l, *a* défavorable.

unfeeling*, onn-fî´-linng,
a insensible.

unfit, onn-fite´, *a*
impropre à.

unflagging, onn-flâgue´-
inng, *a* soutenu.

unflinching, onn-
flinntch´-inng, *a* ferme,
résolu.

unfold, onn-faulde´, *v*
déplier; (reveal)
dévoiler.

unforeseen, onn-fore-
cîne´, *a* imprévu.

unfortunate*, onn-fôr´-
tiou-néte, *a* malheureux.

unfounded, onn-fâ'ounn´-
dedde, *a* sans
fondement.

unfriendly, onn-frennde´-
li, *a* peu amical; hostile.

unfulfilled, onn-foull-
fillde´, *a* inaccompli.

unfurl, onn-feurle´, *v*
déployer.

unfurnished, onn-feur´-
nichte, *a* non meublé.

ungrateful, onn-gréte´-
foull, *a* ingrat.

unguarded, onn-gâre´-
dedde, *a* (*fig*)
inconsidéré.

unhappy, onn-hǎpp´-i, *a*
malheureux.

unhealthy, onn-hêltz´-i, *a*
malsain; (sick) maladif.

unheard, onn-heurde´,
–of, *a* inconnu; inouï.

unheeded, onn-hî´-dedde,
a inaperçu.

unhinge, onn-hinndje´, *v*
démonter; déranger.

unhurt, onn-heurte´, *a*
sain et sauf.

uniform*, ioue´-ni-fôrme,
n & *a* uniforme *m.*

uniformity, ioue-ni-fôr´-
mi-ti, *n* uniformité *f.*

unimaginable, onn-i-
mâdj´-i-na-b'l, *a*
inimaginable.

unimpaired, onn-imm-
pairde´, *a* intact.

unimportant, onn-imm-
por´-t'nt, *a* sans
importance.

uninhabitable, onn-inn-
hǎb´-i-ta-b'l, *a*
inhabitable.

uninhabited, onn-inn-
hǎb´-i-tedde, *a* inhabité.

unintelligible, onn-inn-
tel´-i-dji-b'l, *a*
inintelligible.

unintentional*, onn-inn-
tenn´-ch'n-al, *a*
involontaire.

uninviting, onn-inn-vâï´-
tinng, *a* peu attrayant.

union, ioue´-ni-eune, *n*
union *f.*

unique*, iou-nique´, *a*
unique.

unit, ioue´-nitte, *n* unité *f.*

unite, iou-nâïte´, *v* unir;
s'unir.

unity, ioue´-ni-ti, *n* unité
f; concorde *f.*

universal*, iou-ni-veur´-
s'l, *a* universel.

universe, ioue´-ni-veurce, *n* univers *m.*

university, iou-ni-veur´-ci-ti, *n* université *f.*

unjust*, onn-djosste´, *a* injuste.

unkind*, onn-kâïnnde´, *a* pas gentil; peu aimable.

unknown, onn-naune´, *a* inconnu.

unlawful*, onn-loa´-foull, *a* illégal; illicite.

unleaded, onn-lèdd´-id, *a* sans plomb (gasoline, fuel).

unless, onn-lesse´, *conj* à moins que; à moins de.

unlike, onn-lâïque´, *a* différent; **–ly,** improbable.

unlimited, onn-limm´-i-tedde, *a* illimité.

unload, onn-laude´, *v* décharger.

unlock, onn-loque´, *v* ouvrir; (*fig*) révéler.

unlucky, onn-loque´-i, *a* malheureux; (ill-omened) de mauvais augure; qui porte malheur.

unmanageable, onn-mânn´-idj-*a*-b'l, *a* ingouvernable; intraitable.

unmannerly, onn-mânn´-'r-li, *a* grossier; mal élevé.

unmarried, onn-mãr´-idde, *a* non marié; célibataire.

unmerciful*, onn-meur´-ci-foull, *a* impitoyable.

unmistakable, onn-mice-téque´-*a*-b'l, *a* évident.

unmoved, onn-mouvde´, *a* impassible.

unnatural, onn-nãt´-tiou-r'l, *a* (hard) dénaturé.

unnecessary, onn-nèss´-ess-*a*-ri, *a* inutile.

unnerve, onn-neurve´, *v* effrayer; démonter.

unnoticed, onn-nau´-tisste, *a* inaperçu.

unoccupied, onn-ok´-kiou-pâïde, *a* inoccupé; libre.

unopposed, onn-ŏp-auzde´, *a* sans opposition.

unpack, onn-pãque´, *v* défaire; (case) déballer.

unparalleled, onn-pã´-ral-lelde, *a* sans pareil.

unpardonable, onn-pãr´-donn-*a*-b'l, *a* impardonnable.

unpleasant*, onn-plè´-zannte, *a* déplaisant.

unpopular, onn-pop´-iou-lar, *a* impopulaire.

unprecedented, onn-pré´-sid-enn-tedde, *a* sans précédent.

unprepared, onn-pri-

pérde´, *a* à l'improviste.

unproductive, onn-pro-deuc´-tive, *a* improductif.

unprofitable, onn-prof´-i-ta-b'l, *a* peu profitable.

unprotected, onn-pro-tec´-tedde, *a* sans protection; sans défense.

unprovided, onn-prŏ-vâï´-dedde, *a* dépourvu de.

unpunctual, onn-ponngk´-tiou-*a*l, *a* inexact.

unqualified, onn-couoll´-i-fâïde, *a* non qualifié; incapable de.

unquestionable, onn-couess´-tieunn-*a*-b'l, *a* incontestable.

unravel, onn-rãv´-'l, *v* démêler.

unreadable, onn-rî´-da-b'l, *a* illisible.

unreasonable, onn-rî´-z'n-*a*-b'l, *a* déraisonnable.

unrelenting, onn-ri-lenn´-tinng, *a* implacable.

unreliable, onn-ri-lâï´-*a*-b'l, *a* sur lequel on ne peut pas compter.

unreserved, onn-ri-zeurvde´, *a* non réservé; libre; sans réserve.

unrest, onn-reste´, *n* inquiétude *f*; agitation *f.*

unrestrained, onn-ri-strénnde, *a* sans

contrainte; (unruly) désordonné.

unrestricted, *o*nn-ri-stric´-tedde, *a* sans restriction.

unripe, *o*nn-râïpe´, *a* pas mûr; vert.

unroll, *o*nn-raule´, *v* dérouler.

unruly, *o*nn-roue´-li, *a* indiscipliné.

unsafe, *o*nn-séfe´, *a* peu sûr; dangereux.

unsatisfactory, *o*nn-sătt-iss-făque´-t'ri, *a* peu satisfaisant.

unscrew, *o*nn-scroue´, *v* dévisser.

unscrupulous, *o*nn-scroue´-piou-*le*uce, *a* sans scrupule.

unseasonable, *o*nn-sî´-z'n-a-b'l, *a* hors de saison.

unseemly, *o*nn-sîme´-li, *a* inconvenant.

unseen, *o*nn-sîne´, *a* inaperçu.

unselfish, *o*nn-self´-iche, *a* désintéressé.

unsettled, *o*nn-sett´-'lde, *a* incertain; troublé; (accounts) en suspens.

unshaken, *o*nn-chéque´-'n, *a* inébranlable.

unshrinkable, *o*nn-chrinng´-ka-b'l, *a* irrétrécissable.

unsightly, *o*nn-sâïte´-li, *a* déplaisant; laid.

unskilled, *o*nn-skillde, *a* inexpérimenté (dans).

unsociable, *o*nn-sau´-cha-b'l, *a* insociable.

unsold, *o*nn-saulde´, *a* invendu.

unsolicited, *o*nn´-sŏ-liss´-i-tedde, *a* spontané.

unsound, *o*nn-sâ'ounnde´, *a* défectueux; (mind) dément.

unsparing*, *o*nn-spére´-inng, *a* prodigue; (not merciful) impitoyable.

unsteady, *o*nn-stedd´-i, *a* instable.

unsuccessful, *o*nn-*se*uk-cess´-foull, *a* (person) sans succès; (undertaking) infructueux.

unsuitable, *o*nn-sioue´-ta b'l, *a* déplacé; impropre.

unsupported, *o*nn-*se*up-paur´-tedde, *a* (*fig*) sans appui.

unsurpassed, *o*nn-*se*ur-pâsste´, *a* sans égal.

unsuspecting, *o*nn-*se*uss-pèque´-tinng, *a* confiant.

untamed, *o*nn-témmde´, *a* indompté; sauvage.

untarnished, *o*nn-târe´-nichte, *a* sans tache.

untenable, *o*nn-tenn´-a-b'l, *a* insoutenable.

untidy, *o*nn-tâï´-di, *a* en

désordre; (person) négligé.

untie, *o*nn-tâï´, *v* délier; (a knot) défaire; dénouer.

until, *o*nn-til´, *prep* jusqu'à; jusque. *conj* jusqu'à ce que.

untold, *o*nn-taulde´, *a* non raconté; passé sous silence; (*fig*) inouï.

untouched, *o*nn-tochte´, *a* intact; non ému.

untranslatable, *o*nn-trănnss-lé´-ta-b'l, *a* intraduisible.

untried, *o*nn-trâïde´, *a* non essayé.

untrodden, *o*nn-trode´-'n, *a* non frayé; vierge.

untrue, *o*nn-troue´, *a* faux; pas vrai.

untrustworthy, *o*nn-trosst´-oueur*dz*-i, *a* indigne de confiance.

untruth, *o*nn-trout*s*´, *n* mensonge *m*.

untwist, *o*nn-tou'isste´, *v* détordre.

unusual*, *o*nn-ioue´-joue*u*l, *a* rare; peu commun.

unvaried, *o*nn-vair´-idde, *a* uniforme; constant.

unveil, *o*nn-vaile´, *v* dévoiler; inaugurer.

unwarrantable, *o*nn-ouor´-ann-ta-b'l, *a* injustifiable;

inexcusable.

unwary, onn-ouè´-ri, *a*
imprudent.

unwelcome, onn-ouel´-k'm, *a* importun;
indésirable.

unwell, onn-ouell´, *a*
indisposé; souffrant.

unwholesome, onn-haule´-somme, *a*
malsain; insalubre.

unwieldy, onn-ouîld´-i, *a*
lourd; pesant.

unwilling, onn-ouil´-inng, *a* de mauvaise volonté.

unwind, onn-ouâïnnde´, *v*
dérouler; se relaxer.

unwise, onn-ouâïze´, *a*
peu sage, imprudent.

unwittingly, onn-ouitt´-inng-li, *adv* sans y
penser.

unworthy, onn-oueurdz´-i, *a* indigne.

unwrap, onn-răppe´, *v*
défaire.

unwritten, onn-ritt´-'n, *a*
non écrit; (*fig*)
traditionnel.

unyielding, onn-yîld´-inng, *a* rigide; inflexible.

up, op, *adv* en haut; en
l'air; (stand up) debout;
(prices) en hausse;
(risen) levé; **–and down,**
de haut en bas; **–here,**
ici; **–side down,** sens
dessus dessous; à

l'envers; **–there,** là-haut;
–to, *prep* jusqu'à.

upbraid, op-bréde´, *v*
reprocher à.

upheaval, op-hî´-v'l, *n*
(geological)
soulèvement *m.*

uphill, op´-hill, *a* en
montant; (*fig*) ardu.

uphold, op-haulde´, *v*
soutenir; maintenir.

upholsterer, op-haule´-steur-'r, *n* tapissier *m.*

upkeep, op´-kîpe, *n*
entretien *m;* soutien *m.*

upland, op´-lănnde, *n* pays
élevé *m.*

uplift, op-lifte´, *v* élever.

upon, op-onne´, *prep* sur.

upper, op´-'r, *a* supérieur;
de dessus; **–hand,** *n*
avantage *m,* dessus *m;*
–most, *a* dominant.

upright, op´-râïte, *a* droit;
honorable; (erect)
debout.

uprising, op-râï´-zinng, *n*
soulèvement *m.*

uproar, op´-raure, *n*
tumulte *m;* vacarme *m.*

uproot, op-route´, *v*
déraciner.

upset, op-cette´, *v*
renverser; **to be –,** être
bouleversé.

upstairs, op´-stèrze, *adv* en
haut; **to go –,** *v* aller en
haut.

upstart, op´-stărte, *n*
parvenu, -e *m* & *f;*
nouveau riche *m.*

upwards, op´-oueurdse,
adv en haut; en
montant.

urban, eur´-b'n, *a* urbain.

urchin, eur´-tchinne, *n*
(child) gamin, -e *m* & *f.*

urge, eurdje, *n* désir
ardent *m. v* pousser.

urgency, eur´-djenn-ci, *n*
urgence *f.*

urgent, eur´-djennte, *a*
urgent; pressant.

urine, iou´-râïne, *n* urine
f.

urinate, iou´-ri-néte, *v*
uriner.

urn, eurne, *n* urne *f.*

us, osse, *pron* nous.

use, iouze, *v* user de; se
servir de; employer. *n*
usage *m;* utilité *f;* **–ful*,**
a utile; **–less*,** inutile;
–up, *v* consommer.

usher, och´-'r, *n* (in a
court) huissier *m;* **–in,** *v*
annoncer.

usherette, och-'orette´, *n*
ouvreuse *f.*

usual*, iou´-jou'eul, *a*
usuel; habituel;
ordinaire; **–ly,** *a*
d'habitude; d'ordinaire.

usurer, iou´-jeu-r'r, *n*
usurier,
-ère *m* & *f.*

usurp, iou-zeurpe´, *v*
usurper.

usury, iou´-*jeu*-ri, *n* usure
f.

utensil, iou-tenn´-cil, *n*
ustensile *m*.

utility, iou-til´-i-ti, *n*
utilité *f*.

utilize, ioue´-til-âïze, *v*
utiliser.

utmost, ott´-mauste, *a*
extrême; dernier; *n*
comble *m*; tout son
possible *m*.

utter, ott´-'r, *v* (words)
prononcer; (sound, coin,
etc) émettre; (cry)
pousser. *a** entier;
absolu; total.

utterance, ott´-*eur*-'nce, *n*
expression *f*; émission *f*.

uttermost, (see **utmost**).

a
b
c
d
e
f
g
h
i
j
k
l
m
n
o
p
q
r
s
t
u
v
w
x
y
z

A B C D E F G H I J K L M N O P Q R S T U **V** W X Y Z

vacancy, vé´-k'n-ci, n vacance f; place vacante f; (emptiness) vide m.

vacant*, vé´-k'nt, a (empty) vide; (free) libre; (mind) distrait.

vacate, va-quéte´, v (law) vider; évacuer; quitter.

vacation, va-qué´-ch'n, n vacances fpl; congé m.

vaccinate, văque´-ci-néte, v vacciner.

vacillate, văss´-il-léte, v vaciller.

vacuum, văque´-iou-'m, n vide m; **–cleaner,** aspirateur m; **–-flask,** thermos m.

vagabond, văgue´-a-bonnde, n vagabond, -e m & f.

vagina, va-dji´-na, n vagin m

vague*, végue, a vague.

vain*, véne, a vain; vaniteux; **in –,** adv en vain.

vale, véle, n vallée f; vallon m.

valet, văl´-ette, n valet de chambre m.

valiant*, văl´-i-annte, a vaillant; brave.

valid, văl´-ide, a valable; valide.

valley, văl´-i, n vallée f.

valor, văl´-'r, n bravoure f.

valuable, văl´-iou-a-b'l, a précieux; de valeur.

valuables, văl´-iou-a-b'lze, n objets de valeur mpl.

valuation, văl´-iou-é´-ch'n, n évaluation f.

value, văl´iou, v évaluer; priser. n valeur f.

valuer, văl´-iou-'r, n

(official) commissaire-priseur m.

valve, vălve, n (bot.) valve f; soupape f; (radio) lampe f.

vampire, văm´-pâïre, n vampire m.

van, vănne, n camion m; camionnette f; (train) fourgon m.

vane, véne, n girouette f; (windmill) aile f.

vanilla, va-nil´-a, n vanille f.

vanish, vănn´-iche, v disparaître.

vanity, vănn´-i-ti, n vanité f.

vanquish, vaing´-kouiche, v vaincre.

vapor, vé´-p'r, n vapeur f.

vaporize, vé´-por-âïze, v vaporiser.

variable, vé´-ri-a-b'l, a variable; (fig) inconstant.

variation, vé-ri-é´-ch'n, n variation f; différence f.

varicose vein, văr´-i-kôze véne, n varice f.

varied, vé´-ride, a varié; divers.

variegated, vé´-ri-i-gué-tedde, a (bot.) panaché; bigarré.

variety, va-râï´-i-ti, n variété f, choix m; **–theater,** music-hall m.

various, vè´-ri-*euce, a* divers, différent.

varnish, vâre´-niche, *n* vernis *m. v* vernir.

vary, vé´-ri, *v* varier; changer; dévier.

vase, vâze, *n* vase *m*; (oriental) potiche *f*.

vast, vâsste, *a* vaste; immense.

vat, vătte, *n* cuve *f*; cuvier *m*.

Vatican, văt´-i-k'n, *n* Vatican *m*.

vault, voalte, *n* voûte *f*; (church, etc) crypte *f*; (burial) caveau *m*; (cellar) cave *f. v* (jump) sauter.

veal, vîle, *n* veau *m*.

veer, vi´-*eur, v* tourner; (wind) changer.

vegetable, vedj´-i-t*a*-b'l, *n* (food) légume *m; a* végétal.

vegetarian, vedj-i-té´-ri-an, *n* végétarien, -ne *m* & *f*.

vegetation, vedj-i-té´-ch'n, *n* végétation *f*.

vehement, vî´-hi-m'nt, *a* véhément.

vehicle, vî´-i-k'l, *n* véhicule *m*.

veil, véle, *n* voile *m. v* voiler.

vein, véne, *n* veine *f*; (geological) filon *m*.

vellum, vell´-'m, *n* vélin *m*.

velocity, vi-loss´-i-ti, *n* vélocité *f*; (*mech*) vitesse *f*.

velvet, vell´-vett, *n* velours *m*.

velveteen, vell-vè-tine´, *n* velours de coton *m*.

vending machine, vennd-inng-m*a*-chîne, *n* distributeur automatique *m*.

vendor, venn´-d'r, *n* vendeur, -euse *m* & *f*.

veneer, vi-ni*eur*´, *n* placage *m. v* plaquer.

venerable, venn´-*eur*-*a*-b'l, *a* vénérable.

veneration, venn-*eur*-é´-ch'n, *n* vénération *f*.

venereal, vi-ni´-ri-al, *a* vénérien.

vengeance, venn´-dj'nce, *n* vengeance *f*.

venial*, vî´-ni-al, *a* véniel.

venison, venn´-i-z'n, *n* venaison *f*.

venom, venn-´'m, *n* venin *m*; **–ous,** *a* venimeux.

vent, vennte, *n* issue *f*; (cask) trou de fausset *m*; **give –to,** *v* donner cours à.

ventilate, venn´-ti-léte, *v* aérer.

ventilator, venn´-ti-lé-t'r, *n* ventilateur *m*.

ventriloquist, venn-tril´-ŏ-couiste, *n* ventriloque *m* & *f*.

venture, venn´-tioure, *v* aventurer; risquer; (dare) oser. *n* aventure *f*; entreprise *f*; **–some,** *a* aventureux; (daring) osé.

veracity, vi-răss´-i-ti, *n* authenticité *f*; véracité *f*.

veranda, vi-rănn´-d*a, n* véranda *f*.

verb, veurbe, *n* verbe *m*; **–al*,** *a* verbal; **–atim,** *adv* & *a* mot pour mot.

verbose, veur-bauce´, *a* verbeux; diffus.

verdant, veur´-d*a*nnte, *a* verdoyant.

verdict, veur´-dicte, *n* verdict *m*.

verdigris, veur´-di-gri, *n* vert-de-gris *m*.

verge, veurdje, *v* pencher vers. *n* (brink) bord *m*.

verify, vair´-i-fâï, *v* vérifier.

vermilion, veur-mil´-yonne, *n* & *a* vermillon *m*.

vermin, veur´-minne, *n* vermine *f*.

vernacular, veur-năk´-iou-l'r, *n* & *a* vernaculaire *m*.

versatile, veur´-s*a*-tâïle, *a*

A
B
C
D
E
F
G
H
I
J
K
L
M
N
O
P
Q
R
S
T
U
V
W
X
Y
Z

versatile; apte à tout.

verse, veurce, *n* vers *m*;
(song) couplet *m*;
(Bible) verset *m*.

versed, veursste, *a* versé.

version, veur´-ch'n, *n*
version *f*.

versus, veur´-ceusse, *prep*
contre.

vertical*, veur´-ti-k'l, *a*
vertical.

vertigo, veur´-ti-gau, *n*
vertige *m*,
étourdissement *m*.

very, vèr´-i, *adv* très; fort;
bien; *a* même.

vessel, vess´-'l, *n* vase *m*;
récipient *m*; (*naut*)
vaisseau *m*.

vest, veste, *n* gilet *m*;
(under) tricot de corps
m.

vested, vess´-tedde, *a*
(interest; rights) acquis.

vestige, vess´-tidje, *n*
vestige *m*.

vestment, vesst´-m'nt, *n*
vêtement *m*.

vestry, vess´-tri, *n* (place)
sacristie *f*.

vet, vette, *n* vétérinaire
m/f.

veteran, vett´-e-rǎnn, *n*
vétéran *m*.

veterinarian, vett´-eur-i-
na-ri-an, *n* (*pop*. bet)
vétérinaire *m*.

veterinary, vett´-eur-i-na-

ri, *a* vétérinaire.

veto, vî´-tau, *n* veto *m*. *v*
mettre le veto à.

vex, vexe, *v* vexer;
contrarier.

vexatious, vex-é´-cheuce,
a vexant; contrariant;
irritant; (law) vexatoire.

via, vâï´-a, *prep* via, par.

viaduct, vâï´-a-docte, *n*
viaduc *m*.

vibrate, vâï´-bréte, *v*
vibrer.

vibration, vâï´-bré´-ch'n,
n vibration *f*.

vicar, vik´-'r, *n* (of a
parish) curé *m*;
(protestant) pasteur *m*.

vicarage, vik´-'r-idj, *n*
presbytère *m*.

vice, vâïce, *n* vice *m*;
(*mech*) étau *m*.

vice admiral, vâïce-ǎd´-
mi-ral, *n* vice-amiral *m*.

vice president, vâïce-
prèz´-i-dennte, *n* vice-
president *m*.

viceroy, vâïce´-roa'i, *n*
vice-roi *m*.

vice versa, vâïce-veur-sǎ,
adv vice versa.

vicinity, vi-cinn´-i-ti, *n*
voisinage *m*; proximité *f*.

vicious*, vich´-euce, *a*
vicieux.

viciousness, vich´-euce-
nesse, *n* nature vicieuse
f.

victim, vic´-time, *n*
victime *f*.

victimize, vic´-timm-âïze,
v rendre victime.

victor, vic´-t'r, *n*
vainqueur *m*.

victorious*, vic-tau´-ri-
euce, *a* victorieux.

victory, vic´-tŏr-i, *n*
victoire *f*.

victual, vitt´-'l, *v*
ravitailler; **–s,** *npl* vivres
mpl.

video, vi´-dî-ô *n* vidéo, *f*
(film); *n* vidéo-cassette
(videocassette) *f*; *n*
magnétoscope
(recorder) *m*.

vie, vâï, *v* rivaliser; faire
assaut de.

view, vioue, *n* vue *f*;
opinion *f*. *v* visiter;
examiner.

vigil, vidj´-il, *n* veille *f*;
(*eccl*) vigile *f*.

vigilance, vidj´-i-l'nce, *n*
vigilance *f*.

vigilant, vidj´-i-l'nt, *a*
vigilant.

vigor, vigg´-'r, *n* vigueur *f*;
force *f*.

vigorous*, vigg´-eur-euce,
a vigoureux; fort.

vile*, vâïle, *a* vil; abject.

vilify, vil´-i-fâï, *v* diffamer;
avilir.

villain, vil´-inne, *n*
scélérat *m*; gredin *m*.

villainous, vil´-*a*-ne*u*ce, *a*
vil; infâme.

villainy, vil´-*a*-ni, *n*
infamie *f.*

vindicate, vinn´-dik-éte, *v*
défendre; justifier.

vindication, vinn-di-ké´-
ch'n, *n* justification *f*;
défense *f.*

vindictive*, vinn-dic´-
tive, *a* vindicatif;
rancunier.

vindictiveness, vinn-dic´-
tive-nesse, *n* rancune *f.*

vine, vâïne, *n* vigne *f.*

vinegar, vinn´-i-gue*u*r, *n*
vinaigre *m.*

vineyard, vinn´-ie*u*rde, *n*
vignoble *m.*

vintage, vinn´-tidje, *n*
vendange *f*; (year)
année *f.*

viola, vi-au´-la, *n* alto *m.*

violate, vâï´-ŏ-léte, *v*
violer.

violence, vâï´-ŏ-l'nce, *n*
violence *f.*

violent*, vâï´-ŏ-lennte, *a*
violent.

violet, vâï´-ŏ-lette, *n*
violette *f. n* & *a* violet
m.

violin, vâï-ŏ-linne´, *n*
violon *m.*

violinist, vâï-ŏ-linn´-ist, *n*
violoniste *m* & *f.*

viper, vâï´-p'r, *n* vipère *f.*

virgin, veur´-djinne, *n* &
a vierge *f.*

virile, vi´-râïle, *a* viril.

virtual*, veur´-tiou-*a*l, *a*
virtuel.

virtue, veur´-tiou*e*, *n*
vertu *f.*

virtuous*, veur´-tiou-
e*u*ce, *a* vertueux.

virulent, vir´-iou-lennte,
a virulent.

virus, vî´-reusse, *n* virus
m.

visa, vî´-za, *n* visa *m.*

viscount, vâï´-câ'ounnte,
n vicomte *m.*

viscountess, vâï´-câ'ounn-
tesse, *n* vicomtesse *f.*

visibility, viz-i-bile´-i-ti, *n*
visibilité *f.*

visible, viz´-i-b'l, *a* visible.

visibly, viz´-i-bli, *adv*
visiblement.

vision, vij´-'n, *n* vision *f.*

visit, viz´-itte, *v* visiter;
aller voir; (a person)
rendre visit à. *n* visite *f.*

visitor, viz´-itt-'r, *n*
visiteur,
-euse *m* & *f.*

visual, vij´-iou-'l, *a* visuel.

vital*, vâï´-t'l, *a* essentiel;
vital; –s, *npl* organes
essentiels *mpl.*

vitality, vâï-tăl´-i-ti, *n*
vitalité *f.*

vitamin, vit´-*a*-minn, *n*
vitamine *f.*

vitriol, vite´-ri-ŏle, *n*
vitriol *m.*

vivacious*, vi-vé´-che*u*ce,
a vif; animé.

vivacity, vi-văss´-i-ti, *n*
vivacité *f.*

vivid, viv´-ide, *a* vif;
frappant; (color)
éclatant.

vixen, vic´-senn, *n*
(female fox) renarde *f*;
(*fig*) mégère *f.*

vocabulary, vau-căb´-iou-
la-ri, *n* vocabulaire *m.*

vocal*, vau´-c'l, *a* vocal;
–**chords,** *npl* cordes
vocales *fpl.*

vocalist, vau´-cal-ist, *n*
chanteur *m*; cantatrice *f.*

vocation, vau-qué´-ch'n, *n*
vocation *f*; profession *f.*

vociferous*, vŏ-ci´-feur-
e*u*ce, *a* bruyant.

vogue, vaugue, *n* vogue *f*;
mode *f.*

voice, voa'ice, *n* voix *f.*

void, voa'ide, *a* vide; nul;
dénué de. *n* vide *m.*

volatile, vol´-*a*-tâïle, *a*
volatil; (*fig*) gai.

volcano, vol-qué´-nau, *n*
volcan *m.*

volley, vol´-i, *n* (of
cannon) volée *f*;
(salute) salve *f.*

volt, volte, *n* (electric)
volt *m*; –**age,** tension *f.*

voluble, vol´-iou-b'l, *a*
volubile; loquace.

a
b
c
d
e
f
g
h
i
j
k
l
m
n
o
p
q
r
s
t
u
v
w
x
y
z

A
B
C
D
E
F
G
H
I
J
K
L
M
N
O
P
Q
R
S
T
U
V
W
X
Y
Z

volume, vol´-ioume, *n* volume *m*.

voluminous*, vol-ioue´-mi-*neuce*, *a* volumineux.

voluntary, vol´-*eunn*-ta-ri, *a* volontaire; spontané.

volunteer, vol-*eunn*-tîre´, *n* volontaire *m* & *f*. *v* s'offrir.

voluptuous*, vol-op´-tiou-*euce*, *a* voluptueux.

vomit, vomm´-itte, *v* vomir.

voracious, vŏ-ré´-che*uce*, *a* vorace; dévorant.

vortex, voar´-texe, *n* tourbillon *m*.

vote, vaute, *n* vote *m*; scrutin *m*; voix *f*. *v* voter; **–r,** *n* électeur, -trice *m* & *f*.

vouch, vâ'outche, *v* attester; (persons) répondre de.

voucher, vâ'outch´-'r, *n* pièce justificative *f*; bon *m*.

vow, vâ'ou, *n* vœu *m*. *v* faire vœu de; jurer.

vowel, vâ'ou´-'l, *n* voyelle *f*.

voyage, voa'i´-idj, *n* voyage par mer *m*.

vulgar, vol´-gueur, *a* vulgaire; commun.

vulnerable, vol´-*neur*-a-b'l, *a* vulnérable.

vulture, vol´-tioure, *n* vautour *m*.

W

wad, ouode, *n* (for fire arms, etc.) bourre *f*; (surgical) tampon *m*.

wadding, ouodd´-inng, *n* coton-hydrophile *m*; (padding) ouate *f*.

waddle, ouodd´-'l, *v* se dandiner.

wade, ouéde, *v* marcher dans.

wafer, oué´-f'r, *n* (thin biscuit) gaufrette *f*; (*eccl*) hostie *f*.

wag, ouågue, *v* remuer; secouer. *n* farceur *m*.

wage, ouédje, *v* (war) faire la guerre à.

wager, oué´-dj'r, *n* gageure *f*; pari *m*. *v* parier.

wages, oué´-djize, *npl* (servants) gages *mpl*; (workmen) salaire *m*.

waggle, ouågg´-'l, *v* remuer; **–about,** *v* frétiller.

wagon, ouågg´-'n, *n* chariot *m*.

waif, ouéfe, *n* épave *f*.

wail, ouéle, *v* se lamenter. *n* lamentation *f*.

waist, ouéste, *n* taille *f*; ceinture *f*.

wait, ouéte, *v* attendre; (at table) servir; **–er,** *n* serveur *m*; **–for,** *v* attendre; **–ing,** *n* attente *f*; (service) service *m*; **–ing room,** salle d'attente *f*; **–ress,** serveuse *f*; **–upon,** *v* servir.

waive, ouéve, *v* abandonner; renoncer à.

wake, ouéke, *v* (to awake) se réveiller; (to be called) réveiller. *n* (ship's) sillage *m*.

walk, ou'oak, *v* aller à pied; marcher; (stroll) se promener. *n* promenade *f*.

wall, ou'oal, *n* mur *m*; **–flower,** giroflée *f*; **–paper,** papier peint *m*.

wallet, ouol´-ite, *n* portefeuille *m*.

wallow, ouol´-au, *v* se vautrer.

walnut, ouôl´-notte, *n* noix *f*; (tree) noyer *m*.

walrus, ouôl´-reuce, *n* morse *m*.

waltz, ouôlts, *v* valser. *n* valse *f*.

wan, ou'oanne, *a* pâle; blême.

wander, ou'oann´-d'r, *v* errer; (mentally) délirer.

wane, ouéne, (of the moon) *v* décroître. *n* déclin *m*.

want, ou'oannte, *n* (lack) manque *m*; (distress) dénuement *m*; **for –of,** faute de; *v* vouloir; avoir besoin de; avoir envie de.

wanton, ou'onne´-t'n, *a* (lustful) licencieux; (wicked) criminel; (waste) de gaieté de cœur.

war, ou'oar, *v* faire la guerre à; *n* guerre *f*;

–like, *a* belliqueux; **–office,** ministère de la guerre *m;* **–ship,** vaisseau de guerre *m.*

warble, ou'oar´-b'l, *v* gazouiller.

warbler, ou'oar´-bleur, *n* fauvette *f.*

ward, ou'oarde, *n* (minor) pupille *m* & *f;* (hospital) salle *f;* **–en,** (guard) gardien *m;* **–off,** *v* parer; **–ress,** *n* gardienne *f;* **–robe,** armoire *f;* **–room,** (naval) carré des officiers *m.*

ware, ouère, *n* marchandise *f.*

warehouse, ouère´-hâ'ouce, *n* entrepôt *m;* magasin *m. v* emmagasiner; (furniture, etc) entreposer.

warm, ou'oarme, *a** chaud. *v* chauffer; se chauffer; **–th,** *n* chaleur *f;* (*fig*) ardeur *f.*

warn, ou'oarne, *v* avertir; notifier à; **–ing,** *n* avertissement *m;* (caution) avis *m.*

warp, ou'oarpe, *v* (wood) jouer; (mind) fausser.

warrant, ouor´-'nte, *n* (authority) autorisation *f;* (for arrest) mandat d'arrêt *m;* (voucher) mandat *m;* **–y,** garantie *f.*

warrior, ouor´-ieur, *n* guerrier *m.*

wart, ou'oarte, *n* verrue *f.*

wary, oué´-ri, *a* circonspect, prudent.

wash, ou'oache, *v* laver; se laver; **–basin,** *n* cuvette *f;* **–up,** *v* faire la vaisselle; **–erwoman,** laveuse *f;* **–ing,** blanchissage *m;* **–ing machine,** *n* lave-linge *m;* **–stand,** table de toilette *f.*

washer, ou'oache´-'r, *n* (*mech*) joint *m;* rondelle *f.*

washing machine, ou'oache´-inng-ma-chîne, *m* machine à laver *f.*

wasp, ou'oaspe, *n* guêpe *f.*

waste, ouéste, *n* gaspillage *m;* (refuse) rebut *m;* déchets *mpl* (land) terrain vague *m. v* gaspiller; **–away,** dépérir; **–ful,** *a* gaspilleur; prodigue.

watch, ouotche, *v* (not to sleep) veiller; observer; (vigilance) surveiller. *n* montre *f;* (wrist) montre-bracelet *f;* (*naut*) quart *m;* **–dog,** chien de garde *m;* **–maker,** horloger *m;*

–man, veilleur de nuit *m;* **over,** *v* veiller sur; **–word,** *n* mot d'ordre *m.*

water, ou'oa´-t'r, *v* arroser; (cattle, etc) abreuver. *n* eau *f;* **hot –bottle,** bouillotte *f;* **–color,** aquarelle *f;* **–cress,** cresson *m;* **–fall,** chute d'eau *f;* **–jug,** cruche *f;* **–lily,** nénuphar *m;* **–line,** ligne de flottaison *f;* **–logged,** *a* plein d'eau; **–mark,** *n* niveau des eaux *m;* (paper) filigrane *m;* **–proof,** *a* imperméable; **–tank,** *n* réservoir *m;* **–tight,** *a* étanche; **–skiing,** *n* ski nautique *m;* **–works,** *npl* ouvrages hydrauliques *mpl.*

watering, ou'oa-teur-inng, *n* (of plants, etc.) arrosage *m;* abreuvage *m;* **–can,** arrosoir *m.*

wave, ouéve, *n* (sea, etc) vague *f;* (radio, etc) onde *f. v* (flags, etc) flotter; agiter; (to somebody) faire signe; (sway) se balancer; (hair) onduler; **–length,** *n* longueur d'onde *f.*

waver, ouéve´-'r, *v* hésiter; être indécis.

wavering, ouéve´-eur-inng, *a* indécis; irrésolu.

wavy, ouéve´-i, *a* onduleux; (hair) ondulé.

wax, ouăxe, *v* cirer. *n* cire *f*; **--works,** musée de figures de cire *m*.

way, oué, *n* chemin *m*; manière *f*; façon *f*; **–in,** entrée *f*; **–lay,** *v* dresser un guet-apens; **–out,** *n* sortie *f*; **–through,** passage *m*; **–ward,** *a* entêté; capricieux.

we, oui, *pron* nous.

weak, ouîque, *a** faible; infirme; débile; **–en,** *v* affaiblir; **–ening,** *a* débilitant; **–ling,** *n* être faible *m*; **–ness,** faiblesse *f*.

weal, ouîle, *n* bien-être *m*; (mark) marque *f*.

wealth, ouèl*ts*, *n* richesse *f*; opulence *f*.

wealthy, ouèl*ts*´-i, *a* riche; opulent.

wean, ouîne, *v* sevrer; (*fig*) détacher de.

weapon, ouèp´-'n, *n* arme *f*.

wear, ouère, *n* (by use) usage *m*. *v* (carry) porter; (last) durer; **–able,** *a* mettable; **–out (away),** *v* user; (fatigue) épuiser.

weariness, oui´-ri-nesse, *n* lassitude *f*; (*fig*) ennui *m*.

weary, oui´-ri, *a* las; ennuyé. *v* fatiguer; **–of,** se lasser de.

weasel, oui´-z'l, *n* belette *f*.

weather, ouèd*z*´-'r, *n* temps *m*. *v* surmonter; **--bound,** *a* retenu par le mauvais temps; **–cock,** *n* girouette *f*; **–report,** bulletin météorologique *m*.

weave, ouîve, *v* tisser; **–r,** *n* tisserand *m*.

web, ouèbe, *n* (spider) toile *f*.

webbing, ouèbe´-inng, *n* (of a chair, bed, etc.) sangle *f*.

web-footed, ouèbe-foutt´-èdde, *a* palmé.

wed, ouède, *v* se marier avec; épouser; (perform ceremony) marier.

wedding, ouède´-inng, *n* mariage *m*; **–ring,** alliance *f*.

wedge, ouèdje, *n* coin *m*; (for fixing) cale *f*. *v* caler; **–in,** serrer; presser.

wedlock, ouède´-loque, *n* mariage *m*.

Wednesday, ou'ennze´-dé, *n* mercredi *m*.

weed, ouîde, *n* mauvaise herbe *f*. *v* sarcler.

week, ouîque, *n* semaine *f*; **--day,** jour de semaine *m*; **--end,** fin de semaine *f*; week-end *m*; **–ly,** *a* (of newspapers) hebdomadaire.

weep, ouîpe, *v* pleurer.

weevil, ouî´-v'l, *n* charançon *m*.

weigh, oué, *v* peser; (mentally) considérer.

weight, ouéte, *n* poids *m*; **–y,** *a* pesant; (*fig*) grave.

weir, ouire, *n* barrage *m*.

weird, ouirde, *a* étrange; fantastique.

welcome, ouell´-*keume*, *n* bienvenue *f*. *a* bienvenu. *v* bien recevoir; accueillir.

weld, ouelde, *v* souder.

welfare, ouell´-fére, *n* bien-être *m*; prospérité *f*.

well, ouell, *n* puits *m*. *adv* bien. *a* bon; **--being,** *n* bien-être *m*; **--bred,** *a* bien élevé; **–done,** (meat, etc) bien cuit; **--known,** *a* (bien) connu.

wend, ouennde, *v* aller; se diriger vers.

west, ouesste, *n* ouest *m*; occident *m*.

westerly, ouess´-*teur*-li, *a* d'ouest; occidental.

wet, ouette, *n* humidité *f*. *a* humide; mouillé; (weather) pluvieux. *v* mouiller; **–suit,** *n* combinaison de plongée *f*.

A
B
C
D
E
F
G
H
I
J
K
L
M
N
O
P
Q
R
S
T
U
V
W
X
Y
Z

whack, houăque, *v* rosser; battre.

whale, houéle, *n* baleine *f*; **–bone,** baleine *f*.

whaler, houél´-*eur*, *n* baleinier *m*.

wharf, hou'oarfe, *n* quai *m*; embarcadère *m*.

what, houotte, *pron* ce qui; ce que; que; quoi; qu'est-ce qui; qu'est-ce que. *a* quel; quelle; quels; quelles.

whatever, houotte-èv´-'r, *pron* & *a* tout ce qui; tout ce que; quel que soit; quelque ... que.

wheat, houîte, *n* froment *m*; blé *m*.

wheedle, houîdd´-'l, *v* cajoler; câliner.

wheel, houîle, *n* roue *f*. *v* faire rouler; **spinning– ,***n* rouet *m*; **–barrow,** brouette *f*; **–wright,** charron *m*; **–chair,** *n* fauteuil roulant *m*.

wheezy, houîz´-i, *a* poussif.

when, houenne, *adv* quand; lorsque; où, que; **–ce,** d'où; **–ever,** chaque fois que.

where, houère, *adv* où; **–about (s),** où; **–as,** *conj* tandis que; (law) vu que; **–at,** *adv* sur quoi; *conj* **–by,** par quoi; **–fore,** c'est pourquoi;

–in, dans lequel; **–on,** sur lequel.

wherever, houère-èv´-'r, *adv* partout où.

whet, houette, *v* aiguiser.

whether, houèdz´-'r, *conj* si; soit que; que.

which, houitche, *pron* qui; que; lequel; laquelle; lesquels; lesquelles.

whichever, houitch-èv´-'r, *pron* lequel; laquelle; lesquels; lesquelles.

while, houâïle, *v* passer. *conj* pendant que.

whim, houimme, *n* lubie *f*; caprice *f*; **–sical,** *a* capricieux.

whimper, houimm´-p'r, *v* pleurnicher.

whine, houâïne, *v* gémir; (*fig*) pleurnicher.

whip, houippe, *n* fouet *m*. *v* fouetter; (riding whip) cravacher; (cream) fouetter.

whirl, hou'eurle, *v* faire tourner; **–pool,** *n* tourbillon (d'eau) *m*; **–wind,** tourbillon *m*.

whisk, houisske, *n* (cooking) fouet *m*. *v* (eggs) battre; (cream) fouetter.

whiskers, houissk´-*eur*ze, *npl* favoris *mpl*; (cat) moustaches *fpl*.

whiskey, houiss´-ki, *n*

whisky *m*.

whisper, houiss´-p'r, *v* chuchoter. *n* chuchotement *m*.

whistle, houiss´-'l, *n* sifflet *m*. *v* siffler.

whistling, houiss´-linng, *n* sifflement *m*.

white, houâïte, *n* & *a* blanc *m*; **–ness,** blancheur *f*; **–of egg,** blanc d'œuf *m*; **–wash,** *v* (lime) blanchir à la chaux.

whither, houidz´-'r, *adv* où.

whiting, houâïte´-inng, *n* (fish) merlan *m*.

whiz, houize, *v* siffler.

who, houe, *pron* qui.

whoever, houe-èv´-'r, *pron* quiconque.

whole, haule, *n* tout *m*; total *m*. *a* tout; entier; **–sale,** *n* vente en gros *f*. *a* en gross; **–some*,** sain; salubre.

wholewheat bread, haule-houîte-brède, *a* pain complet *m*.

wholly, haul´-li, *adv* entièrement.

whom, houme, *pron* que; qui; lequel; laquelle; lesquels; lesquelles.

whoop, houpe, *v* huer. *n* cri (de guerre) *m*.

whooping cough, houpe´-

inng-coaf, n coqueluche f.

whose, houze, *pron* dont.

whosoever, (see **whoever**).

why, houâï, *adv* pourquoi.

wick, ouique, n mèche f.

wicked*, ouik´-ide, a méchant; mauvais; criminel.

wickedness, ouik´-ideness, n méchanceté f.

wicker, ouik´-'r, n osier m.

wide, ouâïde, a large; vaste; étendu; **–awake,** bien éveillé; (*fig*) vif; sur ses gardes; **–ly,** *adv* largement; très; **--spread,** a répandu.

widen, ouâïde´-'n, v élargir; s'élargir.

widow, ouid´-au, n veuve f.

widower, ouid´-au-'r, n veuf m.

width, ouid*t*s, n largeur f; (extent) étendue f.

wield, ouilde, v manier; (power) détenir.

wife, ouâïfe, n femme f; femme mariée f; épouse f.

wig, ouigue, n perruque f.

wild*, ouâïlde, a sauvage; farouche; (*fig*) furieux; **–life,** n faune f.

wilderness, ouil´-d'r-ness, n désert m; (*fig*)

solitude f.

wile, ou'âïle, n ruse f; artifice m.

will, ouil, n volonté f; testament m. v vouloir; (bequeath) léguer; **good--,**n (com) clientèle f.

willful*, ouil´-foull, a volontaire; (act) prémédité.

willing, ouil´-inng, a consentant; complaisant; **–ly,** *adv* volontiers; **–ness,** n bonne volonté f.

will-o'-the-wisp, ouil-ŏ-dzi-ouispe´, n feu follet m.

willow, ouil´-au, n saule m; **weeping- --,**saule pleureur m.

wily, ou'âï´-li, a astucieux; malin.

win, ouinne, v gagner; (victory) remporter; **–ner,** n gagnant, -e m & f; **–ning,** a (manners) engageant; but m; **–nings,** gain m.

wince, ouinnce, v (*fig*) reculer; tressaillir.

winch, ouinntche, n treuil m.

wind, ouâïnnde, v enrouler; (road, river, etc) serpenter; **–ing,** a sinueux; (stairs) en colimaçon; **–up,** v

rouler; (clock) remonter; (com) liquider.

wind, ouinnde, n vent m; flatulence f; **–fall,** (luck) aubaine f; **–mill,** moulin à vent m; **–pipe,** trachée- artère f; **–ward,** côté du vent m; **to be –y,** v (weather) faire du vent.

windlass, ouinnde´-lasse, n cabestan m.

window, ouinn´-dau, n fenêtre f, (car, etc) glace f; (shop) vitrine f; **–shopping,** n lèchevitrines m.

windshield, ouinnde´-chîlde, n pare-brise m.

windshield wiper, ouinnde-chîlde-ouâïpeu, n essuie-glace m.

wine, ouâïne, n vin m; **– list,** n carte des vins f.

wineglass, ouâïne´-glâce, n verre à vin m.

wing, ouinng, n aile f; (theatre) coulisse f.

wink, ouinnque, v cligner de l'œil. n clin d'œil m.

winkle, ouinnque´-'l, n bigorneau m.

winter, ouinn´-t'r, n hiver m. v passer l'hiver à; hiverner; **– sports,** *npl* sports d'hiver *mpl*.

wipe, ouâïpe, v essuyer;

a
b
c
d
e
f
g
h
i
j
k
l
m
n
o
p
q
r
s
t
u
v
w
x
y
z

A
B
C
D
E
F
G
H
I
J
K
L
M
N
O
P
Q
R
S
T
U
V
W
X
Y
Z

–off, *v* effacer.

wire, ouâïre, *n* fil de fer *m*; **–less,** sans fil; *n* (radio) radio; T.S.F.

wisdom, ouiz´-d'm, *n* sagesse *f*; prudence *f*.

wise*, ouâïze, *a* sage; prudent.

wish, ouiche, *n* souhait *m*; vœu *m*; désir *m*. *v* souhaiter; désirer; vouloir.

wishful, ouiche´-foull, *a* désireux.

wisp, ouissspe, *n* touffe *f*; (straw) bouchon de paille *m*; (hair) mèche *f*.

wisteria, ouiss-terr´-i'a, *n* glycine *f*.

wistful*, ouisst´-foull, *a* pensif; d'envie; de regret.

wit, ouitte, *n* esprit *m*; **to –,**à savoir; c'est-à-dire.

witch, ouitche, *n* sorcière *f*.

witchcraft, ouitche´-crâfte, *n* sorcellerie *f*.

with, ouidz, *prep* avec; (among) chez; de.

withdraw, ouidz-droa´, *v* retirer; se retirer.

wither, ouidz´-'r, *v* se faner; se flétrir.

withhold, ouidz-haulde´, *v* retenir; (sanction) refuser.

within, ouidz-inne´, *prep* dans; en. *adv* à l'intérieur.

without, ouidz-â'oute´, *prep* (not having) sans; *adv* (outside) dehors.

withstand, ouidz-stännde´, *v* résister à.

witness, ouitt´-nesse, *n* témoin *m*. *v* témoigner.

wits, ouittse, *npl* jugement *m*; **to live by one's –,**vivre d'expédients.

witticism, ouitt´-i-cizme, *n* trait d'esprit *m*.

witty, ouitt´-i, *a* spirituel.

wizard, ouiz´-eurde, *n* sorcier *m*; magicien *m*.

wobble, ou'obbe´-'l, *v* branler; vaciller.

woe, ou'au, *n* malheur *m*; (fig) peine *f*.

woeful*, ou'au´-foull, *a* triste; affligé.

wolf, ou'oulf, *n* loup *m*; **female –,** louve *f*.

woman, ou'oum´-m'n, *n* femme *f*.

womanhood, ou'oum´-m'n-houdde, *n* état de femme *m*.

womanly, ou'oum´-m'n-li, *a* féminin.

womb, ou'oumme, *n* utérus *m*; matrice *f*; (fig) sein *m*.

wonder, ouonn´-d'r, *n* merveille *f*. *v* s'émerveiller de;

s'étonner de; (doubt) se demander.

wonderful, ouonn´-d'r-foull, *a* merveilleux; étonnant.

woo, ou'ou, *v* faire la cour â; **–er,** *n* prétendant *m*.

wood, ou'oude, *n* bois *m*.

woodcock, ou'oude´-coque, *n* bécasse *f*.

wooden, ou'oude´-'n, *a* de bois.

woodpecker, ou'oude-pèque´-'r, *n* pivert *m*.

woody, ou'oud´-i, *a* (trees) boisé.

wool, ou'oul, *n* laine *f*.

woolen, ou'oul´-'n, *a* de laine.

woolly, ou'oul´-i, *a* laineux.

word, oueurde, *n* mot *m*; parole *f*; (news) nouvelles *fpl*. *v* (verbal) exprimer; (written) rédiger; **–of honor,** *n* parole d'honneur *f*.

wording, oueurde´-inng, *n* termes *mpl*; style *m*; rédaction *f*.

work, oueurque, *v* travailler; (mine) exploiter; (mech) fonctionner; marcher. *n* travail *m*; ouvrage *m*; (literary) œuvre *f*.

worker, oueurque´-'r, *n* travailleur, -euse *m* & *f*.

working, oueurque´-inng, *n* (*mech*) fonctionnement *m*; marche *f*; (mine) exploitation *f*; (handling) manœuvre *f*; **–expenses,** frais d'exploitation *mpl*.

workman, oueurque´-m'n, *n* ouvrier *m*; **–ship,** exécution *f*; façon *f*.

works, oueurque'se, *npl* usine *f*; (*mech*) mécanisme *m*.

workshop, oueurque´-choppe, *n* atelier *m*.

world, oueurlde, *n* monde *m*; univers *m*.

worldly, oueurlde´-li, *a* mondain.

worm, oueurme, *n* ver *m*; (screw) filet *m*.

worm-eaten, oueurme´-îtt-'n, *a* vermoulu.

worry, ouorr´-i, *n* tracas *m*; (anxiety) tourment *m*. *v* s'inquiéter; se tracasser; se tourmenter; (bother) ennuyer.

worse, oueurse, *adv* pis. *a* pire.

worship, oueur´-chippe, *v* adorer. *n* adoration *f*; (divine) culte *m*.

worst, oueurste, *a* le pire. *n* le pis *m*.

worsted, ou'ouss´-tèdde, *n* (yarn) fil de laine *m*.

worth, oueurts, *n* valeur *f*; mérite *m*. *a* qui vaut; **to be –,** *v* valoir; mériter; **to be –while,** valoir la peine.

worthily, oueurdz´-i-li, *adv* dignement.

worthless, oueurts´-lesse, *a* sans valeur.

worthy, oueurdz´-i, *a* digne; méritant.

would, ou'oude, *aux v* he w. do (*conditional tense*) il ferait; **he w. have done** il aurait fait; **I w. come every day** (*used to*) je venais chaque jour; **I w. like some tea** je voudrais du thé; **w. you come here?** voulez-vous venir ice? **he w.n't come** il a refusé de venir.

would-be, ou'oude´-bî, *a* soi-disant; prétendu.

wound, ou'ounde, *n* blessure *f*; plaie *f*. *v* blesser.

wrangle, rain´-ng'l, *v* se disputer. *n* querelle *f*.

wrap, răppe, *n* sortie de bal *f*. *v* envelopper; **–up,** (oneself) s'emmitoufler.

wrapper, răppe´-'r, *n* enveloppe *f*; (postal) bande *f*; (book) couverture *f*.

wrapping paper, răppe-inng-pé-p'r, *n* papier d'emballage *m*.

wrath, roats, *n* courroux *m*; colère *f*.

wreath, rits, *n* couronne *f*.

wreathe, ridz, *v* entrelacer.

wreck, rèque, *n* naufrage *m*; (*fig*) ruine *f*. *v* faire naufrage; (*fig*) ruiner; **–age,** *n* (pieces of ship, etc) épaves *fpl*.

wrecked, rèkte, *a* naufragé; ruiné.

wren, rène, *n* roitelet *m*.

wrench, renntche, *n* arrachement violent *m*; (sprain) entorse *f*; (tool) clé anglaise *f*. *v* tordre; (pull) arracher (à or de).

wrestle, ress´-'l, *v* lutter.

wrestler, ress´-l'r, *n* lutteur *m*.

wretch, rètche, *n* misérable *m & f*.

wretched, rétch´-edde, *a* triste; (person) misérable.

wretchedness, rétch´-edde-ness, *n* misère *f*.

wriggle, rigg´-'l, *v* se tortiller; **–through,** se faufiler.

wring, rinng, *v* tordre; (washing) essorer.

wrinkle, rinng´-k'l, *n* ride *f*. *v* rider; (brow) froncer.

wrist, risste, *n* poignet *m*.

writ, rite, *n* assignation *f*;

a
b
c
d
e
f
g
h
i
j
k
l
m
n
o
p
q
r
s
t
u
v
w
x
y

A
B
C
D
E
F
G
H
I
J
K
L
M
N
O
P
Q
R
S
T
U
V

commandement *m*.

write, râïte, *v* écrire.

writer, râïte´-'r, *n* auteur *m*; écrivain *m*.

writhe, râï*dz*, *v* se tordre (de douleur).

writing, râïte´-inng, *n* écriture *f*; inscription *f*; **hand–,**écriture *f*; **in–,** *adv* par écrit.

writing paper, râïte´-inng-pé´-pr, *n* papier à lettres.

written, ritt´-'n, *a* écrit.

wrong, ron-ng, *n* tort *m*; injustice *f*. *v* faire tort à. *a** faux; mauvais; mal; injuste; illégal; **–side,** *n* mauvais côté *m*; (material) envers *m*; **to be –,** avoir tort.

wrought iron, roat âï´-*eu*rne, *n* fer forgé *m*.

wry, râï, *a* désabusé; **–face,** *n* grimace *f*.

Xmas (Christmas), criss´-
meusse, *n* Noël *m.*
x-rays, èkce-réze, *npl*
rayons X *mpl*; (X-ray
photograph)
radiographie *f. v*
radiographier.
xylophone, sâï´-lo-faune,
n xylophone *m.*

a
b
c
d
e
f
g
h
i
j
k
l
m
n
o
p
q
r
s
t
u
v
w
x
y
z

yacht, i'ŏte, n yacht m.

yachting, i'ote´-inng, n yachting m.

yard, i'ârde, n cour f; (measure) yard m; (ship, timber, etc) chantier m.

yarn, i'ârne, n fil m; (story) histoire f.

yawn, i'oanne, v bâiller. n bâillement m.

yawning, i'oann´-inng, n bâillement m. a (fig) béant.

year, i'îre, n an m; année f.

yearly, i'îre´-li, a annuel. adv annuellement.

yearn, i'eurne, v soupirer après; languir pour.

yearning, i'eurne´-innng, n désir m; aspiration f.

yearningly, i'eurne´-inng-li, adv ardemment.

yeast, yi'îste, n levure f; levain m.

yell, c'ell, n hurlement m; cri m. v hurler; crier.

yellow, i'ell´-au, n & a jaune m.

yelp, i'elpe, v glapir, japper. n glapissement m.

yes, i'ess, adv oui; (after negative question) si.

yesterday, i'ess´-t'r-dé, adv & n hier m.

yet, i'ette, adv encore; déjà. conj cependant.

yew, i'oue, n (bot) if m.

yield, yi'îlde, v céder; produire; (bring in) rapporter. n rapport m; produit m; revenu m.

yogurt, i'ŏg´-eurte, n yaourt m.

yoke, i'auke, n joug m; (fig) sujétion f. v mettre au joug; subjuguer.

yokel, i'au´-k'l, n rustre m.

yolk, i'auke, n jaune d'œuf m.

yonder, i'onn´-d'r, adv là-bas. a ce . . . là.

you, i'oue, pron vous; (fam) tu; te; toi.

young, i'onng, a jeune. n (animals) petits mpl.

youngster, i'onng´-st'r, n jeune garçon; fille.

your, i'our, poss a votre; vos.

yours, i'ourze, poss pron le vôtre; la vôtre; les vôtres.

youth, i'outs, n jeunesse f; (lad) jeune homme m; − **hostel,** n auberge de jeunesse f

youthful, i'outs´-foull, a jeune; juvénile.

youthfulness, i'outs´-foull-nesse, n jeunesse f.

yuletide, i'oule´-tâïde, n temps de Noël m.

zap, zap, *v* bombarder, détruire; (TV) changer de chaîne.

zeal, zîle, *n* zéle *m*.

zealous, zèl´-*euce*, *a* zélé; ardent.

zebra, zî´-br*a*, *n* zèbre *m*.

zenith, zenn´-*its*, *n* zénith *m*.

zephyr, zèf´-'r, *n* zéphyr *m*.

zero, zi´-rau, *n* zéro *m*.

zest, zeste, *n* (*fig*) ardeur *f*; (relish) saveur *f*.

zinc, zinnque, *n* zinc *m*. *v* zinguer.

zipper, zip-ar, *n* fermeture-éclair *f*.

zone, zaune, *n* zone *f*.

zoo, zoue, *n* zoo *m*.

zoological, zau-ŏl-odj´-i-c'l, *a* zoologique.

zoology, zau-ol´-odj-i, *n* zoologie *f*.

zoom, zoum, *n* vombrissement *m*; zoom *m*. *v* vombrir; passer en trombe.

a
b
c
d
e
f
g
h
i
j
k
l
m
n
o
p
q
r
s
t
u
v
w
x
y
z